Lecture Notes in Computer Science 9063

Commenced Publication in 1973
Founding and Former Series Editors:
Gerhard Goos, Juris Hartmanis, and Jan van Leeuwen

T0211944

More information about this series at http://www.springer.com/series/7410

Anja Lehmann · Stefan Wolf (Eds.)

Information Theoretic Security

8th International Conference, ICITS 2015
Lugano, Switzerland, May 2–5, 2015
Proceedings

 Springer

Editors
Anja Lehmann
IBM Research Zurich
Rüschlikon
Switzerland

Stefan Wolf
Università della Svizzera italiana (USI)
Lugano
Switzerland

ISSN 0302-9743   ISSN 1611-3349   (electronic)
Lecture Notes in Computer Science
ISBN 978-3-319-17469-3   ISBN 978-3-319-17470-9   (eBook)
DOI 10.1007/978-3-319-17470-9

Library of Congress Control Number: 2015935641

LNCS Sublibrary: SL4 – Security and Cryptology

Springer Cham Heidelberg New York Dordrecht London

Printed on acid-free paper

Springer International Publishing AG Switzerland is part of Springer Science+Business Media
(www.springer.com)

Preface

ICITS 2015, the 8th International Conference on Information-Theoretic Security, was held in Lugano, Ticino, Switzerland, during May 2–5, 2015. The conference took place on the campus of Università della Svizzera italiana (USI) in Molino Nuovo, Lugano. The General and Program Co-chairs were Anja Lehmann (IBM Research – Zurich) and Stefan Wolf (USI Lugano).

The scope of ICITS connects the fields of cryptography, information theory, and quantum physics. More specifically, methods are studied that achieve cryptographic security without computational assumptions, or as "post-quantum schemes" which employ techniques from information theory, *e.g.*, coding.

ICITS 2015 had two tracks, a conference and a workshop track: Conference-track articles also appear in the proceedings, whereas workshop-track contributions were only presented on-site with a talk. This two-track format, which was started with ICITS 2012, has the advantage to promote bringing together researchers from various areas, such as information theory, cryptography, and quantum computing, which have different publication traditions.

There were 57 submitted papers, 48 to the conference track and 9 to the workshop track. In total, 23 submissions were accepted, 17 for the conference track and 6 for the workshop track. All submissions were reviewed by at least 3 (conference track) or 2 (workshop track) members of the Program Committee, who sometimes were assisted by external reviewers. These proceedings contain the accepted papers for the conference track. A full list of the workshop-track papers is given before the table of contents.

The conference program also featured five invited talks:

- "New Developments in Relativistic Quantum Cryptography" by *Adrian Kent*, University of Cambridge, UK
- "Tamper and Leakage Resilient von Neumann Architectures from Continuous Non-Malleable Codes" by *Jesper Buus Nielsen*, Aarhus University, Denmark. (Abstract included in this volume.)
- "Classical Uses of Quantum Complementarity: Leakage Resilient Computation and Semantically-Secure Communication" by *Joseph Renes*, ETH Zurich, Switzerland.
- "Tamper-Detection and Non-Malleable Codes" by *Daniel Wichs*, Northeastern University, USA.
- "Reflections on Quantum Data Hiding" by *Andreas Winter*, Universitat Autònoma de Barcelona, Spain.

First of all, we thank the Steering Committee of ICITS, and in particular Yvo Desmedt as well as Rei Safavi-Naini, for their trust and support. We would like to thank all the people who have contributed to the success of ICITS 2015. First, we thank the authors for submitting their work to our conference. It was a great pleasure to work with such a motivated and professional Program Committee. We would like to thank all

PC members for their contribution, and also thank the external reviewers who assisted the Program Committee during the reviewing process. We are grateful to the General and Program Chairs of previous editions of ICITS for their advice and assistance, in particular Frédérique Oggier, Carles Padro, Adam Smith, and Jürg Wullschleger. We also thank Jan Camenisch for his advice on various questions on how to run a conference. We are indebted to Ämin Baumeler for his most generous support, for instance, in producing these proceedings. Diana Corica was helping us with various administrative matters that pop-up in the organization of such an event; grazie mille! We thank a very motivated and competent Local Organization Committee for their precious help, namely Ämin Baumeler, Diana Corica, Helen Ebbe, Arne Hansen, Elisa Larghi, and Benno Salwey. Finally, ICITS 2015 would not have been possible without the generous financial support we received. In particular, we are most grateful to Albino Zgraggen and Klaus Ensslin. Our sponsors were the Università della Svizzera italiana (USI), the NCCR "Quantum Science and Technology" (QSIT), and the City of Lugano.

February 2015

Anja Lehmann
Stefan Wolf

ICITS 2015

The 8th International Conference on Information-Theoretic Security

May 2–5, 2015, Lugano, Switzerland

in cooperation with
International Association for Cryptologic Research (IACR), and
IEEE Information Theory Society

Program and General Chairs

Anja Lehmann   IBM Research-Zurich, Switzerland
Stefan Wolf   Università della Svizzera italiana, Lugano,
                      Switzerland

Program Committee

Paulo Barreto   University of São Paulo, Brazil
Mario Berta   California Institute of Technology, USA
Anne Broadbent   University of Ottawa, Canada
Roger Colbeck   University of York, UK
Paolo D'Arco   University of Salerno, Italy
Frédéric Dupuis   Masaryk University, Czech Republic
Stefan Dziembowski   University of Warsaw, Poland
Sebastian Faust   École Polytechnique Fédérale de Lausanne,
                       Switzerland
Omar Fawzi   ENS Lyon, France
Peter Gazi   Institute of Science and Technology, Austria
Yuval Ishai   Technion - Israel Institute of Technology, Israel
Keith Martin   Royal Holloway, University of London, UK
Prakash Narayan   University of Maryland, USA
Anderson Nascimento   University of Washington Tacoma, USA
Koji Nuida   Advanced Industrial Science and Technology,
                       Japan
Frédérique Oggier   Nanyang Technological University, Singapore
Claudio Orlandi   Aarhus University, Denmark
Carles Padro   Polytechnic University of Catalonia, Spain
Rei Safavi-Naini   University of Calgary, Canada
Marco Tomamichel   University of Sidney, Australia
Mark Zhandry   Stanford University, USA

Steering Committee

Carlo Blundo	University of Salerno, Italy
Ronald Cramer	CWI Amsterdam and Leiden University, The Netherlands
Yvo Desmedt (Chair)	University of Texas at Dallas, USA
Kaoru Kurosawa	Ibaraki University, Japan
Ueli Maurer	ETH Zurich, Switzerland
C. Pandu Rangan	Indian Institute of Technology Madras, India
Rei Safavi-Naini	University of Calgary, Canada
Junji Shikata	Yokohama National University, Japan
Moti Yung	Google and Columbia University, USA
Yulian Zheng	University of North Carolina, USA

External Reviewers

Divesh Aggarwal	Thomas Holenstein	Edoardo Serra
Diego Aranha	Jedrzej Kaniewski	Maciej Skórski
Shi Bai	Marcel Keller	David Sutter
Elette Boyle	Lucas Kowalczyk	Atsushi Takayasu
Matteo Campanelli	Nelly Huei Ying Ng	Tadanori Teruya
Luigi Catuogno	Maura Paterson	Ivan Visconti
Roberto De Prisco	Angel Perez Del Pozo	Evelyn Wainewright
Gregory Demay	Samuel Ranellucci	Mor Weiss
Alexandre Duc	Joseph M. Renes	Mark Wilde
Oriol Farras	Alfredo Rial	Kazuki Yoneyama
Ryo Fujita	Michal Rybar	
Tommaso Gagliardoni	Volkher Scholz	

Local Organizing Committee

Ämin Baumeler	Università della Svizzera italiana, Lugano, Switzerland
Diana Corica	Università della Svizzera italiana, Lugano, Switzerland
Helen Ebbe	Università della Svizzera italiana, Lugano, Switzerland
Arne Hansen	Università della Svizzera italiana, Lugano, Switzerland
Elisa Larghi	Università della Svizzera italiana, Lugano, Switzerland
Benno Salwey	Università della Svizzera italiana, Lugano, Switzerland

Workshop-Track Papers

The following papers were accepted to the *workshop track* of ICITS 2015. They were presented at the conference but do not appear as papers in these proceedings.

1. Non-Signalling Parallel Repetition Using de Finetti Reductions.
   Rotem Arnon-Friedman, Renato Renner and Thomas Vidick

2. Semidefinite Programs for Randomness Extractors.
   Mario Berta, Omar Fawzi and Volkher B. Scholz

3. A Purification Approach to Input Privacy.
   Anne Broadbent and Serge Fehr

4. Revisiting the Shannon Theory Approach to Cryptography.
   Flavio Calmon, Mayank Varia, Muriel Médard, Mark Christiansen, Ken Duffy, Linda M. Zeger and João Barros

5. Alignment of Polarized Sets.
   Joseph M. Renes, David Sutter and S. Hamed Hassani

6. Approximate Degradable Quantum Channels.
   David Sutter, Volkher B. Scholz and Renato Renner

Tamper and Leakage Resilient von Neumann Architectures from Continuous Non-Malleable Codes

Invited Talk

Jesper Buus Nielsen

Department of Computer Science
Aarhus University

Abstract. We present the notion of continuous non-malleable codes along with an instantiation and we show how to use them to securely compute any keyed cryptographic primitive on a computational architecture with a single constant size untamperable CPU and a tamperable and leaky memory in which both the secret key and the program of the cryptographic primitive is located.

1 Introduction

The notion of non-malleable codes introduced by Dziembowski, Pietrzak and Wichs in [2] is a relaxation of the notions of error correcting and error detecting codes. Informally, a code is non-malleable if an adversary trying to tamper with an encoding of a given message can only leave it unchanged or modify it to the encoding of a completely unrelated value.

Continuous non-malleable codes (CNMC) is an extension of the standard non-malleability security notion, where we allow the adversary to tamper with an encoding several times and use its knowledge of the observed effects of the tampering in the subsequent tampering attacks. This is in contrast to the standard notion of non-malleable codes where the adversary is only allowed to tamper a single time with an encoding.

The notion of continuous non-malleable codes was introduced by Faust, Mukherjee, Nielsen and Venturi in [3] where also the first such code was constructed. We present the code from [3]. The code is based on the inner-product function, collision-resistant hashing and non-interactive zero-knowledge proofs of knowledge. We also touch on later work by Coretti, Maurer, Tackmann and Venturi[1,5] and Jafargholi and Wichs[5] constructing information-theoretically secure continuous non-malleable codes.

We then present how to use continuous non-malleable codes to protect arbitrary cryptographic primitives against tampering attacks. Previous applications of non-malleable codes to this problem required to perfectly erase the entire memory of the computational architecture after each execution. This of course makes it impossible to have the program of the primitive sit in the memory of the computational architecture and forces the program to be hardcoded into the architecture itself, forcing essentially a circuit model of computation. In practice this would mean producing a specialised piece of hardware for each primitive that we would like to compute in a tamper-resilient manner. Continuous non-malleable codes were introduced exactly to avoid this limitation.

We present the tamper and leakage-resilient random-access memory architecture from [4]. The architecture has one CPU that accesses a memory. The memory is subject to leakage and tampering. So is the bus connecting the CPU to the memory. We assume that the computation of the CPU is leakage and tamper free. For a fixed value of the security parameter, the CPU has constant size. Furthermore, the design of the CPU is completely independent of the program to be run and its internal registers are non-persistent, i.e., all secret registers are reset between invocations. The most prominent consequence of having a constant size CPU with no persistent secret memory is that the code of the program must be stored in the memory and so must all secrets. Therefore both program and secrets will be subject to tampering and leakage.

We construct a compiler for this architecture which transforms any keyed cryptographic primitive into a program where the key is encoded and stored in the memory along with the program to evaluate the primitive on that key. This result reduces the problem of shielding arbitrarily complex computations to protecting a single, constant-size component. The compiler only assumes the existence of a continuous non-malleable code and is therefore information-theoretically secure if based on an information-theoretically secure continuous non-malleable code.

References

1. S. Coretti, U. Maurer, B. Tackmann, and D. Venturi. From single-bit to multi-bit public-key encryption via non-malleable codes. In Y. Dodis and J. B. Nielsen, editors, *Theory of Cryptography - 12th Theory of Cryptography Conference, TCC 2014. Proceedings*, Lecture Notes in Computer Science. Springer, 2015.
2. S. Dziembowski, K. Pietrzak, and D. Wichs. Non-malleable codes. In A. C. Yao, editor, *Innovations in Computer Science - ICS 2010. Proceedings*, pages 434–452. Tsinghua University Press, 2010.
3. S. Faust, P. Mukherjee, J. B. Nielsen, and D. Venturi. Continuous non-malleable codes. In Y. Lindell, editor, *Theory of Cryptography - 11th Theory of Cryptography Conference, TCC 2014. Proceedings*, volume 8349 of *Lecture Notes in Computer Science*, pages 465–488. Springer, 2014.
4. S. Faust, P. Mukherjee, J. B. Nielsen, and D. Venturi. Leakage-resilient signatures with graceful degradation. In J. Katz, editor, *Public-Key Cryptography - PKC 2015 - 18th International Conference on Practice and Theory in Public-Key Cryptography. Proceedings*, volume 9020 of *Lecture Notes in Computer Science*, pages 579–603. Springer, 2015.
5. Z. Jafargholi and D. Wichs. Tamper detection and continuous non-malleable codes. In Y. Dodis and J. B. Nielsen, editors, *Theory of Cryptography - 12th Theory of Cryptography Conference, TCC 2014. Proceedings*, Lecture Notes in Computer Science. Springer, 2015.

Contents

Practical Sharing of Quantum Secrets over Untrusted Channels

Damian Markham and Anne Marin

CNRS LTCI, Département Informatique et Réseaux, Telecom ParisTech,
23 avenue d'Italie, 75013 Paris, France

Abstract. In this work we address the issue of sharing a quantum secret over untrusted channels between the dealer and players. Existing
solutions require entanglement over a number of systems which scales
with the security parameter, quickly becoming impractical. We present
protocols (interactive and a non-interactive) where single copy encodings
are sufficient. Our protocols work for all quantum secret sharing schemes
and access structures, and are implementable with current experimental
set ups. For a single authorised player, our protocols act as quantum
authentication protocols.

1 Introduction

In secret sharing a dealer wishes to distribute a secret to a network of players such
that only authorised sets of players can access the secret, and unauthorised sets
of players cannot. After the initial protocols for sharing classical secrets [1, 2],
ones for sharing quantum secrets were later developed [3, 4], and have found uses
including secure multiparty computation [5]. However, these protocols rely on
trusted channels between the dealer and the players. In practice, channels may
be corrupted either by unavoidable noise, or malicious attacks.

One way to resolve this situation would be to use the quantum authentication
protocol [6] to check the channel. However this is highly impractical in that it
uses error correcting codes and which requires encoding each qubit sent from the
dealer into a highly entangled state (or perform entangling measurements, which
would allow the generation of large entangled states), the size of which scale with
the security parameter (this is also true of all other authentication protocols
known to the authors, including the encode-encrypt and trap schemes in [7]).
This difficulty, on a par with the coherences needed for quantum computing,
renders this approach infeasible with current or near future technology.

In this work we present a protocol which is universal (it works for all quantum secret sharing protocols and access structures) and is implementable with
current experimental setups, for example by using graph states. This is possible
because our protocol uses only single copy encodings. As in the authentication
scheme [6], our protocol uses an initial shared secret classical key between the
dealer and receivers. Our protocol is secure against any cheating parties including
unauthorised players and external eavesdroppers. We begin by introducing an

© Springer International Publishing Switzerland 2015
A. Lehmann and S. Wolf (Eds.): ICITS 2015, LNCS 9063, pp. 1–14, 2015.
DOI: 10.1007/978-3-319-17470-9_1

interactive protocol, which will serve as a basis for the non-interactive protocol which follows. We then give an example of an explicit graph state implementation for sharing a secret between five players such that any three can access the secret and fewer cannot. We finish with a discussion on possible variants of the protocol including the possibility of abort, and the merits of graph state implementations [8–11]. One of these was recently implemented experimentally using graph states [12].

2   Protocols

In quantum secret sharing, a secret $|\psi\rangle = \alpha|0\rangle + \beta|1\rangle$ is encoded by the dealer d into some logical basis $|\psi_L\rangle_P = \alpha|0_L\rangle_P + \beta|1_L\rangle_P$ on $|P|$ systems, and distributed to the players P. A set of players $B \subset P$ are *authorised* if they can access the secret. This is equivalent to there existing a pair of logical operators $X_{L,B}$, $Z_{L,B}$ which are nontrivial only over the systems B, and act over the logical basis in the appropriate way $X_{L,B}|i_L\rangle = |i \oplus 1_L\rangle$, $Z_{L,B}|i_L\rangle = (-1)^i|i_L\rangle$ (where $\oplus$ symbolises sum modulo two) [10]. These logical operators are used by authorised set B to access the secret, for example by performing a logical swap onto an ancilla held by B. A set of players $B \subset P$ are *unauthorised* if they can get no information at all about the quantum secret state. The choice of the logical basis determines the authorised and unauthorised sets. Our protocols are built on the existence of these schemes (which exist for all access structures [4]), and we will use this notation in our protocols.

For our first protocol, we use a general entangled based picture of secret sharing [10]. In this picture the dealer and the players share an entangled EPR state

$$|\Phi\rangle_{dP} = \frac{|0\rangle_d|0_L\rangle_P + |1\rangle_d|1_L\rangle_P}{\sqrt{2}}, \tag{1}$$

which is then used to teleport the secret to the players. The interactive protocol presented below essentially verifies that the dealer and any given set of authorised players B share this state (or the associated reduced state), in which case the teleportation will be successful. More explicitly, the dealer generates many (S) copies of the entangled EPR state (1) and uses all but one to test the state (steps 3 and 4 in the protocol below), and one to teleport (step 5). By randomly choosing when to test and when to use the state for teleportation any malicious actions cannot help but be detected. We will see after that this can be translated to a non-interactive protocol by replacing communication by a shared random key in a standard way [13, 6].

When analysing these protocols, several subtleties must be addressed arising from the secret sharing requirements. Firstly it is important that the dealer's behaviour be independent of which authorised set of players wish to access the secret (if the dealer knew before hand which set would access, she could just send directly to them - so there would be no need for secret sharing). Secondly the protocol should be defined for all authorised sets of players. Finally the communication should be in such a way that any unauthorised parties, including cheating players and eavesdroppers, do not get information compromising security. We will see that this can be achieved below, where we define the protocol for all authorsed sets B.

Interactive Protocol

1. Dealer d generates S EPR states, $|\Phi\rangle_{dP}^{\otimes S}$, and sends the shares of each one to P.
2. After P received all their parts, d chooses $r \in [1, ...S]$ at random and sends r to P.
3. For EPR pairs $i \neq r$, d chooses $t_i \in [0, 1]$ and measures X_d if $t_i = 0$ or measures Z_d if $t_i = 1$, and denotes the result y_i, and sends t_i and y_i to P.
4. For EPR pairs $i \neq r$, accessing set B measure $X_{L,B}$ if $t_i = 0$ or measures $Z_{L,B}$ if $t_i = 1$. Denoting result by y_i' if $y_i = y_i'$ ACCEPT, if $y_i \neq y_i'$ REJECT.
5. For $i = r$, d uses EPR pair r to teleport the secret state onto the logical basis, denoting the bell basis measurements x, and sends x to all P. Upon receiving x, B decodes using $X_{L,B}$ and $Z_{L,B}$.

This protocol is effectively a quantum authentication protocol from the dealer to authorised set B, with the additional constraints regarding secret sharing mentioned above. In [6] a framework for quantum authentication is laid out, along with definitions of completeness, soundness and security, which we will adopt here. A general quantum authentication scheme for sending messages from A to B is described by a randomly chosen classical key $k \in \mathcal{K}$ that is shared by A and B, and associated encoding and decoding operations A_k and B_k respectively. At the end of the protocol B has a system which encodes the message, and a classical register which encodes the decision whether to accept or reject in orthogonal states $|ACC\rangle$ and $|REJ\rangle$. A quantum authentication scheme is ϵ-*secure* if for all states $|\psi\rangle$ it satisfies the two conditions.

- **Completeness.** For all keys $k \in \mathcal{K}$

$$B_k(A_k(|\psi\rangle\langle\psi|)) = |\psi\rangle\langle\psi| \otimes |ACC\rangle\langle ACC|. \tag{2}$$

- **Soundness.** For all (possibly malicious) channels O, describing the expected state on Bob's side after the protocol as $\rho_B = \frac{1}{|\mathcal{K}|} \sum_{k \in \mathcal{K}} B_k(O(A_k(|\psi\rangle\langle\psi|)))$, and denoting the two projections $P_{fail}^{|\psi\rangle} := (I - |\psi\rangle\langle\psi|) \otimes |ACC\rangle\langle ACC|$, then

$$Tr\left(P_{fail}^{|\psi\rangle}\rho_B\right) \leq \epsilon. \tag{3}$$

We say that our secret sharing protocols are ϵ-secure if all authorised sets B can authenticate the secret with ϵ-security, and unauthorised sets of players get no information. The latter is guarenteed by the use of the original secret sharing logical operators in our protocol, as is the completeness, we will prove the soundness now.

The left hand side of equation (3) is equal to the probability of accepting multiplied by the fidelity to B's resulting state (averaged over keys) to the space orthogonal to the ideal state $|\psi\rangle$. That is, it represents a failing in the protocol, so we want to make it arbitrarily small (with some security parameter S). In order to prove soundness, we will bound this by considering statements about the entangled states themselves, before the teleportation.

We first introduce the operator $\Pi_{dB} := 1/4(I_d \otimes I_B + X_d \otimes X_{L,B} + Z_d X_d \otimes Z_{L,B} X_{L,B} + Z_d \otimes Z_{L,B})$, which is a projector onto a space where all states are maximally entangled between d and B. More specifically every state in this subspace can be expressed in the form $\frac{|0\rangle_d |0_{L(i)}\rangle_B + |1\rangle_d |1_{L(i)}\rangle_B}{\sqrt{2}}$, where $\{|0_{L(i)}\rangle_B, |1_{L(i)}\rangle_B\}$ are some basis of B such that i represents a possible logical bases, $X_{L,B}|j_{L(i)}\rangle_B = |j \oplus 1_{L(i)}\rangle_B$, $Z_{L,B}|j_{L(i)}\rangle_B = (-1)^j |j_{L(i)}\rangle_B$ and we will use many such bases in (4) such that $\langle j_{L(i)}|k_{L(m)}\rangle_B = \delta_{j,k}\delta_{i,m}$.

Consider the state ρ_{dB}^r which is used to teleport in protocol step 5 (conditioned on accepting on all other pairs, see (6)). Any such state can be purified to $|\Psi\rangle_{dBE}$, which can be expanded

$$
\begin{aligned}
|\Psi\rangle_{dBE} &= (\Pi_{dB} \otimes I_E + (I_{dB} - \Pi_{AB}) \otimes I_E))|\Psi\rangle_{dBE} \\
&= \sqrt{F}\left(\sum_i \alpha_i(|0\rangle_d|0_{L(i)}\rangle_B + |1\rangle_d|1_{L(i)}\rangle_B)|\psi_i\rangle_E\right) \\
&\quad + \sqrt{1-F}|\xi\rangle_{dBE},
\end{aligned}
\tag{4}
$$

where $F = Tr(\Pi_{dB}\rho_{dB}^r)$. If this state is then used to teleport a state $|\psi\rangle$ from d to B, followed by B doing a logical decoding to ancilla system B' (for example B performs a logical swap onto B') the state recovered $\rho_{B'}$ has fidelity $f := \langle\psi|\rho_{B'}|\psi\rangle$ with the original state satisfying $f \geq F$. Furthermore,

$$
\begin{aligned}
Tr\left(P_{fail}^{|\psi\rangle}\rho_B\right) &= Tr\left(((I - |\psi\rangle\langle\psi|) \otimes |ACC\rangle\langle ACC|)\rho_B\right) \\
&\leq Tr\left(\Pi_{dB}^{\perp} \otimes |ACC\rangle\langle ACC|\rho_{dB_{AR}}\right),
\end{aligned}
\tag{5}
$$

where $\Pi_{dB}^{\perp}$ is the projector onto the space orthogonal to Π_{dB} and $\rho_{dB_{AR}} = 1/S\sum_{r=1}^{S} p_{ACC}^r \rho_{dB}^r \otimes |ACC\rangle\langle ACC| + p_{REJ}^r \rho_{dB}^{r,REJ} \otimes |REJ\rangle\langle REJ|$, p_{ACC}^r and p_{REJ}^r are the probability of accepting and rejecting respectively when using r, and $\rho_{dB}^{r,REJ}$ is the state conditioned on rejecting.

Denoting the POVM element associated to accepting the test step 4 for pair i as

$$
M_{ACC_i} = 1/2\left(\frac{I_{d_i} \otimes I_{B_i} + X_{d_i} \otimes X_{L,B_i}}{2} + \frac{I_{d_i} \otimes I_{B_i} + Z_{d_i} \otimes Z_{L,B_i}}{2}\right),
$$

we have $M_{ACC_i} \leq \frac{(I_{d_i} \otimes I_{B_i} + \Pi_{d_i,B_i})}{2}$. Then, if we call the total state shared over all copies of the dealer and the players B, $\rho_{d_1,B_1,...d_S,B_S}$, it follows that

$$
\rho_{dB}^r = \frac{1}{p_{ACC}^r}Tr_{r^c}\left(\bigotimes_{i \neq r} M_{ACC_i}\rho_{d_1,B_1,...d_S,B_S}\right),
\tag{6}
$$

where Tr_{r^c} indicates trace over all systems but r. Putting this together we have,

$$Tr\left(\Pi_{dB}^{\perp}\rho_{dB}\right) = \frac{1}{S}\sum_{r=1}^{S}Tr\left(\Pi_{d_r,B_r}^{\perp}\otimes_{i\neq r}M_{ACC_i}\rho_{d_1,B_1,\ldots d_S,B_S}\right)$$

$$\leq Tr\left(Q\rho_{d_1,B_1,\ldots d_S,B_S}\right), \tag{7}$$

where $Q = \sum_{r=1}^{S}\Pi_{d_r,B_r}^{\perp}\otimes_{i\neq r}\frac{\left(I_{d_i}\otimes I_{B_i}+\Pi_{d_i,B_i}\right)}{2}$. It can easily be seen that Q has maximum eigenvalues of $1/S$, reached by projection $\Pi_{d_j,B_j}^{\perp}\otimes_{i\neq j}\Pi_{d_i,B_i}$ for any j. With this, we arrive at the following theorem.

Theorem 1. *The interactive protocol defined above is ϵ-secure, with scaling $\epsilon = 1/S$.*

Note here that the scaling of the protocol is inverse linear, as compared to exponential in [6]. This can be understood as the cost of making the protocol practical. To get the exponential scaling in [6] they require entangled measurements or encodings over S systems (which quickly becomes infeasible). This is indeed true for any protocol which uses quantum error correcting codes where the size of the code scales with the security parameter, as for example in the trap codes and indeed all encode-encrypt codes in [7]. On the other hand our protocol requires S *copies* of the single round encodings, which adds no difficulty in standard optical implementations, and is implementable with current technology.

The protocol above suffers from two main issues. Firstly, interaction is needed between the dealer and the players. Although this could be allowed in principle, it is more interesting if limited or no interaction is needed. Second, largely due to the interaction, a quantum memory is required by the dealer and players B between steps 1 and 5. The dealer must keep their part of the EPR pairs until the players have recieved their shares, and B must keep their shares until r is announced by the dealer and further until d announces their result x for the teleportation. This is challenging experimentally. These problems can be overcome by replacing communication and the entanglement between the dealer and players with shared random keys, as was done in [6], but with an extra twist - they should be shared using a classical secret sharing protocol, so that the access structure is maintained. In this way, the protocol below requires no interaction after the initial sharing of a random key and the dealer's use of the channel, and similarly no quantum memory is required by B or d and no entanglement is needed between d and P (it is of the 'prepare and measure' type). To encode the randomly chosen r, we define string $q = (q_1, \ldots q_S)$ such that $q_i = 0$ if $i \neq r$, $q_i = 1$ if $i = r$, where r is randomly chosen in $[1, \ldots S]$.

Non-interactive Protocol

1. d and P share random strings q, t, y, x via a classical secret sharing scheme over P (i.e. d knows each string, but it is shared via a classical secret sharing scheme with the relevant access structure over P so that only authorised sets

can access it, and only when they collaborate to do so, and unauthorised sets get no information at all).

2. Going through round by round $i = 1...S$. If $q_i = 0$ the dealer proceeds to step 3, if $q_i = 1$ the dealer proceeds to step 4.

3. For $q_i = 0$

    (a) Dealer prepares and distributes state $H_L^{t_i} Z_L^{y_i} \frac{|0_L\rangle_P + |1_L\rangle_P}{\sqrt{2}}$.

    (b) After receiving the state from the dealer, authorised set B collaborate to find q_i (which is 0), t_i, and y_i.

    (c) Authorised set B measures $X_{L,B}$ if $t_i = 0$ or measures $Z_{L,B}$ if $t_i = 1$. The result is denoted y_i'.
        If $y_i \neq y_i'$ REJECT. If $y_i = y_i'$ ACCEPT.

    (d) If $i = S$, END, otherwise return to step 2.

4. For $q_i = 1$

    (a) d encodes and distrubutes the state $X_L^{x_0} Z_L^{x_1} |\psi_L\rangle_P$.

    (b) After recieving the state from the dealer, authorised set B collaborate to find q_i (which is 1), t_i, y_i and x.

    (c) B decodes using $X_{L,B}, Z_{L,B}$.

    (d) If $i = S$, END, otherwise return to step 2

Replacing the communication by shared random strings in this way does not effect the security [6, 13], and we have the following theorem.

Theorem 2. *The non-interactive protocol defined above is ϵ-secure, with $\epsilon = 1/S$.*

3   Example

In recent years graph states have emerged as a useful framework in which to do secret sharing [8, 9, 11, 10]. As an example, we now illustrate how secret sharing over untrusted channels works for the case of five players, such that any set of three or more players can access the secret and any fewer have none (the so called $(3, 5)$ threshold secret sharing scheme of [8]). To begin, we introduce some notation. A graph state $|G\rangle_{1,...,n}$ is a state on n qubits which is associated to graph G through graph state stabiliser operators $K_i := X_i \otimes_{j \in N(i)} Z_j$ where i is associated to a vertex in the graph and $N(i)$ are the set of its neighbours, and the eigenequations $K_i |G\rangle_{1,...n} = |G\rangle_{1,...n} \ \forall i$.

In our example the logical states are given by $|0_L\rangle_P = |G_P\rangle_P$ for the graph G_P in Fig. 1a), and $|1_L\rangle_P = Z_1 Z_2 Z_3 Z_4 Z_5 |G_P\rangle_P$ with $P = \{1, 2, 3, 4, 5\}$. The entangled state used in the interactive protocol step 1 is

$$|\Phi\rangle_{dP} = \frac{|0\rangle_d |0_L\rangle_P + |1\rangle_d |1_L\rangle_P}{\sqrt{2}}. \tag{8}$$

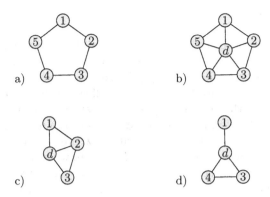

Fig. 1. Graphs for sharing a secret amongst five players such that any majority can access the secret [8]. a) Graph G_P associated to logical encoding. b) Graph G_{dP} for the entangled state between d and P used in step 1 of the protocol. c) Graph G_{dB} associated to the test for players $B = \{1, 2, 3\}$. d) Graph G_{dB} associated to the test for players $B = \{1, 3, 4\}$.

It is not difficult to see that this is itself a graph state associated to the graph in Fig. 1b), $|\Phi\rangle_{dP} = |G_{dP}\rangle_{dP}$.

The choice of logical operators depends on the set $B \subset P$ who are trying to access the secret. Notice that during the protocol the dealers' action does not require knowledge of B - this is essential to secret sharing, so that the players can decide for themselves who access the secret.

If players $B = \{1, 2, 3\}$ wish to act as the authorised set, they can use logical operators $X_L = X_1 Z_2 X_3$ and $Z_L = Z_1 X_2 Z_3$. The logical operators measured in the test step of the protocol (step 4 for the interactive and step 3 for the non-interactive) are graph state stabilisers of the graph G_{dB} given in Fig. 1c), $X_d \otimes X_{L,B} = K_d K_1 K_3$, $Z_d \otimes Z_{L,B} = K_2$. This is no coincidence, and is a general feature of graph state protocols, which gives a simple decomposition of states into the graph state basis as the natural expansion for (4). To decode the secret after teleportation, players 1 and 3 measure in the Bell basis, and the secret is passed onto the qubit of player 2. This is the same decoding procedure for the standard secret sharing protocol [8].

If players $B = \{1, 3, 4\}$ wish to act as the authorised set, they can use logical operators $X_L = Z_1 X_3 X_4$ and $Z_L = X_1 X_3 X_4$. The logical operators measured in the test step of the protocol (4 for the interactive and 3 for the non-interactive) are graph state stabilisers of the graph G_{dB} given in Fig. 1d), $X_d \otimes X_{L,B} = K_d K_3 K_4$, $Z_d \otimes Z_{L,B} = K_1 K_3 K_4$. In this case, to decode the secret after teleportation, players 3 and 4 measure in the Bell basis, and the secret is passed onto the qubit of player 1.

Logical operators can similarly be defined for all sets of three players, and it is easy to see that any two players cannot access the secret by themselves [8].

4   Conclusions

Several variations of these protocols are also possible. In particular, if the quantum secret is precious, the dealer may not want to send the information when the channel is not trusted - i.e. when it fails the test part of the protocols above. To address this one can adapt the protocol to allow for the players to announce abort when they fail the test. It is possible to show an adapted theorem for security, which is only slightly modified. We present the protocol and the theorem in the appendix A. One subtle issue with how this may be used however, is that the protocol is now interactive (albeit limited to when the players announce abort). When the accessing set B announce abort they declare themselves, which may be an issue in some uses of secret sharing as a primitive (one may try to develop ways to overcome this for example using an anonymous announcement of abort). Another alternative protocol with abort can be found if, instead of randomly choosing in a fixed number (S) of rounds, at each round we randomly choose to test or use the channel. This allows for slightly different security statements, as used in [14] for entanglement verification. We consider this simplified unbounded aborting protocol in appendix A.

Note that in all the schemes presented here the entanglement used is only that required for the secret sharing part of the encoding, so that this remains fixed by the demanded access structure. The independence of the the size of entanglement from the security with respect to untrusted dealer to player channels is the main contribution of our protocols.

Using graph state schemes as in the example shown here has several advantages. Firstly they are a common framework for many quantum information processing tasks, including measurement based quantum computation and error correction. This allows these protocols to naturally fit into more general and elaborate network scenarios integrating several of these tasks. Furthermore, this relationship allows us to understand the connection between different protocols. The measurements used for the test part of our protocol are exactly those used for the CQ protocols to establish secure key between the dealer and authorised players [10]. This relationship is general - whenever complementary bases are used to establish a secure key, successful key generation implies the channel works [15, 10].

Secondly graph states are very well suited to implementation. Many schemes exist for the generation and manipulation of graph states in different technologies including linear optics [16], continuous variables [17, 18] and ion traps [24, 25]. Optical implementations of graph states are ideal for the secret sharing protocols presented here, and experiments in this direction are well advanced and optics has been used to implement sophisticated quantum information processing tasks including measurement based quantum computing [19], blind quantum computation [20], and error correction [21]. Indeed a proof of principle experiment implementing our protocol has recently been carried out in the optical setting [12].

All of the results here easily extend to the qudit case, including use for qudit graph state secret sharing [9, 10], which allows our scheme to be used to cover all access structures. One simply extends the states and operators to their natural qudit versions. This is done explicitly in the appendix B. Furthermore, the proofs also follow through for secret sharing protocols using mixed state encodings, as well as the hybrid protocols of [22],[23] where classical secret sharing is used in addition to allow for access structures otherwise forbidden, in this case however authenticated classical channels between the dealer and the players must also be secure.

Quantum secret sharing is one of the underlying sub protocols for secure multiparty quantum computation (as is authentication) [5]. There too large, and scaling (with security parameters), entanglement is required. However, all these schemes can be phrased in the language of graph states. The techniques developed here may be applied to other protocols to make them within reach sooner.

Acknowledgement. We thank Anthony Leverrier, Eleni Diamanti and André Chailloux for many useful discussions and helpful comments. This work was supported by the Ville de Paris Emergences program, project CiQWii.

References

1. Shamir, A.: Commun. ACM 22, 612 (1979)
2. Blakley, G.R.: Proceedings of the National Computer Conference 48, 313–317 (1979)
3. Hillery, M., Bužek, V., Berthiaume, A.: Phys. Rev. A 59, 1829 (1999)
4. Cleve, R., Gottesman, D., Lo, H.K.: Phys. Rev. Lett. 83, 648 (1999)
5. Ben-Or, M., Crépeau, C., Gottesman, D., Hassidim, A., Smith, A.: 47th Annual IEEE Symposium on Foundations of Computer Science, FOCS 2006, pp. 249–260 (2006)
6. Barnum, H., Crépeau, C., Gottesman, D., Smith, A., Tapp, A.: Proc. 43rd Annual IEEE Symposium on the Foundations of Computer Science (FOCS 2002), pp. 449–458. IEEE Press (2002)
7. Broadbent, A., Gutoski, G., Stebila, D.: Quantum One-Time Programs. In: Canetti, R., Garay, J.A. (eds.) CRYPTO 2013, Part II. LNCS, vol. 8043, pp. 344–360. Springer, Heidelberg (2013)
8. Markham, D., Sanders, B.C.: Phys. Rev. A 78(4), 042309 (2008)
9. Keet, A., Fortescue, B., Markham, D., Sanders, B.C.: Phys. Rev. A 82, 062315 (2010)
10. Marin, A., Markham, D.: Phys. Rev. A 88, 042332 (2013)
11. Marin, A., Markham, D., Perdrix, S.: In: TQC 2013. LIPICS, vol. 22, pp. 308–324 (2013)
12. Bell, B.A., Markham, D., Herrera-Martí, D.A., Marin, A., Wadsworth, W.J., Rarity, J.G., Tame, M.S.: Nature Communications 5, 5480 (2014)
13. Shor, P.W., Preskill, J.: Phys. Rev. Lett. 85, 441 (2000)
14. Pappa, A., Chailloux, A., Wehner, S., Diamanti, E., Kerenidis, I.: Phys. Rev. Lett. 108(26), 260502 (2012)
15. Christandl, M., Winter, A.: IEEE Trans. Inf. Theory 51(9), 3159–3165 (2005)
16. Browne, D.E., Rudolph, T.: Physical Review Letters 95, 010501 (2005)

17. Rigas, I., Gabriel, C., Berg-Johansen, S., Aiello, A., van Loock, P., Andersen, U.L., Marquardt, C., Leuchs, G.: Quant-ph/1210.5188
18. Ukai, R., Iwata, N., Shimokawa, Y., Armstrong, S.C., Politi, A., Yoshikawa, J.-I., van Loock, P., Furusawa, A.: Phys. Rev. Lett. 106, 240504 (2011)
19. Walther, P., Resch, K.J., Rudolph, T., Schenck, E., Weinfurter, H., Vedral, V., Aspelmeyer, M., Zeilinger, A.: Nature 434, 169 (2005)
20. Barz, S., Kashefi, E., Broadbent, A., Fitzsimons, J.F., Zeilinger, A., Walther, P.: Science 335, 303 (2012)
21. Bell, B.A., Herrera-Mart, D.A., Tame, M.S., Markham, M.S., Wadsworth, W.J., Rarity, W.J.: Nature Communications 5, 3658 (2014)
22. Broadbent, A., Chouha, P.R., Tapp, A.: Proceedings of the Third International Conference on Quantum, Nano and Micro Technologies (ICQNM 2009), pp. 59–62 (2009)
23. Javelle, J., Mhalla, M., Perdrix, S.: (2011), Preprint at http://arxiv.org/abs/1109.1487
24. Wunderlich, H., Wunderlich, C., Singer, K., Schmidt-Kaler, F.: Physical Review A 79, 052324 (2009)
25. Lanyon, B.P., Jurcevic, P., Zwerger, M., Hempel, C., Martinez, E.A., Briegel, W.H.J., Blatt, R., Roos, C.F.: Measurement-based quantum computation with trapped ions. Physical Review Letters 111, 210501 (2013)
26. Sheridan, L., Scarani, V.: Phys. Rev. A 82, 030301(R) (2010)

A   Aborting Protocols

We first present an adaptation of the non-interactive protocol to include abort.

Protocol with Abort

1. d and P share random strings q, t, y, x via a classical secret sharing scheme over P.
2. Going through round by round $i = 1...S$. Authorised set B collaborate to find q_i. If $q_i = 0$ all proceed to step 3, if $q_i = 1$ all proceed to step 4.
3. For $q_i = 0$
   (a) Dealer prepares and distributes state $H_L^{t_i} Z_L^{y_i} \frac{|0_L\rangle_P + |1_L\rangle_P}{\sqrt{2}}$.
   (b) For authorised set B, if $t_i = 0$, B measures Z_L, if $t_i = 1$, B measures X_L. The result is denoted y_i'.
      If $y_i \neq y_i'$ B announces ABORT, all abort.
   (c) If $y_i = y_i'$ ACCEPT, and return to step 2.
4. For $q_i = 1$
   (a) d encodes and distributes the state $X_L^{x_0} Z_L^{x_1} |\psi_L\rangle_P$.
   (b) B decode.
   (c) END

Theorem 3. *The aborting protocol defined above is ϵ-secure, with $\epsilon < 2/S$.*

The proof follows the same argumentation as before, but in this case the testing stops at round r. This gives a different Q operator (applied as in equation (7)),

$$Q = \frac{1}{S} \sum_{r=1}^{S} \Pi_{d_r, B_r}^{\perp} \bigotimes_{i<r} \frac{(I_{d_i} \otimes I_{B_i} + \Pi_{d_i, B_i})}{2} \bigotimes_{i>r} (I_{d_i} \otimes I_{B_i}). \qquad (9)$$

To find the greatest eigenvalue we can decompose into the $\{\Pi_{d_i, B_i}, \Pi_{d_i, B_i}^{\perp}\}$ basis. Then we have a sum with all strings of products, where each string x, in which Π_{d_i, B_i} appears $|x|$ times, occurs with weight $1/S \sum_{a=0}^{|x|-1} 1/2^a$. Thus, the greatest eigenvalue of Q is $1/S \sum_{a=0}^{S-1} 1/2^a = \frac{2-2^{-S}}{S} < 2/S$, given by the string $\Pi_{d_1, B_1}^{\perp} \otimes \Pi_{d_2, B_2}^{\perp} \otimes ... \Pi_{d_S, B_S}^{\perp}$. In this case we see that the optimal cheat (in terms of maximising the failure of the protocol) is given by the dishonest parties preparing many copies of states all outside the ideal space.

We also present an aborting protocol where the randomness (over whether to test the channel or use it) is inserted each round.

Aborting Protocol, Indefinite Length

1. Dealer d generates EPR state $|\Phi\rangle_{dP}$ and sends the shares to P.
2. After P received all their parts, d chooses $r \in [0, ...S - 1]$ at random and sends r to P. If $r \neq 0$, continue to step 3, otherwise move to step 4.
3. TEST
   (a) d chooses $t \in \{0, 1\}$. If $t = 0$, d measures Z_d, if $t = 1$ d measures X_d. The result is denoted y. d sends t and y to P.
   (b) If $t = 0$, B measures $Z_{L,B}$, if $t = 1$, B measures $X_{L,B}$. The result is denoted y'. If $y_i \neq y_i'$ B announces ABORT, all abort.
   (c) If $y_i = y_i'$ ACCEPT, and return to step 1.
4. USE CHANNEL
   (a) d uses EPR pair to teleport the secret state onto the logical basis, denoting the bell basis measurements x, and sends x to all P. Upon receiving x, B decodes.

This protocol is similar to the use of the verification of GHZ states in [14], and we can present a similar security statement as there. Let C_f be the event that the state is teleported, and that the fidelity of any teleported state ρ and the sent state $|\psi\rangle$ is bounded by $\langle \psi | \rho | \psi \rangle \leq f$, then we have the following theorem.

Theorem 4. *For all f, the probability of event C_f is bounded*

$$P(C_f)) \leq \frac{2}{S(1-f)}. \qquad (10)$$

To prove this, call C_f^N the event that at round $N + 1$ the state is used (which means that all previous rounds have returned accept) and that the fidelity of all states sent satisfies $\langle \psi | \rho | \psi \rangle \leq f$. The probability of this event is given by the probability of using the $N + 1$th round state, times the probability of having tested the previous rounds times the probability of passing all the previous rounds.

$$P(C_f^N) = \frac{1}{S}\left(1 - \frac{1}{S}\right)^N \prod_{i=1}^N p_i \tag{11}$$

where p_i is the probability that round i is accepted. This is given by

$$\begin{aligned} p_i &= Tr(\rho_{d_i,B_i} M_{ACC_i}) \\ &\leq \frac{1 + Tr(\rho_{d_i,B_i}\Pi_{d_i,B_i})}{2} \\ &\leq \frac{1+f}{2}. \end{aligned} \tag{12}$$

The probability of event C_f is then given by taking the limit of the sum over N, which is bounded by taking the integral.

$$\begin{aligned} P(C_F) &\leq \frac{1}{S}\sum_0^\infty \left(1 - \frac{1}{S}\right)^N \left(\frac{1+f}{2}\right)^N \\ &\leq \frac{1}{S}\int_{N=0}^\infty \left(1 - \left(\frac{1-f}{2}\right)\right)^N dN \\ &= \frac{1}{S}\frac{-1}{\log\left(1 - \left(\frac{1-f}{2}\right)\right)} \\ &\leq \frac{2}{S(1-f)}. \end{aligned} \tag{13}$$

The last protocol was implemented recently using graph states [12].

B   Qudit Protocols

The qudit versions work in the same way, by simply replacing states and operators by their generalised high dimensional versions. For simplicity we consider prime dimension q (this is sufficient for allowing for all access structures [6]). Paulis and the computational basis are replaced by their qudit extensions, X, Z, $X|i\rangle = |i \oplus 1\rangle$ (where now $\oplus$ denotes sum modulo q) and $Z|i\rangle = \omega^i|i\rangle$, $\omega = e^{i2\pi/q}$ (analogously for all the possible sets of logical operators and basis states), and the EPR state by its qudit version

$$|\Phi\rangle_{dP} = \frac{1}{\sqrt{q}}\sum_{i=0}^{q-1} |i\rangle_d|i_L\rangle_P. \tag{14}$$

We similarly define the projection operator on d and subset of players $B \subset P$,

$$\Pi_{dB} = \sum_{t\in F_q^2} Z_d^{t^1}X_d^{t^2} \otimes Z_{L,B}^{t^1}X_{L,B}^{t^2}, \tag{15}$$

where $t = \{t^1, t^2\}$, $t^i \in F_q$. This again defines a space of maximally entangled states between the dealer and players B.

For simplicity we present a qudit protocol which includes all the measurements in this projection. This is not necessary for our results, indeed for the qubit case we had fewer and similar results follow using fewer measurements as in the qubit version - it is mostly a matter of taste if one chooses the full set or fewer (similar to the situation for qudit versions of QKD [26]). We adopt it here for its simpler presentation. It allows for analagous statement of Theorems 1, 2 following the same logic as for the qubit version.

Interactive Protocol (qudit)

1. Dealer d generates S qudit EPR states, $|\Phi\rangle_{dP}^{\otimes S}$, and sends the shares of each one to P.
2. After P received all their parts, d chooses $r \in [1, ...S]$ at random and sends r to P.
3. For qudit EPR pairs $i \neq r$, d chooses $t_i \in F_q^2$, and measures $Z_d^{t_i^1} X_d^{t_i^2}$, and denotes the result y_i, and sends t_i and y_i to P.
4. For qudit EPR pairs $i \neq r$, accessing set B measure $Z_{L,B}^{t_i^1} X_{L,B}^{t_i^2}$. Denoting result by y_i' if $y_i = y_i'$ ACCEPT, if $y_i \neq y_i'$ REJECT.
5. For $i = r$, d uses qudit EPR pair r to teleport the secret state onto the logical basis, denoting the qudit bell basis measurements x, and sends x to all P. Upon receiving x, B decodes.

Theorem 5. *Any state ρ_{dB} with fidelity $F = Tr(\Pi_{dB}\rho_{dB})$ to projector Π_{dB} accepts at step 4 of the qudit interactive protocol with probability $Pr = \dfrac{1 + F}{2}$.*

Theorem 6. *The interactive qudit protocol defined above is ϵ-secure, with $\epsilon = 1/S$.*

The non-interactive version follows similarly, as does the Theorem. The state $|\Psi^{t,y}\rangle_P$ denotes the eigenstate of the operator $Z_L^{t_i^1} X_L^{t_i^2}$ with eigenvalue ω^y.

Non-interactive Protocol (qudit)

1. d and P share random strings r, t, y, x via a classical secret sharing scheme over P (i.e. d knows the string, but it is shared via a classical secret sharing scheme with the relevant access structure over P so that only authorised sets can access it, and only when they collaborate to do so, and unauthorised sets get no information at all).
2. Going through round by round $i = 1...S$. If $q_i = 0$ the dealer proceeds to step 3, if $q_i = 1$ the dealer proceeds to step 4.
3. For $q_i = 0$
   (a) Dealer prepares and distributes state $|\Psi^{t,y}\rangle_P$.
   (b) After receiving the state from the dealer, authorised set B collaborate to find q_i (which is 0), t_i and y_i.
   (c) Authorised set B measures $Z_{L,B}^{t_i^1} X_{L,B}^{t_i^2}$. The result is denoted y_i'. If $y_i \neq y_i'$ REJECT. If $y_i = y_i'$ ACCEPT.

(d) If $i = S$, END, otherwise return to step 2.
4. For $q_i = 1$
   (a) d encodes and distrubutes the state $X_L^{x_0} Z_L^{x_1} |\psi_L\rangle_P$.
   (b) After recieving the state from the dealer, authorised set B collaborate to find q_i, which is 1.
   (c) B decodes.
   (d) If $i = S$, END, otherwise return to step 2

Theorem 7. *The non-interactive qudit protocol defined above is ϵ-secure, with $\epsilon = 1/S$.*

The aborting protocol follows similarly.

Generalizing Efficient Multiparty Computation

Bernardo M. David[1,*], Ryo Nishimaki[2], Samuel Ranellucci[1,*], and Alain Tapp[3]

[1] Department of Computer Science, Aarhus University, Denmark
{bernardo,samuel}@cs.au.dk
[2] Secure Platform Laboratories, NTT, Japan
nishimaki.ryo@lab.ntt.co.jp
[3] DIRO, Université de Montréal, Canada
tappa@iro.umontreal.ca

Abstract. We focus on generalizing constructions of Batch Single-Choice Cut-And-Choose Oblivious Transfer and Multi-sender k-out-of-n Oblivious Transfer, which are at the core of efficient secure computation constructions proposed by Lindell *et al.* and the IPS compiler. Our approach consists in showing that such primitives can be based on a much weaker and simpler primitive called Verifiable Oblivious Transfer (VOT) with low overhead. As an intermediate step we construct Generalized Oblivious Transfer from VOT. Finally, we show that Verifiable Oblivious Transfer can be obtained from a structure preserving oblivious transfer protocol (SPOT) through an efficient transformation that uses Groth-Sahai proofs and structure preserving commitments.

1 Introduction

Secure multiparty computation (MPC) allows mutually distrustful parties to compute functions on private data that they hold, without revealing their data to each other. Obtaining efficient multiparty computation is a highly sought after goal of cryptography since it can be employed in a multitude of practical applications, such as auctions, electronic voting and privacy preserving data analysis. Notably, it is known that secure two-party computation can be achieved from the garbled circuits technique first proposed by Yao [Yao86] and that general MPC can be obtained from a basic primitive called oblivious transfer (OT), which was introduced in [Rab81, EGL85]. The basic one-out-of-two oblivious transfer (OT_1^2) is a two-party primitive where a *sender* inputs two messages m_0, m_1 and a *receiver* inputs a bit c, referred to as the *choice bit*. The receiver learns m_c but not m_{1-c} and the sender learns nothing about the receiver's choice (*i.e.* c). This primitive was proven to be sufficient for achieving MPC in [Kil88, GMW87, CvdGT95].

* Bernardo David and Samuel Ranellucci were supported by European Research Council Starting Grant 279447. The authors acknowledge support from the Danish National Research Foundation and The National Science Foundation of China (under the grant 61061130540) for the Sino-Danish Center for the Theory of Interactive Computation, and also from the CFEM research centre (supported by the Danish Strategic Research Council) within which part of this work was performed.

© Springer International Publishing Switzerland 2015
A. Lehmann and S. Wolf (Eds.): ICITS 2015, LNCS 9063, pp. 15–32, 2015.
DOI: 10.1007/978-3-319-17470-9_2

Even though many approaches for constructing MPC exist, only recently methods that can be efficiently instantiated have been proposed. Among these methods, the IPS compiler [IPS08] stands out as an important construction, achieving MPC without honest majority in the OT-hybrid model. In this work, we will focus on the cut-and-choose OT based construction and the improvement of the IPS compiler introduced by Lindell et al. [LP11, LP12, LOP11, Lin13].

In the approaches for obtaining efficient MPC presented in [LP11, Lin13], the authors employ cut-and-choose OT, where the sender inputs s pairs of messages and the receiver can choose to learn both messages b_0, b_1 from $\frac{s}{2}$ input pairs, while he only learns one of the messages in the remaining pairs. A batch version of this primitive is then combined with Yao's protocol to achieve efficient MPC. In the improvement of the IPS compiler, the authors employ Multi-sender k-out-of-n OT, where j senders input a set of n messages out of which a receiver can choose to receive k messages. These complex primitives are usually constructed from specific number-theoretic and algebraic assumptions yielding little insight to their relationship with other generic and potentially simpler primitives.

In parallel to the efforts for obtaining efficient MPC, research has been devoted to obtaining constructions of basic primitives that can be efficiently combined between themselves in order to obtain more complex primitives and protocols. One of the main approach taken towards this goal has been called *structure preserving cryptography*, which aims at constructing primitives where basically all the public information (*e.g.* signatures, public keys, ciphertexts and commitments) are solely composed of bilinear group elements. This allows for the application of efficient Groth-Sahai non-interactive zero knowledge (NIZK) proof systems [GS08] (GS-Proofs) and efficient composition of primitives. Until now, the main results in this area have been structure preserving signature and commitment schemes [AFG+10, AGHO11] and encryption [CHK+11].

Our Contributions: The central goal of this paper is to present general constructions of the primitives used as the main building blocks in the frameworks of [LP11, LOP11, LP12, Lin13] in the universal composability model [Can01]. In contrast to previous works, we present *general* reductions from such complex primitives to simpler variants of OT without relying on specific number theoretic assumptions. We present three main results:

- **General Constructions of Multi-sender k-out-of-n OT (MSOT) and Batch Single Choice Cut-and-Choose OT (CACOT) from Generalized OT (GOT):** We show that MSOT and CACOT can be obtained GOT [IK97] combined with proper access structures. Differently from the original constructions of [LP11, LP12, LOP11, Lin13], our constructions are based on a simple generic primitive, not requiring Committed OT or specific computational assumptions. These constructions can be readily used to instantiate the MPC frameworks presented in [LP11, LP12, LOP11, Lin13].
- **Generalized Oblivious Transfer Based on Verifiable Oblivious Transfer:** Verifiable Oblivious Transfer (VOT) [CC00, JS07, KSV07] is a flavor of 1-out-of-2 OT where the sender can reveal one of his messages at

any point during the protocol execution allowing the receiver to verify that this message is indeed one of the original sender's inputs. We show that GOT can be obtained from VOT, generalizing even more the constructions described before. Our generic construction of GOT may be of independent interest.

– **Structure Preserving Oblivious Transfer (SPOT) and a *Generic Composable Constructions of Verifiable Oblivious Transfer*:** We introduce SPOT, which is basically a 1-out-of-2 OT compatible with GS-Proofs. We then build on this characteristic to provide a generic (non black-box) construction of VOT from any SPOT protocol combined with structure preserving extractable or equivocable commitments and Groth-Sahai NIZKs. Differently from the VOT protocols of [CC00, JS07, KSV07], our constructions are modular and independent of specific assumptions. Moreover, we provide a concrete round optimal SPOT protocol based on a framework by Peikert et al. [PVW08] and observe that the protocols in [CKWZ13] fit our definitions. This notion is also of independent interest in other scenarios besides general MPC.

1.1 Efficiency

Our constructions are as efficient as the underlying NIZK proof system, structure preserving commitment and SPOT. Hence, they can easily take advantage of more efficient constructions of these primitives. In Table 1, we present an estimate of the concrete complexity of our protocols when instantiated with GS-Proofs and commitments [GS08] and our structure preserving variant of the DDH based UC secure OT of [PVW08]. Our general constructions achieve essentially the same round complexity as the previous DDH based constructions of the same funtionalities. Our constructions incur higher communication and computational overheads, which is expected since we do not optimize our protocols for an specific number theoretic assumptions as in previous works. We remark that independently of their concrete efficiency, our protocols are the first to realize MSOT and CACOT from generic primitives without relying on specific number theoretic assumptions.

2 Preliminaries

Notations and Conventions. For any $n \in \mathbb{N} \setminus \{0\}$, let $[n]$ be the set $\{1, \ldots, n\}$. When D is a random variable or distribution, $y \xleftarrow{R} D$ denotes that y is randomly selected from D according to its distribution. If S is a set, then $x \xleftarrow{U} S$ denotes that x is uniformly selected from S. $y := z$ denotes that y is set, defined or substituted by z. When b is a fixed value, $A(x) \rightarrow b$ (e.g., $A(x) \rightarrow 1$) denotes the event that machine (or algorithm) A outputs b on input x. We say that a function $f : \mathbb{N} \rightarrow \mathbb{R}$ is negligible in $\lambda \in \mathbb{N}$ if for every constant $c \in \mathbb{N}$ there exists $k_c \in \mathbb{N}$ such that $f(\lambda) < \lambda^{-c}$ for any $\lambda > k_c$. Hereafter, we use $f < \mathsf{negl}(\lambda)$ to mean that f is negligible in λ. We write $\mathcal{X} \stackrel{c}{\approx} \mathcal{Y}$ to denote that $\mathcal{X}$ and $\mathcal{Y}$ are computationally indistinguishable.

Table 1. Efficiency of our protocols compared to previous constructions based on DDH. The column VOTs shows the number of VOTs needed in our general constructions, "-" marks the previous protocols that do not enjoy general constructions. Exp. stands for exponentiations and Pair. stands for bilinear pairings. n and s express the number of inputs according to each protocol (explained in the respective sections), p is the number of senders in MSOT and k is the number of messages transferred to the receiver. Communication complexity is stated in terms of number of group elements exchanged.

Protocol		VOTs	Rounds	Computational Complexity	Communication Complexity
GOT	Sec. 4	n	6	$23n$ Exp. $+28$ Pair.	$24n + k + 4$
CACOT	Sec. 5	$2ns$	6	$46ns$ Exp. $+56ns$ Pair.	$48.5ns$ $+n+4$
	[LP11]	-	6	$11.5ns + 19n$ $+9s + 5$ Exp.	$5ns + 11n$ $+5s + 5$
Modified CACOT	Sec. 6	$4ns + s$	6	$92ns + 23s$ Exp. $112ns + 28s$ Pair.	$16ns + 16s$ $+k+4$
	[Lin13]	-	21	$10.5ns + 20.5ns$ $+n + 26$ Exp.	$5ns + n$ $+11s + 15$
MSOT	Sec. 7	pn	8	$23pn$ Exp. $+28pn$ Pair.	$24pn + 4p + k$ $p!/(p-3)! + 4$
	[LOP11]	-	7	$4n + 11(p-1)n$ $+k(p-1)$ Exp.	$12pn + 1$

Bilinear Groups. Let $\mathcal{G}$ be a bilinear group generator that takes security parameter 1^λ as input and outputs a description of bilinear groups $\Lambda := (p, \mathbb{G}, \mathbb{H}, \mathbb{G}_T, e, g, \hat{g})$ where $\mathbb{G}$, $\mathbb{H}$ and $\mathbb{G}_T$ are groups of prime order p, g and $\hat{g}$ are generators in $\mathbb{G}$ and $\mathbb{H}$, respectively, e is an efficient and non-degenerate map $e : \mathbb{G} \times \mathbb{H} \to \mathbb{G}_T$. If $\mathbb{G} = \mathbb{H}$, then we call it the symmetric setting. If $\mathbb{G} \neq \mathbb{H}$ and there is no efficient mapping between the groups, then we call it the asymmetric setting.

Symmetric External Decisional Diffie-Hellman Assumption. Intuitively, SXDH is the assumption that the DDH assumption holds for both groups $\mathbb{G}$ and $\mathbb{H}$ in a bilinear group Λ. Let $\mathcal{G}^{\mathsf{DDH1}}(1^\lambda)$ be an algorithm that on input security parameter λ, generates parameters $\Lambda := (p, \mathbb{G}, \mathbb{H}, \mathbb{G}_T, e, g, \hat{g}) \xleftarrow{\text{R}} \mathcal{G}(1^\lambda)$ (where $\mathcal{G}$ is the bilinear group generator introduced in the previous paragraph.), chooses exponents $x, y, z \xleftarrow{\text{U}} \mathbb{Z}_p$, and outputs $\boldsymbol{I} := (\Lambda, g^x, g^y)$ and (x, y, z). When an adversary is given $\boldsymbol{I} \xleftarrow{\text{R}} \mathcal{G}^{\mathsf{DDH1}}(1^\lambda)$ and $T \in \mathbb{G}$, it attempts to distinguish whether $T = g^{xy}$ or $T = g^z$. This is called the DDH1 problem. The advantage $\mathsf{Adv}_{\mathcal{A}}^{\mathsf{DDH1}}(\lambda)$ is defined as follows:

$$\mathsf{Adv}_{\mathcal{A}}^{\mathsf{DDH1}}(\lambda) := \left| \Pr\left[\mathcal{A}(\boldsymbol{I}, g^{xy}) \to 1 \,\middle|\, (\boldsymbol{I}, x, y, z) \xleftarrow{\text{R}} \mathcal{G}^{\mathsf{DDH1}}(1^\lambda); \right] \right.$$
$$\left. - \Pr\left[\mathcal{A}(\boldsymbol{I}, g^z) \to 1 \,\middle|\, (\boldsymbol{I}, x, y, z) \xleftarrow{\text{R}} \mathcal{G}^{\mathsf{DDH1}}(1^\lambda); \right] \right|$$

Definition 1 (DDH1 Assumption). *We say that the DDH1 assumption holds if for all PPT (Probabilistic Polynomial Time) adversaries $\mathcal{A}$,* $\mathsf{Adv}_{\mathcal{A}}^{\mathsf{DDH1}}(\lambda) < \mathsf{negl}(\lambda)$.

The DDH2 assumption is similarly defined in terms of group $\mathbb{H}$. If both DDH1 and DDH2 assumptions hold simultaneously, then we say that the symmetric external Diffie-Hellman (SXDH) assumption holds.

Universal Composability. The Universal Composability framework was introduced by Canetti in [Can01] to analyse the security of cryptographic protocols and primitives under arbitrary composition. In this framework, protocol security is analysed by comparing an ideal world execution and a real world execution under the supervision of an *environment* $\mathcal{Z}$, which is represented by a *PPT* machine and has access to all communication between individual parties. In the ideal world execution, dummy parties (possibly controlled by a *PPT simulator*) interact directly with the ideal functionality $\mathcal{F}$, which works as a fully secure third party that computes the desired function or primitive. In the real world execution, several *PPT* parties (possibly corrupted by a real world adversary $\mathcal{A}$) interact with each other by means of a protocol π that realizes the ideal functionality. The real world execution is represented by the ensemble $\mathrm{EXEC}_{\pi,\mathcal{A},\mathcal{Z}}$, while the ideal execution is represented by the $\mathrm{IDEAL}_{\mathcal{F},\mathcal{S},\mathcal{Z}}$. The rationale behind this framework lies in showing that the environment $\mathcal{Z}$ is not able to efficiently distinguish between $\mathrm{EXEC}_{\pi,\mathcal{A},\mathcal{Z}}$ and $\mathrm{IDEAL}_{\mathcal{F},\mathcal{S},\mathcal{Z}}$, thus implying that the real world protocol is as secure as the ideal functionality. It is known that a setup assumption is needed for UC realizing oblivious transfer as well as most "interesting" ideal functionalities [CF01]. In this work we consider security against static adversaries, *i.e.* the adversary can only corrupt parties before the protocol execution starts. We consider malicious adversaries that may deviate from the protocol in any arbitrary way. See [Can01] for further details.

Definition 2. *A protocol π is said to UC-realize an ideal functionality $\mathcal{F}$ if, for every adversary $\mathcal{A}$, there exists a simulator $\mathcal{S}$ such that, for every environment $\mathcal{Z}$, the following holds:*

$$\mathrm{EXEC}_{\pi,\mathcal{A},\mathcal{Z}} \stackrel{c}{\approx} \mathrm{IDEAL}_{\mathcal{F},\mathcal{S},\mathcal{Z}}$$

We present oblivious transfer ($\mathcal{F}_{OT}$), commitment ($\mathcal{F}_{COM}$), and common reference string ($\mathcal{F}_{CRS}^{\mathcal{D}}$) ideal functionalities in the full version of this paper.

3   Generic Construction of Verifiable OT from Structure Preserving OT

In this section, we introduce Structure Preserving Oblivious Transfer (SPOT) and use it to construct verifiable oblivious transfer (VOT).

Structure Preserving Oblivious Transfer

Basically we require all the SPOT protocol messages (*i.e.* the protocol transcript) and inputs to be composed solely of group elements and the transcript to be generated from the inputs by pairing product equations or multi exponentiation equations, which allows us to apply GS proofs to prove relations between the parties' inputs and the protocol transcript. Further on, our general transformation will rely on GS proofs to show that a given sender input is associated with a specific protocol transcript.

Definition 3 (Structure Preserving Oblivious Transfer). *A structure preserving oblivious transfer protocol taking inputs m_0, m_1 from the sender and c from the receiver defined over a bilinear group $\Lambda := (p, \mathbb{G}, \mathbb{H}, \mathbb{G}_T, e, g, \hat{g})$ must have the following properties:*

1. *Each of the sender's input messages m_0, m_1 consists of elements of $\mathbb{G}$ or $\mathbb{H}$.*
2. *All the messages exchanged between* **S** *and* **R** *(i.e. the protocol transcript) consist of elements of $\mathbb{G}$ and $\mathbb{H}$.*
3. *The relation between the protocol inputs m_0, m_1, c and a given protocol transcript is expressed by a set of pairing product equations or multi exponentiation equations.*

Notice that our general transformations can be applied to any OT protocol in a bit by bit approach, by mapping the binary representation of each element in a given protocol to specific group elements representing 0 and 1 and applying GS proofs individually to each of those elements. However, this trivial approach is extremely inefficient. The number of GS proofs and group elements exchanged between parties would grow polynomially. The first OT protocol to fit this definition was proposed in [GH08], but it relies simultaneously on the SXDH, the DLIN and the q-hidden LSRW assumptions. A recent result by Choi *et. al.* [CKWZ13] also introduced OT protocols based on DLIN and SXDH that match out definition of SPOT. However, these protocols already require a GS proof themselves, introducing extra overhead in applications that combine SPOT with GS proofs.

Obtaining SPOT from Dual-Mode Cryptosystems

The starting point for constructing SPOT is the general framework for universally composable oblivious transfer protocols proposed by Peikert *et al.* [PVW08] (hanceforth called PVW). The PVW framework provides a black-box construction of UC secure OT from dual-mode cryptosystems, which were initially instantiated under the DDH, QR and LWE assumptions. Essentially, this framework relies on an information theoretical reduction from UC secure OT to dual-mode cryptosystems in the CRS model, such that the resulting OT protocol inherits the characteristics of the underlying dual-mode cryptosystem. In order to obtain an OT protocol compatible with GS-proofs, we convert the DDH based dual-mode cryptosystem construction of [PVW08] into a scheme secure under the SXDH assumption (which can also be used to instantiate GS proofs). This scheme is then plugged in the PVW framework to obtain a UC secure OT protocol. Note that, in the resulting protocol, the CRS, all protocol messages and inputs are composed solely by group elements. Moreover, all the protocol messages are generated by pairing product equations. Therefore, we obtain a SPOT protocol whose security follows from the PVW framework. Our SXDH dual-mode cryptosystem is constructed as follows:

- SetupMessy(1^λ) $\Lambda := (p, \mathbb{G}, \mathbb{H}, \mathbb{G}_T, e, g, \hat{g}) \overset{R}{\leftarrow} \mathcal{G}(1^\lambda)$, $g_0, g_1 \overset{U}{\leftarrow} \mathbb{G}$, $x_0, x_1 \overset{U}{\leftarrow} \mathbb{Z}_p$ where $x_0 \neq x_1$. Let $h_b := g_b^{x_b}$ for $b \in \{0,1\}$, crs $:= (g_0, h_0, g_1, h_1)$, and $t := (x_0, x_1)$. It outputs (crs, t).

- SetupDec(1^λ) $\Lambda := (p, \mathbb{G}, \mathbb{H}, \mathbb{G}_T, e, g, \hat{g}) \overset{R}{\leftarrow} \mathcal{G}(1^\lambda)$, $g_0 \overset{U}{\leftarrow} \mathbb{G}$, $y \overset{U}{\leftarrow} \mathbb{Z}_p^*$, $g_1 := g_0^y$, $x \overset{U}{\leftarrow} \mathbb{Z}_p$, $h_b := g_b^x$ for $b \in \{0,1\}$, crs $:= (g_0, h_0, g_1, h_1)$, and $t := y$. It outputs (crs, t).

- Gen(σ) $r \overset{U}{\leftarrow} \mathbb{Z}_p$, $g := g_\sigma^r$, $h := h_\sigma^r$, $pk := (g, h) \in \mathbb{G}^2$, $sk := r$. It outputs (pk, sk).

- Enc(pk, b, m) For $pk = (g, h)$ and message $m \in \mathbb{G}$, reads (g_b, h_b) from crs $= (g_0, h_0, g_1, h_1)$, chooses $s, t \overset{U}{\leftarrow} \mathbb{Z}_p$, and computes $u = g_b^s h_b^t$, $v = g^s h^t$. It outputs ciphertext $(u, v \cdot m) \in \mathbb{G}^2$.

- Dec(sk, c) $c = (c_0, c_1)$, It outputs c_1 / c_0^{sk}.

- FindMessy(t, pk) For input $t = (x_0, x_1)$ where $x_0 \neq x_1$, $pk = (g, h)$, if $h \neq g^{x_0}$, then it outputs $b = 0$ as a messy branch. Otherwise, we have $h = g^{x_0} \neq g^{x_1}$, so it outputs $b = 1$ as a messy branch.

- TrapGen(t) For input $t = y$, it chooses $r \overset{U}{\leftarrow} \mathbb{Z}_p$, computes $pk := (g_0^r, h_0^r)$ and outputs $(pk, sk := r, sk_1 := r/y)$.

Theorem 1. *The cryptosystem described above is a Dual-Mode Cryptosystem according to the definition of [PVW08] under the SXDH Assumption.*

The proof of this theorem and details of the PVW framework can be found in the full version of this paper, where we also describe how to use GS-proofs to prove relations between protocol inputs and transcripts.

Obtaining VOT

Verifiable oblivious transfer is basically a 1-out-of-2 oblivious transfer where the sender may choose to open one of its input messages m_b where $b \in \{0,1\}$ at any time, in such a way that the receiver is able to verify that this message had indeed been provided as input. This notion is formalized by the following ideal functionality:

Functionality $\mathcal{F}_{VOT}$

$\mathcal{F}_{VOT}$ interacts with a sender **S** a receiver **R** and an adversary $\mathcal{S}$.

- Upon receiving (Send, $sid, ssid, x_0, x_1$) from the **S**, if the pair $sid, ssid$ has not been used, store $(sid, ssid, x_0, x_1)$ and send (Receipt, $sid, ssid$) to **S,R** and $\mathcal{S}$.
- Upon receiving (Transfer, $sid, ssid, c$) from **R**, check if a (Transfer, sid, $ssid$) message has already been sent, if not, send (transferred, $sid, ssid$, x_c) to the receiver and (transferred, $sid, ssid,$) to $\mathcal{S}$, otherwise ignore the message.
- Upon receiving (Open, $sid, ssid, b$) from the sender, send (reveal, sid, $ssid, b, x_b$) to the receiver.

We will construct a general protocol π_{VOT} that realizes $\mathcal{F}_{VOT}$ from any universally composable SPOT protocol π_{SPOT} by combining it with a structure preserving commitment π_{COM} (such as the schemes in [GS08][AFG+10]) and Groth-Sahai NIZK proofs. An interesting property of this generic protocol is that even though it was designed for an underlying structure preserving protocol that realizes the 1-out-of-2 OT functionality $\mathcal{F}_{OT}$, it can be applied multiple times to the individual transfers of an adaptive OT protocol in order to obtain verifiable adaptive OT. In this case, the same CRS can be reused for all the individual transfers. Notice that this is the first generic construction of universally composable VOT.

We assume that both parties are running the underlying universally composable structure preserving oblivious transfer protocol $SPOT$ and describe the extra steps needed to obtain VOT. In the context of π_{COM}, we denote commitment to a message m by $\mathsf{Com}(m)$ and the opening of such a commitment by $\mathsf{Open}(m)$.

Protocol π_{VOT}: **S** inputs two messages m_0, m_1 and **R** inputs a choice bit c.

- **Setup:** A common reference string is generated containing the following information:
  - The description of a bilinear group $\Lambda := (p, \mathbb{G}, \mathbb{H}, \mathbb{G}_T, e, g, \hat{g})$.
  - The public parameters for an instance of a Groth-Sahai non-interactive zero knowledge proof system.
  - The CRS for the underlying structure preserving commitment scheme π_{COM}.
  - The CRS for the underlying UC structure preserving OT π_{SPOT}.
- **Commitment Phase:** Before starting π_{SPOT}, **S** commits to m_0 and m_1 by sending $(sid, ssid, \mathsf{Com}(m_0), \mathsf{Com}(m_1))$ to **R**, where $m_0, m_1 \in \{0, 1\}^n$ (Notice that it is possible to efficiently map the messages into corresponding group elements that will serve as inputs to π_{SPOT} [GH08]).

- π_{SPOT} **protocol Execution**: **S** and **R** run π_{SPOT} storing all the messages exchanged during the protocol execution up to the end of π_{SPOT} with **S**'s input (m_0, m_1) and **R**'s input c or until **S** decides to reveal one of its messages.
- **Reveal Phase:** If **S** decides to reveal one of its messages m_b where $b \in \{0, 1\}$ at any point of the protocol execution it sends a decommitment to m_b and a GS-proof ψ that the messages exchanged up to that point of the execution contain a valid transfer of message m_b, sending $(sid, ssid, b, \text{Open}(\mathsf{m_b}), \psi)$ to **R**.
- **Verification Phase:** After receiving the decommitment and the GS-proof, **R** verifies ψ and the decommitment validity. If both are valid, it accepts the revealed bit, otherwise it detects that **S** is cheating. If the protocol π_{SPOT} did not reach its end yet, **S** and **R** continue by executing the next steps, otherwise they halt.

Theorem 2. *For every universally composable structure preserving oblivious transfer protocol π_{SPOT} and every universally composable structure preserving commitment scheme π_{Com}, Protocol π_{VOT} securely realizes the functionality F_{VOT} in the $\mathcal{F}_{CRS}$ hybrid model under the assumption that Groth-Sahai proof systems are Zero Knowledge Proofs of Knowledge.*

Before proceeding to the security proof we show that the protocol works correctly. First of all, notice that since π_{SPOT} is a structure preserving oblivious transfer protocol it is possible to prove statements about the sender's input messages and the protocol transcript using Groth-Sahai NIZK proof systems. Correctness of Protocol π_{VOT} in the case that no Reveal phase happens follows from the correctness of protocol π_{SPOT}. The correctness of the Reveal phase follows from the commitment scheme's security and the GS-proof completeness and soundness. When **S** opens the commitment, **R** is able to check whether the revealed message is indeed one of the messages that **S** used as input in the beginning of the protocol and by verifying the GS-proof, **R** is able to check that the input message m_b is contained in the messages exchanged by both parties meaning that this message is indeed used in the protocol execution. The full proof is presented in the full version of this paper.

4   Generalized Oblivious Transfer

Generalized Oblivious Transfer is an interesting application of Verifiable Oblivious Transfer. An interesting way of describing an OT is by describing the groups of messages that the receiver can get as sets in a collection. In the case of a simple OT, he can learn the values indexed by one of the sets in the collection $\{\{1\}, \{2\}\}$. The k-out-of-n OT is an OT with a collection that contains all the sets of index of k or less elements. This mindset allows us to present a very general form of oblivious transfer. There is an important link between generalized oblivious transfer and general access structures. The notation $\mathcal{F}_{GOT(\mathcal{I})}$ denotes the instance of generalized oblivious transfer associated with the enclosed[1] collection $\mathcal{I}$.

Definition 4. *We define the following basic facts about enclosed collections:*

- Let $I = \{1, 2, ..., n\}$ be a set of indices. A collection $\mathcal{A} \subseteq \mathcal{P}(I)$ is **monotone** if the fact that $\mathcal{B} \in \mathcal{A}$ and $\mathcal{B} \subseteq \mathcal{C}$ implies that $\mathcal{C} \in \mathcal{A}$.
- An **access structure** is a monotone collection $\mathcal{A}$ of non-empty sets of I. A set S is **authorized** if $S \in \mathcal{A}$ and a set S' is **minimal** if there exists no strict subset S'' of S' such that $S'' \in \mathcal{A}$.
- The **complement** of a collection $\mathcal{C}$ is defined as $\mathcal{C}^* = \{B \subseteq I \mid \exists\, C \in \mathcal{C},\ B = I - C\}$.
- We define **Closure**$(\mathcal{C}) = \{C \subseteq C' \mid C' \in \mathcal{C}\}$.
- A collection $\mathcal{C}$ is **enclosed** if $\mathcal{C} = \mathbf{Closure}(\mathcal{C})$.
- An element $C \in \mathcal{C}$ is **maximal** if there exists no $C' \in \mathcal{C}$ such that $C \subseteq C'$ and $C \neq C'$.

Theorem 3. *For every enclosed collection C, there exists a unique access structure $\mathcal{A}$ such that $C^* = \mathcal{A}$*

See [SSR08] for a full proof.

Definition 5. *A **secret sharing scheme** is a triplet of randomized algorithms (Share, Reconstruct, Check) over a message space $\mathcal{M}$ with an access structure $\mathcal{A}$. $Share_{\mathcal{A}}(s)$ always output shares $(s_1, \ldots, s_n)$ such that:*
(1) for all $A \in \mathcal{A}$, $Reconstruct_{\mathcal{A}}(\{(i, s_i) \mid i \in A\}) = s$,
(2) for any $A' \notin \mathcal{A}$, $\{(i, s_i) \mid i \in A'\}$ gives no information about s.
$Check_{\mathcal{A}}(s_1, \ldots, s_n) = 1$ if and only if for all $A \in \mathcal{A}$, $Reconstruct_{\mathcal{A}}(\{(i, s_i) \mid i \in A\}) = s$.

Definition 6. *We say that shares $(s_1, \ldots, s_n)$ are **consistent** if $Check_{\mathcal{A}}(s_1, \ldots, s_n) = 1$.*

Functionality $\mathcal{F}_{GOT}(\mathcal{I})$

$\mathcal{F}_{GOT}(\mathcal{I})$ interacts with a sender **S**, a receiver **R** and an adversary $\mathcal{S}$ and is parametrized by an enclosed collection $\mathcal{I}$.

- Upon receiving (Send, $sid, ssid, m_1, \ldots, m_n$) from the **S**, if the pair $sid, ssid$ has not already been used, store $(sid, ssid, m_1, \ldots, m_n)$ and send (receipt, $sid, ssid$) to **S** and **R**.
- Upon receiving (Choice, $sid, ssid, I$) where I is a set of indices, if no (Choice, $sid, ssid$) message was previously sent and I is in $\mathcal{I}$, then for each $i \in I$, send (Reveal, $sid, ssid, i, m_i$) to **R** and (Reveal, $sid, ssid$) to the adversary $\mathcal{S}$.

---

[1] See definition 1.

4.1   Protocol

In this section, we will present a protocol that implements $\mathcal{F}_{GOT}$ in the $\mathcal{F}_{VOT}$, $\mathcal{F}_{COM}$ − *hybrid* model with the aid of secret sharing. The protocol is inspired by [SSR08] but is secure against a stronger adversary. The fact that every enclosed collection is the complement of an access structure will be key to this construction. The protocol requires n instances of $\mathcal{F}_{VOT}$. The selection of the secret sharing scheme is dictated by the security parameter. Namely, for security parameter s, we require that the message space of the secret sharing scheme must have cardinality greater or equal to 2^s. The size of the elements transferred in the $\mathcal{F}_{VOT}$ is the maximum between the length of the messages and the size of the shares which depends on the underlying access structure. Let $\mathcal{I}$ be the enclosed collection that defines the subsets of messages that are accessible to the receiver.

Protocol: $\pi_{GOT(\mathcal{I})}$ (The sender has input $(m_1, \ldots, m_n)$ and the receiver has input $I \in \mathcal{I}$.)

1. The sender selects $k_1, ..., k_n \xleftarrow{\cup} \{0,1\}^l$ (one-time pads)
2. Let $\mathcal{A} = \mathcal{I}^*$, the sender selects $s \xleftarrow{\cup} \mathcal{M}$ and $(s_1, ..., s_n) = Share_{\mathcal{A}}(s)$.
3. The sender selects a set of n unused ssids, denote these ids as $(ssid_1, \ldots, ssid_n)$ and sends (Ids, $sid, ssid, ssid_1, \ldots, ssid_n)$ to the receiver. For each $i \in [n]$, the sender sends (send, $k_i, s_i, sid, ssid_i$) to $\mathcal{F}_{VOT}$.
4. The receiver awaits (Ids, $sid, ssid, ssid_1, \ldots, ssid_n)$ from the sender. He aborts if any of the ssid are not unused. Let $I \in \mathcal{I}$ be the set of messages that the receiver wishes to receive. He sets $b_i = 0$ when $i \in I$ otherwise he sets $b_i = 1$. For each $i \in [n]$, the receiver sends (Transfer, $b_i, sid, ssid_i$) to $\mathcal{F}_{VOT}$ and records the result.
5. The receiver executes the recover algorithm with the shares he received and obtains S. If the reconstruction failed, he chooses an arbitrary value for S instead. The receiver sends (commit, $sid, ssid, S$) to $\mathcal{F}_{COM}$.
6. The sender awaits (committed, $sid, ssid$) from $\mathcal{F}_{COM}$. Then, for each $i \in [n]$, the sender sends (open, $1, sid, ssid_i$) to $\mathcal{F}_{VOT}$.
7. The receiver awaits for each $i \in [n]$, the message (reveal, $1, s_i, sid, ssid_i$) from $\mathcal{F}_{VOT}$. The receiver aborts if Check$_{\mathcal{A}}(s_1, ..., s_n) \neq 1$.
8. The receiver sends (open, $sid, ssid$) to $\mathcal{F}_{COM}$. The sender on receipt of (reveal, $sid, ssid, S$) verifies that $S = s$ and if not, he aborts the protocol.
9. The sender sends $z_i = m_i \oplus k_i$ to the receiver. ($\{m_i \mid i \in [n]\}$ is the set of messages)
10. The receiver for each $i \in I$, outputs (i, m_i) where $m_i = z_i \oplus k_i$.

Theorem 4. π_{GOT} *securely realizes* $\mathcal{F}_{GOT}$ *in the* $\mathcal{F}_{VOT}$, $\mathcal{F}_{COM}$ *hybrid model.*

The proof of this theorem is presented in the full version of this paper.

4.2   Insecurity of Previously Published GOT Protocols

The GOT protocol presented in this article improves on the one from [SSR08] and [Tas11] significantly. We believe that their protocols are secure against semi-honest adversaries but unfortunately, a malicious sender can easily break the privacy of both schemes.

The protocol of [SSR08] works as follows: first the dealer generates shares for a randomly chosen secret, then the sender and receiver execute n instances of oblivious transfer where the receiver can learn either a share or a key chosen uniformly at random. The receiver then reconstructs the secret and sends it back to the sender. On receipt of a value, the sender checks that it is indeed the secret that he generated shares for. The sender can thus use the keys to encrypt messages and he is guaranteed that the receiver cannot learn a set of messages that is not within the enclosed collection.

However, it is possible for a malicious sender to determine if a specific message was chosen by the receiver. We will now proceed to demonstrate an attack on [SSR08]. An adversary wishes to learn if a receiver learns the message m_c. He selects a secret s and executes the share algorithm resulting in shares $\{s_i\}$. He replaces s_c by s'_c and executes the GOT protocol with those shares. As a result, if the receiver chooses to learn m_c, he will reconstruct s correctly otherwise he will reconstruct an $s' \neq s$. The attack breaks the privacy of the receiver. The same idea can be applied to attack the protocol from [Tas11].

5   Batch Single-Choice Cut-and-Choose OT

The Batch Single-Choice Cut-and-Choose OT ($\mathcal{F}_{CACOT}$) is an an instantiation of $\mathcal{F}_{GOT}$ for a specific enclosed collection. The procedure was introduced in [LP11] and it was used to implement constant round secure function evaluation.

Definition 7 makes formal the enclose collection used $\mathcal{F}_{CACOT}$. Informally, the data that will be transferred has a three dimensional structure; a table of pairs. Each row is composed of s pairs and each column is composed of n pairs. The receiver can learn two categories of element of the table. First he can learn exactly all the pairs for a subset of half the columns. In addition to that, independently for each line, he can either learn the first element of every pair or the second element of every pair.

Definition 7. *Let $T_{i,j,k}$, where $i \in [n], j \in [s]$ and $k \in \{0,1\}$. Let $A(J,\sigma)$ where $J \subseteq [s], \sigma \in \{0,1\}^n$ be the following subset of T: for all i and for all j if $j \in J$ both $T_{i,j,0}$ and $T_{i,j,1}$ are in the set otherwise only $T_{i,j,\sigma(i)}$ belongs to the set. Let $\mathcal{C}' = \bigcup_{|J|=s/2,\sigma} A(J,\sigma)$ then we define $\mathcal{C} = \mathbf{Closure}(\mathcal{C}')$. Furthermore any maximal element of $\mathcal{C}$ can be uniquely specified by some J and σ as defined previously.*

We can now formally define the Batch Single-Choice Cut-and-Choose OT.

Definition 8. $\mathcal{F}_{CACOT} = \mathcal{F}_{GOT(\mathcal{C})}.$

Theorem 5. *Any $\mathcal{F}_{CACOT}$ can be implemented with $2ns$ calls to $\mathcal{F}_{VOT}$ where the elements transferred by $\mathcal{F}_{VOT}$ are the maximum between twice the size of the secret and the value of the messages transferred.*

The proof of this theorem is presented in the full version of this paper.

6   Modified Cut-and-Choose from [Lin13]

The Cut-and-Choose OT from [Lin13] is very similar to the one in [LP11] but there are two important differences. First, the set of indices in J is no longer size restricted (instead of size $s/2$). In addition, for each $j \notin J$, the receiver receives a special string v_j which will allow the receiver to prove that $j \notin J$. Although, we could still use the protocol for generalized oblivious transfer defined above, the complement access structure is very complicated. Instead, we will present a hybrid of the protocols from [Tas11] and [SSR08] to realize this functionality.

The protocol follow the same basic structure as the previous protocol: (1) sharing of a secret, (2) verifiable oblivious transfer, (3) commitment, (4) proof of share validity and finally (5) the message encryption and transmission. Note that the input selection for each row i is still denoted as σ_i.

Construction

Essentially, by reconstructing the secret which has been shared with the secret sharing scheme below, the prover will be able to prove two statements. First, it will show that, for each column, the receiver either didn't learn the verification string or one element from each pair. Second, it demonstrates that for each row, the receiver either learned the first element of all pairs, or the second element of all pairs. The first statement which can be thought of as a proof of ignorance reflects the approach of [SSR08], while the second one, which can be thought as a proof of knowledge, reflects the approach of [Tas11]. The protocol that follows is thus a hybrid of [Tas11] and [SSR08]. Since the protocol is very similar to the GOT protocol, we will only describe how shares are constructed and what is transferred by the verifiable oblivious transfer.

Sharing

This part describes how a sender will generate shares of a secret. The reconstruct procedure of this secret sharing naturally follows from its description. This secret will then be used as in the previous protocols to ensure that the receiver does not learn keys for a set of indices which is not within the enclosed collection. The sharing will first split the secret into two shares, sc and sr. The receiver will be able to extract sc only if for each column, he either did not learn the verification string, or he did not learn one element from each pair. The purpose of sr is to ensure that for each row, for all pairs within that row he learned the first element, or he learned for all pairs the second element. The notation k-n is used as shorthand for $\{S \subset \{1, \ldots, n\} \mid |S| \leq k\}$. In particular, the notation Share$_{k\text{-}n}$ denotes the sharing of a secret using a k-out-of-n secret sharing.

$$(\mathrm{sc}, \mathrm{sr}) = \mathrm{share}_{2\text{-}2}(s)$$
$$(\mathrm{sr}_1, \ldots, \mathrm{sr}_n) = share_{n\text{-}n}(\mathrm{sr})$$
$$(\mathrm{sr}_{i10}, \ldots, \mathrm{sr}_{in0}) = \mathrm{share}_{s\text{-}s}(\mathrm{sr}_i)$$
$$(\mathrm{sr}_{i11}, \ldots, \mathrm{sr}_{in1}) = \mathrm{share}_{s\text{-}s}(\mathrm{sr}_i)$$
$$(\mathrm{sc}_1, \ldots, \mathrm{sc}_s) = \mathrm{share}_{s\text{-}s}(\mathrm{sc})$$
$$(\mathrm{sc}_{1j}, \ldots, \mathrm{sc}_{nj}) = \mathrm{share}_{n\text{-}n}(\mathrm{sc}_j)$$
$$(\mathrm{sc}_{ij0}^0, \mathrm{sc}_{ij0}^1) = \mathrm{share}_{2\text{-}2}(\mathrm{sc}_{ij})$$
$$(\mathrm{sc}_{ij1}^0, \mathrm{sc}_{ij1}^1) = \mathrm{share}_{2\text{-}2}(\mathrm{sc}_{ij})$$

Sender's Input to VOT

This part describes which messages will be sent by the sender to $\mathcal{F}_{VOT}$. We will use $\mathrm{vid}_j, \mathrm{kid}_{i,j,k}, \mathrm{srid}_{i,j,k}$ indexed by variable i, j, k to denote distinct ssids.

$$(\mathsf{Send}, \mathrm{sid}, \mathrm{vid}_j, v_j, \mathrm{sc}_j)$$
$$(\mathsf{Send}, \mathrm{sid}, \mathrm{kid}_{i,j,k}, k_{ijk}, \mathrm{sc}_{ijk}^0)$$
$$(\mathsf{Send}, \mathrm{sid}, \mathrm{srid}_{i,j,k}, \mathrm{sr}_{ijk}, \mathrm{sc}_{ijk}^1)$$

Receiver's Input to VOT

These are the messages that the receiver will send to $\mathcal{F}_{VOT}$. We also add next to them a description of the values learned by the receiver. Note that these values allow the sender to reconstruct both sc and sr as well as get the keys for a set of indices within the enclosed collection.

For each $j \in J$, the receiver sends $(\mathsf{Transfer}, \mathrm{sid}, \mathrm{vid}_j, 1)$ to $\mathcal{F}_{VOT}$, he learns $\{\mathrm{sc}_j \mid j \in J\}$.

For each $j \notin J$, the receiver sends $(\mathsf{Transfer}, \mathrm{sid}, \mathrm{vid}_j, 0)$ to $\mathcal{F}_{VOT}$, he learns $\{v_j \mid j \notin J\}$.

For each $j \in J, i \in [n], k \in \{0,1\}$, the receiver sends to $\mathcal{F}_{VOT}$

    $(\mathsf{Transfer}, \mathrm{sid}, \mathrm{kid}_{i,j,k}, 0)$, he learns $\{(k_{ijk}) \mid j \in J, i \in [n], k \in \{0,1\}\}$.

    $(\mathsf{Transfer}, \mathrm{sid}, \mathrm{srid}_{i,j,k}, 0)$, he learns $\{(\mathrm{sr}_{ijk}) \mid j \in J, i \in [n], k \in \{0,1\}\}$.

For each $j \notin J, i \in [n]$, the receiver sends to $\mathcal{F}_{VOT}$

    $(\mathsf{Transfer}, \mathrm{sid}, \mathrm{kid}_{i,j,\sigma_i}, 0)$, he learns $\{(k_{ij\sigma_i}) \mid j \notin J, i \in [n]\}$.

    $(\mathsf{Transfer}, \mathrm{sid}, \mathrm{srid}_{i,j,\sigma_i}, 0)$, he learns $\{(\mathrm{sr}_{ij\sigma_i}) \mid j \notin J, i \in [n]\}$.

    $(\mathsf{Transfer}, \mathrm{sid}, \mathrm{kid}_{i,j,1-\sigma_i}, 1)$, he learns $\{\mathrm{sc}_{ij(1-\sigma_i)}^0 \mid j \notin J, i \in [n]\}$

    $(\mathsf{Transfer}, \mathrm{sid}, \mathrm{srid}_{i,j,1-\sigma_i}, 1)$, he learns $\{\mathrm{sc}_{ij(1-\sigma_i)}^1 \mid j \notin J, i \in [n]\}$

Share Reconstruction and Commitment

In this phase, the receiver reconstructs a secret using the reconstruction algorithm for the secret sharing described in 6. He then commits to that value.

Proof of Share Validity

The sender sends the messages described below to $\mathcal{F}_{VOT}$. This allows the receiver to check that the shares are consistent relative to the secret sharing defined in 6. If the shares are not consistent, the receiver aborts.

- for each $j \in J$,
  (Reveal, sid, vid_j, 1), the receiver learns sc_j.
- for each $i \in [n], j \in J, k \in \{0,1\}$
  (Reveal, sid, $\mathrm{kid}_{i,j,k}$, 1), the receiver learns $\mathrm{sc}^0_{i,j,k}$.
  (Reveal, sid, $\mathrm{srid}_{i,j,k}$, 0), the receiver learns $\mathrm{sr}_{i,j,k}$.
  (Reveal, sid, $\mathrm{srid}_{i,j,k}$, 1) the receiver learns $\mathrm{sc}^1_{i,j,k}$.

Message Encryption and Transmission

For each $i \in [n], j \in [s], k \in \{0,1\}$, the sender encrypts the message m_{ijk} using k_{ijk} resulting in $z_{i,j,k}$. He then sends $z_{i,j,k}$ to the receiver. For each $i \in [n], j \notin J$, the receiver can decrypt m_{i,j,σ_i} since he knows k_{i,k,σ_i}. For each $i \in [m], j \in J$, the receiver can decrypt $m_{i,j,0}, m_{i,j,1}$ since he knows $k_{i,j,0}$ and $k_{i,j,1}$

7 Multi-sender k-Out-of-n OT

The Multi-sender k-out-of-n OT functionality was defined in [LOP11] where it was used to optimize the IPS compiler. The functionality involves p senders and one receiver. It is essentially many k-out-of-n OT executed in parallel with the same choice made by the receiver in each execution. This OT primitive can be implemented using ideas similar to the ones we presented to implement GOT in conjunction with the appropriate use of linear secret sharing.

The protocol is divided in four phases. In the first phases, the senders will construct/distribute the shares of a special secret sharing with value S. They must commit to this information. In the VOT phase, each sender will transfer a key for each message along with the associated share. The receiver will read the key associated with the messages he wishes to learn and otherwise he will obtain a share. The next phase is a verification phase, the receiver will commit to S which he could only obtain if he was requesting the same k messages from each sender. The senders will open all their commitment so that the shares are validated by the receiver. If the verification phase succeeds, the receiver opens S which proved he only read a legal set of key. In the last phase, the senders will transmit all the messages encrypted with the appropriate key.

The following functionality and protocol involves p senders with n messages of length r each and one receiver. We denote the shares of a a-out-of-b linear secret sharing as $\{B\}_{a\text{-}b}$.

Functionality $\mathcal{F}_{MSOT}$

$\mathcal{F}_{MSOT}$ interacts with senders $P_1, \ldots, P_p$ and receiver P_r

---

- **Inputs:** For $j = 1, \ldots, p$, upon receiving message (Send, sid, $ssid$, $x_{1j}, \ldots, x_{nj}$) from a sender P_j, record all x_{ij}.
- **Outputs:** Upon receiving message (Transfer, sid, $ssid$, $I \subset [n]$), check if $|I| = k$, if not abort. Send to receiver P_r, for each $j = 1, \ldots, p$ and $i \in I$, the message (Receipt, sid, $ssid$, i, j, x_{ij}).

Protocol: (π_{MSOT})

- **Preparation**
  1. Each sender a selects a random secret S_a and broadcasts a non-interactive commitment to S_a. We define $S = \sum_a S_a$.
  2. Each sender a reshares S_a to obtain $\{S_{ab}\}_{(n-k)\text{-}n}$.
  3. Each sender a reshares each S_{ab} to obtain $\{S_{abc}\}_{p\text{-}p}$.
  4. For each j, b and c, sender j sends share S_{jbc} to sender c.
  5. Each sender c computes for each b, $S'_{bc} = \sum_a s_{abc}$.

  We have that $S''_b = \{S'_{bc}\}_{p\text{-}p}$ and $\sum S''_b = S$.
- **VOT's**
  1. Each sender j selects uniformly at random a set of n keys k_{ij} of length r (one-time pads). He also selects n unused ids denoted by $ssid_{ij}$ and sends them to the receiver.
  2. Each sender j, for each $i \in [n]$ sends $\mathcal{F}_{VOT}$ the message (Send, sid, $ssid_{ij}$, k_{ij}, S'_{ij}).
  3. Let $I \in \mathcal{I}$ be the set of messages that the receiver wishes to receive, he sets $b_i = 0$ if $i \in I$ otherwise he sets $b_i = 1$. For each i, for each sender, the receiver sends $\mathcal{F}_{VOT}$ the message (Transfer, sid, $ssid_{ij}$, b_i) and records the result.
- **Verification**
  1. Receiver computes $S''_b = \{S'_{bc}\}_{p\text{-}p}$ then $S = \sum S''_b$ and broadcasts a non-interactive commitment to S. The receiver commits to a random S if he cannot reconstruct S.
  2. Each sender j, for each i, player j sends (open, sid, $ssid_{ij}$, 1) to $\mathcal{F}_{VOT}$, thus revealing his shares to the receiver.
  3. Receiver verifies that the shares are consistent with a legal preparation phase and aborts otherwise.
  4. Receiver reveals S and if the secret is invalid, the senders abort the protocol.
- **Transfer**
  1. Each sender sends $m_{ij} \oplus k_{ij}$ to the receiver who can now calculate m_{ij} for all $i \in I$.

Theorem 6. π_{MSOT} *securely realizes* $\mathcal{F}_{MSOT}$.

The proof of this theorem is presented in the full version of this paper.

References

[AFG+10]   Abe, M., Fuchsbauer, G., Groth, J., Haralambiev, K., Ohkubo, M.:
            Structure-preserving signatures and commitments to group elements. In:
            Rabin, T. (ed.) CRYPTO 2010. LNCS, vol. 6223, pp. 209–236. Springer,
            Heidelberg (2010)
[AGHO11]   Abe, M., Groth, J., Haralambiev, K., Ohkubo, M.: Optimal structure-
            preserving signatures in asymmetric bilinear groups. In: Rogaway, P. (ed.)
            CRYPTO 2011. LNCS, vol. 6841, pp. 649–666. Springer, Heidelberg (2011)
[BCKL08]   Belenkiy, M., Chase, M., Kohlweiss, M., Lysyanskaya, A.: P-signatures
            and noninteractive anonymous credentials. In: Canetti, R. (ed.) TCC 2008.
            LNCS, vol. 4948, pp. 356–374. Springer, Heidelberg (2008)
[Can01]   Canetti, R.: Universally composable security: A new paradigm for cryp-
            tograpic protocols. In: FOCS 2001 (2001), Current Full Version Available
            at Cryptology ePrint Archive, Report 2000/067 (2001)
[CC00]   Cachin, C., Camenisch, J.L.: Optimistic fair secure computation. In:
            Bellare, M. (ed.) CRYPTO 2000. LNCS, vol. 1880, pp. 93–111. Springer,
            Heidelberg (2000)
[CF01]   Canetti, R., Fischlin, M.: Universally composable commitments. In:
            Kilian, J. (ed.) CRYPTO 2001. LNCS, vol. 2139, pp. 19–40. Springer,
            Heidelberg (2001)
[CHK+11]   Camenisch, J., Haralambiev, K., Kohlweiss, M., Lapon, J., Naessens,
            V.: Structure preserving CCA secure encryption and applications. In:
            Lee, D.H., Wang, X. (eds.) ASIACRYPT 2011. LNCS, vol. 7073,
            pp. 89–106. Springer, Heidelberg (2011)
[CKWZ13]   Choi, S.G., Katz, J., Wee, H., Zhou, H.-S.: Efficient, adaptively secure,
            and composable oblivious transfer with a single, global CRS. In: Kurosawa,
            K., Hanaoka, G. (eds.) PKC 2013. LNCS, vol. 7778, pp. 73–88. Springer,
            Heidelberg (2013)
[CS97]   Camenisch, J.L., Stadler, M.A.: Efficient group signature schemes for large
            groups (extended abstract). In: Kaliski Jr., B.S. (ed.) CRYPTO 1997.
            LNCS, vol. 1294, pp. 410–424. Springer, Heidelberg (1997)
[CvdGT95]   Crépeau, C., van de Graaf, J., Tapp, A.: Committed oblivious transfer
            and private multi-party computation. In: Coppersmith, D. (ed.) Advances
            in Cryptology - CRYPT0 1995. LNCS, vol. 963, pp. 110–123. Springer,
            Heidelberg (1995)
[DHLW10]   Dodis, Y., Haralambiev, K., López-Alt, A., Wichs, D.: Cryptography
            against continuous memory attacks. In: FOCS, pp. 511–520. IEEE Com-
            puter Society (2010)
[EGL85]   Even, S., Goldreich, O., Lempel, A.: A randomized protocol for signing
            contracts. Communications of the ACM 28(6), 637–647 (1985)
[GH08]   Green, M., Hohenberger, S.: Universally composable adaptive oblivious
            transfer. In: Pieprzyk, J. (ed.) ASIACRYPT 2008. LNCS, vol. 5350, pp.
            179–197. Springer, Heidelberg (2008)
[GMW87]   Goldreich, O., Micali, S., Wigderson, A.: How to play any mental game
            or a completeness theorem for protocols with honest majority. In: STOC
            1987, pp. 218–229. ACM (1987)
[GS08]   Groth, J., Sahai, A.: Efficient non-interactive proof systems for bilinear
            groups. In: Smart, N.P. (ed.) EUROCRYPT 2008. LNCS, vol. 4965, pp.
            415–432. Springer, Heidelberg (2008)

[GSW10]   Ghadafi, E., Smart, N.P., Warinschi, B.: Groth-Sahai proofs revisited. In: Nguyen, P.Q., Pointcheval, D. (eds.) PKC 2010. LNCS, vol. 6056, pp. 177–192. Springer, Heidelberg (2010)

[IK97]   Ishai, Y., Kushilevitz, E.: Private simultaneous messages protocols with applications. In: Proceedings of the Fifth Israeli Symposium on Theory of Computing and Systems 1997, pp. 174–183. IEEE (1997)

[IPS08]   Ishai, Y., Prabhakaran, M., Sahai, A.: Founding cryptography on oblivious transfer - efficiently. In: Wagner, D. (ed.) CRYPTO 2008. LNCS, vol. 5157, pp. 572–591. Springer, Heidelberg (2008)

[JS07]   Jarecki, S.: Efficient two-party secure computation on committed inputs. In: Naor, M. (ed.) EUROCRYPT 2007. LNCS, vol. 4515, pp. 97–114. Springer, Heidelberg (2007)

[Kil88]   Kilian, J.: Founding crytpography on oblivious transfer. In: Proceedings of the Twentieth Annual ACM Symposium on Theory of Computing, pp. 20–31. ACM (1988)

[KSV07]   Kiraz, M.S., Schoenmakers, B., Villegas, J.: Efficient committed oblivious transfer of bit strings. In: Garay, J.A., Lenstra, A.K., Mambo, M., Peralta, R. (eds.) ISC 2007. LNCS, vol. 4779, pp. 130–144. Springer, Heidelberg (2007)

[Lin13]   Lindell, Y.: Fast cut-and-choose based protocols for malicious and covert adversaries. In: Canetti, R., Garay, J.A. (eds.) CRYPTO 2013, Part II. LNCS, vol. 8043, pp. 1–17. Springer, Heidelberg (2013)

[LOP11]   Lindell, Y., Oxman, E., Pinkas, B.: The IPS compiler: Optimizations, variants and concrete efficiency. In: Rogaway, P. (ed.) CRYPTO 2011. LNCS, vol. 6841, pp. 259–276. Springer, Heidelberg (2011)

[LP11]   Lindell, Y., Pinkas, B.: Secure two-party computation via cut-and-choose oblivious transfer. In: Ishai, Y. (ed.) TCC 2011. LNCS, vol. 6597, pp. 329–346. Springer, Heidelberg (2011)

[LP12]   Lindell, Y., Pinkas, B.: Secure two-party computation via cut-and-choose oblivious transfer. J. Cryptology 25(4), 680–722 (2012)

[PVW08]   Peikert, C., Vaikuntanathan, V., Waters, B.: A framework for efficient and composable oblivious transfer. In: Wagner, D. (ed.) CRYPTO 2008. LNCS, vol. 5157, pp. 554–571. Springer, Heidelberg (2008)

[Rab81]   Rabin, M.O.: How to exchange secrets by oblivious transfer. Technical report, Aiken Compuation Laboratory, Harvard University, TR-81 (1981)

[SSR08]   Shankar, B., Srinathan, K., Rangan, C.P.: Alternative protocols for generalized oblivious transfer. In: Rao, S., Chatterjee, M., Jayanti, P., Murthy, C.S.R., Saha, S.K. (eds.) ICDCN 2008. LNCS, vol. 4904, pp. 304–309. Springer, Heidelberg (2008)

[Tas11]   Tassa, T.: Generalized oblivious transfer by secret sharing. Designs, Codes and Cryptography 58(1), 11–21 (2011)

[Yao86]   Yao, A.C.-C.: How to generate and exchange secrets (extended abstract). In: FOCS 1986, pp. 162–167. IEEE (1986)

Round-Optimal Perfectly Secret Message Transmission with Linear Communication Complexity

Ravi Kishore*, Ashutosh Kumar, Chiranjeevi Vanarasa,
and Srinathan Kannan

International Institute of Information Technology, Hyderabad, India - 500032
{ravikishore.vasala,chiranjeevi.v}@research.iiit.ac.in,
ashutosh.kumar@students.iiit.ac.in, srinathan@iiit.ac.in

Abstract. Consider an arbitrary network of n nodes, up to any t of which are eavesdropped on by an adversary. A sender S wishes to send a message m to a receiver R such that the adversary learns nothing about m (unless it eavesdrops on one among $\{S, R\}$). We prove a necessary and sufficient condition on the (synchronous) network for the existence of r-round protocols for perfect communication, for any given $r > 0$. Our results/protocols are easily adapted to asynchronous networks too and are shown to be optimal in asynchronous "rounds". Further, we show that round-optimality is achieved without trading-off the communication complexity; specifically, our protocols have an overall message complexity of $O(n)$ elements of a finite field to perfectly transmit one field element. Interestingly, optimality (of protocols) also implies: (a) when the shortest path between S and R has $\Omega(n)$ nodes, *perfect secrecy is achieved for "free"*, because any (insecure routing) protocol would also take $O(n)$ rounds and send $O(n)$ messages (one message along each edge in the shortest path) for transmission and (b) it is well-known that $(t + 1)$ vertex disjoint paths from S to R are necessary for a protocol to exist; a consequent folklore is that the length of the $(t + 1)^{th}$ ranked (disjoint shortest) path would dictate the round complexity of protocols; we show that the folklore is false; round-optimal protocols can be substantially faster than the aforementioned length.

1   Introduction

We address the problem of Perfectly Secret Message Transmission(PSMT),[1] defined as follows: A sender S wishes to send a message m to a receiver R such that an adversary, that eavesdrops on no more than t out of the n nodes, learns nothing about m. Our inquiry includes (a) *characterization*: under what conditions is

---

* Financial support from TCS is acknowledged.

[1] In this work, we interchangeably use PSMT to mean both Perfectly *Secret* Message Transmission as well as Perfectly *Secure* Message Transmission; the former when the adversary is passive and the latter when the adversary is Byzantine. At any rate, our technical contributions are only in the passive adversarial case.

© Springer International Publishing Switzerland 2015
A. Lehmann and S. Wolf (Eds.): ICITS 2015, LNCS 9063, pp. 33–50, 2015.
DOI: 10.1007/978-3-319-17470-9_3

a solution possible? (b) *feasibility*: is the characterization efficiently testable and is there an efficient protocol? (c) *round complexity*: what is the *fastest* solution? and (d) *communication complexity*: what is the *cheapest* solution? Intuitively, the above questions are in increasing order of difficulty. Consequently, question '(a)' has been answered in settings that are far more general than those where optimal solutions are, as yet, known.

Although literature on information theoretically secure message transmission is rich, there are settings where answers to none of the aforementioned four questions are, yet, known. For instance, we do not know of a necessary and sufficient condition on digraphs influenced by a Byzantine adversary corrupting up to any t nodes, for the existence of protocols for perfectly secure message transmission from S to R; not to mention, design of optimal protocols for the same are still far-fetched. Researchers have therefore attacked the problem in scenarios that are not as general as mentioned above – harder the inquiry, more specific the chosen setting. Notwithstanding, researchers have also worked on interesting generalizations in some dimensions (while, of course, being more specific in other parameters so that the problem is tractable using contemporary techniques), including hyper-graphs [1], non-threshold adversaries [2], mobile faults [3,4], mixed/hybrid faults [5,6], asynchronous networks [7], to name a few.

The PSMT problem was conceived and first solved by Dolev *et. al* [8]. They assume that the graph is *undirected*. It is proved that PSMT is possible if and only if there are at least $(2t + 1)$ vertex disjoint paths between S and R. Further, the protocols designed in [8] are efficient too. However, designing round optimal protocols for PSMT (even in undirected graphs) still remains a hard open problem. Consequently, results are known only with further restrictions.

A setting where round-optimal protocols have been designed (on arbitrary digraphs) is when a small probability of error is permitted [9] (that is, perfectness is negligibly traded-off). However the design of communication optimal solutions are still open.

A particular setting where communication optimum protocol for PSMT are designed is the following: applying Menger's theorem [10], the undirected graph can be abstracted as a collection of wires (vertex-disjoint paths) between S and R, up to t among which are corrupted by the adversary. In this setting, a two phase protocol for PSMT that is optimal in communication complexity is known [11]. While the notion of phase complexity has been studied [12,11,13], we stress that round complexity is markedly different from phase complexity, even in the case of undirected networks (as illustrated in Section 2.1).

Recently, restricting to passive adversaries, Renault *et. al* [14] characterize the digraphs that enable PSMT. In fact they use a more general non-threshold adversary model, characterized via an adversary structure, which is a collection of subsets of nodes in the graph, where in the adversary may choose to corrupt (passively in this case) the nodes in any one subset among the collection. The protocols of [14] are therefore not always efficient (that is, may be super-polynomial in n).

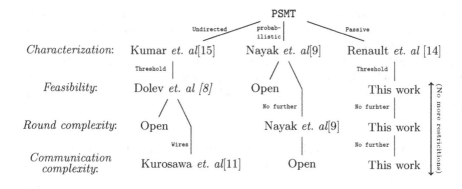

Fig. 1. Restriction based solutions

In summary, as depicted in the Fig. 1, all the four questions in our inquiry, with respect to the problem of PSMT, have remained open in the general case of digraphs influenced by a Byzantine adversary characterized via an adversary structure A. However, (im)possibility results are known if one restricts the setting to either undirected graphs [15] or passive adversary or security with error [14,9]. Nevertheless, efficient protocols are still elusive. To design efficient protocols using contemporary techniques, further restriction (apart from moving to undirected graphs) is required, namely, *threshold* adversary. For instance, Dolev *et. al* [8] give one such efficient protocol, which, however, is neither round optimal nor bit-optimal.

Round-optimal protocols are known only in the case of weaker (not perfect) security models like statistical [9] or computational security [16]. Bit-optimal protocols have been designed in the wires-based abstraction of the undirected graph [11]. While a similar wires-based approach has been used for digraphs too [17], it is known to be inadequate to capture all digraphs on which protocols exists [18].

2 Our Contributions

As depicted in Fig. 1, we ask: *does restricting to the setting of passive* **threshold** *adversaries lead to the design of efficient and round-optimal and/or bit-optimal protocols?* (or, are further restrictions like wires-based abstractions still required?)

Interestingly, we design efficient round/bit optimal protocols, with no further restrictions beyond assuming that the adversary passively corrupt up to t nodes in the digraph. Incidentally, it turns out that our techniques for designing round-optimal protocols are orthogonal to those that entail linear communication complexity – therefore, when applied together, we obtain protocols that are *simultaneously* round optimal as well as bit-optimal.[2] Further, the *simplicity* of our protocol ensures the implementability of highly scalable perfectly secret message transmission.

In a nutshell, we address the PSMT problem in such a way that all the four questions, namely, characterization, feasibility, round and bit optimality, are answered in one-shot. In the subsections below, we briefly describe our results and their significance.

2.1 Complete Characterization of Networks Wherein an r-round Secure Communication is Possible

It is well-known that, for passive threshold adversaries, $(t + 1)$-vertex disjoint paths are necessary and sufficient for PSMT from S to R in undirected graphs [8]. Consequently, as noted in [8] too, without loss of generality, any network (undirected graph) may be abstracted as a set of wires (vertex disjoint paths) between S and R. However, in the design of round optimal PSMT protocols, such an abstraction is inadequate, even if the length of the wires is recorded. Specifically, using the edges across these wires (or practically every edge in the network) it is possible to design *faster* protocols. For example, consider the graph in Fig. 2, the two wires corresponding to two vertex disjoint paths $\langle S, v, R \rangle$ and $\langle S(= v_0), v_1, v_2, v_3, \ldots v_{n-1}, R(= v_n) \rangle$ have length of 2 and n respectively. Following Dolev's protocol, S sends two points on a linear polynomial whose constant term is the secret m, individually through these two wires. R gets the two points and hence the message after n rounds. Can a faster protocol exist? Our answer: *Yes. In fact, a 3-round protocol exists, irrespective of how large n is!* Perhaps it is not conspicuous at first glance and certainly not if we continue to use the wires-based abstraction of the network. As a corollary to our Theorem 3 we know that 3 rounds are necessary and sufficient for PSMT in the graph in Fig. 2. Thus, extant techniques are insufficient to design round optimal protocols and new techniques are necessary to design and more importantly prove round optimality. To summarize, the problem of characterizing round optimal protocols in directed networks is a non-trivial and an interesting problem.

A Remark on Extending to Asynchronous "Rounds". Due to the absence of fail-stop and/or Byzantine corrupt nodes in our setting, it is fairly straight-forward to adapt all our protocols (and hence our characterizations) to the asynchronous setting too. Indeed, several of our protocols are directly designed assuming that the network is asynchronous; this is the reason that commands like **wait** appear in our algorithms (these can be safely ignored in case of full-fledged synchrony). On the other hand in asynchronous networks, there is no formal notion of global round, and therefore our claims of round-optimality have to be understood accordingly. Specifically, we define an asynchronous 'hop'

---

[2] Linear communication complexity is equivalent to bit-optimality only when we consider optimally fault-tolerant protocols, that is, using the maximum t-adversary that is tolerable. Otherwise, *sub-linear* communication complexity is achieved by trading-off fault-tolerance using multi-secret sharing (analogous to [19]).

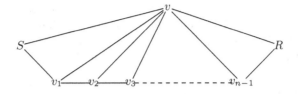

Fig. 2. An undirected graph tolerating one passive fault

as a round with an in-built `wait-for-the-message`. Though, these hops are not globally in lock-step, we may easily use it as a measure of asynchronous round-complexity of a protocol – the length of longest nested hop sequence. We see that our protocol are hop-optimal, and we can derive the same using the same algorithms used for deriving the round optimal protocols.

2.2   Linear Communication Complexity

Folklore suggests that optimizing the number of rounds for a distributed protocol, typically increases the communication complexity (total numbers of bits transferred across all edges in the network during the execution of protocol). In rare cases, round optimality can co-exist with bit-optimality – PSMT is indeed one such case! Specifically, we prove that the number of edges used by our protocol can be brought down to linear in the number of nodes (Section 4.2). We also ensure that an edge is used to send at most one field element (or in general, bits equivalent to the size of the message). At any rate, each of these edges is *critical*, in the sense that, if deleted, PSMT is rendered impossible – hence they need to be used at least once. Thus, we arrive at a surprising protocol for secure communication which is round optimal and at the same time has linear communication complexity. Even more interesting is the case when the shortest path from S to R has $\Omega(n)$ nodes. In such cases, *perfect secrecy is achieved for "free"*, because any (insecure routing) protocol would also take $O(n)$ rounds and send $O(n)$ messages (one message along each edge in the shortest path) for transmission.

2.3   Efficient Discriminant Algorithms

Specifying the necessary and sufficient condition does not imply that there exists an efficient algorithm for checking the same. Indeed, the literature (on possibility of protocols in directed graphs) is replete with several problem specific characterizations, none of which are known to be efficiently testable. For instance, the possibility of reliable/secure message transmission in Byzantine adversarial setting in digraphs is characterized in [18,9]. However, no efficient algorithms to test these conditions are known; in fact they may be NP-hard too, though no such study has been carried out. In contrast, for each of the results in this paper, we have a polynomial time algorithm for testing the same. Algorithm 5.3 is a polynomial-time algorithm for testing the existence of an r-round secure communication protocol in a given network (and if yes, obtaining a round optimal one). All the reductions mentioned in the paper can be easily done in polynomial time, as all of them involve creation of a sub-graph of the given graph.

3   Network Model and Definitions

Definition 1. *Passive Corruption:* *Following [12], a node v is said to be passively corrupted if the adversary has full access to the information and internal state of v. But v will honestly follow the protocol execution.*

Definition 2. *Following [12], define the VIEW of a node $v \in V$ at any point of the execution of a protocol Π, to be the information the node can get from its local input (if any) to the protocol, all the messages that it had earlier sent or received, the protocol code executed by the node and its random coins. VIEW of a set of nodes $W (\subseteq V)$ is the information that the nodes in W can get together from their individual VIEWS and is denoted by $\text{VIEW}_G^\Pi(W)$. The VIEW of an adversary $\mathbb{A}$ is the VIEW of the set of nodes controlled by adversary, denoted by $\text{VIEW}_G^\Pi(\mathbb{A})$.*

Definition 3. *Perfect Security:* *Following [12], a message transmission protocol Π for sending message m from sender S to receiver R is said to be perfectly secure if it satisfies the following two conditions:*

1. *Perfect Reliability: At the end of the protocol Π receiver should learn the correct message m.*
2. *Perfect Secrecy: Adversary should not learn any information about the message m (i.e. adversary should not be able to distinguish whether S sent message m or m' for any two messages m and m').*

Definition 4. *The underlying undirected graph of a directed graph $G(V,E)$ is denoted by $G_u(V,E_u)$, where $E_u = \{(u,v) \mid (u,v) \in E \text{ or } (v,u) \in E\}$.*

Definition 5. *A sequence of nodes $p : \langle v_0(= u), v_1, v_2, \ldots, v_k, v_{k+1}(= v)\rangle$ is said to be a weak path from u to v in a directed graph $G(V,E)$, if $\forall j \in \{0, 1, \ldots, k\}$, either $(v_j, v_{j+1}) \in E$ or $(v_{j+1}, v_j) \in E$.*
We say that path $p' : \langle v_0(= u), v_1, v_2, \ldots, v_k, v_{k+1}(= v)\rangle$ in G_u, is the corresponding path of a weak path $p : \langle v_0(= u), v_1, v_2, \ldots, v_k, v_{k+1}(= v)\rangle$.

Notations:

1. In a directed graph $G(V,E)$
   (a) The set of all corrupted nodes is denoted by $V_C \subseteq V$ and $V \setminus V_C$ denotes the set of honest nodes. We also have $|V_C| \le t$.
   (b) $G[V']$ denotes the induced sub graph of G induced by the vertex set V'.
   (c) V_v denotes the set of vertices from which vertex v is reachable.
2. d_v denotes the length of a shortest path from $v(\in V_R)$ to receiver R.
3. $[l, u] = \{m \in \mathbb{Z} \mid l \le m \le u\}$.

We model our communication network as a directed graph $G(V, E)$, $|V| = n$, where each edge is a private, authentic and reliable channel. Our network is synchronous and every node knows the topology of the network. Communication happens in a sequence of rounds. In any round, a player can receive the messages sent to it by its in-neighbours in the previous round, perform some computation and finally send a message to its out-neighbours. The set of faults in the network is characterized by a central (fictitious) adversary who can eavesdrop or passively corrupt no more than t nodes in the network. Throughout this paper, by a "faulty node" we mean that the node is "passively corrupted by the adversary" and by "secure" we mean "perfectly secure". For brevity, by "PSMT is possible", we mean "PSMT tolerating t-threshold passive adversary is possible". By "a number r is chosen randomly" we mean "r is chosen uniformly at random from field $\mathbb{F}$". Our message space is a large enough field $\langle \mathbb{F}, +, \star \rangle$ and all the calculations are done in this field $\mathbb{F}$ only.

4   Communication Efficient PSMT Protocol in G

In any protocol Π, if there is no path from a node v to receiver R, then v can't convey any information to R. Therefore with out loss of generality we can assume that from every node to R there is at least one path. Once this assumption is made, in this section we present a communication efficient protocol Π_{Eff} in G with communication complexity of $O(n^2)$ whenever PSMT is possible in G_u. First we present a protocol Π_{Sim}, which simulates the corresponding path p' of a weak path p. Then we run protocol Π_{Sim} for simulating the corresponding path of each such weak path, to get protocol Π_{Eff}. We show that if every node in a weak path p is an honest node then protocol Π_{Sim}, securely transmits message m from S to R in G. Thus, executing Π_{Sim} for $t + 1$ (or more) times results in a PSMT protocol.

4.1   Protocol Π_{Sim}

Let $p : \langle S(= u_0), u_1, \ldots, u_l, u_{l+1}(= R) \rangle$ be a weak path in G and m be the message S wants to send to R using the corresponding path p'.

1. if weak path p is a path in G then S simply sends message m using path p.
2. otherwise let $\{u_{i_1}, u_{i_2}, \ldots, u_{i_k}\}$ be the set of all nodes in the weak path p such that $(u_{i_j}, u_{i_j+1}) \notin E$ for $j \in [1, k]$ and without loss of generality assume that $i_m < i_n$ for $m < n$.
   (a) As $(u_{i_j}, u_{i_j+1}) \notin E$, we have (i) $(u_{i_j+1}, u_{i_j}) \in E$ and (ii) a subpath p_{i_j+1} from u_{i_j+1} to $u_{i_{j+1}}$ in G having only nodes of weak path p.
   (b) u_{i_j+1} chooses a random number r_{i_j+1} and sends to $u_{i_{j+1}}$ using path p_{i_j+1} and to u_{i_j} using edge (u_{i_j+1}, u_{i_j}).
   (c) $u_{i_j}(j \neq 1)$ calculates $r_{i_{j-1}+1} + r_{i_j+1}$ and sends to R using some path as there exists at least one path.
3. S will send m to u_{i_1} and u_{i_1} sends $m + r_{i_1+1}$ to R.

4. for $j = k - 1, k - 2, \ldots, 1$; R computes $r_{i_j+1} = (r_{i_j+1} + r_{i_{j+1}+1}) - r_{i_{j+1}+1}$.
5. Once R gets r_{i_1+1} for $j = 1$, it finally computes $m = (m + r_{i_1+1}) - r_{i_1+1}$.

Lemma 1. *In graph G, for three honest nodes u, v, w; if* PSMT *is possible from w to u and w to v then* PSMT *is possible from u to v if there is a path p from u to v(i.e. $u \in V_v$).*

Proof. Let m be the message that u wants to communicate to v secretly. First w chooses a random number r and sends the same to both u and v secretly. Now u masks the message m with r as $m + r$ and sends to v using path p. Finally v unmasks the message m by subtracting r from $m + r$. This protocol is perfectly secure even if path p contains malicious nodes, since in a field $\langle \mathbb{F}, +, * \rangle$; for given $x, z \in \mathbb{F}$, $\exists$ unique $y \in \mathbb{F}$ such that $x + y = z$.

Corollary 1. *Protocol Π_{Sim} for simulating the corresponding path p' of a weak path $p : \langle S(= u_0), u_1, \ldots, u_l, u_{l+1}(= R) \rangle$, securely transmits a message m from S to R if every node u_i in p is an honest node.*

Proof. As i_k is maximum, u_{i_k} is the last node in p such that $(u_{i_k}, u_{i_k+1}) \notin E$, we have (i) Secure edge $(u_{i_k+1}, u_{i_k}) \in E$ and (ii) secure path from u_{i_k+1} to R containing only nodes of weak path p, which implies PSMT from u_{i_k+1} to R is possible in G. Therefore, from Lemma 1, PSMT is possible from u_{i_k} to R.

1. for $j = k - 1, k - 2, \ldots, 1$ we have:
   (a) a secure path p_{i_j+1} from u_{i_j+1} to $u_{i_{j+1}}$ in G containing only nodes of weak path p.
   (b) PSMT is possible from $u_{i_{j+1}}$ to R.
   (c) Above two steps together gives, PSMT is possible from u_{i_j+1} to R.
   (d) Secure edge $(u_{i_j+1}, u_{i_j}) \in E$.
   (e) From Lemma 1, we get, PSMT is possible from u_{i_j} to R.
2. In particular when $j = 1$ we get, PSMT is possible from u_{i_1} to R in G.
3. We have a secure path from S to u_{i_1} containing only nodes of weak path p.
4. From the above two steps we get, PSMT is possible from S to R.

4.2   Efficient Protocol

We now present a PSMT protocol Π_{Eff} in G whenever PSMT is possible in G_u. Dolev *et. al* [8] show that PSMT is possible in G_u if **and only if** there exists $(t + 1)$ vertex disjoint paths from S to R in G_u. Let p'_i be a vertex disjoint path in G_u corresponding to weak path p_i, for each $i \in [1, t + 1]$.

Protocol Π_{Eff}:

1. S chooses a random t-degree polynomial $p(x)$ and replaces constant term $p(0)$ with the message m.
2. S sends $p(i)$ to R by simulating the corresponding path p'_i of a weak path p_i using protocol Π_{Sim}.
3. R reconstructs $p(x)$ once it receives all $(t + 1)$ points to get message m.

Lemma 2. *The protocol Π_{Eff} is reliable and secure.*

Proof. Protocol Π_{Eff} is reliable since the protocol Π_{Sim} is reliable. Protocol Π_{Eff} is secure since there exists at least one secure weak path p_i for some $i \in [1, t+1]$, so $p(i)$ is secure by Corollary 1. On a t-degree polynomial, t or fewer points reveals nothing about constant term [20], which is the message m.

The communication complexity of the above protocol Π_{Eff} is $O(n^2)$ since these $(t+1)$ paths may contain all the n nodes and each node may need to send the masked value to the receiver R using some path which in turn can contain $O(n)$ nodes.

Now we will give one example for the simulation of a corresponding of a weak path using the protocol Π_{Sim}. Consider the graph G in the Fig. 3 which has three disjoint weak paths namely $p_1 : \langle S, v_1, v_2, R \rangle$, $p_2 : \langle S, v_3, v_4, R \rangle$ and $p_3 : \langle S, v_5, v_6, R \rangle$. Therefore it can tolerate up to two faulty nodes. Due to space constraints, we only give the simulation of the corresponding path of weak path p_3, which is as follows:

1. R chooses a random number r_8 and sends to v_6.
2. v_5 chooses a random number r_5 and sends to both S and v_6.
3. v_6 masks r_5 with r_8 as $r_5 + r_8$ and sends to R using the path $\langle v_6, v_4, v_1, v_2, R \rangle$.
4. S sends the masked value $p(3) + r_5$ to R using the path $\langle S, v_3, v_1, v_2, R \rangle$.
5. R first unmasks r_5 by just subtracting r_8 from $r_5 + r_8$ and gets r_5 and then R similarly unmasks $p(3)$.

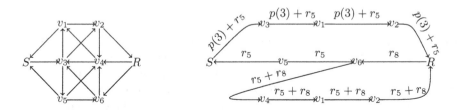

Fig. 3. An example graph G with simulation of the corresponding path of p_3

Theorem 1. PSMT *from S to R is possible in G if and only if in G_u.*

Proof. Run the protocol Π_{Eff} for PSMT in G if PSMT is possible in G_u.

4.3   Polynomial Time Algorithm for Verifying PSMT Possibility in G

1. Compute V_R using Breadth First Search from R, using opposite direction of edges.
2. **if** edge $(S, R) \in E$ or $(R, S) \in E$ **then return** true.

3. `else` create auxiliary graph $G^{aux}(V^{aux}, E^{aux})$ of G as follows :
    (a) split each vertex $v_i \in V$ except S and R, into two vertices v_{i1} and v_{i2} and add an edge from v_{i1} to v_{i2}. $V^{aux} = \{S, R\} \cup_{i=1}^{n} \{v_{i1}, v_{i2}\}$.
    (b) point all incoming edges of v_i to v_{i1} as incoming edges of v_{i1}.
    (c) point all out going edges of v_i as out going edges of v_{i2}.
    (d) for every edge add uniform edge capacity of 1.
4. Run `Max flow algorithm` to find `Max flow` in G_u^{aux}.
5. If `Max flow` $\geq t + 1$ then return `true` else `false`.
6. Note that $(t + 1)$ Vertex disjoint paths also can be found easily.

This is a polynomial time algorithm as breadth first search takes in worst case $O(n^2)$ time [21], construction of graph G^{aux} takes $O(n^2)$ time and max flow takes $O(n^3)$ time [22,23].

5   Round Optimality

In first subsection, we present a `generic round efficient PSMT protocol` in G. In later subsection we bring the notion of `round evolution graph`, a subgraph of G which evolves as number of rounds increases. We show that if `PSMT` is possible in `round evolution graph` then we can simulate the `generic round efficient PSMT protocol` in that `round evolution graph`. Finally we give a polynomial time algorithm for identifying the optimal rounds number. Combing all together, we obtain round optimal protocol as well as the optimal rounds number.

5.1   Round Efficient Protocol

In this section we present a `round efficient` protocol Π_{Rnd_Eff} whenever `PSMT` is possible in G_u. The main idea is every node v in G, will start its computation and/or communication from first round itself and if anything needs to be sent to R directly it will send using a shortest path, so that it conveys the required information to R possibly in least number of rounds. In the first round, for an edge $(u, v) \in E_u$, both nodes u and v chooses random numbers r_u, r_v respectively such that:

1. `if` $(u, v) \in E$ (forward edge with respect to u) then u sends r_u to v and initializes its `Right Value`, $R[u] = r_u$ and v initializes its `Left Value`, $L[v] = r_u$ once it receives r_u from u.
2. `else if`(i.e. there is no forward edge) v sends r_v to u and initializes its `Left Value`, $L[v] = r_v$, this is possible since $(u, v) \in E_u$ and $(u, v) \notin E$; edge (v, u) must be in E(backward edge with respect to u). Node u initializes its `Right Value`, $R[u] = r_v$ once it receives r_v from v.
3. It is clear that in both the cases $R[u] = L[v]$.

Protocol Π_{Rnd_Eff}:

1. Since **PSMT** is possible in G_u, there exists $(t+1)$ vertex disjoint paths from S to R in G_u namely $p_i : \langle u_{i0}(=S), u_{i1}, \ldots, u_{ik_i}, u_{i(k_i+1)}(=R)\rangle$, for $i \in [1, t+1]$. As $u_{ij} \in V_R$, there exists at least one path from u_{ij} to R, for $j \in [0, k_i]$ and let $p_{u_{ij}}$ be a shortest path from u_{ij} to R. Note that for $i \in [1, t+1]$, $u_{i0} = S$ and $u_{i(k_i+1)} = R$.
2. Let m be the message S wants to send to R securely.
3. S chooses a random t degree polynomial $p(x)$ and replaces constant term $p(0)$ with m.
4. For each path p_i, $i \in [1, t+1]$:
   (a) Every node $u_{ij}(\neq u_{i0})$, chooses a random number r_{ij}, for $j \in [1, k_i + 1]$.
   (b) $S(= u_{i0})$ initializes $r_{i0} = p(i)$ and also initializes $L[u_{i0}] = p(i)$.
   (c) For $j \in [1, k_i + 1]$, if $(u_{i(j-1)}, u_{ij}) \in E$ then $u_{i(j-1)}$ sends $r_{i(j-1)}$ to u_{ij} and initializes $R[u_{i(j-1)}] = r_{i(j-1)}$. u_{ij} waits to receive $r_{i(j-1)}$ and initializes $L[u_{ij}] = r_{i(j-1)}$ once it is received.
   (d) For $j \in [1, k_i + 1]$, if $(u_{i(j-1)}, u_{ij}) \notin E$ then u_{ij} sends r_{ij} to $u_{i(j-1)}$ and initializes $L[u_{ij}] = r_{ij}$. $u_{i(j-1)}$ waits to receive r_{ij} and initializes $R[u_{i(j-1)}] = r_{ij}$ once it is received.
   (e) Observe that in both cases $R[u_{i(j-1)}] = L[u_{ij}]$, for $j \in [1, k_i + 1]$.
   (f) For $j \in [0, k_i]$ every node u_{ij} calculates its **Value**, $Val[u_{ij}] = L[u_{ij}] - R[u_{ij}]$ and if it is non-zero(i.e. $L[u_{ij}] \neq R[u_{ij}]$) then it sends $Val[u_{ij}]$ to receiver R using shortest a path $p_{u_{ij}}$. R waits till it receives $Val[u_{ij}]$.
5. R computes $p(i) = \sum_{j=0}^{k_i} Val[u_{ij}] + L[u_{i(k_i+1)}]$. This is possible for R to compute since R knows $L[u_{i(k_i+1)}]$ as $u_{i(k_i+1)} = R$.

Protocol Π_{Rnd_Eff} runs in maximum of $|V|$ rounds. This is because, in first round nodes share their random numbers with neighbours as explained in protocol and then each node u_{ij} sends $Val[u_{ij}]$ to R using shortest path $p_{u_{ij}}$, if required. Sending $Val[u_{ij}]$ can take in worst case(when every node in V appears in path $p_{u_{ij}}$ for some values of i, j) $|V|$-1 rounds. Therefore protocol Π_{Rnd_Eff}, achieves **PSMT** in a total of $|V|$ or fewer rounds.

Lemma 3. *Protocol Π_{Rnd_Eff} for sending message m from S to R is reliable.*

Proof. For each u_{ij}, $(j \neq k_i + 1)$ in path p_i, we have $R[u_{ij}] = L[u_{i(j+1)}]$
Let $Sum = \sum_{j=0}^{k_i} Val[u_{ij}] + L[u_{i(k_i+1)}]$. Now we will show that $Sum = p(i)$.

$$Sum = \sum_{j=0}^{k_i}(L[u_{ij}] - R[u_{ij}]) + L[u_{i(k_i+1)}]$$

$$= \sum_{j=0}^{k_i}(L[u_{ij}] - L[u_{i(j+1)}]) + L[u_{i(k_i+1)}]$$

$$= L[u_{i0}] - L[u_{i(k_i+1)}] + L[u_{i(k_i+1)}] = L[u_{i0}] = p(i)$$

Lemma 4. *Protocol Π_{Rnd_Eff} for sending message m from S to R is secure.*

Proof. As the adversary can corrupt at most t nodes, there exists a path p_i from S to R in $G_u[V \setminus V_C]$ for some $i \in [1, t+1]$ (i.e. path p_i is not under the control of adversary). Each u_{ij} in path p_i except $u_{i(k_i+1)}$ sends $Val[u_{ij}]$ to R using path $p_{u_{ij}}$ if required, which may be under the control of adversary. For $j \in [0, k_i]$, even if adversary gets $Val[u_{ij}]$, in a field $\mathbb{F}$, $\exists$ unique x such that $\sum_{j=0}^{k_i}(\lambda_j * Val[u_{ij}]) + x = p(i)$, for any $\lambda_j \in \mathbb{F}$. Alternatively we can think as adversary gets $k_i + 1$ system of linear independent equations in $k_i + 2$ variables namely for each $j \in [0, k_i]$, $Val[u_{ij}] = L[u_{ij}] - R[u_{ij}] = L[u_{ij}] - L[u_{i(j+1)}]$. Therefore the adversary learns nothing about $p(i)$ and so nothing about m as well [20]. $\quad\square$

5.2   PSMT in Round Evolution Graphs

Graphs have been used as a very powerful abstraction of the network by modelling the physical link from one player to another as a directed edge between the corresponding vertices of the graph. However in this kind of modelling of the network, the edges of the graph only indicate the link between two spatial locations. It does not contain any temporal information. To incorporate the notion of time (rounds) in our graph, we propose a representation named `round evolution graph`, that contains both spatial and temporal information.

Definition 6. *Given the round number r, and a network represented by a directed graph $G(V, E)$, with receiver R, the round evolution graph of order r, $G^{(r)}(V, E^{(r)})$ is defined as subgraph of G, where $E^{(r)} = E \setminus \{(u, v) \in E \mid d_v \geq r\}$. i.e. Remove edges from which R can't receive information in r rounds.*

Theorem 2. PSMT *is possible in $G^{(r)}$ $\iff$ r-round* PSMT *protocol exists in $G^{(r)}$.*

Proof. Sufficiency: It is clear that if r-round protocol exists then PSMT is trivially possible in $G^{(r)}$.
Necessity: Suppose PSMT is possible in $G^{(r)}$, then we show that in r-rounds we can simulate the protocol Π_{Rnd_Eff} given in Section 5.1. Observe that in protocol Π_{Rnd_Eff}, every node u_{ij} in path p_i, in first round sends the chosen random number r_{ij} to its neighbour(s) if required. We have three cases for each u_{ij}:

1. $(u_{i(j-1)}, u_{ij}) \in E^{(r)}$. By our construction of $G^{(r)}$, $d_{u_{ij}} \leq r - 1$, therefore even if in first round u_{ij} waits to receive random numbers from neighbours, it can send $Val[u_{ij}]$ in total of r-rounds.
2. $(u_{ij}, u_{i(j+1)}) \notin E^{(r)}$ which implies $(u_{i(j+1)}, u_{ij}) \in E^{(r)}$. By our construction of $G^{(r)}$, $d_{u_{ij}} \leq r - 1$. Rest follows as in case(1).
3. $(u_{i(j-1)}, u_{ij}) \notin E^{(r)}$ and $(u_{ij}, u_{i(j+1)}) \in E^{(r)}$, In this case u_{ij} is not required to send its `value` to receiver R, since $Val[u_{ij}] = L[u_{ij}] - R[u_{ij}] = r_{ij} - r_{ij} = 0$.

Theorem 3. *r-round* PSMT *protocol exists in* $G \Longleftrightarrow$ PSMT *is possible in* $G^{(r)}$.

Proof. Sufficiency: Suppose PSMT is possible in $G^{(r)}$, from Theorem 2 we know that r-round protocol exists in $G^{(r)}$ and so r-round protocol exists in G since $G^{(r)}$ is a sub graph of G.

Necessity: Suppose r-round protocols exists for G. Note that any node v with $d_v > r$, never conveys any information to R in an r-round protocol(Since it needs at least $r + 1$ send commands to send to R). Therefore in r-round protocol, an edge (u, v) in E but not in $E^{(r)}$, $\forall v \in V$ can be safely ignored when $d_v \geq r$. In other words, at the end of the r-round protocol Π, $\mathbf{VIEW}_G^{\Pi}(\{R\})$ does not change whether these edges are present or not.

Therefore round optimal protocol in G is a protocol in $G^{(r)}$, where r is the minimum number of rounds required for PSMT in G.

5.3 Polynomial Time Algorithm for Identifying the Optimal Number of Rounds

We will find minimum r for which PSMT is possible in $G^{(r)}$ by doing binary search on r for $r \in [1, |V|]$. This can be done in polynomial time since in each iteration:

1. We are constructing sub graph $G^{(r)}$ of G, this can be done in polynomial time.
2. We are checking whether PSMT is possible or not in $G^{(r)}$, this also can be done in polynomial time as explained in Section 4.3.

5.4 An Example of Round Optimal Protocol

In this section we give a round optimal protocol for the graph G given in Fig. 3. In Fig. 4 we can see a shortest path from each node to R and its distance. Fig. 5 represents the round evolution graphs $G^{(3)}$ and $G^{(4)}$ corresponding to the same graph in Fig. 3. Now in graph G we show that 4 is the optimal number of rounds by showing that PSMT is not possible in $G^{(3)}$ but possible in $G^{(4)}$.

Node	Shortest path to R	Shortest distance
S	$p_S : \langle S, v_3, v_2, R \rangle$	3
v_1	$p_{v_1} : \langle v_1, v_2, R \rangle$	2
v_2	$p_{v_2} : \langle v_2, R \rangle$	1
v_3	$p_{v_3} : \langle v_3, v_2, R \rangle$	2
v_4	$p_{v_4} : \langle v_4, v_3, v_2, R \rangle$	3
v_5	$p_{v_5} : \langle v_5, v_4, v_3, v_2, R \rangle$	4
v_6	$p_{v_6} : \langle v_6, v_3, v_2, R \rangle$	3

Fig. 4. A shortest path from each node to receiver R in graph G

As shortest distance from S to R is 3, any protocol will take at least three rounds. Clearly PSMT is not possible in $G^{(3)}$ tolerating 2-adversary as there is

Fig. 5. An example of round evolution graphs $G^{(3)}$ and $G^{(4)}$

only one vertex disjoint path from S to R in $G_u^{(3)}$. In $G_u^{(4)}$ there are 3 vertex disjoint paths from S to R, also R is reachable from each of the nodes in these paths, so by Theorem 1, PSMT is possible in G. Now we present a 4 round protocol in the graph G as an example.

1. **Round 1**:
   (a) Node S chooses a random two degree polynomial $p(x)$ and replaces constant term $p(0)$ with m.
   (b) Every node v except S and R chooses a random number r_v. R chooses three random numbers $r_{R_1}, r_{R_2}, r_{R_3}$.
   (c) Node v_1 sends r_{v_1} to v_2 and $S(= S_1)$; node v_2 sends r_{v_2} to R.
   (d) Node $S(= S_2)$ sends $p(2)$ to v_3; node v_4 sends r_{v_4} to v_3; node R sends r_{R_2} to v_4.
   (e) Node v_5 sends r_{v_5} to v_6 and $S(= S_3)$; node R sends r_{R_3} to v_6.

2. **Round 2, Round 3 and Round 4**:
   (a) Every node v calculates its **value** $Val[v]$: $Val[S_1] = p(1) - r_{v_1}$, $Val[v_1] = r_{v_1} - r_{v_1}$, $Val[v_2] = r_{v_1} - r_{v_2}$, $Val[S_2] = p(2) - p(2)$, $Val[v_3] = p(2) - r_{v_4}$, $Val[v_4] = r_{v_4} - r_{R_2}$, $Val[S_3] = p(3) - r_{v_5}$, $Val[v_5] = r_{v_5} - r_{v_5}$, $Val[v_6] = r_{v_5} - r_{R_3}$
   (b) Every node $v \notin \{v_1, S_2, v_5, R\}$, sends its value $Val[v]$ to R using shortest path p_v from v to R, this is possible since the distance of shortest path p_v is less than or equal to 3.

3. R calculates $p(1) = Val[S_1] + Val[v_1] + Val[v_2] + r_{v_2} = p(1) - r_{v_1} + 0 + r_{v_1} - r_{v_2} + r_{v_2} = p(1)$, $p(2) = Val[S_2] + Val[v_3] + Val[v_4] + r_{R_2} = 0 + p(2) - r_{v_4} + r_{v_4} - r_{R_2} + r_{R_2} = p(2)$ and $p(3) = Val[S_3] + Val[v_5] + Val[v_6] + r_{R_3} = p(3) - r_{v_5} + 0 + r_{v_5} - r_{R_3} + r_{R_3} = p(3)$

All the nodes whose shortest distance to receiver R, is less than or equal to 3 can send their values to R in less than or equal to 4 rounds by simply forwarding via shortest path(they may wait in first round for receiving the random numbers from neighbour). Every node except v_5 is at a distance of less than or equal to 3 so they can send their **values** to R in 4 rounds if required. Since, for node v_5, $Val[v_5] = 0$, it is not required to send any value to R. Therefore, this protocol runs in a total of 4 rounds.

6 Linear Communication Complexity

In Section. 4.2, it has already been noted that, communication complexity of protocol Π_{Eff} is $O(n^2)$. Now we modify our protocol to get a generic $O(n)$ communication protocol. We achieve this by ensuring that PSMT is possible in a sub-graph of G, which has only $O(n)$ edges and no edge is used more than once, for transmitting a single field element. As this is a generic protocol, when we apply in $G^{r_{min}}$ (r_{min} is the minimum number of rounds required for PSMT) we get a round optimal linear communication protocol.

Definition 7. *Spanning tree of a graph G_u is denoted by $T = (V, E_T)$ is defined as a tree with R as its root(which is at 0th level) and node $v \in V_R$ is at i^{th} level(in any order) if $d_v = i$(distance from v to R in digraph). Note that each node in i^{th} level points to only one node in the $(i-1)^{th}$ level, else we get cycles.*

Definition 8. *Suppose if we have k-vertex disjoint weak paths from S to R in G, namely p_i for $i \in [1, k]$. Communication graph of the graph $G(V, E)$ of order k is denoted by $\mathcal{G}^k(V, \mathcal{E})$ and is defined as $\mathcal{E} = E \cap (E_p \cup E_T)$. Where $E_p = \bigcup_{i=1}^{k} E(p_i)$ and E_{p_i} is the set of edges in weak path p_i.*

Theorem 4. PSMT *from S to R is possible in G if* and only if *it is possible in $\mathcal{G}^{(t+1)}$.*

Proof. Sufficiency: Suppose PSMT is possible from S to R in G then from Theorem 1, we have $(t+1)$-vertex disjoint weak paths from S to R in G. By construction of graph $\mathcal{G}^{(t+1)}$, every edge in these paths present in $\mathcal{G}^{(t+1)}$. We now show that we can simulate the protocol Π_{Rnd_Eff} given in Section 5.1. By using the edges in these $t+1$ paths, if required nodes can share their random numbers with neighbours. Also every node $v \in V_R$ is at i^{th} level in spanning tree T for some $i \in [1, n-1]$ and so has a shortest path to R for sending $Val[u_{ij}]$ to R. Necessity: Suppose PSMT is not possible in G then clearly PSMT is not possible in sub graph $\mathcal{G}^{(t+1)}$ of G.

6.1 Round Optimal Protocol with Linear Communication Complexity $\Pi_{Rnd\_Opt\_Lin}$:

1. Every node u_{ij} except $u_{(t+1)0}$, in these $(t+1)$ paths pick a number $r_{ij} \in_R \mathbb{F}$, for $i \in [1, t+1]$ and $j \in [0, k_i+1]$. $S(= u_{(t+1)0})$ computes $r_{(t+1)0} = m - \sum_{i=1}^{t} r_{i0}$, this is possible for S to compute since r_{i0} is chosen by u_{i0} which is S itself.
2. For $i \in [1, t+1]$, $S(= u_{i0})$ initializes $L[u_{i0}] = r_{i0}$.
3. S computes $Val[S] = \sum_{i=1}^{t+1} Val[u_{i0}]$.
4. Let the height of the spanning tree T of G_u is h with root R is at 0th level.
5. For each u_{ij} in path p_i, follow the protocol Π_{Rnd_Eff} exactly as in Section 5.1, except that instead of sending $Val[u_{ij}]$ to R using path $p_{u_{ij}}$ separately:

(a) **If** u_{ij} is at h^{th} level(leaf node), u_{ij} sends $Val[u_{ij}]$ to its parent at $(h-1)^{th}$ level.

(b) **Else** each u_{ij} which is in $k^{th}(k \in [1, h-1])$ level waits till it receives *Values* $Val[u_{ij}]$ from its children in $(k+1)^{th}$ level if required. Once u_{ij} receives *Values* from its children it *adds* all the received values to its **Value** $Val[u_{ij}]$ and sends to its parent which is at $(k-1)^{th}$ level.

6. In last round, R adds all the **values** received from its children which are at level one with its sum of **Left Values**(i.e. $\sum_{i=1}^{t+1} L[u_{i(k_i+1)}]$) to get message m.

Lemma 5. *The protocol $\Pi_{Rnd\_Opt\_Lin}$ is reliable.*

Proof. For each u_{ij}, $(j \neq k_i + 1)$ in path p_i, we have $R[u_{ij}] = L[u_{i(j+1)}]$

Let $Sum = \sum_{i=1}^{t+1} \sum_{j=0}^{k_i} Val[u_{ij}] + \sum_{i=1}^{t+1} L[u_{i(k_i+1)}]$. Now we show that $Sum = m$

$$Sum = \sum_{i=1}^{t+1} \sum_{j=0}^{k_i} (L[u_{ij}] - R[u_{ij}]) + \sum_{i=1}^{t+1} L[u_{i(k_i+1)}]$$

$$= \sum_{i=1}^{t+1} \sum_{j=0}^{k_i} (L[u_{ij}] - L[u_{i(j+1)}]) + \sum_{i=1}^{t+1} L[u_{i(k_i+1)}]$$

$$= \sum_{i=1}^{t+1} (L[u_{i0}] - L[u_{i(k_i+1)}]) + \sum_{i=1}^{t+1} L[u_{i(k_i+1)}]$$

$$= \sum_{i=1}^{t+1} L[u_{i0}] = \sum_{i=1}^{t+1} r_{i0} = m.$$

Lemma 6. *The protocol $\Pi_{Rnd\_Opt\_Lin}$ is secure.*

Proof. Proof is analogous to the proof in Lemma 4. We shown that, in Lemma 4, protocol Π_{Eff} simulates the corresponding path p'_i of a secure weak path p_i, to securely transmit $p(i)$. In protocol $\Pi_{Rnd\_Opt\_Lin}$, $p(i)$ is replaced with r_{i0} and so r_{i0} is secure. This implies m is secure, since $m = r_{i0} + \sum_{j(\neq i)=1}^{t+1} r_{j0}$ and such r_{i0} is unique in any field $\mathbb{F}$.

The communication complexity of the above protocol $\Pi_{Rnd\_Opt\_Lin}$ is linear. Since, in first round as every node u_{ij} sends r_{ij} to its neighbours if require, which is $O(n)$ and each edge in spanning tree T is used only once to send a value from child to parent. We know that in a spanning tree with n nodes can not have more than n-1 edges, therefore total communication complexity is $O(n)$. Suppose shortest distance d_S from S to R is $\Omega(n)$ then we achieve **security for free** since the reliable communication itself requires $O(n)$ communication. We give an example of the protocol $\Pi_{Rnd\_Opt\_Lin}$ in graph G given in Fig. 3. Tree constructed based on the shortest distances from each node to R is given in Fig. 6. S chooses two random numbers r_1, r_2 and initializes $r_3 = m - (r_1 + r_2)$. S replaces $p(i)$ with r_i, for $i \in [1, 3]$.

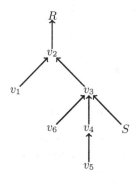

1. **Round 1**: Every node shares their random numbers, exactly as in examle given in section 5.4, except that $p(i)$ is replaced with r_i.
2. **Round 2**: Every node v calculates its value $Val[v]$. Nodes v_4, v_6, S will send $Val[v_4], Val[v_6], Val[S]$ to v_3 respectively.
3. **Round 3**: Node v_3 calculates the sum, $Sum(v_3) = Val[v_3] + Val[v_4] + Val[v_6] + Val[S]$ and sends to v_2.
4. **Round 4**: Node v_2 calculates $sum(v_2) = Sum(v_3) + Val[v_2]$ and sends to R. Finally R computes
$$m = sum(v_2) + r_{v_2} + r_{R_2} + r_{R_3}$$

Fig. 6. An example of protocol $\Pi_{Rnd\_Opt\_Lin}$ in graph G of Fig. 3

7   Conclusions and Open Problems

We have completely characterized the feasibility and optimality of PSMT in arbitrary networks under the influence of passive adversary. Similar characterization for the case of Byzantine and/or Mobile adversary has been left as an interesting open problem.

References

1. Franklin, M.K., Yung, M.: Secure hypergraphs: privacy from partial broadcast (extended abstract). In: Leighton, F.T., Borodin, A. (eds.) STOC, pp. 36–44. ACM (1995)
2. Hirt, M., Maurer, U.: Complete Characterization of Adversaries Tolerable in Secure Multi-party Computation. In: Proceedings of the 16th Symposium on Principles of Distributed Computing (PODC), pp. 25–34. ACM Press (August 1997)
3. Ostrovsky, R., Yung, M.: How to Withstand Mobile Virus Attacks. In: Proceedings of the 10th Symposium on Principles of Distributed Computing (PODC), pp. 51–61. ACM Press (1991)
4. Srinathan, K., Raghavendra, P., Chandrasekaran, P.R.: On proactive perfectly secure message transmission. In: Pieprzyk, J., Ghodosi, H., Dawson, E. (eds.) ACISP 2007. LNCS, vol. 4586, pp. 461–473. Springer, Heidelberg (2007)
5. Fitzi, M., Hirt, M., Maurer, U.M.: Trading Correctness for Privacy in Unconditional multi-party Computation. In: Krawczyk, H. (ed.) CRYPTO 1998. LNCS, vol. 1462, pp. 121–136. Springer, Heidelberg (1998)
6. Choudhary, A., Patra, A., Ashwinkumar, B.V., Srinathan, K., Rangan, C.P.: Perfectly reliable and secure communication tolerating static and mobile mixed adversary. In: Safavi-Naini, R. (ed.) ICITS 2008. LNCS, vol. 5155, pp. 137–155. Springer, Heidelberg (2008)
7. Sayeed, H., Abu-Amara, H.: Perfectly Secure Message Transmission in Asynchronous Networks. In: Seventh IEEE Symposium on Parallel and Distributed Processing (1995)

8. Dolev, D., Dwork, C., Waarts, O., Yung, M.: Perfectly Secure Message Transmission. Journal of the Association for Computing Machinery (JACM) 40(1), 17–47 (1993)
9. Nayak, M., Agrawal, S., Srinathan, K.: Minimal connectivity for unconditionally secure message transmission in synchronous directed networks. In: Fehr, S. (ed.) ICITS 2011. LNCS, vol. 6673, pp. 32–51. Springer, Heidelberg (2011)
10. Menger, K.: Zur allgemeinen kurventheorie. Fundamenta Mathematicae 10, 96–115 (1927)
11. Kurosawa, K., Suzuki, K.: Truly efficient 2-round perfectly secure message transmission scheme. IEEE Trans. Inf. Theor. 55(11), 5223–5232 (2009)
12. Badanidiyuru, A., Patra, A., Choudhury, A., Srinathan, K., Rangan, C.P.: On the trade-off between network connectivity, round complexity, and communication complexity of reliable message transmission. J. ACM 59(5), 22 (2012)
13. Fitzi, M., Franklin, M.K., Garay, J.A., Vardhan, S.H.: Towards optimal and efficient perfectly secure message transmission. In: Vadhan, S.P. (ed.) TCC 2007. LNCS, vol. 4392, pp. 311–322. Springer, Heidelberg (2007)
14. Renault, J., Renou, L., Tomala, T.: Secure message transmission on directed networks. Games and Economic Behavior 85, 1–18 (2014)
15. Kumar, M.V.N.A., Goundan, P.R., Srinathan, K., Pandu Rangan, C.: On perfectly secure communication over arbitrary networks. In: Proceedings of the 21st Symposium on Principles of Distributed Computing (PODC), Monterey, California, USA, pp. 193–202. ACM Press (July 2002)
16. Diffie, W., Hellman, M.E.: New Directions in Cryptography. IEEE Transactions on Information Theory IT-22, 644–654 (1976)
17. Desmedt, Y.G., Wang, Y.: Perfectly Secure Message Transmission Revisited. In: Knudsen, L.R. (ed.) EUROCRYPT 2002. LNCS, vol. 2332, pp. 502–517. Springer, Heidelberg (2002)
18. Srinathan, K., Rangan, C.P.: Possibility and complexity of probabilistic reliable communications in directed networks. In: Proceedings of 25th ACM Symposium on Principles of Distributed Computing, PODC 2006 (2006)
19. Franklin, M.K., Yung, M.: Communication complexity of secure computation (extended abstract). In: Kosaraju, S.R., Fellows, M., Wigderson, A., Ellis, J.A. (eds.) Proceedings of the 24th Annual ACM Symposium on Theory of Computing, Victoria, British Columbia, Canada, May 4-6, pp. 699–710. ACM (1992)
20. Shamir, A.: How to Share a Secret. Communications of the ACM 22, 612–613 (1979)
21. Cormen, T.H., Leiserson, C.E., Rivest, R.L., Stein, C.: Introduction to Algorithms, 3rd edn. MIT Press (2009)
22. Endre Tarjan, R.: Testing graph connectivity. In: Proceedings of the Sixth Annual ACM Symposium on Theory of Computing, STOC 1974, pp. 185–193. ACM, New York (1974)
23. Goldberg, A.V., Tarjan, R.E.: A new approach to the maximum flow problem. Journal of the ACM 35, 921–940 (1988)

On Zero-Knowledge with Strict Polynomial-Time Simulation and Extraction from Differing-Input Obfuscation for Circuits

Ning Ding

Department of Computer Science and Engineering
Shanghai Jiao Tong University, China
NTT Secure Platform Laboratories, Japan
dingning@sjtu.edu.cn

Abstract. This paper investigates the exact round complexity of zero-knowledge arguments of knowledge (ZKAOK) with **strict-polynomial-time simulation and extraction**. Previously, Barak and Lindell [STOC 02] presented a constant-round such ZKAOK. With the parallel technique by Ostrovsky and Visconti [ECCC 12] for implementing Barak's zero-knowledge [FOCS 01] in 6 rounds, the Barak-Lindell ZKAOK can be implemented in, we believe, 7 rounds, which achieves the best exact round complexity for such ZKAOK from reasonable assumptions.

Recently, Pandey *et al.* [ePrint 13] proposed a 4-round (concurrent) ZK with strict-polynomial-time simulation based on differing-input obfuscation for machines. Based on their construction, Ding [ISC 14] presented a 4-round ZKAOK with strict-polynomial-time simulation and extraction. However, the known construction of differing-input obfuscation for machines uses knowledge assumptions which are too strong. So an interesting question is whether we can reduce the round complexity of such ZKAOK without using differing-input obfuscation for machines.

In this paper we show that based on differing-input obfuscation for some circuit samplers and other reasonable assumptions, there exists a 6-round ZKAOK for **NP** with strict-polynomial-time simulation and extraction. Importantly, the assumption of differing-input obfuscation for circuits does not use any knowledge assumption and thus is mild. Moreover, we note that the auxiliary inputs output by the circuit samplers in our construction are public coins and perfectly-hiding commitments, which is quite natural. So this assumption, in our view, could be considered reasonable.

Keywords: Zero Knowledge, Argument of Knowledge, Differing-Input Obfuscation for Circuits.

1 Introduction

Zero-knowledge (ZK) proof systems, introduced by Goldwasser, Micali and Rackoff [23], are a fundamental notion in cryptography. Later Brassard *et al.* [9] suggested the notion of interactive arguments. Since their introduction, there

© Springer International Publishing Switzerland 2015
A. Lehmann and S. Wolf (Eds.): ICITS 2015, LNCS 9063, pp. 51–68, 2015.
DOI: 10.1007/978-3-319-17470-9_4

are many works constructing ZK protocols that satisfy various properties such as constant rounds, proof of knowledge [12,5,23,32] and strict-polynomial-time simulation and extraction etc. We sketch these results as follows.

Positive Results. Goldreich *et al.* [21] shows that every language in **NP** has a ZK proof. Goldreich and Kahan [19] presented a 5-round ZK proof. Lindell [29] presented a 5-round ZK proof of knowledge. Feige and Shamir [13] gave a 4-round ZKAOK. The simulators (resp. extractor if there is) of these protocols use a verifier's code (resp. prover's code) in a black-box way and run in expected-polynomial-time. Hada and Tanaka [24] presented a 3-round ZK argument based on two knowledge-exponent assumptions.

Barak [2] presented a constant-round public-coin non-black-box ZK argument. This is the first construction achieving constant-round and strict-polynomial-time simulation properties from reasonable assumptions. Ostrovsky and Visconti [30] showed a 6-round implementation for this protocol, achieving the best round complexity ever known for it. Although this protocol also admits an extractor, the extractor runs in expected-polynomial-time. Barak and Lindell [4] presented a construction with simultaneous strict-polynomial-time simulation and extraction, which can be implemented in 7 rounds via the technique in [30] as well as some other round parallel techniques (this 7-round conclusion did not appear in literature to the best of our knowledge but we find it doable).

Pandey *et al.* [31] presented a 4-round (concurrent) ZK argument with strict-polynomial-time simulation from differing-input obfuscators diO for machines [1]. Also based on diO for machines, Ding [11] presented a 4-round zero-knowledge argument of knowledge with strict polynomial-time simulation and extraction. Currently, diO for machines is based on diO for circuits (a candidate shown in [16]), fully homomorphic encryption and SNARKs [6] that require knowledge assumptions. So the assumption is very strong. Note that the usage of diO for machines in [31,11] cannot be replaced by diO for circuits because the programs in [31,11] that should be obfuscated have unbounded running-time and cannot be implemented by fixed-size circuits.

Negative Results. Goldreich and Oren [22] showed there is no 1-round or 2-round (auxiliary-input) ZK protocols for any language outside **BPP**. Then Goldreich and Krawczyk [20] showed that 3-round black-box ZK proofs exist only for languages in **BPP** and Katz [26] showed that 4-round black-box ZK proofs exist only for languages whose complement is in **MA**. Barak and Lindell [4] showed that black-box simulators and extractors cannot run in strict-polynomial-time if the protocols are constant-round.

To summarize, now we have 6-round ZKAOK with strict-polynomial-time simulation but expected-polynomial-time extraction and 7-round ZKAOK with strict-polynomial-time simulation and extraction from reasonable assumptions, and 4-round ZKAOK with strict-polynomial-time simulation and extraction from diO for machines. The current state of the art leaves an interesting question, i.e., *does there exist a 6-round ZKAOK for* **NP** *with strict-polynomial-time simulation and extraction without using diO for machines or knowledge assumptions?*

1.1   Our Results

This paper provides an affirmative answer to the above question by making use of $di\mathcal{O}$ for circuits which is not based on knowledge assumptions[1] and thus is more reasonable than $di\mathcal{O}$ for machines.

Generally, an obfuscator is a compiler that on input a circuit outputs a new program of same functionality with some security. Specifically, a $di\mathcal{O}$ for circuits is associated with a randomized sampling algorithm Sampler, which samples (C_0, C_1, z) where C_0, C_1 are two circuits of same size and z is an auxiliary input. We say $di\mathcal{O}$ is a differing-input obfuscator for Sampler as long as if it is hard for any polynomial-size algorithm to find an input x from (C_0, C_1, z) satisfying $C_0(x) \neq C_1(x)$, then $di\mathcal{O}(C_0)$ and $di\mathcal{O}(C_1)$ are indistinguishable for any distinguisher that has z.

Garg *et al.* [17] investigated the plausibility of general $di\mathcal{O}$ and showed that the existence of general $di\mathcal{O}$ conflicts with some special obfuscation. They constructed a contrived sampler that outputs two circuits $C_b, b = 0, 1$ each of which has the verification key vk and outputs b on receiving a message-signature pair (outputs 0 otherwise) and a contrived auxiliary input z that is the specially obfuscated program which has the signing key sk and on input any circuit C outputs $C(h(C), \sigma)$ where h is a hash function and σ is a signature of $h(C)$. Thus z on input any obfuscation of C_b outputs b and thus can distinguish the obfuscation of C_0, C_1. So if z is well specially obfuscated in hiding sk, there is no $di\mathcal{O}$ for this sampler. However, the auxiliary inputs randomly generated by the samplers in this paper are public coins and perfectly-hiding commitments. As suggested in [25] that $di\mathcal{O}$ is plausible for samplers which auxiliary-input outputs are public coins, we take $di\mathcal{O}$ in [1] as a candidate obfuscator for our samplers and achieve the following result.

Theorem 1. *(Informal) Assuming the existence of $di\mathcal{O}$ for some circuit samplers and other reasonable assumptions, there exists a 6-round ZKAOK for* **NP** *with strict polynomial-time simulation and extraction.*

Our Techniques. In a high level, our construction is divided to two steps. First, we construct a 8-round statistically ZKAOK with strict-polynomial-time simulation and extraction. Second, we modify the protocol by additionally in Step 6 letting the prover obfuscate its original next-message function of Step 8 with $di\mathcal{O}$ and send the obfuscated program as well as the original message of

---

[1] We do not treat $di\mathcal{O}$ for circuits itself as a real knowledge assumption. Typically a knowledge assumption says for an algorithm A computing some task, there is another algorithm A' that given A's coins can extract some secret from A's computation which will be used explicitly later. This extraction is specific to A. So we call this a knowledge assumption since A' has some knowledge of A. As for $di\mathcal{O}$ if there is a distinguisher D for the obfuscation of two circuits, there is an algorithm A' that can find a differing-input from the two unobfuscated circuits and the auxiliary input (without knowing the coins of D or the coins of the sampler). This extraction manifests some inherence of A'. So we do not think A' has some knowledge in the computation of some algorithm e.g. the sampler or D.

Step 6 to the verifier, which then finishes the interaction with the obfuscated program locally. Thus the modified protocol uses 6 rounds.

Recall that Barak and Lindell [4] proposed such a constant-round ZKAOK, which essentially makes use of Barak's non-black-box ZK [2] twice in reverse directions, of which one is for simulation and the other is for extraction. Since the best round complexity ever known for implementing Barak's ZK uses 6 rounds [30], Barak-Lindell's protocol uses at least 7 rounds with deliberate parallel techniques. We note that we cannot construct a desired 6-round ZKAOK based on the Barak-Lindell's protocol with diO. The main difficulty for this is that the Barak-Lindell's protocol is computational zero-knowledge and we have no idea on how to design a sampler that outputs the prover's next-message function and simulator's of last step as well as an auxiliary input such that it is hard to find a differing-input from the output of the sampler. Due to the high level description in the previous paragraph, the auxiliary input is probably the view except for the message of last step. Since the protocol is computational zero-knowledge, there may not exist a common such view with which both the two next-message functions are consistent. So it may not be hard to find a differing-input from the output by the sampler. However, to apply diO, the two functions/circuits being obfuscated, sampled by the sampler, should be able of fooling all polynomial-size algorithms having the view that they were of same functionality.

Moreover, in the 7-round Barak-Lindell's protocol, the prover's next-message function can be represented by a fixed polynomial-size circuit, while the simulator's cannot (depending on verifier's size). Thus we cannot use diO to obfuscate the two circuits. One more difficulty is that to use diO, the prover's strategy of last step should typically first verify if the latest verifier's message is valid and then proceed ordinarily if yes and abort otherwise, while the 7-round implementation does not admit this typicalness. Though we believe these two minor difficulties can be bypassed in a 8-round implementation, the above main difficulty is essentially unavoidable.

Our 8-round ZKAOK also uses Barak's ZK twice in the reverse directions for simulation and extraction respectively, but the prover's messages and simulator's output except for the message of last step are identically distributed (when considering the last message, the protocol is statistical zero-knowledge). Thus for a common view except for the last message, there are coins such that the two next-message functions, when having the coins hardwired, are consistent with the view and of same functionality to polynomial-size algorithms, which lets us bypass the main difficulty above.

The protocol basically runs as follows. The prover proves to the verifier in the first Barak's ZK that $x \in L$ using witness w. Recall that Barak's protocol consists of a preamble and a WI universal argument of knowledge (WIUA). The original simulator in [2] can obtain a trapdoor in the preamble and use it as witness in the WIUA and thus achieve the zero-knowledge property. To further achieve strict-polynomial-time extraction, we adopt the following idea. Note that the WIUA consists of an "encrypted" universal argument of knowledge and a 3-round WIAOK and the verifier accepts x if the messages of WIAOK are convincing.

Thus if we can obtain two different transcripts of form (α, β, γ) and $(\alpha, \beta', \gamma')$ of the WIAOK, then we can extract a witness. So instead of sending β we let the verifier encrypt (β, β) with a fully homomorphic encryption scheme and send the encryption to the prover, and further provide a proof that what is encrypted is indeed (β, β). The prover computes the encryption of (γ, γ) with the homomorphism property and sends it back to the verifier, and provides a final proof that the responding encryption is honestly generated. Then the verifier accepts the public input if the final proof is convincing.

In extraction the extractor samples two different β, β' and encrypts (β, β') and sends the encryption to the prover. Then we let the extractor cheat the prover that what is encrypted is (β, β) in the following proof. Actually this can be realized through the second Barak's ZK, in which the verifier proves to the prover that either it knows the trapdoor of the preamble (of this Barak's ZK) or what is encrypted is of form (β, β). Note that the extractor has the trapdoor (which is the prover's code), so it can accomplish the proof by using the trapdoor. Since the messages in extraction are indistinguishable from those in the ordinary interaction, the prover cannot be aware of this. Due to the soundness of the final proof what the prover responds with is an encryption of the answers to (β, β'), denoted (γ, γ'). Thus the extractor can decrypt it to obtain γ, γ' and recover a witness from the two transcripts of WIAOK.

Note that the simulator and extractor both run in non-black-box ways and in strict polynomial-time. By adopting some parallel techniques, we can indeed arrange the protocol in eight rounds. We note the protocol can also bypass the two minor difficulties that arise in directly compressing the rounds of 7-round Barak-Lindell's protocol mentioned above. First the prover's and simulator's next-message functions of last step have had all required information and are fixed polynomial-size. So they can be represented by two circuits of same size. Second the functionality of the two next-message functions is to output an encryption, followed by a proof for its honesty when the verifier's proof is sound for the honesty of the encryption of (β, β). If what the verifier encrypts is indeed (β, β), we can show the two circuits are of same functionality for rightly chosen coins. In the oppositive case, any polynomial-size verifier cannot find a valid proof for the cheating encryption except for negligible probability. That means no polynomial-size algorithm given the view as auxiliary input can find a differing-input for the two circuits with noticeable probability. Thus we can employ $di\mathcal{O}$ to obfuscate them and the two obfuscated circuits are indistinguishable. So let the prover/simulator directly send the obfuscation to the verifier as well as the original message of Step 6, which can reduce the round number of the protocol to six finally.

Organizations. The rest of the paper is arranged as follows. For lack of space we only present the notion of differing-input obfuscation for circuits in Appendix A. In Section 2 we present the 8-round statistically ZKAOK. In Section 3 we present an analysis of the prover's and simulator's next-message functions of last step and their obfuscation. In Section 4 we present the 6-round ZKAOK with obfuscation.

2 A Eight-Round Statistically Zero-Knowledge Argument of Knowledge

In this section we present the 8-round statistically ZKAOK. In Section 2.1 we present the primitives that will be used in the protocol. In Section 2.2 we present an overview of the protocol. In Section 2.3 we present its actual construction.

2.1 The Primitives in Use

Our construction will employ the following primitives.

1. Commitment Schemes. Let HCom denote a 2-round trapdoor perfectly-hiding computationally-binding commitment scheme, of which the binding property holds against $n^{O(\log \log n)}$-size algorithms, referred to [14]. Let Com denote a non-interactive perfectly-binding computationally-hiding commitment scheme from any one-permutation [7]. Let (msg, HCom) denote the two messages of HCom and Trapdoor denote the trapdoor corresponding to msg.

Note that here we require HCom and the following $\{\mathcal{H}_n\}$ are secure against $n^{O(\log \log n)}$-size adversaries. In this paper to claim some properties using the primitives, we will show if the properties cannot be achieved then there are adversaries that can break the security of these primitives. Since the adversaries need to run the extractors of the following WIUA or UA which run within $n^{O(\log \log n)}$-time, these primitives should be secure against $n^{O(\log \log n)}$-time adversaries.

2. Hash Functions. Let $\{\mathcal{H}_n\}$ denote a collision-resistant hash function family and each $h \in \mathcal{H}_n$ maps arbitrarily polynomially long strings to n-bit strings. We assume the collision resistance of $\mathcal{H}_n$ holds against $n^{O(\log \log n)}$-size algorithms.

3. Lapidot-Shamir 3-Round Perfectly WIAOK. Let LS denote this primitive due to Lapidot and Shamir [28], which is a variant of the 3-round Blum's protocol [8] and still public-coin. LS enjoys a key property that the first two messages are independent of the witness and the public input, noted in [30] and also used in [27,10]. In this paper we instantiate LS with HCom, which is thus perfectly WI. If ignoring the first message msg of HCom, LS uses 3 rounds and let $(\mathsf{LS}_1, \mathsf{LS}_2, \mathsf{LS}_3)$ denote the 3 messages.

Let P_{LS} be the algorithm that has coins s and $|y|$ and outputs LS_1 where y is a public input and then later on receiving y and witness W for y (in a specified language) and any two same/different challenges $(\mathsf{LS}_2, \mathsf{LS}_2')$ outputs the corresponding $(\mathsf{LS}_3, \mathsf{LS}_3')$. We denote the two-step computation by $\mathsf{LS}_1 \leftarrow P_{\mathsf{LS}}(|y|; s)$ and $(\mathsf{LS}_3, \mathsf{LS}_3') \leftarrow P_{\mathsf{LS}}(y, W, s, (\mathsf{LS}_2, \mathsf{LS}_2'))$.

Moreover, let LS^* denote another running of the LS system for a different public input. We still instantiate LS^* with HCom and msg, so LS^* is also perfectly WI. If ignoring the first message msg of HCom, let $(\mathsf{LS}_1^*, \mathsf{LS}_2^*, \mathsf{LS}_3^*)$ denote the 3 messages of LS^*.

4. 4-Round Public-Coin Universal Arguments of Knowledge. Let UA denote this primitive shown in [3] constructed from $\{\mathcal{H}_n\}$. It consists of 4 messages and let $(\mathsf{UA}_1, \mathsf{UA}_2, \mathsf{UA}_3, \mathsf{UA}_4)$ denote the 4 messages of UA.

5. 4-Round Public-Coin WI Universal Arguments of Knowledge. Let WIUA denote this primitive shown in [3] constructed from $\{\mathcal{H}_n\}$ and Com. In this paper, WIUA is used to prove a combined statement from an **NP** statement and an **Ntime**$(n^{O(\log \log n)})$ statement. Note that WIUA consists of an "encrypted" UA for the **Ntime**$(n^{O(\log \log n)})$ statement and a WIPOK for that either the plain UA is valid or the **NP** statement is true.

As shown in [30], WIUA can be implemented in 4 rounds and accordingly let (WIUA$_1$, WIUA$_2$, WIUA$_3$, WIUA$_4$) denote the 4 messages of WIUA. The **NP** statement can be determined after WIUA$_1$ is sampled and if the prover uses a witness for it in (the WIPOK of) WIUA, the witness can be extracted in expected-polynomial-time, or else a witness for the **Ntime**$(n^{O(\log \log n)})$ statement can be extracted in $n^{O(\log \log n)}$-time.

6. Fully Homomorphic Encryption. Let FHE = (KeyGen, Enc, Dec, Evaluate) denote a fully homomorphic encryption scheme in e.g. [18].

2.2   Overview

Recall that Barak's preamble consists of three messages in which the verifier first samples a random hash function h and then the prover responds with a commitment Z and lastly the verifier sends a random r. Let L be in **NP** and (x, w) is an instance-witness pair of L. Our protocol for L basically runs as follows.

1. P and V interact of the first Barak's preamble to generate $\lambda_1 = (h_1, Z_1, r_1)$, where Z_1 is computed with HCom. Then the two parties interact of the second preamble of reverse direction to generate $\lambda_2 = (h_2, Z_2, r_2)$. Let Trapdoor be the trapdoor of HCom corresponding to msg.

2. P interacts with V in the "encrypted" UA for proving that there are a program Π of size less than $n^{\log \log n}$ and some coins such that $h_1(\Pi)$ and the coins are an opening of Z_1 and Π (on input some message) outputs r_1 in $n^{\log \log n}$ steps.

3. Then P proves to V in LS that either there is w for $x \in L$ or the committed messages in the "encrypted" UA are a valid proof of UA. In the execution of LS, P first sends LS$_1$. Then V samples LS$_2$ and encrypts (LS$_2$, LS$_2$) with FHE and sends the encryption to P. Then prove to P in WIUA that either there are a program Π' of size less than $n^{\log \log n}$ and some coins such that $h_2(\Pi')$ and the coins are the opening of Z_2 and Π' (on input some message) outputs r_2 in $n^{\log \log n}$ steps, or the encryption is generated as specified and there is Trapdoor that is the trapdoor to msg. Lastly, P responds with the encryption of (LS$_3$, LS$_3$) honestly generated using algorithm Evaluate and witness w.

4. P proves to V in LS* using witness w that its responding encryption is generated honestly. V accepts x if LS* is convincing.

We sketch the intuition of the zero-knowledge and argument of knowledge properties as follows.

Statistical Zero-Knowledge. We present a simulator S for any verifier V^* and $x \in L$. Like Barak's simulator in [2], S knows V^*'s code and thus computes Z_1 as $\mathsf{HCom}(h_1(\Pi))$ in the first preamble where Π denotes V^*'s remainder strategy at this step. Then Π is a witness for λ_1 in UA, which means S can use it as witness to accomplish the UA, LS and LS^*.

Notice that all primitives used by P or S achieve some perfect security, i.e. the perfectly-hiding property of HCom and the perfectly WI properties of $\mathsf{LS}, \mathsf{LS}^*$. So basically, S's output is identically distributed to a real view of V^*. But the perfectly WI property of LS does not hold if the encryption sent by V^* is not as specified but V^* can send valid messages of WIUA. This is so because in this case V^* can receive P/S's responding encryption and thus gain two different transcripts of LS and recover a witness, which can distinguish the ordinary interaction from simulation. However, for such invalid encryption, V^* can convince P/S in WIUA only with negligible probability, since otherwise we can come up with an algorithm to break the collision-resistance of h_2. Therefore, we conclude that S's output is actually statistically close to a real view of V^*. In particular, if ignoring the message of last step, the output of S is identically distributed to a real view of V^*.

Argument of Knowledge. We show there is an extractor E such that if P' is a prover that can convince V of $x \in L$ with noticeable probability ϵ, $E(P', x)$ outputs a witness for x with probability $\epsilon - \mathsf{neg}(n)$. E basically follows V's strategy to interact with P'. Notice that E can obtain a trapdoor in the second preamble i.e. P''s code, that is a witness for λ_2 in WIUA. Then it samples two different $\mathsf{LS}_2, \mathsf{LS}_2'$ and sends the encryption of $(\mathsf{LS}_2, \mathsf{LS}_2')$. Then E can send a valid proof in WIUA using P''s code as witness. Due to the hiding property of Com, the encryption indistinguishability of FHE and the WI property of WIUA, P' can still output valid messages in the remainder interaction. Thus due to the soundness of LS^*, P''s responding encryption is generated as specified. So E can decrypt it to gain two answers, denoted $\mathsf{LS}_3, \mathsf{LS}_3'$ and extract a witness from the two transcripts $(\mathsf{LS}_1, \mathsf{LS}_2, \mathsf{LS}_3)$ and $(\mathsf{LS}_1, \mathsf{LS}_2', \mathsf{LS}_3')$. Lastly, we show what is extracted must be w since otherwise we can come up with an algorithm either to break the collision resistance of h_1 or to break the binding property of HCom.

2.3 Actual Construction

The actual construction of the protocol follows the overview in the previous subsection but with intensive parallel implementations of different phases, shown in Protocol 1. We present the detailed specification as follows.

1. $V \to P$: Sample $h_1 \in \mathcal{H}_n$ and $(msg, \mathsf{Trapdoor})$ of HCom where $\mathsf{Trapdoor}$ is the trapdoor of HCom corresponding to msg. Send h_1, msg to P.
2. $P \to V$: Sample $h_2 \in \mathcal{H}_n$ and compute $Z_1 \leftarrow \mathsf{HCom}(h_1(0^n))$. Send Z_1, h_2 to V.
3. $V \to P$: Sample $r_1 \in \{0, 1\}^n, \mathsf{UA}_1$. Compute $Z_2 \leftarrow \mathsf{Com}(h_2(0^n))$. Send them to P.

Public input: x (statement to be proved is "$x \in L$");
Prover's auxiliary input: w, (a witness for $x \in L$).

---

1. $V \to P$: Send $h_1 \in \mathcal{H}_n$, msg.
2. $P \to V$: Send $Z_1 \leftarrow \mathsf{HCom}(h_1(0^n))$, $h_2 \in \mathcal{H}_n$.
3. $V \to P$: Send $r_1 \in \{0,1\}^n$, $Z_2 \leftarrow \mathsf{Com}(h_2(0^n))$, UA_1.
4. $P \to V$: Send $r_2 \in \{0,1\}^n$, $C_1 \leftarrow \mathsf{HCom}(0^{|\mathsf{UA}_2|})$, LS_1, WIUA_1, LS_1^*.
5. $V \to P$: Send UA_3, WIUA_2, LS_2^*, pk, $X_1 \leftarrow \mathsf{Enc}(pk, \mathsf{LS}_2, \mathsf{LS}_2)$.
6. $P \to V$: Send $C_2 \leftarrow \mathsf{HCom}(0^{|\mathsf{UA}_4|})$, WIUA_3.
7. $V \to P$: Send WIUA_4.
8. $P \to V$: Send X_2 (imagine it is of form $\mathsf{Enc}(pk, \mathsf{LS}_3, \mathsf{LS}_3)$), LS_3^*.

Protocol 1. *The zero-knowledge argument of knowledge (P, V) for L*

- The UA system is to prove that there are a program Π of size less than $n^{\log \log n}$ and some coins such that $h_1(\Pi)$ and the coins are an opening of Z_1 and Π on input the message of Step 2 outputs r_1 in $n^{\log \log n}$ steps.

4. $P \to V$: Sample $r_2 \in \{0,1\}^n$, WIUA_1. Generate $\mathsf{LS}_1 \leftarrow P_{\mathsf{LS}}(|y|; s)$ where y denotes the public input that LS is proving and s is the coins, and $C_1 \leftarrow \mathsf{Com}(0^{|\mathsf{UA}_2|})$ and LS_1^* (which is the first message of LS^* interpreted below). Send them to P.

   - The LS system is to prove that either there is w for $x \in L$ or there are openings of C_1, C_2, in which let $\mathsf{UA}_2, \mathsf{UA}_4$ denote the committed messages and then $(\mathsf{UA}_1, \mathsf{UA}_2, \mathsf{UA}_3, \mathsf{UA}_4)$ is a valid transcript of UA. Note that at this step UA_3, C_2 have not been generated yet, but their lengths are known and thus LS_1 can be computed.

   - The WIUA system is to prove that either there are LS_2, coins s' and Trapdoor such that $X_1 = \mathsf{Enc}_{s'}(pk, \mathsf{LS}_2, \mathsf{LS}_2)$ and Trapdoor is the trapdoor to msg, or there are a program Π' of size less than $n^{\log \log n}$ and some coins such that $h_2(\Pi')$ and the coins are the opening of Z_2 and Π' on input the message of Step 3 outputs r_2 in $n^{\log \log n}$ steps.
   Note that at this step X_1 has not been generated yet, but the first statement of WIUA is of **NP** type and thus it can be determined after WIUA_1 is sampled.

5. $V \to P$: Sample UA_3, LS_2^*, LS_2 and $(pk, sk) \leftarrow \mathsf{KeyGen}(1^n)$. Compute $X_1 \leftarrow \mathsf{Enc}(pk, \mathsf{LS}_2, \mathsf{LS}_2)$, and WIUA_2 using witness LS_2, Trapdoor (and the coins). Send them (excluding sk) to P.

   - The LS^* system is to prove that there are a witness W for y (where y denotes the public input that LS is proving) and coins s such that $\mathsf{LS}_1 = P_{\mathsf{LS}}(|y|; s)$ and $X_2 = \mathsf{Evaluate}(pk, P_{\mathsf{LS}}, y, W, s, X_1)$. Note that at Step 4 although some messages involved in LS^* have not been generated yet, their lengths are known and thus LS_1^* can be computed at Step 4 (and in Step 8 P will generate LS_3^* using witness w).

6. $P \to V$: Compute $C_2 \leftarrow \mathsf{Com}(0^{|\mathsf{UA}_4|})$. Sample WIUA_3. Send them to V.

7. $V \to P$: Compute WIUA_4 (still using witness LS_2, Trapdoor). Send it to P.
8. $P \to V$: Compute $X_2 \leftarrow \mathsf{Evaluate}(pk, P_{\mathsf{LS}}, y, w, s, X_1)$. Also compute LS_3^* with witness w. Send them to V. V accepts x if $(\mathsf{LS}_1^*, \mathsf{LS}_2^*, \mathsf{LS}_3^*)$ is convincing.

Claim 1. *Protocol 1 is an interactive argument for L.*

Proof. It can be seen that the honest prover can always use witness w to convince the honest verifier and thus the completeness holds. The computational soundness follows from Claim 3. □

Claim 2. *Assuming the existence of $\mathcal{H}_n$, Com, HCom, Protocol 1 is statistical zero-knowledge. (In particular, when ignoring the message of Step 8, Protocol 1 is perfect zero-knowledge.)*

Proof. (Sketch.) We construct a simulator S for any polynomial-size verifier V^* and $x \in L$. $S(x, V^*)$ works as follows.

1. Emulate V^* to send out h_1, msg. Then sample h_2 and compute $Z_1 \leftarrow \mathsf{HCom}(h_1(\Pi))$ where Π denotes the remainder strategy of V^*. Send Z_1, h_2 to V^*.
2. Emulate V^* to send out r_1, Z_2, UA_1. Sample r_2, WIUA_1. Compute $\mathsf{LS}_1, \mathsf{LS}_1^*$ honestly. Compute UA_2 with witness Π (and the coins) and further $C_1 \leftarrow \mathsf{HCom}(\mathsf{UA}_2)$. Send them to V^*.
3. Emulate V^* to send out $\mathsf{UA}_3, \mathsf{WIUA}_2, \mathsf{LS}_2^*, pk, X_1$. Compute UA_4 still with Π and $C_2 \leftarrow \mathsf{HCom}(\mathsf{UA}_4)$. Lastly, sample WIUA_3. Send them to V^*.
4. Emulate V^* to send out WIUA_4. Adopt P's strategy to compute X_2 but with witness $(\mathsf{UA}_2, \mathsf{UA}_4)$ (and some coins) with algorithm $\mathsf{Evaluate}$. Compute LS_3^* with witness $(\mathsf{UA}_2, \mathsf{UA}_4)$.

Since Π is a witness for the public input to UA, S can use it to finish the interaction and run in polynomial-time. We now show S's output is statistically close to V^*'s real view interacting with $P(w)$. Briefly, the statistical indistinguishability follows from the perfectly-hiding property of HCom and the perfectly WI properties of $\mathsf{LS}, \mathsf{LS}^*$. Actually, the output of S is identically distributed to a real view of V^* if ignoring the message of Step 8. It can be seen that in Step 7, V^* may send a valid WIUA_4 even when X_1 is not as specified. If this happens, S's message of Step 8 differs from P's. Otherwise, they are also identically distributed. In the following we show this bad event occurs with negligible probability. Thus S's message and P's are statistically close.

Suppose, on the contrary, V^* can send a valid proof with noticeable probability for an invalid X_1. Then by running the extractor of WIUA we can generate a witness for the public input of WIUA. Since X_1 is not as specified, this witness must be a program for λ_2, denoted Π_1'. Then with a similar argument in [2], we can re-execute the above process independently one more time by rewinding V^* to Step 4, and also extract a witness for λ_2, denoted Π_2'. Note that the extraction of Π_1', Π_2' costs $n^{O(\log \log n)}$-time with noticeable probability.

Since on input a same message of Step 3, Π_1' and Π_2' both outputs r_2 but the two r_2 are different with probability $1 - 2^{-n}$, Π_1' and Π_2' are different programs.

Due to the perfectly-binding property of Com, $h_2(\Pi_1') = h_2(\Pi_2')$, which means we find a collision of h_2. It is impossible. So X_1 is indeed as specified except for an negligible probability. Thus the statistical zero-knowledge property holds.   □

Claim 3. *Assuming the existence of $\mathcal{H}_n$, FHE, Com, Protocol 1 is an argument of knowledge.*

Proof. (Sketch.) We show there is an extractor E such that if P' is a polynomial-size prover that can convince V of $x \in L$ with noticeable probability ϵ, $E(P', x)$ outputs a witness for x in polynomial-time with probability $\epsilon - \mathsf{neg}(n)$. E works as follows.

1. Sample h_1, msg. Send them to P'. Then emulate P' to send out Z_1, h_2.
2. Sample r_1, UA_1, but compute $Z_2 \leftarrow \mathsf{Com}(h_2(\Pi'))$, where Π' denotes the remainder strategy of P'. Send them to P' and emulate it to send out $r_2, C_1, \mathsf{LS}_1, \mathsf{WIUA}_1, \mathsf{LS}_1^*$.
3. Sample UA_3 and LS_2^*. Compute WIUA_2 using witness Π' (and the coins). Sample $(pk, sk) \leftarrow \mathsf{KeyGen}(1^n)$. Sample $\mathsf{LS}_2, \mathsf{LS}_2'$ and compute $X_1 \leftarrow \mathsf{Enc}(pk, \mathsf{LS}_2, \mathsf{LS}_2')$. Send them to P' and emulate it to output C_2, WIUA_3.
4. Compute WIUA_4 still using witness Π'. Send it to P' and emulate it to output X_2, LS_3^*.
5. If LS_3^* is invalid or $\mathsf{LS}_2 = \mathsf{LS}_2'$ output nothing. Otherwise, decrypt X_2 with sk to gain $\mathsf{LS}_3, \mathsf{LS}_3'$. Compute a witness from $(\mathsf{LS}_1, \mathsf{LS}_2, \mathsf{LS}_3)$ and $(\mathsf{LS}_1, \mathsf{LS}_2', \mathsf{LS}_3')$ and output it.

Note that Π' is a witness for the public input to WIUA and E can use it to finish the interaction. Note that the difference between the ordinary interaction and extraction is the message committed in Z_2, the message encrypted in X_1 and the witness used in WIUA. So due to the hiding property of Com, the encryption indistinguishability of FHE and the WI property of WIUA, Z_2, X_1 and the messages of WIUA in extraction and the ordinary interaction are indistinguishable. Thus P''s messages are still convincing except for an negligible probability. Thus E can extract a witness from $(\mathsf{LS}_1, \mathsf{LS}_2, \mathsf{LS}_3)$ and $(\mathsf{LS}_1, \mathsf{LS}_2', \mathsf{LS}_3')$.

We claim the output by E is w for $x \in L$ except for negligible probability. Suppose, on the contrary, what is extracted is $(\mathsf{UA}_2, \mathsf{UA}_4)$ with non-negligible probability. Then there is a prover P^* of UA such that when having λ_1 as public input (precisely it is (λ_1, h_2) since h_2 is a message in Step 2) it can convince the honest verifier of UA with noticeable probability.

We sketch P^* as follows. It plays as verifier of Protocol 1 to interact with P' of the first three steps (excluding UA_1) and also invokes an interaction with the honest verifier V_{UA} of UA, in which P^* tries to convince V_{UA} of the knowledge of Π for λ_1. On receiving UA_1 from V_{UA}, P^* transfers UA_1 to P' and finishes the remainder interaction with E's strategy to extract UA_2 (as well as some UA_4 corresponding to UA_3 it samples). Then P^* sends UA_2 to V_{UA}. On receiving the real UA_3 from V_{UA}, P^* rewinds P' to Step 5 and sends the UA_3 as well as other messages to P' and then extracts $(\mathsf{UA}_2, \mathsf{UA}_4)$. Note that the UA_2 must be identical to that one extracted previously due to the binding property of

HCom (note that E does not use Trapdoor as part of the witness, so the binding property of HCom is not compromised at all). Then P^* sends the UA_4 to V_{UA}.

The above means by running the extractor of UA, we can generate a program Π for λ_1 in $n^{O(\log \log n)}$-time.

Then with a similar argument in [2], we can run the extraction process twice from Step 3 in which the two r_1 are different and obtain two programs, denoted Π_1, Π_2, with noticeable probability. This costs $n^{O(\log \log n)}$-time. Since the two r_1 are different, $\Pi_1 \neq \Pi_2$, which either breaks the collision-resistance of h_1 or breaks the binding property of HCom. This is impossible. So we conclude what is extracted is indeed w for $x \in L$.   □

So combining the three claims, we have proved the following proposition.

Proposition 1. *Assuming all the underlying primitives, Protocol 1 is a 8-round statistically ZKAOK for* **NP** *with strict-polynomial-time simulation and extraction.*

3   Differing-Input Obfuscation of P/S's Next-Message Functions

In this section we investigate the functionalities of the next-message functions of the honest prover P and S of last step of Protocol 1. The result is that when having independently random coins, the differing-input obfuscation of the circuits of the two next-message functions are indistinguishable, which will be used to compress the last three rounds to one round in the next section.

Let $P_{x,w,u}$ denote the honest prover $P(x,w)$ with randomness u hardwired and $S_{x,V^*,v}$ denote $S(x,V^*)$ with randomness v hardwired. For each u used by the prover, parse $u = (u_1, u_2)$, where u_1 is used for computing the messages of Steps 2, 4, 6 and u_2 is used for Step 8. Similarly, for each v used by S, parse $v = (v_1, v_2)$, where v_1 is used for Steps 2, 4, 6 and v_2 is used for Step 8. Then we divide a view of V^* to two parts $\mathsf{view}_1 \circ \mathsf{view}_2$, where view_1 denotes V^*'s view up to Step 6 (excluding x) and view_2 denotes its view of Step 8. Thus view_1 is determined by u_1 for P or by v_1 for S and view_2 is determined by u_2 for P or by v_2 for S. W.l.o.g. assume $|u| = |v|$.

Due to Claim 2, for each fixed view_1 P and S have the equal-probability to generate it. Thus each u_1 corresponds to a v_1 such that both $P_{x,w,u}$ and $S_{x,V^*,v}$ generate a same view_1. Moreover, since Protocol 1 is statistical zero-knowledge, for each fixed view_1, if X_1 is as specified, each u_2 corresponds to a v_2 such that $P_{x,w,u}$ and $S_{x,V^*,v}$ generate a same view_2. That is, let P_{view_1,u_2} be $P_{x,w,u}$'s next-message function of last step and S_{view_1,v_2} be $S_{x,V^*,v}$'s next-message function of last step. When X_1 is as specified, for each corresponding pair (u,v), two view_1 generated in the ordinary interaction and simulation are same and P_{view_1,u_2} and S_{view_1,v_2} are of same functionality.

Let us then consider the size of P_{view_1,u_2} and S_{view_1,v_2}. Notice that at Step 5 where V^* interacts with $S_{V^*,x,v}$, the challenge UA_3 is chosen and then fixed. So $\mathsf{UA}_2, \mathsf{UA}_4$ are fixed. Then S_{view_1,v_2} can be represented by a circuit of fixed polynomial-size. The circuit has the public inputs and the existing transcripts of the $\mathsf{WIUA}, \mathsf{LS}^*$, and $\mathsf{UA}_2, \mathsf{UA}_4$ and some coins hardwired. On input WIUA_4, the circuit adopts S's strategy of Step 8 to output X_2, LS_3^*. We use Q_{view_1, v_2} to denote this circuit. So Q_{view_1, v_2} has the same functionality as S_{view_1, v_2}. (Q_{view_1, v_2} does not store those leaves of the PCP witness of UA which are not related to UA_3 and thus is fixed polynomial-size.)

Therefore, we can implement P_{view_1, u_2} and Q_{view_1, v_2} with circuits of same polynomial size. So we conclude that if X_1 is as specified, the two circuits are not only of same functionality, but also of same size. In the following we summarize this by presenting explicitly a sampler Sampler.

Algorithm 2. *The circuit sampler* $\mathsf{Sampler}(1^n)$ *which has* V^*'s *code and* (x, w) *hardwired.*
Input: *the system parameter* n.
Output: $(P_{\mathsf{view}_1}, Q_{\mathsf{view}_1}, \mathsf{view}_1)$.

- *Sample u and invokes an interaction between $P_{x,w,u}$ and V^* through the first six steps. Let view_1 denote the current view to V^*. Let P_{view_1, u_2} denote the circuit of P's next-message function of last step.*
- *Run the extractor of WIUA to extract a witness for the public input for WIUA. Due to the collision-resistance of h_2, the witness cannot be a desired program Π'. So it must be $(\mathsf{LS}_2, s', \mathsf{Trapdoor})$, extracted in expected polynomial-time.*
- *Follow S's strategy to compute all right messages that should be committed in all prover's commitments (i.e. $\Pi, \mathsf{UA}_2, \mathsf{UA}_4, \mathsf{LS}_1^*$) in simulation. Find $v = v(u)$ corresponding to u using $\mathsf{Trapdoor}$ such that $P_{x,w,u}$ and $S_{x,V^*,v}$ result in the same view_1 and $P_{\mathsf{view}_1, u_2}, Q_{\mathsf{view}_1, v_2}$ are of same functionality (supposing X_1 is as specified). Lastly, output $(P_{\mathsf{view}_1, u_2}, Q_{\mathsf{view}_1, v_2}, \mathsf{view}_1)$.*

Let $di\mathcal{O}$ be the differing-input obfuscator for circuits in [1] and we assume it works for Sampler with any (V^*, x, w). Then we have the following result.

Claim 4. *Let* $(P_{\mathsf{view}_1, u_2}, Q_{\mathsf{view}_1, v_2}, \mathsf{view}_1) \leftarrow \mathsf{Sampler}(1^n)$, $\mathcal{P}_{\mathsf{view}_1, u_2} \leftarrow di\mathcal{O}(P_{\mathsf{view}_1, u_2})$, $\mathcal{Q}_{\mathsf{view}_1, v_2} \leftarrow di\mathcal{O}(Q_{\mathsf{view}_1, v_2})$. *Then* $\mathcal{P}_{\mathsf{view}_1, u_2}$ *and* $\mathcal{Q}_{\mathsf{view}_1, v_2}$ *are indistinguishable for any polynomial-size distinguisher even having* view_1.

Proof. If we can show no polynomial-size algorithm given $(P_{\mathsf{view}_1, u_2}, Q_{\mathsf{view}_1, v_2}, \mathsf{view}_1)$ can with noticeable probability output a differing-input input for P_{view_1, u_2} and Q_{view_1, v_2}, then the claim holds. So in the following we show this.

First consider the case X_1 in view_1 is as specified, according to Sampler's strategy, P_{view_1, u_2} and Q_{view_1, v_2} are of same functionality. Second consider the case X_1 is not as specified. In this case, if there is a polynomial-size algorithm A that can find a convincing WIUA_4 with noticeable probability as input to the two circuits, the two circuits are not of same functionality. However, as we showed in Claim 3 that the existence of A implies the collision-resistance of h_2 can be broken. For any invalid WIUA_4, the two circuits both abort. This shows except for negligible probability, A cannot find a differing-input. Thus the claim holds. $\square$

Note that the indistinguishability in Claim 4 holds when the two circuits as well as view_1 are sampled by Sampler. In the following, we show for independent running of P and S, the indistinguishability also holds (remark that we do not need to truly run Sampler in the protocol).

Proposition 2. *For any $V^*, x \in L$, for any polynomial-size distinguisher D, for independently random u, v, $|\Pr[D(\mathsf{view}_1, \mathcal{P}_{\mathsf{view}_1, u_2}) = 1] - \Pr[D(\mathsf{view}_1, \mathcal{Q}_{\mathsf{view}_1, v_2}) = 1]| = \mathsf{neg}(n)$, where the probabilities are taken over all values of u, v and $di\mathcal{O}$'s independent coins in generating $\mathcal{P}_{\mathsf{view}_1, u_2}$ and $\mathcal{Q}_{\mathsf{view}_1, v_2}$ (note that the two view_1 are independently generated).*

Proof. For random u, let $v(u)$ denote the v corresponding to u such that the view_1 in the ordinary interaction and simulation are same, and the tripe of $(\mathcal{P}_{\mathsf{view}_1, u_2}, \mathcal{Q}_{\mathsf{view}_1, v_2}, \mathsf{view}_1)$ is identically distributed to the output of $\mathsf{Sampler}(1^n)$. For this triple, Claim 4 shows

$$|\Pr_{u, di\mathcal{O}'\text{s coins}}[D(\mathsf{view}_1, \mathcal{P}_{\mathsf{view}_1, u_2}) = 1]$$

$$- \Pr_{v(u), di\mathcal{O}'\text{s coins}}[D(\mathsf{view}_1, \mathcal{Q}_{\mathsf{view}_1, v_2}) = 1]| = \mathsf{neg}(n)$$

Thus

$$|\Pr_{u, di\mathcal{O}'\text{s coins}}[D(\mathsf{view}_1, \mathcal{P}_{\mathsf{view}_1, u_2}) = 1] - \Pr_{v, di\mathcal{O}'\text{s coins}}[D(\mathsf{view}_1, \mathcal{Q}_{\mathsf{view}_1, v_2}) = 1]|$$

$$= |\Pr_{u, di\mathcal{O}'\text{s coins}}[D(\mathsf{view}_1, \mathcal{P}_{\mathsf{view}_1, u_2}) = 1] - \Pr_{v(u), di\mathcal{O}'\text{s coins}}[D(\mathsf{view}_1, \mathcal{Q}_{\mathsf{view}_1, v_2}) = 1]|$$

$$= \mathsf{neg}(n)$$

$\square$

4   The Six-Round Zero-Knowledge Argument of Knowledge

In this section we present the 6-round ZKAOK for any **NP** language L. In Section 4.1, we present the construction idea. In Section 4.2 we present the protocol and show it satisfies all the properties claimed in the main theorem.

4.1   Construction Idea

Our idea of constructing the 6-round protocol is to compress the last three rounds of Protocol 1 to one round. Notice that in the previous section we show that Protocol 1 is statistical zero-knowledge with strict polynomial-time simulation and extraction. With the notations used in the previous section, let P_{view_1, u_2} (resp. Q_{view_1, v_2}) denote the prover's (resp. simulator's) next-message function of last step, $\mathcal{P}_{\mathsf{view}_1, u_2}$ and $\mathcal{Q}_{\mathsf{view}_1, v_2}$ be their differing-input obfuscation with $di\mathcal{O}$. Our idea to compress the last three rounds is to let P (resp. S) send $\mathcal{P}_{\mathsf{view}_1, u_2}$ (resp. $\mathcal{Q}_{\mathsf{view}_1, v_2}$) in Step 6 with the original message. Then the verifier on receiving the message can adopt the original honest verifier's algorithm to interact with

---

Public input: x (statement to be proved is "$x \in L$");
Prover's auxiliary input: w, (a witness for $x \in L$).

---

1. $V \to P$: Send $h_1 \in \mathcal{H}_n$, msg.
2. $P \to V$: Send $Z_1 \leftarrow \mathsf{HCom}(h_1(0^n))$, $h_2 \in \mathcal{H}_n$.
3. $V \to P$: Send $r_1 \in \{0,1\}^n$, $Z_2 \leftarrow \mathsf{Com}(h_2(0^n))$, UA_1.
4. $P \to V$: Send $r_2 \in \{0,1\}^n$, $C_1 \leftarrow \mathsf{HCom}(0^{|\mathsf{UA}_2|})$, LS_1, WIUA_1 and LS_1^*.
5. $V \to P$: Send UA_3, WIUA_2, LS_2^*, pk, $X_1 \leftarrow \mathsf{Enc}(pk, \mathsf{LS}_2, \mathsf{LS}_2)$.
6. $P \to V$: Send $C_2 \leftarrow \mathsf{HCom}(0^{|\mathsf{UA}_4|})$, WIUA_3, $\mathcal{P}_{\mathsf{view}_1, u_2}$.

Protocol 2. *The 6-round zero-knowledge argument of knowledge for L*

the obfuscated program locally to make a decision. Then due to Proposition 2, $(\mathsf{view}_1, \mathcal{P}_{\mathsf{view}_1, u_2})$ and $(\mathsf{view}_1, \mathcal{Q}_{\mathsf{view}_1, v_2})$ are indistinguishable for all polynomial-size distinguisher (that can have x), where the two random elements are independently generated, which ensures the modified protocol is zero-knowledge.

4.2   The Protocol

Let $di\mathcal{O}$ be the differing-input obfuscator for Sampler. Our 6-round ZKAOK for L is shown in Protocol 2, in which P and V follow the honest prover's and verifier's strategies of Protocol 1. The exception is that in the sixth step P additionally computes $\mathcal{P}_{\mathsf{view}_1, u_2} \leftarrow di\mathcal{O}(P_{\mathsf{view}_1, u_2})$ for random u_2 and sends V this obfuscation as well as the original message of Step 6. When V receives the last message, it adopts the honest verifier's strategy of Step 7 of Protocol 1 to send WIUA_4 to $\mathcal{P}_{\mathsf{view}_1, u_2}$ and runs the program. When $\mathcal{P}_{\mathsf{view}_1, u_2}$ sends out X_2, LS_3^*, V adopts the honest verifier's strategy to make the decision. Then we have the following claims.

Claim 5. *Protocol 2 is an interactive argument for L.*

Proof. The completeness is straightforward and the computational soundness follows from Claim 7. $\square$

Claim 6. *Assuming the existence of $\mathcal{H}_n$, Com, HCom, $di\mathcal{O}$, Protocol 2 is zero-knowledge.*

Proof. Now we construct a polynomial-time simulator Sim for Protocol 2 for any polynomial-size verifier V^* and $x \in L$. Sim adopts the simulator's strategy of Protocol 1 in the first fix steps. Let view_1 be the view up to Step 6. Then Sim samples random coins v_2. Let Q_{view_1, v_2} be S's strategy at Step 8 of Protocol 1. Then compute $\mathcal{Q}_{\mathsf{view}_1, v_2} \leftarrow di\mathcal{O}(Q_{\mathsf{view}_1, v_2})$. Output $(\mathsf{view}_1, \mathcal{Q}_{\mathsf{view}_1, v_2})$.

For each V^* and each $x \in L$, Proposition 2 ensures that $(\mathsf{view}_1, \mathcal{P}_{\mathsf{view}_1, u_2})$ and $(\mathsf{view}_1, \mathcal{Q}_{\mathsf{view}_1, v_2})$ are indistinguishable for any polynomial-size distinguisher that has x. So the zero-knowledge property holds. $\square$

Claim 7. *Assuming the existence of $\mathcal{H}_n$, FHE, Com, Protocol 2 admits a knowledge extractor.*

Proof. We show there is an extractor E such that if P' is a polynomial-size prover that can convince V of $x \in L$ with probability ϵ, $E(P', x)$ outputs a witness for x in polynomial-time with probability $\epsilon - \mathsf{neg}(n)$. Actually, E's strategy is identical to that of Protocol 1 except that in the last step on receiving the obfuscated program, denoted $\mathcal{Q}$, E interacts with $\mathcal{Q}$ and extracts a witness similarly.

It can be seen that if $\mathcal{Q}$ can output X_2 and a valid LS_3^*, what E obtains and decrypts from X_2 is indeed $(\mathsf{LS}_3, \mathsf{LS}_3')$. Then it can recover a witness from $(\mathsf{LS}_1, \mathsf{LS}_2, \mathsf{LS}_3)$ and $(\mathsf{LS}_1, \mathsf{LS}_2', \mathsf{LS}_3')$, which is either w for $x \in L$ or $(\mathsf{UA}_2, \mathsf{UA}_4)$. For a similar reason shown in the proof of Claim 3, what E extracts is indeed w except for negligible probability. $\square$

Combining these claims, we have the following formal restatement of the main theorem.

Theorem 3. *Assuming the existence of HCom, $di\mathcal{O}$, $\mathcal{H}_n$, FHE, Com, Protocol 2 is a 6-round ZKAOK for NP with strict polynomial-time simulation and extraction.*

Acknowledgments. I am grateful to the reviewers of ICITS 2015 for their detailed comments, which help improve the presentation of this paper a lot. This work is supported by the National Natural Science Foundation of China (Grant No. 61100209) and Doctoral Fund of Ministry of Education of China (Grant No. 20120073110094).

References

1. Ananth, P., Boneh, D., Garg, S., Sahai, A., Zhandry, M.: Differing-inputs obfuscation and applications. IACR Cryptology ePrint Archive 2013, 689 (2013)
2. Barak, B.: How to go beyond the black-box simulation barrier. In: FOCS, pp. 106–115 (2001)
3. Barak, B., Goldreich, O.: Universal arguments and their applications. In: IEEE Conference on Computational Complexity, pp. 194–203 (2002)
4. Barak, B., Lindell, Y.: Strict polynomial-time in simulation and extraction. In: Reif, J.H. (ed.) STOC, pp. 484–493. ACM (2002)
5. Bellare, M., Goldreich, O.: On defining proofs of knowledge. In: Brickell, E.F. (ed.) Advances in Cryptology - CRYPTO 1992. LNCS, vol. 740, pp. 390–420. Springer, Heidelberg (1993)
6. Bitansky, N., Canetti, R., Chiesa, A., Tromer, E.: Recursive composition and bootstrapping for snarks and proof-carrying data. In: Boneh, D., Roughgarden, T., Feigenbaum, J. (eds.) STOC, pp. 111–120. ACM (2013)
7. Blum, M.: Coin flipping by telephone. In: Gersho, A., (ed.) CRYPTO, pp. 11–15. U. C. Santa Barbara, Dept. of Elec. and Computer Eng., ECE Report No 82-04 (1981)
8. Blum, M.: How to prove a theorem so no one else can claim it. In: Proceedings of the International Congress of Mathematicians, pp. 1444–1451 (1987)

9. Brassard, G., Chaum, D., Crépeau, C.: Minimum disclosure proofs of knowledge. J. Comput. Syst. Sci. 37(2), 156–189 (1988)

10. Crescenzo, G.D., Persiano, G., Visconti, I.: Constant-round resettable zero knowledge with concurrent soundness in the bare public-key model. In: Franklin [15], pp. 237–253, http://dx.doi.org/10.1007/978-3-540-28628-8_15

11. Ding, N.: Obfuscation-based non-black-box extraction and constant-round zero-knowledge arguments of knowledge. In: Chow, S.S.M., Camenisch, J., Hui, L.C.K., Yiu, S.M. (eds.) ISC 2014. LNCS, vol. 8783, pp. 120–139. Springer, Heidelberg (2014)

12. Feige, U., Fiat, A., Shamir, A.: Zero knowledge proofs of identity. In: Aho, A.V. (ed.) STOC, pp. 210–217. ACM (1987)

13. Feige, U., Shamir, A.: Witness indistinguishable and witness hiding protocols. In: Ortiz, H. (ed.) STOC, pp. 416–426. ACM (1990)

14. Fischlin, M.: Trapdoor Commitment Schemes and Their Applications. Ph.D. thesis, Fachbereich Mathematik Johann Wolfgang Goethe-Universit at Frankfurt am Main (2001)

15. Franklin, M. (ed.): CRYPTO 2004. LNCS, vol. 3152. Springer, Heidelberg (2004)

16. Garg, S., Gentry, C., Halevi, S., Raykova, M., Sahai, A., Waters, B.: Candidate indistinguishability obfuscation and functional encryption for all circuits. In: FOCS, pp. 40–49. IEEE Computer Society (2013)

17. Garg, S., Gentry, C., Halevi, S., Wichs, D.: On the implausibility of differing-inputs obfuscation and extractable witness encryption with auxiliary input. In: Garay, J.A., Gennaro, R. (eds.) CRYPTO 2014, Part I. LNCS, vol. 8616, pp. 518–535. Springer, Heidelberg (2014),
http://dx.doi.org/10.1007/978-3-662-44371-2_29

18. Gentry, C.: Fully homomorphic encryption using ideal lattices. In: Mitzenmacher, M. (ed.) STOC, pp. 169–178. ACM (2009)

19. Goldreich, O., Kahan, A.: How to construct constant-round zero-knowledge proof systems for NP. J. Cryptology 9(3), 167–190 (1996)

20. Goldreich, O., Krawczyk, H.: On the composition of zero-knowledge proof systems. SIAM J. Comput. 25(1), 169–192 (1996)

21. Goldreich, O., Micali, S., Wigderson, A.: Proofs that yield nothing but their validity and a methodology of cryptographic protocol design (extended abstract). In: FOCS, pp. 174–187. IEEE Computer Society (1986)

22. Goldreich, O., Ostrovsky, R.: Software protection and simulation on oblivious rams. J. ACM 43(3), 431–473 (1996)

23. Goldwasser, S., Micali, S., Rackoff, C.: The knowledge complexity of interactive proof systems. SIAM J. Comput. 18(1), 186–208 (1989)

24. Hada, S., Tanaka, T.: On the existence of 3-round zero-knowledge protocols. In: Krawczyk, H. (ed.) CRYPTO 1998. LNCS, vol. 1462, pp. 408–423. Springer, Heidelberg (1998)

25. Ishai, Y., Pandey, O., Sahai, A.: Public-coin differing-inputs obfuscation and its applications. Cryptology ePrint Archive, Report 2014/942 (2014), http://eprint.iacr.org/

26. Katz, J.: Which languages have 4-round zero-knowledge proofs? In: Canetti, R. (ed.) TCC 2008. LNCS, vol. 4948, pp. 73–88. Springer, Heidelberg (2008)

27. Katz, J., Ostrovsky, R.: Round-optimal secure two-party computation. In: Franklin [15], pp. 335–354,
http://dx.doi.org/10.1007/978-3-540-28628-8_21

28. Lapidot, D., Shamir, A.: Publicly verifiable non-interactive zero-knowledge proofs. In: Menezes, A.J., Vanstone, S.A. (eds.) CRYPTO 1990. LNCS, vol. 537, pp. 353–365. Springer, Heidelberg (1991)
29. Lindell, Y.: A note on constant-round zero-knowledge proofs of knowledge. J. Cryptology 26(4), 638–654 (2013)
30. Ostrovsky, R., Visconti, I.: Simultaneous resettability from collision resistance. Electronic Colloquium on Computational Complexity (ECCC) 19, 164 (2012)
31. Pandey, O., Prabhakaran, M., Sahai, A.: Obfuscation-based non-black-box simulation and four message concurrent zero knowledge for np. Cryptology ePrint Archive, Report 2013/754 (2013), http://eprint.iacr.org/
32. Tompa, M., Woll, H.: Random self-reducibility and zero knowledge interactive proofs of possession of information. In: FOCS, pp. 472–482. IEEE Computer Society (1987)

A Preliminaries

A.1 Differing-Input Obfuscation for Circuits

Recall the notion of differing-input obfuscation for circuits in [1].

Definition 1. *A circuit family $\mathcal{C}$ associated with a PPT (or expected PPT) sampler Sampler is said to be a differing-input circuit family if for every polynomial-size adversary A such that:*

$$\Pr[C_0(x) \neq C_1(x) : (C_0, C_1, \text{aux}) \leftarrow \text{Sampler}(1^n), x \leftarrow A(1^n; C_0, C_1, \text{aux}] = \text{neg}(n)$$

Definition 2. *(Differing-input Obfuscators for Circuits) A uniform PPT machine $di\mathcal{O}$ is called a differing-input Obfuscator for a differing-input circuit family $\mathcal{C}$, if the following conditions are satisfied:*

- *Correctness. for every input x and all $C \in \mathcal{C}$, $C(x) = di\mathcal{O}(C)$.*
- *Polynomial slowdown. There exists a universal polynomial p such that for any circuit C, we have $|C'| \leq p(|C|)$, where $C' \leftarrow di\mathcal{O}(C)$.*
- *Differing-input: For any (not necessarily uniform) PPT distinguisher D such that the following holds: For all security parameters $n \in N$, for $(C_0, C_1, \text{aux}) \leftarrow \text{Sampler}(1^n)$, we have that*

$$|\Pr[D(di\mathcal{O}(C_0), \text{aux}) = 1] - \Pr[D(di\mathcal{O}(C_1), \text{aux}) = 1] = \text{neg}(n)$$

A candidate construction for this primitive appears in the work of [1]. We note that this primitive does not use any knowledge assumption, while a generalized notion of differing-input obfuscation for machines needs knowledge assumptions.

Unifying Leakage Classes: Simulatable Leakage and Pseudoentropy[*]

Benjamin Fuller[1,2] and Ariel Hamlin[2]

[1] Boston University, 244 Wood Street, Lexington, MA 02420, USA
[2] MIT Lincoln Laboratory, One Silber Way, Boston, MA 02215, USA

Abstract. Leakage resilient cryptography designs systems to withstand partial adversary knowledge of secret state. Ideally, leakage-resilient systems withstand current and future attacks; restoring confidence in the security of implemented cryptographic systems. Understanding the relation between classes of leakage functions is an important aspect.

In this work, we consider the memory leakage model, where the leakage class contains functions over the system's entire secret state. Standard limitations include functions with bounded output length, functions that retain (pseudo) entropy in the secret, and functions that leave the secret computationally unpredictable.

Standaert, Pereira, and Yu (Crypto, 2013) introduced a new class of leakage functions they call simulatable leakage. A leakage function is *simulatable* if a simulator can produce indistinguishable leakage without access to the true secret state. We extend their notion to general applications and consider two versions. For *weak* simulatability: the simulated leakage must be indistinguishable from the true leakage in the presence of public information. For *strong* simulatability, this requirement must also hold when the distinguisher has access to the true secret state. We show the following:

- Weakly simulatable functions retain computational unpredictability.
- Strongly simulatability functions retain pseudoentropy.
- There are bounded length functions that are not weakly simulatable.
- There are weakly simulatable functions that remove pseudoentropy.
- There are leakage functions that retain computational unpredictability are not weakly simulatable.

1 Introduction

Cryptography relies on secret randomness, such as keys. It is crucial to properly model how an adversary can interact with and observe this secret state. As an example, when defining security of a block cipher, an adversary may ask for

---

[*] The Lincoln Laboratory portion of this work was sponsored by the Department of the Air Force under Air Force Contract #FA8721-05-C-0002. Opinions, interpretations, conclusions and recommendations are those of the author and are not necessarily endorsed by the United States Government.

© Springer International Publishing Switzerland 2015
A. Lehmann and S. Wolf (Eds.): ICITS 2015, LNCS 9063, pp. 69–86, 2015.
DOI: 10.1007/978-3-319-17470-9_5

encryption of arbitrary plaintexts and see the corresponding ciphertext. The secret key and randomness used by the algorithm are assumed to be hidden from the adversary.

Unfortunately, the adversary rarely uses cryptographic systems as black-boxes, exploiting side-channel information when possible. As many works have shown, side-channel attacks have been devastating to existing deployed cryptosystems [Koc96,KJJ99,BB05,BM06,OST06,TOS10,GST13].

Completely eliminating side-channel attacks seems hopeless. The cryptographic community began designing systems that remain secure in the presence of side-channel attacks. In the theoretical community, the work of Ishai, Sahai, and Wagner [ISW03] showed how to transform any circuit into one that withstood adversarial knowledge of some constant fraction of the wire values. The work of Micali and Reyzin [MR04] considered arbitrary leakage functions of bounded output length.

There are two crucial aspects to defining a leakage function: what the function computes on, and what type of computations the function can perform. We refer to these aspects as the leakage *model* and leakage *class* respectively.

Leakage Models. There are two commons models: *circuit leakage* assumes the leakage function operates on a particular circuit implementation of a computation. The leakage function is allowed (with restrictions) to compute on individual gates and wires in the circuit. *Memory leakage* allows the leakage function to leak on secret state and ignores the intermediate states of computation specific to the implementation of the algorithm.[1] Circuit leakage is used in conjunction with leakage classes restricted to local computations. Memory leakage is used in conjunction with functions that access all state simultaneously (but with some restriction on the output). Results in these models are not easily compared. We focus on the memory leakage model but briefly discuss simulatable leakage in the context of circuit leakage in Appendix A.

Leakage Classes. We now describe common leakage classes in the memory leakage model.

- **Bounded Length** [MR04]. The leakage function is an arbitrary function $\mathcal{L}$ of input, secret state and randomness. The only limitation on the function is a bounded output length. A natural broadening of this class is the set of all functions that preserve min-entropy of the secret state.[2] We denote this class of leakage functions by bLEN.

- **Indistinguishable** [DP08]. Bounded length leakage is easy to reason about because secret state has entropy conditioned on the output of the leakage function. Unfortunately, many leakage functions (such as the power

---

[1] If the leakage class is sufficiently powerful, the particular implementation of an algorithm is irrelevant. The leakage function can recompute a given implementation of the functionality. This is the case for all leakage classes we consider in the memory leakage model.

[2] If the output length of the leakage function is significantly less than the entropy of the secret state, then bounded length leakage functions retain average min-entropy.

trace of computation) are quite long. Furthermore, in many applications the secret key does not have information-theoretic entropy (for example, a Diffie-Hellman key conditioned on the public transcript). A leakage function $\mathcal{L}$ is an *indistinguishable leakage function* if the secret state looks like it has entropy conditioned on $\mathcal{L}$ (we use HILL entropy [HILL99]). Note this class contains bounded length functions. We denote this class of leakage functions by Indist. We also use a weaker notion of pseudoentropy called relaxed HILL entropy [Rey11] and denote the class of leakage functions that preserve relaxed HILL entropy as rIndist.

- **Hard-to-invert** [DKL09]. The indistinguishable leakage model is too restrictive for many applications. As an example, a symmetric cipher key is often uniquely determined conditioned on a few plaintext/ciphertext pairs. It is usually possible to verify a guess for the key and thus, it is not indistinguishable from any high entropy distribution. A minimum condition is that secret state is hard to guess given leakage. This is known as *hard-to-invert* leakage. We denote this class of functions as hINV.

- **Simulatable** [SPY13]. Standaert, Pereira, and Yu recently introduced simulatable leakage. Consider some private state K with some public information Y (such as a public key or plaintext/ciphertex pairs). A leakage function is simulatable if a simulator S can create a random variable $S(Y)$ that is indistinguishable from $\mathcal{L}(K)$. Simulatable leakage is a combination of ideas from practice and theory. It allows simulators to be proposed for actual leakage functions. Then practitioners can try and distinguish simulator output from the true leakage. Indeed, the simulator proposed by Standaert et al. was subsequently broken [LMO⁺14]. The work of Standaert, Pereira, and Yu also shows how to construct a stream cipher that withstands simulatable leakage from a pseudorandom generator that withstands simulatable leakage.

Containments between the first three leakage classes are understood. (bLEN ⊂ Indist ⊂ hINV.) Simulatable leakage is a natural definition. Ideally, simulatable leakage would preserve security as an adversary could use the simulated leakage (and execute their attack with similar success probability) and therefore leakage would not harm application security. The goal of this work is to clarify this intuition.

We consider two versions of simulatable leakage: first where the simulated leakage must be consistent with only the public system state, and second where the simulated leakage must be consistent with both the public and private system state. We call these classes weakly simulatable (wSIM) and strongly simulatable (sSIM) respectively.

Meaningfulness of Weakly Simulatable Leakage Weakly simulatable leakage is not always meaningful. As example, consider an adversary trying to guess a private key K with no public information. The identity function is a weakly simulatable. A simulator for the leakage can sample a uniform random key K'. We call this situation *leak-and-resample*. To prevent this, we assume it is difficult to sample a key that is consistent with the public information (Definition 12).

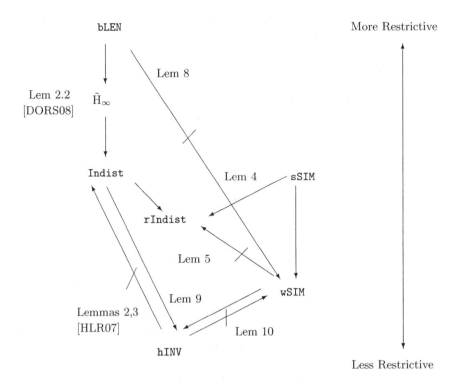

Fig. 1. Containment between difference leakage notions. The relations between simulatable leakage are shown in this work. Arrows imply containment and arrows with slashes imply there is a function in one class not contained in the other class.

This is the case in many applications but not all. We call this setting—borrowing terminology from zero knowledge—*witness hiding.*

Our contribution: We connect the notion of simulatable leakage to standard leakage models. A graphical description of our results is in Figure 1. We show five results:

- Lemma 4: Strong simulatability implies relaxed HILL entropy. That is, sSIM ⊆ rIndist.
- Lemma 5: There are simulatable leakage functions that remove all pseudoentropy from private state. That is, wSIM ⊄ rIndist.
- Lemma 8: There are bounded-length leakage functions that are not simulatable. bLEN ⊄ wSIM.
- Lemma 9: Simulatable leakage preserves unpredictability. wSIM ⊂ hINV.
- Lemma 10: There are hard-to-invert leakage functions that are not simulatable. hINV ⊄ wSIM.

Discussion: These results show that weakly simulatable leakage is properly contained in hard-to-invert leakage. This suggests it may be possible to build cryptographic primitives for weakly simulatable leakage that have eluded hard-to-invert leakage. Building crypto systems secure against hard-to-invert leakage been difficult, suggesting that simulatable leakage is a promising alternative.

This work places simulatable leakage in the context of other memory leakage classes. The complementary question is how simulatable leakage fits with previously considered leakage classes in the circuit model. We discuss definitional considerations for simulatable leakage in the circuit model in Appendix A. Providing results in the circuit model is more complicated as one must consider the implementation of a functionality. We leave this an open problem.

In this work we show that sSIM is contained in rIndist. It seems natural that simulatable leakage is related to indistinguishability (since it is an indistinguishability based definition). Settling the containment with Indist is an interesting question.

Organization: The remainder of the paper is organized as follows. We begin by covering preliminaries and definitions of memory leakage classes in Section 2. In Section 3, we define simulatable leakage and extend it to general applications (the definition of [SPY13] is specific to symmetric ciphers). In Section 4, we discuss strong simulatability and pseudoentropy. In Sections 5 and 6, we connect weakly simulatable leakage to indistinguishable and hard-to-invert leakage respectively.

2   Preliminaries

We usually use upper case letters for random variables and lower case letters for particular outcomes. U_n denotes the uniformly distributed random variable on $\{0,1\}^n$. Unless otherwise noted logarithms are base 2.

Entropy Notions. The *min-entropy* of X is $H_\infty(X) = -\log(\max_x \Pr[X = x])$. Let $|W|$ be the size of the support of W that is $|W| = |\{w|\Pr[W = w] > 0\}|$.

Definition 1. *[DORS08, Section 2.4] The average (conditional) min-entropy of X given Y is*

$$\tilde{H}_\infty(X|Y) = -\log(\mathop{\mathbb{E}}_{y \in Y} \max_x \Pr[X = x|Y = y]).$$

Distance Notions. The *statistical distance* between random variables X and Y with the same domain is $\Delta(X, Y) = \frac{1}{2}\sum_x |\Pr[X = x] - \Pr[Y = x]|$. For a distinguisher D (or a class of distinguishers $\mathcal{D}$) we write the *computational distance* between X and Y as $\delta^D(X, Y) = |\mathbb{E}[D(X)] - \mathbb{E}[D(Y)]|$. We denote by $\mathcal{D}_{s_{sec}}$ the class of randomized circuits which output a single bit and have size at most s_{sec}.

We use a slightly nonstandard notion of a one-way function is hard on a particular input distribution (instead of the uniform distribution).

Definition 2. *Let K be a distribution over space $\mathcal{M}$ and let $f : \mathcal{M} \to \{0,1\}^*$. We say that f is (s, ϵ, K)-one-way if for all A of size at most s,*

$$\Pr_{x \leftarrow K}[f(A(f(x))) = f(x)] \leq \epsilon.$$

2.1 Pseudoentropy

In this section, we present notions of pseudoentropy that are used to describe leakage classes. Pseudoentropy is the computational analogue of min-entropy. In general, a pseudoentropy notion describes how much entropy a random variable has to computationally bounded adversaries. The most common notions of pseudoentropy consider indistinguishability from a high entropy random variable and unpredictability.[3]

Indistinguishability. We use the common notion of HILL entropy [HILL99] extended to the conditional setting [HLR07].

Definition 3. *[HLR07] Let (K, Y) be a pair of random variables. K has* relaxed HILL entropy *at least k conditioned on Y, denoted $H^{\mathrm{HILL}}_{\epsilon_{ent}, s_{ent}}(K|Y) \geq k$ if for each $y \in Y$ there exists distributions Z_y giving rise to a joint distribution (Z, Y), such that $\tilde{H}_\infty(Z|Y) \geq k$ and $\delta^{\mathcal{D}_{sent}}(K, Y), (Z, Y)) \leq \epsilon_{ent}$.*

One of the primary uses of HILL entropy is that applying a randomness extractor [NZ93] yields pseudorandom bits [BSW03, Lemma 4.2]. There are many notions of indistinguishability based pseudoentropy [BSW03,Sko14]. One significant drawback of conditional HILL entropy is that revealing one bit can significantly decrease HILL entropy [KPW13]. Relaxed HILL entropy allows replacement of the condition as well in the indistinguishability game.

Definition 4. *[GW11,Rey11] Let (K, Y) be a pair of random variables. K has* relaxed HILL entropy *at least k conditioned on Y, denoted $H^{\mathrm{HILL-rlx}}_{\epsilon_{ent}, s_{ent}}(K|Y) \geq k$ if there exists a joint distribution (K', Y') such that $\tilde{H}_\infty(K'|Y') \geq k$ and $\delta^{\mathcal{D}_{sent}}(K, Y), (K', Y')) \leq \epsilon_{ent}$.*

Relaxed HILL entropy is a weaker notion than HILL entropy (by restricting to the joint distributions (K', Y') where $Y' = Y$).

Proposition 1. $H^{\mathrm{HILL-rlx}}_{\epsilon_{ent}, s_{ent}}(K|Y) \geq H^{\mathrm{HILL}}_{\epsilon_{ent}, s_{ent}}(K|Y).$

However, it is still useful as applying a randomness extractor still yields a pseudorandom output [Ful15, Theorem 2.2.4]. Furthermore, relaxed HILL entropy obeys a chain rule unlike traditional HILL entropy [GW11,Rey11].

---

[3] There are also notions of pseudoentropy that consider compressibility of a random variable. We do not discuss this notion in this work. See [Yao82,BSW03,HLR07].

Unpredictability. One can also consider the unpredictability of a random variable by computationally bounded adversaries. This is captured by the following definition [HLR07]:

Definition 5. *Let (K, Y) be a pair of random variables. We say that K has unpredictability entropy at least k conditioned on Y, denoted by $H_{\epsilon_{unp}, s_{unp}}^{\mathrm{unp}}(K|Y) \geq k$, if for all joint distributions (Z, Y) such that $\delta^{\mathcal{D}_{s_{unp}}}((K, Y), (Z, Y)) \leq \epsilon_{unp}$, and for all circuits $\mathcal{I}$ of size s_{unp},*

$$\Pr[\mathcal{I}(Y) = Z] \leq 2^{-k}.$$

HILL entropy is at least as large as unpredictability entropy.

Proposition 2. *[HLR07, Lemma 8] $H_{\epsilon,s}^{\mathrm{HILL}}(K|Y) \geq H_{\epsilon,s}^{\mathrm{unp}}(K|Y)$.*

The work of Hsiao, Lu, and Reyzin shows they can be separated by an arbitrary polynomial case in the conditional case [HLR07, Lemmas 2 and 3]. However, it is possible extract from unpredictability entropy using a randomness extractor with a reconstruction procedure [HLR07, Lemma 6].

In our results, we use of the fact that HILL and unpredictability entropy are unchanged if a polynomial size circuit is applied to the condition. In the information theoretic setting this is known as the data processing inequality.

Lemma 1. *Let S be a circuit of size s_{sim}. Then*

$$H_{\epsilon_{ent}, s_{ent} - s_{sim}}^{\mathrm{HILL}}(K|S(Y)) \geq H_{\epsilon_{ent}, s_{ent}}^{\mathrm{HILL}}(K|Y).$$

Proof. Let $H_{\epsilon_{ent}, s_{ent}}^{\mathrm{HILL}}(K|Y) = k$. Suppose for the sake of contradiction that for all joint distributions $Z, S(Y)$ such that $\tilde{H}_\infty(Z|Y) \geq k$ there exists $D \in \mathcal{D}_{s_{ent} - s_{sim}}$ such that

$$D((Z, S(Y)), (K, S(Y))) > \epsilon_{ent}.$$

Let Z', Y be a distribution such that $\tilde{H}_\infty(Z'|Y) \geq k$. By the information-theoretic data-processing inequality, $\tilde{H}_\infty(Z'|S(Y)) \geq k$. Thus, there exists a $D \in \mathcal{D}_{s_{ent} - s_{sim}}$ such that $D((Z, S(Y)), (K, S(Y))) > \epsilon_{ent}$. Fix one such D. Consider the distinguisher $D'(z, y) = D(z, S(y))$ (of size at most s_{ent}). Then $D'((K, Y), (Z', Y)) \geq D((K, S(Y)), (Z', S(Y))) \geq \epsilon_{ent}$. This is a contradiction and completes the proof.

This fact also holds for relaxed HILL entropy and unpredictability entropy. We present these lemmas without proof.

Lemma 2. *Let S be a circuit of size s_{sim}. Then*

$$H_{\epsilon_{ent}, s_{ent} - s_{sim}}^{\mathrm{HILL\text{-}rlx}}(K|S(Y)) \geq H_{\epsilon_{ent}, s_{ent}}^{\mathrm{HILL\text{-}rlx}}(K|Y).$$

Lemma 3. *Let S be a circuit of size s_{sim}. Then*

$$H_{\epsilon_{ent}, s_{ent} - s_{sim}}^{\mathrm{unp}}(K|S(Y)) \geq H_{\epsilon_{ent}, s_{ent}}^{\mathrm{unp}}(K|Y).$$

2.2   Leakage Models

In this section we focus on memory leakage models – the models in which our results focus. We briefly review circuit leakage models in Appendix A.

Bounded Leakage: This leakage class allows an arbitrary $\mathcal{L}$ with limited output length [DP08].

Definition 6. *Let K be a discrete random variable over space χ_1. The randomized map $\mathcal{L} : \chi_1 \to \{0,1\}^*$ is an ℓ-bounded leakage function if for $\mathcal{L}(x)$ takes at most 2^ℓ values for any choice $x \in \chi_1$ and any choice of random coins of $\mathcal{L}$.*

For convenience, we refer to this class of leakage as bLEN. Bounded leakage is a natural definition. If a random variables starts with min-entropy k, we know that after ℓ bits of leakage it has remaining min-entropy $k - \ell$ [DORS08, Lemma 2.2]. That is, if $\mathrm{H}_\infty(K) \geq k$, then $\tilde{\mathrm{H}}_\infty(K|\mathcal{L}(K)) \geq k - \ell$. Unfortunately, bounded length leakage is not representative of reality. Many side channels take values in a universe larger than the key itself.

Indistinguishable Leakage. In many applications, the secret state has no true information conditioned on the public state of the algorithm. For example, the secret key of a symmetric cipher has little entropy after a few plaintext/ciphertext pairs. However, it often has pseudoentropy. Dziembowski and Pietrzak construct a pseudorandom generator secure against this type of leakage [DP08]. Indistinguishability leakage retains high entropy (we refer to this class of functions as Indist):

Definition 7. *Let K be a random variable and let $\mathcal{L}$ be a randomized map. $\mathcal{L}$ is a $(k, \epsilon_{ent}, s_{ent})$-indistinguishable leakage function if $H^{\mathtt{HILL}}_{\epsilon_{ent}, s_{ent}}(K|\mathcal{L}(K)) \geq k$.*

We refer to leakage functions that retain relaxed HILL entropy as rIndist.

Hard to invert leakage. For a scheme with secret key K, the minimal notion of security is that an adversary should not be able to predict the value of K. This is model is known as the auxiliary input [DKL09] or hard-to-invert leakage [FHN+12]. We refer to this class of functions as hINV:

Definition 8. *Let K be a random variable over space χ_1. The randomized map $\mathcal{L}$ is a $(k, \epsilon_{unp}, s_{unp})$-hard-to-invert leakage if $H^{\mathtt{unp}}_{\epsilon_{unp}, s_{unp}}(K|\mathcal{L}(K)) \geq k$.*

We make no condition in the above definition about K unconditionally. For K to be unpredictable with $\mathcal{L}(K)$ it must have unconditional unpredictability at least k.[4] Hard-to-invert leakage seems like the weakest leakage class for which applications can retain security.

---

[4] In the unconditional setting, there is a polynomial time circuit that predicts K with probability $2^{-\mathrm{H}_\infty(K)}$. That is, $\mathrm{H}_\infty(W) = H^{\mathtt{unp}}_{\epsilon_{unp}, s_{unp}}(K)$.

3   Simulatable Leakage

Standaert, Pereira, and Yu [SPY13] introduce a new leakage class designed to be achievable and verifiable. Simulatable leakage is leakage that can be simulated without access to the true secret state. We first present the definition of Standaert, Pereira, and Yu [SPY13]. This definition is specific to the setting of a block cipher (denoted BC) in the presence of leakage function $\mathcal{L}$. For more information on block ciphers and the definition see [SPY13].

Game $sim(q, D, BC, \mathcal{L}, S, b)$.			
The challenger selects two random keys k and k^* in $\{0,1\}^n$. The output of the game is a bit b' computed by D based on the challenger responses to a total of at most q adversarial queries of the following type:			
Query	Response if $b = 0$	Response if $b = 1$	
$Enc(x)$	$BC_k(x), \mathcal{L}(k, x)$	$BC_k(x), S(k^*, x, BC_k(x))$	
and one query of the following type:			
Query	Response if $b = 0$	Response if $b = 1$	
$Gen(z, x)$	$S(z, x, k)$	$S(z, x, k^*)$	

Definition 9. *[SPY13, Definition 1] A block cipher BC with leakage function $\mathcal{L}$ has $(\epsilon, s_{sim}, s_{sec})$ q-simulatable leakages if there is a simulator S, of size s_{sim}, for every D, of size s_{sec}, , we have:*

$$\delta(sim(q, D, BC, \mathcal{L}, S, 1), sim(q, D, BC, \mathcal{L}, S, 0)) \leq \epsilon.$$

3.1   Extending Simulatable Leakage to General Applications

Definition 9 is specialized to the setting of symmetric-key cryptography. In particular, the second type of query exists because the authors argue that symmetric keys are often derived from sources that themselves have leakage. It is not clear how to generalize this type of query to arbitrary leakage settings. In addition, providing a single key to S as consistent state is limiting, it is not clear why the simulator should not be allowed to keep state between leakage queries. Furthermore, the fact that leakage is provided with each output of the block cipher is not a necessary requirement. There may multiple leakage queries for each block cipher output or vice versa. Furthermore, the distinguisher does not have any access to k when trying to decide if the leakage is legitimate. In different applications, the distinguisher may have partial access to the secret state k. We present two definitions modeling the two extremes, one where the distinguisher has full access to the secret and one the secret is completely hidden. Our definitions consider two random variables K and Y that represent the private and public state of the cryptosystem (but we do not include this distinction in the definitions).

Definition 10. *Let (K, Y) be a pair of random variables over $\chi_1 \times \chi_2$. The randomized map $\mathcal{L}$ is an $(\epsilon, s_{sim}, s_{sec})$-weakly simulatable leakage function if there exists a simulator S of size at most s_{sim} such that*

$$\delta^{\mathcal{D}_{ssec}}\left((Y, \mathcal{L}(K)), (Y, S(Y))\right) \leq \epsilon.$$

Definition 11. *Let (K, Y) be a pair of random variables over $\chi_1 \times \chi_2$. The randomized map $\mathcal{L}$ is an $(\epsilon, s_{sim}, s_{sec})$-strongly simulatable leakage function if there exists a simulator S of size at most s_{sim} such that*

$$\delta^{\mathcal{D}_{ssec}}\left((K, Y, \mathcal{L}(K)), (K, Y, S(Y))\right) \leq \epsilon.$$

We use wSIM and sSIM as shorthand for weakly and strongly simulatable classes respectively.

Proposition 3. *If $\mathcal{L}$ is $(\epsilon, s_{sim}, s_{sec})$-strongly simulatable leakage function, then $\mathcal{L}$ is a $(\epsilon, s_{sim}, s_{sec})$-weakly simulatable. That is, wSIM $\subseteq$ sSIM.*

Notes: These definitions do not model secret key updates. We assume a single leakage query. Alternatively, we can think of an adversary that prepares all of their multiple leakage queries simultaneously. This is slightly weaker than the definition of Standaert et al.

We also assume that Y incorporates all public values of the scheme. This may include a public-key, ciphertexts, signatures, etc. In the work of Standaert et al., this is assumed to be the input and output of the block cipher with the true key.

Meaningfulness of Weakly Simulatable Leakage. Some restriction on Y is necessary to make weakly simulatable leakage meaningful. If Y is empty, the leakage $\mathcal{L}(K) = K$ is simulatable by sampling a fresh secret key K'. However, there is no security remaining in the system. In particular, in this setting, there is no min-entropy, HILL entropy, or unpredictability entropy remaining in the key. Indeed, when there is no public Y, any polynomial time function is simulatable (by sampling a fresh $k \leftarrow K$ and outputting $f(k)$). This gives us the following proposition:

Proposition 4. *Let K be a random variable over χ_1 samplable by procedure Sample of size s_{sam} and let Y be empty. Let $f : \chi_1 \to \{0, 1\}^*$ be a function computable by a circuit of size $|f|$. Then f is a $(0, s_{sim}, \infty)$-weakly simulatable leakage if $s_{sim} \geq |f| + s_{sam}$.*

It is not just empty Y that presents a problem to weakly simulatable leakage. It may be possible to leak the entire secret even when it is information-theoretically determined by the condition Y. For example, if the public state is a Diffie-Hellman exchange g^a, g^b, then the key g^{ab} can be leaked (since a fresh g^c is indistinguishable).

To prevent these *leak-and-resample* simulators, we assume it is hard to find k values consistent with the public information. We use the notation of witness hiding from zero-knowledge.

Definition 12. *Let K, Y be random variables and let R be a relation (computable by a circuit of size s_{rel}) where $\Pr[R(K, Y) = 1] = 1$. The public state Y is a $(s_{rel}, s_{inv}, \epsilon_{rel})$-witness hiding relation if for all $\mathcal{I}$ of size at most s_{inv}, $\Pr[R(\mathcal{I}(Y), Y) = 1] \le \epsilon_{rel}$.*

Note: If it is hard to find keys that are consistent with plaintext/ciphertext pairs, then the definition of Standaert et al. also has a witness hiding condition.

When discussing weakly simulatable leakage, we consider public information that is witness hiding of the secret state K. Witness hiding implies unpredictability of $H_{0,s_{inv}}^{\text{unp}}(K|Y) \ge -\log(\epsilon_{rel})$. We first discuss strongly simulatable leakage and then weakly simulatable leakage. We discuss how to apply simulatable leakage to the circuit leakage model in Appendix A.

4   Strongly Simulatable Leakage

In this section, we show that all strongly simulatable leakages preserve indistinguishability. We use the relaxed notion of HILL entropy. We show that sSIM $\subseteq$ rIndist. In the next section, we show that bLEN $\not\subseteq$ wSIM which implies that bLEN (and thus rIndist)) are not contained in sSIM.

Lemma 4 (sSIM $\Rightarrow$ rIndist). *Let K be a distribution over χ and let Y be some public information. Let $H_{\epsilon_{ent}, s_{ent}}^{\text{HILL-rlx}}(K|Y) \ge k$ and let $\mathcal{L}$ be a $(\epsilon_{sim}, s_{sim}, s_{sec})$-strongly simulatable leakage function. Then $H_{\epsilon', s'}^{\text{HILL-rlx}}(K|Y, \mathcal{L}(K)) \ge k$ for $\epsilon' = \epsilon_{ent} + \epsilon_{sim}, s' = \min\{s_{sec}, s_{ent} - s_{sim}\}$.*

Proof. Fix $\mathcal{L}$ and let S be a simulator of size at most s_{ent}. Define the circuit S' that on input y outputs $y, S(y)$ and note that S' is of size s_{sim}. Then by Lemma 2 the simulator does not decrease relaxed HILL entropy,

$$H_{\epsilon_{ent}, s_{ent} - s_{sim}}^{\text{HILL-rlx}}(K|Y, S(Y)) = H_{\epsilon_{ent}, s_{ent} - s_{sim}}^{\text{HILL-rlx}}(K|S'(Y)) \ge k.$$

Thus, there exists some K', Y', Z' where $\tilde{H}_{\infty}(K'|S', Y') \ge k$ such that

$$\delta^{\mathcal{D}_{s_{ent} - s_{sim}}}((K, Y, S(Y)), (K', Y', Z'))) \le \epsilon_{ent}.$$

By simulatability, we have that

$$\delta^{\mathcal{D}_{s_{sec}}}((K, Y, \mathcal{L}(K)), (K, Y, S(Y))) \le \epsilon_{sim}.$$

Finally, by the triangle inequality,

$$\delta^{\mathcal{D}_{\min\{s_{sec}, s_{ent} - s_{sim}\}}}((K, Y, \mathcal{L}(K)), (K', Y', Z'))) \le \epsilon_{sim} + \epsilon_{ent}.$$

5   wSIM and rIndist

In the previous section, we showed that strong simulatability of a leakage function implied relaxed HILL entropy. However, this does not carry over to the setting of weak simulatability. In this section we show that simulatable leakage is incomparable with indistinguishable leakage functions. We show a bounded leakage function that is not simulatable (bLEN $\not\subseteq$ wSIM) and a simulatable leakage function that removes all relaxed pseudoentropy from the secret (rIndist $\not\subseteq$ wSIM). Since bounded length leakage functions are contained in Indist (and rIndist) this also shows that rIndist $\not\subseteq$ wSIM. In this section, we assume that the public information is witness hiding of the secret state (Definition 12).

5.1   wSIM $\not\subseteq$ rIndist

There are simulatable leakage functions that remove all HILL-rlx.

Lemma 5 (wSIM $\not\subseteq$ rIndist). *Let $K = (K_1, K_2)$ where $K_1 \in \{0,1\}^{\ell_1}$ and $K_2 \in \{0,1\}^{\ell_2}$ be uniformly distributed. Let f be an $(\epsilon_{owp}, s_{owp})$-injective one-way function from $\{0,1\}^{\ell_1} \to \{0,1\}^{\ell_3}$ computable in size $|f|$. Let $Y = f(K_1)$. Then $H_\infty(K|Y) = \ell_2$. The function $\mathcal{L}(K) = K_2$ is $(0, \ell_2, \infty)$-weakly simulatable and $H_{\epsilon,s_{sec}}^{\text{HILL-rlx}}(K|Y, \mathcal{L}(K)) \leq -\log(1-\epsilon)$ if $s_{sec} \geq s_{owf} + \ell_1 + \ell_2$.*

Proof. We first prove that for K, Y where $Y = f(K)$ and f is a function computable in size $|f|$, $K|Y$ has almost no min-entropy remaining. We first show that $Y, \mathcal{L}(K)$ removes all HILL-rlx from K.

Lemma 6. *Let K be a random variable over $\{0,1\}^\ell, \{0,1\}^{\ell_2}$ and let $f : \{0,1\}^{\ell_1} \to \{0,1\}^{\ell_2}$ be an injective function computable by a circuit of size $|f|$. Then*

$$H_{\epsilon,|f|+\ell_1+\ell_2}^{\text{HILL-rlx}}(K|f(K)) \leq -\log(1-\epsilon).$$

Proof. Let K', Z' be a distribution

$$\delta^{\mathcal{D}^{s_{sec}}}((K, f(K)), (K', Z')) \leq \epsilon.$$

Consider the distinguisher

$$D(k, z) = 1 \text{ if and only if } f(k) = z.$$

Clearly $\mathbb{E}[D(K, f(K))] = 1$. By indistinguishability, $\mathbb{E}[D(K', Z')] \geq 1 - \epsilon$. This means that

$$\mathbb{E}_{z \leftarrow Z'} D(K'|Z' = z, z) \geq 1 - \epsilon.$$

For all z there is a unique $k \in \{0,1\}^{\ell_1}$ such that $D(k, z) = 1$, denote this value by k_z. This means that $\mathbb{E}_{z \leftarrow Z'} \Pr[K' = k_z|Z' = z] \geq 1 - \epsilon$. We then have the following:

$$\mathbb{E}_{z \leftarrow Z'} \max_k \Pr[K' = k'|Z' = z] \geq \mathbb{E}_{z \leftarrow Z'} \Pr[K = k_z|Z' = z] \geq 1 - \epsilon.$$

Taking the negative logarithm of each side yields that $\tilde{H}_\infty(K'|Z') \leq -\log(1-\epsilon)$. This completes the proof of Lemma 6.

Lemma 6 implies that $H_{\epsilon,s_{sec}}^{\text{HILL-rlx}}(K|Y, \mathcal{L}(K)) \leq -\log(1-\epsilon)$.

Y is a $(|f|, s_{owp}, \epsilon_{owp})$, witness hiding relation of K where the relation is $R(k_1, k_2, y) = (f(k_1) \overset{?}{=} y)$. The simulator S for $\mathcal{L}$ computes a uniform sample from $\{0,1\}^{\ell_2}$. This is identically distributed to $\mathcal{L}(K)$ and takes ℓ_2 size to compute. Since there is a unique k_1 for each y, $\tilde{H}_\infty(K|Y) = \tilde{H}_\infty(K_2|Y) = H_\infty(K_2)$.

5.2   bLEN ⊄ wSIM

We now show a leakage function of bounded length that cannot be simulated.[5] We will use a secure signature scheme and leak a valid signature. This leakage function has been used previously to demonstrate the difficult of constructing leakage resilient signature schemes [FHN+12]. We need a signature scheme that is hard to forge and a signature does not determine the secret key completely. We begin by describing the EU-RMA notion of signatures from Goldwasser, Micali, and Rivest [GMR88].

Definition 13 (EU-RMA). *A signature scheme* $\Sigma = (\mathsf{Gen}, \mathsf{Sig}, \mathsf{Ver})$ *is* (q, s_{sec}, ϵ)-*existential unforgeable against random message attacks if for all circuits A of size s_{sec} the following holds:*

$$\Pr_{(pk,sk) \leftarrow \mathsf{Gen}(\cdot)} [m_1, ..., m_q \leftarrow \mathcal{M} \wedge \sigma_i \leftarrow \mathsf{Sig}(m_i, \mathsf{sk}) \wedge$$
$$(m^*, \sigma^*) \leftarrow A(m_1, ..., m_q, \sigma_1, ..., \sigma_q, \mathsf{pk})$$
$$\wedge m^* \neq m_i \wedge \mathsf{Ver}(pk, m^*, \sigma^*) = 1] < \epsilon$$

Under this definition a signature must not be simulatable. To ensure that the secret key still has high entropy we need a signature scheme where multiple private keys exist for each public key. We use a scheme where it is hard to find a candidate private key for each public key (making the public key witness hiding). We use Lamport's one-time secure signature scheme [Lam79].[6]

Construction 1. *Let f be a $(\epsilon_{owf}, s_{owf})$-one-way function mapping $\{0,1\}^{k^c} \to \{0,1\}^k$ for $c > 1$:*

Key Generation: *Choose random $x_{i,0}, x_{i,1} \leftarrow \{0,1\}^{k^c}$ for $i = 1, ..., \ell$. Compute $y_{i,b} \leftarrow f(x_{i,b})$ for $i \in \{1, ..., \ell\}$ and $b \in \{0,1\}$. The public key is $pk = \{y_{i,b}\}$ and the secret key is $\{x_{i,b}\}$.*

Signing: *The signature on a k-bit message $m = m_1, ..., m_k$ consists of the k values $x_{1,m_1}, ..., x_{k,m_k}$.*

Verification: *Given $x_1, ..., x_k$ and $m = m_1, .., m_k$ and $pk = (s, \{y_{i,b}\})$, output 1 iff $y_{i,m_i} \overset{?}{=} f(x_i)$ for all i.*

Lemma 7. *Construction 1 is a $(1, \epsilon_{owf}, s_{owf})$-secure signature scheme. Furthermore $\tilde{\mathrm{H}}_\infty(SK|PK) \geq 2\ell k^c - 2\ell k$. Furthermore for any message m,*

$$\tilde{\mathrm{H}}_\infty(SK|PK, \mathsf{Sig}_{PK}(m)) \geq \ell k^c - 2\ell k.$$

---

[5] This also shows that Indist ⊄ wSIM and rIndist ⊄ wSIM.

[6] This scheme was used in the setting of leakage-resilient cryptography by Katz and Vaikunatanathan [KV09]. They extend Lamport's scheme making the function collision resistant and using error correcting codes. Lamport's original scheme suffices for our purposes.

Proof. We omit the proof that the scheme is secure (and that $Y = PK$ is witness hiding of X). We have the following for the entropy calculations by [DORS08, Lemma 2.2], $\tilde{H}_\infty(SK|PK) \geq 2\ell k^c - 2\ell k$. Similarly, for any m $\tilde{H}_\infty(SK|PK, \mathrm{Sig}_{PK}(m)) \geq 2\ell k^c - 2\ell k - \ell k^c \geq \ell k^c - 2\ell k$.

Lemma 8. *Let* $(\mathrm{Gen}, \mathrm{Sig}, \mathrm{Ver})$ *be as above for some* $c > 1$, *let* $K = SK, Y = PK$. *Then for any message* m *the function* $\mathcal{L}(K) = \mathrm{Sig}_{SK}(m)$ *is not simulatable by any* S *of size* $s_{sec} \leq s_{owf}$ *with* $\epsilon \leq \epsilon_{owf}$. *Furthermore,* $\tilde{H}_\infty(SK|PK, \mathcal{L}(K)) \geq \ell k^c - 2\ell k$ *(and thus,* $H_{0,\infty}^{\mathrm{HILL}}(SK|PK, \mathcal{L}(K)) \geq \ell k^c - 2\ell k$).

Proof. The lack of a simulator follows from the one-time security of the signature scheme. The remaining entropy follows from Lemma 7.

6   wSIM $\subsetneq$ hINV

In the previous section, we showed that weakly simulatable leakage and indistinguishable leakage are incomparable. In this section, we turn to hard-to-invert leakage. We show that weakly simulatable leakage preserves unpredictability but there are leakage functions that preserve unpredictability that are not simulatable. Our results assume Y is witness hiding.

6.1   wSIM $\subseteq$ hINV

We show the ability to predict K given both Y and $\mathcal{L}(K)$ is not significantly different than the ability to predict the witness given just Y.

Lemma 9. *Let* K, Y *be a pair of random variables. Let* R *be a* $(s_{rel}, s_{inv}, \epsilon_{rel})$-*witness hiding relation on* K, Y. *If* $\mathcal{L}$ *be a* $(\epsilon_{sim}, s_{sim}, s_{sec})$-*weakly simulatable leakage for* (K, Y). *Then* $H_{0, s'_{inv}}^{\mathrm{unp}}(K|Y, \mathcal{L}(K)) \geq -\log(\epsilon_{rel} + \epsilon_{sim})$ *for* $s'_{inv} = \min\{s_{sec} - s_{rel}, s_{inv} - s_{rel}\}$.

Proof. Let S be a simulator of size s_{sim} for $\mathcal{L}$. Suppose there exists an inverter $\mathcal{I}$ of size s'_{inv} such that $\Pr[\mathcal{I}(Y, \mathcal{L}(K)) = K] > \epsilon_{rel} + \epsilon_{sim}$. To arrive at a contradiction it suffices to show there exists an inverter $\mathcal{I}'(Y)$ of size $s'_{inv} + s_{sim} \leq s_{inv}$ and succeeds with probability $> \epsilon_{rel}$. Define $\mathcal{I}'(y) = \mathcal{I}(y, S(y))$.

Claim. $\Pr[R(\mathcal{I}(Y, S(Y)), Y) = 1] \geq \Pr[R(\mathcal{I}(Y, \mathcal{L}(K)), K) = 1] - \epsilon_{sim} \geq \epsilon_{rel}$.

Proof. Recall that $\delta^{\mathcal{D}_{s_{sec}}}((Y, \mathcal{L}(K)), (Y, S(Y))) \leq \epsilon_{sim}$. Suppose for contradiction that

$$\Pr[R(\mathcal{I}'(Y, S(Y)), K) = 1] < \Pr[R(\mathcal{I}'(Y, \mathcal{L}(K)), K) = 1] - \epsilon_{sim}.$$

We present a distinguisher D of size $s'_{inv} + s_{rel} \leq s_{sec}$:

- On input y, z.
- Run $x \leftarrow \mathcal{I}'(y, z)$.
- Output 1 if and only if $R(x, y) = 1$.

Then

$$\Pr[D(Y, \mathcal{L}(K)) = 1] - \Pr[D(Y, S(Y)) = 1]$$
$$= \Pr[R(\mathcal{I}(Y, \mathcal{L}(K)), K) = 1] - \Pr[R(\mathcal{I}(Y, S(Y)), K) = 1] > \epsilon_{sim}.$$

This is a contradiction. This completes the proof of the claim and the proof of the lemma.

6.2 hINV $\not\subseteq$ wSIM

In the previous section, we saw that simulatable leakage preserves unpredictability. In this section, we show this containment is tight.

Lemma 10. *Let $f_1 : \{0,1\}^{\ell_1} \to \{0,1\}^{\ell_2}$ be $(s_1, \epsilon_1, U_{\ell_1})$-one way and let $f_2 : \{0,1\}^{\ell_2} \to \{0,1\}^{\ell_3}$ be $s_2, \epsilon_2, f(U_{\ell_1})$-one way. Then for $K = U_{\ell_1}, Y = f_2(f_1(K)), \mathcal{L}(K) = f_1(K)$ the following hold:*

1. $H_{0,s_1 - |f_2|}^{\mathrm{unp}}(K | Y, \mathcal{L}(K)) \geq -\log(\epsilon_{owf,1})$.
2. *$\mathcal{L}$ is not $(|f_2|, s_2, 1 - \epsilon_2)$-weakly simulatable.*

Proof. We prove each statement in turn. Suppose Statement *1* is not true, that is, there exists an inverter $\mathcal{I}'$ of size $s_1 - |f_1|$ that inverts $f_2 \circ f_1 | f_1$. Then $\mathcal{I}(y) = \mathcal{I}'(y, f_2(y))$ is an inverter for f_1.

Now suppose that Statement *2* is not true. Then there exists a simulator S of size s_2 that simulates $f_1(K)$. That is, $\delta^{\mathcal{D}_{ssec}}((Y, \mathcal{L}(K)), (Y, S(Y))) < 1 - \epsilon_2$. Consider the following distinguisher D (of size $|f_2|$):

- Input y, z.
- Output 1 if and only if $y = f_2(z)$.

Clearly, $\mathbb{E}[D(Y, \mathcal{L}(K))] = 1$. Thus, by indistinguishability, $\mathbb{E}[D(Y, S(K))] \geq 1 - (1 - \epsilon_2) \geq \epsilon_2$, this is a contradiction.

Acknowledgements. The authors wish to thank Olivier Pereira, Krzysztof Pietrzak, Leonid Reyzin, François-Xavier Standaert, and Sophia Yakoubov for their helpful and insightful discussion. In addition, the authors wish to thank the anonymous reviewers for their constructive and astute comments. The work of Benjamin Fuller is sponsored in part by US NSF grants 1012910 and 1012798.

References

BB05.   Brumley, D., Boneh, D.: Remote timing attacks are practical. Computer Networks 48(5), 701–716 (2005)

BM06.   Bonneau, J., Mironov, I.: Cache-collision timing attacks against AES. In: Goubin, L., Matsui, M. (eds.) CHES 2006. LNCS, vol. 4249, pp. 201–215. Springer, Heidelberg (2006)

BSW03.   Barak, B., Shaltiel, R., Wigderson, A.: Computational analogues of entropy. In: Arora, S., Jansen, K., Rolim, J.D.P., Sahai, A. (eds.) RANDOM 2003 and APPROX 2003. LNCS, vol. 2764, pp. 200–215. Springer, Heidelberg (2003)

CJRR99.   Chari, S., Jutla, C.S., Rao, J.R., Rohatgi, P.: Towards sound approaches to counteract power-analysis attacks. In: Wiener, M. (ed.) CRYPTO 1999. LNCS, vol. 1666, pp. 398–412. Springer, Heidelberg (1999)

DDF14.   Duc, A., Dziembowski, S., Faust, S.: Unifying leakage models: From probing attacks to noisy leakage. In: Nguyen, P.Q., Oswald, E. (eds.) EUROCRYPT 2014. LNCS, vol. 8441, pp. 423–440. Springer, Heidelberg (2014)

DKL09.   Dodis, Y., Kalai, Y.T., Lovett, S.: On cryptography with auxiliary input. In: Proceedings of the 41st Annual ACM Symposium on Theory of Computing, pp. 621–630. ACM (2009)

DORS08.   Dodis, Y., Ostrovsky, R., Reyzin, L., Smith, A.: Fuzzy extractors: How to generate strong keys from biometrics and other noisy data. SIAM Journal on Computing 38(1), 97–139 (2008)

DP08.   Dziembowski, S., Pietrzak, K.: Leakage-resilient cryptography. In: FOCS, pp. 293–302 (2008)

FHN+12.   Faust, S., Hazay, C., Nielsen, J.B., Nordholt, P.S., Zottarel, A.: Signature schemes secure against hard-to-invert leakage. In: Wang, X., Sako, K. (eds.) ASIACRYPT 2012. LNCS, vol. 7658, pp. 98–115. Springer, Heidelberg (2012)

FRR+10.   Faust, S., Rabin, T., Reyzin, L., Tromer, E., Vaikuntanathan, V.: Protecting circuits from leakage: the computationally-bounded and noisy cases. In: Gilbert, H. (ed.) EUROCRYPT 2010. LNCS, vol. 6110, pp. 135–156. Springer, Heidelberg (2010)

Ful15.   Fuller, B.: Strong Key Derivation from Noisy Sources. PhD thesis, Boston University, 111 Cummington Ave, Boston, MA 02215 (January 2015)

GMR88.   Goldwasser, S., Micali, S., Rivest, R.L.: A digital signature scheme secure against adaptive chosen-message attacks. SIAM J. Comput. 17(2), 281–308 (1984), Preliminary version in FOCS 1984

GST13.   Genkin, D., Shamir, A., Tromer, E.: RSA key extraction via low-bandwidth acoustic cryptanalysis. IACR Cryptology ePrint Archive, 2013:857 (2013)

GW11.   Gentry, C., Wichs, D.: Separating succinct non-interactive arguments from all falsifiable assumptions. In: STOC 2011, pp. 99–108. ACM, New York (2011)

HILL99.   Håstad, J., Impagliazzo, R., Levin, L.A., Luby, M.: A pseudorandom generator from any one-way function. SIAM Journal on Computing 28(4), 1364–1396 (1999)

HLR07.   Hsiao, C.-Y., Lu, C.-J., Reyzin, L.: Conditional computational entropy, or toward separating pseudoentropy from compressibility. In: Naor, M. (ed.) EUROCRYPT 2007. LNCS, vol. 4515, pp. 169–186. Springer, Heidelberg (2007)

ISW03.   Ishai, Y., Sahai, A., Wagner, D.: Private circuits: Securing hardware against probing attacks. In: Boneh, D. (ed.) CRYPTO 2003. LNCS, vol. 2729, pp. 463–481. Springer, Heidelberg (2003)

KJJ99.   Kocher, P.C., Jaffe, J., Jun, B.: Differential power analysis. In: Wiener, M. (ed.) CRYPTO 1999. LNCS, vol. 1666, pp. 388–397. Springer, Heidelberg (1999)

Koc96.   Kocher, P.C.: Timing attacks on implementations of Diffie-Hellman, RSA, DSS, and other systems. In: Koblitz, N. (ed.) Advances in Cryptology - CRYPTO 1996. LNCS, vol. 1109, pp. 104–113. Springer, Heidelberg (1996)

KPW13.   Krenn, S., Pietrzak, K., Wadia, A.: A counterexample to the chain rule for
          conditional hill entropy. In: Sahai, A. (ed.) TCC 2013. LNCS, vol. 7785,
          pp. 23–39. Springer, Heidelberg (2013)
KV09.   Katz, J., Vaikuntanathan, V.: Signature schemes with bounded leakage
          resilience. In: Matsui, M. (ed.) ASIACRYPT 2009. LNCS, vol. 5912,
          pp. 703–720. Springer, Heidelberg (2009)
Lam79.   Lamport, L.: Constructing digital signatures from a one-way function. Tech-
          nical report, Technical Report CSL-98, SRI International (1979)
LMO+14.   Longo, J., Martin, D.P., Oswald, E., Page, D., Stam, M., Tunstall, M.J.:
          Simulatable leakage: Analysis, pitfalls, and new constructions. In: Sarkar,
          P., Iwata, T. (eds.) ASIACRYPT 2014. LNCS, vol. 8873, pp. 223–242.
          Springer, Heidelberg (2014)
MR04.   Micali, S., Reyzin, L.: Physically observable cryptography (extended ab-
          stract). In: Naor, M. (ed.) TCC 2004. LNCS, vol. 2951, pp. 278–296.
          Springer, Heidelberg (2004)
NZ93.   Nisan, N., Zuckerman, D.: Randomness is linear in space. Journal of Com-
          puter and System Sciences, 43–52 (1993)
OST06.   Osvik, D.A., Shamir, A., Tromer, E.: Cache attacks and countermeasures:
          The case of AES. In: Pointcheval, D. (ed.) CT-RSA 2006. LNCS, vol. 3860,
          pp. 1–20. Springer, Heidelberg (2006)
Rey11.   Reyzin, L.: Some notions of entropy for cryptography. In: Fehr, S. (ed.)
          ICITS 2011. LNCS, vol. 6673, pp. 138–142. Springer, Heidelberg (2011)
Sko14.   Skórski, M.: Modulus computational entropy. In: Padró, C. (ed.) ICITS
          2013. LNCS, vol. 8317, pp. 179–199. Springer, Heidelberg (2014)
SPY13.   Standaert, F.-X., Pereira, O., Yu, Y.: Leakage-resilient symmetric cryp-
          tography under empirically verifiable assumptions. In: Canetti, R., Garay,
          J.A. (eds.) CRYPTO 2013, Part I. LNCS, vol. 8042, pp. 335–352. Springer,
          Heidelberg (2013)
TOS10.   Tromer, E., Osvik, D.A., Shamir, A.: Efficient cache attacks on AES, and
          countermeasures. Journal of Cryptology 23(1), 37–71 (2010)
Yao82.   Yao, A.C.-C.: Theory and applications of trapdoor functions (extended ab-
          stract). In: FOCS, pp. 80–91 (1982)

A   Extending Simulatable Leakage to the Circuit Model

A.1   Leakage Classes in the Circuit Model

In this section we provide a brief introduction to the circuit leakage model and discuss the applicability of simulatable leakage to the circuit leakage model. The main difference between the circuit and memory leakage model is that the leakage function leaks on a particular implementation of a cryptographic primitive. (In the memory leakage model, leakage is only on the private state.) Most circuit leakage classes assume leakage is "local" to the computation. This makes the leakage class sensitive to the implementation. C represent a circuit with wires $C_1, ..., C_k$ (with the first wires representing the inputs and final wires representing the outputs).

- **Probing** [ISW03]. Let The adversary specifies a subset $\mathcal{L} \subset C_1, ..., C_k$ (of bounded size) and sees the values of all wires in $\mathcal{L}$. $\mathcal{L}$ may include some of the secret input, intermediate values, and output values. However, the leakage function is not allowed to compute on parts of the computation simultaneously, the leakage function can only learn the value of individual wires.

- **Computationally Bounded** [FRR+10]. Faust et al. [FRR+10] hypothesize that leakage can be modeled by low complexity circuits. As an example, they show how to protect circuits against leakage in $\mathtt{AC}^0$. They secret share state, security critically relies on the inability of $\mathtt{AC}^0$ circuits to compute parity.
- **Noisy** [CJRR99,FRR+10]. It is not clear how to precisely determine the computational complexity of a side-channel attack. However, most side-channel attacks are known to contain significant noise. The work of Faust et al. [FRR+10] also proposed modeling leakage function as an arbitrary function $\mathcal{L}$ applied to the secret state with an additive noise term $\mathcal{N}$.

Recent work of Duc, Dziembowski, and Faust [DDF14] shows how to simulate a noisy leakage function using a probing leakage function.

A.2 Adapting Simulatable Leakage to the Circuit Model

We now provide a definition of simulatable leakage that can be used in either the memory or circuit leakage models. As before, we can define both a weak and strong version. We present only a weak version for simplicity.

Definition 14. *Let (K, Y) be a pair of random variables over $\chi_1 \times \chi_2$ and $\mathcal{C}$ be a encoding function such that $\mathcal{C} : \chi_1 \to \zeta$. The randomized map $\mathcal{L}$ is an $(\epsilon, s_{sim}, s_{sec}, \mathcal{C})$-weakly simulatable leakage function if there exists a simulator S of size at most s_{sim} such that*

$$\delta^{\mathcal{D}_{s_{sec}}} \left((Y, \mathcal{L}(\mathcal{C}(K))), (Y, S(Y)) \right) \le \epsilon.$$

Notes: Taking the encoding function to be the identity function yields the memory leakage model. The above definition depends on the encoding function and the leakage class. As an example, for a fixed leakage function, there may be a simulator for only some encoding functions. The work of Ishai, Sahai, and Wagner [ISW03] builds an encoding function where the probing side-channel is simulatable (security of the encoded circuit is shown through simulation).

On the Orthogonal Vector Problem and the Feasibility of Unconditionally Secure Leakage-Resilient Computation

Ivan Damgård[1,*], Frédéric Dupuis[2,**], and Jesper Buus Nielsen[1,***]

[1] Department of Computer Science, Aarhus University, Aarhus, Denmark
{ivan,jbn}@cs.au.dk
[2] Faculty of Informatics, Masaryk University, Brno, Czech Republic
dupuis@fi.muni.cz

Abstract. We consider unconditionally secure leakage resilient two-party computation. Security means that the leakage obtained by an adversary can be simulated using a similar amount of leakage from the private inputs or outputs. A related problem is known as circuit compilation, where there is only one device doing a computation on public input and output. Here the goal is to ensure that the adversary learns only the input/output behaviour of the computation, even given leakage from the internal state of the device. We study these problems in an enhanced version of the "only computation leaks" model, where the adversary is additionally allowed a bounded amount of *global* leakage from the state of the entity under attack. In this model, we show the first unconditionally secure leakage resilient two-party computation protocol. The protocol assumes access to correlated randomness in the form of a functionality f_{ORT} that outputs pairs of orthogonal vectors $(\boldsymbol{u}, \boldsymbol{v})$ over some finite field, where the adversary can leak independently from $\boldsymbol{u}$ and from $\boldsymbol{v}$. We also construct a general circuit compiler secure in the same leakage model. Our constructions work, even if the adversary is allowed to corrupt a constant fraction of the calls to f_{ORT} and decide which vectors should be output. On the negative side, we show that unconditionally secure two-party computation and circuit compilation are in general impossible in the plain version of our model. It follows that even a somewhat unreliable version of f_{ORT} cannot be implemented with unconditional security in the plain leakage model, using

---

[*] Acknowledges support from the Danish National Research Foundation and The National Science Foundation of China (under the grant 61061130540) for the Sino-Danish Center for the Theory of Interactive Computation and also from the CFEM research center (supported by the Danish Strategic Research Council).

[**] FD was supported by the Czech Science Foundation GA CR project P202/12/1142 and the EU FP7 under grant agreement no 323970 (RAQUEL). Part of this work was performed while the author was at Aarhus University, where he was supported by the Danish National Research Foundation and The National Science Foundation of China (under the grant 61061130540) for the Sino-Danish Center for the Theory of Interactive Computation, and also by the CFEM research centre (supported by the Danish Strategic Research Council).

[***] Supported by European Research Council Starting Grant 279447.

© Springer International Publishing Switzerland 2015
A. Lehmann and S. Wolf (Eds.): ICITS 2015, LNCS 9063, pp. 87–104, 2015.
DOI: 10.1007/978-3-319-17470-9_6

classical communication. However, we show that an implementation using quantum communication does exist. In particular, we propose a simple "prepare-and-measure" type protocol which we show secure using a new result on sampling from a quantum population. Although the protocol may produce a small number of incorrect pairs, this is sufficient for leakage resilient computation by our other results. To the best of our knowledge, this is the first time a quantum protocol is used constructively for leakage resilience.

Note that the full version of this paper is available at [6].

1   Introduction

In this paper, we consider secure leakage-resilient computation, more precisely solutions to two different types of problems, known as leakage resilient two-party computation (LR2PC) and leakage resilient circuit compilation (LRCC).

In LR2PC, two parties A and B want to compute a (possibly probabilistic) function securely on private inputs. Both parties are assumed to follow the protocol. There is an adversary who may obtain leakage from the internal state of the players, say by some side channel attack, but we still want to keep the private inputs and outputs "as private as possible".

In the closely related problem of LRCC, there is only a single device that carries out a computation (usually given as a Boolean circuit) on public input and output. The goal is to make sure that an adversary who gets to choose the input and is given the output, will learn nothing more than the input/output behaviour, even if he can leak from the internal state of the device. The computation may in addition depend on some secret data that should be completely protected. Think, for instance, of a device that uses a secret key to decrypt or sign data: we are fine with revealing the output but want to hide the secret key.

We need, of course, a meaningful notion of security for protocols claiming to solve such problems. For this, we clearly need to somehow limit the leakage that the adversary can get, and there is a lot of previous work considering various types of restrictions. In this paper we consider a new and enhanced version of the "only computation leaks" model proposed by Micalin and Reyzin in [11]. They assume that the computation of a party under attack is split into several smaller parts. The adversary may submit one or more leakage functions, where each function must address a certain part of the computation. The function is applied to only the data that is actually used during this part of the computation, and the result is returned to the adversary. It is assumed that only some bounded number of bits can leak from each part of the computation.

Our enhancement to the model is to allow not only leakage from sub-computations, but also a bounded amount of leakage from the *global* state of the party under attack. Typically, the allowed amount of global leakage will be comparable to what is allowed from a single part of the computation. This clearly makes the adversary stronger, but also more realistic: in a real life, an adversary might use a combination of several side channel attacks, and completely avoiding global leakage in such a case may be extremely difficult.

Security for LR2PC now means that the leakage obtained by the adversary can be (efficiently) simulated, however, when the adversary leaks from a part where private inputs or outputs are touched, the simulator is allowed to leak the same number of bits from those inputs/outputs. For LRCC, we require that the leakage can be simulated given only the public inputs and outputs. We emphasize that we consider throughout unbounded adversaries and leakage functions, nevertheless we demand that all simulators and honest parties be efficient.

For LR2PC, a UC based definition of leakage resilience was given in [2]. Also a few examples were given of two party protocols for specific functionalities (based on various computational assumptions). In [3], generic leakage resilient multiparty computation protocols were constructed, again under a computational assumption.

For LRCC, Dziembowski and Faust in [8] (see also [7]) have shown a general unconditionally secure method. As they explain in their paper, their construction can be interpreted in a natural way as being derived from a two-party protocol for parties A and B in the only-computation-leaks model (where two physically separated parts of the device plays the parts of A and B). They assume that so-called leak-free gates are available, or equivalently, parties are given access to an ideal functionality f_{ORT} which will on request produce a random pair of vectors u, v over some finite field, subject to $u \cdot v = 0$ and give u to A and v to B. It is assumed that nothing about the internal computation of f_{ORT} leaks to the adversary. The idea is to use the vectors from the leak-free gates to refresh the state in between different parts of the computation, such that leakage from different parts will become (essentially) uncorrelated. The drawback of this solution is that an implementation will require secure hardware components, even if these are much simpler than the device we want to protect. Goldwasser and Rothblum [9] improve this using a different method that does not use leak-free gates during the computation, but instead assumes that the device initially has a randomised state, a so-called ciphertext bank. They then use this as well as fresh randomness as a source for refreshing. Also this construction is in the only-computation-leaks model. The adversary does not get leakage from the computation that generates the ciphertext bank, so one can think of this as allowing access once and for all to a leak-free component (with output size depending only on the security parameter) before the computation starts.

It is of course natural to ask if we can make do with no leak-free components at all? In particular, can we securely implement f_{ORT} by a two-party leakage resilient protocol?

Our Contribution. In this paper, we make the following contributions:

- We generalise the protocol in [8] to show that we can do, not just LRCC, but general LR2PC given access to f_{ORT}. To the best of our knowledge, this is the first result of its kind. On the way, we propose a new framework for defining security of LR2PC where global leakage from the entire view of the party under attack is (also) allowed. This is a strictly stronger leakage model than that of [8, 9]. The definition is much simpler than the UC based definition of [2] while still supporting modular composition.

- Our construction works even given a partially corrupted version of f_{ORT} where the adversary is allowed to corrupt a constant fraction of the calls to f_{ORT} and choose the output vectors himself. The result improves on [8] and is incomparable to [9]: we need a (partially) leak-free source during the computation but on the other hand we allow active corruption of it under a stronger leakage model.
- We show that general LR2PC is impossible in the plain version of our model, where no auxiliary functionalities are assumed.
- We show that also general LRCC is impossible in the plain model. For this result, we need a computational assumption to exhibit a function that cannot be computed securely. The result rules out only protocols with perfect correctness. On the other hand, impossibility holds even if the simulation for the protocol is only computationally close to the real view. All constructions we are aware of have perfect correctness.
- From the results mentioned, it follows easily that there is no unconditionally secure and leakage-resilient implementation of f_{ORT}, not even for a somewhat unreliable version. It also follows that the ciphertext bank of [9] cannot be securely created, starting from scratch (except if the implementation produces incorrect output with non-zero probability).
- We show that the orthogonal vector problem does have an unconditional solution using quantum communication, in particular we provide a relatively simple "prepare-and-measure" type protocol. We show security using a new technical result of independent interest on sampling from a quantum population. This gives us LR2PC for an adversary whose quantum memory lasts only a bounded amount of time, and we get LRCC for a completely unbounded quantum adversary. To the best of our knowledge, this is the first time a quantum protocol is used constructively for leakage resilience.

It should be noted that the impossibility of LR2PC from scratch follows because a secure protocol in our model is also passively secure in the standard (non-leakage) model (see the following section for details). Not only does this show that correlated randomness is necessary, it also follows that the amount of such randomness must depend on the size of the secure computation: if we had a generic two-party computation protocol using a fixed amount of randomness, we could use it to implement any number of oblivious transfers from such fixed-size randomness, and this is well known to be impossible. In our protocol, the number of calls we make to f_{ORT} is proportional to the circuit size of the function we compute, so the argument we just gave says that this is in some sense necessary. Note that the result of [9] does not contradict this as it is does only circuit compilation in a weaker leakage model.

2   Techniques and Ideas

In this section, we explain the techniques used in the paper and how they fit together.

The classical results. In Section 3, we define a framework for secure LR2PC. In order to support modular composition we require so-called full-view simulation. This is a notion inspired by leakage oblivious simulation as defined in [2], and it means that the simulator must produce a full simulated view for a given player, and leakage is then simulated by applying the adversary's function to that view[1].

An important observation is then that a secure protocol for general LR2PC in our model is also a passively secure general protocol for 2-party computation in the *standard model* [4]. We prove this in Lemma 1 of the full version. This is because the computation of a passive adversary D can be emulated by a leakage adversary: it can hardwire D's algorithm into a leakage function that will be applied to the full view of the player under attack. This works because we allow a small amount of global leakage, and here we just need to get one bit back, namely D's guess at whether it looks at a real or a simulated view. It follows that this leakage adversary together with the leakage simulator can act as an ideal model adversary in the model from [4].

This observation is important because it immediately implies that unconditionally secure LR2PC in the plain model (with no auxiliary functionalities) is impossible, and this paves the way for our negative result: in Sections 2.2–2.4 of the full version, we extend the LRCC protocol from [8] to a protocol for general LR2PC, assuming access to f_{ORT}. This construction allows us to conclude that an unconditionally secure implementation of f_{ORT} is impossible: any such implementation could be plugged into our LR2PC protocol and would result in secure LR2PC from scratch which is impossible. The technical contribution is to modify the protocol and proof of [8] to ensure that the simulator does not need to leak from a party unless the adversary does so. In particular, the simulator in [8] uses one bit of leakage when simulating the so-called refresh protocol, even if the adversary requests no leakage. This is fine for LRCC but will not work for LR2PC. For instance, it might force the simulator to leak from the inputs of both parties even if the adversary only asked for leakage from one party.

In Section 3.1, we show that unconditionally secure LRCC is also impossible in general without set-up assumptions, assuming the protocol always outputs correct results. The idea is to show that we cannot have an LRCC protocol for computing a pseudorandom generator on a secret key. For this, we consider an LRCC protocol as a multi-player protocol where we think of each unit of computation that can be leaked from as a player, and where the data that is passed between units is thought of as messages sent between players. The technical idea is to define a leakage adversary in a clever way: once the computation is done, it will first force the simulator S to commit to all the communication between

---

[1] We argue in Section 2.6 of the full version that this is in some sense the right simulation notion and is anyway often implied by seemingly weaker requirements.

players by leaking from each player P_i a set of hash values, namely for each P_j the hash of messages exchanged between P_i and P_j (of course the same hash-value must be output from P_j). Finally, the adversary will leak from each P_i a succinct proof of knowledge that it knows a complete view for P_i (input, random coins and messages) that is consistent with the hash values and the public output y. Say y is *good* if it is a possible output from the PRG. Now, in real life y is always good and acceptable proofs would always be produced, so for a good y, S must succeed in giving acceptable proofs with overwhelming probability. But for a bad y, S has to fail: if it succeeds, we could extract from S a complete view of the entire computation resulting in y being output, but no such view exists for a bad y, by perfect correctness. It follows that S is breaking the security of the PRG. Note that this argument works, even if S produces output that is only computationally close to real leakage, so it is only correctness that needs to be perfect. All protocols we are aware of are perfectly correct.

Section 4 shows that we can have unconditionally secure LR2PC even given an unreliable version of f_{ORT}, where the adversary has corrupted a constant fraction of the calls. This is motivated by the fact that our quantum protocol can only emulate such an unreliable functionality. The main technical idea of the construction is to not compute directly a circuit C for the desired function, but instead a fault tolerant circuit C' computing the some result. We start from a perfectly secure MPC protocol that computes securely the same function as C. The protocol should have $3k + 1$ players and be secure against corruption of k players, for instance [1]. Write down the computation done by the protocol as a circuit C'. There will be a sub-circuit corresponding to the local computation done by each player and wires between sub-circuits for the messages exchanged. We now use our LR2PC protocol to compute C', and we show that if we apply some extra tests to the output from the unreliable f_{ORT} and do some extra refreshing, the adversary can effectively only corrupt or leak from at most k of the sub-circuits of C'. Security then follows from security of the MPC protocol.

The quantum result. For the quantum part of our results, our basic observation is as follows: if we consider two (physically separated) sets of particles, quantum mechanics allows the entire system to be in an *entangled* state, and this means that if we give one set to A and the other to B and ask them both do a measurement on what they received, then the results they get will be highly correlated. In particular, if we put $2n$ particles in the right state and give A and B n particles each, then the measurements are guaranteed to output 2 orthogonal n-vectors $\boldsymbol{u}, \boldsymbol{v}$. Moreover, the mere fact that the particles of A and B are in a pure entangled state implies that no third party can obtain any information on the measurement results. Therefore, to solve our problem, we "only" need to design a protocol that can supply A and B with enough copies of the right state. As we explain shortly, this can be done using known methods, but this imposes rather unrealistic demands on the technology A and B must use. We therefore suggest a different protocol that is simpler to implement but technically much more challenging to prove secure.

In more detail, the quantum result works as follows: we introduce an extra component Q that one may think of as a replacement for f_{ORT}. Q will prepare quantum states and send them to A and B. However, we do not assume secure hardware so we allow the (unbounded) adversary to remove Q and instead prepare himself the states to be sent[2]. We must therefore allow for the possibility that the protocol terminates with no output. Finally, all random choices by A or B during the protocol are leaked to the adversary as soon as they are made[3]. In this model, we obtain solutions that leak no information on the output $\boldsymbol{u}, \boldsymbol{v}$.

One such solution can be designed as follows: one can use a quantum key distribution protocol to generate a set of essentially perfect EPR pairs shared by A and B, where in particular the adversary is essentially unentangled with the state held by A and B. We then ask A to prepare a bipartite state that is a superposition over all pairs of orthogonal vectors. Then we use the EPR pairs to teleport one part of this state to B, which only requires local quantum operations and classical communication. Finally, measuring the state on both sides will produce exactly the output we need. However, this is not a satisfactory solution: it requires quantum storage and computation, and so is very far from what current technology allows. Also, if A and B store and compute on a quantum state for some time, it makes sense to ask what happens if the adversary can leak from the quantum state. It is not entirely clear what this should mean and how to protect against it.

In Section 5.1, we therefore propose a new protocol in which A and B measure immediately the states they receive. Although the required states may be non-trivial to prepare, this is certainly much closer to current technology than the first solution. Note that in this case, the only edge we have on the adversary is that he must choose the states to send before seeing the random choices A and B use later. This is a minimal assumption: if the adversary knows all random choices in advance, A and B have no chance to verify the states they receive.

Similarly to QKD protocols, what we need to make this idea work is a test that A and B can use to make sure that they have copies of the right state. The test we use is not surprising: A and B measure some of the copies in the computational basis, others in the Hadamard basis. If the results match the statistics we expect from the right state(s), we would like to conclude that the untested states are (mostly) correct. In QKD we typically use EPR pairs,, and then A and B can expect to always get the same measurement results if they have correct states. However, for our states, the measurement results that we expect from the correct states are probabilitistic mixtures (i.e. we do not expect to always get the same answer even if the adversary is not cheating), and hence A and B can only compare their results in a probabilistic sense. This means that known results on quantum sampling are not sufficient. So the main technical challenge we solve here is to obtain a new and

---

[2] Equivalently, we could let A prepare the states and send them to B, but allow the adversary to tamper arbitrarily with the quantum communication.

[3] This is similar to the standard model for quantum key distribution, where these choices are sent on a classical channel that the adversary can observe but not tamper with.

more general sampling result, see Theorem 5. We strongly believe that this result is of independent interest.

By combining this with our classical results, we immediately obtain general LR2PC for a quantum adversary whose quantum memory "dies" after a certain time, and with additional work, we obtain LRCC for a completely unbounded quantum adversary, in Section 5.

To summarise, this gives us a way to do LRCC even if Q is replaced by an arbitrary adversarial (quantum) component, assuming (as usual) that the adversary can only leak independently from different parts of the actual computation. Of course, we do not mean to suggest that this is more practical than using leak-free classical gates or ciphertext banks, but we do claim that the solution is fundamentally different since we need no leak-free components at all. Finally we also want to emphasise that by showing that the orthogonal vector problem has a quantum solution but no classical solution, we enhance our understanding of which extra power quantum communication can buy us. We believe this is of fundamental interest, independently of leakage resilience.

3 Leakage-Resilient Two-Party Computation from Orthogonal Vectors

Due to space restrictions, we cannot give the detailed description here, of our model for leakage resilient 2-party computation. All details and proofs of results can be found in Section 2 of the full version.

An adversary attacking the protocol may submit leakage functions that will be applied to a designated part of the view of one of the parties. It is assumed that at most a bounded number of bits leak from each part.

The security definition follows the real/ideal world paradigm and negl(k)-leakage resilience means that the simulation has statistical distance negl(k) to the real view, where negl() is a negligible function and k is the security parameter. We require separate simulators (sharing a source of randomness) for simulating the view of each party. In the ideal process, the leakage functions submitted by the adversary are then applied to these views. We call this full-view simulation. We require this in order to be able to prove (in Theorem 1 of the full version) that our security notion composes sequentially. We also prove (in Lemma 1 of the full version), that a protocol computing a function f securely in our model is also a semi-honestly secure implementation of f in the standard sense according to the definition from [4].

When we construct concrete protocols, we will consider what we call a $\lambda/2$-adversary, who is allowed to leak at most $\lambda/2$ bits from each part of a player's view. A similar amount of global leakage is also allowed. The parameter λ comes from the way our protocols represent secret bits, namely each party holds a binary vector such that the inner product is the bit in question. By choosing long enough vectors, λ can be linear in the security parameter.

Our first main positive result is that there exist leakage resilient 2-party protocol for computing any function f if the parties are given oracle access to a function f_{ORT} that outputs a pair of orthogonal vectors, one to each party.

Theorem 1. *There exists a protocol $\pi_f^{f_{\text{ORT}}}$ that is a full-view $\text{negl}(k)$-leakage resilient implementation of f against the $\lambda/2$-class of adversaries in the f_{ORT}-hybrid model.*

We can then consider replacing the calls to f_{ORT} in $\pi_f^{f_{\text{ORT}}}$ by calls to a full-view leakage-resilient implementation π_{ORT}, resulting in a protocol we will call π_f. This is mainly for later proving certain such implementations impossible.

Theorem 2. *If π_{ORT} is a full-view $\text{negl}(k)$-leakage resilient implementation of f_{ORT} secure against an adversary leaking at most $\lambda(n)/2$ bits on each share, then π_f is a full-view $\text{negl}(k)$-leakage-resilient implementation of f against the $\lambda/2$-class of adversaries.*

3.1 Negative Results

It follows directly from the above theorem and Lemma 1 of the full version that there exists no full-view negl-leakage resilient implementation π_{ORT} of f_{ORT}, as we would have for all f a protocol π securely realizing f in the sense of [4] against a computationally unbounded adversary corrupting any one party in the model with secure communication. It is well known that we cannot have such a thing.

We now prove that also unconditionally secure circuit compilation is impossible in the plain model with only secure communication. In circuit compilation there are no secret inputs or outputs, so the output is known to all parties, but there might be a hidden secret state, like a key. To simplify matters, consider a function g_{PRG} which ignores the inputs from the parties and the state, it is only a function of the first k bits of its own random tape, r say. Furthermore, it gives no secret outputs. It gives a public output $y = f(r)$ for a pseudo-random generator f. We show that it is impossible to securely compute this function in the plain model with an implementation which is perfectly correct.

When we prove impossibility of circuit compilation, it seems we have to give up on getting an unconditional result. Instead, we show impossibility under reasonable computational assumptions, namely those used in [10]. We assume there exists a collision resistant hash function and a succinct proof of knowledge with soundness $1/2$, where the communication is $\tilde{O}(k)$, see e.g. [10]. It might seem odd that we need computational assumptions to prove that an unconditionally secure protocol is impossible. However, for an intuition why this might be needed, consider the case where P=NP. In that case it might be possible to compute all functions with no secret inputs and outputs in a leakage resilient manner,[4]

Theorem 3. *Under the computational assumptions in [10], there exists no perfectly correct and negl-leakage-resilient implementation of g_{PRG} against an adversary class allowing global leakage of $\tilde{O}(k)$ bits, in the plain model with only secure communication.*

---

[4] Consider, e.g., a function like g_{PRG} but for an easy to invert f. If one can compute r from $s = f(r)$ efficiently, then one might just implement this function by letting party 1 sample r uniformly at random and send $s = f(r)$ to party 2 – technically this is leakage resilient. If, on the other hand, f is a one-way function, then sampling s in a leakage resilient manner appears much harder.

Proof. We can assume that the length of the output of the collision resistant hash function H plus the communication of the succinct proof of knowledge is within the leakage-bound by setting n high enough. We prove that $\pi_{g_{\text{PRG}}}$ has the property that there exist an expected poly-time extractor X which given just the output $s = f(r)$ will produce, except with negligible probability, randomness r_1 and r_2 for parties 1 and 2, such that running $\pi_{g_{\text{PRG}}}$ with this randomness will result in output s. Since our protocol is perfectly correct, it follows that s then is also an output of f. Hence X is an almost perfect distinguisher of outputs from f from random strings, which breaks the pseudo-randomness.

We conclude by sketching how X works. It starts with a leakage adversary, and it works as follows: Given leakage access to $\pi_{g_{\text{PRG}}}$ it will ask each party to leak a hash $h = H(M)$ of the transcript M of all messages exchanged with the other party. These hashes will of course be the same, as we assume the parties have noiseless communication and thus the same transcripts. Then it will ask party i to leak a proof of knowledge of a string r_i and a communication transcript M' with the properties that $H(M') = h$ and that if party i runs the protocol with random string r_i and the incoming message in M' it will produce the outgoing messages in M'. The proof might be interactive, but this is not a problem as it can be simulated by one leakage query per round in the protocol. The communication of the proof is within the leakage bound, so by assumption we can simulate the view of X given just s. Call the simulator P. We can assume we have P. By assumption the simulation cannot be distinguished from the real execution, so in particular the proof will be accepting except with negligible probability, which is bounded far away from the knowledge error of $1/2$. So, from black-box access to $P(s)$ we can extract the proofs in poly-time. So, from the soundness of the proofs we can extract r_1, M'_1 from party 1 and r_2, M'_2 from party 2. By the soundness of the proof and collision resistance, we have that $H(M'_1) = h = H(M'_2)$ except with negligible probability. By soundness we have except with negligible probability that r_1 and r_2 are consistent with M'_1 respectively M'_2. So, we can let the output of X be (r_1, r_2).   □

Note that the same proof technique can be applied to show impossibility of protocols satisfying the standard only-computation-leaks definition, i.e., only independent leakage from each unit is allowed (and the protocol is not necessarily derived from a 2-party protocol).

More specifically, we assume that: 1) Each unit which exchanges data with c other units should allow adaptive leakage of $O(c)\tilde{O}(k)$ bits. Furthermore, 2) the protocol should be perfectly correct. Finally, 3) the protocol should allow to compute a PRG on a secret state and give the expanded string as public output and 4) the leakage should be efficiently simulatable given just this output.

In that case we build an adversary that leaks from each unit a hash of the communication with each of the units with which it communicates, plus a succinct proof of knowledge of the hashed transcripts and a proof of knowledge of a random tape consistent with the hashed transcripts. Since these leaked values can be simulated given just the public inputs and outputs, we can turn the efficient simulator into an efficient and successful prover in the argument system.

Then we can extract all the proofs, and we will get a consistent run of the protocol as in the above argument, which in particular will allow to verify that the output is a pseudo-randomly generated string. So we have

Corollary 1. *There exists no protocol for computing g_{PRG} satisfying conditions 1–4 above.*

The protocol from [9] does allow leakage of $\tilde{O}(k)$ bits from each unit but is not of the specified form because it assumes that the ciphertext bank is already given. However, the above corollary rules out implementing the ciphertext bank perfectly correctly from scratch in a way suitable for plugging into [9], as this would result in a protocol contradicting the corollary[5].

4   Leakage Resilient Computation from an Imperfect Source of Orthogonal Vectors

In this section we consider again a Boolean circuit C that computes a two-party function $(y_1, y_2) = f_C(x_1, x_2)$. We first show how to compile C into a new circuit C' that computes the same function but is more resilient to errors and specific forms of information leakage. We then show how to use a partial corrupted source of orthogonal vectors together with the previous construction applied to C' to get full leakage resilience against an adversary who may both leak information and corrupt some of the pairs received from f_{ORT}.

Securing against Faults and Some Leakage. We now compile C into a circuit C'. The compilation takes the security parameter k as input and the size of C' will be polynomial in the size of C and in k.

It is well known that there exists a perfectly secure MPC protocol, computing any function for $3k+1$ players tolerating k actively corrupted players. We might take the protocol from [1], for instance which is based on Shamir secret sharing. More precisely, we will use a protocol σ_C that takes as input Shamir shares of x_1, x_2 and computes securely Shamir-shares of the output $(y_1, y_2) = C(x_1, x_2)$ for all players, that is, each player gets as input a share of each of the bits in x_1, x_2 and will output a share of each of the bits in y_1 and y_2. The total computational complexity of σ_C is polynomial in k and the size of C. We let C' be the circuit we get by specifying the internal computation of each player as a circuit, and putting wires between players at each point where a message is to be sent. Since in σ_C each player outputs a share of each bit in the result y_1, y_2, C' will output all such shares. We specify all wires carrying a share of y_1 as output wires for player 1 and wires carrying a share of y_2 as output for player 2.

---

[5] Note that it does not matter how many units communicate in the construction of [9]: we could choose the security parameter for g_{PRG} and the hash function so small (but polynomially related to k) such that even if all units communicate, we can still leak enough for the proof to go through.

Let N be the number of players in σ_C, and let C'_i denote that part of C' that corresponds to the i'th player in σ_C.

Note that, by security of σ_C, the outputs of corrupt players reveal nothing beyond $C(x_1, x_2)$. In fact, much more is true: even if the parts of C' corresponding to at most k players malfunction and/or leak information, we would still get the correct result and nothing beyond $C(x, y)$ would be revealed.

Getting Full Leakage Resilience. We now show how we can compile C' into a fully leakage resilient computation, however, we now consider a more adversarial setting than in the previous section. Namely, we still assume access to f_{ORT}, but we allow the adversary to initially point out a set D of the calls to f_{ORT}. For these calls, he will be allowed to choose the output vectors in any way he wants. Assuming there are m calls in total, the set D can be of size at most ϵm for a constant $0 \le \epsilon < 1$. In addition, he may leak η bits in each leakage query. Such an adversary is called a (η, ϵ)-adversary.

Our protocol works as follows:

Leakage Resilient Protocol for C: Π_C

1. Invoke f_{ORT} $m = 2|C'|k$ times, where $|C'|$ is the size of C'. The output vectors are stored by A and B.
2. A chooses a random test subset of the pairs of size $m/2$ and sends it to B. The parties exchange the vectors in the test set and check that they are orthogonal. If a non-orthogonal pair is found, the protocol aborts. Otherwise the pairs in the test set are discarded.
3. A chooses a random permutation ξ on $m/2 = k|C'|$ elements and sends it to B. We think of ξ as defining a random division of the remaining pairs into $|C|$ groups of k pairs each. Starting indices from 0, group j consists of pairs number $\xi(jk), \xi(jk+1), ..., \xi(jk+k-1)$.
4. We now start the actual computation: party i secret-shares the bits in his input x_i and uses the shares as input in the protocol we run in the following step.
5. Run the protocol $\pi_{f_{C'}}^{f_{\text{ORT}}}$, where $f_{C'}$ is the function computed by C', with the following modification: Recall that the protocol runs in the f_{ORT}-hybrid model. When the protocol makes call number j to do a refresh operations (which happens once for every gate) we will instead do k refresh operations sequentially using each pair in group j as input.
6. For each bit in y_i, party i receives $3k+1$ shares from the protocol in the previous step. He considers these shares as a Reed-Solomon codeword with at most k errors, decodes and outputs the result.

Theorem 4. Π_C *is a* negl(k)-*leakage resilient implementation of the function computed by C, against the $(\lambda/4, \epsilon)$-class of adversaries, where* negl() *is a negligible function.*

The proof of this theorem can be found in the full version (labelled Theorem 6).

5   A Quantum Solution for the Orthogonal Vector Problem

In this section, we present a quantum protocol that allows us to generate pairs of random orthogonal vectors, with the guarantee that a malicious adversary cannot succeed in introducing more than a small fraction of bad pairs except with negligible probability. Intuitively, this is possible essentially for the same reason that quantum key distribution is possible: by conducting checks on a joint quantum state in two different bases, A and B can test not only the correctness (which they could also do classically), but also the privacy of their state. The privacy is guaranteed by the principle of "monogamy of entanglement": if a state has a certain amount of entanglement between A and B, then it can only have a limited amount of entanglement with any other party.

As a warm-up, we first argue that a solution to the orthogonal vector problem can be constructed from standard results if one neglects efficiency issues: One can use a quantum key distribution protocol to generate a set of essentially perfect EPR pairs shared by A and B, where in particular the adversary is essentially unentangled with the state held by A and B. We then ask A to prepare a bipartite state that is a superposition over all pairs of orthogonal vectors. Then we use the EPR pairs to teleport one part of this state to B, this only requires local quantum operations and classical communication. A and B now hold the state

$$|\psi\rangle_{\mathsf{AB}} := \frac{1}{\sqrt{K}} \sum_{\boldsymbol{u},\boldsymbol{v}\in\mathbb{F}^n,\boldsymbol{u}\cdot\boldsymbol{v}=0} |\boldsymbol{u}\rangle_{\mathsf{A}} \otimes |\boldsymbol{v}\rangle_{\mathsf{B}} \quad \left(\text{where } K = (|\mathbb{F}|^n - 1)|\mathbb{F}|^{n-1} + |\mathbb{F}|^n\right),$$

(1)

where A and B are Hilbert spaces of dimension $|\mathbb{F}|^n$. This state contains a superposition of all pairs of orthogonal vectors, so measuring on both sides produces the result we want.

5.1   A Simple Quantum Protocol

While the protocol described above will work, it would require A and B to perform rather complex quantum operations: already the entanglement-based quantum key distribution part (to generate the EPR pairs) requires full-scale quantum error correction and storage. It would therefore be desirable to come up with a protocol that limits the amount of quantum processing required. Ideally, one would want a prepare-and-measure protocol, in the spirit of quantum key distribution, which would only require A and B to prepare individual qubits, send them to the other side, and then measure the received qubits immediately upon reception. While we will not quite achieve this level of simplicity, we can get much closer to this ideal than the protocol from the last section.

Basic Protocol. Like the EPR-based protocol outlined above, this protocol works by trying to get A and B to share multiple copies of the state $|\psi\rangle_{\mathsf{AB}}$

(see Equation 1). In this protocol, however, instead of starting with EPR pairs, A and B receive their respective shares of this state directly from an untrusted source. After A and B get their possibly corrupted copies of $|\psi\rangle$, they sample some of them using a checking procedure that will ensure that the error rate is sufficiently low. Once this is done, A and B measure the remaining states in the computational basis and use the measurement results as their orthogonal vectors. The checking procedure ensures that the vast majority of the vectors they have are indeed orthogonal and secret.

The protocol for distributing and checking copies of $|\psi\rangle$ is described in Fig. 1.

Generate-Pairs:
1. A and B receive a state $\rho_{A^{\otimes m+2\ell}B^{\otimes m+2\ell}}$ from an untrusted adversary.
2. A and B choose two disjoint random subsets $T_1, T_2 \subseteq \{1, \ldots, m+2\ell\}$, each of size ℓ, to test.
3. (Test 1) For all states in T_1, A and B measure them in the computational basis and reject if any of the results are not orthogonal vectors.
4. (Test 2) For all states in T_2, A and B measure them in the Hadamard basis, and accept only if at least $\frac{\ell K}{|\mathbb{F}|^{2n}}(1-\delta)$ measurement results are $|0^{tn}\rangle|0^{tn}\rangle$.
5. If both tests succeed, then output the remaining m states.

Fig. 1. A simpler quantum protocol

In the protocol, Test 1 ensures that the input is supported on a subspace which contains very few non-orthogonal pairs, and Test 2 ensures that the state contains coherent superpositions of at least a roughly $1/|\mathbb{F}|$ fraction of all possible pairs of vectors. Since only about a fraction $1/|\mathbb{F}|$ of the pairs are orthogonal, the only states that can pass both tests with non-negligible probability are those that contain the state $|\psi\rangle$ in most positions. In the next section, we analyze the sampling procedure being used here, and then apply the results to our specific protocol in Section 5.3 of the full version.

A Quantum Sampling Theorem. To analyze the protocol, we will first rephrase it in more general language as a type of sampling procedure that may be of independent interest. We describe the procedure in Fig.2. Like our protocol, this procedure takes an arbitrary state as input, and the goal is to accept if it contains a large fraction of some pure state $|\varphi\rangle$. To ensure this, we again perform two tests: the first test ensures that the vast majority of the positions are in the support of some projector M, and the second test ensures that if we measure the POVM $\{|\theta\rangle\langle\theta|, \mathrm{id} - |\theta\rangle\langle\theta|\}$ for some pure state $|\theta\rangle$ such that $M|\theta\rangle = \sqrt{\gamma}|\varphi\rangle$, then roughly a fraction γ of the sample comes out as $|\theta\rangle$. Our goal will be to show that if the input has a non-negligible probability of passing both tests, then the output will with high probability contain at least $m(1-\epsilon)$ copies of the state $|\varphi\rangle$, for an appropriate choice of ϵ.

To formalize this statement, we will view the whole sampling procedure as a completely positive, trace-preserving map $\mathcal{S}$ from the Hilbert space $\mathsf{H}^{\otimes m+2\ell}$

Sampling operation $\mathcal{S}$:
1. Input: An unknown state ρ on $\mathsf{H}^{\otimes m+2\ell}$.
2. Choose two disjoint random subsets $T_1, T_2 \subseteq \{1, \ldots, m + 2\ell\}$, each of size ℓ, to test.
3. (Test 1) For all states in T_1, measure them with the POVM $\{M, \mathrm{id} - M\}$, accept only if the result is M for all of them.
4. (Test 2) For all states in T_2, measure them using POVM $\{|\theta\rangle\langle\theta|, \mathrm{id} - |\theta\rangle\langle\theta|\}$, and accept only if at least $\gamma\ell(1 - \delta)$ measurement results are $|\theta\rangle\langle\theta|$, where γ is such that $M|\theta\rangle = \sqrt{\gamma}|\varphi\rangle$.
5. If both tests succeed, then output the remaining m states.

Fig. 2. The sampling operation analyzed in Section 5.1

to $\mathsf{H}^{\otimes m} \oplus \mathrm{span}\{|\mathrm{fail}\rangle\}$, the $|\mathrm{fail}\rangle$ flag being used to denote the case when the sampling procedure aborts due to a failed test. We also define the projector $\Pi_{\epsilon,\mathrm{good}}$, which projects onto the subspace of $\mathsf{H}^{\otimes m}$ spanned by vectors containing at least $m(1 - \epsilon)$ copies of $|\varphi\rangle$, along with $|\mathrm{fail}\rangle$:

$$\Pi_{\epsilon,\mathrm{good}} := |\mathrm{fail}\rangle\langle\mathrm{fail}| + \sum_{x \in \{0,1\}^m, |x| \leqslant \epsilon m} \Pi_{x_1} \otimes \cdots \otimes \Pi_{x_m},$$

where $\Pi_0 = |\varphi\rangle\langle\varphi|$, $\Pi_1 = \mathrm{id} - \Pi_0$, and $|x|$ denotes the Hamming weight of x. The statement we will prove will be that the sampling procedure $\mathcal{S}$ is almost indistinguishable from an "ideal" procedure $\mathcal{S}_{\mathrm{ideal}}$ that can never output anything outside of the support of $\Pi_{\epsilon,\mathrm{good}}$. This ideal procedure is defined as

$$\mathcal{S}_{\mathrm{ideal}}(\rho) := \Pi_{\epsilon,\mathrm{good}}\mathcal{S}(\rho)\Pi_{\epsilon,\mathrm{good}} + \mathrm{tr}[\Pi_{\epsilon,\mathrm{good}}^{\perp}\rho]|\mathrm{fail}\rangle\langle\mathrm{fail}|,$$

where $\Pi_{\epsilon,\mathrm{good}}^{\perp} := \mathrm{id} - \Pi_{\epsilon,\mathrm{good}}$ In other words, the ideal procedure first applies $\mathcal{S}$ and then measures whether the output is in the support of $\Pi_{\epsilon,\mathrm{good}}$ or not; if it is, then it outputs the result as usual, and otherwise it simply outputs the $|\mathrm{fail}\rangle$ flag, as if the test had failed. It is clear that this procedure can never output a state with less than $m(1 - \epsilon)$ copies of $|\varphi\rangle$.

The theorem we will use is the following; its proof can be found in the full version (labelled Theorem 7), along with the details of how to apply it to the situation at hand:

Theorem 5. *Let $\mathcal{S}_{\mathrm{ideal}}$ be defined as above, and let $\epsilon = 4\delta + 8\gamma^{-1}\sqrt{\delta}$. Then, we have that*

$$\|\mathcal{S} - \mathcal{S}_{\mathrm{ideal}}\|_{\diamond} \leqslant \exp(-\Omega(\min(\ell, m))). \tag{2}$$

Furthermore, if we run on the protocol on the honest input $|\varphi\rangle^{\otimes m+2\ell}$, then the probability of outputting $|\mathrm{fail}\rangle$ is at most $\ell \exp(-\ell\gamma^2\delta^2)$.

Note that the diamond norm $\|\cdot\|_{\diamond}$ can be interpreted as follows: if we are given a box that implements either $\mathcal{E}$ or $\mathcal{F}$ and we must distinguish which of the two using the box only once, the probability that we will guess correctly using the best strategy is given by $\frac{1}{2} + \frac{1}{4}\|\mathcal{E} - \mathcal{F}\|_\diamond$. Hence, the above theorem means that one cannot distinguish the real sampling protocol from the "ideal" protocol that never outputs something outside of the support of $\Pi_{\epsilon,\text{good}}$ except with negligible probability. The proof strategy will be as follows: we will first show that it is sufficient to consider inputs of the form $\rho_{\mathsf{H}^{\otimes m+2\ell}} = \sigma_{\mathsf{H}}^{\otimes m+2\ell}$ using a variant of the "postselection" technique from [5], and we then show that the only σ's that survive both tests have a high fidelity with $|\varphi\rangle$.

5.2   Leakage Resilience against a Quantum Adversary

Security for Bounded-Time Quantum Memory. It might seem natural to expect that we could immediately get leakage resilience for a quantum adversary by using the protocol from the previous section as an implementation of a source of orthogonal pairs, and then run our classical protocol Π_C from Theorem 4, which was designed to tolerate a constant fraction of corrupted pairs. Indeed, the parameters of the quantum protocol can be chosen such that the state created is very close to an ideal state where at most a constant fraction of the pairs come from measuring an incorrect state.

However, the problem is that the adversary may be in superposition of having corrupted several different sets of pairs, and therefore we cannot assume that one single set of pairs is bad, as we did in the proof of Theorem 4[6].

On the other hand, if the adversary cannot keep a coherent state alive until the computation is done, his superposition will collapse, and then Theorem 4 can indeed be applied. The only price we pay is an added term in the statistical distance between simulation and real execution that comes from the distance between real and ideal state in the quantum protocol. Since long-term quantum memory is well beyond current technology, and we don't assume quantum memory for honest parties, limiting the adversary's memory in this way can be a reasonable assumption.

Security against Unbounded Quantum Adversaries. In this section, we show that by designing the protocol slightly differently, we can prove security against an unbounded adversary. For this case, we will only be able to get a circuit compilation type of result, rather than a 2-party computation protocol.

We recall informally the notion of leakage resilient circuit compilation: here a Boolean circuit C is given that takes a secret input y and a public input x chosen by the adversary. The output $C(x,y)$ is given to the adversary. The goal is now to compile C into a leakage resilient computation that is split in several parts where the adversary is allowed to leak independently from each parts, as well as a small amount of global leakage, as defined in our model. The secret input y is assumed to be given in some specially encoded form. A simulator must exist that simulates the adversary's view given only $x, C(x,y)$, i.e., a public-input-output simulator as described earlier. This is a special case of our model of two-party

---

[6] Of course, each pair we generate is either orthogonal or not, but we cannot point out a single set of pairs that are known to the adversary.

computation, namely we will give x as input to both parties and both parties get $C(x, y)$ as output. Furthermore, we assume that the protocol is given access to an oracle function $g_y()$ that takes no input, and outputs y to the parties encoded in some form that is suitable for the protocol. In an implementation there would be a single device executing all parts of the computation, but here we will stick to the interpretation as a two-player protocol for consistency with the rest of the paper.

We now define an oracle function $g_y()$, which will fit into the way our protocol Π_C represents data. It will make $3k + 1$ Shamir secret shares of each bit in y and output leakage resilient encodings of these shares to the two parties.

We can then construct a protocol called $\Pi_{C,y}$ which we define to be our protocol Π_C (which will compute $C(x, y)$), except that instead of getting an encoding of shares of y from the parties, it calls $g_y()$ initially and otherwise evaluates C as usual, assuming access to f_{ORT}. While $\Pi_{C,y}$ is only secure against a classical adversary, we can still use it to construct a protocol that is secure against a quantum adversary.

The idea is as follows: we build from C a new circuit $\bar{C}$ taking inputs $x, \bar{y}$, which works as follows: It parses $\bar{y}$ as the concatenation of a bit b and a string y. If $b = 0$, it outputs $C(x, y)$, while if $b = 1$ it outputs y. One may think of $\bar{C}$ as being like C but with a built-in trapdoor: it "usually" works like C, but if you can choose the secret input, you can force the output value. The idea is now to run $\Pi_{\bar{C},\bar{y}}$ instead of $\Pi_{C,y}$. That is, the same protocol is run, but we replace C by $\bar{C}$. This also means that the protocol will call initially an oracle function $g_{\bar{y}}()$ that will produce leakage resilient encodings of Shamir shares in $\bar{y}$. Finally, note that the protocol will construct a new circuit $\bar{C}'$ from $\bar{C}$, just as we built C' from C earlier, based on an MPC protocol secure against k corrupted players.

Our protocol will be used only with secret inputs of form $\bar{y} = (0, y)$. The other option is something we only need for the proof. Our leakage resilient protocol now works as follows:

Quantum Leakage Resilient Protocol for C: $Q_{C,\bar{y}}$

1. Invoke the quantum protocol to obtain $m = 2|\bar{C}'|k$ pairs of (hopefully) orthogonal vectors. For each pair, the process of measuring and storing the pair is defined to be a separate part of the computation from which the adversary can leak a bounded amount of information.
2. Run $\Pi_{\bar{C},\bar{y}}$ based on the list of pairs of vectors from the quantum protocol (instead of getting the list from f_{ORT}). Output whatever $\Pi_{\bar{C},\bar{y}}$ outputs.

Definition 1. *Consider a protocol π for computing circuit C on public input x chosen by adversary E and secret input y. The adversary may issue a leakage query for every separate part of the computation. Let Φ_E^{real} be the state of the adversary after executing π. We say that π is leakage resilient against an adversary E if there exists a simulator S that interacts with E (where, after E sends the public input x, S is given $C(x, y)$). This interaction results in state Φ_E^{sim} for E. We require that the trace norm distance between Φ_E^{real} and Φ_E^{sim} be negligible in the security parameter.*

The proof of the following theorem can be found in the full version (labelled Theorem 8).

Theorem 6. $Q_{f_C, \bar{y}}$ *is leakage resilient against a quantum unbounded* $\lambda/4$-*adversary.*

References

[1] Ben-Or, M., Goldwasser, S., Wigderson, A.: Completeness theorems for non-cryptographic fault-tolerant distributed computation. In: Proc. STOC 1988, pp. 1–10 (1988)

[2] Bitansky, N., Canetti, R., Halevi, S.: Leakage-tolerant interactive protocols. In: Cramer, R. (ed.) TCC 2012. LNCS, vol. 7194, pp. 266–284. Springer, Heidelberg (2012)

[3] Boyle, E., Goldwasser, S., Jain, A., Kalai, Y.T.: Multiparty computation secure against continual memory leakage. In: Proc. STOC 2012, pp. 1235–1254. ACM (2012)

[4] Canetti, R.: Security and composition of multiparty cryptographic protocols. J. Cryptology 13(1), 143–202 (2000)

[5] Christandl, M., König, R., Renner, R.: Postselection technique for quantum channels with applications to quantum cryptography. Phys. Rev. Lett. 102, 020504 (2009)

[6] Damgård, I., Dupuis, F., Nielsen, J.B.: On the orthogonal vector problem and the feasibility of unconditionally secure leakage resilient computation. Cryptology ePrint Archive, Report 2014/282 (2014)

[7] Dziembowski, S., Faust, S.: Leakage-resilient cryptography from the inner-product extractor. In: Lee, D.H., Wang, X. (eds.) ASIACRYPT 2011. LNCS, vol. 7073, pp. 702–721. Springer, Heidelberg (2011)

[8] Dziembowski, S., Faust, S.: Leakage-resilient circuits without computational assumptions. In: Cramer, R. (ed.) TCC 2012. LNCS, vol. 7194, pp. 230–247. Springer, Heidelberg (2012)

[9] Goldwasser, S., Rothblum, G.N.: How to compute in the presence of leakage. In: Proc. FOCS 2012, pp. 31–40. IEEE (2012)

[10] Kilian, J.: A note on efficient zero-knowledge proofs and arguments (extended abstract). In: Kosaraju, S.R., Fellows, M., Wigderson, A., Ellis, J.A. (eds.) STOC, pp. 723–732. ACM (1992)

[11] Micali, S., Reyzin, L.: Physically observable cryptography. In: Naor, M. (ed.) TCC 2004. LNCS, vol. 2951, pp. 278–296. Springer, Heidelberg (2004)

Metric Pseudoentropy: Characterizations, Transformations and Applications*

Maciej Skorski**

Cryptology and Data Security Group, University of Warsaw, Warsaw, Poland
`maciej.skorski@mimuw.edu.pl`

Abstract. Metric entropy is a computational variant of entropy, often used as a convenient substitute of HILL Entropy which is the standard notion of entropy in many cryptographic applications, like leakage-resilient cryptography, deterministic encryption or memory delegation. In this paper we develop a general method to characterize metric-type computational variants of entropy, in a way depending only on properties of a chosen class of test functions (adversaries). As a consequence, we obtain a nice and elegant geometric interpretation of metric entropy. We apply these characterizations to simplify and modularize proofs of some important results, in particular: (a) computational dense model theorem (FOCS'08), (b) a variant of the Leftover Hash Lemma with improvements for square-friendly applications (CRYPTO'11) and (c) equivalence between unpredictability entropy and HILL entropy over small domains (STOC'12). We also give a new tight transformation between HILL and metric pseudoentropy, which implies the dense model theorem with best possible parameters.

1 Introduction

1.1 Computational Entropy

ENTROPY. Entropy, as a measure of uncertainty or randomness, is a fundamental notion in information-theory. The most known metric of entropy is Shannon Entropy [Sha48]. For cryptographic applications such as *extracting randomness*, it is more convenient to work with so called min-entropy, which gives an upper bound on the probability that computationally unbounded adversary can guess a value sampled according to a given distribution. A slightly weaker but also very useful, especially in the context of *hashing*, is the notion of collision entropy which upperbounds the probability that two independent samples of a given distribution collide.

COMPUTATIONAL VARIANTS OF ENTROPY. The motivation for computational analogues of entropy is the fact that in cryptographic applications we often

---

* Preliminary versions of this work appeared in the Proceedings of Student Research Forum Papers and Posters at SOFSEM 2015.
** This work was partly supported by the WELCOME/2010-4/2 grant founded within the framework of the EU Innovative Economy Operational Programme.

© Springer International Publishing Switzerland 2015
A. Lehmann and S. Wolf (Eds.): ICITS 2015, LNCS 9063, pp. 105–122, 2015.
DOI: 10.1007/978-3-319-17470-9_7

consider only computationally bounded attackers. Computational variants of entropy found many important applications, like leakage-resilient cryptography [DP08], deterministic encryption [FOR12], memory-delegation [CKLR11], computational complexity [RTTV] and foundations of cryptography [HRV10]. Computational variants can be defined in different ways. In any case, we need to formalize what it means that a distribution behaves, from a computational point of view, like a distribution having "true" information-theoretic entropy. This might be based on hardness of *compressing-decompressing*, hardness of *unpredictability* or hardness of *distinguishing*. In this paper we follow the last approach, which is most widely used. A good survey of different entropy notions and their properties can be found in [BSW03] and [Rey11]. We stress that, contrarily to the information-theoretic case, for computational entropy it's not only the *amount* of entropy that matters but also its *quality* is important.

COMPUTATIONAL INDISTINGUISHABILITY. Indistinguishability is a fundamental concept in computational complexity and cryptography. For two distributions X, Y taking values in the same space, a class $\mathcal{D}$ of $[0, 1]$-valued functions (refereed to as the "attacker's class") and a parameter ϵ (refereed to as the "distinguishing advantage"), we say that X and Y are $(\mathcal{D}, \epsilon)$-indistinguishable if for all $D \in \mathcal{D}$ we have $|\mathbf{E}\,D(X) - \mathbf{E}\,D(Y)| \leqslant \epsilon$. An attacker D can distinguish X and Y if $\mathbf{E}\,D(X) - \mathbf{E}\,D(Y) > 0$ or $\mathbf{E}\,D(X) - \mathbf{E}\,D(Y) < 0$; the bigger the gap from 0 is, the better "advantage" he achieves. Sometimes we want to define indistinguishability between two sets $\mathbb{X}$ and $\mathbb{Y}$ of probability distributions. We can formalize this by saying that no single adversary D can achieve bigger than ϵ advantage for *every* pair (X, Y) where X comes from $\mathbb{X}$ and Y comes from $\mathbb{Y}$. Since the expectation $\mathbf{E}\,D(X)$ can be thought as the scalar product of the vectors representing D and the distribution of X, the concept of indistinguishability is *exactly* the same concept as the idea of *separating hyperplanes*.

DEFINING COMPUTATIONAL ENTROPY. Having formalized the concept of "computational closeness", one can define the "computational" entropy, called also pseudoentropy, of a distribution X by one of the following ways:

(a) (stronger) X is computationally indistinguishable from a *single* distribution having required amount of information-theoretic entropy (min-entropy, Shannon Entropy etc.)

(b) (weaker) is computationally indistinguishable from a *set* of all distributions having required amount of information-theoretic entropy.

Both approaches turn out to be useful. Setting the underlying information-theoretic entropy measure to be the min-entropy, for case (a) we obtain the notion of HILL entropy [HILL99] which directly generalizes the notion of pseudorandomness, whereas for case (b) we get the notion of the so called Metric Entropy [BSW03]. Roughly speaking, with HILL entropy one generalizes most of information-theoretic facts about entropy, into the computational setting. Metric entropy is commonly thought as a less intuitive and understood notion than HILL entropy. Surprisingly, it is quite often more convenient to work with.

ADVANTAGES OF METRIC ENTROPY AND APPLICATIONS. There are very good reasons to introduce and study metric entropy: quite often it is much easier to prove a statement for metric-entropy and then pass to the HILL version. Actually, this strategy is unavoidable for the standard proof technique which uses the min-max theorem to switch the order of players in a game. Therefore, many facts about HILL entropy use metric entropy explicitly or implicitly [VZ12, FOR12, CKLR11, RTTV, DP08, BSW03]. Perhaps the most spectacular example is the efficient version of the Dense Model Theorem [RTTV, DP08], being the key ingredient of the famous result of Tao and Ziegler on primes in arithmetic progressions [TZ08]. The efficient version, which found many interesting applications in complexity theory and cryptography, was originally proved using the idea of metric computational entropy in [RTTV] and independently in [DP08]. A much simpler proof with significant improvements in quality was given later in [FOR12]. It uses only very basic properties of Metric entropy!

CONVERSIONS BETWEEN HILL AND METRIC ENTROPY. The following result, due to Barak, Shaltiel and Widgerson, states that metric and HILL computational entropy are equivalent up to some loss in quality.

Theorem 1 (From Metric to HILL Entropy [BSW03]). *Let X and Z be, respectively, n-bit and m-bit correlated random variables. Then*

$$\mathbf{H}^{\mathrm{HILL},(s',\epsilon')}\left(X|Z\right) \geqslant \mathbf{H}^{\mathrm{M,det}[0,1],(s,\epsilon)}\left(X|Z\right)$$

where $s' = O\left(s \cdot \delta^2/(n+m)\right)$ and $\epsilon' = \epsilon + \delta$ for arbitrary $\delta \in (0,1)$.

Remark 1. The conversion in the other direction is lossless.

WORST CASE DISTRIBUTIONS. In problems which involve computational indistinguishability it is often convenient to know the distributions which makes the attacker's advantage minimal. This distribution is typically subjected to some entropy restrictions. In particular, one might ask the following question

> Given D and X, what is the best (minimal) attacker advantage $|\Delta^D| = |\mathbf{E}\,\mathrm{D}(X) - \mathbf{E}\,\mathrm{D}(Y)|$ over all distributions Y of entropy as least k?

An answer to this question yields a bound on how (computationaly) close is X to the set of all distributions of entropy k. Such problems arises where one uses HILL and Metric entropy, see for instance [BSW03, CKLR11, FOR12, RTTV].

1.2 Our Contribution

IMPROVED TRANSFORMATIONS. We improve Theorem 1 in the following way:

Theorem 2 (From Metric to HILL Entropy, tight bounds). *For any n-bit random variable X and a correlated random variable Z we have*

$$\mathbf{H}^{\mathrm{HILL},(s',\epsilon')}\left(X|Z\right) \geqslant \mathbf{H}^{\mathrm{M,det}[0,1],(s,\epsilon)}\left(X|Z\right)$$

where $\delta \in (0,1)$ is arbitrary, $s' = O\left(s \cdot \delta^2/(\Delta+1)\right)$, $\epsilon' = \epsilon + \delta$ and $\Delta = n - \mathbf{H}^{\mathrm{M,det}[0,1],(s,\epsilon)}\left(X|Z\right)$.

In comparison to Theorem 1 we replace the factor $n + m$ by $\Delta + 1$. Hence, the conversion does not depended on the dimension of the domain of X and Z but *only* on the entropy deficiency Δ. The proof technique, based on approximating convex hulls in L_p-norms, might be of independent interests. There is a lot of research focused on achieving better rates of convex approximations in L^p-spaces for some restricted class of functions. In case of metric-to-HILL transformations (or similar results) it might be possible to obtain some further improvements for restricted classes of adversaries.

APPLICATION: DENSE MODEL THEOREM Our transformation implies the efficient dense model theorem with the best possible parameters due to Zhang [Zha11], which is not the case of the bound in Theorem 1.

MINIMIZING ATTACKER'S ADVANTAGE. As mentioned, the concept of characterizing the "worst case" distribution which optimizes the attacker advantage is very common, thought not always explicitly stated. In this paper we give a uniform treatment of this idea, in terms of convex optimization, and use it to obtain characterizations for pseudoentropy and other interesting corollaries.

CHARACTERIZING METRIC PSEUDOENTROPY VIA OPTIMIZING ATTACKER'S ADVANTAGE. Using standard constrained optimization techniques, we develop a general method to characterize metric-type pseudoentropy. A characterization is based on *explicitly* building the distribution which minimizes the attacker's advantage, subject to entropy constraints. These characterizations could be used in studying properties of variants of pseudoentropy based on different notions than min-entropy. In particular, they could be applied in studying the problem of comparing the amount of metric pseudoentropy against *deterministic* and *randomized* adversaries, or verifying the so called "chain rule". Our characterizations unify the definitions of metric and HILL entropy in a geometric way.

APPLICATION: THE POWER OF PSEUDOENTROPY CHARACTERIZATIONS. Our technique leads to interesting corollaries besides the basic properties of pseudoentropy. From the characterization of metric pseudo-entropy we immediately obtain the computational Dense Model Theorem [RTTV, DP08, FOR12] Extending our characterization into the conditional case when side information is available to the attacker, we reprove equivalence between unpredictability and indistinguishability based definition of pseudoentropy for short strings [VZ12]. Finally, from the characterization of collision-pseudoentropy we derive the improved Leftover Hash Lemma [BDK+11] for square-friendly applications. This shows that metric entropy is a powerful tool which deserves a systematic study.

1.3   Organization of the Paper

In Section 2 we explain basic notions and definitions. The proofs of our main technical results appear in Section 3 and Section 4. In Section 5 we discuss some applications. The conclusion in Section 6 contains some ideas for future research.

2 Preliminaries

PROBABILITIES, MEASURES AND INTEGRALS. By μ_X or $\mathbf{P}_X$ we denote the probability mass function (distribution) of X. A measure ν on a finite set Ω is a function $\mu : \Omega \to \mathbb{R}^+ \cup \{0\}$. For notational convenience, we use the signs of sums and integrals interchangeably. The integral of a function D on E with respect to a measure ν is defined as $\int_E \mathrm{D}\,d\nu = \sum_{x \in E} \mathrm{D}(x)\nu(x)$. For the integral over the entire domain we omit the subscript E.

ENTROPY NOTIONS. The min-entropy of a distribution X equals $\mathbf{H}_\infty(X) = -\log(\max_x \Pr[X = x])$. The collision entropy of X is $\mathbf{H}_2(X) = -\log(\sum_x \Pr[X = x]^2)$. If there is side information Z, we define the average conditional min-entropy [DORS08] of X given Z by $\widetilde{\mathbf{H}}_\infty(X|Z) = -\log(\mathbf{E}_{z \leftarrow Z} \max_x \Pr[X = x|Z = z])$.

COMPUTATIONAL ADVANTAGE. The advantage of an attacker D in distinguishing random variables X and Y, equals $\Delta^\mathrm{D}(X; Y) = \mathbf{E}\,\mathrm{D}(X) - \mathbf{E}\,\mathrm{D}(Y)$.

COMPUTATIONAL ENTROPY. Often we assume that information Z correlated to X might be available to an adversary. That's why we work with the notion of conditional pseudoentropy. The unconditional case is simply $Z = \mathrm{const}$.

Definition 1 (Conditional HILL Pseudoentropy [HLR07]). *Let X, Z be a joint distribution with the following property: there exists Y of average conditional min-entropy at least k given Z such that for all circuits D of size at most s we have $|\Delta^\mathrm{D}(X, Z; Y, Z)| \leqslant \epsilon$. Then we say that X given Z has k bits of HILL min-entropy of quality (s, ϵ) and denote by $\mathbf{H}_\infty^{\mathrm{HILL},(s,\epsilon)}(X|Z) \geqslant k$.*

Remark 2 (HILL entropy against different circuits classes). For HILL entropy all kinds of circuits: deterministic boolean, deterministic real valued and randomized boolean, are equivalent (for the same size s).

Definition 2 (Conditional Metric Pseudoentropy [FOR12]). *Let X, Z be a joint distribution with the following property: for every deterministic boolean (respectively: deterministic real valued or boolean randomized) circuit D of size at most s there exists Y of average conditional min-entropy at least k given Z such that $|\Delta^\mathrm{D}(X, Z; Y, Z)| \leqslant \epsilon$. Then we say that X given Z has k bits of deterministic (respectively: deterministic real valued or boolean randomized) metric min-entropy of quality (s, ϵ) and denote by $\mathbf{H}_\infty^{\mathrm{M,det}\{0,1\},(s,\epsilon)}(X|Z)$ (respectively: $\mathbf{H}_\infty^{\mathrm{M,det}[0,1],(s,\epsilon)}(X|Z)$ and $\mathbf{H}_\infty^{\mathrm{M,rand}\{0,1\},(s,\epsilon)}(X|Z)$).*

Remark 3. For unconditional metric min-entropy, it doesn't matter if the deterministic circuits are boolean or real valued (see [RTTV] and the errata of [BSW03]). This is not true for the conditional case.

There is a variant of conditional pseudoentropy where (X, Z) is required to be computationally close to (Y, Z') but Z' is not necessarily the same as Z. This notion is called the "relaxed" HILL entropy [Rey11] Typically we want Z to be the same as Z'[1] but this relaxed notion is also useful [GW11a, Rey11, KPW13].

---

[1] For instance, when Z represents information that adversary might have learned.

L^p SPACES. Given a finite set Ω and a measure μ on Ω one defines the p-th norm of a real-valued function D defined on Ω as $\|D\|_p = \int_\Omega D\mathrm{d}\mu$

CONVEX COMBINATIONS. Given a set of real-valued functions $\mathcal{C}$ defined on the same domain, by $\mathrm{conv}_t(\mathcal{C})$ we denote the set of all convex combinations of length at most t of members of $\mathcal{C}$.

3   Transformations

In this section we prove our main technical result which immediately implies Theorem 2. It is a constrained version of the standard approximation result.

Lemma 1 (Approximating Long Convex Combinations with Respect to All High-min-entropy Distributions). *Let X be an n-bit random variable, be Z be a correlated m-bit random variable, and let $\mathcal{C}$ be a class of $[0,1]$-valued function on $\{0,1\}^n \times \{0,1\}^m$. Let $D \in \mathrm{conv}(\mathcal{C})$. Then for $\ell = 49(n+1-k)/\delta^2$ there exists $D_\ell \in \mathrm{conv}_\ell(\mathcal{C})$ such that*

$$\mathbf{E}\,|D(X) - D_\ell(X)| \leqslant \delta \tag{1}$$

and simultaneously

$$\mathbf{E}\,|D(X) - D_\ell(Y)| \leqslant \delta \tag{2}$$

for every distribution Y jointly distributed with Z such that $\mathbf{H}_\infty(Y|Z) \geqslant k$.

Corollary 1. *Lemma 1 implies Theorem 2*

Proof (of Corollary 1). If $\mathbf{H}_\infty^{\mathrm{HILL},(s',\epsilon')}(X|Z) < k$ then for every Y satisfying $\widetilde{\mathbf{H}}_\infty(Y|Z) \geqslant k$ we find D of size at most s' such that $|\mathbf{E}\,D(X,Z) - \mathbf{E}\,D(Y,Z)| \geqslant \epsilon'$. Replacing D by D^c of necessary we can assume that $\mathbf{E}\,D(X,Z) - \mathbf{E}\,D(Y,Z) \geqslant \epsilon$ for some D of size $s'+1$. By applying the min-max theorem we get that there exists a convex combination D' of circuits of size at most $s'+1$ such that

$$\mathbf{E}\,D(X,Z) - \mathbf{E}\,D(Y,Z) \geqslant \epsilon' \quad \forall Y : \widetilde{\mathbf{H}}_\infty(Y|Z) \geqslant k$$

That combination might be very long. But applying Lemma 1 we can approximate it by a combination D' of at most $O\left((n+1-k)/\delta^2\right)$ circuits of size $s'+1$ in such a way that the expectations with respect to X, Z and Y, Z differs at most by $\delta/2$. This way we obtain

$$\mathbf{E}\,D'(X,Z) - \mathbf{E}\,D'(Y,Z) \geqslant \epsilon' - 2 \cdot \delta/2 \quad \forall Y : \widetilde{\mathbf{H}}_\infty(Y|Z) \geqslant k$$

which finishes the proof.   □

Now we prove our main approximation result

Proof (of Lemma 1). Consider the space of all functions on $\{0,1\}^{n+m}$. We start by the following trivial observation

Claim 1. It suffices to show that for some $D' \in \mathrm{conv}_\ell(\mathcal{C})$ we have $\int |D - D'| \cdot \mathrm{d}(\mu_X + \mu_Y) \leqslant \delta$ for all Y such that $\widetilde{\mathbf{H}}_\infty (Y|Z) \geqslant k$.

By applying the Hölder Inequality, we immediately get

Claim 2. For every functions D, D' and every $p, q > 1$ such that $\frac{1}{p} + \frac{1}{q} = 1$ we have

$$\int |D - D'| \cdot \mathrm{d}(\mu_X + \mu_Y) \leqslant \|D - D'\|_p \cdot \left\| \frac{\mu_{X,Z} + \mu_{Y,Z}}{\mu} \right\|_q \tag{3}$$

Now we give estimates on both factors on the right hand side of Equation (3).

Claim 3. If $q \in [1, 2]$ then for any Y such that $\widetilde{\mathbf{H}}_\infty (Y|Z) \geqslant k$ we have

$$\left\| \frac{\mu_{X,Z} + \mu_{Y,Z}}{\mu} \right\|_q \leqslant \left(2^q + 2^{(q-1)(n+1-k)} \right)^{1/q} \tag{4}$$

Proof (Of Claim 3). Recall the well-known inequality

Proposition 1. *If $a, b > 0$ and $q \geqslant 1$ then $(a + b)^q \leqslant 2^{q-1}(a^q + b^q)$.*

From Proposition 1 it follows now that

$$\left\| \frac{\mu_{X,Z} + \mu_{Y,Z}}{\mu} \right\|_q \leqslant 2^{q-1} \left(\left\| \frac{\mu_{X,Z}}{\mu} \right\|_q + \left\| \frac{\mu_{Y,Z}}{\mu} \right\|_q \right) \tag{5}$$

We shall estimate two terms in Equation (4) separately. Since $\mu_{X,Z}(x, z) < \mu_{X,Z}(x, z) + \mu_{U,Z}(x, z) = \mu(x, z)$ for all x, z we have

$$\left\| \frac{\mu_{X,Z}}{\mu} \right\|_q < \int 1 \mathrm{d}\mu = 2 \tag{6}$$

To bound the second term note that the functional $\mu_{Y,Z} \rightarrow \left\| \frac{\mu_{X,Z} + \mu_{Y,Z}}{\mu} \right\|_q$ is convex as a function of $\mu_{Y,Z}$ (being a composition of an affine function and the p-th norm). Therefore, the maximum over the convex set of distributions Y, Z satisfying $\widetilde{\mathbf{H}}_\infty (Y|Z) \geqslant k$ is attained at an extreme point. This means that the maximum is attained for a distribution (Y^*, Z) such that the distribution $Y^*|_{Z=z}$ is flat for every z and the conditional min-entropy of Y given Z is exactly k. Since $\mu(x, z) = \mu_U(x)\mu_Z(z)$ and $\mu_{Y^*,Z}(x, z) = \mu_{Y^*|_{Z=z}}(x)\mu_Z(z)$ we obtain

$$\left\| \frac{\mu_{Y,Z}}{\mu} \right\|_q^q \leqslant \int \left(\frac{\mu_{Y^*,Z}}{\mu} \right)^q \mathrm{d}\mu$$

$$= \int \left(\int \left(\frac{\mu_{Y^*_{Z=z}}}{\mu_U} \right)^q \mathrm{d}\mu_U \right) \mathrm{d}\mu_Z$$

$$= \int \left(2^{(q-1)(n-\mathbf{H}_\infty (Y^*|Z=z))} \right) \mathrm{d}\mu_Z$$

$$= 2^{(q-1)n} \int 2^{-(q-1) \mathbf{H}_\infty (Y^*|Z=z)} \mathrm{d}\mu_Z$$

By applying the Jensen Inequality to the function $u \to u^{q-1}$ (which is concave by the assumption on q) we get

$$\left\| \frac{\mu_{Y,Z}}{\mu} \right\|_q^q \leqslant 2^{(q-1)n} \left(\int 2^{-\mathbf{H}_\infty (Y^*|Z=z)} d\mu_Z \right)^{q-1}$$

$$\leqslant 2^{(q-1)n} \left(2^{-\tilde{\mathbf{H}}_\infty (Y|Z)} \right)^{q-1} = 2^{(q-1)(n-k)} \qquad (7)$$

Plugin Equation (7) and Equation (6) into Equation (5) yields

$$\left\| \frac{\mu_{X,Z} + \mu_{Y,Z}}{\mu} \right\|_q^q \leqslant 2^{q-1} \left(2 + 2^{(q-1)(n-k)} \right) = 2^q + 2^{(q-1)(n+1-k)}.$$

and Equation (4) follows. $\square$

Claim 4. Suppose that $p \geqslant 2$. Then for any $D \in \text{conv}(\mathcal{C})$ and $\ell \geqslant 1$ there exists $D_\ell \in \text{conv}_\ell(D)$ such that $\|D - D_\ell\|_p < 1.74\sqrt{p/\ell}$.

Proof. The proof relies on the following approximation result on rates of convex approximation, which generalizes the famous Maurey-Johnes-Barron Theorem.

Lemma 2 (Convex Approximation in L^p Spaces [DDGS97]). *Let E be an L^p space with $1 \leqslant p < +\infty$. Suppose that $S \subset E$, $f \in \text{conv}(S)$ and let $K > 0$ be such that for all $g \in S$ we have $\|g - f\|_p \leqslant K$. Then for any ℓ we have*

$$\min_{s \in \text{conv}_\ell(S)} \|f - s\|_p \leqslant \frac{K C_p}{\ell^{1-\frac{1}{t}}}$$

where $t = \min(2, p)$ and $C_p = 1$ if $1 \leqslant p \leqslant 2$, $C_p = \sqrt{2}[\Gamma((p+1)/2)/\sqrt{\pi}]^{1/p}$ for $2 < p < +\infty$.

Remark 4. The constant C_p can be estimated using the following approximation for the gamma function [Mor11], valid for $x \geqslant 1$:

$$\sqrt{\pi}(x/e)^x \sqrt{2x + 0.33} < \Gamma(x+1) < \sqrt{\pi}(x/e)^x \sqrt{2x + 0.36}$$

From this we find that $C_p < 0.87\sqrt{p}$ for all $p > 2$.

The claim follows by setting E to be the space of $[0,1]$-valued functions on $\{0,1\}^n \times \{0,1\}^m$ and $K = \int 1 d\mu = 2$. $\square$

By Claim 3 and Claim 4 combined with Claim 2 and Claim 1 it suffices to find $p \geqslant 2$ (which automatically ensures $q \in [1,2]$) and ℓ such that

$$1.74\sqrt{p/\ell} \cdot \left(2^q + 2^{(q-1)(n+1-k)} \right)^{1/q} \leqslant \delta.$$

If $k \geqslant n-1$ then we put $p = q = 2$. Then it suffices to ensure that $1.74\sqrt{2/\ell}(2^2 + 2^2)^{1/2} \leqslant \delta$ which is equivalent to $6.96\sqrt{\ell} \leqslant \delta$. Suppose that $k \leqslant n - 1$. By the inequality $(a+b)^r \leqslant a^r + b^r$ valid for $a, b > 0$ and $0 < r \leqslant 1$, we see that it suffices if $1.74\sqrt{p/\ell} \left(2 + 2^{(n+1-k)/p} \right) \leqslant \delta$. For $p = n+1-k$ we obtain $6.96\sqrt{\ell} \leqslant \delta$. $\square$

4 Characterizing Metric Pseudoentropy

In what follows we assume that **H** is a concave entropy notion (like min-entropy or collision entropy), and that all distributions and distinguishers are over $\{0,1\}^n$.

4.1 Connections to Separating Hyperplanes

We start with the following simple observation, which gives a nice geometrical formulation of the definition of pseudo-entropy. We say that the sets $\mathbb{X}$ and $\mathbb{Y}$ of probability distributions are $(\mathcal{D}, \epsilon)$-indistinguishable if there exists *no* adversary D such that $|\mathbf{E}\,\mathrm{D}(X) - \mathbf{E}\,\mathrm{D}(Y)| \geqslant \epsilon$ for all $X \in \mathbb{X}$ and all $Y \in \mathbb{Y}$. It is easy to see that if $\mathbb{X}$ and $\mathbb{Y}$ are convex and if $\mathcal{D}$ is closed under complements (that is $\mathrm{D} \in \mathcal{D}$ implies $1 - \mathrm{D} \in \mathcal{D}$) then this is equivalent to

There is no $\mathrm{D} \in \mathcal{D}$ such that: $\mathbf{E}\,\mathrm{D}(X) - \mathbf{E}\,\mathrm{D}(Y) \geqslant \epsilon$ for all $X \in \mathbb{X}, Y \in \mathbb{Y}$.

We can interpret the expectation $\mathbf{E}\,\mathrm{D}(X)$ as the scalar product $\langle \mathrm{D}, \mathbf{P}_X \rangle$ by identifying D and distributions of X with the vectors in $\mathbb{R}^{2^n}$. Hence we can write the above condition as

There is no $\mathrm{D} \in \mathcal{D}$ such that: $\langle \mathrm{D}, \mathbf{P}_X - \mathbf{P}_Y \rangle \geqslant \epsilon$ for all $X \in \mathbb{X}, Y \in \mathbb{Y}$,

which means that the distinguisher D is precisely a *separating hyperplane*. If $\mathcal{D}$ is a circuit class, $\mathbb{X} = \{X\}$ and $\mathbb{Y} = \{Y : \mathbf{H}(Y) \geqslant k\}$ we obtain[2]

Corollary 2 (Geometric Definitions of Metric and HILL Entropy). *Let X be an n-bit random variable and let* **H** *be a concave entropy notion. Then*

(a) $\mathbf{H}^{\mathrm{HILL},(s,\epsilon)}(X) \geqslant k$ *iff X is $(\mathcal{D}, \epsilon)$-indistinguishable from some Y of entropy* **H** *at least k, where $\mathcal{D}$ is the class of boolean circuits[3] of size s with n-inputs.*
(b) $\mathbf{H}^{\mathrm{M},\det\{0,1\},(s,\epsilon)}(X) \geqslant k$ *iff X is $(\mathcal{D}, \epsilon)$-indistinguishable from the set of all Y of entropy* **H** *at least k,*

where $\mathcal{D}$ is the class of all deterministic boolean circuits of size s with n-inputs (analogously for randomized and deterministic real valued circuits).

4.2 Reduction to Constrained Optimization

By the "geometric" view on pseudoentropy, given in Corollary 2, we obtain the following characterization of pseudoentropy.

---

[2] We can assume that the class circuits of size at most s is closed under complements because every complement is of size at most $s + 1$. Formally we need to start with size $s' = s + 1$ but we omit this negligible difference.
[3] Randomized or deterministic- it makes no difference.

Lemma 3 (Characterization of Metric Pseudoentropy). *Let X and $\mathbf{H}$ be as in Corollary 2. Then* $\mathbf{H}^{M,\det\{0,1\},(s,\epsilon)}(X) \geqslant k$, *respectively* $\mathbf{H}^{M,\det[0,1],(s,\epsilon)}(X) \geqslant k$ *if and only if for every boolean (respectively real valued) deterministic circuit* D *of size at most s we have*

$$\mathbf{E}\,\mathrm{D}(X) \leqslant \mathbf{E}\,\mathrm{D}(Y^*) + \epsilon,$$

where Y^* is optimal to the following optimization problem

$$\begin{array}{ll} \underset{Y}{\text{maximize}} & \mathbf{E}\,\mathrm{D}(Y) \\ \text{s.t.} & \mathbf{H}(Y) \geqslant k \end{array} \tag{8}$$

This results is useful if we can solve the optimization problem in Equation (8). In the next subsections we explain how to solve it in general and discuss the two concrete and simple cases: min-entropy and collision entropy.

4.3 Maximizing Expectations Under Convex Constraints

We can characterize optimal solutions of (8) in terms of Lagrange multipliers. Due to convexity, the characterization is both: necessary and sufficient.

Lemma 4 (Maximizing Expectation Under Convex Constraints). *Let f be a differentiable convex real-valued function on $\mathbb{R}^d$. Assume that a is a number such that $\min_p f(p) < a$ where the minimum is over all probability vectors, and consider the following optimization program*

$$\begin{array}{ll} \underset{(p_i)_i}{\text{maximize}} & \sum_i \mathrm{D}_i p_i \\ \\ \text{s.t.} & \left\{ \begin{array}{l} f(p) \leqslant a \\ -p_i \leqslant 0 \\ \sum_i p_i = 1 \end{array} \right. \end{array} \tag{9}$$

Then a feasible point $p = p^*$ is optimal to (9) if and only if there exist $\lambda_1 \geqslant 0, \lambda_2 \geqslant 0$ and $\lambda_{3i} \in \mathbb{R}$ for $i = 1, \ldots, m$ such that the following relations hold

$$\mathrm{D}_i = \lambda_1 (\nabla f(p^*))_i - \lambda_{3i} + \lambda_2 \quad \text{for } i = 1, \ldots, m \tag{10}$$

and the following complementary condition is satisfied:

$$p_i \cdot \lambda_{3i} = 0 \tag{11}$$

Proof. The Slater Constraint Qualification holds, by the assumption on a, and we have strong duality. In other words, the first order Karush-Kuhn-Tucker condition is sufficient and necessary [BV04]. The numbers $\lambda_1, \lambda_2, \lambda_{3i}$ are exactly KKT multipliers for the convex program in Equation (9), and Equation (10) states that the gradient of the objective function is a combination of gradients of constraints. The condition in Equation (11) means that we take only active constraints into account. Finally, to the inequality constraints we assign non-negative multipliers which explains the requirement $\lambda_1 \geqslant 0$ and $\lambda_{3i} \geqslant 0$. □

Remark 5. If f is not differentiable, we replace the gradient of f in optimality conditions by the *subdifferential* of f, which always exists for a convex function.

4.4 Characterization of Metric Min Entropy

For $\mathbf{H} = \mathbf{H}_\infty$ we obtain from Lemma 4 the following simple characterization of pseudoentropy based on min-entropy (see [BSW03] for a restricted variant)

Theorem 3 (Characterization of Metric Min-entropy). *Let X be an n-bit r.v.. Then* $\mathbf{H}_\infty^{M,\det\{0,1\},(s,\epsilon)}(X) \geqslant k$, *respectively* $\mathbf{H}_\infty^{M,\det[0,1],(s,\epsilon)}(X) \geqslant k$ *if and only if for every boolean (respectively real valued) deterministic circuit D of size at most s with n inputs we have*

$$\mathbf{E}\,D(X) \leqslant \mathbf{E}\,D(Y^*) + \epsilon,$$

where Y^* is uniform over 2^k values x corresponding to the biggest values of $D(x)$.

Extending Lemma 4 by adding additional constraints, to cover the case of side information, we can obtain the characterization of conditional metric entropy

Theorem 4 (Characterization of Conditional Metric Min-entropy). *Let X and Z be, respectively, n and m-bit random variables. Then* $\mathbf{H}_\infty^{M,\det\{0,1\},(s,\epsilon)}(X|Z)$ $\geqslant k$ *(respectively* $\mathbf{H}_\infty^{M,\det[0,1],(s,\epsilon)}(X|Z) \geqslant k$*) iff for every boolean (respectively real valued) deterministic circuit D of size at most s on $\{0,1\}^{n+m}$ we have*

$$\mathbf{E}\,D(X,Z) \leqslant \mathbf{E}\,D(Y^*,Z) + \epsilon,$$

for Y^* such that $Y^*|Z = z$ is uniform over the set $\{D(x,z) \geqslant t(z)\}$ for every z, where the thresholds $t(z)$ satisfy the following two conditions

$$\mathop{\mathbf{E}}_{x \leftarrow U_n} \max(D(x,z) - t(z), 0) = \text{const} \quad \text{for every } z$$

$$\mathop{\mathbf{E}}_{z \leftarrow Z}\left[1/\#\left\{x : D(x,z) \geqslant t(z)\right\}\right] \leqslant 2^{-k} \leqslant \mathbf{E}\left[1/\#\left\{x : D(x,z) > t(z)\right\}\right].$$

4.5 Characterization of Metric Collision Entropy

The characterization of the worst-case collision entropy distribution is slightly different. It is *proportional* to a distinguisher, after taking a threshold.

Theorem 5 (Characterization of Metric Collision Entropy). *Let X be an n-bit r.v.. Then* $\mathbf{H}_2^{M,\det\{0,1\},(s,\epsilon)}(X) \geqslant k$, *respectively* $\mathbf{H}_2^{M,\det[0,1],(s,\epsilon)}(X) \geqslant k$ *if and only if for every boolean (respectively real valued) deterministic circuit D of size at most s with n inputs we have*

$$\mathbf{E}\,D(X) \leqslant \mathbf{E}\,D(Y^*) + \epsilon,$$

where Y^* satisfies $\lambda \cdot \mathbf{P}_{Y^*}(x) = \max(D(x) - t, 0)$ for some $t \in \mathbb{R}$ and $\lambda \geqslant 0$.

Remark 6. Note that t is a solution of $\mathbf{E}\,D'(U)^2 = 2^{n-k}\left(\mathbf{E}\,D'(U)\right)^2$ where $D'(x) = \max(D(x) - t, 0)$ and $\lambda = 2^n\,\mathbf{E}\,D'(U)$. It follows that $\mathbf{E}\,D'(Y^*) = 2^{n-k}\,\mathbf{E}\,D'(U) = \mathbf{E}\,D'(U) + \sqrt{\mathrm{Var}D'(U)} \cdot \sqrt{2^{n-k} - 1}$.

5   Applications

5.1   A Short Proof of the Efficient Dense Model Theorem

DENSE MODEL THEOREM AND ITS APPLICATIONS. Given a pair of two distributions W and V over the same finite domain we say that W is δ-dense in V if and only if $\Pr[W = x] \leqslant \Pr[V = x]/\delta^4$. The dense model theorem [TZ08], specialized to the boolean case, can be formulated as follows:

Theorem 6 (Dense Model Theorem). *Let $\mathcal{D}'$ be a class of n-bit boolean functions, R be uniform over $\{0, 1\}^n$, X be an n-bit random variable and let X' be δ-dense in X. If X and R are $(\mathcal{D}, \epsilon)$-indistinguishable then there exists a distribution R' which is δ-dense in R such that X' and R' are $(\mathcal{D}', \epsilon')$-indistinguishable, where $\epsilon' = (\epsilon/\delta)^{O(1)}$ and $\mathcal{D}$ consists of all functions of the form $g(D_1, \ldots, D_\ell)$ where $D_i \in \mathcal{D}'$, $\ell = \mathrm{poly}(1/\delta, 1/\epsilon)$ and g is some' function.*

Informally, this statement reads as follows: if a distribution X' is dense in a pseudorandom distribution X, then X' must be indistinguishable from a distribution dense in the uniform distribution. Note that the indistinguishability parameters for X' are worse than for X: to achieve $(\mathcal{D}', \epsilon')$-indistinguishably we need to start with ϵ smaller than ϵ' and a class $\mathcal{D}$ sufficiently more complicated than $\mathcal{D}'$. Note also that for this statement to be computationally meaningful we need g to be efficient. Efficient versions of the Dense Model Theorem have found applications in differential privacy [MPRV], pseudoentropy and leakage-resilient cryptography [DP08, CKLR11], graph decompositions [RTTV], and further applications in additive combinatorics [GW11b]. We refer the reader to [Tre11] for a survey. In Table 1 below we give a brief overview of different bounds.

A SUPER-SIMPLE PROOF. The dense model theorem is in fact a statement about HILL entropy with "leakage". This follows from the following observation

Claim 5. X' is δ-dense in X if and only if X' can be written as $X|A$ for some event A of probability δ.

Now we see that the following "leakage lemma" is a version of the dense model theorem, stated in language of pseudoentropy.

Theorem 7 (Leakage Lemma [DP08, FOR12]). *Let X be an n-bit random variable such that $\mathbf{H}_\infty^{\mathrm{HILL}, (s, \epsilon)}(X) \geqslant k$ and let Z be correlated with X. Then we have $\mathbf{H}_\infty^{\mathrm{HILL}, (s', \epsilon')}(X|_{Z=z}) \geqslant k'$ where $k' = k - \log(1/\Pr[Z = z])$, $s' = \mathcal{O}\left(s \cdot \delta^2/n\right)$ and $\epsilon' = \epsilon/\Pr[Z = z] + \delta$, for any $\delta \in (0, 1)$.*

The lemma states that the amount of pseudoentropy due to leakage of t bits of information decreases roughly by t, hence its name. The original proof was simplified by the use of metric entropy [FOR12]. We show how it can be simplified even further: just few lines using the basic facts about metric entropy!

---

[4] The term "δ-dense" comes from the fact that V can be written as a convex combination of W with weight δ and some other distribution with weight $1 - \delta$.

Table 1. Different versions of the Dense Model Theorem

Author	Technique	Function g	ℓ as complexity of $\mathcal{D}'$ w.r.t $\mathcal{D}$	ϵ' vs ϵ
[TZ08]	Complicated	Inefficient	$\ell = \text{poly}(1/(\epsilon/\delta), \log(1/\delta))$	$\epsilon' = O(\epsilon/\delta)$
[RTTV, Gow08]	Min-Max Theorem	Linear threshold	$\text{poly}(1/(\epsilon/\delta), \log(1/\delta))$	$\epsilon' = O(\epsilon/\delta)$
[FOR12], [DP08]	Metric Entropy	Linear threshold	$\ell = O(n/(\epsilon/\delta)^2)$	$\epsilon' = O(\epsilon/\delta)$
[Zha11]	Boosting	Linear threshold	$\ell = O(\log(1/\delta)/(\epsilon/\delta)^2$	$\epsilon' = O(\epsilon/\delta)$
This paper	Metric Entropy	Linear threshold	$\ell = O(\log(1/\delta)/(\epsilon/\delta)^2$	$\epsilon' = O(\epsilon/\delta)$

Proof. If we can prove that

$$\mathbf{H}_\infty^{M,\det\{0,1\},(s,\epsilon/\Pr[Z=z]))}\left(X|_{Z=z}\right) \geqslant \mathbf{H}_\infty^{M,\det\{0,1\},(s,\epsilon)}\left(X\right) - \log(1/\Pr[Z=z])$$

then the result will follow by Theorem 1 and Remark 3. Note that by Theorem 3 for any X we have $\mathbf{H}_\infty^{M,\det\{0,1\},(s,\epsilon)}\left(X\right) \geqslant k$ if and only if $\mathbf{E}\,D(X) \leqslant \frac{|D|}{2^k} + \epsilon$ for all boolean D of size at most s. From this we get

$$\mathbf{E}\,D(X|_{Z=z}) \leqslant \mathbf{E}\,D(X)/\Pr[Z=z] \leqslant |D|/2^k \Pr[Z=z] + \epsilon/\Pr[Z=z]$$

for any D. Since the characterization is also sufficient, the results follows. □

5.2   The Optimal Efficient Dense Model Theorem

THE DENSE MODEL THEOREM WITH OPTIMAL PARAMETERS. Below we derive from our Lemma 1 the optimal Dense Model Theorem due to Zhang [Zha11].

Corollary 3. *Dense Model Theorem (Theorem 6) holds with $\epsilon' = O(\epsilon/\delta)$, g being a linear threshold and $\ell = O(\log(1/\delta)/(\epsilon/\delta)^2$.*

Proof. We need Claim 5 and the following version of the leakage lemma

Lemma 5 ([FOR12], Reformulated). *Let X be a random variable and A be an event of probability δ. Suppose that there exists D such that $\mathbf{E}\,D(X|A) - \mathbf{E}\,D(Y) \geqslant \epsilon'$ for all Y of min-entropy at least $k - \log(1/\Pr[A])$ and $\epsilon' = \epsilon/\Pr[A] > 0$. Then there exists a a function D' being a threshold of D such that $\mathbf{E}\,D'(X) - \mathbf{E}\,D'(Y) \geqslant \epsilon$ for all Y of min-entropy at least k.*

The name "leakage lemma" is because for $s' \approx s$ the lemma implies

$$\mathbf{H}_\infty^{M,\det[0,1],s,\epsilon)}\left(X|A\right) \geqslant \mathbf{H}_\infty^{M,\mathcal{D},s'\epsilon/\Pr[A])}\left(X\right) - \log(1/\Pr[A]).$$

Now we are ready to give the proof. Suppose that the Dense Model Theorem is not true with the claimed parameters. Then for some event A of probability δ, some ϵ' and every distribution Y of min-entropy $n - \log(1/\delta)$ (equivalently: δ-dense in the uniform distribution) there exists $D \in \mathcal{D}$ or $D \in 1 - \mathcal{D}$ such that

$$\mathbf{E}\,D(X|A) - \mathbf{E}\,D(Y) \geqslant \epsilon'$$

By applying the min-max theorem we get that there exists a long convex combination $\bar{D}$ of functions from $\mathcal{D} \cup (1 - \mathcal{D})$ such that

$$\mathbf{E}\,\bar{D}(X|A) - \mathbf{E}\,\bar{D}(Y) \geqslant \epsilon' \quad \forall Y: \mathbf{H}_\infty(Y) \geqslant n - \log(1/\delta).$$

We apply Lemma 1, to the class $\mathcal{D} \cup (1-\mathcal{D})$ and δ replaced by $\epsilon'/3$, approximating $\bar{D}$ by a convex combination D' of length $\ell = O\left(\log(1/\delta)/\epsilon'^2\right)$. We get

$$\mathbf{E}\, D'(X|A) - \mathbf{E}\, D'(Y) \geqslant \epsilon'/3 \quad \forall Y:\ \mathbf{H}_\infty(Y) \geqslant n - \log(1/\delta).$$

Note that D' is a linear threshold of ℓ functions from $\mathcal{D}$. By Lemma 5 we replace D' by D'' which is again a linear threshold of ℓ functions from $\mathcal{D}$ and satisfies

$$\mathbf{E}\, D''(X) - \mathbf{E}\, D''(Y) \geqslant \epsilon'\delta/3 \quad \forall Y:\ \mathbf{H}_\infty(Y) \geqslant n.$$

Hence, with any $\epsilon' > 3\epsilon/\delta$ we get a contradiction. □

5.3   Equivalence of HILL Entropy and Unpredictability Entropy for Short Strings

UNPREDICTABILITY ENTROPY. The notion of unpredictability entropy is based on the (assumed) hardness of guessing X given auxiliary information Z. More formally, we have $\mathbf{H}^{\mathrm{Unp},s}(X|Z) \geqslant k$ if and only if no adversary of size at most s can predict X given Z better than with probability 2^{-k}. For Z independent of X or of the relatively short length, this reduces to the min-entropy of X[5].

SEPERATION FROM HILL ENTROPY. If f is a one-way function, U is the uniform distribution and $X = U, Z = f(U)$ then we see that $X|Z$ has large amount of unpredictability. It is also easy to see that $X|Z$ has almost no HILL entropy.

EQUIVALENCE FOR SHORT STRINGS. On the positive side, using metric entropy and the characterization in Theorem 4, we reprove the following result of Vadhan and Zheng who established the equivalence when X is short[6]

Theorem 8 ([VZ12]). *Suppose that X and Z are, respectively, n and m-bit random variables. Then $\mathbf{H}_\infty^{\mathrm{HILL},(s',\epsilon)}(X|Z) \gtrsim \mathbf{H}^{\mathrm{Unp},s}(X|Z)$ with $s' = \frac{s}{\mathrm{poly}(2^n,1/\epsilon)}$.*

The original proof is based on a result similar to Theorem 4 proved in a much more complicated way. We note that this part is a trivial consequence of KKT optimality conditions and also simplify the rest of the proof.

Proof (Sketch). We prove that $\mathbf{H}_\infty^{\mathrm{M},\det[0,1],(s',\epsilon)}(X|Z) < k$ implies $\mathbf{H}^{\mathrm{Unp},s}(X|Z) < k$. Suppose not, then we have $\mathbf{E}\, D(X,Z) - \mathbf{E}\, D(Y,Z) \geqslant \epsilon$ for all Y such that $\widetilde{\mathbf{H}}_\infty(X|Z) \geqslant k$. Let Y^* be the distribution which minimizes this expression, that is which maximizes $\mathbf{E}\, D(Y,Z)$. Let $t(z)$ be as in Theorem 4 and denote $D'(x,z) = \max(D(x,z) - t(z), 0)$ and let $\lambda = \sum_x D'(x,z)$ (according to Theorem 4 this sum does not depend on z). Consider the following predictor A:

On input z sample x according to the probability $\Pr[A(z) = x] = D'(x,z)/\lambda$

Note that $Y^*|_{Z=z}$ is uniform over the set $\{x : D'(x,z) > 0\}$. By Theorem 4 (the sufficiency part) it follows that Y^* is also maximal for D. For every z we have

---

[5] Provided that $s > 2^m n$ so that the adversary can hardcore his best guess.

[6] Logarithmically in the security parameter.

$\mathbf{E} D'(Y^*|_{Z=z}, z) = \mathbf{E} D(Y^*|Z = z, z) - t(z)$. We have also $\mathbf{E} D'(X|_{Z=z}, z) \geqslant \mathbf{E} D(X|_{Z=z}, z) - t(z)$ by the definition of D'. This proves

$$\mathbf{E} D'(X, Z) - \mathbf{E} D'(Y, Z) \geqslant \epsilon \text{ for all } Y \text{ such that } \widetilde{\mathbf{H}}_\infty(X|Z) \geqslant k.$$

It is easy to observe that

$$\Pr_{z \leftarrow Z}[A(Z) = X] = \frac{\mathbf{E} D'(X, Z)}{\lambda} > \mathop{\mathbf{E}}_{z \leftarrow} \left[\frac{\mathbf{E} D'(Y|_{Z=z}, z)}{\sum_x D'(x, z)} \right] \geqslant \mathop{\mathbf{E}}_{z \leftarrow Z} 2^{-\mathbf{H}_\infty(Y^*|_{Z=z})}$$

which is at least 2^{-k}. The circuit $D'(x, z)$ is of complexity $2^m \cdot \text{size}(D)$, which is too big. However, if the domain of x is small, we can approximate the numbers $t(z)$ given λ from relations in Theorem 4 (and even λ, from the second relation, for the uniform setting). Indeed, knowing that $\mathbf{E} \max(D(U, z) - t(z)) = \lambda$, we estimate $\mathbf{E} \max(D(U, z) - t)$ for fixed t and then find a "right" value $t = t(z)$ by the binary search. This way for every z we can approximate $D'(\cdot, z)$, and hence the distribution $\Pr[A(z) = x]$, up to a maximal error $\delta \ll 2^{-k}$ and with overwhelming probability $1 - \exp(-\text{poly}(1/\delta))$, using $\text{poly}(1/\delta)$ samples of D. On average over z we predict X with probability $2^{-k} - \delta \approx 2^{-k}$.   □

5.4   Improved Leftover Hash Lemma for Square-Secure Applications

In the key derivation problem we want to derive a secure m-bit key for some application P from an *imperfect* source of randomness X. The generic approach is to use a randomness extractor. However, as implied by the RT-bounds [RTS00], the min-entropy in X needs to be at least $m + 2\log(1/\epsilon)$ if we want the derived key to be ϵ-secure. Fortunately, as shown by Barak et. al [BDK+11], for many cryptographic applications, one can reduce this loss by half, that is to $L = \log(1/\epsilon)$. To this end, they introduce the class of *square-secure* applications, where the squared advantage, over the uniform choice of keys, of every bounded attacker is small[7]. This class contains for example all unpredictability applications, stateless chosen plaintext attack secure encryption and weak pseudo-random functions. The reduction of entropy loss follows by combining universal hashing with the following lemma

Lemma 6 ([BDK+11]). *For a function* $D : \{0,1\}^\ell \to [-1, 1]$ *and* $X \in \{0,1\}^\ell$ *of collision entropy k we have*

$$\mathbf{E} D(X) \leqslant \mathbf{E} D(U_\ell) + \sqrt{\text{Var} D(U_\ell)} \cdot \sqrt{2^{\ell-k} - 1}.$$

To see this, let $\text{Win}_A(r, h)$, for arbitrary attacker $A \in \mathcal{A}$, be the probability that A breaks the key r given in addition[8] h and let $D_{\mathcal{A}}(r, h) = \text{Win}_A(r, h) - \frac{1}{2}$ be its advantage. Let X be any n-bit random variable of min-entropy $m + \log(1/\epsilon)$. We

---

[7] Essentially the probability that an attacker break the key is concentrated over keys.
[8] For the uniform key this doesn't help the adversary, at least in the nonuniform model.

apply a randomly chosen universal hash function[9] H from n to m bits. It is easy to see that $H(X), H$ is a distribution with collision entropy $m + \log |\mathcal{H}| - \log(1+\epsilon)$. From the lemma it follows now that

$$\mathbf{E}\,\mathrm{D_A}(H(X), H) \leqslant \mathbf{E}\,\mathrm{D_A}(U, H) + \sqrt{\mathrm{Var}\mathrm{D_A}(U, H)} \cdot \sqrt{\epsilon}$$

If we assume that $\max_h \mathbf{E}\,\mathrm{D_A}(U, h) \leqslant \epsilon$ (which means ϵ-security against $\mathcal{A}$ with the uniform key) and that $\max_h \mathbf{E}\,\mathrm{D_A}(U, h)^2 \leqslant \sigma$ with $\sigma = \mathcal{O}(\epsilon)$ (which means σ-square-security against $\mathcal{A}$ with the uniform key) then we achieve $\mathcal{O}(\epsilon)$ security for the *extracted* key, with entropy loss only $\log(1/\epsilon)$.

AN ALTERNATIVE PROOF. We show that Theorem 5 implies Lemma 6. Indeed, set $k = \ell$ and $\epsilon = 0$ in Theorem 5. Let Y^* be the distribution of collision entropy at least $k = \ell$ which maximizes $\mathbf{E}\,\mathrm{D}(Y)$, and let t, λ and D' be as in the characterization. Denote $S = \{x : \mathrm{D}(x) \geqslant t\}$ and let $\mathrm{D}|_S$ be the restriction of D to the set S. Note that $Y^*|S \stackrel{d}{=} Y^*$ maximizes $\mathrm{D}|_S$ and $\mathrm{D}|_S(x) = \mathrm{D}'|_S(X) + t$ for every $x \in S$. By Remark 6 we get

$$\mathbf{E}\,\mathrm{D}(X) \leqslant \mathbf{E}\,\mathrm{D}(Y^*) = \mathbf{E}\,\mathrm{D}|_S(Y^*|S) \quad = \mathbf{E}\,\mathrm{D}|_S(U_S) + \sqrt{\mathrm{Var}\mathrm{D}_S(U_S)} \cdot \sqrt{|S|2^{-k} - 1}.$$

We can replace S by the $\{0,1\}^\ell$. This follows by the following general lemma

Lemma 7. *Let X be a random variable, $c > 1$ be a constant and S be an event of probability $\mathbf{P}(S) > c^{-1}$. Then*

$$\mathbf{E}[X|S] + \sqrt{\mathrm{Var}[X|S]} \cdot \sqrt{c\mathbf{P}(S) - 1} \leqslant \mathbf{E}[X] + \sqrt{\mathrm{Var}[X]} \cdot \sqrt{c - 1} \qquad (12)$$

The proof follows by a few algebraic manipulations and is given in Appendix A.

5.5 Some Further Applications

LOWER BOUNDS ON SQUARE SECURITY. Using Theorem 5 one can derive some non-trivial lower bounds on square-security needed for key derivation. We discuss this problem in a separate paper (see also a full version of this paper on ePrint).

6 Conclusion

In this paper we develop a general tool to characterize metric-type pseudoentropy and prove a tight transformation between conditional Metric and HILL entropy. A question we want to address in our future work is to find more applications of metric pseudoentropy characterizations, especially for key derivation.

Acknowledgments. The author would like to thank Krzysztof Pietrzak for helpful discussions.

---

[9] A family $\mathcal{H}$ functions from n to m bits is universal if $\mathrm{Pr}_{h \leftarrow \mathcal{H}}[h(x) = h(x')] = 2^{-m}$ for $x \neq x'$.

References

BDK+11. Barak, B., Dodis, Y., Krawczyk, H., Pereira, O., Pietrzak, K., Standaert, F.-X., Yu, Y.: Leftover hash lemma, revisited. In: Rogaway, P. (ed.) CRYPTO 2011. LNCS, vol. 6841, pp. 1–20. Springer, Heidelberg (2011)

BSW03. Barak, B., Shaltiel, R., Wigderson, A.: Computational analogues of entropy. In: Arora, S., Jansen, K., Rolim, J.D.P., Sahai, A. (eds.) RANDOM 2003 and APPROX 2003. LNCS, vol. 2764, pp. 200–215. Springer, Heidelberg (2003)

BV04. Boyd, S., Vandenberghe, L.: Convex optimization. Cambridge University Press, New York (2004)

CKLR11. Chung, K.-M., Kalai, Y.T., Liu, F.-H., Raz, R.: Memory delegation. In: Rogaway, P. (ed.) CRYPTO 2011. LNCS, vol. 6841, pp. 151–168. Springer, Heidelberg (2011)

DDGS97. Donahue, M.J., Darken, C., Gurvits, L., Sontag, E.: Rates of convex approximation in non-hilbert spaces. Constructive Approximation 13(2), 187–220 (1997)

DORS08. Dodis, Y., Ostrovsky, R., Reyzin, L., Smith, A.: Fuzzy extractors: How to generate strong keys from biometrics and other noisy data. SIAM J. Comput. 38(1), 97–139 (2008)

DP08. Dziembowski, S., Pietrzak, K.: Leakage-resilient cryptography. In: FOCS 2008, pp. 293–302. IEEE Computer Society (2008)

FOR12. Fuller, B., O'Neill, A., Reyzin, L.: A unified approach to deterministic encryption: New constructions and a connection to computational entropy. In: Cramer, R. (ed.) TCC 2012. LNCS, vol. 7194, pp. 582–599. Springer, Heidelberg (2012)

Gow08. Gowers, W.T.: Decompositions, approximate structure, transference, and the Hahn-Banach theorem, ArXiv e-prints (2008)

GW11a. Gentry, C., Wichs, D.: Separating succinct non-interactive arguments from all falsifiable assumptions. In: STOC 2011, pp. 99–108. ACM (2011)

GW11b. Gowers, W.T., Wolf, J.: Linear forms and higher-degree uniformity for functions on $\mathbb{F}_p^n$. Geometric and Functional Analysis 21(1), 36–69 (2011)

HILL99. Hastad, J., Impagliazzo, R., Levin, L.A., Luby, M.: A pseudorandom generator from any one-way function. SIAM J. Comput. 28(4), 1364–1396 (1999)

HLR07. Hsiao, C.-Y., Lu, C.-J., Reyzin, L.: Conditional computational entropy, or toward separating pseudoentropy from compressibility. In: Naor, M. (ed.) EUROCRYPT 2007. LNCS, vol. 4515, pp. 169–186. Springer, Heidelberg (2007)

HRV10. Haitner, I., Reingold, O., Vadhan, S.: Efficiency improvements in constructing pseudorandom generators from one-way functions. In: STOC 2010, pp. 437–446. ACM (2010)

KPW13. Krenn, S., Pietrzak, K., Wadia, A.: A counterexample to the chain rule for conditional hill entropy. In: Sahai, A. (ed.) TCC 2013. LNCS, vol. 7785, pp. 23–39. Springer, Heidelberg (2013)

Mor11. Mortici, C.: Journal of Mathematical Inequalities 5(4), 611–614 (2011)

MPRV. Mironov, I., Pandey, O., Reingold, O., Vadhan, S.: Computational differential privacy. In: Halevi, S. (ed.) CRYPTO 2009. LNCS, vol. 5677, pp. 126–142. Springer, Heidelberg (2009)

Rey11. Reyzin, L.: Some notions of entropy for cryptography. In: Fehr, S. (ed.) ICITS 2011. LNCS, vol. 6673, pp. 138–142. Springer, Heidelberg (2011)

RTS00. Radhakrishnan, J., Ta-Shma, A.: Bounds for dispersers, extractors, and depth-two superconcentrators. SIAM Journal on Discrete Mathematics 13 2000 (2000)

RTTV.   Reingold, O., Trevisan, L., Tulsiani, M., Vadhan, S.: Dense subsets of pseudorandom sets. In: FOCS 2008, pp. 76–85. IEEE Computer Society (2008)

Sha48.   Shannon, C.E.: A mathematical theory of communication. Bell System Technical Journal 27 (1948)

Tre11.   Trevisan, L.: Dense model theorems and their applications. In: Ishai, Y. (ed.) TCC 2011. LNCS, vol. 6597, pp. 55–57. Springer, Heidelberg (2011)

TZ08.   Tao, T., Ziegler, T.: The primes contain arbitrarily long polynomial progressions. Acta Mathematica 201(2), 213–305 (2008)

VZ12.   Vadhan, S., Zheng, C.J.: Characterizing pseudoentropy and simplifying pseudorandom generator constructions. In: STOC 2012, pp. 817–836. ACM (2012)

Zha11.   Zhang, J.: On the query complexity for showing dense model. Electronic Colloquium on Computational Complexity (ECCC) 18, 38 (2011)

A   Proof of Lemma 7

Proof (Proof of Lemma 7). Denote $p = \mathbf{P}(S), q = 1 - p$ and $a = \mathbf{E}[X|S], b = \mathbf{E}[X|S^c], v = \mathrm{Var}[X|S]$. Applying the Jensen's Inequality we obtain

$$\mathrm{Var}X = \mathbf{E}\left(X - \mathbf{E}X\right)^2$$

$$= \mathbf{P}(S)\mathbf{E}\left[(X - \mathbf{E}X)^2 \,\middle|\, X \in S\right] + \mathbf{P}(S^c)\mathbf{E}\left[(X - \mathbf{E}X)^2 \,\middle|\, X \in S^c\right]$$

$$\geqslant \mathbf{P}(S)\mathbf{E}\left[(X - \mathbf{E}X)^2 \,|\, X \in S\right] + \mathbf{P}(S^c)\left(\mathbf{E}[X|S^c] - \mathbf{E}X\right)^2$$

Observe that

$$\mathbf{E}\left[(X - \mathbf{E}X)^2 \,|\, X \in S\right] = \mathbf{E}\left[((X - \mathbf{E}[X|S]) + (\mathbf{E}[X|S] - \mathbf{E}X))^2 \,|\, X \in S\right]$$

$$= \mathbf{E}\left[(X - \mathbf{E}[X|S])^2 \,\middle|\, X \in S\right] + (\mathbf{E}[X|S] - \mathbf{E}X)^2$$

$$= \mathrm{Var}[X|S] + (\mathbf{E}[X|S] - \mathbf{E}X)^2$$

By the total probability law we obtain

$$\mathbf{E}[X|S] - \mathbf{E}X = \mathbf{P}(S^c)(\mathbf{E}[X|S] - \mathbf{E}[X|S^c])$$

$$\mathbf{E}[X|S^c] - \mathbf{E}X = \mathbf{P}(S)(\mathbf{E}[X|S^c] - \mathbf{E}[X|S]).$$

Putting this all together we see that it is enough to prove the following inequality

$$a + \sqrt{v} \cdot \sqrt{cp - 1} \leqslant pa + (1 - p)b + \sqrt{c - 1} \cdot \sqrt{\begin{array}{l} pv + p(1 - p)^2(a - b)^2 + \\ (1 - p)^2 p(a - b)^2 \end{array}}$$

which after introducing $u = a - b \in (-1, 1)$ becomes

$$(1 - p)u + \sqrt{v} \cdot \sqrt{cp - 1} \leqslant \sqrt{v + (1 - p)u^2} \cdot \sqrt{cp - p}$$

Setting $A = v$, $B = cp - 1$, $C = u^2$ and $D = 1 - p$ we rewrite it as

$$D\sqrt{C} + \sqrt{AB} \leqslant \sqrt{A + CD} \cdot \sqrt{B + D}$$

(where we assume $A, B, C \in [0, 1]$ and $B \geqslant 0$). This inequality, by taking the squares of both side, is equivalent to $0 \leqslant (\sqrt{BC} - \sqrt{A})^2$, which finishes the proof.

$\square$

Nonuniform Indistinguishability and Unpredictability Hardcore Lemmas: New Proofs and Applications to Pseudoentropy[*]

Maciej Skorski[**]

Cryptology and Data Security Group, University of Warsaw, Warsaw, Poland
maciej.skorski@mimuw.edu.pl

Abstract. Hardcore lemmas are results in complexity theory which state that average-case hardness must have a very hard "kernel", that is a subset of instances where the given problem is extremely hard. They find important applications in hardness amplification. In this paper we revisit the following two fundamental results:

(a) The hardcore lemma for unpredictability, due to Impagliazzo (FOCS '95). It states that if a boolean function f is "moderately" hard to predict on average, then there must be a set of noticeable size on which f is "extremely" hard to predict.

(b) The hardcore lemma for indistinguishability, proved by Maurer and Tesaro (TCC'10), states that for two random variables X and Y which are ϵ-computationally close, there are events A and B of probability $1 - \epsilon$ such that the distributions of $X|A$ and $Y|B$ are "computationally" identical.

Using only the standard min-max theorem and some basic facts about convex approximations in L_p spaces, we provide alternative modular proofs and some generalizations of these results in the nonuniform setting, achieving best possible bounds for (a) and slightly improving the known bounds for (b). As an interesting application, we show a strengthening of the transformation between two most popular pseudoentropy variants: HILL and Metric Entropy, and apply it to show how to extract pseudorandomness from a sequence of metric-entropy sources of poor quality. In this case we significantly improve security parameters, comparing to the best known techniques.

1 Introduction

1.1 Hardcore Lemmas and Their Applications

UNPREDICTABILITY HARDCORE LEMMA. Suppose that we have a function $f : \{0,1\}^n \to \{0,1\}$ that is mildly hard to predict by a class of circuits; for every

---

[*] A preliminary version of this work appeared in the Proceedings of Student Research Forum Papers and Posters at SOFSEM 2015.

[**] This work was partly supported by the WELCOME/2010-4/2 grant founded within the framework of the EU Innovative Economy Operational Programme.

© Springer International Publishing Switzerland 2015
A. Lehmann and S. Wolf (Eds.): ICITS 2015, LNCS 9063, pp. 123–140, 2015.
DOI: 10.1007/978-3-319-17470-9_8

circuit D from our class, D(x) and $f(x)$ agree on at most, say, a 0.99 fraction of inputs x. One of the reasons for that, which could intuitively explain this behavior, is the existence of a "kernel" for this hardness: a set of noticeable size on which f is extremely hard to predict, meaning that there is (almost) no advantage over a random guess. How big this set should be? The intuitive answer is a $0.02 = 2(1 - 0.99)$ fraction of input. Indeed, if f cannot be guessed better than with probability $\frac{1}{2}$ on this set, then the probability that D agrees with f is at most $0.02 \cdot \frac{1}{2} + 0.98 \cdot 1 = 0.99$, by the total probability law.

Quite surprisingly, this intuitive characterization is true. The first such result was proved by Impagliazzo [Imp95]. An improved version with the optimal density of the hardcore set was found by Holenstein [Hol05]. Below we present the best possible result due to Klivans and Servedio.

Theorem 1 (Nonuniform Unpredictability Hardcore Lemma [KS03]).
Let $f : \{0,1\}^n \to \{0,1\}$ be ϵ-unpredictable by circuits of size s, that is

$$\Pr_{x \leftarrow \{0,1\}^n}[D(x) = f(x)] \leqslant 1 - \frac{\epsilon}{2}$$

holds for all boolean circuits D over n bits of size at most s. Then for any $\delta \in (0,1)$ there exists a "hardcore" set S of size $\epsilon 2^n$ such that f on S is $1 - \delta$ unpredictable by circuits of size $s' = O\left(s\delta^2/\log(1/\epsilon)\right)$, that is

$$\Pr_{x \leftarrow S}[D(x) = f(x)] \leqslant \frac{1 + \delta}{2}, \quad \text{for every D of size at most } s'.$$

Remark 1 (Conventions). Some authors define ϵ-unpredictability in a different manner. We follow the approach of [Hol05]. The definition above is quite intuitive, since 1-unpredictability means that f is totally unpredictable.

Remark 2 (Trade-off between the Loss in Complexity and Quality of the Hardcore Set). Ideally we want $\delta = 0$ but then we get nothing nontrivial about the indistnguishability. In fact, we cannot guarantee that f on the hardcore is perfectly unpredictable. The loss of $\delta^2/\log(1/\epsilon)$ in complexity is necessary (the matching lower bound is due to Lu, Tsai, and Wu [LTW07]).

Remark 3 (Hardcore for any Sampling Distribution). Klivans and Servedio proved in fact a more general result, where one samples x from arbitrary distribution V. The hardcore set is replaced then by a distribution "dense" in V. See Theorem 3.

Note that the size of the hardcore set, guaranteed to be at least $2^n\epsilon$, is tight. Indeed, if the second part of the theorem is satisfied, i.e. f is almost unpredictable on a set of size ϵ, it implies that f, on average over the whole domain, cannot be predicted better than $1 - \frac{\epsilon+\delta}{2} \approx 1 - \frac{\epsilon}{2}$ (provided that $\delta \ll \epsilon$). A uniform version, with the tight hardcore density, is given also in [Hol05] and [VZ12]. Constructive versions of the hardcore lemma can be obtained by any boosting algorithm [KS99,BHK09], however such results are not necessarily tight without additional optimization.

INDISTINGUISHABILITY HARDCORE LEMMA. It is well known that if two distributions X_1, X_2 have the statistical distance at most ϵ, then there exist events A_1, A_2 of probability at least $1 - \epsilon$ such that the distributions $X_1|A_1$ and $X_2|A_2$ are *identical*. Based on the reduction to the unpredictability hardcore lemma, Maurer and Tessaro proved the following computational generalization of this fact in the nonuniform setting.

Theorem 2 (Indistinguishability Hardcore Lemma [MT10]). *Let X_1 and X_2 be distributions on $\{0,1\}^n$, with the computational distance ϵ against circuits of size s, that is*

$$|\mathbf{E}\,D(X_1) - \mathbf{E}\,D(X_2)| < \epsilon \quad \text{for all } D \text{ of size } s.$$

Then there exist events A_1 and A_2 of probability $1 - \epsilon$ such that A_1 and A_2 are computationally indistinguishable, that is

$$|\mathbf{E}\,D(X_1|A_1) - \mathbf{E}\,D(X_2|A_2)| \leqslant \delta \quad \text{for every } D \text{ of size } s = s\delta^2/128n.$$

which states that if two distributions are (computationally) not too far away from each other, then after conditioning on an event of noticeable probability they are almost completely indistinguishable. Since the lower bound $1 - \epsilon$ on the probabilities of hardcore events is tight[1], this theorem can be viewed as a characterization of computational indistinguishability.

APPLICATIONS OF HARDCORE LEMMAS. Hardcore lemmas are fundamental result in complexity theory and find applications in cryptography and learning theory. They are particularly important in the context of hardness amplification, i.e. transforming somewhat hard problems into hard problems. See for instance [LT13, GNW11, MT10, Hol05, Imp95].

1.2 Our Results

AN UNPREDICTABILITY HARDCORE LEMMA FROM STANDARD MIN-MAX THEOREM. We reprove Theorem 1 in its full generality developing a few new ideas. Our approach has the following advantages:

(a) *A new modular proof technique.* Our approach is very simple and natural. We observe that it is straightforward to construct a hardcore for any fixed circuit of size s. Then we show that this is possible for any *real-valued circuit* of the same size. The third step (the only one which loses in complexity) is an approximation argument which shows that there exists a hardcore for any convex combination of circuits of size s. Finally we trivially "switch" the quantifiers by the standard min-max theorem. See Figure 1 for an overview.

(b) *Tight bounds from the standard min-max theorem.* In our proof the weight of the hardcore event[2] for ϵ-unpredictability is guaranteed to be ϵ and

---

[1] By the similar reasoning as in the unpredictability case.

[2] The hardcore is then understood as the sampling distribution conditioned on an appropriate event of sufficiently big probability.

we loss a factor of $O\left(\log(1/\epsilon)/\delta^2\right)$ in complexity for the hardcore to be $1 - \delta$ unpredictable, which matches the lower bound [LTW07]. The previous proofs which achieve optimal parameters required involved iterative arguments [KS03] or dedicated versions of the min-max theorem [VZ12]. Some authors even suggested that it might be impossible to get the tight parameters using the standard min-max theorem [VZ12].

(c) *New ideas of independent interests.* The only technical difficulties in our proof are steps 2 and 3. The tools we have developed to overcome them allows us to give a direct proof (without reduction!) of the indistinguishability hardcore lemma and a variant of the indistinguishability hardcore lemma dedicated for computational entropy.

Below, in Figure 1, we sketch our proof strategy. We have managed to separate a lossless use of the min-max theorem from a standard approximaiton argument which is responsible for the only loss in complexity.

Fig. 1. An overview of our proof technique

A quantitative comparison with versions of Theorem 1 is given in Table 1.

Table 1. Our unpredictability hardcore lemma compared to previous works

Result	Author	Proof technique	Complexity loss	Sampling distribution
Unpredictability Hardcore	[Hol05]	standard min-max theorem hardcore density optimization	$O(n/\delta^2)$	Uniform
	[KS03]	boosting	$O\left(\frac{\log(1/\epsilon)}{\delta^2}\right)$	Arbitrary
	[VZ12]	dedicated min-max theorem hardcore density optimization	$O\left(\frac{\log(1/\epsilon)}{\delta^2}\right)$	Arbitrary
	This paper Theorem 3	standard min-max theorem convex approximation	$O\left(\min\left(\frac{n}{\delta^2}, \frac{\log(1/\epsilon)}{\delta^2}\right)\right)$	Arbitrary

A SIMPLIFIED AND IMPROVED REDUCTION FROM TO UNPREDICTABILITY HARD-CORES. We show an alternative proof for the indistinguishability hardcore lemma of Maurer and Tessaro. In [MT10] the non-trivial reduction goes from the indistinguishablity hardcore lemma to the "standard" unpredictability hardcore lemma, that is where inputs are sampled from the uniform distribution. On the contrary, we find it much easier and natural to reduce it to unpredictability of some predicate which explicitly depends on the distributions X_1, X_2 (it is simply equal to the sign of the difference between probability mass functions). In our reduction we achieve better numerical constants and improve the factor depending on the dimension, replacing n by $\Delta^2 \log(1/\delta)$ where Δ is the statistical distance of X_1 and X_2. The comparison with Theorem 2 is given in Table 2.

Table 2. Our indistinguishability hardcore lemma compared to previous works

Result	Author	Proof technique	Complexity loss
Indistinguishability	[MT10]	Reduction (to unpredictability hardcore)	$O(n/\delta^2)$
Hardcore	**This paper** Theorem 4	Simpler Reduction (general unpredictability hardcore)	$O\left(\min\left(\frac{\Delta^2 n}{\delta^2}, \frac{\Delta^2 \log(\Delta/\epsilon)}{\delta^2}\right)\right)$

A DIRECT PROOF OF THE INDISTINGUISHABILITY HARDCORE LEMMA. Adapting the proof given for the unpredictability case, we derive the (nonuniform) Indistinguishability Hardcore Lemma of Maurer and Tessaro *directly*, that is *without reducing* it to unpredictability hardcore lemmas. This might be important for lower bounds. Indeed, lower bounds on unpredictability hardcore lemmas do not imply lower bounds for the indistinguishability. For more details, see Corollary 3 in Section 4.

AN INDISTINGUISHABILITY HARDCORE LEMMA FOR PSEUDOENTROPY. In some situations, for instance in extracting entropy, we do not really need our distribution X to be indistinguishable from a *particular* Y but rather from a *class* of distributions Y (which is a weaker requirement). In particular, consider the following alternatives to formalize the statement "X almost has min-entropy k":

(i) X is (s, δ)-close to having property P, if there exists a distribution Y with min-entropy k such that for every circuit D of size s, we have $\Delta^D(X; Y) \leqslant \delta$

(ii) X is (s, δ)-close to having property P, if for every D of size s there exists a distribution Y with min-entropy k such that we have $\Delta^D(X; Y) \leqslant \delta$.

where $\Delta^D(X; Y) = \mathbf{E} D(X) - \mathbf{E} D(Y)$ is the advantage of the attacker D. For case (i), we obtain the notion of the HILL entropy [HILL99]. In case (ii) we obtain a relaxed notion called metric pseudoentropy [BSW03]. Metric pseudoentropy is widely used as a convenient substitute of HILL entropy and find many application in studying pseudorandomness [VZ12, FOR12, DP08, BSW03]. It is known [BSW03] that metric entropy with parameters (s, ϵ) can be converted into HILL entropy with no loss in the amount and the parameters $(s', \epsilon') = (O\left(s \cdot \delta^2/n\right), \epsilon + \delta)$ for any δ. We obtain a nice and much stronger version of this transformation: if X has metric entropy of quality (s, ϵ) (even against weakest deterministic circuits) then after conditioning on an event of probability $1 - \epsilon$, it has the same amount of HILL entropy of quality $(O\left(s \cdot \delta^2/n\right), \delta)$.

APPLICATION: EXTRACTING PSEUDORANDOMNESS FROM PSEUDOENTROPY OF POOR QUALITY. Using our generalized indistinguishability hardcore lemma, we prove that for a sequence of independent distributions $X_1, \ldots, X_\ell$, each having metric-entropy k with parameters (s, ϵ) for some *large* ϵ and against *deterministic* circuits of size s, the concatenated string $X = X_1, X_2, \ldots, X_\ell$ has HILL entropy roughly $(1 - \epsilon)\ell k$ with parameters $(s', \delta') = (\delta, s\delta^2 \ell^{-2}/n)$. In other words, for a metric pseudoentropy source of quality (s, ϵ) we achieve, sampling many times, the entropy extraction rate $\alpha = 1 - \epsilon^3$ with good security. Comparing to the state of art we save a quite large factor δ^2 in security[4].

1.3   Outline of the Paper

Section 2 provides necessary definitions for hardness of unpredictability, computational indistinguishabilty and computational entropy. In Section 3 we present a generalization of the unpredictability hardcore lemma and a slightly simplified proof of the indistinguishability hardcore lemma. A hardcore lemma dedicated for pseudoentropy is given in Section 4. An application to the problem of extracting from a pseudoentropy source of very bad quality is discussed in Section 5.

2   Preliminaries

COMPUTATIONAL AND STATISTICAL INDISTINGUISHABILITY. Let X and Y be two random variables taking values in the same space. The advantage of D in distinguishing between X and Y is defined to be $\Delta^{\mathrm{D}}(X;Y) = \mathbf{E}\,\mathrm{D}(X) - \mathbf{E}\,\mathrm{D}(Y)$. The statistical distance between two random variables X and Y, is defined as $\Delta(X;Y) = \frac{1}{2}\sum_x |\Pr[X = x] - \Pr[Y = x]|$ and is equal to the maximum of $\Delta^{\mathrm{D}}(X;Y)$ over all $[0,1]$-valued functions D. The computational distance between X and Y is defined as $\max_{\mathrm{D} \in \mathcal{D}} |\Delta^{\mathrm{D}}(X;Y)|$ where $\mathcal{D}$ is a fixed class of boolean functions. We say that X and Y are (s,ϵ)-close or (s,ϵ)-indistinguishable if $\Delta^{\mathrm{D}}(X;Y) \leqslant \epsilon$ for all D of size at most s.

HARDNESS OF UNPREDICTABILITY. A boolean funciton $f : \{0,1\}^n \to \{0,1\}$ is said to be (s,δ)-unpredictable if $\Pr_{x \leftarrow \{0,1\}^n}[\mathrm{D}(x) = f(x)] \leqslant 1 - \delta/2$ for all D of size at most s. We also say that f is δ-hard against circuits of size s. We say that that f is (s,δ)-unpredictable under the distribution V if $\Pr_{x \leftarrow V}[\mathrm{D}(x) = f(x)] \leqslant 1 - \delta/2$ for all D of size at most s.

MEASURES AND DENSE DISTRIBUTIONS. X is δ-dense in Y if $\Pr[X = x] \leqslant \Pr[Y = x]/\delta$ for all x.

CIRCUITS. By $\mathcal{D}^{\{0,1\},s}$ and $\mathcal{D}^{[0,1],s}$ we denote the set of boolean and, respectively, real-valued circuits of size at most s.

COMPUTATIONAL ENTROPY. There are many ways to define computational analogues of entropy. We follow the most popular approach, which is based on the concept of computational indistinguishability.

Definition 1 (HILL Pseudoentropy [HILL99]). *Let X be a distribution with the following property: there exists Y of min-entropy at least k such that for all circuits D of size at most s we have $|\Delta^{\mathrm{D}}(X;Y)| \leqslant \epsilon$. Then we say that X has k bits of HILL entropy of quality (s,ϵ) and denote by $\mathbf{H}^{\mathrm{HILL}}_{s,\epsilon}(X) \geqslant k$.*

---

[3] Understood as the ratio of the number of extracted bit to the length of the input.

[4] We note that the following issues makes this problem challenging: (a) since ϵ is large, no hybrid technique can be applied and (b) pseudoentropy is *only* against deterministic adversaries so no extractor can be directly applied.

It is known that for HILL Entropy all kind of circuits: deterministic boolean, deterministic real valued and randomized boolean, are equivalent (with the same size s). The following definition differs in the order of quantifiers

Definition 2 (Metric Pseudoentropy [BSW03]). *Let X be a distribution with the following property: for every deterministic boolean (respectively: deterministic real valued or boolean randomized) circuit D of size at most s there exists Y of min-entropy at least k such that $|\Delta^D(X;Y)| \leqslant \epsilon$. Then we say that X has k bits of deterministic (respectively: deterministic real valued or boolean randomized) metric entropy of quality (s, ϵ) and denote by $\mathbf{H}_{s,\epsilon}^{\mathrm{Metric,det}\{0,1\}}(X) \geqslant k$ (respectively: $\mathbf{H}_{s,\epsilon}^{\mathrm{Metric,det}[0,1]}(X)$ and $\mathbf{H}_{s,\epsilon}^{\mathrm{Metric,rand}}(X)$).*

APPROXIMATING CONVEX HULLS. The following facts are useful when we want to approximate possibly long convex combinations of functions by a combination of few functions; in particular, when we use the min-max theorem and need to approximate any mixed strategy by an efficient strategy.

Lemma 1 ([BSW03]). *Let $\mathcal{X}$ be a finite domain, ν be a distribution on $\mathcal{X}$ and let $\mathcal{G}$ be any set of functions $g : \mathcal{X} \to [-1,1]$ and let $\bar{g}$ be a convex combinations of functions from $\mathcal{G}$. Then for any $\epsilon \in (0,1)$ and for some $k \leqslant \frac{\log|\mathcal{X}|}{2\epsilon^2}$, there exist functions $g_1, \ldots, g_k$ such that*

$$\max_{x \in \mathcal{X}} \left| \bar{g}(x) - \left(\frac{1}{k} \sum_{i=1}^{k} g_i(x) \right) \right| \leqslant \epsilon$$

Lemma 2 (Convex approximation in L^p spaces [DDGS97]). *Let $\mathcal{X}$ be a finite domain, ν be a distribution on $\mathcal{X}$. Fix a number $1 \leqslant p < +\infty$ and for any function f on $\mathcal{X}$ define $\|f\|_p = (\mathbf{E}_{x \leftarrow \nu} |f(x)|^p)^{\frac{1}{p}}$. Let $\mathcal{G}$ be any set of real functions on $\mathcal{X}$, let $\bar{g}$ be a convex combinations of functions from $\mathcal{G}$ and $K > 0$ be such that for all $g \in \mathcal{G}$ we have $\|\bar{g} - g\|_p \leqslant K$. Then for any $\ell > 0$ there exists a convex combination $g' = \sum_{i=1}^{\ell} \alpha_i g_i$ of functions $g_1, \ldots, g_k \in \mathcal{G}$ such that*

$$\|\bar{g} - g'\|_p \leqslant \frac{K C_p}{\ell^{1 - \frac{1}{t}}}$$

where $t = \min(2, p)$ and $C_p = 1$ if $1 \leqslant p \leqslant 2$, $C_p = \sqrt{2}[\Gamma((p+1)/2)/\sqrt{\pi}]^{1/p}$ for $2 < p < +\infty$.

3 Hardcore Lemmas

3.1 Hardcore Lemma for Unpredictability

Below we prove a general hardcore lemma for unpredictability.

Theorem 3 (Unpredictability Hardcore Lemma for arbitrary distributions). *Let V be an arbitrary distribution on $\{0,1\}^n$ and suppose that an n-bit boolean function f is (s, ϵ)-unpredictable under V. Then for any δ there exists an event A of probability at least 2ϵ such that f is $(s', 1 - \delta)$-unpredictable under $V|A$, where $s' = O\left(s\delta^2 \cdot \max\left(1/n, 1/\log(1/\epsilon)\right)\right)$.*

Note that f is essentially *almost* unbiased under $V|A$: by applying trivial distinguishers $D \equiv 1$ and $D \equiv 0$ we get $\frac{1}{2} - \delta \leqslant \Pr[f(V|A) = 1] \leqslant \frac{1}{2} + \delta$. For some technical reasons we need the following observation, which states that the hardcore event "preserves" unbiased predicates.

Corollary 1 (Unpredictability Hardcore Lemma for Unbiased Predicates). *Suppose that Theorem 3 holds for f and V such that $\mathbf{P}\left(f(V) = -1\right) = \frac{1}{2} = \mathbf{P}\left(f(V) = 1\right)$. Then the hardcore event A can be chosen in such a way that $\mathbf{P}\left(f(V|A) = -1\right) = \mathbf{P}\left(f(V|A) = 1\right) = \frac{1}{2}$, with the additional loss of a factor $O(1)$ in circuit size.*

The proof of Corollary 1 appears in Appendix A. It is relatively simple and uses the idea of "mass-shifting". The proof of Theorem 3 appears in Appendix B.

3.2 Hardcore Lemma for Indistinguishability - Reduction to Unpredictability Case

The following lemma shows that indistinguishability of two distributions is equivalent to the hardness of predicting some boolean function, which explicitly depends on these distributions. This function is quite natural: it equals the sign of the difference between the probability mass functions.

Lemma 3. *Let $\mathcal{D}$ be a class of boolean functions, $X, Y \in \{0,1\}^n$ be random variables, and let $\Delta = \Delta(X,Y)$ be different than 0. Then the following are equivalent:*

(a) X and Y are $(\mathcal{D}, \epsilon)$-indistinguishable
(b) $f(x)$ is $(\mathcal{D}, 1 - \epsilon/\Delta)$-unpredictable under V, where $f(x)$ is the indicator of the set $\{x : \mathbf{P}_X(x) > \mathbf{P}_Y(x)\}$ and the distribution of V is given by $\mathbf{P}_V(x) = |\mathbf{P}_X(x) - \mathbf{P}_Y(x)|/2\Delta$.

Proof. For any boolean D we obtain

$$\mathbf{E}\,D(X) - \mathbf{E}\,D(Y) = \sum_x (\mathbf{P}_X(x) - \mathbf{P}_Y(x))D(x)$$

$$= 2\Delta\left(\Pr[f(V) = 1]\,\mathbf{E}[D(V)|f(V) = 1] - \Pr[f(V) = 0]\,\mathbf{E}[D(V)|f(V) = 0]\right)$$

Observe that $\Pr[f(V) = 1] = \Pr[f(V) = 0] = \frac{1}{2}$. Therefore

$$\mathbf{E}\,D(X) - \mathbf{E}\,D(Y) = 2\Delta\left(-\frac{1}{2} + \frac{1}{2}\mathbf{E}[D(V)|f(V){=}1] + \frac{1}{2}\mathbf{E}[(1{-}D(V))|f(V){=}0]\right).$$

Since D is boolean, the last equation is equivalent to

$$\mathbf{E}\,D(X) - \mathbf{E}\,D(Y) = 2\Delta\left(\Pr[D(V) = f(V)] - \frac{1}{2}\right),$$

which finishes the proof. □

Based on Lemma 3 we prove the following result

Theorem 4 (Indistinguishability Hardcore Lemma). *Suppose that X and Y are distributions (s, ϵ)-indistinguishable by boolean circuits Then for any $\delta > 0$ there exist events $A(X), A(Y)$, both of equal probability at least $1 - \epsilon$, such that $X|A(X)$ and $Y|A(Y)$ are $(O\left(s \cdot \delta^2 / \log(\Delta(X;Y)/\epsilon)\right), \Delta(X;Y) \cdot \delta)$ indistinguishable.*

Proof. From the construction of V, we obtain that f is $(s, 1 - \epsilon/\Delta(X,Y))$-unpredictable under V. From Theorem 3 we obtain that there exists a hardcore A with probability at least $1 - \epsilon/\Delta(X,Y)$ such that f is *extremely* unpredictable under $V|A$. This hardcore event can be described as follows: there exists a measure $M = M_A$ that satisfies $M(x) \leqslant \mathbf{P}_V(x)$ and $\mathbf{P}(A) = \mu(M) \geqslant 1 - \epsilon/\Delta(X,Y)$ and such that $f(x)$ is unpredictable for sampling according to M, i.e. $\mathbf{P}_{x \leftarrow M}\left(D(x) = f(x)\right) < 1/2 + \delta$. The distribution $V|A$ is then defined by $\mathbf{P}_{V|A} = \mathbf{P}_M$. Consider the events $S^- = \{x : f(x) = 0\}$ and $S^+ = \{x : f(x) = 1\}$. From the definition of V and f it follows that $\mathbf{P}_V(S^-) = \mathbf{P}_V(S^+) = \frac{1}{2}$. As shown in Corollary 1, the sets S^+, S^- can be assumed to be *perfectly unbiased* also under $V|A$. Define now two measures $M_0 = M_X$ and $M_1 = M_Y$ as follows:

$$M_0(x) = \begin{cases} \mathbf{P}_X(x) - 2\Delta(X,Y)\left(\mathbf{P}_V(x) - M'(x)\right) & \text{if } \mathbf{P}_X(x) > \mathbf{P}_Y(x) \\ \mathbf{P}_X(x) & \text{otherwise} \end{cases} \tag{1}$$

and similarly,

$$M_1(x) = \begin{cases} \mathbf{P}_Y(x) - 2\Delta(X,Y)\left(\mathbf{P}_V(x) - M'(x)\right) & \text{if } \mathbf{P}_X(x) < \mathbf{P}_Y(x) \\ \mathbf{P}_Y(x) & \text{otherwise} \end{cases} \tag{2}$$

Note that both measures are well defined since $\mathbf{P}_V(x) = |\mathbf{P}_X(x) - \mathbf{P}_Y(x)| / 2\Delta(X,Y)$ and $M'(x) \leqslant \mathbf{P}_V(x)$. Then from the definition of (V, A) and the definition of f it follows that

$$\mu(M_0) = 1 - 2\Delta(X,Y) \sum_{x: f(x)=1} \mathbf{P}_V(x) + 2\Delta(X,Y) \sum_{x: f(x)=1} M'(x)$$
$$= 1 - \Delta(X,Y) + 2\Delta(X,Y)\mathbf{P}(A) \cdot \mathbf{P}_{V|A}\left(S^+\right)$$
$$= 1 - \Delta(X,Y)\mathbf{P}(A^c)$$
$$\geqslant 1 - \epsilon \tag{3}$$

and similarly that the same estimate holds for $\mu(M_1)$. Observe also that since S^+ and S^- are perfectly unbiased with respect to M', and since the same holds for V, we have $\mu(M_0) = \mu(M_1)$. These measures give rise to the joint distributions $X, A(X)$ and $Y, A(Y)$ for some events $A(X), A(Y)$ with probabilities at least $\mu(M_0) = \mu(M_1)$. It remains to calculate the advantage in distinguishing. Let V' and f' be a distribution and a predicate corresponding to $X|A(X)$ and $Y|A(Y)$ according to the statement of Lemma 3. Observe that $M_0(x) > M_1(x)$ if and only if $f(x) = 1$, hence $f'(x) = f(x)$. Since $|M_0(x) - M_1(x)| = 2\Delta(X,Y)M'(x)$ for every x, we get $\mathbf{P}_V(x) = M'(x)/\mu(M') = \mathbf{P}_{V|A}(x)$ and $\Delta(X|A(X), Y|A(Y)) = \Delta(X, Y)$. Therefore

$$\Delta^D(X|A(X), Y|A(Y)) = \Delta(X, Y) \cdot (2\mathbf{P}_{x \leftarrow V'}(D(x) = f'(x)) - 1)$$
$$= \Delta(X, Y) \cdot (2\mathbf{P}_{x \leftarrow V|A'}(D(x) = f(x)) - 1)$$
$$< \Delta(X, Y) \cdot \delta, \tag{4}$$

and we have finished the proof.   □

Remark 4. We note that without Corollary 1 we would obtain a slightly weaker version of the indistinguishability hardcore lemma where the probability of the hardcore events is guaranteed to be at least $1 - \epsilon - \delta$, which is very close to the optimal $1 - \epsilon$ and equally good in applications.

4   Indistinguishability Hardcore Lemma for Pseudoentropy

In this section we prove the following theorem, which gives the existence of a "HILL-entropy-hardcore" for metric pseudoentropy.

Theorem 5 (Indistinguishability Hardcore Lemma for Pseudoentropy).
Suppose that $\mathbf{H}_{s,\epsilon}^{\mathrm{Metric,det}\{0,1\}}(X) \geqslant k$. *Then for any* δ *and* $s' = O(s \cdot \delta^2/n)$ *there exists an event* A *of probability* $1 - \epsilon$ *such that* $\mathbf{H}_{s',\delta}^{\mathrm{HILL}}(X|A) \geqslant k - \log(1/(1 - \epsilon))$.

This theorem shows that metric entropy not only can be converted to HILL entropy with the loss of factor δ in advantage and δ^2 in circuit size; It has a hardcore of HILL entropy with the same quality parameters. Before we give the proof, let us observe that this result implies the transformation between metric and HILL entropy (up to the lose of at most one bit)

Corollary 2 (Metric Entropy - HILL Entropy Transformation [BSW03]).
Suppose that $\mathbf{H}_{s,\epsilon}^{\mathrm{Metric,det}\{0,1\}}(X) \geqslant k$. *Then* $\mathbf{H}_{s',\epsilon'}^{\mathrm{HILL}}(X) \geqslant k$ *where* $s' = O(s \cdot \delta^2/n)$ *and* $\epsilon' = \epsilon + \delta$.

Proof (Proof of Corollary 2). We apply Theorem 5 obtaining a distribution $Y|A$ which is (s', δ)-indistinguishable from $X|A$, and then we define $\Pr[Y' = x] = \Pr[A] \cdot \Pr[Y = x|A] + 2^{-n} \Pr[A^c]$. Note that $\mathbf{H}_\infty(Y') \geqslant k - 1$ and Y' is $(s', \epsilon + \delta)$-indistinguishable from X. We remark that one can actually show without the loss of 1 bit, because Theorem 5 actually is slightly stronger that stated, namely $\mathbf{H}_{s',\delta}^{\mathrm{HILL}}(X|A) \geqslant k - \log(1/(1 - \epsilon))$ can be replaced by the following: $X|A$ is (s', δ)-indistinguishable from $Y|A$ where Y has k bits of min-entropy.   □

The proof strategy for Theorem 5 is exactly the same as in the case of Theorem 3. The full proof is given in Appendix C. Note that the result in Theorem 5 with much worse parameters follows by converting metric-entropy into HILL entropy using Corollary 2 and then applying Theorem 2. This way we lose δ^4 in circuit size.

Corollary 3 (Direct Proof of the Indistinguishability Hardcore Lemma).
The proof of Theorem 5 can be easily adapted to give a direct proof of Theorem 4 without reducing it to Theorem 3. Namely, in the proof we replace the condition $M_2 \leqslant 2^{-k}$ by $M_2 \leqslant \mathbf{P}_Y$.

5 Applications: Extracting from Metric Pseudoentropy of Poor Quality

Suppose that we have a source of metric pseudoentropy that produces samples secure against deterministic adversaries of high complexity but only with a very big advantage ϵ (for instance, $\epsilon = 0.25$). Since the metric entropy is only against deterministic adversaries, for which it is not known [FOR12] if we can extract pseudorandomness directly[5], one needs to convert in into the HILL entropy. However, it still does not solve the problem of large ϵ. In the next step one can use Theorem 2 to prove that a concatenated sequence of many samples has large HILL entropy[6]., with the rate of roughly $1 - \epsilon$. This approach loses $O\left(\delta^4\right)$ in security. Below we show that these two steps can be done *at the same time* which allows us to save a factor of $O\left(\delta^2\right)$ in security.

Theorem 6. *Suppose that X_i, for $i = 1, \dots, \ell$, are independent n-bit random variables such that $\mathbf{H}_{s,\epsilon}^{\text{Metric,det}\{0,1\}}(X) \geqslant k$. Then for any $\gamma > 0$ we have*

$$\mathbf{H}_{s',\delta'}^{\text{HILL}}(X) \geqslant (1 - \epsilon - \gamma)\ell\left(k - \log(1/(1 - \epsilon))\right),$$

where $s' = O\left(s \cdot \delta^2/n\ell^2\right)$ and $\delta' = \delta + 2\exp(-2\ell\gamma^2)$

Proof. Fix δ and let $s' = O\left(s \cdot \delta^2/n\right)$. We apply Theorem 5 to X_i, for $i = 1,, \dots, \ell$, obtaining hardcore events A_i of probability at least $1 - \epsilon$ such that $\mathbf{H}_{s',\delta}^{\text{HILL}}(X_i|A_i) \geqslant k - \log(1/(1 - \epsilon))$. By the Chernoff Bound we know that the probability that $m = \ell(1 - \epsilon - \gamma)$ of them happen simultaneously, is at least $1 - 2\exp(-2\ell\gamma^2)$. The result follows now by the observation that concatenating ℓ random variables $Y_1, \dots, Y_\ell$ of HILL entropy $k_1, \dots, k_\ell$ with parameters (s', δ) yields a distribution of HILL entropy $k_1 + k_2 + \dots + k_\ell$ with parameters $(s', \ell\delta)$ (the proof follows by a standard hybrid argument). $\qquad\square$

6 Conclusion

An interesting open problem is to check if the indistinguishability hardcore lemma can be derived from the unpredictability hardcore lemma, that is show the reduction in other direction than in [MT10] and this paper. Another problem worth of mentioning is the question about lower bounds on the necessary loss in security for indistinguishability hardcore lemma.

---

[5] The problem of randomized vs deterministic adversaries is the matter of metric entropy only; for the HILL entropy all kind of circuits are equivalent.

[6] Maurer and Tessaro construct in the same way a PRG from a weak PRG.

Acknowledgments. The author would like to thank Krzysztof Pietrzak for helpful discussions, and the anonymous referee for valuable criticism.

References

BHK09. Barak, B., Hardt, M., Kale, S.: The uniform hardcore lemma via approximate bregman projections. In: SODA 2009. Society for Industrial and Applied Mathematics, pp. 1193–1200 (2009)

BSW03. Barak, B., Shaltiel, R., Wigderson, A.: Computational analogues of entropy. In: Arora, S., Jansen, K., Rolim, J.D.P., Sahai, A. (eds.) RANDOM 2003 and APPROX 2003. LNCS, vol. 2764, pp. 200–215. Springer, Heidelberg (2003)

DDGS97. Donahue, M.J., Darken, C., Gurvits, L., Sontag, E.: Rates of convex approximation in non-hilbert spaces. Constructive Approximation 13(2), 187–220 (1997)

DP08. Dziembowski, S., Pietrzak, K.: Leakage-resilient cryptography. In: FOCS 2008, pp. 293–302. IEEE Computer Society (2008)

FOR12. Fuller, B., O'Neill, A., Reyzin, L.: A unified approach to deterministic encryption: New constructions and a connection to computational entropy. In: Cramer, R. (ed.) TCC 2012. LNCS, vol. 7194, pp. 582–599. Springer, Heidelberg (2012)

GNW11. Goldreich, O., Nisan, N., Wigderson, A.: On Yao's XOR-lemma. In: Goldreich, O. (ed.) Studies in Complexity and Cryptography. LNCS, vol. 6650, pp. 273–301. Springer, Heidelberg (2011)

HILL99. Hastad, J., Impagliazzo, R., Levin, L.A., Luby, M.: A pseudorandom generator from any one-way function. SIAM J. Comput. 28(4), 1364–1396 (1999)

Hol05. Holenstein, T.: Key agreement from weak bit agreement. In: STOC 2005, pp. 664–673. ACM (2005)

Imp95. Impagliazzo, R.: Hard-core distributions for somewhat hard problems. In: FOCS 1995, pp. 538–545. IEEE Computer Society (1995)

KS99. Klivans, A.R., Servedio, R.A.: Boosting and hard-core sets. In: FOCS 1999, pp. 624–633. IEEE Computer Society (1999)

KS03. Klivans, A.R., Servedio, R.A.: Boosting and hard-core set construction. Mach. Learn. 51(3), 217–238 (2003)

LT13. Lin, H., Tessaro, S.: Amplification of chosen-ciphertext security. In: Johansson, T., Nguyen, P.Q. (eds.) EUROCRYPT 2013. LNCS, vol. 7881, pp. 503–519. Springer, Heidelberg (2013)

LTW07. Lu, C.-J., Tsai, S.-C., Wu, H.-L.: On the complexity of hard-core set constructions. In: Arge, L., Cachin, C., Jurdziński, T., Tarlecki, A. (eds.) ICALP 2007. LNCS, vol. 4596, pp. 183–194. Springer, Heidelberg (2007)

MT10. Maurer, U., Tessaro, S.: A hardcore lemma for computational indistinguishability. In: Micciancio, D. (ed.) TCC 2010. LNCS, vol. 5978, pp. 237–254. Springer, Heidelberg (2010)

VZ12. Vadhan, S., Zheng, C.J.: Characterizing pseudoentropy and simplifying pseudorandom generator constructions. In: STOC 2012, pp. 817–836. ACM (2012)

A   Proof of Corollary 1

Proof (Proof of Corollary 1). Let $M(x) = \Pr[V = x, A]$. Since $M(x) \leqslant \mathbf{P}_V(x)$ and we have $M(S^-), M(S^+) \leqslant \frac{1}{2}$. Suppose that $M(S^+) - M(S^-) = 2\delta_0$. Then $M(S^-) = \frac{\mu(M)}{2} - \delta_0$ and $M(S^+) = \frac{\mu(M)}{2} + \delta_0$. Suppose $\delta_0 > 0$. Since $M(S^-) \leqslant \mathbf{P}(S^-) - \delta_0$ and $M(S^+) \geqslant \delta_0$, we can define the measure M' by decreasing the mass of S^+ by δ_0 and moving it to S^- in such a way that $M'(x) \leqslant \mathbf{P}_V(x)$ still holds on S^-. For the case $\delta_0 < 0$ observe that $M(S^+) \leqslant \mathbf{P}(S^+) - (-\delta_0)$ and $M(S^-) \geqslant -\delta_0$ thus we proceed similarly by decreasing the mass of S^- by $(-\delta_0)$ and moving it to S^+ in such a way that $M'(x) \leqslant \mathbf{P}_V(x)$ holds on S^+. Therefore, in both cases we have $M'(x) \leqslant \mathbf{P}_V(x)$. Clearly $M'(S^+) = M'(S^-)$. Thus the measure M' gives rise to a distribution V, A'. While constructing M' from M we only shift a mass between disjoint sets, hence $\mu(M) = \mu(M')$ and $\mathbf{P}(A) = \mathbf{P}(A')$. It remains to show, that under distribution $V|A'$ the function f is still unpredictable. Applying trivial distinguishers $D = 1$ and $D = -1$ to unpredictability under $V|A$, we get $M(S^+), M(S^-) \leqslant (1/2 + \delta)\mathbf{P}(A)$. Since $M(S^+) + M(S^-) = \mathbf{P}(A)$ it follows then that $2|\delta_0| = |M(S^+) - M(S^-)| \leqslant 2\delta\mathbf{P}(A)$. Since the total mass that of M that is shifted to M' is equal to δ_0, we have $\|M' - M\|_1 = \sum_x |M'(x) - M(x)| \leqslant 2|\delta_0| \leqslant 2\delta\mathbf{P}(A)$. Since $\mathbf{P}(A') = \mathbf{P}(A)$, this implies $\Delta(V|A, V|A') \leqslant 2\delta$. Therefore, for every D of size s' we obtain $\mathbf{P}_{x \leftarrow V|A'}(D(x) = f(x)) < \frac{1}{2} + \delta + 2\delta$. Replacing δ with $\delta/3$ changes the circuit size only by a (small) constant factor.   □

B   Proof of Theorem 3

Proof. In this proof, for convenience, we assume that boolean functions take values in $\{-1, 1\}$.

Step 1. We extended the concept of unpredictability to all real-valued functions. The following straightforward but very useful property is easy to check:

Lemma 4. *Let f and D be boolean. Then f is ϵ-unpredictable by D under V if and only if $\mathbf{E}_{x \leftarrow V} D(x)f(x) \leqslant 1 - \epsilon$.*

Step 2. We show how to construct a hardcore for a *single boolean* attacker D. For some technical reasons, we need actually a slightly stronger statement, namely a construction for a function D which takes values $-1, 0, 1$.

Lemma 5. *Suppose that for a distribution V, a function D with values in $\{-1, 0, 1\}$ and a boolean function f we have $\mathbf{E}_{x \leftarrow V} D(x)f(x) = \pm\delta$. Then there is a measure M such that $M(x) \leqslant \mathbf{P}_V(x)$, $\mu(M) \geqslant 1 - \delta$ and $\mathbf{E}_{x \leftarrow M} D(x)f(x) = 0$.*

Proof. By replacing D by $-D$ we can assume that $\mathbf{E}_{x \leftarrow V} D(x)f(x) = \delta > 0$. Let $S_1 = \{x : D(x)f(x) > 0\}$. If follows that $\Pr[V \in S_1] = \sum_{x \in S_1} \mathbf{P}_V(x)D(x) \geqslant \delta$. Now we define $M(x) = \mathbf{P}_V(x) \cdot (\Pr[V \in S^1] - \delta)/\Pr[V \in S_1]$ for $x \in S_1$ and $M(x) = \mathbf{P}_V(x)$ otherwise. M satisfies the required properties.   □

Step 3. We argue that the same is true for *real-valued* functions D.

Lemma 6. *Suppose that f is ϵ-unpredictable by boolean circuits of size s under a distribution V. Then for every real-valued D of size $s' \approx s$ there exists a measure M such that $M(x) \leqslant \mathbf{P}_V(x)$ for every x, $\mu(M) \geqslant \epsilon$ and $\mathbf{E}_{x \leftarrow M} D(x) f(x) = 0$.*

Proof. Suppose not. Since the set of feasible measures M is convex, this is we must have either $\mathbf{E}_{x \leftarrow M} D(x) f(x) > 0$ for all M or $\mathbf{E}_{x \leftarrow M} D(x) f(x) < 0$ for all M. By eventually replacing D with $-D$ we obtain that there exists a real-valued circuit D of size s such that for all measures M satisfying the constraints

$$\sum_x D(x) f(x) M(x) > 0.$$

Now we give a characterization of the measure that minimizes the left-hand side in the inequality above.

Claim 1. Let M_0 be an optimal solution of the following problem

$$\underset{M}{\text{minimize}} \quad \sum_x D(x) f(x) M(x)$$

$$\text{s.t.} \quad \begin{cases} M(x) \leqslant \mathbf{P}_V(x) \\ \mu(M) \geqslant \epsilon \end{cases}$$

Define $S = \{x : \operatorname{sgn} D(x) = f(x)\}$ and let $p = \mathbf{P}(V \in S)$. Let x_i for $i = 1, \ldots, M$ be the elements of S, enumerated in such a way that $|D(x_i)| \geqslant |D(x_{i+1})|$. Let N be the maximal number such that $N \leqslant M$ and $\sum_{i=1}^{N} \mathbf{P}_V(x_i) \leqslant \min(1 - \epsilon, p)$. Then the measure M_0 defined by $M_0(x) = 0$ if $x = x_i$ for some $i \in [1, N]$ and $M_0(x) = \mathbf{P}_V(x)$ otherwise, is the minimizer.

Proof. It is clear that for the optimal measure M_0, the mass of $\mathbf{P}_V(x)$ is decreased only if $f(x) D(x) > 0$ and keeps unchanged if $f(x) D(x) < 0$. Thus, the total mass we cut is equal to at most

$$\sum_{x:\, D(x) f(x) > 0} \mathbf{P}_V(x) = p$$

In the other hand, it is bounded from above by $1 - \epsilon$ due to the constraint $\mu(M) \geqslant \epsilon$. The last observation is that if $D(x) f(x) > 0$, the greater the absolute value of $D(x)$ is, the more mass we cut. $\square$

As a conclusion from Claim 1 we get that $\mu(M_0) = \max(\epsilon, 1 - p)$. From the definition of M_0 we have that

$$\min_{\substack{M:\, M \leqslant \mathbf{P}_V \\ \mu(M) \geqslant \epsilon}} \sum_x D(x) f(x) M(x) = \sum_x D(x) f(x) M_0(x)$$

Let $D_1(x) := D(x) \cdot \mathbf{1}_{\{f > 0\}}$ and $D_2(x) := D(x) \cdot \mathbf{1}_{\{f < 0\}}$. Then we have

$$\mathbf{E}_{x \leftarrow M_0} D(x) f(x) = \mathbf{E}_{x \leftarrow M_0} D_1^+(x) - \mathbf{E}_{x \leftarrow M_0} D_1^-(x) - \mathbf{E}_{x \leftarrow M_0} D_2^+(x)$$
$$+ \mathbf{E}_{x \leftarrow M_0} D_2^-(x)$$

By applying the formula $\mathbf{E}Y = \int_{t \in [0,1]} \mathbf{P}(Y > t)\, dt$ (valid for any random variable $Y \in [0, 1]$) to $Y = \mathbf{P}_{M_0}$ we obtain that for some $t = t_0 \in (0, 1)$ and D' defined by $D'(x) = \mathrm{sgn}D(x) \cdot \mathbf{1}_{|D(x)| > t_0}$ we get

$$\Pr[D_1^+(Y) > t_0] - \Pr[D_1^-(Y) > t_0] - \Pr[D_2^+(Y) > t_0] + \Pr[D_2^-(Y) > t_0] > 0,$$

which is equivalent to

$$\mathbf{E}_{x \leftarrow M_0} D'(x) f(x) > 0.$$

Observe that, by the construction, $\mathrm{sgn}D' = \mathrm{sgn}D$ and $|D(x_1)| \geqslant |D(x_2)|$ is equivalent to $|D'(x_1)| \geqslant |D'(x_2)|$. Therefore, applying the characterization given by Claim 1 to the two cases: D, M_0 and D', M_0, we obtain that M_0 is a minimizer for both circuits. Therefore

$$\min_{\substack{M : \substack{M \leqslant \mathbf{P}_V \\ \mu(M) \geqslant \epsilon}}} \sum_x D'(x) f(x) M(x) = \sum_x D'(x) f(x) M_0(x) > 0$$

which gives us a contraddiction to Lemma 5. $\square$

Step 4. We argue that Lemma 6 holds *approximately* for *all convex combinations* of circuits of size comparable to s. Let D'' be a convex combination of real-valued circuits of size $s'' = O\left(s\delta^2 / \log(1/\epsilon)\right)$. From Lemma 2 applied to D'', we obtain that for some real-valued circuit D' of size $s' \approx s$ we have

$$\left(\mathbf{E}_{x \leftarrow V} |D''(x) - D'(x)|^p\right)^{\frac{1}{p}} = O\left(\delta \cdot \sqrt{p / \log(1/\epsilon)}\right) \tag{5}$$

Let M be the "hardcore" measure corresponding to D' according to Lemma 6. Since $|f| = 1$ and $\mathbf{E}_{x \leftarrow M} D'(x) f(x) = 0$, we obtain

$$\mathbf{E}_{x \leftarrow M} D''(x) f(x) \leqslant \mathbf{E}_{x \leftarrow M} |D''(x) - D'(x)| \tag{6}$$

By the Hölder Inequality we obtain

$$\mathbf{E}_{x \leftarrow M} |D''(x) - D'(x)| \leqslant \left(\mathbf{E}_{x \leftarrow V} \left(\frac{\mathbf{P}_M(x)}{\mathbf{P}_V(x)}\right)^q\right)^{\frac{1}{q}} \cdot \left(\mathbf{E}_{x \leftarrow V} |D''(x) - D'(x)|^p\right)^{\frac{1}{p}} \tag{7}$$

We will show that

$$\left(\mathbf{E}_{x \leftarrow V} (\mathbf{P}_M(x)/\mathbf{P}_V(x))^q\right)^{\frac{1}{q}} \leqslant (1/\epsilon)^{\frac{1}{p}} \tag{8}$$

Indeed, consider the set $\mathcal{M}$ of all distributions ϵ-dense in V. By definition, we have $\mathbf{P}_M \in \mathcal{M}$. Since the expression on the left-hand side of Equation (8) is convex with respect to $\mathbf{P}_M$, its maximum over $\mathcal{M}$ is achieved on one of *extreme points* of the set $\mathcal{M}$. It is easy to check that the extreme points $\mathbf{P}$ of $\mathcal{M}$ satisfy $\mathbf{P}(x) = \mathbf{P}_V(x)/\epsilon$ for all but at most one $x \in \text{supp}(\mathbf{P})$.[7] For any such $\mathbf{P}$ we have

$$\mathop{\mathbf{E}}_{x \leftarrow V} \left(\frac{\mathbf{P}(x)}{\mathbf{P}_V(x)} \right)^q \leqslant \frac{1}{\epsilon^q} \cdot \epsilon \cdot (1 - \mathbf{P}(x')) + \left(\frac{\mathbf{P}(x')}{\mathbf{P}_V(x')} \right)^q \cdot \mathbf{P}_V(x')$$

where x' is the point such that $0 < \mathbf{P}(x') \leqslant \mathbf{P}_V(x)/\epsilon$. Since the right-hand is convex with respect to $\mathbf{P}(x')$, it is maximized either for $\mathbf{P}(x') = 0$ or $\mathbf{P}(x') = \mathbf{P}_V(x)/\epsilon$. In any case, it is at most ϵ^{1-q}. Let $p = 2\log(1/\epsilon)$. Combining Equation (6), Equation (7), Equation (8) and Equation (5) we get

$$\mathop{\mathbf{E}}_{x \leftarrow M} D''(x) f(x) \leqslant \delta. \tag{9}$$

Alternatively, we can use of Lemma 1, with $s'' = O\left(s\delta^2/n\right)$.

Step 5. By applying the min-max theorem we reverse the order of quantifiers: we obtain that there exists a measure M satisfying $\mu(M) \geqslant \epsilon$ and $M(x) \leqslant \mathbf{P}_V(x)$ such that Equation (9) hold for all circuits D'' of size s. By replacing D'' with $-D''$ we see that these inequalities hold in absolute values. It remains to observe that the measure M gives rise to a joint distribution (V, A) where $M(x) = \Pr[V = x, A = 1]$. In particular, $\Pr[A = 1] = \mu(M) \geqslant \epsilon$.   □

C   Proof of Theorem 5

Proof (Proof of Theorem 5). By considering the functions $\mathbf{P}(X = x, A_1)$ and $\mathbf{P}(Y = x, A_2)$ for some events A_1, A_2, it is easy to see that, equivalently, we need to find measures M_1, M_2 which satisfy the following conditions:

(a) $M_1 \leqslant \mathbf{P}_X(x)$ and $M_2 \leqslant 2^{-k}$
(b) $\mu(M_1) = \mu(M_2) \geqslant 1 - \epsilon$
(c) $\Delta^D\left(\mathbf{P}_{M_1}, \mathbf{P}_{M_2}\right) \leqslant \delta$ for every D of size s'.

First, we show how to construct measures satisfying these conditions only for one fixed boolean circuit D

Claim 2. Let $\mathcal{X}$ be a finite domain. Suppose that we are given a boolean function D and two probability distributions μ_1, μ_2 on $\mathcal{X}$, such that $\Delta^D(\mu_1, \mu_2) = \epsilon$. Then there exist measures M_1, M_2 such that:

(a) $M_i(x) \leqslant \mu_i(x)$ for every x and i,
(b) $\mu(M_1) = \mu(M_2) = 1 - \epsilon$,
(c) $\sum_x D(x) M_1(x) = \sum_x D(x) M_2(x)$.

Proof. Assume $\sum_x D(x)\mu_1(x) - \sum_x D(x)\mu_2(x) = \epsilon$ (the other case is symmetric). By decreasing the measure μ_1 on the set $\{x : D(x) = 1\}$ we define a measure M_1 such that $M_1(x) \leqslant \mu_1(x)$ and $\mu(M_1) = 1 - \epsilon$ and $\sum_x D(x) M_1(x) = \sum_x D(x)\mu_2(x)$. Now consider $\{x : D(x) = 0\}$ and proceed similarly to obtain M_2 from μ_2.   □

---

[7] This observation can be viewed as a generalization of the well-known fact that the extreme points for the set of all high min-entropy distributions are flat distributions.

Next we argue that the same is also possible for a real-valued circuit. This is the main technical difficulty in the proof.

Claim 3. Suppose that for any boolean D of size s there exist measures M_1, M_2 such that $M_1(x) \leqslant \mathbf{P}_X(x)$ and $M_2(x) \leqslant 2^{-k}$ for every x and $\mu(M_1) = \mu(M_2) \geqslant 1 - \epsilon$ and $\left| \sum_x D(x)M_1(x) - \sum_x D(x)M_2(x) \right| \leqslant \delta$. Then the same is true for *real-valued* circuits of size D.

Proof. Suppose not. Since feasible measure M_1, M_2 form convex sets, we have either $\sum_x D(x)M_1(x) - \sum_x D(x)M_2(x) < -\delta$ for all feasible M_1, M_2 or $\sum_x D(x) M_1(x) - \sum_x D(x)M_2(x) > \delta$ for all feasible M_1, M_2. Replacing D with D^c if necessary we can assume that for all measures M_1, M_2 satisfying the corresponding constraints, the following inequality holds

$$\sum_x D(x)M_1(x) - \sum_x D(x)M_2(x) > \delta. \qquad (10)$$

We will characterize the measures $M_1 = M_1^+, M_2 = M_2^+$ which maximize the left-hand side of Equation (10), similarly as in Claim 1 in the proof of Theorem 3.

Claim 4. Suppose that the measures $M_1 = M_1^+, M_2 = M_2^+$ minimize

$$\sum_x D(x)M_1(x) - \sum_x D(x)M_2(x) > \delta,$$

subject to constraints $M_1(x) \geqslant 0$ and $M_2(x) \geqslant 0$ for all x, $\sum_x M_1(x) = 1 - \epsilon = \sum_x M_2(x)$, $M_1(x) \leqslant \mathbf{P}_X(x)$ and $M_2(x) \leqslant a$ for all x. Let $x_1, \dots, x_N$, where $N = 2^n$, be all the elements of $\{0,1\}^n$ sorted such that $D(x_i) \geqslant D(x_{i+1})$ and let T be the maximal number such that $\sum_{i=1}^T \mathbf{P}_X(x) \leqslant \epsilon$. The optimal measures M_1^+, M_2^+ can be characterized as follows: $M_1^+(x_i) = 0$ for $i = 1, 2 \dots, T$, $M_1^+(x_{T+1}) = \epsilon - \sum_{i=1}^T \mathbf{P}_X(x)$, and $M_1^+(x_i) = \mathbf{P}_X(x_i)$ for $i > T + 1$; $M_2^+(x_i) = a$ for $i = 1, \dots, \lfloor (1-\epsilon)/a \rfloor$, $M_2^+(x_{2^k+1}) = (1 - \epsilon)/a - a\lfloor (1-\epsilon)/a \rfloor$.

Proof (Proof of Claim). The characterization of M_1^+ follows from the simple observation that if we have $D(x') \geqslant D(x)$, $0 < M(x')$ and $M(x) < \mathbf{P}_X(x)$, then we can decrease $M(x')$ by δ and increase $M(x)$ by $\delta = \min(M(x'), \mathbf{P}_X(x) - M(x))$ decreasing (or at least not increasing) the value of $\sum_x M(x)D(x)$. Consider now M_2^+. Suppose that $D(x') \geqslant D(x)$, $M(x') < a$ and $0 < M(x)$. Then we increase M on x' by δ and decrease M on x by δ, where $\delta = \min(a - M(x'), M(x))$, and increasing (or at least not decreasing) the value of $\sum_x D(x)M(x)$. □

Since for every x we have $D(x) = \int_0^1 [D(x) \geqslant t]dt$, for some positive number t_0 and $D'(x) = [D(x) > t_0]$ we obtain

$$\sum_x D'(x)M_1^+(x) - \sum_x D'(x)M_2^+(x) \geqslant \delta.$$

The circuit D' is comparable in size to D and is boolean. Observe now that M_1^+ and M_2^- are also minimizers for D'. This follows by Claim 4 since the extreme measures depends only on the *ordering* of the values $\{D(x)\}_x$ and D', as a threshold, is a monotone transform of D.   □

Finally, by an approximation argument, we show that suitable measures exist for every D being a convex combination of circuit of size s'.

Claim 5. For any $D \in \mathrm{conv}\left(\mathcal{D}^{\mathrm{det},\{0,1\},s'}\right)$ there exist measures M_1, M_2 such that $M_1(x) \leqslant \mathbf{P}_X(x)$ and $M_2(x) \leqslant 2^{-k}$ for every x and $\mu(M_1) = \mu(M_2) \geqslant 1 - \epsilon$ and $\left|\sum_x D(x)M_1(x) - \sum_x D(x)M_2(x)\right| \leqslant \delta$.

Proof (Proof of Claim). We know by Lemma 1 that any convex combination of circuits of size at most s' can be approximated up to the error δ by a convex combination of $\ell = O\left(n/\delta^2\right)$ of them. Let $D' = \sum_{i=1}^{m} a_i D_i$ be such a convex combination approximating D. Define M_1, M_2 as a measures corresponding to the real-valued circuit D'.   □

Claim 6. There exist measures M_1 and M_2 such that $M_1(x) \leqslant \mathbf{P}_X(x)$ and $M_2(x) \leqslant 2^{-k}$ for every x and $\mu(M_1) = \mu(M_2) \geqslant 1 - \epsilon$ and such that for every D of size at most s' we have $\left|\sum_x D(x)M_1(x) - \sum_x D(x)M_2(x)\right| \leqslant \delta$.

Proof. Consider a game where one player choses a cricuit D of size at most s' and the second choses a pair of measures (M_1, M_2) where M_1, M_2 satisfy $M_i(x) \leqslant \mathbf{P}_{X_i}(x)$ for every x and $\mu(M_1) = \mu(M_2) \geqslant 1 - \epsilon$. Let the payoff matrix be given by $\sum_x D(x)M_1(x) - \sum_x D(x)M_2(x)$. By combining the claim with the min-max theorem we get measures M_1, M_2 satisfying the same conditions and such that for every D of size at most s' we have

$$\sum_x D(x)M_1(x) - \sum_x D(x)M_2(x) \leqslant \delta. \qquad (11)$$

Applying this to D^c and using $\mu(M_1) = \mu(M_2)$ we get also

$$\sum_x D(x)M_1(x) - \sum_x D(x)M_2(x) \geqslant -\delta. \qquad (12)$$

for all circuits of size at most $s' - 1$. Thus the proof is finished.   □

Define $\mathbf{P}(X_i = x, A_i) = M_i(x)$. Since $M_i(x) \leqslant \mathbf{P}(X_i = x)$ the events A_i are well defined. We have $\mathbf{P}(A_i) = \mu(M_i) \geqslant 1 - \epsilon$. Finally note that since $\mu(M_1) = \mu(M_2)$ we have $\mathbf{E}D(X_1|A_1) - \mathbf{E}D(X_2|A_2) = \left(\sum_x D(x)M_1(x) - \sum_x D(x)M_2(x)\right)/\mu(M_1)$. Therefore, the result follows.   □

Gambling, Computational Information and Encryption Security

Mohammad Hajiabadi and Bruce M. Kapron

Department of Computer Science, University of Victoria,
Victoria, BC, CANADA V8W 3P6
{mhaji,bmkapron}@uvic.ca

Abstract. We revisit the question, originally posed by Yao (1982), of whether encryption security may be characterized using computational information. Yao provided an affirmative answer, using a compression-based notion of computational information to give a characterization equivalent to the standard computational notion of semantic security. We give two other equivalent characterizations. The first uses a computational formulation of Kelly's (1957) model for "gambling with inside information", leading to an encryption notion which is similar to Yao's but where encrypted data is used by an adversary to place bets maximizing the rate of growth of total wealth over a sequence of independent, identically distributed events. The difficulty of this gambling task is closely related to Vadhan and Zheng's (2011) notion of KL-hardness, which in certain cases is equivalent to a conditional form of the pseudoentropy introduced by Hastad et. al. (1999). Using techniques introduced to prove this equivalence, we are also able to give a characterization of encryption security in terms of conditional pseudoentropy. Finally, we will reconsider the gambling model with respect to "risk-neutral" adversaries in an attempt to understand whether assumptions about the rationality of adversaries may impact the level of security achieved by an encryption scheme.

Keywords: Kelly criterion, KL-hardness, computational entropy, semantic security, rational adversaries.

1 Introduction

The first rigorous characterization of encryption security was given by Shannon in [14], using a formulation based on probability and information theory. The space of plaintexts is equipped with a probability distribution, which along with a distribution on keys induces a distribution on ciphertexts. An encryption scheme is said to be secure if the mutual information between plaintexts and ciphertexts is zero, capturing the intuition that ciphertexts should not "leak information" about plaintexts. A drawback of Shannon's approach is that it does not account for the computational difficulty of extracting information, and so it sets a very high bar [4]. It took a quarter of a century before a definition of encryption security which accounts for computation was given by Goldwasser

© Springer International Publishing Switzerland 2015
A. Lehmann and S. Wolf (Eds.): ICITS 2015, LNCS 9063, pp. 141–158, 2015.
DOI: 10.1007/978-3-319-17470-9_9

and Micali [8], where a scheme is proposed which has that property that "whatever is efficiently computable about the cleartext given the ciphertext, is also efficiently computable without the ciphertext." This notion, dubbed *semantic security*, may be viewed as a computational version of Shannon's definition, at least in an intuitive sense where *computational information* is identified with "whatever is efficiently computable about the plaintext". Nevertheless, Shannon uses a specific entropy-based notion of *mutual information*, and it is natural to ask whether one could formulate a notion of encryption security by first formulating a computational version of mutual information. In fact, such a question was posed, and answered by Yao [16,17], who gave definitions of computational entropy and computational mutual information, based on the relationship between entropy and compressibility, and used this to characterize encryption security. In particular, an encryption scheme is secure if no efficient compression scheme in which the decoding function has access to an encryption of the corresponding message can achieve an expected length more than negligibly better than the optimal that can be achieved by any efficient scheme without such access. Yao [17] and Micali, Rackoff and Sloan [12] show that this notion is equivalent to semantic security.

This paper presents a new approach to characterizing encryption security via computational information. Rather than relying on the machinery of data compression, our approach uses a characterization of mutual information given by Kelly in [11], which considers the optimal rate of return for a gambler who has noisy inside information on the outcome of an event. When we take the very natural steps of replacing "noisy" with "encrypted" and considering a computationally bounded gambler, we are led immediately to a definition of encryption security which we dub *gambling security*. We then show (Theorem 1)

An encryption scheme is semantically secure iff it is gambling secure

While Yao's characterization of encryption security using computational information is not widely used, his introduction of a notion of computational entropy based on compression is one foundation of computational information theory. Another important contribution in this direction was made by Håstad et. al. in [9], which introduces the notion of *pseudoentropy*. Unfortunately, the relationship between various forms of computational entropy is not well understood. In some cases (e.g. with respect to conditional distributions), Yao's entropy and HILL entropy are not equivalent [10].[1] We may wonder what this means in the setting of encryption security. Do these different notions of computational information lead to different forms of encryption security? We show that this is not the case (Theorem 2)

An encryption scheme is semantically secure iff access to the ciphertext does not reduce the pseudoentropy of the plaintext.

The gambling framework allows us to consider gamblers with different utilities. We also consider security against gamblers who are trying to maximize

---

[1] The cited result considers versions based on min-entropy rather than Shannon entropy.

a one-shot payout. Perhaps not surprisingly, in this setting we obtain a much tighter equivalence with semantic security. But this does raise an interesting question. Namely, what can we say about the relationship between security and assumptions about an adversary's rationality?

2 Preliminaries

We assume standard facts and definitions about discrete probability spaces, but we will begin by clarifying our notational conventions and use of terminology. A *probability distribution on* a finite set $\mathcal{X}$ is specified by a *probability mass function* $X : \mathcal{X} \to [0,1]$ which satisfies $\sum_{x \in \mathcal{X}} X(x) = 1$. We will abuse terminology and use the term random variable as a synonym for distribution, so that for a distribution with mass function X we have $\Pr[X = x] = X(x)$. In general, we follow the convention of [7] regarding random variables, i.e., multiple occurrences of a variable in a probability expression denote multiple occurrences of a single sampled value. If X is distributed jointly with Y, we write $X|Y$ to denote the corresponding conditional distribution, and X, Y to denote the joint distribution. We write log and ln, respectively, for logarithm base 2 and base e.

Definition 1. *Suppose that X and Y are jointly distributed random variables on $\mathcal{X}$ and $\mathcal{Y}$, respectively. The* entropy $\mathrm{H}(X)$ *of X is defined by*

$$\mathrm{H}(X) = -\sum_x \Pr[X = x] \log \Pr[X = x].$$

The conditional entropy $\mathrm{H}(X|Y)$ *of X given Y is defined by*

$$\mathrm{H}(X|Y) = -\sum_{y,x} \Pr[Y = y \wedge X = x] \log \Pr[X = x|Y = y]$$

The mutual information $\mathrm{I}(X;Y)$ *between X and Y is defined by*

$$\mathrm{I}(X;Y) = \sum_{y,x} \Pr[Y = y \wedge X = x] \log \frac{\Pr[Y = y \wedge X = x]}{\Pr[Y = y] \Pr[X = x]}$$

Note that $\mathrm{I}(X;Y) = \mathrm{H}(X) - \mathrm{H}(X|Y)$. *For a random variable X', the* KL *divergence from X to X' is defined by*

$$\mathrm{KL}(X\|X') = \sum_m \Pr[X = x] \log \frac{\Pr[X = x]}{\Pr[X' = x]}$$

If X' jointly distributed with Y'. The conditional KL *divergence from $X|Y$ to $X'|Y'$ is defined by*

$$\mathrm{KL}(X|Y\|X'|Y') = \sum_{y,x} \Pr[Y = y \wedge X = x] \log \frac{\Pr[X = x|Y = y]}{\Pr[X' = x|Y' = y]}$$

We recall the following facts:

Proposition 1 (Chain Rule for KL-divergence)

$$KL(Y, X \| Y', X') = KL(Y \| Y') + KL(X | Y \| X' | Y').$$

In particular $KL(X | Y \| X' | Y) = KL(Y, X \| Y, X')$.

Proposition 2 (Gibb's Inequality). $KL(X \| X') \geq 0$, *with equality when* X' *is distributed identically to* X.

3   Proportional Betting with Noisy Inside Information

We begin by recalling the model of Kelly, proposed in his seminal paper [11]. Kelly considers the problem of maximizing the expected *rate* at which a gambler can accumulate wealth over repeated independent, identically-distributed plays of a game such as a coin flip, or horse race. In this scenario each play of the game results in an outcome from a fixed set of outcomes, according to an *a priori* fixed probability distribution known to the gambler. In particular, Kelly considers the advantage that an *eavesdropping gambler* who is given access to a channel providing a "noisy" version of the outcome of each event has over an *honest gambler*, who may only use *a priori* probabilities when placing bets. Kelly shows that the eavesdropping gambler's optimal strategy is proportional betting conditioned on the outcome observed on the noisy channel, and that the advantage of the best eavesdropping gambler over the best honest gambler is equal to the mutual information between the event and its noisy version.

Definition 2. *Let* X *be a distribution over a set* $\mathcal{X}$ *of* outcomes, *i.e., the outcome of each play of the game is independently determined according to* X. *An* honest gambler *is given by a* betting function $b : \mathcal{X} \to [0, 1]$ *which satisfies* $\sum_{x \in \mathcal{X}} b(x) = 1$.

The value $b(x)$ is the fraction of total wealth that the gambler bets on outcome x. Note that we are assuming that the gambler distributes all his wealth over the possible outcomes. The amount paid on a given outcome is determined by an odds function o. In particular, with an odds function o, and a betting function b, after outcome x the gambler's new wealth is $o(x)b(x)$ times his current wealth. In this paper, we will only consider odds functions which satisfy $\sum_{x \in \mathcal{X}} \frac{1}{o(x)} = 1$, in which case the assumption that the gambler bets all his wealth in each race is without loss of generality, because withholding can be simulated by spreading the witheld amount across outcomes in inverse proportion to o. While is it natural to consider more general odds functions, the analysis in this setting is much less tractable, and moreover it is not clear how to interpret such a setting from a security perspective.

Notation. A betting function $b : \mathcal{X} \to [0, 1]$ may be viewed as the mass function of a distribution on $\mathcal{X}$. We will abuse notation somewhat and write b to also denote the random variable corresponding to the distribution with this mass function and also writing $b(X)$ for the value of b on x chosen randomly according to X.

Kelly considers a gambler who is trying to maximize the expected rate at which his wealth grows over a sequence of identically distributed independent random events. Asymptotically, this is equivalent to maximizing $\mathrm{E}[\log o(X)b(X)]$ (see [3], Theorem 6.1.1.) In this setting, for an honest gambler we have:

Proposition 3. *The maximum over all betting functions b of $\mathrm{E}[\log o(X)b(X)]$ is $\mathrm{E}[\log o(X)] - \mathrm{H}(X)$, and is achieved by b^* where $b^*(x) = \Pr[X = x]$.*

Note that $\mathrm{E}[\log o(X)]$ is the theoretical maximum, achieved by a "clairvoyant" gambler who always has all wealth placed on the winning outcome.

Proof. For any b we have

$$\mathrm{E}[\log o(X)b(X)] = \mathrm{E}[\log o(X)] + \mathrm{E}[\log b(X)] = \mathrm{E}[\log o(X)] - \mathrm{H}(X) - \mathrm{KL}(X\|b)$$

Now recall by Proposition 2 that $\mathrm{KL}(X\|b) \geq 0$, with equality when $b = X$. □

An *eavesdropping gambler* has access to the outcome of each race before betting takes place, but the access is noisy. This "noisy inside knowledge" is modeled by a random variable Y, jointly distributed with X.

Definition 3. *An eavesdropping gambler is given by a conditional betting function, where $b(x|y)$ is the fraction of wealth bet on outcome x when y is observed.*

We will write Y, b for the joint random variable induced by the conditional betting function b and distribution Y on observations, and $b|Y$ for the corresponding conditional random variable.

Definition 4. *For any honest gambler b' the advantage over b' of an eavesdropping gambler b is equal to*

$$\mathrm{E}[\log o(X)b(X|Y)] - \mathrm{E}[\log o(X)b'(X)],$$

The eavesdropper's advantage is its advantage over the best honest gambler b^*.

By the preceding Proposition, an eavesdropping gambler's advantage is equal to

$$\mathrm{E}[\log o(X)] + \mathrm{E}[\log b(X|Y)] - (\mathrm{E}[\log o(X)] - \mathrm{H}(X)) = \mathrm{H}(X) + \mathrm{E}[\log b(X|Y)]$$

Proposition 4. *An eavesdropping gambler's maximum advantage is $\mathrm{I}(X;Y)$ and is achieved by $\hat{b}$ where $\hat{b}(x|y) = \Pr[X = x|Y = y]$*

Proof. For any eavesdropping b we have

$$\mathrm{H}(X) + \mathrm{E}[\log b(X|Y)] = \mathrm{H}(X) - \mathrm{H}(X|Y) - \mathrm{KL}(X|Y\|b|Y)$$
$$= \mathrm{I}(X;Y) - \mathrm{KL}(X|Y\|b|Y)$$

We now use the properties of KL-divergence to obtain the optimal strategy and value. □

Relation to Information-theoretic Security. While Kelly did not explicitly consider an encrypted channel, it is clear that with this approach, we obtain an alternate characterization of perfect secrecy. In particular suppose that Y is just $\mathcal{E}(K, X)$ where $(\mathcal{E}, \mathcal{D})$ is an encryption scheme (and K denotes a distribution over keys.) According to Shannon's definition, this encryption scheme has perfect secrecy exactly when $I(X; Y) = 0$. In other words, any eavesdropping gambler using inside information encrypted by $\mathcal{E}$ has at best zero advantage. One advantage of this characterization of encryption security, as opposed to Shannon's characterization in [14] is the explicit introduction of an adversary (i.e. the eavesdropping gambler.) By considering resource bounded adversaries, we are led naturally to a version of Shannon security in the computational setting.

4   Computational Setting

We have seen that Kelly's model of gambling with inside information may be used to give a characterization of information-theoretic encryption security which is equivalent to Shannon's. Our goal now is to use Kelly's model to give a computational defintion of encryption security by considering computationally limited gamblers. We begin by reviewing some basic definitions regarding private-key encryption and security in the computational setting.

Definition 5. *A private-key encryption scheme $\langle \mathcal{E}, \mathcal{D} \rangle$ is a probabilistic polytime function ensemble $\langle \mathcal{E}_n, \mathcal{D}_n \rangle$ satisfying the following properties, for every n:*

1. $\mathcal{E}_n : \{0,1\}^n \times \{0,1\}^{\ell(n)} \to \{0,1\}^{q(n)}$
2. $\mathcal{D}_n : \{0,1\}^n \times \{0,1\}^{q(n)} \to \{0,1\}^{\ell(n)}$
3. *For any $k \in \{0,1\}^n$ and $m \in \{0,1\}^{\ell(n)}$, $\mathcal{D}_n(k, \mathcal{E}_n(k,m)) = m$,*

where ℓ, q are poly-bounded functions such that $q(n) \geq \ell(n) \geq n$. The value n is the securty parameter of the scheme.

Without loss of generality, we have dispensed with the specification of a *key generation* function. We may assume that keys are just uniformly generated random strings, as such strings could indeed be viewed as the randomness used in key generation. In what follows, we will write U_n to denote the uniform distribution over keys of length n. We will typically write M_n for an arbitrary distribution over messages of length $\ell(n)$.

In this paper, we limit our attention to *single message* security, that is, definitions of security in which an attacker has only has access to a single ciphertext c drawn from $\mathcal{E}_n(U_n, M_n)$. While it is possible to adapt some of our results to more comprehensive notions of security (e.g. CPA security) we will focus on the conceptual foundations of the notion of attacker success rather than attack models. We will consider the possibility of more "intrinsic" notions of multiple message security in Section 7. We will also only consider *non-uniform* definitions of security. That is, efficient adversaries will be modeled as poly-bounded families of circuits. While most of our results may be transferred to the uniform setting we will retain a non-uniform approach for the sake of conceptual clarity.

We now introduce a notion of encryption security using a resource-bounded formulation of Kelly's model. In this setting, we consider betting functions which are computed by poly-size families of circuits (which are defined in the obvious way.)

Definition 6 (Gambling Security). *An encryption scheme* $(\mathcal{E}, \mathcal{D})$ *is* gambling secure *if for every* k, *every distribution ensemble* $\{M_n\}$, *where* M_n *is a distribution over* $\{0,1\}^{\ell(n)}$, *every* poly-*size family of betting circuits* $\{b_n\}$, *and all sufficiently large* n

$$\mathrm{H}(M_n) + \mathrm{E}[\log b_n(M_n | \mathcal{E}_n(U_n, M_n))] \leq \frac{1}{n^k}.$$

Note: Our definition of gambling security measures the advantage of a computationally bounded eavesdropping gambler versus the *best* honest gambler. This is without loss of generality for our results, unless we do not admit honest gamblers whose complexity is polynomial in that of the eavesdropping gambler.

We would like to compare gambling security to the more familiar notion of *message indistinguishability*. To do so, we first recall some definitions.

Definition 7. *A* distinguisher *is a function* $D : \{0,1\}^\ell \to \{0,1\}$. *If* X, X' *are distributions defined on* $\{0,1\}^\ell$, *the* advantage of D in distinguishing between X and X', *denoted* $\mathrm{Adv}_D(X, X')$, *is defined by*

$$\mathrm{Adv}_D(X, X') = \Pr[D(X) = 1] - \Pr[D(X') = 1]$$

We will also consider generalized distinguishers *which take values in* $[0,1]$.[2] *For such a* D, Adv_D *is defined by*

$$\mathrm{Adv}_D(X, X') = \mathrm{E}[D(X)] - \mathrm{E}[D(X')]$$

We say that a (generalized) distinguisher is size t *if it is computed by a circuit of size* t.

In the case of size-bounded generalized distinguishers, the circuit D outputs the binary representation of a (rational) value in $[0,1]$. Note that the size restriction means that the actual range of D's output is contained in $\{0\} \cup [2^{-d}, 1]$. Using standard techniques, with polynomial overhead and at most d bits of randomness, we may transform a generalized distinguisher D into a distinguisher D' such that $\mathrm{E}[D(X)] = \mathrm{E}[D'(X)] = \Pr[D'(X) = 1]$, so that $\mathrm{Adv}_{D'}(X, X') = \mathrm{Adv}_D(X, X')$ for any X and X'. In particular, on input x, D' flips t coins and interprets the result as a value δ in $\{0\} \cup [2^{-t}, 1)$. If $\delta < D(x)$ then $D'(x)$ returns 1. Otherwise it returns 0. We also recall the following.

---

[2] We use the same terminology here as [15], but note that in their setting, generalized distinguishers take values in $\mathbb{R}^+$.

Proposition 5. *For any distinguisher D and distributions X_0, X_1,*

$$\text{Adv}_D(X_0, X_1) \leq \epsilon \quad \text{iff} \quad \Pr[D(X_z) = z] \leq \frac{1}{2} + \frac{\epsilon}{2}$$

where z is selected uniformly at random from $\{0, 1\}$.

Definition 8. *Let ℓ be a poly-bounded function. A distribution ensemble is a sequence $\mathbf{X} = \{X_n\}$ of distributions, where X_n is a distribution on $\{0, 1\}^{\ell(n)}$. A poly-size family of distinguishing circuits is a sequence $\{D_n\}$ of circuits, where $D_n : \{0, 1\}^{\ell(n)} \to \{0, 1\}$ has size $n^{O(1)}$. Distribution ensembles $\{X_n\}$ and $\{Y_n\}$ are computationally indistinguishable if for every k, poly-size family $\{D_n\}$ of distinguishing circuits, and sufficiently large n,*

$$\text{Adv}_{D_n}(X_n, Y_n) \leq \frac{1}{n^k}$$

We recall the following standard definition of encryption security (equivalent to semantic security [8]):

Definition 9 (Message Indistinguishability). *An encryption scheme $(\mathcal{E}, \mathcal{D})$ has* indistinguishable messages *if for any k and poly-size family of distinguishing circuits $\{D_n\}$, for all sufficiently large n and pair of messages $m_0, m_1 \in \{0, 1\}^{\ell(n)}$*

$$\text{Adv}_{D_n}(\mathcal{E}_n(U_n, m_1)), \mathcal{E}_n(U_n, m_0)) \leq \frac{1}{n^k}$$

Let $\langle \mathcal{E}, \mathcal{D} \rangle$ be an encryption scheme. The equivalence of message indistinguishability and gambling security for $\langle \mathcal{E}, \mathcal{D} \rangle$ is established using the following two lemmas

Lemma 1. *For any n, $0 < \delta < \frac{1}{2}$, size t distinguishing circuit D, and messages $m_0, m_1 \in \{0, 1\}^{\ell(n)}$, such that $\text{Adv}_D(\mathcal{E}_n(U_n, m_0), \mathcal{E}_n(U_n, m_1)) > 2\delta$, there is a size $poly(t, \log(1/\delta), \ell(n), q(n))$ betting circuit b and a distribution M on $\{0, 1\}^{\ell(n)}$ such that*

$$H(M) + \text{E}[\log b(M|\mathcal{E}_n(U_n, M))] > \frac{2}{\ln 2}\delta^2$$

Proof. By assumption and Proposition 5, for uniformly chosen $z \in \{0, 1\}$,

$$\Pr[D(\mathcal{E}_n(U_n, m_z)) = z] > \tfrac{1}{2} + \delta$$

Define b with size $t + poly(\log(1/\delta), \ell(n), q(n))$ as follows

$$b(m|c) = \begin{cases} 0 & \text{if } m \notin \{m_0, m_1\}; \\ \frac{1}{2} + \delta & \text{if } m = m_z \text{ and } D(c) = z; \\ \frac{1}{2} - \delta & \text{otherwise.} \end{cases}$$

Let M be the distribution which assigns m_0 and m_1 probability $\frac{1}{2}$ and all other messages probability 0. Then $H(M) = 1$, while

$$\text{E}[\log b(M|\mathcal{E}_n(U_n, M))] > (\tfrac{1}{2} + \delta) \log(\tfrac{1}{2} + \delta) + (\tfrac{1}{2} - \delta) \log(\tfrac{1}{2} - \delta)$$

which is just $-h(\frac{1}{2}+\delta)$, where h is the binary entropy function. So it suffices to show that for $0 \le \delta < \frac{1}{2}$

$$1 - h\left(\frac{1}{2}+\delta\right) \ge \frac{2}{\ln 2}\delta^2$$

Using a Taylor series expansion we have

$$1 - h\left(\frac{1}{2}+\delta\right) = 1 - \left(1 - \frac{1}{2\ln 2}\sum_{t=1}^{\infty}\frac{(2\delta)^{2t}}{t(2t-1)}\right)$$

$$= \frac{1}{2\ln 2}\sum_{t=1}^{\infty}\frac{(2\delta)^{2t}}{t(2t-1)} \ge \frac{1}{2\ln 2}4\delta^2 = \frac{2}{\ln 2}\delta^2.$$

$\square$

Lemma 2. *For any n, any $\delta \ge 0$, any size t betting circuit b and distribution M on $\{0,1\}^{\ell(n)}$, such that $H(M) + E[\log b(M|\mathcal{E}_n(U_n,M))] > \delta$, there is a size $poly(t, \log(1/\delta), \ell(n), q(n))$ distinguishing circuit D and and messages $m_0, m_1 \in \{0,1\}^{\ell(n)}$ such that*

$$\mathrm{Adv}_D(\mathcal{E}_n(U_n,m_0), \mathcal{E}_n(U_n,m_1)) > \frac{\delta}{2t}$$

Proof. By Proposition 3, we have $E[\log b'(M)] \le -H(M)$ for any betting function b', so that

$$E[\log b(M|\mathcal{E}_n(U_n,M))] - \max_{b'} E[\log b'(M)] > \delta$$

In particular, define b' by $b'(m) = b(m|\mathcal{E}_n(U_n,m_0))$ for some fixed message m_0 (note that b''s complexity is polynomial in b's, assuming $\mathcal{E}$ is poly-time.) Then we have $E[\log b(M|\mathcal{E}_n(U_n,M))] - E[\log b(M|\mathcal{E}_n(U_n,m_0))] > \delta$. By averaging, we conclude that that there must be some fixed m_1 for which $E[\log b(m_1|\mathcal{E}_n(U_n,m_1))] - E[\log b(m_1|\mathcal{E}_n(U_n,m_0))] > \delta$. Define D' as follows

$$D'(c) = \begin{cases} \frac{1}{t}(\log b(m_1,c)+t) & \text{if } b(m_1|c) > 0; \\ 0 & \text{otherwise.} \end{cases}$$

Then $D'(c) \in [0,1]$, and

$$\mathrm{Adv}_{D'}(\mathcal{E}_n(U_n,m_1), \mathcal{E}_n(U_n,m_0)) > \frac{\delta}{t}.$$

As shown in [15] (Theorem 3.22), D' may be approximated using a Taylor series to precision $\frac{\delta}{2}$ by a circuit D of size $poly(t, \log(1/\delta), \ell(n), q(n))$ such that

$$\mathrm{Adv}_D(\mathcal{E}_n(U_n,m_1), \mathcal{E}_n(U_n,m_0)) > \frac{\delta - \delta/2}{t} = \frac{\delta}{2t}$$

As discussed previously, we may assume that, with polynomial overhead, instead of outputting a value $p \in [0,1]$, D outputs 1 with probability p and 0 with probability $1 - p$, so that D is a distinguisher.

$\square$

We may combine the preceding results to obtain the desired equivalence between gambling security and semantic security in the asymptotic setting. Note this is simply a matter of applying the appropriate lemma at every n at which the corresponding security property fails, and then "stitching together" the results.

Theorem 1. $(\mathcal{E}, \mathcal{D})$ *is gambling secure iff it has indistinguishable messages.*

We conclude by noting that the concrete reductions given by the lemmas are quite far from being tight, but are adequate to obtain polynomial equivalence.

5   A Characterization Based on Pseudoentropy

The notion of *KL-hardness*, introduced by Vadhan and Zheng in [15], characterizes the difficulty of approximating a distribution with respect to KL-divergence. In the nonuniform setting, they show that a conditional distribution is KL-hard if and only if it has high conditional pseudoentropy.[3] KL-hardness is closely related to gambling security: as we have already seen in the information-theoretic setting, an eavesdropping gambler b maximizes its advantage by minimizing $KL(M|C\|b|C)$. Moving to the computational setting, things are less straightforward. In particular, the definition of KL-hardness given in [15] depends on the notion of a *KL-predictor*, which does not correspond exactly to a betting function. A KL-predictor is obtained by normalizing a *measure*, which is a function from the space of outcomes to $(0, +\infty)$. Nevertheless, the results of [15] and the preceding section suggest that we should be able to give a characterization of encryption security based on conditional pseudoentropy. We will do this directly, relying heavily on techniques introduced in [15]. We could also first establish an equivalence between KL-hardness for gambling functions and KL-hardness for normalized measures and then appeal directly to the main result of Vadhan and Zheng; this approach is discussed in Appendix A.

Definition 10. *Suppose* $\mathbf{X} = \{X_n\}$, $\mathbf{Y} = \{Y_n\}$ *are distribution ensembles.* $\mathbf{X}$ *has* conditional pseudoentropy *at least* k *given* $\mathbf{Y}$, *written* $\tilde{H}(\mathbf{X}|\mathbf{Y}) \geq k$, *if there is a distribution ensemble* $\{X'_n\}$ *such that* $\{(Y_n, X_n)\})$ *and* $\{(Y_n, X'_n)\}$ *are computationally indistinguishable and for all* c *and sufficiently large* n $H(X'_n|Y_n) \geq k - \frac{1}{n^c}$.

We recall that according to Shannon [14], an encryption scheme is perfectly secure if $I(M; C) = H(M) - H(M|C) = 0$. In our setting, then, it seems natural to characterize an adversary's advantage as $H(M) - \tilde{H}(M|C)$. Before showing that the corresponding security notion corresponds to message indistinguishability, we must consider a general relationship between conditional betting functions and distinguishers, required in the proof of Lemma 5 below. We will limit our attention to betting functions which are nonzero, taking values in $[2^{-t}, 1]$ (any nonzero size t betting function will take values in this range.) Any such function b determines a generalized distinguisher D_b, which we now define.

---

[3] Results are obtained in the uniform setting as well, but only for joint distributions of the form X, B over $\{0, 1\}^n \times [q]$, where q is poly(n).

Definition 11. *Suppose b is a conditional betting function taking values in $[2^{-t}, 1]$. Define the generalized distinguisher D_b, taking values in $[0, 1]$, as follows:*

$$D_b(y, x) = \frac{1}{t}(\log b(x|y) + t)$$

Note that $\log b(x|y) = tD_b(y, x) - t$. We have the following (information theoretic) relationships between b and D_b.

Lemma 3. *Suppose b is a conditional betting function taking values in $[2^{-t}, 1]$. Then for any distribution X on $\mathcal{X}$ and Y on $\mathcal{Y}$,*

$$KL((Y, X)\|(Y, b)) = H(b|Y) - H(X|Y) - tAdv_{D_b}((Y, X), (Y, b))$$

Proof. This is just a reformulation of [15], Lemma 3.13 in our setting.

$KL((Y, X)\|(Y, b))$

$$= E_Y\left[\sum_x X(x|Y) \log \frac{X(x|Y)}{b(x|Y)}\right]$$

$$= H(b|Y) - H(X|Y) + E_Y\left[\sum_x (X(x|Y) - b(x|Y)) \log \frac{1}{b(x|y)}\right]$$

$$= H(b|Y) - H(X|Y) + E_Y\left[\sum_x (X(x|Y) - b(x|Y))(t - tD_b(Y, x))\right]$$

$$= H(b|Y) - H(X|Y) + tE_Y\left[(1 - 1) - \sum_x D_b(Y, x)(X(x|Y) - b(x|Y))\right]$$

$$= H(b|Y) - H(X|Y) - tAdv_{D_b}((Y, X), (Y, b))$$

$\square$

Lemma 4. *Suppose b is a conditional betting function taking values in $[2^{-t}, 1]$. Then for all distributions X, X' on $\mathcal{X}$ and Y on $\mathcal{Y}$,*

$$Adv_{D_b}((Y, X), (Y, X')) \geq (H(X'|Y) + E[\log b(X|Y)])/t$$

Proof. By Lemma 3 we have

$$H(b|Y) - H(X'|Y) - tAdv_{D_b}((Y, X'), (Y, b)) = KL((Y, X')\|(Y, b))$$

since $KL((Y, X')\|(Y, b)) \geq 0$, it follows that

$$Adv_{D_b}((Y, X'), (Y, b)) \leq \frac{H(b|Y) - H(X'|Y)}{t} \tag{$\dagger$}$$

Applying Lemma 3 again, we obtain

$$H(b|Y) - H(X|Y) - tAdv_{D_b}((Y, X), (Y, b)) = KL((Y, X)\|(Y, b))$$

But

$$KL((Y, X) \| (Y, b)) = I(X; Y) - H(X) - E[\log b(X|Y)]$$
$$= -H(X|Y) - E[\log b(X|Y)]$$

so that

$$\text{Adv}_{D_b}((Y, X), (Y, b)) = \frac{H(b|Y) + E[\log b(X|Y)]}{t} \qquad (\dagger\dagger)$$

But then

$$\text{Adv}_{D_b}((Y, X), (Y, X')) = \text{Adv}_{D_b}((Y, X), (Y, b)) - \text{Adv}_{D_b}((Y, X'), (Y, b))$$
$$\geq (H(X'|Y) + E[\log b(X|Y)])/t \qquad \text{by } (\dagger) \text{ and } (\dagger\dagger)$$

$\square$

Lemma 5. *For any* n, $0 \leq \delta < \frac{1}{4}$, *size* t *distinguishing circuit* D, *and messages* $m_0, m_1 \in \{0, 1\}^{\ell(n)}$, *such that* $\text{Adv}_D(\mathcal{E}_n(U_n, m_0), \mathcal{E}_n(U_n, m_1)) > 2\delta$, *there is a distinguishing circuit* D_b *of size* $poly(t, \log(1/\delta), \ell(n), q(n))$ *and distribution* M *on* $\{0, 1\}^{\ell(n)}$ *such that for any* $\gamma \geq 0$ *and any* M' *such that* $H(M'|\mathcal{E}_n(U_n, M)) \geq H(M) - \gamma$

$$\text{Adv}_{D_b}((\mathcal{E}_n(U_n, M), M), (\mathcal{E}_n(U_n, M), M')) > \frac{\delta^2}{t \ln 2} - \frac{\gamma}{t}$$

Proof. By Proposition 5, for uniformly chosen $z \in \{0, 1\}$,

$$\Pr[D(\mathcal{E}_n(U_n, m_z)) = z] > \frac{1}{2} + \delta$$

Let M be the distribution which assigns m_0 and m_1 probability $\frac{1}{2}$ and all other messages probability 0. We now define a betting function b such that D_b is a distinguisher between M and any M' such that $H(M'|\mathcal{E}_n(U_n, M)) > H(M) - \gamma$. For any $\sigma > 0$, we define b as follows:

$$b(m|c) = \begin{cases} \frac{\sigma}{2^{\ell(n)} - 2} & \text{if } m \notin \{m_0, m_1\}; \\ 1/2 + \delta & \text{if } m = m_z \text{ and } D(c) = z; \\ 1/2 - \delta - \sigma & \text{otherwise.} \end{cases}$$

Let $D_b(y, x) = \frac{1}{t}(\log b(x|y) + t)$ be the associated distinguisher given in Definition 11. Let C denote $\mathcal{E}_n(U_n, M)$. Consider any M' for which $H(M'|C) \geq H(M) - \gamma$. By Lemma 4

$$\text{Adv}_{D_b}((C, M), (C, M')) \geq (H(M'|C) + E[\log b(M|C)])/t$$
$$\geq (H(M) + E[\log b(M|C)] - \gamma)/t$$

Now $H(M) = 1$, while we have, assuming $\delta < \frac{1}{4}$ and $\sigma < \frac{2}{9}$,

$$E[\log b(M|\mathcal{E}_n(U_n, M))] > (\tfrac{1}{2} + \delta) \log(\tfrac{1}{2} + \delta) + (\tfrac{1}{2} - \delta) \log(\tfrac{1}{2} - \delta - \sigma)$$
$$= -h(\tfrac{1}{2} + \delta) - \tfrac{1}{\ln 2} \sum_{j=1}^{\infty} \frac{2^{j-1} \delta^j}{j(1 - 2\gamma)^{j-1}}$$
$$\geq -h(\tfrac{1}{2} + \delta) - \tfrac{1}{4 \ln 2} \sum_{s=1}^{\infty} 4^j \sigma^j$$
$$= -h(\tfrac{1}{2} + \delta) - \frac{4\sigma}{(4 \ln 2)(1 - 4\sigma)}$$
$$\geq -h(\tfrac{1}{2} + \delta) - \tfrac{2}{\ln 2} \sigma$$

As demonstrated previously, $1 - h(\frac{1}{2} + \delta) \geq \frac{2}{\ln 2}\delta^2$, so that, setting $\sigma = \delta^2/2$ we have

$$H(M) + E[\log b(M|\mathcal{E}_n(U_n, M))] \geq \frac{\delta^2}{\ln 2}$$

and

$$\text{Adv}_{D_b}((\mathcal{E}_n(U_n, M), M), (\mathcal{E}_n(U_n, M), M')) > \frac{\delta^2}{t \ln 2} - \frac{\gamma}{t}$$

Finally, we note that D_b has size $poly(t, \log(1/\delta), \ell(n), q(n))$ □

Lemma 6. *For any n, $\delta \geq 0$, and distribution M on $\{0,1\}^{\ell(n)}$ which has the property that for any distribution M' on $\{0,1\}^{\ell(n)}$ with $H(M'|\mathcal{E}_n(U_n, M)) \geq H(M)$, there is a size t distinguishing circuit D such that*

$$\Pr[D(\mathcal{E}_n(U_n, M), M')) = 1] - \Pr[D(\mathcal{E}_n(U_n, M), M) = 1] > \delta,$$

there is a size t distinguisher D' and messages $m_0, m_1 \in \{0,1\}^{\ell(n)}$ such that

$$\text{Adv}_D(\mathcal{E}_n(U_n, m_0), \mathcal{E}_n(U_n, m_1)) > \delta.$$

Proof. Take M' which is independent of M but identically distributed. Then

$$H(M'|\mathcal{E}_n(U_n, M)) = H(M') = H(M)$$

and so by assumption there is a size t distinguisher D such that

$$\Pr[D(\mathcal{E}_n(U_n, M), M')) = 1] - \Pr[D(\mathcal{E}_n(U_n, M), M) = 1] > \delta$$

But then there are messages m_0, m_1 such that

$$\Pr[D(\mathcal{E}_n(U_n, m_0), m_1) = 1] - \Pr[D(\mathcal{E}_n(U_n, m_1), m_1) = 1] > \delta \qquad (\dagger)$$

Defining $D'(c) = D(c, m_1)$ completes the proof. To obtain the required m_0, m_1, we apply an averaging argument twice. The first application allows us to conclude that

$$\Pr[D(\mathcal{E}_n(U_n, M), m_1) = 1] - \Pr[D(\mathcal{E}_n(U_n, m_1), m_1) = 1] > \delta.$$

We then average again to obtain ($\dagger$).   □

From the preceding lemmas, we immediately obtain

Theorem 2. *$(\mathcal{E}, \mathcal{D})$ has indistinguishable messages iff for any message distribution ensemble $\mathbf{M} = \{M_n\}$, $\tilde{H}(\mathbf{M}|\mathbf{C}) \geq H(\mathbf{M})$, where $\mathbf{C} = \{C_n\}$ is the distribution ensemble such that for each n, $C_n = \mathcal{E}_n(U_n, M_n)$.*

6 Risk-Neutral Adversaries

We now revisit the model proposed by Kelly. Kelly's gambler may be viewed as trying to maximize the rate of return over repeated plays or, alternately, as just having a logarithmic utility for total wealth. What happens if we consider gamblers with different utility functions? We will now consider the case of linear utility. Such gamblers are typically referred to as being *risk-neutral*. Clearly, in this case, if no inside information is available the optimal strategy is to bet everything on the outcome which gives the maximum expected payout. An important difference in this setting is that the odds now make a difference, and the advantage of an eavesdropping gambler over the best honest gambler will be

$$\mathrm{E}[o(X)b(X|Y)] - \max_{x \in \mathcal{X}}(o(x)\Pr[X = x])$$

While in a more realistic setting we would want to take the odds function into account, as a first step we just assume constant odds, say $o(x) = \frac{1}{|\mathcal{X}|}$ for all x. In this way we remove consideration of odds from the gambler's strategy, leading to the following

Definition 12 (Risk-Neutral Gambling Security). *An encryption scheme $(\mathcal{E}, \mathcal{D})$ is gambling secure against risk-neutral adversaries if for every k, every distribution ensemble $\{M_n\}$, where M_n is a distribution over $\{0, 1\}^{\ell(n)}$, and every poly-size family of betting circuits $\{b_n\}$, for all sufficiently large n*

$$\mathrm{E}[b_n(M_n|\mathcal{E}_n(U_n, M_n))] - \max_{m \in \{0,1\}^{\ell(n)}} \Pr[M_n = m] \le \frac{1}{n^k}.$$

Lemma 7. *For any n, $0 \le \delta < \frac{1}{2}$, size t distinguishing circuit D, and messages $m_0, m_1 \in \{0, 1\}^{\ell(n)}$, such that $\mathrm{Adv}_D(\mathcal{E}_n(U_n, m_0), \mathcal{E}_n(U_n, m_1)) > 2\delta$, there is a size $poly(t, \log(1/\delta), \ell(n))$ betting circuit b and a distribution M on $\{0, 1\}^{\ell(n)}$ such that*

$$\mathrm{E}[\log b(M|\mathcal{E}_n(U_n, M))] - \max_{m \in \{0,1\}^{\ell(n)}} \Pr[M = m] > \delta$$

Proof. By Proposition 5, for uniformly chosen $z \in \{0, 1\}$

$$\Pr[D(\mathcal{E}_n(U_n, m_z)) = z] > \frac{1}{2} + \delta$$

Define b with size $t + poly(\ell(n), q(n))$ as follows

$$b(m|c) = \begin{cases} 1 \text{ if } m = m_z \text{ and } D(c) = z; \\ 0 \text{ otherwise.} \end{cases}$$

Let M be the distribution which assigns m_0 and m_1 probability $\frac{1}{2}$ and all other messages probability 0. Clearly,

$$\mathrm{E}[b(M|\mathcal{E}_n(U_n, M))] > (\tfrac{1}{2} + \delta) \cdot 1 + (\tfrac{1}{2} - \delta) \cdot 0 = \tfrac{1}{2} + \delta$$

The result follows by observing that $\max_{m \in \{0,1\}^{\ell(n)}} \Pr[M_n = m] = \frac{1}{2}$. $\square$

Lemma 8. *For any n, any $\delta \geq 0$, any size t betting circuit b and distribution M on $\{0,1\}^{\ell(n)}$, such that $\mathrm{E}[b(M|\mathcal{E}_n(U_n, M))] - \max_{m \in \{0,1\}^{\ell(n)}} \Pr[M_n = m] > \delta$, there is a size $poly(t, \log(1/\delta), \ell(n), q(n))$ circuit D and messages $m_0, m_1 \in \{0,1\}^{\ell(n)}$ such that $\mathrm{Adv}_D(\mathcal{E}_n(U_n, m_0), \mathcal{E}_n(U_n, m_1)) > \delta$.*

Proof. As we have argued above, for any honest b', $\mathrm{E}[b(M_n|\mathcal{E}_n(U_n, M_n))] - \mathrm{E}[b'(M_n)] > \delta$. In particular, define b' by $b'(m) = b(m, \mathcal{E}_n(U_n, m_0))$ for some fixed message m_0. Then $\mathrm{E}[b(M_n|\mathcal{E}_n(U_n, M))] - \mathrm{E}[b(M_n|\mathcal{E}_n(U_n, m_0))] > \delta$, and so there is some m_1 such that

$$\mathrm{E}[b(m_1|\mathcal{E}_n(U_n, m_1))] - \mathrm{E}[b(m_1|\mathcal{E}_n(U_n, m_0))] > \delta$$

Define the generalized distinguisher D' by $D'(c) = b(m_1|c)$ and use D' to obtain a distinguisher D for which

$$\mathrm{Adv}_D(\mathcal{E}_n(U_n, m_0), \mathcal{E}_n(U_n, m_1)) > \delta \qquad \square$$

Theorem 3. *$(\mathcal{E}, \mathcal{D})$ is gambling secure against risk-neutral adversaries iff it has indistinguishable messages.*

7 Conclusions and Future Work

We have revisited Yao'a program of characterizing encryption security via computational information, providing two new equivalent characterizations based on different approaches to computational entropy. In some sense this is more of a contribution to computational information theory than to cryptography, as we have shown that, at least in the setting of encryption security, various notions coincide. This of course raises the question of how these notions are related in more general settings. We now have another notion of computational entropy, based on Kelly's model, although this is closely related to Vadhan and Zheng's notion of KL-hardness, which in turn is closely related to pseudoentropy. Indeed, in a general setting, KL-hardness and pseudoentropy coincide for nonuniform adversaries ([15], Corollary 3.10.) There are still numerous open questions regarding the relationship Yao and HILL entropy; a broader view involving notions such as KL-hardness and gambling entropy may be useful here. We can also look at relationships to other notions such as the *unpredictability entropy* of [10], and also consider the relationship between computational entropy and Kolmogorov complexity [13].

In the information-theoretic setting, gambling and data compression are equivalent. In [3], Section 6.5, a reduction from compression to gambling is given, using the gambling function to construct a cumulative distribution function which is then used in an arithmetic coding scheme, but this reduction is not efficient. We conjecture that under an appropriate complexity-theoretic assumption, no such efficient reduction is possible.

Our results only concern single-message security. We could easily give a version of CPA security, by considering the usual CPA-game, but replacing the challenge phase with one in which the adversary is a gambler rather than a distinguisher. On the other hand, Kelly's model suggests forms of multiple-message security which are ostensibly weaker than CPA, but stronger than standard multiple-message security. In particular, we could consider a situation in which the same key is used to encrypt the results of multiple races in an on-line fashion, and where the gambler is able to use information about his success in each round to place future bets. This is very similar to the setting of on-line prediction (see, e.g. [2]). We would like to consider adversaries performing this sort of on-line prediction task, or on-line game playing as introduced in [5].

Our results imply that ϵ-gambling security implies $\sqrt{\epsilon}$-gambling security against risk neutral adversaries (or, equivalently, $\sqrt{\epsilon}$-message indistinguishability.) We may ask whether there is an inherent loss of security entailed by assuming adversaries have logarithmic utility, i.e., are there encryption schemes which are ϵ-gambling secure, but not ϵ'-message indistinguishable for some $\epsilon' \geq \epsilon$? In general, we would like to understand how assumptions about an adversary's utility impact security. This has the potential to contribute to a decision-theoretic approach to security (cf. *rational protocol design* as presented in [6].)

Finally, we note that our work may be viewed as complementary to recent work by Bellare et. al. [1], which considers a version of message indistinguishability and its relationship with entropy-based definitions of security in the information-theoretic setting. Dodis ([4], Lemma 2) states upper and lower bounds on mutual-information-based security in terms of message indistinguishability which are implicit in [1]. Our Lemmas 1 and 2 may be viewed as computational versions of Dodis' bounds.

Acknowledgements. We would like to thank Salil Vadhan and Colin Jia Zheng for their suggestions, and John Mitchell for asking the questions that led to this work.

References

1. Bellare, M., Tessaro, S., Vardy, A.: Semantic security for the wiretap channel. In: Safavi-Naini, R., Canetti, R. (eds.) CRYPTO 2012. LNCS, vol. 7417, pp. 294–311. Springer, Heidelberg (2012)
2. Cesa-Bianchi, N., Lugosi, G.: Prediction, learning, and games. Cambridge University Press (2006)
3. Cover, T.M., Thomas, J.A.: Elements of Information Theory, 2nd edn. Wiley (2006)
4. Dodis, Y.: Shannon impossibility, revisited. In: Smith, A. (ed.) ICITS 2012. LNCS, vol. 7412, pp. 100–110. Springer, Heidelberg (2012)
5. Freund, Y., Schapire, R.E.: Adaptive game playing using multiplicative weights. Games and Economic Behavior 29(1-2), 79–103 (1999)
6. Garay, J.A., Katz, J., Maurer, U., Tackmann, B., Zikas, V.: Rational protocol design: Cryptography against incentive-driven adversaries. In: 54th Annual IEEE Symposium on Foundations of Computer Science, FOCS 2013, pp. 648–657 (2013)
7. Goldreich, O.: The Foundations of Cryptography. Basic Techniques, vol. 1. Cambridge University Press, Cambridge (2001)

8. Goldwasser, S., Micali, S.: Probabilistic encryption. J. Comput. Syst. Sci. 28(2), 270–299 (1984)
9. Håstad, J., Impagliazzo, R., Levin, L.A., Luby, M.: A pseudorandom generator from any one-way function. SIAM J. Comput. 28(4), 1364–1396 (1999)
10. Hsiao, C.-Y., Lu, C.-J., Reyzin, L.: Conditional computational entropy, or toward separating pseudoentropy from compressibility. In: Naor, M. (ed.) EUROCRYPT 2007. LNCS, vol. 4515, pp. 169–186. Springer, Heidelberg (2007)
11. Kelly Jr., J.L.: A new interpretation of information rate. Bell System Technical Journal 35(4), 917–926 (1956)
12. Micali, S., Rackoff, C., Sloan, B.: The notion of security for probabilistic cryptosystems. SIAM J. Comput. 17(2), 412–426 (1988)
13. Pinto, A.: Comparing notions of computational entropy. Theory Comput. Syst. 45(4), 944–962 (2009)
14. Shannon, C.E.: Communication theory of secrecy systems. Bell System Technical Journal 28(4), 656–715 (1949)
15. Vadhan, S.P., Zheng, C.J.: Characterizing pseudoentropy and simplifying pseudorandom generator constructions. Electronic Colloquium on Computational Complexity (ECCC) 18, 141 (2011)
16. Yao, A.C.-C.: Theory and applications of trapdoor functions (Extended abstract). In: 23rd Annual Symposium on Foundations of Computer Science, Chicago, Illinois, USA, 1982, November 3-5, pp. 80–91 (1982)
17. Yao, A.C.-C.: Computational information theory. In: Abu-Mostafa, Y.B. (eds.) Complexity in Information Theory, pp. 1–15. Springer (1988)

A   An Alternate Proof of Lemma 5

Here we outline an alternate approach to proving a version of Lemma 5, using one of the main results of [15].

Suppose $\mathcal{X}, \mathcal{Y}$ are finite sets. A *measure* is a mapping $P : \mathcal{Y} \times \mathcal{X} \to (0, +\infty)$. Associated with P is a conditional mass function C_P defined by $C_P(x|y) = P(y, x)/\sum_{z \in \mathcal{X}} P(y, z)$. Suppose X, Y respectively are distributions on $\mathcal{X}, \mathcal{Y}$. X is (t, δ) *KL-hard given* Y if for any measure P computed by a circuit of size t, $\mathrm{KL}(Y, X \| Y, C_P) > \delta$.

Theorem 4 ([15], Theorem 3.8(2)). *Let* (Y, X) *be a* $\mathcal{Y} \times \mathcal{X}$-*valued random variable,* $\delta, \epsilon > 0$. *If* X *has nonuniform* (t, ϵ) *conditional pseudoentropy at least* $H(X|Y) + \delta$ *given* Y, *then for every* $\sigma > 0$, X *is* $(t', \delta - \sigma)$ *KL-hard given* Y, *for* $t' = \min\{t^{\Omega(1)}/\mathrm{polylog}(1/\sigma), \Omega(\sigma/\epsilon)\}$

We now note that the betting function b defined in the proof of Lemma 5 is strictly positive, so it is a measure. Moreover $C_b = b$. We have

$$H(M) + \mathrm{E}[\log b(M|\mathcal{E}_n(U_n, M))] \geq \tfrac{\delta^2}{\ln 2}$$

Now

$$H(M) + \mathrm{E}[\log b(M|\mathcal{E}_n(U_n, M))] =$$
$$H(M) - H(M|\mathcal{E}_n(U_n, M)) - \mathrm{KL}(M|\mathcal{E}_n(U_n, M)\|b|\mathcal{E}_n(U_n, M))$$

so that

$$\mathrm{KL}(M|\mathcal{E}_n(U_n, M)\|b|\mathcal{E}_n(U_n, M))) \leq \mathrm{H}(M) - \mathrm{H}(M|\mathcal{E}_n(U_n, M)) - \frac{\delta^2}{\ln 2}$$

Applying the above-cited result, we can conclude that given $\mathcal{E}_n(U_n, M)$, M does not have conditional pseudoentropy at least $\mathrm{H}(M)$, as required for the "if" direction of Theorem 2.

By appealing to the result of [15], we have made Lemmas 3 and 4 redundant. On the other hand, the work of Vadhan and Zheng involves considerable machinery beyond what is needed for Lemma 5.

Query-Complexity Amplification
for Random Oracles

Grégory Demay[1], Peter Gaži[2], Ueli Maurer[1], and Björn Tackmann[3,⋆]

[1] Department of Computer Science, ETH Zürich, Switzerland
{gregory.demay,maurer}@inf.ethz.ch
[2] Institute of Science and Technology, Austria
peter.gazi@ist.ac.at
[3] Computer Science and Engineering, University of California, San Diego
btackmann@eng.ucsd.edu

Abstract. Increasing the computational complexity of evaluating a hash function, both for the honest users as well as for an adversary, is a useful technique employed for example in password-based cryptographic schemes to impede brute-force attacks, and also in so-called proofs of work (used in protocols like Bitcoin) to show that a certain amount of computation was performed by a legitimate user. A natural approach to adjust the complexity of a hash function is to iterate it c times, for some parameter c, in the hope that any query to the scheme requires c evaluations of the underlying hash function. However, results by Dodis et al. (Crypto 2012) imply that plain iteration falls short of achieving this goal, and designing schemes which provably have such a desirable property remained an open problem.

This paper formalizes explicitly what it means for a given scheme to amplify the query complexity of a hash function. In the random oracle model, the goal of a secure query-complexity amplifier (QCA) scheme is captured as transforming, in the sense of indifferentiability, a random oracle allowing R queries (for the adversary) into one provably allowing only $r < R$ queries. Turned around, this means that making r queries to the scheme requires at least R queries to the actual random oracle. Second, a new scheme, called collision-free iteration, is proposed and proven to achieve c-fold QCA for both the honest parties and the adversary, for any fixed parameter c.

Keywords: hash functions, random oracle, indifferentiability, moderately hard functions.

1 Introduction

1.1 Motivation of This Work

Moderately Hard Hashing. Hash functions are one of the most basic and widely used building blocks in practically deployed cryptographic protocols. Their use in different contexts puts diverse requirements on their properties.

⋆ Work partially done while author was at ETH Zürich.

© Springer International Publishing Switzerland 2015
A. Lehmann and S. Wolf (Eds.): ICITS 2015, LNCS 9063, pp. 159–180, 2015.
DOI: 10.1007/978-3-319-17470-9_10

There is a vast body of literature exploring various desirable properties of cryptographic hash functions such as collision resistance, (second-) preimage resistance, indifferentiability from a random oracle, and several others.

A seemingly orthogonal property of a hash function is its efficiency—the amount of computational resources that is required to evaluate it. Naturally, the typical design goal is to provide hash functions that are as efficient as possible, while still maintaining the desired security requirements mentioned above. As a result of the long-term design effort with this motivation, the currently standardized and used cryptographic hash functions such as SHA-1, SHA-2 [25] and SHA-3 [26] are extremely efficient: for example, a software implementation of SHA-2 can process data at (very roughly) about 100 MB/s on a typical PC.

However, in several application scenarios the efficiency of the hash function actually has serious *security* implications, and these motivate design efforts going in the opposite direction. Namely, sometimes hash functions are used to perform computation by the honest parties that would need to be repeated on a significantly higher scale by an adversary trying to compromise the security of the system. One example of such a setting is any non-interactive password-based scheme where the hash function is used to, say, derive a key from this password. Here, increasing the complexity of the hash-function evaluation, while slightly increasing the computational burden for the honest user, also significantly increases the cost of a brute-force and password-guessing (dictionary) attack. Another setting that could benefit from an adjustable complexity of a hash function is a proof of work [9] where a legitimate protocol participant shows that he performed a certain amount of computation. This concept was proposed, among other uses, as a countermeasure against denial-of-service attacks or junk mail. Similar ideas are used in the now widely used Bitcoin system [21] and other cryptocurrencies basing their security on proofs of work.

The common denominator of all the settings mentioned above is that it would be desirable to employ hash functions that are, loosely speaking, *moderately hard* to compute [22]. While the occasional evaluation of such a function by an honest user needs to still remain feasible, at the same time the scaling resulting from a brute-force attack must be prohibitive for any adversary.

Complexity Amplification. Since designing new cryptographic hash functions from scratch is a long and intricate process (e.g., the SHA-3 competition spanned over almost 5 years), to answer the above-described demand it would be preferable to give *generic schemes* that would instead turn an existing hash function h into a new function H with moderately increased evaluation complexity. A natural first candidate for such a scheme is the simple *c-iteration* (or plain iteration), i.e., letting

$$H(\cdot) := h^c(\cdot) := \underbrace{h(\ldots h(\cdot)\ldots)}_{c \text{ times}}$$

for some integer $c > 1$.

Indeed, many password-hashing schemes are based on some form of iteration. Historically, the earliest implementations of crypt(3) used several iterations of (a variant of) the block cipher DES to hash users' passwords on Unix systems [20], the more recent bcrypt [23] iterates the block cipher Blowfish instead. Iteration is also used in the password-based key derivation function PBKDF2 standardized in PKCS#5 [12] and recommended by NIST [28].

However, when it comes to assessing the security of any such generic scheme for increasing evaluation complexity (for example to justify the choice of plain iteration), it turns out that merely *defining* the security requirement formally is a surprisingly subtle task. This is especially true if one asks for a composable definition that then allows every scheme secure under this definition to be plugged into any possible application, so that proving a scheme secure according to this single definition immediately implies that it can be used in, e.g., key derivation, proofs of work, or other applications that make use of the query complexity. One of our main contributions will be to give such a composable definition by modeling the underlying hash function h as a random oracle and exploiting the power of the well-established concept of indifferentiability. Before inspecting it in greater detail, let us first mention a surprising observation given in recent work that is very relevant in our context.

The Caveats of Plain Iteration. Dodis et al. [8] studied the structural differences between a random oracle and its second iterate: more precisely, they investigated the indifferentiability of the 2-iteration of a random oracle from a plain random oracle. Interestingly, they showed that such indifferentiability *does* hold, but only with poor parameters. Namely (and very roughly), any simulator in this indifferentiability statement, if asked r queries during the distinguishing experiment, would itself have to issue a large number of queries $\Omega(\ell r)$ to the underlying random oracle in order to succeed in simulation, where ℓ denotes (an upper bound on) the number of honest queries. (We show in Section 4 that the result extends to higher-order iterates.) On a high level, this large number of simulator queries means that if one uses the c-iterate of a hash function in some application, then the *concrete* security statement obtained through the composition theorem of indifferentiability is weaker than intuitively expected. Therefore, any strong security guarantee could only be obtained through an ad-hoc security analysis depending on the particular scenario considered, as done by Bellare et al. [1].

Let us recall an example of Dodis et al. [8] to illustrate this last point. In the hash-then-sign paradigm, a signature scheme SS_n signing n-bit messages and a hash function $h : \{0,1\}^* \to \{0,1\}^n$ are combined into a signature scheme $SS_* (h)$ for arbitrary length messages by signing the hash $h(m)$ of the message instead of the message m itself. Forging a signature for the extended scheme $SS_* (h)$ requires either to find a collision for the hash function h or to find a forgery for the original fixed-length signature scheme SS_n. If the hash function h is modelled as a random oracle, then its second iterate h^2 is indifferentiable from h [8, Thm. 2], and the composition theorem of indifferentiability [18,24] implies that the security of $SS_* \left(h^2 \right)$ can be reduced to that of $SS_* (h)$. However, such a reductionist argument, which is standard in any composable cryptographic framework such as indifferentiability, consists of obtaining an adversary against $SS_* (h)$ from an adversary against $SS_*\left(h^2\right)$ which *additionally* performs the job of the simulator given in the indifferentiability statement. Due to the blow-up in simulator queries mentioned above, this concretely means that one relates an adversary trying to forge a signature for $SS_*\left(h^2\right)$ with at most ℓ signing queries and r random oracle queries, to an adversary trying to forge a signature for $SS_*\left(h\right)$ also with ℓ signing queries, but with $\ell \cdot r$ random oracle queries. Thus, although $SS_*\left(h\right)$ is secure as long as the collision probability $(\ell+r)^2/2^n$ is sufficiently small (assuming that the original length-restricted signature scheme SS_n is secure within ℓ queries), the security of $SS_*\left(h^2\right)$ derived through composition depends instead on the much higher collision probability $(\ell \cdot r)^2/2^n$, corresponding roughly to a quadratic decrease of security.

1.2   Contributions of This Paper

In this work, we develop a new formal framework for treating the amplification of the evaluation complexity for random oracles (which are often used to model hash functions in practical scenarios). We first develop a security definition that tightly captures how well a given scheme increases the computational burden for an adversary in evaluating the function. Being based on indifferentiability, our definition is naturally composable and hence guarantees the desired universal applicability of any scheme meeting it. Secondly, guided by the observations of Dodis et al. [8] about the second iterate, we show that plain iteration, regardless of the number of iterations employed, fails to achieve the amplification of the hash-function complexity in the above sense. In response, we develop a modification of the plain-iteration scheme, called collision-free iteration, that does provably and generically achieve the desired amplification. Let us now discuss the details of each of these contributions.

Composable Security for Hash-Complexity Amplification. Employing the random oracle model (ROM) [2], we model hash functions as random oracles. A random oracle can be viewed as a resource that is available to all parties in a given setting, and allows each of them to evaluate the oracle by querying it—this corresponds to the party internally computing the output of the hash function. A restriction on the computational resources of the adversary hence naturally translates to a restriction on the number of queries it is allowed to ask the random oracle. In a typical security proof in the ROM, one establishes that the scheme in question is secure unless the ROM-adversary performs a huge number of queries to the random oracle. This then suggests that the adversary against the real implementation has to evaluate the hash function on a prohibitive number of inputs. Following this intuition, we model the increase in evaluation complexity of a hash function by a decrease in the number of queries that the adversary is allowed to issue to the random oracle (before its computational resources are exhausted).

  As a starting point, we make explicit the number of queries that such an oracle allows to each party: for two integers L and R, a random oracle that allows up to L queries at the left (honest user's) interface and up to R queries at the right (adversary's) interface formalizes the guarantee that the honest user has sufficient resources to evaluate the hash function (at least) L times, whereas the resources of the adversary are bounded to (at most) R evaluations. Naturally, a desirable guarantee for the honest user is that the number L is large enough to execute higher-level protocols, whereas the number R must be small enough to prevent the adversary from attacking those protocols with significant probability. The goal of a protocol for the *amplification of query complexity* is hence to reduce the number R, while at the same time not affecting the number L more than necessary.

Following the paradigm of constructive cryptography [17], we understand a cryptographic protocol or scheme as a way to *construct*, in a well-defined sense, a certain desired resource from one or more assumed resources. In the context of query-complexity amplification (QCA), this means that the goal is to construct, from a random oracle that allows the adversary to do some number R of queries, a random oracle that allows the adversary only a smaller number $r < R$ of queries. Intuitively, such a construction means that an adversary with the same computational resources can evaluate the random oracle less often, which will generally reduce his success in attacking higher-level protocols.

This constructive way of stating security definitions comes with a natural notion of composition. Denoting the statement that a protocol π constructs the desired resource $\mathbf{S}$ from the assumed resource $\mathbf{R}$ as $\mathbf{R} \xrightarrow{\pi} \mathbf{S}$, any two such construction steps that "syntactically" match can be composed: If we consider another protocol ψ that assumes the resource $\mathbf{S}$ and constructs a resource $\mathbf{T}$, the composition theorem immediately implies that

$$\mathbf{R} \xrightarrow{\pi} \mathbf{S} \quad \wedge \quad \mathbf{S} \xrightarrow{\psi} \mathbf{T} \quad \Longrightarrow \quad \mathbf{R} \xrightarrow{\psi \circ \pi} \mathbf{T},$$

where $\psi \circ \pi$ denotes the composed protocol. For example, let π in the above represent a protocol for hash-complexity amplification that is capable of transforming a random oracle $\mathbf{R}$ that can be evaluated R times within the adversary's resources into a ("much harder") random oracle $\mathbf{S}$ that the adversary can only evaluate $r \ll R$ times. Then, for *any* higher-level construction ψ of some useful resource $\mathbf{T}$ that uses an underlying random oracle $\mathbf{S}$ and guarantees that $\mathbf{T}$ will be secure as long as the adversary is not capable of evaluating S more than r times, we can instead start from the oracle $\mathbf{R}$ and amplify its complexity using π before using it to construct $\mathbf{T}$. The security will not be compromised by this as long as the adversary cannot evaluate $\mathbf{R}$ more than R times; and this guarantee then heuristically translates into the setting where we use an efficient hash function instead of $\mathbf{R}$.

Finally, while aiming for a formalization of hash-complexity amplification, we also arrive at a new formalism of parameterized construction statements, as detailed in Section 3. We believe that this formalism will be useful also in many other settings, such as secure communication as discussed in [27], and consider it an additional contribution of this paper of independent interest.

A Scheme for Hash-Complexity Amplification. As our second contribution, we present a simple scheme, called collision-free iteration, that achieves query-complexity amplification in the sense of our new definition discussed above.

One would naturally expect that the c-iteration of a random oracle for some $c \geq 2$ would lead to a reduction of adversary queries from R to R/c, at the cost of simultaneously reducing the honest party's queries from L to L/c. However, we show in Section 4 that c-iteration, much like the second iterate studied by Dodis et al. [8], suffers from the blow-up in the number of simulator queries and therefore falls short of achieving this goal.

We show that modifying the c-iterate of a random oracle by a proper encoding of the queries will indeed lead to the desired (and expected) result. The high-level idea is to make sure that each query will access a distinct part of the random oracle and hence the "shifted chains" of queries that caused problems for the plain iteration will not occur. In greater detail, collision-free iteration works almost like the plain iteration, but each query to the underlying function $h(\cdot)$ during the computation of $H(x)$ is prefixed by a prefix-free encoding $\lfloor x \rceil$ of the original query x, as well as the sequence number within the iterative process. Formally, we define $W_0(x)$ to be the empty string and

$$W_j(x) := h(\lfloor x \rceil \,\|\, \langle j \rangle \,\|\, W_{j-1}(x)) \text{ for all } j \in \{1, \ldots, c\},$$

where $\lfloor \cdot \rceil$ and $\langle \cdot \rangle$ denote a prefix-free encoding and an injective encoding of an integer over $\lceil \log c \rceil$ bits, respectively. Finally, we simply let $H(x) := W_c(x)$. We prove in Section 5 that this construction reduces the number of adversary queries from R to R/c, at the cost of simultaneously reducing the honest party's queries from L to L/c.

TOWARDS PROVING OPTIMALITY. In the full version of this paper we study whether this simultaneous reduction of the honest-party queries is inherent to any query-complexity amplification scheme. Based on the observation that the adversary can always choose to evaluate the honest scheme, we can show that our construction, which reduces the adversary's queries exactly as much as the honest party's queries, is optimal with respect to a natural, albeit restricted, class of simulators.

We aimed for simplicity in the design of our construction and did not tailor it to minimize query lengths. In particular, extending the length of each sub-query by the length of $\lfloor x \rceil$ is most likely not necessary. We leave the question of improving the lengths of the honest-user queries open for future work.

2   Preliminaries

2.1   Basic Notation

We denote sets by calligraphic letters or capital Greek letters (e.g., $\mathcal{X}$, Σ). Throughout this paper, we consider only discrete random variables. A discrete random variable will be denoted by an upper-case letter X, its range by the corresponding calligraphic letter $\mathcal{X}$, and a realization of the random variable X

will be denoted by the corresponding lower-case letter x. Unless stated otherwise, $X \xleftarrow{\$} \mathcal{X}$ denotes a random variable X selected independently and uniformly at random in $\mathcal{X}$. A tuple of n random variables $(X_1, \ldots, X_n)$ is denoted by X^n. Similarly, x^n denotes a tuple of n values $(x_1, \ldots, x_n)$. The set of bit strings of finite length is denoted $\{0,1\}^*$ and λ denotes the empty bit string.

2.2 Random Systems

Many cryptographic primitives like block ciphers, MAC schemes, random functions, etc., can be described as $(\mathcal{X}, \mathcal{Y})$-random systems [14] taking inputs X_1, $X_2, \ldots \in \mathcal{X}$ and generating for each input X_k an output $Y_k \in \mathcal{Y}$. In full generality, such an output Y_k depends probabilistically on all the previous inputs X^k as well as all the previous outputs Y^{k-1}. For an $(\mathcal{X}, \mathcal{Y})$-random system $\mathbf{S}$, such a dependency is captured by a (possibly infinite) sequence of functions $\mathsf{p}^{\mathbf{S}}_{Y_k|X^k Y^{k-1}} : \mathcal{Y} \times \mathcal{X}^k \times \mathcal{Y}^{k-1} \to [0,1]$ such that for all choices of the arguments x^k and y^{k-1} the sum of the function values over the choices of y_k equals 1, and where the superscript indicates the considered system. Random systems are usually denoted by upper-case boldface letters such as $\mathbf{R}$ or $\mathbf{S}$. An $(\mathcal{X}, \mathcal{Y})$-random system $\mathbf{S}$ considered in isolation does not define a random experiment since the distribution of the inputs to the system $\mathbf{S}$ is not defined. For this reason, the function $\mathsf{p}^{\mathbf{S}}_{Y_k|X^k Y^{k-1}}$, which is called a *conditional* probability distribution, is denoted by a lower-case letter p instead of an upper-case letter P, which we use for probability distributions in a fully specified random experiment.

A random system $\mathbf{S}$ can alternatively be described by the sequence of conditional distributions $\mathsf{p}^{\mathbf{S}}_{Y^k|X^k}$, where $\mathsf{p}^{\mathbf{S}}_{Y^k|X^k} := \prod_{j=1}^{k} \mathsf{p}^{\mathbf{S}}_{Y_j|X^j Y^{j-1}}$. Note that the conditional distribution $\mathsf{p}^{\mathbf{S}}_{Y^k|X^k}$ contains the conditional distribution $\mathsf{p}^{\mathbf{S}}_{Y^j|X^j}$ for all $j < k$ and hence the above description of a system is redundant. The conditional distribution $\mathsf{p}^{\mathbf{S}}_{Y^k|X^k}$ must satisfy a consistency condition which ensures that Y_j does not depend on $X_{j+1}, \ldots, X_k$. Two random systems $\mathbf{R}$ and $\mathbf{S}$ are said to be *equivalent*, denoted $\mathbf{R} \equiv \mathbf{S}$, if they behave identically, i.e., $\mathsf{p}^{\mathbf{R}}_{Y^k|X^k} = \mathsf{p}^{\mathbf{S}}_{Y^k|X^k}$, for all $k \geq 1$.

Distinguishers and a Distance Measure on Random Systems. A natural notion of similarity for random systems can be based on the concept of *distinguishers*. Intuitively, a distinguisher can be viewed as a system that connects to a random system, interacts with this system, and at some point outputs a single bit. In the case of $(\mathcal{X}, \mathcal{Y})$-random systems, a distinguisher $\mathbf{D}$ that makes some arbitrary but fixed number $q \in \mathbb{N}$ of queries corresponds to a finite $(\mathcal{Y}, \mathcal{X})$-random system which is one query ahead [16], i.e., distributions $\mathsf{p}^{\mathbf{D}}_{X_i|Y^{i-1} X^{i-1}}$ for $i \in \{1, \ldots, q\}$, and an additional distribution $\mathsf{p}^{\mathbf{D}}_{Z|Y^q X^q}$. The distinguisher interacts with an $(\mathcal{X}, \mathcal{Y})$-random system $\mathbf{R}$ by providing inputs $X_1, X_2, \ldots \in \mathcal{X}$ to $\mathbf{R}$ and by receiving its corresponding outputs $Y_1, Y_2, \ldots \in \mathcal{Y}$. Connecting a distinguisher $\mathbf{D}$ to an $(\mathcal{X}, \mathcal{Y})$-random system $\mathbf{R}$ defines a binary random variable (the output bit Z of the distinguisher), denoted $\mathbf{DR}$. For two $(\mathcal{X}, \mathcal{Y})$-random systems $\mathbf{R}$ and $\mathbf{S}$, the distinguishing advantage of a distinguisher $\mathbf{D}$ in telling apart $\mathbf{R}$ from $\mathbf{S}$ is then defined as

$$\Delta^{\mathbf{D}}(\mathbf{R}, \mathbf{S}) \quad := \quad |\mathsf{P}(\mathbf{DR} = 1) - \mathsf{P}(\mathbf{DS} = 1)| \ .$$

For a class $\mathcal{D}$ of distinguishers, we define $\Delta^{\mathcal{D}}(\mathbf{R}, \mathbf{S}) := \sup_{\mathbf{D} \in \mathcal{D}} \Delta^{\mathbf{D}}(\mathbf{R}, \mathbf{S})$. (The only classes we are interested in are the class of *all* distinguishers, in which case we omit the superscript and write $\Delta(\mathbf{R}, \mathbf{S})$, and the class NA of all *non-adaptive* distinguishers.)

Games. A central tool in deriving an indistinguishability proof between two systems is to characterize both systems as being equivalent until a certain condition arises [14,3]. Thus, being able to distinguish both systems requires to provoke this condition, and one is then interested in upper-bounding the probability of this event. Interacting with a random system in order to provoke a certain condition is naturally modeled by defining an additional *monotone binary output (MBO)* on the original system, where the binary output is monotone in the sense that it is initially set to 0 and that, once it has turned to 1, it can not turn back to 0. An $(\mathcal{X}, \mathcal{Y} \times \{0, 1\})$-system where the second output component is monotone is often indicated by using a system symbol with a hat, such as $\widehat{\mathbf{R}}$.

For an $(\mathcal{X}, \mathcal{Y} \times \{0, 1\})$-system $\widehat{\mathbf{R}}$ with an MBO, we consider two particular $(\mathcal{X}, \mathcal{Y})$-systems which are derived from $\widehat{\mathbf{R}}$, following Maurer et al. [16]:

1. $\widehat{\mathbf{R}}^-$ is the $(\mathcal{X}, \mathcal{Y})$-system obtained from $\widehat{\mathbf{R}}$ by ignoring the MBO, we usually refer to this system as $\mathbf{R}$ (i.e., we simply omit the hat);
2. $\widehat{\mathbf{R}}^{\dashv}$ is the $(\mathcal{X}, \mathcal{Y} \cup \{\diamond\})$-system which masks the $\mathcal{Y}$-output to a dummy symbol $\diamond \notin \mathcal{Y}$ as soon as the MBO turns 1, and in addition, it does not output the MBO itself.[1]

We will alternatively refer to an $(\mathcal{X}, \mathcal{Y} \times \{0, 1\})$-random system $\widehat{\mathbf{R}}$ with an MBO as an $(\mathcal{X}, \mathcal{Y})$-*game*, in particular if we are interested in the probability with which the MBO can be provoked. More formally, we are then interested in the probability that some $(\mathcal{X}, \mathcal{Y})$-game winner $\mathbf{W}$ (which, like a distinguisher, can be viewed as a finite $(\mathcal{Y}, \mathcal{X})$-random system that is one query ahead) provokes the MBO of a game $\widehat{\mathbf{R}}$ to be 1. As in a distinguishing experiment, the game winner $\mathbf{W}$ and the game $\widehat{\mathbf{R}}$ define a binary random variable, the value of the MBO of $\widehat{\mathbf{R}}$ after $\mathbf{W}$ stops, which we denote as $\mathbf{W}\widehat{\mathbf{R}}$. Hence, the *winning probability of $\mathbf{W}$ in the game $\widehat{\mathbf{R}}$* is defined as

$$\Gamma^{\mathbf{W}}(\widehat{\mathbf{R}}) \quad := \quad \Pr[\mathbf{W}\widehat{\mathbf{R}} = 1] \ .$$

Similarly to $\Delta^{\mathcal{D}}$, the supremum of $\Gamma^{\mathbf{D}}(\widehat{\mathbf{R}})$ over $\mathcal{D}$ is denoted $\Gamma^{\mathcal{D}}(\widehat{\mathbf{R}})$.

---

[1] This definition deviates from the one used by Maurer et al. [16], where the MBO is still output by $\widehat{\mathbf{R}}^{\dashv}$. The difference between the definitions is irrelevant because the output is $\diamond$ if and only if the MBO is 1.

Restricted Systems and Games. The concept of a blocked system $\widehat{\mathbf{R}}^\dashv$, derived from a given system $\widehat{\mathbf{R}}$ with MBO, is particularly useful if $\widehat{\mathbf{R}}$ is in turn derived from some underlying system $\mathbf{R}$ (i.e., $\widehat{\mathbf{R}}^- = \mathbf{R}$, where $\mathbf{R}$ is of interest to us) by adding an MBO representing some *restriction* on $\mathbf{R}$ (e.g., an upper bound on the number of queries than can be made to this system). In this case, the *restricted distinguishing advantage* of a distinguisher $\mathbf{D}$ in distinguishing the two systems with MBO $\widehat{\mathbf{R}}$ and $\widehat{\mathbf{S}}$ is defined as

$$\widehat{\Delta}^{\mathbf{D}}(\widehat{\mathbf{R}}, \widehat{\mathbf{S}}) \quad := \quad \Delta^{\mathbf{D}}(\widehat{\mathbf{R}}^\dashv, \widehat{\mathbf{S}}^\dashv) \ . \tag{1}$$

The concept of restricting a system via an additional MBO can also be applied to the case of games and game winning. In such a case, we consider a system restricted by some MBO $A_1, A_2, \ldots$ with an additional MBO $B_1, B_2, \ldots$ specifying when the game is won. Formally, this is an $(\mathcal{X}, \mathcal{Y} \times \{0,1\} \times \{0,1\})$-random system $\mathbf{R}$, where the outputs are triples (Y_j, A_j, B_j) and the latter two components are monotone. Then, we can consider the task of winning the restricted game, i.e., provoking the event modelled by the MBO $B_1, B_2, \ldots$ *before* violating the restriction modelled by the MBO $A_1, A_2, \ldots$, as the task of winning the game with the MBO $C_1, C_2, \ldots$ with $C_j = C_{j-1} \vee (\neg A_j \wedge B_j)$. Denoting the system with the single MBO $C_1, C_2, \ldots$ as $\mathbf{R}^<$, we define the restricted game-winning advantage as

$$\widehat{\Gamma}^{\mathbf{W}}(\mathbf{R}) \quad := \quad \Gamma^{\mathbf{W}}(\mathbf{R}^<) \ .$$

Conditional Equivalence. The notion of *conditional equivalence* has been introduced by Maurer [14,13] and is a useful tool in deriving indistinguishability proofs. An $(\mathcal{X}, \mathcal{Y})$-game $\widehat{\mathbf{R}}$ with MBO $B_1, B_2, \ldots$ is said to be *conditionally equivalent* to an $(\mathcal{X}, \mathcal{Y})$-random system $\mathbf{S}$, denoted $\widehat{\mathbf{R}} \models \mathbf{S}$, if $\mathsf{p}^{\widehat{\mathbf{R}}}_{Y_j|X^j B_j = 0} = \mathsf{p}^{\mathbf{S}}_{Y_j|X^j}$, for all $j \geq 1$ and for all arguments for which $\mathsf{p}^{\widehat{\mathbf{R}}}_{Y_j|X^j B_j = 0}$ is defined. If a game $\widehat{\mathbf{R}}$ is conditionally equivalent to a system $\mathbf{S}$, then the distinguishing advantage between the systems $\mathbf{R}$ and $\mathbf{S}$ is upper bounded by the probability of winning the game $\widehat{\mathbf{R}}$ in a *non-adaptive* manner, a statement which was first presented by Maurer [14] and was studied more extensively later by Jetchev et al. [11] and Maurer [13].

2.3   Two-Interface Systems and Converters

Two-Interface Systems. Systems that can be accessed by multiple parties can be viewed as systems with multiple interfaces and formalized as random systems by making the interface identifier an explicit part of the input (or output) of the system. In this work, we focus on systems with two interfaces, which we naturally label by elements of the set $\mathcal{I} := \{\mathsf{left}, \mathsf{right}\}$.

We restrict our considerations to the particular class of two-interface systems that only produce an output (from some set $\mathcal{Y}$) in response to an input (from $\mathcal{X}$) and on the same interface where the input was received, and hence we omit the interface label from the output. Then, such a two-interface system $\mathbf{S}$ takes as input a pair $(I_k, X_k) \in \mathcal{I} \times \mathcal{X}$, where the kth query X_k was input at the I_k-interface, and produces as output $Y_k \in \mathcal{Y}$, where it is understood that the response Y_k of the system $\mathbf{S}$ is output at the same interface I_k that the query X_k was input. In other words, a two-interface system corresponds (due to our restrictions) to an $(\mathcal{I} \times \mathcal{X}, \mathcal{Y})$-random system and can be described by a sequence of conditional probability distributions $\mathsf{p}^{\mathbf{S}}_{Y_k | I^k X^k Y^{k-1}}$, $k \geq 1$. Moreover, we will usually consider two-interface systems which have an additional MBO, this is defined exactly as above and will be used to restrict the access of the distinguisher as in equation (1).

In this work, we focus on variants of the arbitrary input-length random oracle **RO** with output length n, which we understand as two-interface systems with one interface for the honest party and one interface for the adversary, and which are thus formally seen as $(\mathcal{I} \times \{0,1\}^*, \{0,1\}^n)$-random systems.

Converters. Strategies employed locally by a party are modeled by a *converter*[2], which can also be viewed as a system with two interfaces: an *inside* interface and an *outside* interface, denoted by in and out, respectively. In this view, the inside interface is attached to the i-interface of a resource and models how the scheme makes use of this resource, where $i \in \mathcal{I}$, while the outside interface of the converter becomes the i-interface of the composite system and models how the scheme can be used in applications and higher-level protocols.

We consider that a converter is always invoked by queries $X_1, X_2, \ldots \in \mathcal{X}$ at the out-interface. For each such query, it (adaptively) makes zero or more[3] queries $X'_1, \ldots, X'_{j_1}$ (resp., $X'_{j_1+1}, \ldots, X'_{j_2}$ etc.) at the inside interface, i.e., to the two-interface system whose i-interface is attached to the in-interface of the converter. After having received the corresponding answers $Y'_1, \ldots, Y'_{j_1}$ (resp., $Y'_{j_1+1}, \ldots, Y'_{j_2}$ etc.), it finally produces an output $Y_1 \in \mathcal{Y}$ (resp., Y_2 etc.) at the out-interface. As it is always clear at which interface the input to the converter is obtained (it is the same interface where the converter produced the last output), it need not be explicitly specified. Finally, we will usually consider converters which have an additional MBO, also for the purpose of restricting the distinguisher's access. Summarizing the above, such a converter can be formalized as a $(\mathcal{X} \cup \mathcal{Y}, ((\{\mathsf{out}\} \times \mathcal{Y}) \cup (\{\mathsf{in}\} \times \mathcal{X})) \times \{0,1\})$-random system.

Attaching a converter to the i-interface of a two-interface system with label set $\mathcal{I}$, where $i \in \mathcal{I}$, results in a two-interface system that can be described as follows.[4] Inputs to interfaces $i' \neq i$ are processed by the system as before. Whenever an input is given to the i-interface of the combined system, the converter is evaluated on this input. If the output of the converter (without the MBO) is of the form (in, x) for some $x \in \mathcal{X}$, the resource is evaluated on (i, x) and provides

---

[2] We use the term converter here although it is only fully appropriate once we consider the object within a cryptographic algebra [17].

[3] We assume that, for each converter, there is some (constant) upper bound on the number of inside queries it makes per outside query.

[4] The described process can be written as a closed formula to formally obtain a random system.

an output $y \in \mathcal{Y}$ (and an MBO). Then, the converter is evaluated on y. This process continues until the output of the converter is of the form (out, y') for some $y' \in \mathcal{Y}$, and this value y' is then considered the output of the composed system. This process leads to a well-defined random system because the number of inside queries is bounded for each query to the random system. The MBO of the overall system is defined to be the disjunction of the MBOs of the two-interface system and the converter.

Converters are denoted by lower-case Greek letters (e.g., α, π, σ) or by sans-serif fonts (e.g., amp_c). The set of all converters is denoted as Σ. To denote the composition of converters and two-interface systems, we will understand the left and the right side of the symbol $\mathbf{R}$ as representing the left- and right-interface of the system $\mathbf{R}$, respectively. Hence, attaching a converter π to the left-interface of a two-interface system $\mathbf{R}$ results in a two-interface system $\pi\mathbf{R}$ while attaching a converter σ to the right-interface of a two-interface system $\mathbf{S}$ results in a two-interface system $\mathbf{S}\sigma$.

2.4   Indifferentiability

Indifferentiability was introduced by Maurer et al. [18] as a generalization of indistinguishability for settings where some access to the internal state of the considered resources is available publicly, within reach of any potential adversary. In such a scenario, the left-interface of a two-interface system $\mathbf{R}$ models interaction with honest users and is referred to as the "private" interface, while the right-interface formalizes adversarial access and is referred to as the "public" interface. For a protocol $\pi \in \Sigma$ and $\varepsilon \in [0, 1]$, the system $\pi\mathbf{R}$ is said to be (strongly) ε-indifferentiable from the system $\mathbf{S}$ if there exists a converter $\sigma \in \Sigma$ such that $\Delta^{\mathbf{D}}(\pi\mathbf{R}, \mathbf{S}\sigma) \leq \varepsilon$ for all distinguishers $\mathbf{D} \in \mathcal{D}$. We usually refer to the converter σ as the *simulator*. Indifferentiability has been widely applied, especially in the context of hash functions [6,4] and reductions among idealized primitives [10].

3   Parameterized Constructions and QCA

As outlined in Section 1, we formalize query-complexity amplification as a construction of random oracles which only allow for a limited number of queries from random oracles which allow more queries, both at the (honest user's) left and at the (adversary's) right interface. That is, we consider a random oracle as a resource, and the "quality" of a certain QCA scheme will be captured by the translation of restrictions (in the numbers of queries) that it achieves at both the honest and the adversarial interface. In this section we formalize the above intuition.

Query-Restricted Systems. We are interested in two-interface systems that only allow a certain number of queries that can be made to their left- or right-interface.[5] This is formalized by extending the considered system **R** with an MBO that captures when the system is exhausted. Notationally, for some integers $L, R \in \mathbb{N}$, we denote by $\mathbf{S}^{|R}$ the system **S** with an MBO that becomes 1 as soon as more than R queries have been made at the right-interface of the system **S**, and similarly $^{L|}\mathbf{S}$ denotes the system **S** with an MBO that becomes 1 as soon as more than L queries have been made at the left-interface of **S**. If a system has both types of restrictions, we consider the MBO which is the disjunction of the two individual MBOs described above, i.e., $^{L|}\mathbf{S}^{|R}$ denotes the restricted system allowing at most L queries at the left-interface *and* at most R queries at the right-interface. We use the same notation for restricting the number of queries at the outside interface of a converter (i.e., we write $^{L|}\alpha$ for $\alpha \in \Sigma$ and $L \in \mathbb{N}$), and it is easy to see that for a converter α and a system **S** we have $^{L|}(\alpha \mathbf{S}) \equiv (^{L|}\alpha)\mathbf{S}$ and hence we typically drop the parentheses.

Parameterized Families of Construction Statements. We recall the definition of a construction statement for the case where there is only a single (external) adversary as described originally by Maurer et al. [17,15,19].[6] This construction notion, specialized to two-interface resources, is equivalent to (strong) indifferentiability as described in Section 2.4.[7] The described construction notion is composable if the pseudo-metric on the set of resources (i.e., the distinguishing advantage) is non-expanding. We defer the simple proof that $\widehat{\Delta}(\cdot, \cdot)$ is non-expanding to the full version of this paper.

Definition 1. *A protocol* $\pi \in \Sigma$ *constructs a restricted resource* **S** *from an assumed restricted resource* **R** *relative to a simulator* $\sigma \in \Sigma$ *and within* $\varepsilon \in [0, 1]$, *denoted* $\mathbf{R} \xrightarrow{(\pi, \sigma, \varepsilon)} \mathbf{S}$, *if*

$$\mathbf{R} \xrightarrow{(\pi, \sigma, \varepsilon)} \mathbf{S} \quad :\Longleftrightarrow \quad \widehat{\Delta}(\pi \mathbf{R}, \mathbf{S}\sigma) \leq \varepsilon .$$

In the distinguishing advantage $\widehat{\Delta}(\cdot, \cdot)$ that we consider, the outputs of a system are blocked once the MBO of the system becomes 1. In the particular case of query-restricted systems this means that the distinguisher does not obtain further outputs from the system once the specified number of queries is exhausted.

We extend the "arrow notation" from Definition 1 to the case where we consider parameterized families of construction statements, where we require that all of the individual statements must hold. More formally, given a space $\mathcal{K}$ of parameters, a family of protocols $\boldsymbol{\pi} := \{\pi_k\}_{k \in \mathcal{K}}$ constructs a family of restricted

---

[5] In contrast to most other definitional approaches, we restrict the number of queries in a distinguishing experiment by restricting the *system*, not the *distinguisher*.

[6] The exact form we describe here, which considers the simulator to be an explicit parameter of the construction, has appeared in the work of Coretti et al. [5]. However, we formalize the definition only for the information-theoretic case where ε is a constant.

[7] The statement that $\pi \mathbf{R}$ is indifferentiable from **S** corresponds to the statement that π constructs **S** from **R**.

resources $\{\mathbf{S}_k\}_{k \in \mathcal{K}}$ from an assumed family of restricted resources $\{\mathbf{R}_k\}_{k \in \mathcal{K}}$, relative to a family of simulators $\boldsymbol{\sigma} := \{\sigma_k\}_{k \in \mathcal{K}}$ and within $\boldsymbol{\varepsilon} : \mathcal{K} \to [0,1]$, denoted $\{\mathbf{R}_k\}_{k \in \mathcal{K}} \xrightarrow{(\pi, \sigma, \varepsilon)} \{\mathbf{S}_k\}_{k \in \mathcal{K}}$, if

$$\{\mathbf{R}_k\}_{k \in \mathcal{K}} \xrightarrow{(\pi, \sigma, \varepsilon)} \{\mathbf{S}_k\}_{k \in \mathcal{K}} \quad :\Longleftrightarrow \quad \forall k \in \mathcal{K}: \ \mathbf{R}_k \xrightarrow{(\pi_k, \sigma_k, \varepsilon(k))} \mathbf{S}_k \ .$$

Uniform Protocols. A family of converters $\boldsymbol{\alpha} = \{\alpha_k\}_{k \in \mathcal{K}}$ is said to be *uniform* if all the converters in the family are identical without their MBO, i.e., $\alpha_k^- = \alpha_{k'}^-$, for all $k, k' \in \mathcal{K}$. Thus, in a uniform parameterized family of converters, the parameter can only influence the MBO of each converter in the family and can therefore only influence the end of a random experiment (and not the values of the random variables). The reason to consider uniform families of converters is that (semantically) a protocol shall not depend on the number of queries that are made to it, since the restriction is a parameter of the environment in which the protocol is used (and not of the protocol itself). We often denote uniform families of converters only by a symbol that denotes a single converter which has no specified MBO, with the implicit understanding that for each single instance of the construction statement, the converter is amended by an MBO that formalizes the suitable restriction of queries.

Query-Complexity Amplifiers. The construction notion in Definition 1 induces a definition of ε-security for protocols, with respect to a given simulator, if one considers a specific assumed resource $\mathbf{R}$ and a specific desired resource $\mathbf{S}$. In our case, both resources $\mathbf{R}$ and $\mathbf{S}$ will be variants of the random oracle $\mathbf{RO}$.

Definition 2. *Consider two functions $\varphi : \mathbb{N} \times \mathbb{N} \to \mathbb{N} \times \mathbb{N}$ and $\varepsilon : \mathbb{N} \times \mathbb{N} \to [0,1]$. Then, a uniform family of protocols $\{\pi_{L,R}\}_{L,R \in \mathbb{N}}$, where $\pi_{L,R}^- = \pi$ for all $L, R \in \mathbb{N}$ and for some protocol $\pi \in \Sigma$, is said to be a (φ, ε)-query-complexity amplifier, with respect to a family of simulators $\boldsymbol{\sigma} := \{\sigma_{L,R}\}_{L,R \in \mathbb{N}}$, if*

$$\left\{ {}^{L|}\mathbf{RO}^{|R} \right\}_{L,R \in \mathbb{N}} \xrightarrow{(\pi, \sigma, \varepsilon)} \left\{ {}^{\ell|}\mathbf{RO}^{|r} \right\}_{L,R \in \mathbb{N}},$$

where $(\ell, r) := \varphi(L, R)$ and $r < R$, for all $L, R \in \mathbb{N}$.

Thus, proving that a protocol π is a (φ, ε)-query-complexity amplifier requires in particular to show that the system $\pi \ {}^{L|}\mathbf{RO}^{|R}$ is within $\varepsilon(L, R)$ from the system ${}^{\ell|}\mathbf{RO}^{|r} \ \sigma_{L,R}$, and where $(\ell, r) := \varphi(L, R)$ quantifies the exact amplification achieved for all $L, R \in \mathbb{N}$. Both resources are depicted in Fig. 1. Since schemes for query-complexity amplification are often used in contexts where they are evaluated independently by several parties, we will restrict ourselves to the case of *deterministic* and *stateless* protocols[8] to assure that the results remain consistent for all parties.

---

[8] A converter is said to be stateless if it does not keep a state between answering outer queries, i.e., its behavior for a particular outer query depends only on the query itself and the ongoing interaction at the inside interface. We refer to [7, Def. 1] for a more formal treatment.

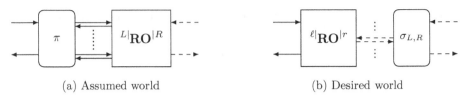

(a) Assumed world   (b) Desired world

Fig. 1. A (φ, ε)-query-complexity amplifier π: For any number of queries L, R, the resource on the left is within $\varepsilon(L, R)$ from the resource on the right and the simulator $\sigma_{L,R}$ does at most $r < R$ inner queries, where $(\ell, r) := \varphi(L, R)$

4   The Caveats of Plain Iterated Hashing

We show in this section that the protocol consisting of iterating c times a random oracle, denoted iter_c, is *not* a query-complexity amplifier, for *any* number $c \geq 2$ of iteration. To do so, we generalize some of the results of Dodis et al [8], who specifically focused on the case $c = 2$, to deal with a higher number of iterations. The next theorem shows that if one assumes a random oracle with only 2 adversarial queries, then the random oracle constructed by the c-iteration protocol iter_c must allow at least ℓ adversarial queries, where ℓ roughly corresponds to the number of honest queries in the constructed random oracle. For example, this implies that the c-iteration protocol iter_c cannot construct the random oracle $^{4|}\mathbf{RO}^{|1}$ from $^{4c|}\mathbf{RO}^{|2}$ (unless the distinguishing advantage becomes trivial), and therefore iter_c is not a query-complexity amplifier according to Definition 2.

To give some intuition behind this result, consider the c-iteration of a random oracle $\mathrm{iter}_c \mathbf{RO}$ and a chain $\left(y^{(0)}, y^{(c)}, \ldots, y^{(c\ell)}\right)$ of ℓ hashes, where $y^{(cj)}$ denotes the output of the c-iteration protocol iter_c when queried on the previous chain element $y^{(c(j-1))}$. The key observation here is that $y^{(c\ell+1)}$, the output of the random oracle $\mathbf{RO}$ when queried on the last chain element $y^{(c\ell)}$, forms the end of another chain of ℓ hashes starting with $y^{(1)}$, the output of $\mathbf{RO}$ when queried on the first element $y^{(0)}$ of the previous chain, *and* that both chains do not have any element in common (with overwhelming probability). In contrast, such shifted chains of queries cannot occur in the system $\mathbf{RO}\,\sigma$, unless the simulator σ does at least ℓ inner queries to its underlying random oracle.

Note that if the assumed random oracle in Theorem 3 had more adversarial queries, say R instead of 2, then one could force the simulator to make in total in the order of $\Omega(\ell R)$ queries to the underlying random oracle by "hiding" the query on the last chain element $y^{(c\ell)}$ among $R - 2$ random queries. A similar technique was used in [8, Th. 1]. The proof of Theorem 3 appears in the full version of this work.

Theorem 3. *The protocol* iter_c, *consisting of iterating c times a random oracle, where $c \geq 2$, is such that for any number ℓ of queries and any simulator σ,*

$$^{2c\ell|}\mathbf{RO}^{|2} \xrightarrow{(\mathrm{iter}_c, \sigma, \varepsilon)} {}^{2\ell|}\mathbf{RO}^{|r} \quad \Longrightarrow \quad r \geq \ell \ \lor \ \varepsilon \geq 1 - \mu,$$

where $\mu := 2^{-n} \cdot f(c, \ell)$ *and* $f \in \mathcal{O}((c\ell)^2)$.

A Vulnerable Application. There are concrete applications where the fact that the plain iteration protocol iter_c fails to be a query-complexity amplifier is problematic. One example of such a vulnerable application is the setting of mutual proofs of work, introduced by Dodis et al. [8], which is secure if a monolithic random oracle **RO** is employed, but becomes insecure if the c-iterate iter_c **RO** is used instead, for any $c \geq 2$. This fact was already known for the special case $c = 2$ [8] and it is easy to show, with the same kind of arguments as used to prove Theorem 3, that it generalizes to higher iteration counts.

Recall that in mutual proofs of work, two parties aim at proving to each other that they did a certain amount of computation. In the protocol proposed by Dodis et al. [8], both parties exchange in the first round a nonce and then compute a chain of hashes of a certain length (chosen by the computing party) starting with the received nonce. In the second round, both parties exchange the length and the last element of their computed chain. Then, each party checks that the other party actually did the claimed amount of computation by first computing a chain of hashes of the asserted length starting with the nonce that was originally sent, and second, by checking that both computed chains do not have any common element.

Note that such a scheme is insecure if the parties use iter_c **RO** to compute their chain of hashes. Indeed, a malicious party can simply "shift" the chain of hashes computed by the honest party and needs therefore only two hash evaluations to compute the beginning and the end of a valid chain of hashes (which with overwhelming probability has no common element with the chain computed by the honest party). In contrast, this protocol for mutual proofs of work is secure if the parties use the monolithic random oracle **RO** to compute their chain of hashes. We refer to the full version of this paper for more details.

5   Complexity Amplification via Collision-Free Iteration

The main result of this section is to present the collision-free iteration protocol, denoted amp_c, for amplifying the query complexity of a random oracle by a constant factor c, for some fixed parameter $c \in \mathbb{N}$. We present the (uniform) protocol amp_c and the corresponding (uniform) simulator sim in Section 5.1 and prove the actual construction stated below in Section 5.2.

Theorem 4. *The collision-free iteration protocol* amp_c *described in Fig. 2 is an* $\left((L, R) \mapsto \left(\lfloor \frac{L}{c} \rfloor, \lfloor \frac{R}{c} \rfloor\right), \delta\right)$*-query-complexity amplifier with respect to the simulator* sim *described below in Alg. 1, i.e.,*

$$\left\{ {}^L|\mathbf{RO}|^R \right\}_{L,R \in \mathbb{N}} \xrightarrow{(\text{amp}_c, \text{sim}, \delta)} \left\{ {}^{\lfloor \frac{L}{c} \rfloor}|\mathbf{RO}|^{\lfloor \frac{R}{c} \rfloor} \right\}_{L,R \in \mathbb{N}},$$

where $\delta(L, R) := R \cdot 2^{-n}$ *and* n *is the output length of the random oracle* **RO***, for all* $L, R \in \mathbb{N}$.

Notice that the upper bound δ on the distinguishing advantage in the previous theorem is independent of the number L of queries made to the left-interface and also

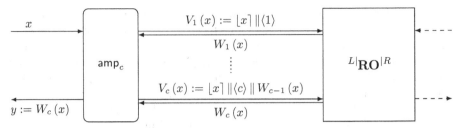

Fig. 2. Protocol amp_c for amplifying the complexity of a random oracle by a factor c. A prefix-free encoding of a bit-string x is denoted by $\lfloor x \rceil$, and an encoding of an integer j over $\lceil \log_2 c \rceil$-bit strings is denoted by $\langle j \rangle$.

of the factor c, which also corresponds to the number of iterations in the protocol amp_c given in Fig. 2 above. Throughout this section, we will denote by ℓ and r the two integers corresponding to $\lfloor \frac{L}{c} \rfloor$ and $\lfloor \frac{R}{c} \rfloor$, respectively, for all $L, R \in \mathbb{N}$.

5.1   The Protocol and the Simulator

Protocol amp_c. Consider the collision-free iteration protocol amp_c attached to the left-interface of a random oracle as described in Fig. 2. When queried on an input $x \in \{0,1\}^*$ (at its outside interface), the protocol amp_c does c queries $V_1(x), \ldots, V_c(x)$ to the random oracle, where the query $V_j(x)$ contains the answer of the random oracle on the previous query $V_{j-1}(x)$. In addition, amp_c uses prefixing to ensure that there is no collision among the queries asked, i.e., $V_j(x) \neq V_{j'}(x')$ whenever $(j, x) \neq (j', x')$. Namely, amp_c prefixes each query $V_j(x)$ with a prefix-free encoding $\lfloor x \rceil$ of x and with an iteration counter $\langle j \rangle$ where $\langle \cdot \rangle : \{1, \ldots, c\} \rightarrow \{0,1\}^{\lceil \log_2 c \rceil}$ denotes an arbitrary *injective* function from $\{1, \ldots, c\}$ to the set of $\lceil \log_2 c \rceil$-bit strings. The former guarantees no overlap between the queries for two different inputs x and x', while the second prevents collisions within the sequence of queries for the same input x. More generally, letting $W_0(x)$ be the empty bit string and $W_j(x)$ be the inner response of the connected resource to the inner query $V_j(x)$, we then define iteratively

$$V_j(x) := \lfloor x \rceil \, \| \langle j \rangle \, \| \, W_{j-1}(x)$$
$$W_j(x) := \textbf{result of querying } V_j(x) \text{ at the in-interface,}$$

for all $j \in \{1, \ldots, c\}$. Finally, we simply let $W_c(x)$, the response of the connected resource to the final query, be the output of the protocol.

PREFIX-FREE ENCODINGS. A prefix-free encoding function $\lfloor \cdot \rceil : \{0,1\}^* \rightarrow \{0,1\}^*$ is a function ensuring that $\lfloor \tilde{x} \rceil$ is not a prefix of $\lfloor x \rceil$ whenever $x \neq \tilde{x}$. We also assume it can be easily decided whether a bit string $y \in \{0,1\}^*$ is in the range of $\lfloor \cdot \rceil$, and in that case the (unique) pre-image of y can be efficiently recovered. Our results are independent of which such prefix-free encoding function is used. A simple example of such a prefix-free encoding is the function $\lfloor \, \rceil : \{0,1\}^* \rightarrow \{0,1\}^*; (b_1, \ldots, b_n) \mapsto (1, b_1, 1, b_2, \ldots, 1, b_n, 0)$. Many other (more efficient) examples exist, such as those described by Coron et al. [6].

Simulator sim. Before describing the behavior of the simulator sim defined in Alg. 1, let us first characterize more precisely the different types of queries we will consider. A query v is said to be well-formed, denoted isWellFormed(v), if it contains the prefixes as used by the protocol amp_c, i.e., $v \in \mathcal{V} \subseteq \{0,1\}^*$, where $\mathcal{V} := \bigcup_{\substack{x \in \{0,1\}^* \\ j \in \{1,\ldots,c\}}} \mathcal{V}_j(x)$, with

$$\mathcal{V}_1(x) := \{\lfloor x \rfloor \| \langle 1 \rangle\} \quad \text{and} \quad \mathcal{V}_j(x) := \{\lfloor x \rfloor \| \langle j \rangle \| z : z \in \{0,1\}^n\} \quad \text{for} \quad j \geq 2 .$$

An element of $\mathcal{V}_j(x)$ will be called a well-formed query of level j with prefix x. We denote by parse$(\cdot) : \mathcal{V} \to \{0,1\}^* \times \{1,\ldots,c\}$ the function which, given a well-formed query v, returns the pair (x,j) corresponding to the prefix and level associated with this query, respectively. Given an arbitrary subset of well-formed queries $\tilde{\mathcal{V}} \subseteq \mathcal{V}$, a prefix $x \in \{0,1\}^*$ is declared to be "fresh", denoted isPrefixFresh$(x, \tilde{\mathcal{V}})$, if it was never encountered, i.e.,

$$\text{isPrefixFresh}(x, \tilde{\mathcal{V}}) \quad :\Longleftrightarrow \quad \forall v \in \tilde{\mathcal{V}} \; \forall j \in \{1,\ldots,c\} : (x,j) \neq \text{parse}(v) .$$

The simulator sim works as follows: whenever it receives a well-formed query $v \in \{0,1\}^*$ of some level $j \in \{1,\ldots,c\}$ with a "fresh" prefix $x \in \{0,1\}^*$, it emulates the behavior of the protocol amp_c on input x by generating a "fake" chain of queries $\tilde{V}_1(x), \tilde{W}_1(x), \ldots, \tilde{V}_{c-1}(x), \tilde{W}_{c-1}(x), \tilde{V}_c(x)$, where the emulated answers $\tilde{W}_k(x)$ are simply uniform n-bit strings *locally* sampled by the simulator. Then, the simulator sim returns the answer of the random oracle ${}^{\ell|}\mathbf{RO}^{|r}$ when queried on the prefix x, only if the outer query v matches the last chain element $\tilde{V}_c(x)$ and all previous chain elements $\tilde{V}_1(x), \ldots, \tilde{V}_{c-1}(x)$ were already queried. On the other hand, if the query v matches one of the lower-level chain elements, i.e., $v = \tilde{V}_j(x)$ with $j < c$ and all previous chain elements were already queried, then the simulator sim replies with the answer $\tilde{W}_j(x)$ that was already chosen earlier (when generating the chain for the prefix x). In the (unlikely) case where a distinguisher happens to have guessed the value of $\tilde{V}_j(x)$, i.e., $v = \tilde{V}_j(x)$ but the previous chain element $\tilde{V}_{j-1}(x)$ was never queried, the simulator sim gives up on simulation by outputting the all zero bit string 0^n and setting internally the event hit to 1 in order to prevent any further inner query to the random oracle. Finally, if the query v considered is not well-formed, then the simulator sim replies with a fresh uniform n-bit string. We refer to Alg. 1 for a precise description of the simulator sim. Note that it maintains a state over all invocations, keeping track of the set $\tilde{\mathcal{V}}$ of well-formed queries received, the values $\tilde{V}_j(x)$ and $\tilde{W}_j(x)$ corresponding to the locally generated chains of queries, and the mapping g to be able to reply consistently to any repeated query.

5.2 Indistinguishability Proof

Recall that the statement of Theorem 4 considers a construction between an assumed random oracle ${}^{L|}\mathbf{RO}^{|R}$ and a desired random oracle ${}^{\ell|}\mathbf{RO}^{|r}$, for all integers L, R. If the number of queries that can be made to the left-interface of the

Algorithm 1. Simulator sim

$g(v) := \lambda$, for all $v \in \{0,1\}^*$ // λ denotes the empty bit string
$\tilde{\mathcal{V}} = \emptyset$ and hit $:= 0$
on input $v \in \{0,1\}^*$ at the out-interface
   if $g(v) = \lambda$ **then**   // v was never queried before
     if isWellFormed (v) **then**
      $(x,j) :=$ parse (v)
      if isPrefixFresh$(x, \tilde{\mathcal{V}})$ **then** // generate a "fake" chain of queries
       $(\tilde{V}_1(x), \tilde{W}_1(x), \dots, \tilde{V}_{c-1}(x), \tilde{W}_{c-1}(x)) :=$ GenerateChain$(x, c-1)$
       $\tilde{V}_c(x) := \lfloor x \rceil \| \langle c \rangle \| \tilde{W}_{c-1}(x)$
      if $v = \tilde{V}_j(x)$ **then**
       if $j > 1 \wedge g(\tilde{V}_{j-1}(x)) = \lambda$ **then**   // previous chain element was
       not queried
        hit $:= 1$
        $\tilde{Y} := 0^n$
       else if $j = c \wedge$ hit $= 0$ **then**
        $\tilde{Y} :=$ **result of querying** x at the in-interface
       else if $j = c \wedge$ hit $= 1$ **then**
        $\tilde{Y} := 0^n$
       else $\tilde{Y} := \tilde{W}_j(x)$
      else $\tilde{Y} \xleftarrow{\$} \{0,1\}^n$
      $\tilde{\mathcal{V}} \leftarrow \tilde{\mathcal{V}} \cup \{v\}$
     else $\tilde{Y} \xleftarrow{\$} \{0,1\}^n$
     $g(v) := \tilde{Y}$
   output: $g(v)$ at the out-interface

Procedure GenerateChain(x, m)
  $\tilde{W}_0(x) := \lambda$
  for $j = 1$ **to** m **do**
   $\tilde{V}_k(x) := \lfloor x \rceil \| \langle k \rangle \| \tilde{W}_{k-1}(x)$
   $\tilde{W}_k(x) \xleftarrow{\$} \{0,1\}^n$
  return $(\tilde{V}_1(x), \tilde{W}_1(x), \dots, \tilde{V}_m(x), \tilde{W}_m(x))$

---

desired random oracle is limited to ℓ, then so should also be restricted the number of queries that can be made to the outside interface of the protocol. Similarly, restricting the assumed random oracle to at most R queries at its right-interface implies the same restriction on the number of queries that can be made to the outside interface of the simulator. Thus, we will prove Theorem 4 for the uniform family of protocols $\{\ell|\text{amp}_c\}_{L,R \in \mathbb{N}}$ and for the uniform family of simulators $\{\text{sim}^{|R}\}_{L,R \in \mathbb{N}}$. We therefore need to upper bound the distinguishing advantage between the query-restricted systems $\ell|\text{amp}_c \ ^{L|}\mathbf{RO}^{|R}$ and $\ell|\mathbf{RO}^{|r} \text{sim}^{|R}$, for all $L, R \in \mathbb{N}$. The idea for upper bounding this distinguishing advantage is to first transform the system $\mathbf{RO}$ sim into a game $\overline{\mathbf{RO} \text{ sim}}$, where the latter is defined to be won if the event hit is provoked in the simulator sim described in Alg. 1; and second, to show that this game $\lceil\mathbf{RO}\ \mathsf{sim}\rceil$ is conditionally equivalent to the system $\mathsf{amp}_c\ \mathbf{RO}$. Before proving the corresponding conditional equivalence statement in Lemma 5 below, we start by describing informally how it implies Theorem 4. A more formal treatment appears in the full version.

Query Complexity. The protocol amp_c makes exactly c inner queries for every query it receives at its outside interface. Consequently, the protocol amp_c does in total at most L inner queries if it is queried at most ℓ times at its outside interface. The simulator sim makes a query x at its inside interface only if it receives a chain of c (distinct) queries $\tilde{V}_1(x), \ldots, \tilde{V}_c(x)$. The simulator sim keeps in memory the previous interaction, so that when such a chain of c queries is received, at most one query is made to the inside interface of sim. Furthermore, the prefix scheme employed prevents any form of collision among the queries so that making multiple, say k, such chains of c queries requires at least $k \cdot c$ queries. Hence, any tuple of R queries contains at most r such chains of c queries, and thus the simulator does in total at most r inner queries if it is queried at most R times at its outside interface. Thus, the protocol amp_c and the simulator sim are such that

$$\left[{}^{\ell|}\mathsf{amp}_c\ \mathbf{RO}^{|R}\right]^{\dashv} \equiv \left[{}^{\ell|}\mathsf{amp}_c\ {}^{L|}\mathbf{RO}^{|R}\right]^{\dashv} \text{ and } \left[{}^{\ell|}\mathbf{RO}\ \mathsf{sim}^{|R}\right]^{\dashv} \equiv \left[{}^{\ell|}\mathbf{RO}^{|r}\ \mathsf{sim}^{|R}\right]^{\dashv}.$$

It is therefore sufficient to upper bound the restricted distinguishing advantage between the query-restricted systems ${}^{\ell|}\mathsf{amp}_c\ \mathbf{RO}^{|R}$ and ${}^{\ell|}\mathbf{RO}\ \mathsf{sim}^{|R}$. To do so, we consider two games $\lceil\mathbf{RO}\ \mathsf{sim}\rceil$ and $\lceil{}^{\ell|}\mathbf{RO}\ \mathsf{sim}^{|R}\rceil$, where both games are won if and only if the event hit in the simulator sim is provoked. We show in Lemma 5 below that the game $\lceil\mathbf{RO}\ \mathsf{sim}\rceil$ is conditionally equivalent to the system $\mathsf{amp}_c\ \mathbf{RO}$, which then implies that the restricted game $\lceil{}^{\ell|}\mathbf{RO}\ \mathsf{sim}^{|R}\rceil$ is conditionally equivalent to the restricted system ${}^{\ell|}\mathsf{amp}_c\ \mathbf{RO}^{|R}$, since the added MBO, corresponding to a restriction on the number of queries, is simply a deterministic function of the inputs. Similarly to [13, Th. 3], this conditional equivalence statement between query-restricted systems implies that the restricted distinguishing advantage between ${}^{\ell|}\mathsf{amp}_c\ \mathbf{RO}^{|R}$ and ${}^{\ell|}\mathbf{RO}\ \mathsf{sim}^{|R}$ is upper bounded by the probability for non-adaptive game winners to win the query-restricted game $\lceil{}^{\ell|}\mathbf{RO}\ \mathsf{sim}^{|R}\rceil$. Such a game can only be won if the event hit in the simulator sim is provoked within R (well-formed) queries. Any well-formed query has a certain prefix x and level j, where $x \in \{0,1\}^*$ and $j \in \{1, \ldots, c\}$, and the probability for such a query to win the game is therefore at most 2^{-n} since it requires to guess the value of $\tilde{W}_{j-1}(x)$, an independent and uniformly distributed n-bit string. By applying the union bound it follows that the probability of winning the query-restricted game $\lceil{}^{\ell|}\mathbf{RO}\ \mathsf{sim}^{|R}\rceil$ is at most $R \cdot 2^{-n}$. Overall, we thus have for all integers $L, R \in \mathbb{N}$ that

$$\widehat{\Delta}\left({}^{\ell|}\mathsf{amp}_c \; {}^{L|}\mathbf{RO}^{|R}, {}^{\ell|}\mathbf{RO}^{|r} \; \mathsf{sim}^{|R}\right) = \widehat{\Delta}\left({}^{\ell|}\mathsf{amp}_c \; \mathbf{RO}^{|R}, {}^{\ell|}\mathbf{RO} \; \mathsf{sim}^{|R}\right)$$
$$\leq \widehat{\Gamma}^{\mathsf{NA}}\left(\overline{{}^{\lceil\ell|}\mathbf{RO} \; \mathsf{sim}^{|R\rceil}}\right)$$
$$\leq R \cdot 2^{-n} .$$

The proof of the following lemma completes the proof of Theorem 4.

Lemma 5. *Consider the protocol* amp_c *and the simulator* sim *defined in Fig. 2 and Alg. 1, respectively. Let* $\lceil\mathbf{RO} \; \mathsf{sim}\rceil$ *denote the game which is won if and only if the event* hit *in* sim *is provoked. Then,*

$$\lceil\mathbf{RO} \; \mathsf{sim}\rceil \; \models \; \mathsf{amp}_c \; \mathbf{RO} .$$

Proof. Let us denote by $\mathbf{R}$ and $\widehat{\mathbf{S}}$ the systems $\mathsf{amp}_c \; \mathbf{RO}$ and $\lceil\mathbf{RO} \; \mathsf{sim}\rceil$, respectively (where $\widehat{\mathbf{S}}$ is actually a game). We need to show that $\widehat{\mathbf{S}} \models \mathbf{R}$. We are going to argue that as long as the game $\widehat{\mathbf{S}}$ is not won, the probability distribution of the response to any possible query is the same in both $\mathbf{R}$ and $\widehat{\mathbf{S}}^{\dashv}$. Both systems reply consistently to any repeated queries, let us hence without loss of generality only consider fresh queries. To analyze the sampling process of responses, note that we can see both $\mathbf{R}$ and $\widehat{\mathbf{S}}^{\dashv}$ as generating the responses to all possible queries in advance (according to distributions described below) and then using the pre-generated responses to answer all actual queries. To describe these distributions, let us denote by $Left(x)$ and $Right(v)$ the responses of the system in question (either $\mathbf{R}$ or $\widehat{\mathbf{S}}^{\dashv}$) to queries (left, x) and (right, v), respectively. The (inefficient) sampling processes for the systems $\mathbf{R}$ and $\widehat{\mathbf{S}}^{\dashv}$ (as long as the game is not won) are described in Alg. 2 and 3, respectively. It is now easy to see that these two sampling processes result in the same distribution of all the random variables $Left(x)$ and $Right(v)$. $\qquad\square$

Algorithm 2. Sampling for $\mathbf{R}$

1. **foreach** $x \in \{0,1\}^*$ **do**
   $U_1, \ldots, U_c \xleftarrow{\$} \{0,1\}^n$
   $Right(\lfloor x \rceil \| \langle 1 \rangle) := U_1$
   $Right(\lfloor x \rceil \| \langle j \rangle \| U_{j-1}) := U_j$,
   for all $j \in \{1, \ldots, c\}$
   $Left(x) := U_c$
2. Sample all remaining values
   $Right(v) \xleftarrow{\$} \{0,1\}^n$

Algorithm 3. Sampling for $\widehat{\mathbf{S}}^{\dashv}$

1. **foreach** $x \in \{0,1\}^*$ **do**
   $Left(x) \xleftarrow{\$} \{0,1\}^n$
   $U_1, \ldots, U_{c-1} \xleftarrow{\$} \{0,1\}^n$
   $Right(\lfloor x \rceil \| \langle 1 \rangle) := U_1$
   $Right(\lfloor x \rceil \| \langle j \rangle \| U_{j-1}) := U_j$,
   for all $j \in \{1, \ldots, c-1\}$
   $Right(\lfloor x \rceil \| \langle c \rangle \| U_{c-1}) :=$
   $Left(x)$
2. Sample all remaining values
   $Right(v) \xleftarrow{\$} \{0,1\}^n$

Acknowledgments. The authors wish to thank Philip Rogaway and the anonymous reviewers for their valuable comments.

Grégory Demay is supported by the Zurich Information Security and Privacy Center (ZISC). Peter Gaži is supported by the European Research Council under an ERC Starting Grant (259668-PSPC). Björn Tackmann is supported by the Swiss National Science Foundation (SNF).

References

1. Bellare, M., Ristenpart, T., Tessaro, S.: Multi-instance Security and Its Application to Password-Based Cryptography. In: Safavi-Naini, R., Canetti, R. (eds.) CRYPTO 2012. LNCS, vol. 7417, pp. 312–329. Springer, Heidelberg (2012)
2. Bellare, M., Rogaway, P.: Random Oracles Are Practical: A Paradigm for Designing Efficient Protocols. In: Proceedings of the 1st ACM Conference on Computer and Communications Security, CCS 1993, pp. 62–73. ACM, New York (1993)
3. Bellare, M., Rogaway, P.: The Security of Triple Encryption and a Framework for Code-Based Game-Playing Proofs. In: Vaudenay, S. (ed.) EUROCRYPT 2006. LNCS, vol. 4004, pp. 409–426. Springer, Heidelberg (2006)
4. Bertoni, G., Daemen, J., Peeters, M., Van Assche, G.: On the Indifferentiability of the Sponge Construction. In: Smart, N.P. (ed.) EUROCRYPT 2008. LNCS, vol. 4965, pp. 181–197. Springer, Heidelberg (2008)
5. Coretti, S., Maurer, U., Tackmann, B., Venturi, D.: From Single-Bit to Multi-Bit Public-Key Encryption via Non-Malleable Codes. In: Dodis, Y., Nielsen, J.B. (eds.) TCC 2015, Part I. LNCS, vol. 9014, pp. 532–560. Springer, Heidelberg (2015)
6. Coron, J.-S., Dodis, Y., Malinaud, C., Puniya, P.: Merkle-Damgård Revisited: How to Construct a Hash Function. In: Shoup, V. (ed.) CRYPTO 2005. LNCS, vol. 3621, pp. 430–448. Springer, Heidelberg (2005)
7. Demay, G., Gaži, P., Hirt, M., Maurer, U.: Resource-Restricted Indifferentiability. In: Johansson, T., Nguyen, P.Q. (eds.) EUROCRYPT 2013. LNCS, vol. 7881, pp. 664–683. Springer, Heidelberg (2013)
8. Dodis, Y., Ristenpart, T., Steinberger, J., Tessaro, S.: To Hash or Not to Hash Again (In)Differentiability Results for H^2 and HMAC. In: Safavi-Naini, R., Canetti, R. (eds.) CRYPTO 2012. LNCS, vol. 7417, pp. 348–366. Springer, Heidelberg (2012)
9. Dwork, C., Naor, M.: Pricing via Processing or Combatting Junk Mail. In: Brickell, E.F. (ed.) CRYPTO 1992. LNCS, vol. 740, pp. 139–147. Springer, Heidelberg (1993)
10. Holenstein, T., Künzler, R., Tessaro, S.: The Equivalence of the Random Oracle Model and the Ideal Cipher Model, Revisited. In: Proceedings of the Forty-third Annual ACM Symposium on Theory of Computing, STOC 2011, pp. 89–98. ACM, New York (2011)
11. Jetchev, D., Özen, O., Stam, M.: Understanding Adaptivity: Random Systems Revisited. In: Wang, X., Sako, K. (eds.) ASIACRYPT 2012. LNCS, vol. 7658, pp. 313–330. Springer, Heidelberg (2012)
12. Kaliski, B.: PKCS #5: Password-Based Cryptography Specification Version 2.0. RFC 2898, RFC Editor (September 2000)
13. Maurer, U.: Conditional Equivalence of Random Systems and Indistinguishability Proofs. In: 2013 IEEE International Symposium on Information Theory Proceedings (ISIT), pp. 3150–3154 (July 2013)
14. Maurer, U.M.: Indistinguishability of Random Systems. In: Knudsen, L.R. (ed.) EUROCRYPT 2002. LNCS, vol. 2332, pp. 110–132. Springer, Heidelberg (2002)

15. Maurer, U.: Constructive Cryptography – A New Paradigm for Security Definitions and Proofs. In: Mödersheim, S., Palamidessi, C. (eds.) TOSCA 2011. LNCS, vol. 6993, pp. 33–56. Springer, Heidelberg (2012)
16. Maurer, U., Pietrzak, K., Renner, R.S.: Indistinguishability Amplification. In: Menezes, A. (ed.) CRYPTO 2007. LNCS, vol. 4622, pp. 130–149. Springer, Heidelberg (2007)
17. Maurer, U., Renner, R.: Abstract Cryptography. In: Chazelle, B. (ed.) The Second Symposium in Innovations in Computer Science, ICS 2011, pp. 1–21. Tsinghua University Press (January 2011)
18. Maurer, U.M., Renner, R.S., Holenstein, C.: Indifferentiability, Impossibility Results on Reductions, and Applications to the Random Oracle Methodology. In: Naor, M. (ed.) TCC 2004. LNCS, vol. 2951, pp. 21–39. Springer, Heidelberg (2004)
19. Maurer, U., Tackmann, B.: On the Soundness of Authenticate-then-encrypt: Formalizing the Malleability of Symmetric Encryption. In: Proceedings of the 17th ACM Conference on Computer and Communications Security, CCS 2010, pp. 505–515. ACM, New York (2010)
20. Morris, R., Thompson, K.: Password Security: A Case History. Commun. ACM 22(11), 594–597 (1979)
21. Nakamoto, S.: Bitcoin: A peer-to-peer electronic cash system (2008)
22. Naor, M.: Moderately Hard Functions: From Complexity to Spam Fighting. In: Pandya, P.K., Radhakrishnan, J. (eds.) FSTTCS 2003. LNCS, vol. 2914, pp. 434–442. Springer, Heidelberg (2003)
23. Provos, N., Mazieres, D.: A Future-Adaptable Password Scheme. In: USENIX Annual Technical Conference, FREENIX Track, pp. 81–91 (1999)
24. Ristenpart, T., Shacham, H., Shrimpton, T.: Careful with Composition: Limitations of the Indifferentiability Framework. In: Paterson, K.G. (ed.) EUROCRYPT 2011. LNCS, vol. 6632, pp. 487–506. Springer, Heidelberg (2011)
25. Secure Hash Standard. National Institute of Standards and Technology, NIST FIPS PUB 180-4, U.S. Department of Commerce (2012)
26. SHA-3 Standard. National Institute of Standards and Technology (NIST), Draft FIPS Publication 202, U.S. Department of Commerce (April 2014)
27. Tackmann, B.: A Theory of Secure Communication. Ph.D. thesis, ETH Zürich (August 2014)
28. Turan, M.S., Barker, E., Burr, W., Chen, L.: Recommendation for Password-Based Key Derivation. NIST Special Publication 800-132, National Institute of Standards and Technology (December 2010)

The Chaining Lemma and Its Application

Ivan Damgård[1,*], Sebastian Faust[2,**], Pratyay Mukherjee[1,***],
and Daniele Venturi[3]

[1] Aarhus University
[2] EPFL
[3] Sapienza University of Rome

Abstract. We present a new information-theoretic result which we call
the Chaining Lemma. It considers a so-called "chain" of random variables, defined by a source distribution $X^{(0)}$ with high min-entropy and a
number (say, t in total) of arbitrary functions $(T_1, \ldots, T_t)$ which are applied in succession to that source to generate the chain $X^{(0)} \xrightarrow{T_1} X^{(1)} \xrightarrow{T_2}$
$X^{(2)} \ldots \xrightarrow{T_t} X^{(t)}$. Intuitively, the Chaining Lemma guarantees that, if
the chain is not too long, then either (i) the entire chain is "highly random", in that every variable has high min-entropy; or (ii) it is possible
to find a point j ($1 \leq j \leq t$) in the chain such that, conditioned on the
end of the chain i.e. $X^{(j)} \xrightarrow{T_{j+1}} X^{(j+1)} \ldots \xrightarrow{T_t} X^{(t)}$, the preceding part
$X^{(0)} \xrightarrow{T_1} X^{(1)} \ldots \xrightarrow{T_j} X^{(j)}$ remains highly random. We think this is an
interesting information-theoretic result which is intuitive but neverthe-
less requires rigorous case-analysis to prove.

We believe that the above lemma will find applications in cryptography. We give an example of this, namely we show an application of the
lemma to protect essentially any cryptographic scheme against memory-
tampering attacks. We allow several tampering requests, the tampering
functions can be arbitrary, however, they must be chosen from a bounded
size set of functions that is fixed a priori.

1 Introduction

Assume that we have a uniform random distribution over some finite set $\mathcal{X}$,
represented by a discrete random variable X. Let us now apply an arbitrary
(deterministic) function T to X and denote the output random variable by
$X' = T(X)$. Since T is an arbitrary function, the variable X' can also be arbitrarily distributed. Consider now the case where X' is "easy to predict", or
more concretely where X' has "low" min-entropy. A natural question, in this
case, is *how much information can X' reveal about X?* or more formally, *how
much min-entropy can X have if we condition on X'?*

* Partially supported by Danish Council for Independent Research via DFF Starting
  Grant 10-081612.
** Supported by the Marie Curie IEF/FP7 project GAPS, grant number: 626467.
*** Partially supported by Danish Council for Independent Research via DFF Starting
  Grant 10-081612. Partially supported by the ERC Starting Grant 279447.

© Springer International Publishing Switzerland 2015
A. Lehmann and S. Wolf (Eds.): ICITS 2015, LNCS 9063, pp. 181–196, 2015.
DOI: 10.1007/978-3-319-17470-9_11

Intuitively, one might expect that since X' has low entropy, it cannot tell us much about X, so X should still be "close to random" and hence have high entropy. While this would be true for Shannon entropy, it turns out to be completely false for min-entropy. This may seem a bit counter-intuitive at first, but is actually easy to see from an example: Let T be the function which maps half of the elements in $\mathcal{X}$ to one "heavy" point but is injective on all the other elements. For this T, the variable X' has very small min-entropy (namely 1) because the heavy point occurs with probability $1/2$. But on the other hand, X' reveals everything about X half the time, and so the entropy of X in fact decreases very significantly (on average) when X' is given. So despite having very low min-entropy, $X' = T(X)$ does reveal a lot about X.

There is, however, a more refined statement that will be true for min-entropy: Let E be the event that X takes one of the values that are *not* mapped to the "heavy point" by T, while $\bar{E}$ is the event that X is mapped to the heavy point. Now, conditioned on E, both $X_{|E}$ and $X'_{|E}$ have high min-entropy. On the other hand, conditioned on $\bar{E}$, $X_{|\bar{E}}$ will clearly have the same (high) min-entropy whether we are given $X'_{|E}$ or not.

This simple observation leads to the following conjecture: there always exists an event E such that: (i) Conditioned on E, both X and X' have "high" min-entropy, (ii) conditioned on $\bar{E}$, X' reveals "little" about X. In this paper, from a very high-level, we mainly focus into settling (a generalization of) this conjecture, which results in our main contribution: the information-theoretic lemma which we call the Chaining Lemma.

Main Question. Towards generalizing the above setting let us rename, for notational convenience, the above symbols as follows: $X^{(0)} \equiv X$, $T_1 \equiv T$ and $X^{(1)} \equiv X'$. We consider t (deterministic) functions $T_1, T_2, \ldots, T_t$ which are applied to the the variables sequentially starting from $X^{(0)}$. In particular, each T_i is applied to $X^{(i-1)}$ to produce a new variable $X^{(i)} = T_i(X^{(i-1)})$ for $i \in [t]$. We call the sequence of variables $(X^{(0)}, \ldots, X^{(t)})$ a "chain" which is completely defined by the "source" distribution $X^{(0)}$ and the sequence of t functions $(T_1, \ldots, T_t)$. It can be presented more vividly as follows: $X^{(0)} \xrightarrow{T_1} X^{(1)} \xrightarrow{T_2} X^{(2)} \ldots \xrightarrow{T_t} X^{(t)}$.

We are now interested in the min-entropy of $X^{(1)}, \ldots, X^{(t)}$. Of course, each variable $X^{(i)}$ has min-entropy less than (or equal to) the preceding variable $X^{(i-1)}$ (as a deterministic function can not generate randomness). Assume now that we fix some threshold value u and consider any value of min-entropy less than u to be "low". Assume further that the source has min-entropy much larger than u. As a motivation, one may think of a setting where each $X^{(i)}$ is used as key in some cryptographic application, where, as long $X^{(i)}$ has high min-entropy we are fine and the adversary will not learn something he should not. But if $X^{(i)}$ has low min-entropy, things might go wrong and the adversary might learn $X^{(i)}$.

Now, there are two possible scenarios for the above chain: either (i) all the variables (hence the last variable $X^{(t)}$) in the chain have high min-entropy; or (ii) one or more variable (obviously including the last variable $X^{(t)}$) has low min-entropy. In case (i), everything is fine. But in case (ii), things might go wrong at a certain point. We now want to ask if we can at least "save" some part of the chain, i.e., *can we find a point in the chain such that if we condition on all the variables after that point, all the preceding variables (obviously including the source $X^{(0)}$) would still have high min-entropy?* This hope might be justified if t is small enough compared to the entropy of $X^{(0)}$: since the entropy drops below u after a small number of steps, there must be a point (say j) where the entropy falls "sharply", i.e., $X^{(j)}$ has much smaller min-entropy than $X^{(j-1)}$. However, as the above example shows, even if there is a large gap in min-entropy between two successive variables ($X^{(j)}$ and $X^{(j-1)}$ in this case), the succeeding one ($X^{(j)}$) might actually reveal a lot about the preceding one ($X^{(j-1)}$) on average. So it is not clear that we can use j as the point we are looking for. However, one could hope that a generalised version of the above conjecture might be true, namely there might exist some event, further conditioning on which, all variables would have high min-entropy, and on the other hand, conditioning on the complement, $X^{(j-1)}$ (and hence the entire preceding chain) would have high min-entropy. Essentially that is what our Chaining Lemma says, which we present next although in an informal way. We give the formal statement and proof of the lemma in Section 3.

Lemma 1 (The Chaining Lemma, Informal). *Let $X^{(0)}$ be a uniform random variable over $\mathcal{X}$ and $(T_0, \ldots, T_t)$ be arbitrary functions mapping $\mathcal{X} \to \mathcal{X}$ and defining a chain $X^{(0)} \xrightarrow{T_1} X^{(1)} \xrightarrow{T_2} X^{(2)} \ldots \xrightarrow{T_t} X^{(t)}$. If the chain is "sufficiently short", there exists an event E such that (i) if E happens, then all the variables $(X^{(0)}, \ldots, X^{(t)})$ (conditioned on E) have "high" min-entropy; otherwise (ii) if E does not happen there is an index j such that conditioning on $X^{(j)}$ (and also on $\bar{E}$) all the previous variables namely $X^{(0)}, \ldots, X^{(j-1)}$ have "high" min-entropy.*

Application to Tamper-resilient Cryptography. Although we think that the Chaining Lemma is interesting in its own right, in this paper we provide an application in cryptography, precisely in tamper-resilient cryptography. In tamper-resilient cryptography the main goal is to "theoretically" protect cryptographic schemes against so-called fault attacks which are found to be devastating (as shown by [5,12] and many more). In this model, the adversary, in addition to standard black-box access to a primitive, is allowed to change its secret state [9,28,23,32,8], or its internals [30,27,18,19], and observes the effect of such changes at the output. In this paper we restrict ourselves to the model where the adversary is not allowed to alter the computation, but only the secret state (i.e. only the memory of the device, but not the circuitry, is subject to tampering).

To illustrate such memory tampering, consider a digital signature scheme Sign with public/secret key pair (pk, sk). The tampering adversary obtains pk and can replace sk with $T(sk)$ for arbitrary tampering function T. Then, the adversary gets access to an oracle $\mathsf{Sign}(T(sk), \cdot)$, i.e., to a signing oracle running with the tampered key $T(sk)$. As usual the adversary wins the game by outputting a valid forgery with respect to the original public key pk.[1] In the most general setting, the adversary is allowed to ask an arbitrary polynomial number of tampering queries. However, a general impossibility result by Gennaro et al. [28] shows that the above flavour of tamper resistance is unachievable without further assumptions. To overcome this impossibility one usually relies on self-destruct (e.g., [23,15,1,14,13,24,25,26,17,2,3,4,16,31]), or limits the power of the tampering function (e.g., [9,33,7,6,29,34,36,10,11,31,35]).

Recently Damgård et al. [20] proposed a different approach where, instead of limiting the type of allowed modifications, one assumes an upper bound on the number of tampering queries that the adversary can ask, so that now the attacker can issue some a-priori fixed number t of *arbitrary* tampering queries. As argued by [20], this limitation is more likely to capture realistic tampering attacks. They also show how to construct public key encryption and identification schemes secure against bounded leakage[2] and tampering (BLT) attacks.

The above model fits perfectly with the setting of the Chaining Lemma, as we consider a limited number of tampering functions $(T_1, \ldots, T_t)$, for some fixed bound t, applied on a uniform (or close to uniform) secret-state $X^{(0)}$. Now recall that Lemma 1 guarantees that, for "small enough" t, the source distribution stays unpredictable in essentially "any" case. Therefore, the source can be used as a "highly unpredictable" secret-key resisting t arbitrary tampering attacks. As a basic application of the Chaining Lemma, we show in Section 4 that *any* cryptographic scheme can be made secure in the BLT model. To the best of our knowledge, this is the first such general result that holds for arbitrary tampering functions and multiple tampering queries. The price we pay for this is that the tampering functions must be chosen from a bounded-size set that is fixed a priori.

Previous work by Faust et al. [26], shows how to protect generically against tampering using a new primitive called *non-malleable key-derivation*. This result also works for arbitrary tampering functions, does not require that a small set of functions is fixed in advance, but works only for one-time tampering.

2   Preliminaries

2.1   Notation

For $n \in \mathbb{N}$, we write $[n] := \{1, \ldots, n\}$. Given a set $\mathcal{S}$, we write $s \leftarrow \mathcal{S}$ to denote that element s is sampled uniformly from $\mathcal{S}$. If A is an algorithm, $y \leftarrow \mathsf{A}(x)$ denotes an execution of A with input x and output y; if A is randomized, then y is a random variable.

We denote with k the security parameter. A machine A is called *probabilistic polynomial time* (PPT) if for any input $x \in \{0,1\}^*$ the computation of $\mathsf{A}(x)$ terminates in at most $poly(|x|)$ steps and A is probabilistic (i.e., it uses randomness

---

[1] Notice that T may be the identity function, in which case we get the standard security notion of digital signature scheme as a special case.

[2] The adversary is also allowed to leak a bounded—yet arbitrary—amount of information on the secret key; we refer the reader to Section 4 for the details.

as part of its logic). Random variables are usually denoted by capital letters. We sometimes abuse notation and denote a distribution and the corresponding random variable with the same capital letter, say X. We write $\mathsf{sup}(X)$ for the support of X. Given an event E, we let $X_{|E}$ be the conditional distribution of X conditioned on E happening. The statistical distance of two random variables X and Y, defined over a common set $\mathcal{S}$ is $\Delta(X;Y) = \frac{1}{2}\sum_{s\in\mathcal{S}}|\Pr[X=s] - \Pr[Y=s]|$. Given a random variable Z, the statistical distance of X and Y conditioned on Z is defined as $\Delta(X;Y|Z) = \Delta((X,Z);(Y,Z))$.

2.2   Information Theory Basics

The min-entropy of a random variable X over a set $\mathcal{X}$ is defined as $\mathbf{H}_\infty(X) := -\log\max_x \Pr[X=x]$, and measures how X can be predicted by the best (unbounded) predictor. The conditional average min-entropy [22] of X given a random variable Z (over a set $\mathcal{Z}$) possibly dependent on X, is defined as

$$\widetilde{\mathbf{H}}_\infty(X|Z) := -\log\mathbb{E}_{z\leftarrow Z}[2^{-\mathbf{H}_\infty(X|Z=z)}] = -\log\sum_{z\in\mathcal{Z}}\Pr[Z=z]\cdot 2^{-\mathbf{H}_\infty(X|Z=z)}.$$

We say that a distribution X over a set $\mathcal{X}$ of size $|\mathcal{X}| = 2^n$ is (α, n)-good if $\mathbf{H}_\infty(X) \geq \alpha$ and $\Pr[X=x] \geq 2^{-n}$ for all $x \in \mathsf{sup}(X)$.

We will rely on the following basic property (see [22, Lemma 2.2]).

Lemma 2. *For all random variables X, Z and Λ over sets $\mathcal{X}$, $\mathcal{Z}$ and $\{0,1\}^\lambda$ such that $\widetilde{\mathbf{H}}_\infty(X|Z) \geq \alpha$, we have that*

$$\widetilde{\mathbf{H}}_\infty(X|Z,\Lambda) \geq \widetilde{\mathbf{H}}_\infty(X|Z) - \lambda \geq \alpha - \lambda.$$

The above lemma can be easily extended to the case of random variables Λ with bounded support, i.e., $\widetilde{\mathbf{H}}_\infty(X|Z,\Lambda) \geq \widetilde{\mathbf{H}}_\infty(X|Z) - \log|\mathsf{sup}(\Lambda)|$.

3   The Chaining Lemma

Before presenting the statement and proof of the Chaining Lemma, we state and prove two sub-lemmas. We do not provide any intuitions at this point regarding the whole proof of the Chaining Lemma due to involvement of rigorous case-analysis. Instead, we take a modular approach presenting intuitions step-by-step for each of the sub-lemmas and finally providing an intuition of the Chaining Lemma after the proof of these sub-lemmas.

The first lemma states that if the support of a distribution is sufficiently large then there always exists an event E such that, conditioned on E, the conditional distribution has high min-entropy.

Lemma 3. *For $n \in \mathbb{N}_{>1}$ let c be some parameter such that $\sqrt{n} < c < n$. Let $\mathcal{X}$ be a set of size $2^n = |\mathcal{X}|$ and X be a distribution over $\mathcal{X}$ with $|\mathsf{sup}(X)| > 2^c$ such that for all $x \in \mathsf{sup}(X)$ we have $\Pr[X=x] \geq \frac{1}{2^n}$. There exists an event E such that:*

(i) $\mathbf{H}_\infty(X_{|E}) > c - 2\sqrt{n}$, and
(ii) $|\sup(X_{|\overline{E}})| < |\sup(X)|$.

Proof. Intuitively, the lemma is proven by showing that if a distribution has sufficiently large support, then over a large subset of the support the distribution must be "almost" flat. We will describe below what it means for a distribution to be "almost flat". We then define an event E that occurs when X takes some value in the almost flat area. Clearly, X conditioned on E must be "almost" uniformly distributed, and if furthermore the support of X conditioned on E is still sufficiently large, we get that $\mathbf{H}_\infty(X_{|E})$ must be large. We proceed with the formal proof.

We introduce a parameter b which is a positive integer such that $c > n/b$. We explain how to set the value of b later. For ease of description we assume that n is a multiple of b. We start by defining what it means for an area to be flat. For some probability distribution X we define $k \in [2^{n/b} - 1]$ sets as follows:

- $I_k := \left\{ x \in \sup(X) : \frac{k^b}{2^n} \leq \Pr[X = x] < \frac{(k+1)^b}{2^n} \right\}$, for $k \in [2^{n/b} - 1]$ and
- $I_{2^{n/b}} := \{ x \in \sup(X) : \Pr[X = x] = 1 \}$.

These sets characterize the (potential) flat areas in the distribution X as the probability of all values in some set I_k lies in a certain range that is bounded from below and above. Clearly, the sets I_k are pairwise disjoint and cover the whole space between $1/2^n$ and 1. Therefore, each $x \in \sup(X)$ with some probability $\Pr[X = x]$ must fall into some unique set I_k.

We denote by I_m the set that contains the most elements among all sets I_k, and define the event E as the event that occurs when $x \in \sup(X)$ falls into I_m, i.e., X takes a value that falls in the largest set I_m. We now lower bound the probability that E occurs.

$$\Pr[E] \geq |I_m| \frac{m^b}{2^n} \tag{1}$$

$$\geq 2^{c-n/b} \frac{m^b}{2^n}. \tag{2}$$

Inequality (1) holds as for all $x \in I_m$ we have $\Pr[X = x] \geq \frac{m^b}{2^n}$. (2) follows from the fact that I_m must have size at least $2^{c-n/b}$, as there are $2^{n/b}$ sets and there are at least 2^c elements in the support of X.

As $\mathbf{H}_\infty(X_{|E}) = -\log \max_x \Pr[X = x|E]$, we can give a lower bound for the min entropy of $X_{|E}$ by upper bounding $\Pr[X = x|E]$. More precisely,

$$\Pr[X = x|E] = \frac{\Pr[X = x \wedge E]}{\Pr[E]}$$

$$< \frac{(m+1)^b/2^n}{2^{(c-n/b)}m^b/2^n} \tag{3}$$

$$= \left(1 + \frac{1}{m}\right)^b 2^{-c+n/b}$$

$$\leq 2^{b-c+n/b}. \tag{4}$$

Inequality (3) uses (2) and the fact that $\Pr[X = x \wedge E] < \frac{(m+1)^b}{2^n}$ by definition of I_m. (4) follows from $m \geq 1$. This implies that $\mathbf{H}_\infty(X_{|E}) > c - n/b - b$. Now we observe that the loss in min-entropy, given by $(b + n/b)$ is minimum when $b = \sqrt{n}$. Since b is a free parameter, we fix $b := \sqrt{n}$ (note that, since $c > \sqrt{n}$, the constraint $c > n/b$ holds) to get $\mathbf{H}_\infty(X_{|E}) > n - 2\sqrt{n}$ as stated in part (i) of the lemma.

For part (ii), it is easy to see from the definition of E that the support of the conditional probability distribution $X_{|\overline{E}}$ decreases by at least $2^{(c-n/b)}$ points (as these points belong to E). Clearly, $|\mathsf{sup}(X_{|\overline{E}})| \leq |\mathsf{sup}(X)| - 2^{c-n/b} < |\mathsf{sup}(X)|$ as stated in the lemma. □

In the following lemma we consider an arbitrary distribution X with sufficiently high min-entropy and some arbitrary function T. We show that if the support of $Y = T(X)$ is sufficiently large, then there exists an event E such that one of the following happens:

(i) The min-entropy of Y conditioned on the event E is high, i.e., Y conditioned on E has an almost flat area with large support;

(ii) If $\overline{E}$ happens, then the average min-entropy of X given Y is high. Intuitively, this means that Y conditioned on $\overline{E}$ has small support as then it does not "reveal" too much about X.

We formalize this statement in the lemma below.

Lemma 4. *For $n \in \mathbb{N}_{>1}$ let c, α be some parameters such that $\sqrt{n} < c < \alpha \leq n$. Let $\mathcal{X}$ be some set of size $2^n = |\mathcal{X}|$ and X be an (α, n)-good distribution over $\mathcal{X}$. For any function $T : \mathcal{X} \to \mathcal{X}$, let $Y = T(X)$ be such that $|\mathsf{sup}(Y)| > 2^c$. There exists an event E such that the following holds:*

(i) $\mathbf{H}_\infty(Y_{|E}) > c - 2\sqrt{n}$.

(ii) $\widetilde{\mathbf{H}}_\infty(X_{|\overline{E}}|Y_{|\overline{E}}) \geq \alpha - c - \log \frac{1}{1-\Pr[E]}$.

Proof. Intuitively, in the proof below we apply Lemma 3 iteratively to the distribution Y to find flat areas in Y. We "cut off" these flat areas until we have a distribution (derived from Y) which has sufficiently small support. Clearly such restricted Y cannot reveal too much information about X. To formalize this approach, we construct iteratively an event E by combining the events E_i obtained by applying Lemma 3 to Y. If E happens then Y takes values that lie in a large flat area. On the other hand $\overline{E}$ characterizes only a relatively small support, and hence giving such Y does not reveal much information (on average) about X. The formal proof with an explicit calculation of the parameters follows.

We will define the event E depending on events $\{E_i, E_i', E_i''\}_{i \in \{0,\ldots,m-1\}}$ (for some integer m) which we will specify later. These events partition the probability space as follows (cf. Figure 1):

$$E_i' := \bigwedge_{j=0}^{i} \overline{E}_j = \overline{E}_i \wedge E_{i-1}' \qquad E_i'' := E_i \wedge \left(\bigwedge_{j=0}^{i-1} \overline{E}_j \right) = E_i \wedge E_{i-1}'. \quad (5)$$

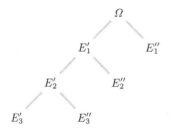
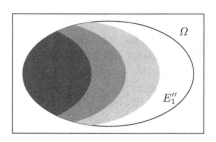

Fig. 1. Events covering the probability space in the proof of Lemma 4 and Lemma 5

We will rely on some properties of the above partition. In particular, note that for all $i \in \{0, \ldots, m-1\}$ we have

$$E'_i \vee E''_i = E'_{i-1} \qquad E'_i \wedge E''_i = \emptyset. \tag{6}$$

We start by constructing the events $\{E_i, E'_i, E''_i\}$ and conditional probability distributions $Y^{(i)}$ that are derived from Y by applying Lemma 3. Lemma 3 requires the following two conditions:

- $|\mathsf{sup}(Y^{(i)})| > 2^c$, and
- $\Pr[Y^{(i)} = y] \geq 2^{-n}$, for all $y \in \mathsf{sup}(Y^{(i)})$.

Clearly these two conditions are satisfied by $Y^{(0)} = Y$, since $Y^{(0)}$ is computed from X by applying a function T and for all $x \in \mathsf{sup}(X)$ the statement assumes $\Pr[X = x] \geq 2^{-n}$. Hence, Lemma 3 gives us an event E_0. We set and we define $Y^{(1)} = Y^{(0)}_{|\overline{E}_0}$. For all $i \geq 1$ we proceed to construct events E_i and conditional distributions $Y^{(i+1)} = Y^{(i)}_{|\overline{E}_i}$ as long as the requirements from above are satisfied. Notice that by applying Lemma 3 to distribution $Y^{(i)}$ we get for each event E_i:

- $\mathbf{H}_\infty(Y^{(i)}_{|E_i}) > c - 2\sqrt{n}$, and
- $|\mathsf{sup}(Y^{(i+1)})| < |\mathsf{sup}(Y^{(i)})|$.

Clearly, there are only finitely many (say m) events before we stop the iteration as the size of the support is strictly decreasing. At the stopping point we have $|\mathsf{sup}(Y^{(m-1)})| > 2^c$ and $|\mathsf{sup}(Y^{(m)})| \leq 2^c$. We define $E = \bigvee_{i=0}^{m-1} E_i = \bigvee_{i=0}^{m-1} E''_i$ and $\overline{E} = \bigwedge_{i=0}^{m-1} \overline{E}_i = E'_{m-1}$ and show in the claims below that they satisfy conditions (i) and (ii) of the lemma.

Claim. $\mathbf{H}_\infty(Y_{|E}) > c - 2\sqrt{n}$.

Proof. Recall that for each $0 \leq i \leq m-1$ we have

$$Y^{(i)}_{|E_i} = Y_{|E_i \wedge \overline{E}_{i-1} \ldots \wedge \overline{E}_0} \tag{7}$$

$$= Y_{|E''_i} \tag{8}$$

Eq. (7) follows from the definition of the conditional probability distribution $Y^{(i)}_{|E_i}$. Eq. (8) from the definition of the constructed events. From Eq. (8) and Lemma 3 we have for each $0 \le i \le m-1$ that $\mathbf{H}_\infty(Y_{|E''_i}) > c - 2\sqrt{n}$. As for each $0 \le i \le m-1$ we have $|\mathsf{sup}(Y_{|E})| \ge |\mathsf{sup}(Y_{|E''_i})|$ we get that $\mathbf{H}_\infty(Y_{|E}) > c - 2\sqrt{n}$. This concludes the proof of this claim. $\square$

Claim. $\widetilde{\mathbf{H}}_\infty(X_{|\overline{E}}|Y_{|\overline{E}}) \ge \alpha - c - \log \frac{1}{1 - \Pr[E]}$.

Proof. We first lower bound $\mathbf{H}_\infty(X_{|\overline{E}})$.

$$\mathbf{H}_\infty(X_{|\overline{E}}) = -\log\left(\max_x \frac{\Pr[X = x \wedge \overline{E}]}{\Pr[\overline{E}]}\right) \tag{9}$$

$$\ge -\log\left(\frac{1}{\Pr[\overline{E}]} \max_x \Pr[X = x]\right) \tag{10}$$

$$= \mathbf{H}_\infty(X) - \log \frac{1}{\Pr[\overline{E}]} \ge \alpha - \log \frac{1}{1 - \Pr[E]}. \tag{11}$$

Eq. (9) follows from the definition of min-entropy and the definition of conditional probability. Eq. (10) follows from the basic fact that for any two events $\Pr[E \wedge E'] \le \Pr[E]$. Finally, we get Eq. (11) from our assumption that $\mathbf{H}_\infty(X) \ge \alpha$. To conclude the claim we compute:

$$\widetilde{\mathbf{H}}_\infty(X_{|\overline{E}}|Y_{|\overline{E}}) \ge \mathbf{H}_\infty(X_{|\overline{E}}, Y_{|\overline{E}}) - \log|\mathsf{sup}(Y_{|\overline{E}})| \tag{12}$$

$$= \mathbf{H}_\infty(X_{|\overline{E}}) - \log|\mathsf{sup}(Y_{|\overline{E}})| \tag{13}$$

$$\ge \alpha - \log \frac{1}{1 - \Pr[E]} - c = \alpha - c - \log \frac{1}{1 - \Pr[E]}. \tag{14}$$

Eq. (12) follows from Lemma 2 and (13) from the fact that $Y_{|\overline{E}}$ is computed as a function from $X_{|\overline{E}}$. Inequality (14) follows from (11) and the fact that the size of $\mathsf{sup}(Y_{|\overline{E}})$ is at most c. The latter follows from the definition of the event $\overline{E} = E'_{m-1}$ which in turn implies that $|\mathsf{sup}(Y_{|\overline{E}})| = |\mathsf{sup}(Y_{|E'_{m-1}})| = |\mathsf{sup}(Y^{(m-1)}_{|\overline{E}_{m-1}})| = |\mathsf{sup}(Y^{(m)})| \le 2^c$, which concludes the proof. $\square$

The above two claims finish the proof. $\square$

We now turn to state and prove the Chaining Lemma.

Lemma 5 (The Chaining Lemma). *For $n \in \mathbb{N}_{>1}$ let $\alpha, \beta, t, \epsilon$ be some parameters where $t \in \mathbb{N}$, $0 < \alpha \le n$, $\beta > 0$, $\epsilon \in (0, 1]$ and $t \le \frac{\alpha - \beta}{\beta + 2\sqrt{n}}$. Let $\mathcal{X}$ be some set of size $|\mathcal{X}| = 2^n$ and let $X^{(0)}$ be a (α, n)-good distribution over $\mathcal{X}$. For $i \in [t]$ let $T_i : \mathcal{X} \to \mathcal{X}$ be arbitrary functions and $X^{(i)} = T_i(X^{(i-1)})$. There exists an event E such that:*

(i) If $\Pr[E] > 0$, *for all* $i \in [t]$, $\mathbf{H}_\infty(X_{|E}^{(i)}) \geq \beta$.

(ii) If $\Pr[\overline{E}] \geq \epsilon$ *there exists an index* $j \in [t]$ *such that*

$$\widetilde{\mathbf{H}}_\infty(X_{|\overline{E}}^{(j-1)}|X_{|\overline{E}}^{(j)}) \geq \beta - \log\frac{t}{\epsilon}.$$

Proof. Consider the chain of random variables $X^{(0)} \xrightarrow{T_1} X^{(1)} \xrightarrow{T_2} \ldots \xrightarrow{T_t} X^{(t)}$. Given a pair of random variables in the chain, we refer to $X^{(i-1)}$ as the "source distribution" and to $X^{(i)}$ as the "target distribution". The main idea is to consider different cases depending on the characteristics of the target distribution. In case the min-entropy of $X^{(i)}$ is high enough to start with, we get immediately property (i) of the statement and we can immediately move to the next pair of random variables in the chain. In case the min-entropy of $X^{(i)}$ is small, we further consider two different sub-cases depending on some bound on the support of the variable. If the support of $X^{(i)}$ happens to be "small", intuitively we can condition on the target distribution since this cannot reveal much about the source; roughly this implies property (ii) of the statement. On the other hand, if the support happens to be not small enough, we are not in a position which allows us to condition on $X^{(i)}$.

In the latter case, we will invoke Lemma 4. Roughly this guarantees that there exists some event such that, conditioned on this event happening, the target lies in a large "flat" area and the conditional distribution has high min-entropy; this yields property (i) of the statement. If instead the event does not happen, then conditioning on the event not happening we get a "restricted" distribution with small enough support which leads again to property (ii) of the statement.

Whenever we are in those cases where (possibly conditioning on some event) the target distribution has high min-entropy, we move forward in the chain by considering $X^{(i)}$ as the source and $X^{(i+1)}$ as the target. However, when we reach a situation where we can "reveal" the target distribution we do not proceed further, since the remaining values can be computed as a deterministic function of the revealed distribution and, as such, do not constrain the min-entropy further. We now proceed with the formal proof.

Similar to Lemma 4, we will define the event E depending on events $\{E_i, E_i', E_i''\}_{i \in [t]}$ which we will specify later. These events partition the probability space as follows (cf. Figure 1):

$$E_i' := \bigwedge_{j=1}^{i} E_j = E_i \wedge E_{i-1}' \qquad E_i'' := \overline{E}_i \wedge \left(\bigwedge_{j=1}^{i-1} E_j\right) = \overline{E}_i \wedge E_{i-1}'. \quad (15)$$

We will rely on some properties of the above partition. In particular, note that for all $i \in [t]$ we have

$$E_i' \vee E_i'' = E_{i-1}' \qquad\qquad E_i' \wedge E_i'' = \emptyset. \quad (16)$$

For all $i \in [t+1]$, define the following parameters:

$$s_i = (t - i + 1)(\beta + 2\sqrt{n}) \quad (17)$$

$$\alpha_{i-1} = \beta + s_i. \quad (18)$$

Note that using the bound on t from the statement of the lemma, we get $\alpha \geq \alpha_0$; moreover, it is easy to verify that $\alpha_{i-1} > s_i > \sqrt{n}$ for all $i \in [t]$.

In the next claim we construct the events $\{E_i, E_i', E_i''\}_{i \in [t]}$.

Claim. For all $i = 0, \ldots, t - 1$, there exist events E_{i+1}' and E_{i+1}'' (as given in Eq. (16)) such that the following hold:

(*) If $\Pr\left[E_{i+1}'\right] > 0$, $\mathbf{H}_\infty(X_{|E_{i+1}'}^{(i+1)}) \geq \alpha_{i+1}$.

(**) If $\Pr\left[E_{i+1}''\right] \geq \epsilon'$, $\widetilde{\mathbf{H}}_\infty(X_{|E_{i+1}''}^{(i)} | X_{|E_{i+1}''}^{(i+1)}) \geq \beta - \log \frac{1}{\epsilon'}$. where $0 < \epsilon' \leq 1$.

Proof. We prove the claim by induction.

<u>*Base Case:*</u> In this case we let E_0 denote the whole probability space and thus $\Pr[E_0] = 1$. Note that $\mathbf{H}_\infty(X_{|E_0}^{(0)}) = \mathbf{H}_\infty(X^{(0)}) = \alpha \geq \alpha_0$. The rest of the proof for the base case is almost the same to that of the inductive step except the use of the above property instead of the induction hypothesis. Therefore we only prove the induction step in detail here. The proof details for the base case are a straightforward adaptation, with some notational changes.

<u>*Induction Step:*</u> The following holds by the *induction hypothesis*:

(*) If $\Pr\left[E_i'\right] > 0$, then $\mathbf{H}_\infty(X_{|E_i'}^{(i)}) \geq \alpha_i$.

(**) If $\Pr\left[E_i''\right] \geq \epsilon'$ then, $\widetilde{\mathbf{H}}_\infty(X_{|E_i''}^{(i-1)} | X_{|E_i''}^{(i)}) \geq \beta - \log \frac{1}{\epsilon'}$ where $0 < \epsilon' \leq 1$.

By construction of the events, E_i' is partitioned into two sub-events E_{i+1}' and E_{i+1}'' (cf. Eq. 16). From the statement of the claim we observe that, since we are assuming $\Pr\left[E_{i+1}'\right] > 0$ in (*) and $\Pr\left[E_{i+1}''\right] \geq \epsilon' > 0$ in (**), in both cases we have $\Pr\left[E_i'\right] > 0$. Hence, property (*) from the induction hypothesis holds: $\mathbf{H}_\infty(X_{|E_i'}^{(i)}) \geq \alpha_i$, which we use to prove the inductive step. We will define the events E_{i+1}' and E_{i+1}'' differently depending on several (complete) cases. For each of these cases we will show that property (*) and (**) hold.

Suppose first that $\mathbf{H}_\infty(X_{|E_i'}^{(i+1)}) \geq \alpha_{i+1}$. In this case we define E_{i+1}' to be E_i', which implies $E_{i+1}'' = \emptyset$ by Eq. (16). Moreover property (*) holds since, if $\Pr\left[E_{i+1}'\right] > 0$, then $\Pr\left[E_i'\right] > 0$ and $\mathbf{H}_\infty(X_{|E_{i+1}'}^{(i+1)}) = \mathbf{H}_\infty(X_{|E_i'}^{(i+1)}) \geq \alpha_{i+1}$; as for property (**) there is nothing to prove, since $\Pr\left[E_{i+1}''\right] = 0$ in this case.

Consider now the case that $\mathbf{H}_\infty(X_{|E_i'}^{(i+1)}) < \alpha_{i+1}$. Here we consider two sub-cases, depending on the support size of $X^{(i+1)}$.

1. $|\mathsf{sup}(X_{|E_i'}^{(i+1)})| \leq 2^{s_{i+1}}$. We define $E_{i+1}'' = E_i'$, which implies $E_{i+1}' = \emptyset$ by Eq. (16). As for property (*) there is nothing to prove, since $\Pr\left[E_{i+1}'\right] = 0$. To prove property (**) we observe that if $\Pr\left[E_{i+1}''\right] \geq \epsilon' > 0$, then

$\Pr\left[E_i'\right] > 0$. Hence,

$$\widetilde{\mathbf{H}}_\infty(X^{(i)}_{|E''_{i+1}}|X^{(i+1)}_{|E''_{i+1}}) = \widetilde{\mathbf{H}}_\infty(X^{(i)}_{|E'_i}|X^{(i+1)}_{|E'_i}) \tag{19}$$

$$\geq \mathbf{H}_\infty(X^{(i)}_{|E'_i}, X^{(i+1)}_{|E'_i}) - \log(|\mathsf{sup}(X^{(i+1)}_{|E'_i})|) \tag{20}$$

$$\geq \alpha_i - s_{i+1} \tag{21}$$

$$= \beta + s_{i+1} - s_{i+1} = \beta.$$

Eq. (19) follows as $E''_{i+1} = E'_i$. Eq. (20) follows from Lemma 2. Eq. (21) follows from two facts: (i) $X^{(i+1)}$ is a deterministic function of $X^{(i)}$, which means $\mathbf{H}_\infty(X^{(i)}_{|E'_i}, X^{(i+1)}_{|E'_i}) = \mathbf{H}_\infty(X^{(i)}_{|E'_i}) \geq \alpha_i$ (plugging-in the value from induction hypothesis), and (ii) $|\mathsf{sup}(X^{(i+1)}_{|E'_i})| \leq 2^{s_{i+1}}$.

2. $|\mathsf{sup}(X^{(i+1)}_{|E'_i})| > 2^{s_{i+1}}$. By the induction hypothesis $\mathbf{H}_\infty(X^{(i)}_{|E'_i}) \geq \alpha_i$; we now invoke Lemma 4 on the distribution $X^{(i+1)}_{|E'_i}$ (recall that $\alpha_i > s_{i+1} > \sqrt{n}$), to obtain the event E_{i+1} such that:

$$\mathbf{H}_\infty(X^{(i+1)}_{|E'_i \wedge E_{i+1}}) > s_{i+1} - 2\sqrt{n} \tag{22}$$

$$\widetilde{\mathbf{H}}_\infty(X^{(i)}_{|E'_i \wedge \overline{E}_{i+1}}|X^{(i+1)}_{|E'_i \wedge \overline{E}_{i+1}}) > \alpha_i - s_{i+1} - \log \frac{1}{1 - \Pr\left[E_{i+1}\right]}. \tag{23}$$

Note that by our definitions of the events E'_i, E''_i (cf. Eq. (15)), we have $E'_i \wedge E_{i+1} = E'_{i+1}$ and $E'_i \wedge \overline{E}_{i+1} = E''_{i+1}$.
To prove (*) we consider that if $\Pr\left[E'_{i+1}\right] > 0$, then $\Pr\left[E'_i\right] > 0$ and $\Pr\left[E_{i+1}\right] > 0$. Plugging the values of α_i and s_{i+1} from Eq. (18) and (17) into Eq. (22), we get

$$\mathbf{H}_\infty(X^{(i+1)}_{|E'_{i+1}}) > s_{i+1} - 2\sqrt{n}$$

$$= (t - i)(\beta + 2\sqrt{n}) - 2\sqrt{n}$$

$$= \beta + (t - i - 1)(\beta + 2\sqrt{n})$$

$$= \beta + s_{i+2} = \alpha_{i+1},$$

Similarly, to prove (**), we consider that if $\Pr\left[E''_{i+1}\right] \geq \epsilon'$, then $\Pr\left[E'_i\right] \geq \epsilon' > 0$ and $\Pr\left[\overline{E}_{i+1}\right] \geq \epsilon'$. Using Eq. (23), we obtain:

$$\widetilde{\mathbf{H}}_\infty(X^{(i)}_{|E''_{i+1}}|X^{(i+1)}_{|E''_{i+1}}) > \alpha_i - s_{i+1} - \log \frac{1}{\Pr\left[\overline{E}_{i+1}\right]}$$

$$= \beta - \log \frac{1}{\Pr\left[\overline{E}_{i+1}\right]}$$

$$\geq \beta - \log \frac{1}{\epsilon'},$$

This concludes the proof of the claim.   □

We define the event E to be $E = E'_t = \bigwedge_{i=1}^{t} E_i = \bigwedge_{i=1}^{t} E'_i$. It is easy to verify that this implies $\overline{E} = \bigvee_{i=1}^{t} E''_i$. We distinguish two cases:

- If $\Pr[E] > 0$, by definition of E we get that $\Pr[E'_i] > 0$ for all $i \in [t]$. In particular, $\Pr[E'_t] > 0$. Hence, $\mathbf{H}_\infty(X^{(t)}_{|E}) = \mathbf{H}_\infty(X^{(t)}_{|E'_t}) \geq \alpha_t = \beta$, where the last inequality follows from property (*) of the above Claim, using $i = t - 1$. Also, we observe that for all $i \in [t]$, $\mathbf{H}_\infty(X^{(i-1)}_{|E}) \geq \mathbf{H}_\infty(X^{(i)}_{|E})$. This proves property (i) of the lemma.
- If $\Pr[\overline{E}] \geq \epsilon$, then we get

$$\Pr\left[\bigvee_{i=1}^{t} E''_i\right] \geq \epsilon. \tag{24}$$

$$\sum_{i=1}^{t} \Pr[E''_i] \geq \epsilon. \tag{25}$$

Eq. (24) follows from the definition of E and Eq. (25) follows applying union bound. Clearly, from Eq. (25), there must exists some j such that $\Pr[E''_j] \geq \epsilon/t$.

Hence, putting $i = j - 1$ and $\epsilon' = \epsilon/t$ in property (**) of the above Claim, we get:

$$\widetilde{\mathbf{H}}_\infty(X^{(j-1)}_{|E''_j} | X^{(j)}_{|E''_j}) \geq \beta - \log \frac{t}{\epsilon}.$$

From the definition of E, E''_j implies $\overline{E}$ and hence property (ii) of the lemma follows.

$\square$

4   Application to Tamper-Resilient Cryptography

We show that *any* cryptographic primitive where the secret key can be chosen as a uniformly random string can be made secure in the BLT model of [20] by a simple and efficient transformation. Our result therefore covers pseudorandom functions, block ciphers, and many encryption and signature schemes. However, the result holds in a restricted model of tampering: the adversary first selects an arbitrary set of tampering functions of bounded size and, as he interacts with the scheme, he must choose every tampering function from the set that was specified initially. We call this the *semi-adaptive* BLT model. Our result holds only when the set of functions is "small enough".[3]

The basic intuition behind the construction using the Chaining Lemma is easy to explain. We use a random string X_0 as secret key, and a universal hash function h as public (and tamper proof) parameter. The construction then computes

---

[3] In particular, the adversary can choose a "short enough" sequence of tampering functions, from a set containing polynomially many such sequences.

$K_0 = h(X_0)$, and uses K_0 as secret key for the original primitive. The intuitive reason why one might hope this would work is as follows: each tampering query changes the key, so we get a chain of keys $X_0, X_1, \ldots, X_t$ where $X_i = T_i(X_{i-1})$ for some tampering function T_i. Recall that the chaining lemma guarantees that for such a chain, there exists an event E such that: (i) when E takes place then all X_i have high min-entropy, and, by a suitable choice of h, all the hash values $K_0 = h(X_0), K_1 = h(X_1), \ldots, K_t = h(X_t)$ are statistically close to uniformly and independently chosen keys; (ii) when E does not happen, for some index $j \in [t]$ we are able to reveal the value of X_j to the adversary as the X_i's with $i < j$ still have high entropy, and hence hash to independent values. On the other hand the X_i's with $i \geq j$ are a deterministic function of X_j and hence the tampering queries corresponding to any subsequent key can be simulated easily.

Due to its generality the above result suffers from two limitations. First, as already mentioned above, the tampering has to satisfy a somewhat limited form of adaptivity. Second, the number of tampering queries one can tolerate is upper bounded by the length n of the secret key. While this is true in general for schemes without key update, for our general result the limitation is rather strong. More concretely, with appropriately chosen parameters our transformation yields schemes that can tolerate up to $O(\sqrt[3]{n})$ tampering queries. We discuss the application in full detail in the full version of this paper [21].

Comparison with Faust et al. *[26].* Very recently, Faust *et al.* [26] introduced the concept of non-malleable key derivation which is similar in spirit to our application of the Chaining Lemma. Intuitively a function h is a non-malleable key derivation function if $h(X)$ is close to uniform even given the output of h applied to a related input $T(X)$, as long as $T(X) \neq X$. They show that a random t-wise independent hash function already meets this property, and moreover that such a function can be used to protect arbitrary cryptographic schemes (with a uniform key) against "one-time" tampering attacks (i.e., the adversary is allowed a single tampering query) albeit against a much bigger class of functions.[4]

We stress that the novelty of our result is in discovering the Chaining Lemma rather than this application, which can be instead thought of as a new technique, fundamentally different from that of [26], to achieve security in the BLT model. We believe that the Chaining Lemma is interesting in its own right, and might find more applications in cryptography in the future.

References

1. Aggarwal, D., Dodis, Y., Lovett, S.: Non-malleable codes from additive combinatorics. Electronic Colloquium on Computational Complexity (ECCC) 20, 81 (2013), To appear in STOC 2014
2. Agrawal, S., Gupta, D., Maji, H.K., Pandey, O., Prabhakaran, M.: Explicit non-malleable codes resistant to permutations. IACR Cryptology ePrint Archive, 2014:316 (2014)

---

[4] It might be possible to extend the analysis of [26] to bounded tampering, but this seems not straightforward.

3. Agrawal, S., Gupta, D., Maji, H.K., Pandey, O., Prabhakaran, M.: Explicit non-malleable codes resistant to permutations and perturbations. IACR Cryptology ePrint Archive, 2014:841 (2014)
4. Agrawal, S., Gupta, D., Maji, H.K., Pandey, O., Prabhakaran, M.: Explicit optimal-rate non-malleable codes against bit-wise tampering and permutations. IACR Cryptology ePrint Archive, 2014:842 (2014)
5. Anderson, R., Kuhn, M.: Tamper resistance: A cautionary note. In: WOEC 1996: Proceedings of the 2nd Conference on Proceedings of the Second USENIX Workshop on Electronic Commerce, pp. 1–1. USENIX Association, Berkeley (1996)
6. Applebaum, B., Harnik, D., Ishai, Y.: Semantic security under related-key attacks and applications. In: ICS, pp. 45–60 (2011)
7. Bellare, M., Cash, D.: Pseudorandom functions and permutations provably secure against related-key attacks. In: Rabin, T. (ed.) CRYPTO 2010. LNCS, vol. 6223, pp. 666–684. Springer, Heidelberg (2010)
8. Bellare, M., Cash, D., Miller, R.: Cryptography secure against related-key attacks and tampering. In: Lee, D.H., Wang, X. (eds.) ASIACRYPT 2011. LNCS, vol. 7073, pp. 486–503. Springer, Heidelberg (2011)
9. Bellare, M., Kohno, T.: A theoretical treatment of related-key attacks: RkA-PRPs, RkA-PRFs, and applications. In: Biham, E. (ed.) EUROCRYPT 2003. LNCS, vol. 2656, pp. 491–506. Springer, Heidelberg (2003)
10. Bellare, M., Paterson, K.G., Thomson, S.: RKA security beyond the linear barrier: IBE, encryption and signatures. In: Wang, X., Sako, K. (eds.) ASIACRYPT 2012. LNCS, vol. 7658, pp. 331–348. Springer, Heidelberg (2012)
11. Bhattacharyya, R., Roy, A.: Secure message authentication against related key attack. In: Moriai, S. (ed.) FSE 2013. LNCS, vol. 8424, pp. 305–324. Springer, Heidelberg (2014)
12. Boneh, D., DeMillo, R.A., Lipton, R.J.: On the importance of eliminating errors in cryptographic computations. J. Cryptology 14(2), 101–119 (2001)
13. Cheraghchi, M., Guruswami, V.: Capacity of non-malleable codes. In: ITCS, pp. 155–168 (2014)
14. Cheraghchi, M., Guruswami, V.: Non-malleable coding against bit-wise and split-state tampering. In: Lindell, Y. (ed.) TCC 2014. LNCS, vol. 8349, pp. 440–464. Springer, Heidelberg (2014)
15. Choi, S.G., Kiayias, A., Malkin, T.: BiTR: Built-in tamper resilience. In: Lee, D.H., Wang, X. (eds.) ASIACRYPT 2011. LNCS, vol. 7073, pp. 740–758. Springer, Heidelberg (2011)
16. Coretti, S., Dodis, Y., Tackmann, B., Venturi, D.: Self-destruct non-malleability. IACR Cryptology ePrint Archive, 2014:866 (2014)
17. Coretti, S., Maurer, U., Tackmann, B., Venturi, D.: From single-bit to multi-bit public-key encryption via non-malleable codes. IACR Cryptology ePrint Archive, 2014:324 (2014)
18. Dachman-Soled, D., Kalai, Y.T.: Securing circuits against constant-rate tampering. In: Safavi-Naini, R., Canetti, R. (eds.) CRYPTO 2012. LNCS, vol. 7417, pp. 533–551. Springer, Heidelberg (2012)
19. Dachman-Soled, D., Kalai, Y.T.: Securing circuits and protocols against $1/\mathrm{poly}(k)$ tampering rate. In: Lindell, Y. (ed.) TCC 2014. LNCS, vol. 8349, pp. 540–565. Springer, Heidelberg (2014)
20. Damgård, I., Faust, S., Mukherjee, P., Venturi, D.: Bounded tamper resilience: How to go beyond the algebraic barrier. In: Sako, K., Sarkar, P. (eds.) ASIACRYPT 2013, Part II. LNCS, vol. 8270, pp. 140–160. Springer, Heidelberg (2013)

21. Damgård, I., Faust, S., Mukherjee, P., Venturi, D.: The chaining lemma and its application. IACR Cryptology ePrint Archive, 2014:979 (2014)
22. Dodis, Y., Ostrovsky, R., Reyzin, L., Smith, A.: Fuzzy extractors: How to generate strong keys from biometrics and other noisy data. SIAM J. Comput. 38(1), 97–139 (2008)
23. Dziembowski, S., Pietrzak, K., Wichs, D.: Non-malleable codes. In: ICS, pp. 434–452 (2010)
24. Faust, S., Mukherjee, P., Nielsen, J.B., Venturi, D.: Continuous non-malleable codes. In: Lindell, Y. (ed.) TCC 2014. LNCS, vol. 8349, pp. 465–488. Springer, Heidelberg (2014)
25. Faust, S., Mukherjee, P., Nielsen, J.B., Venturi, D.: A tamper and leakage resilient von Neumann architecture. IACR Cryptology ePrint Archive, 2014:338 (2014)
26. Faust, S., Mukherjee, P., Venturi, D., Wichs, D.: Efficient non-malleable codes and key-derivation for poly-size tampering circuits. In: Nguyen, P.Q., Oswald, E. (eds.) EUROCRYPT 2014. LNCS, vol. 8441, pp. 111–128. Springer, Heidelberg (2014)
27. Faust, S., Pietrzak, K., Venturi, D.: Tamper-proof circuits: How to trade leakage for tamper-resilience. In: Aceto, L., Henzinger, M., Sgall, J. (eds.) ICALP 2011, Part I. LNCS, vol. 6755, pp. 391–402. Springer, Heidelberg (2011)
28. Gennaro, R., Lysyanskaya, A., Malkin, T., Micali, S., Rabin, T.: Algorithmic tamper-proof (ATP) security: Theoretical foundations for security against hardware tampering. In: Naor, M. (ed.) TCC 2004. LNCS, vol. 2951, pp. 258–277. Springer, Heidelberg (2004)
29. Goyal, V., O'Neill, A., Rao, V.: Correlated-input secure hash functions. In: Ishai, Y. (ed.) TCC 2011. LNCS, vol. 6597, pp. 182–200. Springer, Heidelberg (2011)
30. Ishai, Y., Prabhakaran, M., Sahai, A., Wagner, D.: Private circuits II: Keeping secrets in tamperable circuits. In: Vaudenay, S. (ed.) EUROCRYPT 2006. LNCS, vol. 4004, pp. 308–327. Springer, Heidelberg (2006)
31. Jafargholi, Z., Wichs, D.: Tamper detection and continuous non-malleable codes. Cryptology ePrint Archive, Report 2014/956 (2014), http://eprint.iacr.org/
32. Kalai, Y.T., Kanukurthi, B., Sahai, A.: Cryptography with tamperable and leaky memory. In: Rogaway, P. (ed.) CRYPTO 2011. LNCS, vol. 6841, pp. 373–390. Springer, Heidelberg (2011)
33. Lucks, S.: Ciphers secure against related-key attacks. In: Roy, B., Meier, W. (eds.) FSE 2004. LNCS, vol. 3017, pp. 359–370. Springer, Heidelberg (2004)
34. Pietrzak, K.: Subspace LWE. In: Cramer, R. (ed.) TCC 2012. LNCS, vol. 7194, pp. 548–563. Springer, Heidelberg (2012)
35. Qin, B., Liu, S., Yuen, T.H., Deng, R.H., Chen, K.: Continuous non-malleable key derivation and its application to related-key security. Cryptology ePrint Archive, Report 2015/003 (2015), http://eprint.iacr.org/
36. Wee, H.: Public key encryption against related key attacks. In: Fischlin, M., Buchmann, J., Manulis, M. (eds.) PKC 2012. LNCS, vol. 7293, pp. 262–279. Springer, Heidelberg (2012)

Weakening the Isolation Assumption of Tamper-Proof Hardware Tokens

Rafael Dowsley, Jörn Müller-Quade, and Tobias Nilges

Institute of Theoretical Informatics
Karlsruhe Institute of Technology
Am Fasanengarten 5, Geb. 50.34, 76131 Karlsruhe, Germany
{rafael.dowsley,mueller-quade,tobias.nilges}@kit.edu

Abstract. Recent results have shown the usefulness of tamper-proof hardware tokens as a setup assumption for building UC-secure two-party computation protocols, thus providing broad security guarantees and allowing the use of such protocols as buildings blocks in the modular design of complex cryptography protocols. All these works have in common that they assume the tokens to be completely isolated from their creator, but this is a strong assumption. In this work we investigate the feasibility of cryptographic protocols in the setting where the isolation of the hardware token is weakened.

We consider two cases: (1) the token can relay messages to its creator, or (2) the creator can send messages to the token after it is sent to the receiver. We provide a detailed characterization for both settings, presenting both impossibilities and information-theoretically secure solutions.

Keywords: Hardware Tokens, Isolation Assumption, UC security, One-Time Memory, Oblivious Transfer.

1 Introduction

Tamper-proof hardware tokens are a valuable resource for designing cryptographic protocols. It was shown in a series of recent papers that tamper-proof hardware tokens can be used as a cryptographic setup assumption to obtain Universally Composable (UC) [5] secure two-party computation protocols [20,22,18,17,13], thus achieving solutions that are secure according to one of the most stringent cryptographic models and can be used as buildings blocks in the modular design of complex cryptography protocols. Döttling et al. [13] showed that even a single tamper-proof hardware token generated by one of the mutually distrusting parties is enough to obtain information-theoretical security in the UC framework.

All these works have in common that the tokens are assumed to be completely isolated from their creator. In light of recent events this assumption becomes questionable at the least, apart from the fact that the tokens could contain internal clocks, which can be exploited in conjunction with the activation time to send information into the device (or to make the abort behavior dependent on the

© Springer International Publishing Switzerland 2015
A. Lehmann and S. Wolf (Eds.): ICITS 2015, LNCS 9063, pp. 197–213, 2015.
DOI: 10.1007/978-3-319-17470-9_12

activation time, which is not modeled in the UC framework). We highlight that this problem lies skew to leakage and side-channel attacks, e.g. [2,26], where a malicious token receiver tries to extract some of the contents of the token, i.e. the *tamper-resilience assumption* is weakened. In contrast, we consider a weakened *isolation assumption*. A similar scenario was studied by Damgård et al. [11], but only for a bandwidth-restricted channel and computational security. They showed that a partial physical separation of parties, e.g. in a token with a low-bandwidth covert channel, allows to perform UC-secure multiparty computation under standard cryptographic assumptions.

We consider an *unrestricted* channel and information-theoretical security. In this scenario, communication in both directions between the token and its creator without any restriction obviously renders the token useless as a setup assumption. Thus, there remain two different kinds of communication that can be considered to weaken the isolation assumption: either the tokens' creator can send messages to the tokens, or the tokens can send messages to their creator. While we deem the first case to be more realistic, we consider both cases. We emphasize that these one-way channels are available only for malicious parties and thus are not used by the honest parties during the protocol execution. This scenario is not directly comparable with the one by Damgård et al. [11], since here a broadband communication channel is available, but it is only one-way. This leads to the following question:

Is it possible to obtain UC-secure protocols even if there exists a broadband one-way communication channel between the tokens and their creator?

In this work, we provide a broad characterization from a feasibility standpoint for both malicious incoming and outgoing communication between the tokens and their creator. For our solutions, we only require that one party can create hardware tokens. We thus call this party Goliath, while the receiver of the token is called David and cannot create tokens of its own.

In more detail, we show that with one-way channels into the tokens, it is possible to basically use the One-Time Memory (OTM) protocol using two tokens of Döttling et al. [13] to obtain an information-theoretically UC-secure OTM with aborts (i.e., a malicious token creator can change the abort behavior of the token at runtime, which is unavoidable if one-way channels into the tokens are available) and we also provide a computationally UC-secure OTM protocol from a single token. Additionally, it is possible to obtain information-theoretically UC-secure Oblivious Transfer (OT) from a single hardware token. We prove an impossibility result for unconditionally secure OTM with a single token.

Concerning one-way channels from the tokens to their creator, we show that it is impossible to obtain even information-theoretically secure OT. We provide an information-theoretically UC-secure commitment scheme, which can then be used to obtain a computationally UC-secure OTM protocol with known techniques [25].

Further Related Work. Apart from the model of tamper-proof hardware as formalized by Katz [20], also weaker models such as resettable hardware tokens were proposed, e.g. [18]. With resettable hardware, it is not possible to obtain information-theoretically secure oblivious transfer [17], while commitments are still possible [17,12]. Thus, the main focus of this research direction are efficient protocols based on computational assumptions while minimizing the amount of communication and tokens [6,18,21,2,14,8]. Further results about hardware tokens can be founded in [7,3,9,19,15,1].

Another UC hardware setup assumption are physically uncloneable functions (PUFs) [24,4,23], which have recently gained increasing interest. It was shown that PUFs can be used to achieve oblivious transfer [27] and UC-secure commitments [12]. However, if the PUFs can be created maliciously, oblivious transfer is impossible [10].

2   Preliminaries

2.1   Notation

We use standard information-theoretic measures: by $H(\cdot)$ we denote Shannon entropy, $H(\cdot|\cdot)$ denotes conditional entropy and $I(\cdot;\cdot)$ denotes the mutual information. Let in the following λ denote a security parameter. We use the cryptographic standard notions of negligible functions, as well as computational/ statistical/perfect indistinguishability.

2.2   Model

We state and prove our results in the Universal Composability (UC) framework of Canetti [5] that allows for arbitrary composition of protocols. In this framework an ideal functionality $\mathcal{F}$ that captures the desired security requirements has to be modeled. A protocol Π that is supposed to instantiate $\mathcal{F}$ runs in the real world, where an adversary $\mathcal{A}$ can corrupt protocol parties. To prove the UC-security of Π, it has to be shown that there exists a simulator $\mathcal{S}$ that only interacts with the ideal functionality and simulates the behavior of any $\mathcal{A}$ in such a way that any environment $\mathcal{Z}$ that is plugged either into the real protocol or the simulated protocol cannot distinguish the real protocol run of Π from a simulated one.[1] For our results we assume static corruption, i.e. the adversary cannot adaptively corrupt protocol parties.

Target Functionalities. Ideally one would like to use tamper-proof hardware tokens to realize One-Time Memory (OTM) [16], as in the case where the token is modeled as being completely isolated from its creator [13]. See Fig. 1 for the OTM functionality definition. This primitive resembles oblivious transfer, but the receiver can make his choice at any point in time and the sender is not notified about this event. OTM allows to build One-Time Programs [16,18].

---

[1] In the case of computational security we allow the simulator to be expected polynomial time.

Functionality $\mathcal{F}^{\mathrm{OTM}}$

Parametrized by a security parameter λ. The variable F_{state} is initialized with wait.

Creation. Upon receiving a message (create, sid, $\mathcal{G}, \mathcal{D}, s_0, s_1$) from $\mathcal{G}$ verify if $F_{state} =$ wait and $s_0, s_1 \in \{0, 1\}^{\lambda}$; else abort. Next, set $F_{state} \leftarrow$ sent, store (sid, $\mathcal{G}, \mathcal{D}, s_0, s_1$) and send the message (created, sid, $\mathcal{G}, \mathcal{D}$) to the adversary.

Deliver. Upon receiving a message (deliver, sid, $\mathcal{G}, \mathcal{D}$) from the adversary, verify that $F_{state} =$ sent; else abort. Next, set $F_{state} \leftarrow$ ready, and send (ready, sid, $\mathcal{G}, \mathcal{D}$) to $\mathcal{D}$.

Choice. Upon receiving a message (choice, sid, $\mathcal{G}, \mathcal{D}, c$) from $\mathcal{D}$ check if $F_{state} =$ ready; else abort. Next, set $F_{state} \leftarrow$ dead and send (output, sid, $\mathcal{G}, \mathcal{D}, s_c$) to $\mathcal{D}$.

Fig. 1. The One-Time Memory functionality

Impossibility of Realizing OTMs. Note that in the hybrid execution with a token and a channel into the token, a dishonest sender $\mathcal{G}$ has the ability to send an abortion message to $\mathcal{T}$ at any time, thus changing its abort behavior. In the ideal execution on the other hand, once the OTM functionality goes to the ready state, it is not possible to change its output/abort behavior anymore. Therefore it is not possible to realize the OTM functionality based on tokens that can receive communication from a malicious $\mathcal{G}$.

OTM with Abort. Given the above fact that online changes in the abort behavior are inherent in the setting with one-way communication into the token, we introduce an OTM functionality with abort, see Fig. 2. For such a functionality, there is an initial delivering phase after which the adversary can only let the execution proceed correctly or switch off the functionality whenever he wants (independent of David inputs); but he cannot change the values stored in the functionality.

3   The Case of Incoming Communication

We first show that the existing solution of Döttling, Kraschewski and Müller-Quade [13] for OTM with 2 tokens can be modified to UC-realize OTM with abort. Then we show that using a single token, it is impossible to obtain an information-theoretically secure OTM protocol, if Goliath can send messages to the token. We sketch how a information-theoretically UC-secure OT protocol from a single token can be obtained and give a construction of a compuational UC-secure OTM protocol from a single hardware token.

The formalization of the ideal functionality for stateful tamper-proof hardware tokens in this section uses a wrapper functionality as in the previous

---

Functionality $\mathcal{F}^{\text{OTM-with-Abort}}$

Parametrized by a security parameter λ. The variable F_{state} is initialized with wait and F_{abort} with $\top$. If any message other than (switch on, sid, $\mathcal{G}, \mathcal{D}$) is received while $F_{abort} = \bot$, the functionality aborts.

Creation. Upon receiving a message (create, sid, $\mathcal{G}, \mathcal{D}, s_0, s_1$) from $\mathcal{G}$ verify if $F_{state} =$ wait and $s_0, s_1 \in \{0, 1\}^\lambda$; else abort. Next, set $F_{state} \leftarrow$ sent, store (sid, $\mathcal{G}, \mathcal{D}, s_0, s_1$) and send the message (created, sid, $\mathcal{G}, \mathcal{D}$) to the adversary.

Overwrite. Upon receiving a message (overwrite, sid, $\mathcal{G}, \mathcal{D}, s_0', s_1'$) from $\mathcal{A}$ verify if $F_{state} =$ sent and $s_0', s_1' \in \{0, 1\}^\lambda$; else abort. Set $s_0 \leftarrow s_0'$; $s_1 \leftarrow s_1'$.

Deliver. Upon receiving a message (deliver, sid, $\mathcal{G}, \mathcal{D}$) from the adversary, verify that $F_{state} =$ sent; else abort. Next, set $F_{state} \leftarrow$ ready, and send (ready, sid, $\mathcal{G}, \mathcal{D}$) to $\mathcal{D}$.

Choice. Upon receiving a message (choice, sid, $\mathcal{G}, \mathcal{D}, c$) from $\mathcal{D}$ check if $F_{state} =$ ready; else abort. Next, set $F_{state} \leftarrow$ dead and send (output, sid, $\mathcal{G}, \mathcal{D}, s_c$) to $\mathcal{D}$.

Switch Off. Upon receiving a message (switch off, sid, $\mathcal{G}, \mathcal{D}$) from $\mathcal{A}$ set $F_{abort} \leftarrow \bot$.

Switch On. Upon receiving a message (switch on, sid, $\mathcal{G}, \mathcal{D}$) from $\mathcal{A}$, set $F_{abort} \leftarrow \top$.

Fig. 2. The One-Time Memory with Abort functionality

works [20,22,13], but as one-way communication from the token issuer to the token is now allowed, the wrapper functionality needs to be modified to capture this fact. A sender $\mathcal{G}$ (Goliath) provides as input to $\mathcal{F}^{\text{stateful}}_{\text{wrap-owc}}$ a deterministic Turing machine $\mathcal{T}$ (the token). Note that stateful tokens can be hard-coded with sufficiently long randomness tapes. The receiver $\mathcal{D}$ (David) can query $\mathcal{F}^{\text{stateful}}_{\text{wrap-owc}}$ to run $\mathcal{T}$ with inputs of his choice and receives the output produced by the token. The current state of $\mathcal{T}$ is stored between consecutive queries. In addition, and in order to capture the one-way communication property, we add the possibility of Goliath sending messages to the token, in which case $\mathcal{T}$ is run on the received string and changes to a new state. The complete description of the functionality is shown in Fig. 3. This model captures the fact that on the one hand the token cannot send messages to its creator, and on the other hand David cannot access the code or the internal state of $\mathcal{T}$.

3.1 Unconditionally Secure OTM with Two Tokens

Our solution is to use the non-interactive version of the protocol due to Döttling, Kraschewski and Müller-Quade [13]. The only function of Goliath in this protocol is creating the two tokens and sending them to David. David, on the other

---

Functionality $\mathcal{F}_{\text{wrap-owc}}^{\text{stateful}}$

Parametrized by a security parameter λ and a polynomial upper bound on the runtime $t(\cdot)$. The variable F_{state} is initialized with wait.

Creation. Upon receiving a message (create, sid, $\mathcal{G}, \mathcal{D}, \mathcal{T}$) from $\mathcal{G}$ where $\mathcal{T}$ is a deterministic Turing machine, verify if $F_{state} = $ wait; else ignore the input. Next, store (sid, $\mathcal{G}, \mathcal{D}, \mathcal{T}, T_{state}$) where T_{state} is the initial state of $\mathcal{T}$, set $F_{state} \leftarrow$ sent and send the message (created, sid, $\mathcal{G}, \mathcal{D}$) to the adversary.

Deliver. Upon receiving a message (deliver, sid, $\mathcal{G}, \mathcal{D}$) from the adversary, verify that $F_{state} = $ sent; else ignore the input. Next, set $F_{state} \leftarrow$ ready, and send (ready, sid, $\mathcal{G}, \mathcal{D}$) to $\mathcal{D}$.

Execution. Upon receiving a message (execute, sid, $\mathcal{G}, \mathcal{D}, x$) from $\mathcal{D}$ where x is an input, check if $F_{state} = $ ready and if it is, then run $\mathcal{T}(T_{state}, x)$ for at most $t(\lambda)$ steps. Save the new state of $\mathcal{T}$ in T_{state}, read the output y from its output tape and send (output, sid, $\mathcal{G}, \mathcal{D}, y$) to $\mathcal{D}$.

Incoming Communication. Upon receiving a message (communication, sid, $\mathcal{G}, \mathcal{D}, m$) from $\mathcal{A}$, run $\mathcal{T}(T_{state}, m)$ for at most $t(\lambda)$ steps. Save the new state of $\mathcal{T}$.

Fig. 3. The wrapper functionality allowing one-way communication

hand, interacts with both tokens in order to obtain his output and to check the correctness of the protocol execution. Intuitively, one of the tokens is used to generate a commitment to the input values and to send the input values encrypted using one-time pads. The second token only contains a random affine function which can be evaluated only a single time and allows David to recover the one-time pad key corresponding to one of the inputs. The specifications of the tokens can be found in Fig. 4 and Fig. 5. In the protocol David initially interacts with the token which has the inputs in order to obtain the commitments and the ciphertexts. After this point David considers the OTM as delivered. Then, whenever he wants to choose the input to be received, he simply queries the token that has the affine function on the appropriate input and obtains the one-time pad that he needs in order to recover his desired value. The description of the protocol is presented in Fig. 6.

The fact that the protocol securely realizes $\mathcal{F}^{\text{OTM-with-Abort}}$ follows from a straightforward modification of the original security proof by Döttling et al. [13], which considered the same protocol but with isolated tokens and proved that it realizes $\mathcal{F}^{\text{OTM}}$ (i.e., without aborts) in such scenario.

Theorem 1. *In the model where a malicious Goliath is allowed to send messages to the token, the protocol presented in Fig. 6 UC-realizes the functionality*

Token - Random Values $\mathcal{T}_{\text{Random}}$

Parametrized by a security parameter λ. The token is hardwired with a random vector $a \xleftarrow{\$} \mathbb{F}_2^{2\lambda}$ and a random matrix $B \xleftarrow{\$} \mathbb{F}_2^{2\lambda \times 2\lambda}$. It is initialized with state $T_{state} = $ ready.

Output. Upon receiving a message (choice, z) from $\mathcal{D}$ check if $T_{state} = $ ready; else abort. Next, set $T_{state} \leftarrow $ dead, compute $V \leftarrow a \otimes z + B$ and send the message (output, V) to $\mathcal{D}$.

Fig. 4. The first token, which only contains random values

$\mathcal{F}^{OTM\text{-}with\text{-}Abort}$ *with statistical security against a corrupted Goliath and perfect security against a corrupted David.*

Proof. (Sketch) The correctness as well as the security against a corrupted David follow directly from Döttling's et al. proof of security. In the case of the security against a corrupted Goliath, note that the OTM is considered delivered at the point in which David has received $(G, \tilde{a}, \tilde{B}, \tilde{s}_0, \tilde{s}_1)$ from $\mathcal{T}_{\text{Inputs}}$. From that point on, $\mathcal{T}_{\text{Inputs}}$ does not participate in the protocol anymore and it cannot send messages to the outside world. Hence neither Goliath nor $\mathcal{T}_{\text{Random}}$ know the matrix C which is used for the commitments, so they can cheat in the commitment's opening phase only with negligible probability. Both of them also do not know the value h, which is necessary together with z in order to determine David's input x. So the proof proceeds as in [13], the only difference here is that Goliath can still send messages to $\mathcal{T}_{\text{Random}}$ at any point, and thus he can modify the abort behavior. This can be dealt with by running Döttling's et al. procedure to verify whether the token is going to abort or not (i.e., running a copy of the token in its current state with random inputs) after each incoming message from Goliath to the token. If the simulator notices that the abort behavior changed, he can make the appropriate change in $\mathcal{F}^{OTM\text{-}with\text{-}Abort}$ by using the Switch Off/Switch On commands.

Sequential OTM with Abort. As done by Döttling et al. [13] for the OTM functionality, it is also possible to define a sequential version of the OTM-with-Abort functionality where there are many pairs of Goliath's inputs (i.e., there are multiple stages) which can only be queried sequentially by David. The functionality only needs to be modified to take pairs of inputs which can be queried sequentially by David and to allow an adversary to specify which stages are active/inactive at any time (if an inactive stage is queried by David, then the functionality aborts). In this case the two token solution of Döttling et al. [13] for sequential OTMs can be used. The security proof would be a straightforward modification of Döttling et al.'s proof in the same line as done above.

Token - Inputs $\mathcal{T}_{\text{Inputs}}$

Parametrized by a security parameter λ. The token is initialized with Goliath's inputs s_0, s_1, and the vector a and matrix B that are used by $\mathcal{T}_{\text{Random}}$. It is initialized in state $T_{state} = $ ready.

Matrix Choice. Upon receiving a message (matrix choice, C) from $\mathcal{D}$ check if $T_{state} = $ ready and $C \in \mathbb{F}_2^{\lambda \times 2\lambda}$; else abort. Next, compute a matrix $G \in \mathbb{F}_2^{\lambda \times 2\lambda}$ that is complementary to C (i.e., G is determined by λ vectors of length 2λ which are linearly independent and G spans a subspace of the kernel of C), and also compute $\tilde{a} \leftarrow Ca$, $\tilde{B} \leftarrow CB$. Set $T_{state} \leftarrow $ committed and send the message (commitment, $G, \tilde{a}, \tilde{B}$) to $\mathcal{D}$.

Ciphertexts. Upon receiving a message (vector choice, h) from $\mathcal{D}$ check if $T_{state} = $ committed and $h \in \mathbb{F}_2^{2\lambda} \setminus \{0\}$; else abort. Next, compute $\tilde{s}_0 \leftarrow s_0 + GBh$ and $\tilde{s}_1 \leftarrow s_1 + GBh + Ga$, set $T_{state} \leftarrow $ dead and send the message (output, $\tilde{s}_0, \tilde{s}_1$) to $\mathcal{D}$.

Fig. 5. The second token, which stores Goliath's inputs

3.2   Impossibility of Unconditionally Secure OTM from a Single Token

Lemma 2. *Assume that there is only one token and that a malicious token is not computationally bounded. If a malicious Goliath is allowed to send messages to the token, then there is no protocol Π that realizes OTM with information-theoretic security from this single token.*

Proof. For the sake of contradiction assume that a correct and information-theoretically secure OTM protocol Π from a single stateful token exists. Assume that the parties' inputs are chosen as $s_0, s_1 \xleftarrow{\$} \{0,1\}^\lambda$ and $c \xleftarrow{\$} \{0,1\}$. The sender's privacy of the OTM protocol should hold, i.e.

$$I(\text{view}_\mathcal{D}; s_{1-c}) \leq \varepsilon \Leftrightarrow H(s_{1-c}) - H(s_{1-c}|\text{view}_\mathcal{D}) \leq \varepsilon$$

$$\Leftrightarrow H(s_{1-c}|\text{view}_\mathcal{D}) \geq \lambda - \varepsilon,$$

where $\text{view}_\mathcal{D}$ is David's view of the protocol execution and ε is a function that is negligible in the security parameter.

By definition of the OTM functionality David can choose his input c at any time after he receives the token and Goliath should not learn when David queried the OTM functionality. So David can choose his input c at a point in the future far after receiving the token, when all initial communication between the parties is already finished, and then he interacts with the token to receive s_c. But then, at the moment right before David's choice c is made, its entropy is still 1 from the point of view of all parties. Therefore, due to the sender's privacy, at this

---

Protocol

Parametrized by a security parameter λ.

Deliver. $\mathcal{D}$ waits until $\mathcal{G}$ send the tokens $\mathcal{T}_{\text{Random}}$ and $\mathcal{T}_{\text{Inputs}}$. Then he chooses a random matrix $C \in \mathbb{F}_2^{\lambda \times 2\lambda}$ and sends the message (matrix choice, C) to $\mathcal{T}_{\text{Inputs}}$ in order to get the answer (commitment, $G, \tilde{a}, \tilde{B}$). After that, $\mathcal{D}$ picks a random vector $h \in \mathbb{F}_2^{2\lambda} \setminus \{0\}$ and sends the message (vector choice, h) to $\mathcal{T}_{\text{Inputs}}$ in order to get the output (output, $\tilde{s}_0, \tilde{s}_1$).

Choice Phase. When $\mathcal{D}$ gets his input $c \in \mathbb{F}_2$, he chooses $z \xleftarrow{\$} \mathbb{F}_2^{2\lambda}$ such that $z^T h = c$ and sends the message (choice, z) to $\mathcal{T}_{\text{Random}}$ to get the output (output, V). Then $\mathcal{D}$ checks if $CV = \tilde{a}z^T + \tilde{B}$. If it is not, $\mathcal{D}$ aborts; otherwise, he outputs $s_c = \tilde{s}_c + GVh$.

Fig. 6. The unconditionally secure protocol that realizes $\mathcal{F}^{\text{OTM-with-Abort}}$

point it should hold that

$$H(s_0 \,|\, \text{view}'_{\mathcal{D}}) \geq \lambda - \varepsilon$$

and

$$H(s_1 \,|\, \text{view}'_{\mathcal{D}}) \geq \lambda - \varepsilon,$$

where $\text{view}'_{\mathcal{D}}$ is David's view of the protocol execution until this point. But if a malicious Goliath is allowed to send messages to the token, he can forward his complete view to the token. The token then gets to know all protocol interactions so far and due to the correctness of the OTM protocol (i.e., it should work for any pair of inputs in $\{0,1\}^{\lambda}$) he is able, for almost any $s'_c \in \{0,1\}^{\lambda}$, to find a strategy to follow for the rest of the protocol that makes David accept s'_c. Hence the values s_0 and s_1 are not fixed up to the point when David inputs c. But in the OTM functionality the values s_0 and s_1 are fixed once it is sent, and thus we get a contradiction.

3.3 Unconditionally Secure OT with a Single Token

Döttling et al. [13] also presented an unconditionally secure solution with one token only, in which the interactions which are performed between David and $\mathcal{T}_{\text{Inputs}}$ in the previously described protocol are instead performed between David and Goliath in an initial interactive phase that is used to send the commitments and the ciphertexts. Note that such a version of the protocol would not be secure in the setting where one-way communication is allowed into the token since Goliath could simply forward the matrix C to $\mathcal{T}_{\text{Random}}$, which would then be able to open the commitments to any value and thus be able to change the outputs at any time. But we should mention that it is possible to obtain an

---

Token $\mathcal{T}$

Parametrized by a security parameter λ. The token is hardwired with the shares $(v_{i,0}, v_{i,1})$ for $i = 1, \ldots, \lambda$, the inputs s_0, s_1 and Goliath's public key pk. It is initialized with state $T_{state} = $ ready and $j = 0$.

Message Commitment. Upon receiving a message (challenge, k_j) from $\mathcal{D}$ check if $T_{state} = $ ready and k_j is a bit; else abort Set $j \leftarrow j + 1$. If $j = \lambda$, then set $T_{state} \leftarrow$ message committed. Send the message (message commitment, v_{j,k_j}) to $\mathcal{D}$.

Inputs Commitment. Upon receiving a message (commit, crs, σ) from $\mathcal{D}$ check if $T_{state} = $ message committed and if σ is a valid signature of $\mathcal{G}$ on crs; else abort. Set $T_{state} \leftarrow$ inputs committed. Commit to the values s_0, s_1 using a computationally UC-secure commitment protocol that uses the common reference string crs and send the commitments to $\mathcal{D}$. Let d_0, d_1 denote the information to open the commitments.

Output. Upon receiving the message output from $\mathcal{D}$ check if $T_{state} = $ inputs committed; else abort. Next, set $T_{state} \leftarrow$ dead and execute with $\mathcal{D}$ a computationally UC-secure oblivious transfer protocol using the common reference string crs and with inputs $(s_0 \| d_0, s_1 \| d_1)$.

Fig. 7. The token for a computationally secure OTM protocol with a single token

oblivious transfer protocol with only one token by letting the single token act like $\mathcal{T}_{\text{Inputs}}$ in the above protocol and letting the interactions between David and $\mathcal{T}_{\text{Random}}$ be replaced by identical interactions between David and Goliath. The proof of security would follow in the same line as before since Goliath would never get to know C and h. Note that the drawback of having to know the OT inputs before sending the token can be easily overcome by performing the OTs with random inputs and derandomizing them afterwards.

3.4   Computationally Secure OTM from a Single Token

If one considers the scenario where only one token is available, it is possible to obtain a protocol that realizes $\mathcal{F}^{\text{OTM-with-Abort}}$ with computational security. The idea is to compute as an initial step (i.e. during the delivery phase) the commitment functionality by using the token and interactions between Goliath and David. With access to this commitment functionality it is possible to obtain a common reference string between David and the token[2], which in turn allows to run a computationally secure UC-commitment protocol between them in order

---

[2] The common reference string is actually obtained by Goliath and David, but can be forwarded from Goliath to the token via David by using a digital signature to ensure that the value that the token obtains is exactly the same one that Goliath sent.

Protocol

Parametrized by a security parameter λ.

Deliver. $\mathcal{G}$ generates a pair of signing sk and public pk keys for a signature scheme. Then he picks a random message $m' \xleftarrow{\$} \mathbb{F}_2^\lambda$ and random vectors $v_{i,0} \xleftarrow{\$} \mathbb{F}_2^\lambda$ for $i = 1, \ldots, \lambda$ and sets $v_{i,1} = m' - v_{i,0}$. He creates the token $\mathcal{T}$ (described in Fig. 7) with the hardwired vectors $(v_{i,0}, v_{i,1})$, s_0, s_1 and pk, and sends it to $\mathcal{D}$. Upon receiving the token $\mathcal{T}$, $\mathcal{D}$ queries it with random bits k_i for $i = 1, \ldots, \lambda$ in order to get v_{i,k_i}. $\mathcal{D}$ picks a random message $m'' \xleftarrow{\$} \mathbb{F}_2^\lambda$ and sends it to $\mathcal{G}$. Then $\mathcal{G}$ opens the commitment to m' by sending all the shares $(v_{i,0}, v_{i,1})$ to $\mathcal{D}$. $\mathcal{D}$ checks if $m' = v_{i,0} + v_{i,1}$ for all $i = 1, \ldots, \lambda$, aborting the protocol if this is not the case. Both $\mathcal{G}$ and $\mathcal{D}$ use $m = m' + m''$ to generate a common reference string crs. $\mathcal{G}$ signs crs with his signing key sk and sends the signature σ to $\mathcal{D}$. $\mathcal{D}$ sends crs and σ to $\mathcal{T}$ in order to receive the commitments to s_0 and s_1.

Choice Phase. When $\mathcal{D}$ gets his input $c \in \mathbb{F}_2$, he sends the message output to $\mathcal{T}$ and executes a computationally UC-secure oblivious transfer protocol with the token using the common reference string crs and with input c in order to get the output $s_c \| d_c$, where $\|$ denotes concatenation. $\mathcal{D}$ checks the correctness of s_c using the commitment that he received previously and the opening information d_c.

Fig. 8. The computationally secure OTM protocol using one token

to commit to the input values. After receiving from the token the commitments to the input values, David considers the delivery complete, and whenever he wants to get his output he just executes an oblivious transfer protocol with the token with his desired choice bit as input. He checks the correctness of the output using the commitment. The crucial point for the simulation to go through is that the simulator should be able to extract the first commitment before its opening, so that he can choose the common reference string as he wishes. In order to accomplish that in face of a potentially malicious token which possibly only correctly answers queries to certain values, we will commit to a message m by using λ pairs of random shares $(v_{i,0}, v_{i,1})$ where for each pair $v_{i,0} + v_{i,1} = m$. During the committing phase, $\mathcal{D}$ interacts with the token and can choose to receive either $v_{i,0}$ or $v_{i,1}$ for each pair. To open the commitment, $\mathcal{G}$ reveals all the shares. The specification of the token can be found in Fig. 7 and of the protocol in Fig. 8.

Theorem 3. *In the model where a malicious Goliath is allowed to send messages to the token, the protocol presented in Fig. 8 UC-realizes the functionality* $\mathcal{F}^{OTM\text{-}with\text{-}Abort}$ *with computational security.*

Proof. The correctness of the protocol can be trivially verified. The simulation for the cases that both parties are corrupted or no parties are corrupted are trivial. We describe below how the simulation proceeds in the other cases.

Corrupted Sender: If Goliath is corrupted (and thus also the token), the simulator will simulate an interaction of the protocol with the adversary and has to extract both s_0 and s_1 from this interaction in order to give them as input for the OTM functionality. The main reason to do this is that the simulator should be able to extract the value m' before sending m'', so that he can choose the common reference string crs as he wishes, thus being able to create a trapdoor to extract s_0 and s_1 from the committed values.

We have that only Goliath can program the token, so the environment machine will provide the code to Goliath (and hence to the simulator). To extract the value m' the simulator does the following. When the commitment step happens, whenever David sends a valid message (challenge, k_j) to receive a share $\tilde{v}_{j,k_j}$, the simulator first executes the token with the input $1 - k_j$, obtaining an answer $\tilde{v}_{j,1-k_j}$, and then resets the token to the point before this query and executes the token with input k_j to obtain $\tilde{v}_{j,k_j}$ and forward it to David. Let $\tilde{m}'_j = \tilde{v}_{j,0} + \tilde{v}_{j,1}$. After all the λ challenges are done, the simulator fixes $\tilde{m}'$ as the value that appeared more often in the tuple $(\tilde{m}'_1, \ldots, \tilde{m}'_\lambda)$. He then chooses $m'' = m - \tilde{m}'$ for any m he wants. Lets now analyze this extraction procedure. Let $(\hat{v}_{j,0}, \hat{v}_{j,1})$ denote the values that Goliath reveals in the opening phase. Note that the protocol will be aborted unless $\hat{v}_{j,0} + \hat{v}_{j,1} = \hat{m}'$ for all j and some fixed message $\hat{m}'$. For any j, if $\hat{v}_{j,0} \neq \tilde{v}_{j,0}$ and $\hat{v}_{j,1} \neq \tilde{v}_{j,1}$ then the protocol will be aborted anyway and we do not need to worry about the extracted value. If for the majority of the j's it holds that $\hat{v}_{j,0} = \tilde{v}_{j,0}$ and $\hat{v}_{j,1} = \tilde{v}_{j,1}$, then $\tilde{m}' = \hat{m}'$ and thus the extraction procedure works properly. The remaining case is the one in which at least half of the j's are such that either $\hat{v}_{j,0} = \tilde{v}_{j,0}$ or $\hat{v}_{j,1} = \tilde{v}_{j,1}$, but not both equalities hold. For each such j the probability that the opening check succeeds for this pair of vectors is $1/2$ since Goliath cannot get any information from the token. Therefore if half or more of the j's are in this condition, the protocol will abort with overwhelming probability in the security parameter λ.

Given that the extraction worked properly, the simulator can create the common reference string as he wishes and so he is able to have a trapdoor to extract the values s_0 and s_1 from the commitments and give them as input to the OTM functionality. To learn the abort behavior, the simulator simulates, at onset and also after each incoming message from Goliath to the token, a choice phase execution between David and the token. The simulator can then use the Switch Off/Switch On commands to adapt $\mathcal{F}^{\text{OTM-with-Abort}}$'s abort behavior properly.

Corrupted Receiver: If David is corrupted, the simulator gets to know all David's challenges k_j in the first commitment. Hence, after seeing m'', he can choose any m' he wants (and thus any resulting m and crs) and appropriate shares $(\hat{v}_{j,0}, \hat{v}_{j,1})$ that are correct from David's point of view. By picking a common reference string together with an appropriate trapdoor, the simulator can learn the choice bit c and query it to the functionality $\mathcal{F}^{\text{OTM-with-Abort}}$ to learn s_c. Using the equivocability of the UC-commitment the simulator can find an appropriate opening information d_c and feed $s_c \| d_c$ to David in the OT protocol.

Note that the above protocol can be trivially extended to the case of sequential OTMs.

4   The Case of Outgoing Communication

In the complementary problem, we consider tokens which have a one-way channel that allow them to send messages to Goliath, but which cannot receive any information from Goliath. In this scenario we would like to implement $\mathcal{F}^{\text{OTM}}$. Note that in this case Goliath cannot control online the abort behavior of the token. We first show an impossibility result for unconditionally secure protocols and then present a computationally secure protocol using a single token.

4.1   Impossibility of Information-Theoretically Secure OT(M)

Lemma 4. *If the tokens can send messages to Goliath, then there is no protocol Π that realizes OTM, or even oblivious transfer, with information-theoretic security.*

Proof. (Sketch) The basic idea is that the malicious tokens send their complete view to Goliath after each interaction with David. Thus, independently of whether Goliath or some token receive the last protocol message, the combined view of Goliath and the tokens is available to a malicious Goliath. This directly implies that an OT protocol with information-theoretical security is not possible, because the whole model collapses to the two-party case in the stand-alone setting. Either the complete transcript of the exchanged messages (which is available to a malicious Goliath) uniquely determines the choice-bit c of David or a malicious David can obtain both input bits (s_0, s_1), and in both cases the oblivious transfer security is broken.

We remark that the crucial point here is that for oblivious transfer, it does not matter at which time Goliath gets the complete view, i.e. it does not matter whether some token or Goliath receive the last message. As soon as he learns the choice bit, the protocol is broken. This argumentation, however, does not rule out information-theoretically UC-secure commitments.

4.2   Unconditionally Secure Commitment with a Single Token

The idea here is to commit to a message m by using pairs of random shares $(v_{i,0}, v_{i,1})$ such that for each pair $v_{i,0} + v_{i,1} = m$, the shares are known to both the token and Goliath. The commitment phase is done by interactions between

---

Token $\mathcal{T}$

Parametrized by a security parameter λ. The token is hardwired with the shares $(v_{n,i,0}, v_{n,i,1})$ for $i = 1,\ldots,2\lambda, n = 1,\ldots,\lambda$ and an opening key $\mathsf{cok} \in \{0,1\}^\lambda$. It is initialized with state $T_{state} = \mathsf{ready}$.

Shares Opening. Upon receiving a message ($\mathsf{challenge}, n_1,\ldots,n_{\lambda/2}$) from $\mathcal{D}$ check if $T_{state} = \mathsf{ready}$ and $\{n_1,\ldots,n_{\lambda/2}\} \subset \{1,\ldots,\lambda\}$ are the specifications of the shares $\mathcal{D}$ wants to be revealed; else abort. Set $T_{state} \leftarrow \mathsf{message\ committed}$. Send the message ($\mathsf{shares\ opening}, (v_{n_j,i,0}, v_{n_j,i,1})_{j=1,\ldots,\lambda/2,i=1,\ldots,2\lambda}$) to $\mathcal{D}$.

Message Opening. Upon receiving a message ($\mathsf{reveal\ message}, \overline{\mathsf{cok}}$) from $\mathcal{D}$ check if $T_{state} = \mathsf{message\ committed}$ and $\overline{\mathsf{cok}} = \mathsf{cok}$; else abort. Set $T_{state} \leftarrow \mathsf{message\ opened}$. Send the message ($\mathsf{opening}, (v_{n,i,0}, v_{n,i,1})_{n=1,\ldots,\lambda,i=1,\ldots,2\lambda}$) to $\mathcal{D}$.

Fig. 9. The token for the commitment protocol with outgoing communication

David and Goliath, where for each pair David can choose to receive either $v_{i,0}$ or $v_{i,1}$. In order to guarantee the binding property, the opening phase is executed between David and the token: David receives an opening key from Goliath and forwards it to the token, who checks it and reveals all the shares to David. To guarantee that on the one hand David cannot guess the opening key correctly (and thus open the commitment whenever he wants), but on the other hand the opening key does not contain enough information to allow the token to learn David's choices during the commitment phase (and thus successfully open the commitment to any value), we have opening keys that are random λ-bit strings and we use 2λ pairs of random shares. This commitment scheme is secure, but not yet extractable. In order to get extractability, instead of committing to the message itself, we first use the $(\lambda, \lambda/2 + 1)$-Shamir's secret share scheme to create λ shares $(m_1,\ldots,m_\lambda)$ of the message, then commit to each share using the above scheme (in the opening phase a single opening key of λ-bits is given to the token in order to open all the commitments), but we additionally make David ask the token to open $\lambda/2$ shares $m_{n_1},\ldots m_{n_{\lambda/2}}$ (without sending the opening key) already in the commitment phase, which do not reveal any information about m. The specification of the token can be found in Fig. 9 and of the protocol in Fig. 10.

Theorem 5. *In the model where malicious tokens are allowed to send messages to Goliath, the protocol presented in Fig. 10 UC-realizes the commitment functionality $\mathcal{F}^{COM}$ with unconditional security.*

The proof will be included in the full version.

Commitment Protocol

Parametrized by a security parameter λ.

Commitment Phase. $\mathcal{G}$ generates an opening key $\mathsf{cok} \xleftarrow{\$} \mathbb{F}_2^\lambda$. Then he generates λ shares $(m_1, \ldots, m_\lambda)$ of the message m using Shamir's secret sharing scheme. For each share m_n, $\mathcal{G}$ picks random vectors $v_{n,i,0} \xleftarrow{\$} \mathbb{F}_2^\lambda$ for $i = 1, \ldots, 2\lambda$ and sets $v_{n,i,1} = m_n - v_{n,i,0}$. He creates the token $\mathcal{T}$ (described in Fig. 9) with the hardwired cok and vectors $(v_{n,i,0}, v_{n,i,1})$ for $n = 1, \ldots, \lambda, i = 1, \ldots, 2\lambda$, and sends it to $\mathcal{D}$. Upon receiving the token $\mathcal{T}$, $\mathcal{D}$ queries $\mathcal{G}$ with random bits $k_{n,i}$ for $n = 1, \ldots, \lambda, i = 1, \ldots, 2\lambda$ in order to get $v_{n,i,k_{n,i}}$. Then $\mathcal{D}$ picks a random subset $\{n_1, \ldots, n_{\lambda/2}\} \subset \{1, \ldots, \lambda\}$ and asks the token to reveal $(v_{n_j,i,0}, v_{n_j,i,1})$ for $j = 1, \ldots, \lambda/2, i = 1, \ldots, 2\lambda$, which he checks against the information he received from $\mathcal{G}$; aborting if they do not match.

Opening Phase. $\mathcal{G}$ sends to $\mathcal{D}$ the message shares $(m_1, \ldots, m_\lambda)$ and also the commitment opening key cok, which $\mathcal{D}$ forwards to $\mathcal{T}$ in order to get all the shares $(v_{n,i,0}, v_{n,i,1})$. $\mathcal{D}$ checks if $m_n = v_{n,i,0} + v_{n,i,1}$ for all i and n, aborting the protocol if this is not the case. Then he reconstructs m from the shares; aborting if m is not uniquely determined by the shares.

Fig. 10. The unconditionally secure commitment protocol using one token for the case of outgoing communication

4.3 Computationally Secure OTM with a Single Token

For the case of computational security, it is possible to obtain an OTM protocol which uses only one token. The approach is briefly described below. Using the ideas from the previous section the parties can compute the commitment functionality, which can then be used to establish a common reference string between David and the token. The common reference string in turn can be used to run computationally UC-secure commitments and OT protocols between the token and David. The token commits to the input values using the computationally UC-secure commitment protocol, at which point David considers the deliver complete. Afterwards, whenever David wants to obtain his output, he engages in a computationally UC-secure OT protocol with the token in order to get the desired output and the commitment verification information.

Theorem 6. *In the model where malicious tokens are allowed to send messages to Goliath, there is a protocol using a single token which UC-realizes the functionality $\mathcal{F}^{OTM}$ with computational security.*

The description of the token and the protocol, as well as the security proof will be included in the full version.

5 Conclusion

In this work we investigated a weaker isolation model for tamper-proof hardware, namely one-way (broadband) communication channels are allowed either for the token creator to the tokens or in the opposite direction. In the case that the tokens can receive incoming communication from their creators we showed the following: (1) there is an unconditionally secure One-Time Memory (OTM) protocol using two tokens, (2) it is impossible to realize OTM with unconditional security from a single token, (3) there is an unconditionally secure oblivious transfer protocol using a single token, (4) there is a computationally secure OTM protocol using a single token. In the case that the tokens can send outgoing communication to their creator we showed the following: (1) it is impossible to realize OTM or oblivious transfer with unconditional security, (2) there is an unconditionally secure commitment protocol using a single token, (3) there is a computationally secure OTM protocol using a single token.

References

1. Agrawal, S., Ananth, P., Goyal, V., Prabhakaran, M., Rosen, A.: Lower bounds in the hardware token model. In: Lindell, Y. (ed.) TCC 2014. LNCS, vol. 8349, pp. 663–687. Springer, Heidelberg (2014)
2. Bitansky, N., Canetti, R., Goldwasser, S., Halevi, S., Kalai, Y.T., Rothblum, G.N.: Program obfuscation with leaky hardware. In: Lee, D.H., Wang, X. (eds.) ASIACRYPT 2011. LNCS, vol. 7073, pp. 722–739. Springer, Heidelberg (2011)
3. Brands, S.: Untraceable off-line cash in wallets with observers (extended abstract). In: Stinson, D.R. (ed.) CRYPTO 1993. LNCS, vol. 773, pp. 302–318. Springer, Heidelberg (1994)
4. Brzuska, C., Fischlin, M., Schröder, H., Katzenbeisser, S.: Physically uncloneable functions in the universal composition framework. In: Rogaway, P. (ed.) CRYPTO 2011. LNCS, vol. 6841, pp. 51–70. Springer, Heidelberg (2011)
5. Canetti, R.: Universally composable security: A new paradigm for cryptographic protocols. In: 42nd Annual Symposium on Foundations of Computer Science, Las Vegas, Nevada, USA, October 14–17, pp. 136–145. IEEE Computer Society Press (2001)
6. Chandran, N., Goyal, V., Sahai, A.: New constructions for UC secure computation using tamper-proof hardware. In: Smart, N.P. (ed.) EUROCRYPT 2008. LNCS, vol. 4965, pp. 545–562. Springer, Heidelberg (2008)
7. Chaum, D., Pedersen, T.P.: Wallet databases with observers. In: Brickell, E.F. (ed.) CRYPTO 1992. LNCS, vol. 740, pp. 89–105. Springer, Heidelberg (1993)
8. Choi, S.G., Katz, J., Schröder, D., Yerukhimovich, A., Zhou, H.-S. (Efficient) universally composable oblivious transfer using a minimal number of stateless tokens. In: Lindell, Y. (ed.) TCC 2014. LNCS, vol. 8349, pp. 638–662. Springer, Heidelberg (2014)
9. Cramer, R., Pedersen, T.P.: Improved privacy in wallets with observers (extended abstract). In: Helleseth, T. (ed.) EUROCRYPT 1993. LNCS, vol. 765, pp. 329–343. Springer, Heidelberg (1994)
10. Dachman-Soled, D., Fleischhacker, N., Katz, J., Lysyanskaya, A., Schröder, D.: Feasibility and infeasibility of secure computation with malicious PUFs. In: Garay, J.A., Gennaro, R. (eds.) CRYPTO 2014, Part II. LNCS, vol. 8617, pp. 405–420. Springer, Heidelberg (2014)

11. Damgård, I., Nielsen, J.B., Wichs, D.: Universally composable multiparty computation with partially isolated parties. In: Reingold, O. (ed.) TCC 2009. LNCS, vol. 5444, pp. 315–331. Springer, Heidelberg (2009)
12. Damgård, I., Scafuro, A.: Unconditionally secure and universally composable commitments from physical assumptions. In: Sako, K., Sarkar, P. (eds.) ASIACRYPT 2013, Part II. LNCS, vol. 8270, pp. 100–119. Springer, Heidelberg (2013)
13. Döttling, N., Kraschewski, D., Müller-Quade, J.: Unconditional and composable security using a single stateful tamper-proof hardware token. In: Ishai, Y. (ed.) TCC 2011. LNCS, vol. 6597, pp. 164–181. Springer, Heidelberg (2011)
14. Döttling, N., Mie, T., Müller-Quade, J., Nilges, T.: Implementing resettable UC-functionalities with untrusted tamper-proof hardware-tokens. In: Sahai, A. (ed.) TCC 2013. LNCS, vol. 7785, pp. 642–661. Springer, Heidelberg (2013)
15. Gennaro, R., Lysyanskaya, A., Malkin, T., Micali, S., Rabin, T.: Algorithmic tamper-proof (ATP) security: Theoretical foundations for security against hardware tampering. In: Naor, M. (ed.) TCC 2004. LNCS, vol. 2951, pp. 258–277. Springer, Heidelberg (2004)
16. Goldwasser, S., Kalai, Y.T., Rothblum, G.N.: One-time programs. In: Wagner, D. (ed.) CRYPTO 2008. LNCS, vol. 5157, pp. 39–56. Springer, Heidelberg (2008)
17. Goyal, V., Ishai, Y., Mahmoody, M., Sahai, A.: Interactive locking, zero-knowledge PCPs, and unconditional cryptography. In: Rabin, T. (ed.) CRYPTO 2010. LNCS, vol. 6223, pp. 173–190. Springer, Heidelberg (2010)
18. Goyal, V., Ishai, Y., Sahai, A., Venkatesan, R., Wadia, A.: Founding cryptography on tamper-proof hardware tokens. In: Micciancio, D. (ed.) TCC 2010. LNCS, vol. 5978, pp. 308–326. Springer, Heidelberg (2010)
19. Ishai, Y., Sahai, A., Wagner, D.: Private circuits: Securing hardware against probing attacks. In: Boneh, D. (ed.) CRYPTO 2003. LNCS, vol. 2729, pp. 463–481. Springer, Heidelberg (2003)
20. Katz, J.: Universally composable multi-party computation using tamper-proof hardware. In: Naor, M. (ed.) EUROCRYPT 2007. LNCS, vol. 4515, pp. 115–128. Springer, Heidelberg (2007)
21. Kolesnikov, V.: Truly efficient string oblivious transfer using resettable tamper-proof tokens. In: Micciancio, D. (ed.) TCC 2010. LNCS, vol. 5978, pp. 327–342. Springer, Heidelberg (2010)
22. Moran, T., Segev, G.: David and Goliath commitments: UC computation for asymmetric parties using tamper-proof hardware. In: Smart, N.P. (ed.) EUROCRYPT 2008. LNCS, vol. 4965, pp. 527–544. Springer, Heidelberg (2008)
23. Ostrovsky, R., Scafuro, A., Visconti, I., Wadia, A.: Universally composable secure computation with (malicious) physically uncloneable functions. In: Johansson, T., Nguyen, P.Q. (eds.) EUROCRYPT 2013. LNCS, vol. 7881, pp. 702–718. Springer, Heidelberg (2013)
24. Pappu, R.S.: Physical One-Way Functions. PhD thesis, MIT (2001)
25. Peikert, C., Vaikuntanathan, V., Waters, B.: A framework for efficient and composable oblivious transfer. In: Wagner, D. (ed.) CRYPTO 2008. LNCS, vol. 5157, pp. 554–571. Springer, Heidelberg (2008)
26. Prabhakaran, M., Sahai, A., Wadia, A.: Secure computation using leaky tokens. In: Esparza, J., Fraigniaud, P., Husfeldt, T., Koutsoupias, E. (eds.) ICALP 2014. LNCS, vol. 8572, pp. 907–918. Springer, Heidelberg (2014)
27. Rührmair, U.: Oblivious transfer based on physical unclonable functions. In: Acquisti, A., Smith, S.W., Sadeghi, A.-R. (eds.) TRUST 2010. LNCS, vol. 6101, pp. 430–440. Springer, Heidelberg (2010)

Limited View Adversary Codes: Bounds, Constructions and Applications

Pengwei Wang and Reihaneh Safavi-Naini

Department of Computer Science, University of Calgary, Canada

Abstract. Limited View Adversary Codes (LV codes) provide protection against an adversary who has partial view of the communication channel and can use this view to corrupt the sent codeword by constructing an adversarial error vector that will be added to the codeword. For a codeword of length N, the adversary sees a subset of $\rho_r N$ of the codeword components and adds an adversarial error vector of weight $\rho_w N$ to the codeword. A δ-LV code ensures correct recovery of the sent message with probability at least $1-\delta$. The motivation for studying these codes is modelling adversarial corruptions in wireless communications as well as networks that are partially controlled by an adversary, with the aim of providing reliable communication.

This paper makes the following contributions. First we prove an upper bound on the rate of LV codes and extend it to a bound on the rate of a code family. Second, we give an explicit construction of an LV code family that achieves the bound (over large alphabets) for certain range of ρ_r, and hence obtain the capacity of LV adversarial channels for that range of ρ_r. The construction has efficient encoding and decoding. Finally we show the relationship between LV codes and a cryptographic primitive known as Reliable Message Transmission (RMT), and use this relation to obtain a new bound on the transmission rate of 1-round δ-RMT protocols, and construct an optimal 1-round RMT protocol family. We discuss our results, give their relations to other works and primitives including list decodable codes, and suggest directions for future research.

1 Introduction

Reliable communication in presence of adversarial error has been first considered in Hamming model [14] of error where the adversary sees the whole codeword and arbitrarily corrupts ρN symbols, where N is the length of the codeword and ρ is a constant. More recently weaker adversarial models have been introduced to capture real-life communication scenarios where the adversary's access to the codeword (read, write or both) is limited because of reasons such as their inadequate transceiver in capturing and corrupting wireless communications [15], or that the channel observation and corruption must be is realtime [5,17]. A different line of work [13,19,25] models adversarial channels where the error is generated by a computationally bounded process.

We consider a model of adversarial channel, called *Limited View Adversary Channel (LVAC)*, that was introduced in [23]. In this model the adversary is

© Springer International Publishing Switzerland 2015
A. Lehmann and S. Wolf (Eds.): ICITS 2015, LNCS 9063, pp. 214–235, 2015.
DOI: 10.1007/978-3-319-17470-9_13

computationally unlimited but their access to the channel (codeword) is limited as follows: for a codeword of length N, the adversary can adaptively choose $\rho_r N$ components to "see" and $\rho_w N$ components to modify, and the modification is by "adding" to the codeword an error vector of weight at most $\rho_w N$. Here (ρ_r, ρ_w) is the pair of constants that specify the channel. A Limited View Adversary Codes (LV code) provides reliable communication over an LVAC. There is no shared secret key between the communicants.

The Hamming error model with error fraction ρ can be seen as an LVAC with $\rho_r = 1$[1] and $\rho_w = \rho$. It is known that perfect (no error) unique decoding in Hamming model is only possible when $\rho \leq \frac{1-R}{2}$. Using Hamming error model and allowing *list decoding* where the decoder outputs a list of possible codewords, one can increase the fraction of correctable errors to $\rho \leq 1 - R$. LVAC can provide unique decoding for error rate $\rho \leq 1 - R$ as long as the fraction of the codeword seen by the adversary is bounded. That is, by limiting the view of the adversary the fraction of uniquely decodable error increases to the list decoding capacity of the channel.

1.1   Motivations for This Work and Previous Results

A wireless adversary with a typical transceiver may not be able to "see" (correctly receive) the whole codeword or "write" (introduce strong noise) over the whole codeword. Moreover, the adversary's goal may in fact be to partially corrupt the codeword so that the decoder outputs a different message. This would be feasible by targeting and changing specific symbols in a codeword. By decoupling the read and the write sets of the adversary, one allows the adversary to use powerful strategies for modifying codewords. Compared with the models in [5,17], LV codes do not require causality and allow the adversary to select its read and write sets freely subject to the bound on their sizes. LV adversary channels and LV codes with deterministic and probabilistic encoding have been defined in [23]. Decoding in both cases was deterministic. Two constructions have also been presented: a deterministic construction with $\rho_r = \rho_w = \min(R - \frac{1}{2N}, 1 - R - \frac{1}{2N})$, and a probabilistic one with $S_w = S_r$ and $\rho_r = \rho_w < 1/2$, where S_w and S_r are the adversary's write and read sets, respectively. These showed that unique decodability for $\rho_w > \frac{1-R}{2}$ is possible if the view of the adversary (ρ_r) is limited. However no upper bound on the rate of LV code was given and the relation between ρ_r and ρ_w was left open. A motivation of this work is to study how the adversary's limited view of the codeword can affect its corruption power.

A second motivation for the study of LV codes is to establish a relationship between adversarial channels and RMT protocols. Reliable Message Transmission (RMT) [9] is a well studied cryptographic primitives for reliable communication in networks. In RMT setting Alice is connected to Bob through a set of N node disjoint paths (wires) in a network such that a subset of paths is controlled by a computationally unlimited adversary. RMT protocols provide reliability for communication in the above setting. A δ-RMT protocol ensures that the probability

---

[1] As we point out in Section 6 when $\rho_r = 1$, any general corruption can be modelled as an additive error.

that the receiver receives a message different from the sent one is bounded by δ. In *threshold RMT* the adversary controls a subset of size t of the N wires. *In the rest of this paper we consider threshold RMT only and refer to it as simply RMT.* The relation between LV codes and 1-round RMT allows a unified treatment of these two apparently different problems and relates and enriches the results in the two settings.

1.2   Our Results

In this paper we consider (ρ_r, ρ_w)-LVACs and δ-LV codes that guarantee reliable message transmission over these channels with probability at least $1 - \delta$. We use a definition of reliability that allows the decoder to output an incorrect message. This is a weaker definition of reliability compared to the definition used in [23,24], where the decoder only outputs a correct message or outputs an error symbol. We have the following results.

1) Upper bound on the code rate. For an LV code for a (ρ_r, ρ_w)-LVAC and an arbitrary message distribution $\Pr(M)$, we derive an upper bound on $\mathbf{H}(M)$ (See Eq. (9)), and use it to obtain an upper bound on the rate of LV codes. Using this bound for a code family results in an upper bound on the rate of a code families, and so the the following bound on the capacity of (ρ_r, ρ_w)-LVACs,

$$\mathbf{C} \leq 1 - \rho_w. \tag{1}$$

The bound is similar to the list decoding capacity of codes in Hamming error model. In LVAC model however, the decoder outputs a single codeword and not a list of codewords. The bound holds independent of the value of ρ_r and (intuitively) is the maximum possible rate because the corrupted fraction (ρ_w) of a codeword is not recoverable.

2) An efficient LV code family that achieves the bound for $\rho_r < 1 - \rho_w$. We construct an efficient probabilistic LV code family whose rate R achieves the bound (Eq. 1) with equality, $R = 1 - \rho_w$, as the code length N approaches infinity, assuming $\rho_r + \rho_w < 1$. The construction thus achieves the channel capacity for $\rho_r < 1 - \rho_w$. The capacity of (ρ_r, ρ_w)-LVAC for higher values of ρ_r remains an open question.

The decoding algorithm of the code always outputs a correct message, or outputs $\perp$ and satisfies the stronger definition of reliability. The construction of the efficient LV code family uses three building blocks: a list decodable code [7], a message authentication code (referred to as authentication code) [26,10] and a $(0, \delta)$-Adversarial Wiretap Code $((0, \delta)$-AWTP code)[28].

A MAC is a symmetric key cryptographic primitive that allows detection of message tampering. A MAC algorithm appends a cryptographic checksum (tag) to the message. The verifier checks if a message and its appended tag are consistent under the shared key.

To correct the ρ_w fraction of adversarial error, the message must be encoded using a capacity achieving (ρ_w, ℓ)- list decodable code. The decoder of this code will output a list of possible codewords that will also include the codeword corresponding to the message. To be able to identify the correct codeword in the output list, a MAC algorithm is used to generate a tag that will be appended to the message before it is encoded using the list decodable code. The decoder can check the message part of every codeword in the decoded list to see if it satisfies the required structure. This however needs the key for the MAC algorithm to be sent securely and reliably over the LVAC. This is done by encoding the key using the AWTP code in [28]. A $(0, \delta)$-AWTP code is a code that provides perfect secrecy and δ-reliability for communication over LV adversary channels, guaranteeing that the probability of decoding error is bounded by δ. The code family that is used in our construction achieves the secrecy capacity of the AWTP channel.

In summary, to encode a message block $\mathbf{m}$, Alice (Sender) first authenticates the message $\mathbf{m}$ using a random key block $\mathbf{r}$ to generate a tagged message $(\mathbf{m}, \mathbf{t})$, which is then encoded using a list decodable code. The key block $\mathbf{r}$ is encoded by an AWTP code. Finally the ith component of the LV code will consist of the ith component of the AWTP code concatenated with the ith component of the list decodable code. The receiver decodes the corrupted list decodable codeword and generates a list of possible codewords; it also decodes the corrupted codeword of the AWTP code to find the MAC key and uses it to identify the sent codeword in the list. Details of the construction is in Section 5.

Note that the requirement $\rho_r < 1 - \rho_w$ is because of using a capacity achieving $(0, \delta)$-AWTP code. In [29] it is proved that non-zero rate for these codes implies $\rho_r + \rho_w < 1$ and so for this construction we will have $\rho_r < 1 - \rho_w$. It is however an open question to find capacity of the channel when $\rho_r > 1 - \rho_w$.

3) Relation with RMT. We show a one-to-one correspondence between *symmetric* 1-round RMTs and LV codes: a construction of an LV code gives a construction of a symmetric 1-round RMT with the same δ, and vice versa. Symmetric RMTs are RMTs with the added requirement that the set of transmissions on each wire is the same for all wires. All known RMTs are symmetric and so we simply refer to these protocols as RMT protocols. Efficiency of RMT protocols is measured by their *transmission rate* which is the number of transmitted bits for a single message bit. We give a new lower bound on the transmission rate of RMTs that holds for the more relaxed definition of reliability that is used in this paper and allows the decoder to output incorrect messages also. Previous lower bound on transmission rate of RMT was for the stronger definition of reliability where the decoder outputs only correct messages. The relation between the bounds are discussed in Section 6.2.

We will also use the LV code construction in Section 5 to construct a family of 1-RMT protocols when $N = (2 + c)t$, for which error probability δ decreases exponentially with the number of wires. A comparison between this construction and the only other existing construction of 1-round RMT protocol for $N = (2 + c)t$ is given in Table 2. The field size in the two constructions satisfy the requirements of the underlying FRS codes and are of similar size.

1.3   Related Work

Previous constructions of LV adversary channels and LV code are [23,24]. In these constructions the decoder outputs either the correct message or an error symbol. The probabilistic LV code construction in [24] is for *restricted LV codes* where the set of components that the adversary reads is the same as the set that they write to (modify); that is $S_r = S_w$. The deterministic LV code in [23] does not have this restriction but the decoding algorithm is exponential in the code length N. No rate bound was known for LV codes.

Adversarial channels have been widely studied in the literature [4], [18]. Our model of adversarial channel has similarity with the model of *binary* oblivious channels in [16]. In oblivious channels the adversary sees the codeword and depending on the level of obliviousness denoted by γ, uses a probability distribution, from a set π of $2^{(1-\gamma)n}$ distributions, on possible error vectors $e \in \{0,1\}^N$. Obliviousness in effect makes the errors less dependent on the sent codeword. A similar effect is created in LV adversary channels where the adversary's limited view of a codeword prevents the adversary from distinguishing between codewords that have the same values on the read set S_r.

Error detection against additive tampering has been considered in [3,1]. Using LV adversary channel notations, the adversary's capabilities in [3] is given by $\rho_r = 0$, and $\rho_w = 1$. In [1] again $\rho_r = 0$ but some leakage is allowed. However the amount of leakage is in terms of the randomness of encoding and so cannot be described in terms of the ρ_r parameter. In both cases the goal is detection of tampering. In LV codes however the goal is recovery of the message.

1.4   Organization

In Section 2, we recall list decodable codes, adversarial wiretap codes and message authentication codes that provide the necessary building blocks of our construction. In Section 3, we introduce LV adversary codes with the new definition of reliability that allows decoder to output incorrect messages. In Section 4, we give an upper bound on rate of limited view adversary codes and in Section 5, describe a construction of LV adversary code family that achieves the bound for a specific range of ρ_r. In section 6, we show the relation between limited view adversary code and RMT and in Section 7, discuss our results, open problems and future works.

2   Preliminaries

Notions. We use calligraphic symbols $\mathcal{X}$ to denote sets, $\mathbf{Pr}(X)$ to denote a probability distribution over $\mathcal{X}$, and X to denote a random variable that takes values from $\mathcal{X}$ with probability $\mathbf{Pr}(X)$. The conditional probability of X given Y is denote by $\mathbf{Pr}(X = x|Y = y)$. We use $\log(\cdot)$ to show logarithm in base two. *Shannon entropy* of a random variable X is $\mathbf{H}(X) = -\sum_x \mathbf{Pr}(x) \log \mathbf{Pr}(x)$, and *conditional entropy* of X given a second random variable Y, and the *mutual information* between the two, are given by $\mathbf{H}(X|Y) = -\sum_{x,y} \mathbf{Pr}(x,y) \log \mathbf{Pr}(x|y)$

and $\mathbf{I}(X,Y) = \mathbf{H}(X) - \mathbf{H}(X|Y)$, respectively. For a vector e, *Hamming weight* of a vector e is denoted by be $wt(e)$.

2.1 List Decodable Codes

A code $\mathcal{C}^N$ of length N and *rate* R is $(\rho, \ell_{\mathsf{List}})$-list decodable if the number of codewords within distance ρN from a received word is at most ℓ_{List}. It is assumed that ℓ_{List} is a polynomial function of the code length. It can be proved [8,30] that for list decodable codes, $\rho \le 1 - R$. The limit $1 - R$ on the number of correctable errors for a list decodable code, is twice the unique decoding capability of the code (using Singleton bound) and is equal to the absolute limit of reliable communication when R is the information rate.

Folded Reed-Solomon (FRS) codes are proposed by Guruswami *et al.* [12,11] with explicit construction and forming a subset of Reed-Solomon codes that achieve the list decoding capacity. FRS codes have efficient polynomial time encoding and decoding algorithms. The list size of FRS codes however is exponential in the code length N. A construction of FRS codes that uses subspace evasive sets [7] has constant list size while maintaining efficient encoding and decoding.

Lemma 1. *(Theorem 2 [7]) There exists an explicit family of codes $\{\mathcal{C}^N \subset \Sigma^N\}^{N \in \mathbb{N}}$ such that for every ξ there exists N_0 and codes of length $N > N_0$ and rate $R(\mathcal{C}^N)$ over alphabet $\Sigma = \mathbb{F}_q^{\frac{1}{\xi^2}}$, that can list decode a fraction $\rho = 1 - R(\mathcal{C}^N) - \xi$ of errors in quadratic time. The list size is at most $\mathcal{O}((1/\xi)^{1/\xi})$.*

2.2 Adversarial Wiretap Code (AWTP Code)

Adversarial wiretap codes [27] provide secure and reliable transmission from Alice to Bob over a (ρ_r, ρ_w)-adversarial wiretap channel. The adversary in an adversarial wiretap channel can read a fraction ρ_r of a codeword components, and add error to a fraction ρ_w of the components. This adversary has the same reading and writing capability of the adversary in LV adversarial channels, however the goal of the communicants in adversarial wiretap channel is to achieve secure and reliable transmission, while in LV channels only reliability is required. It is proved that capacity of these channels is $1 - \rho_r - \rho_w$. Wang *et al.* [27] gave an explicit construction of a capacity achieving code for adversarial wiretap channels with polynomial time encoding and decoding time. This AWTP code achieves perfect security and bounds decoding error probability to δ.

Theorem 1. *(Theorem 3 [27]) For any sufficient small $\xi > 0$, there is a perfectly secure adversarial wiretap code $\mathcal{C}^N$ with length N over a (ρ_r, ρ_w) adversarial wiretap channel, such that the informant rate is $R(\mathcal{C}^N) = 1 - \rho_r - \rho_w - \xi$, the alphabet is $\Sigma = \mathbb{F}_q^{\frac{1}{\xi^2}}$, and the decoding error satisfies $\delta \le \frac{(1/\xi)^{D/\xi \log\log(1/\xi)}}{q^N}$.*

2.3   Message Authentication Code (MAC)

A message authentication code (MAC)[26] is a cryptographic primitive that allows a sender who shares a secret key with the receiver to construct authenticated messages to be sent over a channel that is tampered by an adversary, and the receiver to be able to verify the integrity of the received message.

Definition 1. *A message authentication code consists of two algorithms* (MAC, Ver) *that are used for authetication and verification, respectively. For a message* m *an* authentication tag, *or simply a* tag, *is computed,*

$$t = \mathsf{MAC}(m, r),$$

and a tagged message (m, t) *is constructed. The verifier accepts a tagged pair* (m, t) *if* $\mathsf{Ver}((m, t), r)) = 1$. *Security of a one-time MAC is defined as,*

$$\Pr[(m', t'), \mathsf{Ver}((m', t'), r) = 1 | (m, t), t = \mathsf{MAC}(m, r)] \leq \delta$$

We use a MAC construction that uses polynomials over $\mathbb{F}_q$. Let $\mathbf{m}$ be a vector of length ℓN, and $\mathbf{r}$, $\mathbf{t}$ be vectors of length N over $\mathbb{F}_q$. Let ϕ be a bijection between vectors of length N over $\mathbb{F}_q$, and elements of $\mathbb{F}_{q^N}$. Define the MAC generation function $\mathsf{MAC} : \mathbb{F}_q^{\ell N} \times \mathbb{F}_q^N \to \mathbb{F}_q^N$, where $\mathsf{MAC}(\mathbf{m}, \mathbf{r}) = \mathbf{t}$ as,

$$\mathbf{t} = \mathsf{MAC}(\mathbf{m}, \mathbf{r}) = \phi^{-1}(\sum_{i=0}^{\ell-1} \phi(\mathbf{x}_i)\phi(\mathbf{r})^i).$$

Lemma 2. *For the MAC construction above, the success probability of the adversary in forging a tagged message* $(\mathbf{m}', \mathbf{r}')$ *that pass MAC verification is no more than* $\frac{\ell}{q^N}$.

The proof is a direct extension of the proof in [20].

3   Model and Definitions

3.1   Limited View Adversarial Channels

Let $[N] = \{1, \cdots, N\}$, and $S_r = \{i_1, \cdots, i_{\rho_r N}\} \subset [N]$ and $S_w = \{j_1, \cdots, j_{\rho_w N}\} \subset [N]$ denote two subsets of $[N]$, and $\mathsf{SUPP}(x)$ of vector $x \in \Sigma^N$ be the set of positions where the component $x_i \neq 0$.

Definition 2. *A* (ρ_r, ρ_w)-*Limited View Adversarial channel (or a* (ρ_r, ρ_w)-*LVAC), is a communication channel between Alice and Bob, that is partially controlled by Eve with two capabilities: Reading and Writing. For a codeword* $c \in \Sigma^N$ *where* Σ *is an additive group, the capabilities of Eve are,*

- *Reading: Eve can select a subset* $S_r \subseteq [N]$ *of size at most* $\rho_r N$ *and read the components of the codeword* c *on positions associated with* S_r. *Eve's view of the codeword is given by,* $\mathsf{View}_\mathcal{A}(\mathsf{LVACenc}(m), r_\mathcal{A}) = \{c_{i_1}, \cdots, c_{i_{\rho_r N}}\}$, *and consists of all the components that are read (observed).*

- *Writing: Eve can choose a subset $S_w \subseteq [N]$ of size at most $\rho_w N$, for "writing". This is by adding an error vector e to the codeword c, where the addition is component-wise over Σ and $\mathsf{SUPP}(e) \subseteq S_w$. The corrupted components of c are $\{y_{j_1}, \cdots, y_{j_{\rho_w N}}\}$ and $y_{j_\ell} = c_{j_\ell} + e_{j_\ell}$. The error e is generated according to Eve's best strategy for making Bob's decoder to output in error.*

We assume the adversary is *adaptive* and can select the components for reading and writing one by one, at each step using their knowledge of the codeword at that time.

The LVAC is called *restricted* if the reading and writing sets of the adversary are same, that is $S_r = S_w$. For a restricted ρ-LV adversary channel the reading and writing parameters satisfy $\rho = \rho_r = \rho_w$.

3.2 Limited View Adversary Code

Alice and Bob will use a *limited view adversary code* to provide reliability for communication.

Definition 3. *A Limited View Adversary Code (or LV code) for a (ρ_r, ρ_w)-LV adversary channel $((\rho_r, \rho_w)$-LVAC) consists of an encoding $\mathsf{LVACenc} : \mathcal{M} \to \mathcal{C}^N$ from the message space $\mathcal{M}$ to the codeword space $\mathcal{C}^N \subset \Sigma^N$, and a deterministic decoding algorithm $\mathsf{LVACdec} : \Sigma^N \to \mathcal{M}$. For a message m that is encoded to c by the sender and corrupted to $y = c + e$ by the (ρ_r, ρ_w)-LVAC, the probability that the receiver outputs the message $m' \neq m$ with probability is no more than δ. That is for any $m \in \mathcal{M}$, and adversary's observation z we have,*

$$\mathbf{Pr}(\mathsf{LVACdec}(\mathsf{LVACenc}(m) + \mathsf{Adv}(z)) \neq m) \leq \delta.$$

The above definition of reliability is for strong LV codes. In weak LV codes the decoding error probability is averaged over all messages in the message space, and the reliability requirement is,

$$\mathbf{Pr}(M_\mathcal{S} \neq M_\mathcal{R}) \leq \delta.$$

In other words the reliability requirement is for a random message $m \in \mathcal{M}$.

The above definition of reliability allows the decoder to output incorrect messages and is weaker than the one in [24]. More specifically, a decoder that bounds error probability to δ using the definition in [24] will also have the same bound on decoding error using the above definition, but the inverse is not true in general.

An LV code is deterministic if the $\mathsf{LVACenc}(\cdot)$ is deterministic, and LV code is probabilistic if the $\mathsf{LVACenc}(\cdot)$ is probabilistic. A LV code family $\mathbb{C} = \{\mathcal{C}^N\}_{N \in \mathbb{N}}$ for (ρ_r, ρ_w)-LVAC is a family of LV codes indexed by the code length $N \in \mathbb{N}$.

Definition 4. *The rate $R(\mathbb{C})$ is achievable by a code family $\mathbb{C}$ if for any $\xi > 0$ there exists N_0 such that for any $N > N_0$, we have $\frac{1}{N} \log_{|\Sigma|} |\mathcal{M}| \geq R(\mathbb{C}) - \xi$, and the probability of decoding error satisfies $\delta \leq \xi$.*

We use achievable rate of LV code families over a LVAC to define capacity of these channels.

Definition 5. *The capacity* **C** *of a* (ρ_r, ρ_w) *LVAC is the highest achievable rate of all LV code families* $\mathbb{C}$ *for the channel.*

4   An Upper Bound on the Rate of LV Codes

We derive an upper bound on the rate of an LV code and use the bound to find an upper bound on the highest achievable rate of a code family for a (ρ_r, ρ_w)-LV adversary channel. The rate upper bound only depends on the parameter ρ_w. However achieving the bound would impose condition on ρ_r.

Theorem 2. *The rate of an LV code* $\mathcal{C}^N$ *over a* (ρ_r, ρ_w)-*LVAC is bounded as,*

$$R(\mathcal{C}^N) = \frac{\mathbf{H}(M)}{N \log |\Sigma|} \leq 1 - \rho_w + 2\mathbf{H}(\delta). \tag{2}$$

The highest achievable rate of an LV code family for a (ρ_r, ρ_w)-*LVAC is bounded as,*

$$\mathbf{C} \leq 1 - \rho_w. \tag{3}$$

Proof is in Appendix A.

In restricted LVACs, the adversary is restricted in their choice of S_r and S_w and so one may expect a different upper bound. However we prove the same upper bound holds in this case also.

Proposition 1. *The rate of an LV code family for a* restricted ρ-LVAC *is bounded as,*

$$\mathbf{C} \leq 1 - \rho_w$$

Note that this proposition does not follow from Theorem 2 as the adversary in restricted LVAC is less powerful and one may expect a different upper bound. One however can use the same proof method to derive the bound for codes over restricted LVACs.

Achievable Rate of LVAC

LV codes provide unique decoding for bounded number of additive errors, guaranteeing error probability bounded by δ. The upper bound (3) on the rate of LV codes may not be achievable for all values of ρ_r. In particular for $\rho_r = 1$, the full codeword will be visible to the adversary and so LVAC error model reduces to the Hamming error model for which it is well known that perfect (zero error) unique decodeability is possible only for rates up to $1 - 2\rho_w$. For the same error model, allowing decoder error probability to be bounded by δ (instead of perfect unique decoding) one could expect the rate to slightly increase. However the rate

$1 - \rho_w$ is the list decoding capacity in Hamming error model and so one cannot expect small (δ) error probability for unique decoding at such rates. (We are not aware of any relevant bound on the list size that can be used here.)

Our construction in Section 5 achieves the bound $1 - \rho_w$ for $\rho_r < 1 - \rho_w$ and so is capacity achieving for this range of ρ_r. The best achievable rate of LV codes when $1 - \rho_w < \rho_r < 1$ remains an open problem.

5 An LV Code Family that Achieves the Bound for $\rho_r < 1 - \rho_w$

We construct an efficient LV code family $\mathbb{C} = \{\mathcal{C}^N\}_{N \in \mathbb{N}}$ for a (ρ_r, ρ_w)-LVAC. The encoding and decoding algorithms of the LV code family $\mathbb{C}$ are denoted by LVACenc and LVACdec, respectively. The construction employs a construction of Folded Reed-Solomon codes that uses subspace evasive sets, a message authentication code, and an adversarial wiretap code, with the following parameters:

– FRS codes using subspace evasive sets: From Lemma 1, there is an FRS code $\mathcal{C}_{\mathsf{FRS}}$ over alphabet $\Sigma_{\mathsf{FRS}} = \mathbb{F}_q^{\frac{1}{\xi^4}}$, with rate $R_{\mathsf{FRS}} = 1 - \rho_w - \xi^2$. The construction uses subspace evasive sets and has the decoder list size bounded by $(1/\xi^2)^{\frac{D}{\xi^2} \log \log \frac{1}{\xi^2}}$.
– MAC: From Lemma 2, there is a MAC function $\mathsf{MAC} : \mathbb{F}_q^{uRN} \times \mathbb{F}_q^N \to \mathbb{F}_q^N$, with the probability of failure to detect a forged tagged message bounded by $\delta_{\mathsf{MAC}} \leq \frac{uR}{q^N}$.
– AWTP code: From Theorem 1, there is an AWTP code $\mathcal{C}_{\mathsf{AWTP}}$ over alphabet $\Sigma_{\mathsf{AWTP}} = \mathbb{F}_q^{\frac{1}{\xi^2}}$, whose rate is $R_{\mathsf{AWTP}} = 1 - \rho_r - \rho_w - \xi$, and has decoding error bounded by $\delta_{\mathsf{AWTP}} \leq \frac{(1/\xi)^{\frac{D}{\xi} \log \log(\frac{1}{\xi})}}{q^N}$.

The construction of the LV code is as follows.

LV code Construction

Encoding: Alice does the following:

1. For an information block $\mathbf{m}$ of length uRN with $u = \log |\Sigma|$ and $\Sigma = \mathbb{F}_q^{\frac{1}{\xi^2}+\frac{1}{\xi^4}}$, do the following. Generate a random vector $\mathbf{r} \in \mathbb{F}_q^N$ and use it to find the MAC tag for the message $\mathbf{m}$, using the MAC construction in Section 2.3,

$$\mathsf{MAC}(\mathbf{m}, \mathbf{r}) = \mathbf{t}.$$

The tagged message is of length $uRN + N$ over $\mathbb{F}_q$.

2. Encode the randomness $\mathbf{r}$ into a codeword c_{AWTP} of an AWTP code of length N,

$$c_{\mathsf{AWTP}} = \mathsf{AWTPenc}(\mathbf{r}).$$

---

3. Encode the vector $(\mathbf{m}, \mathbf{t})$ into a codeword c_{FRS} of an Folded Reed-Solomon of length N that uses subspace evasive sets for efficient decoding. That is,

$$c_{\mathsf{FRS}} = \mathsf{FRSenc}(\mathbf{m}, \mathbf{t}).$$

4. The codeword c of the LV code has the ith component, $c_i = (c_{\mathsf{AWTP},i}, c_{\mathsf{FRS},i}) \in \Sigma, i = 1, \cdots, N$.
   Alice sends c to Bob over the LVAC.

Decoding: Bob does the following:

1. Bob receives a corrupted word y. The word y can be separated into Each component of y is broken into two parts to reconstruct the (corrupted) AWTP codeword y_{AWTP}, and the (corrupted) FRS codeword y_{FRS}, of the sender.
2. Bob uses AWTP decoding algorithm to decode y_{AWTP} and obtain the randomness vector $\mathbf{r}$. The decoding error of AWTP code is bounded by δ_{AWTP}.
3. Bob uses the FRS codeword decoding algorithm to decode y_{FRS}, and outputs a list $\mathcal{L}_{\mathsf{FRS}}$ of size $|\mathcal{L}_{\mathsf{FRS}}| \leq (1/\xi^2)^{\frac{D}{\xi^2} \log \log \frac{1}{\xi^2}}$. Each element in the list $\mathcal{L}_{\mathsf{FRS}}$ is a potential tagged message $(\mathbf{m}_i, \mathbf{t}_i)$.
4. Bob checks whether the $(\mathbf{m}_i, \mathbf{t}_i)$ is a correctly formed tagged message by verifying,

$$\mathbf{t}_i = \mathsf{MAC}(\mathbf{m}_i, \mathbf{r}_i).$$

If there is a unique valid tagged message, then Bob outputs the message $\mathbf{m}$ corresponding to the tagged message. Otherwise, outputs $\perp$.

Reliability of LV Codes

Lemma 3. *The probability of decoding error (strong reliability) for the LV code is bounded by* $\delta \leq \dfrac{2(1/\xi^2)^{(2+\frac{D}{\xi^2} \log \log \frac{1}{\xi^2})}}{q^N}$.

Proof is in Appendix B.

Rate of an LV Code Family

Theorem 3. *The information rate of the probabilistic LV code family* $\mathbb{C} = \{\mathcal{C}^N\}^{N \in \mathbb{N}}$ *over a* (ρ_r, ρ_w)-*LVAC is* $R(\mathbb{C}) = 1 - \rho_w$. *The read and write parameters must satisfy* $\rho_r + \rho_w < 1$. *The encoding and decoding algorithms are polynomial time in* N.

Proof is in Appendix C.

A Comparison of LV Code Constructions

We compare the LV code construction in this paper with previous constructions. LV code I is deterministic while the latter two are probabilistic. LV code I and LV code III are both capacity achieving and allow $S_r \neq S_w$. LV code I has $\rho_r + \rho_w < 1 - 1/N$ and has the restriction that $\rho_r = \rho_w$. LV code III has efficient decoding and has the requirement that $\rho_r + \rho_w < 1$

Table 1. LV code Construction

Code	Rate $R(\mathcal{C}^N)$	Comp.	Σ	Adversary capability	Achieves the bound
LV code I [23]	$1 - \rho_w - \xi$	$\mathrm{Exp}(N)$	$\mathbb{F}_q^2$	$\rho_r = \rho_w =$ $\min(R - \frac{1}{2N}, 1 - R - \frac{1}{2N})$	Yes
LV code II [24]	$\frac{1 - \rho_w - N\xi^4 - N^2\xi^6}{1 + N\xi^2}$	$\mathrm{Poly}(N)$	$\mathcal{O}(\mathbb{F}_q^{\frac{N^2}{\xi^4}})$	$S_r = S_w,\ \rho < 1/2$	No
LV code III (this work)	$1 - \rho_w - \xi$	$\mathrm{Poly}(N)$	$\mathcal{O}(\mathbb{F}_q^{\frac{1}{\xi^4}})$	$\rho_r + \rho_w < 1$	Yes

6   Reliable Message Transmission and LV Codes

6.1   Reliable Message Transmission (RMT)

A cryptographic primitive that is closely related to LV codes is RMT [6,9], that is introduced to provide reliability for communication in a partially corrupted network.

In the RMT setting (recalled in Section 1.2) Alice uses the *encoding algorithm* of the RMT protocol to encode the message m into a vector $(w_1, w_2 \cdots w_N)$, referred to a *protocol transcript*, and sends w_i over wire i. A transcript may be corrupted by the adversary, and will be received by Bob as $(w_1', w_2' \cdots w_N')$. Bob uses the *decoding algorithm* of the RMT protocol to output a message m'.

Definition 6. *A reliable message transmission protocol is called δ−reliable (δ−RMT) protocol if for any message m, $\mathcal{R}$ receives the message m correctly with probability $\geq 1 - \delta$. That is,*

$$\Pr[M_\mathcal{R} \neq M_\mathcal{S}] \leq \delta$$

Here the probability is over the randomness of the encoding and holds for any message. A stronger reliability requirement is requiring the decoder to output correct messages only. That is the decoder outputs either the correct message, or a special symbol $\perp$.

It has been proved [9] that for 1-round δ-RMT, $\delta < \frac{1}{2}(1 - \frac{1}{|\mathcal{M}|})$ is possible only if $N \geq 2t + 1$. Let $\mathcal{W}_i$ denote the set of possible transmissions over wire i. *Transmission rate of an RMT protocol* is defined as, $\tau(\mathsf{RMT}) = \frac{\text{Length of Transmissions over All Wires}}{\text{Length of Message}} = \frac{\sum_i \log_2 |\mathcal{W}_i|}{\log_2 |\mathcal{M}|}$.

For 1-round δ-RMT protocols, the lower bound on transmission rate, *assuming does not output incorrect message (stronger definition of reliability)* is $\frac{N}{N-t}$ [21]. A δ-RMT protocol whose transmission rate is of order $\mathcal{O}(\frac{N}{N-t})$ is called transmission *optimal*.

6.2   1-round RMT from LV Codes

LV codes are defined over an alphabet Σ and so all components of a codeword are elements of Σ. In RMT protocols however, the set of transmissions over each wire may be different.

Definition 7 (Symmetric RMT). *Let $\mathcal{W}_j^i, j = 1 \cdots N, i = 1 \cdots r$, denote the set of possible transmissions over wire j in an r-round RMT protocol. An RMT protocol is called a* symmetric *RMT protocol if $\mathcal{W}_j^i = \mathcal{W}^i$ is independent of j.*

All known constructions of threshold RMT protocols are symmetric.

Proposition 2. *There is a one-to-one correspondence between LV codes $\mathcal{C}^N$ of length N that provide δ-reliability for restricted ρ-LVACs, and 1-round symmetric δ_{RMT}-RMT protocols for N wires with security against a (t, N) threshold adversary, where $t = \rho N$.*

An LV code can be used to construct a 1-round symmetric δ_{RMT}-RMT, where $\delta_{\mathsf{RMT}} = \delta$. The converse is also true.

Proof is in Appendix D.

The upper bound on the rate (Theorem 2) of LV codes for ρ-restricted LVAC, gives a lower bound on the transmission rate of 1-round symmetric δ-RMT protocols.

Theorem 4. *Transmission rate of 1-round symmetric δ-RMT protocols is lower bounded by,*

$$\tau(\mathsf{RMT}) \geq \frac{N}{N - t + 2N\mathbf{H}(\delta)}.$$

Proof is in Appendix E.

Since $\delta \geq 0$, the right hand side of the bound is smaller than the known bound $\frac{N}{N-t}$. This is expected as the definition of reliability used here us weaker than the one used derivation of this latter bound (Theorem 4, [21]) requiring decoder to output correct messages only.

Corollary 1. *For $N = 2t + 1$, we have,*

$$\tau(\mathsf{RMT}) = \frac{1}{R(\mathcal{C}^N)} \geq \frac{2t + 1}{t + 1 + 2(2t + 1)\mathbf{H}(\delta)}.$$

Since $\delta \geq 0$, the right hand side of the bound is less than the known bound $\frac{2t+1}{1+t}$ that is for the stronger definition of reliability. An explanation similar to what is given for Theorem (4) applies here also.

Corollary 2. *For $N = 2t + ct$, we will have the following.*

1.

$$\tau(\mathsf{RMT}) = \frac{1}{R(\mathcal{C}^N)} \geq \frac{2 + c}{1 + c + 2(2 + c)\mathbf{H}(\delta)}.$$

2. *The RMT construction obtained from the LV code in Section 5 is efficient and optimal, and the failure probability $\delta \leq \mathcal{O}(\frac{1}{q^N})$.*

Proof is in Appendix F.

6.3 Comparing RMT Constructions

Table 2 compares the protocol in this paper with the other known 1-round δ-RMT protocols. The protocol in [22] is for $N = 2t + 1$ but can be easily extended to $N = 2t + ct$ with the same failure probability δ. The last construction allows the read and write sets of the adversary be different: that is $S_r \neq S_w$.

Table 2. Comparison with 1-round δ-RMT protocols for $N = 2t + ct$

RMT	Comp.	δ	Optimality	S_r, S_w	Outputs Incorrect Message
Protocol I, Safavi-Naini *et al.*[22]	*Poly.*	$\leq \mathcal{O}(\frac{N}{q})$	Yes	$S_r = S_w$	No
Protocol II, this Work	*Poly.*	$\leq \mathcal{O}(\frac{1}{q^N})$	Yes	$S_r \neq S_w$	No

7 Conclusions

We revisited the definition of LV codes and gave an upper bound on the rate of LV code families. The bound holds for deterministic and probabilistic codes both. We gave an efficient construction of an LV code family that achieves the bound with equality when $\rho_r < 1 - \rho_w$ and so is capacity achieving.

Construction of LV code families with $\rho_r > 1 - \rho_w$ and small designed δ, for example $\delta < 1/2$, is an open question. A list decodable code corrects errors up to $1 - \rho_w$ where ρ_w is the fraction of errors and assuming the adversary can see the whole codeword ($\rho_r = 1$) before constructing the error vector. We showed that unique decoding for this fraction error is possible if the read fraction ρ_r is bounded. Finding the relationship between the list size and ρ_r is an open question.

Extending this work to include other resources such as extra channels, or allowing interaction are future works.

LV codes provide a coding theoretic framework for the study of 1-round symmetric δ-RMT. The construction of RMT protocol obtained from the LV code in this paper has the lowest δ, and provides security for the case that $S_r \neq S_w$.

Acknowledgement. This research is in part supported by Alberta Innovates Technology Future in the province of Alberta, Canada, and National Science and Engineering Research Council of Canada.

References

1. Ahmadi, H., Safavi-Naini, R.: Detection of algebraic manipulation in the presence of leakage. In: Padró, C. (ed.) ICITS 2013. LNCS, vol. 8317, pp. 238–258. Springer, Heidelberg (2014)
2. Cover, T.M., Thomas, J.A.: Elements of information theory, 2nd edn. Wiley (2006)
3. Cramer, R., Dodis, Y., Fehr, S., Padró, C., Wichs, D.: Detection of algebraic manipulation with applications to robust secret sharing and fuzzy extractors. In: Smart, N.P. (ed.) EUROCRYPT 2008. LNCS, vol. 4965, pp. 471–488. Springer, Heidelberg (2008)
4. Csiszár, I., Narayan, P.: The capacity of the arbitrarily varying channel revisited: Positivity, constraints. IEEE Transactions on Information Theory 34(2), 181–193 (1988)
5. Dey, B.K., Jaggi, S., Langberg, M.: Codes against online adversaries. In: 47th Annual Allerton Conference on Communication, Control, and Computing, Allerton 2009, pp. 1169–1176. IEEE (2009)
6. Dolev, D., Dwork, C., Waarts, O., Yung, M.: Perfectly secure message transmission. J. ACM 40(1), 17–47 (1993)
7. Dvir, Z., Lovett, S.: Subspace evasive sets. In: Proceedings of the Forty-fourth Annual ACM Symposium on Theory of Computing, STOC 2012, pp. 351–358. ACM, New York (2012)
8. Elias, P.: Error-correcting codes for list decoding. IEEE Transactions on Information Theory 37(1), 5–12 (1991)
9. Franklin, M.K., Wright, R.N.: Secure communication in minimal connectivity models. J. Cryptology 13(1), 9–30 (2000)
10. Gilbert, E.N., MacWilliams, F.J., Sloane, N.J.A.: Codes which detect deception. Bell System Technical Journal 53(3), 405–424 (1974)
11. Guruswami, V.: Linear-algebraic list decoding of folded reed-solomon codes. In: Proceedings of the 26th Annual IEEE Conference on Computational Complexity, CCC 2011, San Jose, California, June 8-10, pp. 77–85. IEEE Computer Society (2011)
12. Guruswami, V., Rudra, A.: Explicit capacity-achieving list-decodable codes. In: Kleinberg, J.M. (ed.) Proceedings of the 38th Annual ACM Symposium on Theory of Computing, Seattle, WA, USA, May 21-23, pp. 1–10. ACM (2006)
13. Guruswami, V., Smith, A.: Codes for computationally simple channels: Explicit constructions with optimal rate. In: 51th Annual IEEE Symposium on Foundations of Computer Science, FOCS 2010, Las Vegas, Nevada, USA, October 23-26, pp. 723–732. IEEE Computer Society (2010)
14. Hamming, R.W.: Error detecting and error correcting codes. Bell System Technical Journal 29(2), 147–160 (1950)
15. Langberg, M.: Oblivious communication channels and their capacity. IEEE Transactions on Information Theory 54(1), 424–429 (2008)
16. Langberg, M.: Oblivious communication channels and their capacity. IEEE Transactions on Information Theory 54(1), 424–429 (2008)

17. Langberg, M., Jaggi, S., Dey, B.K.: Binary causal-adversary channels. In: IEEE International Symposium on Information Theory, ISIT 2009, pp. 2723–2727. IEEE (2009)
18. Lapidoth, A., Narayan, P.: Reliable communication under channel uncertainty. IEEE Transactions on Information Theory 44(6), 2148–2177 (1998)
19. Lipton, R.J.: A new approach to information theory. In: Enjalbert, P., Mayr, E.W., Wagner, K.W. (eds.) STACS 1994. LNCS, vol. 775, pp. 699–708. Springer, Heidelberg (1994)
20. Dietzfelbinger, M., Gil, J., Matias, Y., Pippenger, N.: Polynomial hash functions are reliable. In: Kuich, W. (ed.) ICALP 1992. LNCS, vol. 623, pp. 235–246. Springer, Heidelberg (1992)
21. Patra, A., Choudhury, A., Rangan, C.P., Srinathan, K.: Unconditionally reliable and secure message transmission in undirected synchronous networks: possibility, feasibility and optimality. IJACT 2(2), 159–197 (2010)
22. Safavi-Naini, R., Tuhin, M.A.A., Wang, P.: A general construction for 1-round δ-RMT and $(0, \delta)$-SMT. In: Bao, F., Samarati, P., Zhou, J. (eds.) ACNS 2012. LNCS, vol. 7341, pp. 344–362. Springer, Heidelberg (2012)
23. Safavi-Naini, R., Wang, P.: Codes for limited view adversarial channels. In: Proceedings of the 2013 IEEE International Symposium on Information Theory, Istanbul, Turkey, July 7-12, pp. 266–270. IEEE (2013)
24. Safavi-Naini, R., Wang, P.: Efficient codes for limited view adversarial channels. In: 2013 IEEE Conference on Communications and Network Security (CNS), pp. 215–223 (October 2013)
25. Micali, S., Peikert, C., Sudan, M., Wilson, D.A.: Optimal error correction against computationally bounded noise. In: Kilian, J. (ed.) TCC 2005. LNCS, vol. 3378, pp. 1–16. Springer, Heidelberg (2005)
26. Simmons, G.J.: Authentication theory/coding theory. In: Blakely, G.R., Chaum, D. (eds.) CRYPTO 1984. LNCS, vol. 196, pp. 411–431. Springer, Heidelberg (1985)
27. Wang, P., Safavi-Naini, R.: Adversarial wiretap channel with public discussion. CoRR abs/1403.5598 (2014)
28. Wang, P., Safavi-Naini, R.: An efficient code for adversarial wiretap channel. In: Proceedings of the 2014 IEEE Information Theory Workshop, Hobart, Australia, November 2-5, pp. 40–44. IEEE (2014)
29. Wang, P., Safavi-Naini, R.: Efficient codes for adversarial wiretap channels. CoRR abs/1401.4633 (2014)
30. Zyablov, V., Pinsker, M.: List cascade decoding. Problems of Information Transmission 17(4), 29–34 (1981)

A   Proof of Theorem 2

Proof. We prove an upper bound on the rate of weak LV codes for (ρ_r, ρ_w)-LVACs. For these codes error probability is averaged over all codewords. The rate upper bound for strong LV codes cannot be more than this upper bound as for these latter codes error probability of decoding for any message is bounded by δ.

The bound is for the rate of an arbitrary code and is derived for a special strategy of the adversary given below. Noting that the adversary can always use this strategy, it follows that the code rate cannot be higher than the bound that is derived for this special strategy. The adversary's strategy is the following.

1. Adversary selects a reading set S_r and a writing set S_w before the LV code transmission.
2. After the codeword is transmitted, the adversary 1) reads the $\rho_r N$ components of the codeword on the set S_r; 2) chooses an error vector e with $\mathsf{SUPP}(e) \in S_w$, randomly and with uniform distribution, and adds it component-wise to the codeword.

Let M denote the random variable associated with the message space, C denote the random variable associated with the LV codeword sent by Alice, Y denote the random variable associated with the received word of Bob, and E denote the random variable associated with the error generated by the Adversary. We associate a random variable C_i to the ith component of the code. Distribution of this variable can be obtained from the distribution of C. Let Y_{S_w} and $Y_{\overline{S_w}}$ denote the components of a codeword on the sets S_w and $\overline{S_w} = [N]/S_w$ of a word Y, respectively. The proof has three steps.

STEP 1. First, we give an upper bound on $\mathbf{H}(M|Y)$.
From the weak LV codes we have,

$$\mathbf{Pr}(M_{\mathcal{S}} \neq M_{\mathcal{R}}) \leq \delta.$$

From Fano's inequality (Theorem 2.10.1, Page 38, [2]), the decoding error probability δ implies,

$$\mathbf{H}(M|Y) \leq \mathbf{H}(M_{\mathcal{R}}|M_{\mathcal{S}}) \leq \mathbf{H}(\delta) + \delta \log |\mathcal{M}|. \tag{4}$$

Since $\log |\mathcal{M}| \leq N \log |\Sigma|$, we have

$$\mathbf{H}(M|Y) \leq \mathbf{H}(\delta) + \delta N \log |\Sigma|. \tag{5}$$

STEP 2. We give an upper bound on the rate $R(\mathcal{C}^N)$ of an LV code $\mathcal{C}^N$ of length N.
We have,

$$\mathbf{H}(M) = \mathbf{H}(M|Y) + \mathbf{H}(Y) - \mathbf{H}(Y|M). \tag{6}$$

In the following, we will bound the three terms on the right side of Eq. (6). The first term has been bounded by Eq. (5). The second term is bounded by,

$$\mathbf{H}(Y) \leq \log |\mathcal{Y}| \leq N \log |\Sigma|. \tag{7}$$

The last term is bounded as follow,

$$\begin{aligned}
\mathbf{H}(Y|M) &= \mathbf{H}(Y_{S_w} Y_{\overline{S_w}}|M) \\
&\geq \mathbf{H}(Y_{S_w}|M) \\
&\geq \mathbf{H}(Y_{S_w}|MC) \\
&\overset{(1)}{=} \mathbf{H}(E) \\
&= \rho_w N \log |\Sigma|.
\end{aligned} \tag{8}$$

Here (1) is because the adversary's error is selected uniformly and independent of the message and the codeword.

From Eq. (5) (7) (8), we have,

$$\mathbf{H}(M) \leq (1 - \rho_w)N \log |\Sigma| + \mathbf{H}(\delta) + \delta N \log |\Sigma|. \tag{9}$$

The bound (9) holds for any distribution on $\mathcal{M}$. In particular for uniform message distribution, we have the bound $R(\mathcal{C}^N)$ on the code rate,

$$R(\mathcal{C}^N) = \frac{\mathbf{H}(M)}{N \log |\Sigma|} \leq 1 - \rho_w + 2\mathbf{H}(\delta). \tag{10}$$

STEP 3. Let $\mathbf{C}$ denote the highest achievable rate of an LV code family for a (ρ_r, ρ_w)-LVAC. We show the upper bound on $\mathbf{C}$. Suppose there is an LV code family $\mathbb{C}$ for a (ρ_r, ρ_w)-LVAC with rate $R(\mathbb{C}) = 1 - \rho_w + \hat{\xi}$, for some small constant $0 < \hat{\xi} < \frac{1}{2}$.

Let $\mathbf{H}(p_0) = \frac{\hat{\xi}}{4}$. So for any $\hat{\xi}' \leq p_0$, we have $2\mathbf{H}(\hat{\xi}') \leq \frac{\hat{\xi}}{2}$ and $\hat{\xi}' \leq \mathbf{H}(\hat{\xi}') \leq \frac{\hat{\xi}}{4}$. From Definition 4, for any $0 < \hat{\xi}' \leq p_0$, there is an N_0 such that for any $N > N_0$, we have $\delta < \hat{\xi}'$ and,

$$\begin{aligned} R(\mathcal{C}^N) &\geq R(\mathbb{C}) - \hat{\xi}' \\ &= 1 - \rho_w + \hat{\xi} - \hat{\xi}' \\ &\overset{(1)}{=} 1 - \rho_w + 2\mathbf{H}(\delta) + \frac{\hat{\xi}}{2} - \hat{\xi}' \\ &\overset{(2)}{>} 1 - \rho_w + 2\mathbf{H}(\delta). \end{aligned}$$

Here (1) is from $\mathbf{H}(\delta) \leq \mathbf{H}(\hat{\xi}') < \frac{\hat{\xi}}{4}$; and (2) is from $\hat{\xi}' < \frac{\hat{\xi}}{2}$.

This contradicts the bound on $R(\mathcal{C}^N)$ in Eq. (10). So the upper bound on the rate of an LV code family over a (ρ_r, ρ_w)-LVAC is,

$$\mathbf{C} = \max_{\mathbb{C}} R(\mathbb{C}) \leq 1 - \rho_w$$

□

B Proof of Lemma 3

Proof. The decoding error happens in the following cases.

1. The AWTP decoding algorithm outputs the wrong randomness vector $\mathbf{r}'$.
   This probability is bounded by $\delta_{\mathsf{AWTP}} \leq \frac{(1/\xi)^{\frac{D}{\xi} \log \log(\frac{1}{\xi})}}{q^N}$.

2. If the AWTP decoding algorithm outputs the correct randomness $\mathbf{r}'$, there exists a tagged message $(\mathbf{m}', \mathbf{t}')$ in the decoding list $\mathcal{L}_{\mathsf{FRS}}$ with $\mathbf{m}' \neq \mathbf{m}$ that passes the MAC verification algorithm. Since the AWTP code is perfectly secure, the randomness $\mathbf{r}$ is received by Bob with perfect security. So Bob can use $\mathbf{r}$ to verify the validity of the tagged message $(\mathbf{m}', \mathbf{t}')$. For each $(\mathbf{m}', \mathbf{t}')$ with $\mathbf{m}' \neq \mathbf{m}$, the probability of passing MAC verification is bounded by $\delta_{\mathsf{MAC}} \leq \frac{uR}{q^N}$. Since the size of the list containing $(\mathbf{m}', \mathbf{r}') \in \mathcal{L}_{\mathsf{FRS}}$ is bounded by $|\mathcal{L}_{\mathsf{FRS}}| \leq (1/\xi^2)^{\frac{D}{\xi^2} \log \log \frac{1}{\xi^2}}$, the probability that the decoder outputs the message $\mathbf{m}'$, such that the corresponding tagged message $(\mathbf{m}', \mathbf{r}')$ passes the MAC verification and $(\mathbf{m}', \mathbf{r}') \in \mathcal{L}_{\mathsf{FRS}}$, is bounded by $\delta_{\mathsf{FRS}} \leq \frac{uR|\mathcal{L}|}{q^N} \leq \frac{uR(1/\xi^2)^{\frac{D}{\xi^2} \log \log \frac{1}{\xi^2}}}{q^N}$.

So the total probability of decoding error is bounded as follows,

$$\delta = \delta_{\mathsf{AWTP}} + \delta_{\mathsf{FRS}} \leq \frac{2(1/\xi^2)^{(2 + \frac{D}{\xi^2} \log \log \frac{1}{\xi^2})}}{q^N}.$$

$\square$

C   Proof of Theorem 3

Proof. 1). First we show that the rate of the LV code family is $R(\mathbb{C}) = 1 - \rho_w$.

Let $0 \leq \xi \leq \frac{1}{2}$, and $N_0 \geq (2 + \frac{D}{\xi^2} \log \log \frac{1}{\xi^2})(1 + 2\log \frac{1}{\xi}) + \log \frac{1}{\xi}$. From $u_2 R_2 N = uRN$, we have,

$$R_2 = \frac{u}{u_2} R = (1 + \frac{1}{u_2}) R \leq R + \xi^4.$$

Since $R_2 = 1 - \rho_w - \xi^2$, we have,

$$R \geq R_2 - \xi^4 \geq 1 - \rho_w - 2\xi^2 \geq 1 - \rho_w - \xi,$$

and,

$$\delta \leq \frac{2(1/\xi^2)^{(2 + \frac{D}{\xi^2} \log \log \frac{1}{\xi^2})}}{q^N} \leq \xi.$$

So the rate of LV code family is $R(\mathbb{C}) = 1 - \rho_w$.

2). Second we show that the reading and writing parameter must satisfy $\rho_r + \rho_w < 1$.

To transmit the randomness $\mathbf{r}$ securely and reliably, the maximum length of $\mathbf{r}$ must be no more than the maximum information that can be transmitted by the AWTP code. Lemma 1 implies that the length of the randomness $\mathbf{r}$ is bounded as,

$$N \leq (1 - \rho_r - \rho_w - \xi) \log |\Sigma_1| N.$$

Since $\Sigma_1 = \mathbb{F}_q^{\frac{1}{\xi^2}}$, we have,

$$1 - \xi - \xi^2 \geq \rho_r + \rho_w.$$

So the reading and writing sets must satisfy $1 - \xi - \xi^2 \geq \rho_r + \rho_w$. Since ξ approaches zero as N goes to infinity, we have $\rho_r + \rho_w < 1$.

3). The encoding algorithm is efficient since both adversarial wiretap codes and FRS codes (with subspace evasive set message coding), have polynomial (in N) time encoding algorithms (in $\text{Poly}(N)$); also the MAC function MAC is polynomial time $\text{Poly}(N)$. The decoding algorithm is efficient because decoding function of the first two primitives are efficient, and the output list size of the FRS code with subspace evasive set message coding is constant size. Finally, the MAC verification algorithm is in $\text{Poly}(N)$. □

D   Proof of Proposition 2

Proof. Consider an LV code $\mathcal{C}^N$ with decoding error δ for a restricted ρ-LVAC. By associating each component of a codeword with a distinct wire, one can construct a 1-round symmetric δ_{RMT}-RMT protocol for N wires. The protocol security is against a threshold (t, N) adversary with $t = \rho N$. The RMT encoding and decoding are obtained from the corresponding functions in the LV code; that is, $\text{RMTenc}(m) = \text{LVACenc}(m)$ and $\text{RMTdec}(y) = \text{LVACdec}(y)$. To relate the reliability of the RMT protocol to that of the LVAC-code, we note the following:

1. Decoding error is both cases requires the decoder to output the correct message with probability at least $1 - \delta$.
2. The corruption of a codeword in a restricted ρ-LVAC is by additive error while in RMT the adversary can arbitrarily modify the $|S| = t$ corrupted wires. However in restricted ρ-LVACs, $S = S_r = S_w, |S| = \rho N$ and so modifying the components $(c_{i_1}, \cdots c_{i_t})$ to $(c'_{i_1}, \cdots c'_{i_t})$ is equivalent to calculating an error e with $\text{SUPP}(e) = S$ and $(e_{i_1}, \cdots e_{i_t}) = ((c'_{i_1} - c_{i_1}), \cdots (c'_{i_t} - c_{i_t}))$, and adding it to the codeword. This means that for these channels additive error can be used to generate all possible adversarial tamperings.

The theorem follows by constructing a restricted LV code with $S = S_r = S_w$ from a 1-round symmetric δ_{RMT}-RMT, using the same correspondence between the code components and the wires. We will have $\delta = \delta_{\text{RMT}}$. □

E   Proof of Theorem 4

Proof. Let $R(\mathcal{C}^N)$ be the rate of a δ-LV code $\mathcal{C}^N$ for a restricted ρ-LVAC. From Proposition 2, the transmission rate of the associated 1-round symmetric δ-RMT is given by, $\tau(\text{RMT}) = \frac{N \log |\mathcal{V}|}{\log |\mathcal{M}|} = \frac{1}{R(\mathcal{C}^N)}$.

Now consider a 1-round symmetric δ-RMT for N wires and $t = \rho N$. Using Theorem 2, we have an LV code for a restricted LVAC with $S = S_r = S_w$ whose information rate is upper bounded by,

$$R(\mathcal{C}^N) \leq 1 - \rho + 2\mathbf{H}(\delta).$$

Since the transmission rate of a symmetric δ-RMT protocol is the inverse of the information rate of the corresponding LV code, we have,

$$\tau(\mathsf{RMT}) = \frac{1}{R(\mathcal{C}^N)} \geq \frac{1}{1 - \rho + 2\mathbf{H}(\delta)} = \frac{N}{N - t + 2N\mathbf{H}(\delta)}.$$

$\square$

F   Proof of Corollary 2

Proof. Item 1, follows directly from Theorem 4 by substituting $N = (2 + c)t$.

For item 2, we need to choose parameters $R(\mathcal{C}^N), \rho, \xi$ of the LV code such that the corresponding 1-round RMT is optimal. The selection is as follows.

1. We choose $\rho_r = \rho_w = \rho = \frac{1}{2+c}$.
2. Rate $R(\mathcal{C}^N)$: we have the LV code rate $R(\mathcal{C}^N) = \frac{1}{2+c}$. The transmission rate τ of the corresponding RMT is $\tau = \frac{1}{R(\mathcal{C}^N)} = 2 + c = \mathcal{O}(\frac{N}{N-t})$ which is a constant and so the RMT protocol is optimal.
3. Parameter ξ: the code family is capacity achieving and parameter ξ determines that the code rate is at most ξ less than the capacity.

   The parameter must be chosen with two considerations: the FRS code with the subspace evasive set used for the encoding of the message (appended with MAC), and the AWTP code used for transfering the MAC key.

   (a) FRS with subspace evasive set message coding: From Section 5, for the LV code we have $\Sigma_{\mathsf{FRS}} = \mathbb{F}_q^{\frac{1}{\xi^4}}$ and $\Sigma = \mathbb{F}_q^{\frac{1}{\xi^4} + \frac{1}{\xi^2}}$. Let $\rho = \frac{1}{2+c}$ and $R(\mathcal{C}^N) = \frac{1}{2+c}$. From,

   $$\log |\mathcal{M}| = R_{\mathsf{FRS}}(\mathcal{C}^N) N \log |\Sigma_{\mathsf{FRS}}| = R(\mathcal{C}^N) N \log |\Sigma|,$$

   we have,

   $$R(\mathcal{C}^N) \leq R_{\mathsf{FRS}}(\mathcal{C}^N).$$

   Since $R_{\mathsf{FRS}}(\mathcal{C}^N) = 1 - \rho - \xi$, it implies that,

   $$R(\mathcal{C}^N) \leq R_{\mathsf{FRS}}(\mathcal{C}^N) = 1 - \rho - \xi,$$

   and so ξ must satisfy,

   $$\xi \leq 1 - \rho - R(\mathcal{C}^N) = 1 - \frac{1}{2+c} - \frac{1}{2+c} = \frac{c}{2+c}. \tag{11}$$

   (b) AWTP code: We have $R_{\mathsf{AWTP}}(\mathcal{C}^N) = 1 - \rho - \rho - \xi$ and $\rho = \frac{1}{2+c}$, and so,

   $$R_{\mathsf{AWTP}}(\mathcal{C}^N) = 1 - 2\rho - \xi.$$

   Let

   $$\xi \leq \frac{c}{2(2+c)}. \tag{12}$$

From Section 5 the alphabet of AWTP is $\Sigma_{\text{AWTP}} = \mathbb{F}_q^{\frac{1}{\xi^2}}$ and so the rate of the AWTP code is,

$$R_{\text{AWTP}}(\mathcal{C}^N) = 1 - 2\rho - \xi = \frac{c}{2+c} - \xi = \frac{c}{2(2+c)}. \tag{13}$$

The required randomness vector $\mathbf{r}$ h for the LV code has length N. Since,

$$\frac{\log |\mathbf{r}|}{N \log |\Sigma_{\text{AWTP}}|} = \frac{N}{N \log |\Sigma_{\text{AWTP}}|} = \left(\frac{c}{2(2+c)}\right)^2$$

is less than the information rate of the AWTP code with the chosen parameters, if we choose $\xi = \frac{c}{2(2+c)}$, then $\mathbf{r}$ can be sent securely and reliably using the AWTP code.

To satisfy both above conditions, Eq. (11) and AWTP code Eq. (12), we will choose,

$$\xi \leq \frac{c}{2(2+c)}.$$

From the LV code parameter $R(\mathcal{C}^N), \rho, \xi$ above, we can determine the parameters of the δ-RMT scheme obtained from the LV code:

1. Transmission rate: $\tau = \mathcal{O}(\frac{N}{N-t})$ and so the RMT is optimal.
2. Computational time: Since $\xi = \frac{c}{2(2+c)}$ is constant, the list size of the FRS code with subspace evasive set encoding is constant and so the decoding algorithms of the AWTP code and the FRS code with subspace evasive set encoding, are polynomial in N and so the decoding algorithm of the RMT is polynomial time.

3. Decoding error: the LV code decoding error is $\delta \leq \frac{2(1/\xi^2)^{(2+\frac{D}{\xi^2} \log \log \frac{1}{\xi^2})}}{q^N}$ and ξ is constant. This means that the decoding error of RMT is bounded by $\delta \leq \mathcal{O}(\frac{1}{q^N})$.

$\square$

Locally Decodable Codes for Edit Distance

Rafail Ostrovsky[1,*] and Anat Paskin-Cherniavsky[2,**]

[1] Department of Computer Science and Mathematics, UCLA
rafail@cs.ucla.edu
[2] Department of Computer Science and Mathematics,
Ariel University and Department of Computer Science, UCLA
anatpc@ariel.ac.il

Abstract. Locally decodable codes (LDC) [1,9] are error correcting codes that allow decoding (any) individual symbol of the message, by reading only few symbols of the codeword. LDC's, originally considered in the setting of PCP's [1], have found other additional applications in theory of CS, such as PIR in cryptography, generating a lot of fascinating work (see [12] and references within). In one straightforward practical application to storage, such codes provide enormous efficiency gains over standard error correcting codes (ECCs), that need to read the entire encoded message to learn even a single bit of the encoded message. Typically, LDC's, as well as standard ECC's are designed to decode the encoded message if up to some bounded fraction of the symbols had been modified. This corresponds to decoding strings of bounded Hamming distance from a valid codeword. A stronger natural metric is the edit distance, measuring the shortest sequence of insertions and deletions (*indel.*) of symbols leading from one word to another. [1]Standard ECC's for edit distance have been previously considered [11]. Furthermore, [11] devised codes with rate and distance (error tolerance) optimal up to constants, with efficient encoding and decoding procedures. However, combining these two useful settings of LDC, and robustness against indel. errors has never been considered.

---

* Work supported in part by NSF grants 09165174, 1065276, 1118126 and 1136174, US-Israel BSF grant 2008411, OKAWA Foundation Research Award, IBM Faculty Research Award, Xerox Faculty Research Award, B. John Garrick Foundation Award, Teradata Research Award, and Lockheed-Martin Corporation Research Award. This material is based upon work supported by the Defense Advanced Research Projects Agency through the U.S. Office of Naval Research under Contract N00014 -11 -1-0392. The views expressed are those of the author and do not reflect the official policy or position of the Department of Defense or the U.S. Government.
** Work supported in part by NSF grants 09165174, 1065276, 1118126 and 1136174. This material is based upon work supported by the Defense Advanced Research Projects Agency through the U.S. Office of Naval Research under Contract N00014 -11 -1-0392. The views expressed are those of the author and do not reflect the official policy or position of the Department of Defense or the U.S. Government.
[1] Edit distance is "more expressive" than Hamming distance in the sense that $dist_E(x, y) \leq 2dist_H(x, y)$ always holds, while edit distance 2 may translate to Hamming distance n. For instance, consider $x = 1010 \ldots 10, y = 0101 \ldots 1$.

A. Lehmann and S. Wolf (Eds.): ICITS 2015, LNCS 9063, pp. 236–249, 2015.
DOI: 10.1007/978-3-319-17470-9_14

In this work, we study the question of constructing LDC's for edit distance. We demonstrate a strong positive result - LDC's for edit distance can be achieved, with similar parameters to LDC's for Hamming distance. More precisely, we devise a generic transformation from LDC for Hamming distance to LDC for edit distance with related parameters. Besides the theoretical appeal of such a primitive, we put forward a cryptographic application to secure property testing over storage prone to indel. errors (such as DNA-based storage).

1   Introduction

In this work, we define and study the feasibility of locally decodable codes (LDC) for edit distance. Standard LDC codes are defined over the Hamming distance, allowing to decode individual symbols of the message by reading few symbols of the codeword. This provides enormous efficiency gains over standard error correcting codes (ECCs), that need to read the entire encoded message to learn even a single bit of information. There exist many scenarios where edit distance, rather than the more traditional Hamming distance, is the appropriate metric.

Let us give an example of a cryptographic application to efficient secure property testing over unreliable storage. See full version for details. Consider a setting where a storage system prone to insertion and deletion errors is employed. For instance, consider a DNA-based storage system (prototypes of such systems have already been constructed, and have the advantage of high information density [2]). In such systems, it makes sense to store information encoded via ECC for edit distance. Now, consider a scenario where two (or more) users want to securely and efficiently compute whether their joint input (x_1, x_2) satisfies some property, or is far from it (otherwise we don't care about the output). In the world of property testing, the primary goal is to make a sublinear (as small as possible) number of queries into the input [6]. As a simple example, consider a pair of users who wish to securely check whether a pair of strings they hold are equal or 0.2-far from being equal in Hamming distance (but reveal nothing else about their inputs). There exists a simple (not secure) protocol for the task, that makes t queries into the strings at random locations j, and checks whether $x_{1,j} = x_{2,j}$. Accept iff. all comparisons succeed. Clearly, this protocol has one-sided error of $\leq 0.8^t$, so taking $t = \log^2(n)$ results in a negligible error. Observe that (an oracle) to the randomized functionality computed by the protocol, allows for privacy in the sense that the probability of outputting 0 or 1 depends only on whether the input has the property or has distance ≥ 0.2 from the property, but not on the particular distance (upto negligible differences). Thus, to securely evaluate the property if not for the issue of unreliable storage, the parties could run MPC (secure multi-party computation) for the functionality and achieve $polylog(n) \cdot$ security-param work load.[2]

---

[2] Note that to meet the efficiency requirements when using the typical circuit-based protocols form the literature, the parties first agree on randomness for the sampling, and let each party locally derive the sublinear sampling circuit at the first step.

Now consider unreliable storage, and assume upto an ϵ-fraction of insertion or deletion errors (mutations) may occur in the storage devise (except for with negligible probability - see the full version for a treatment of the setting where the mutation rate can be large with non-negligible probability). We modify the above solution to read input symbols by decoding them from the corresponding codewords.[3] If the LDC has a small enough decoding error (assuming few corruptions), it is easy to show that every symbol has a very low (albeit higher and 2-sided) simulation error. The overhead in work is not too great because the code is an LDC, and grows roughly by the query complexity of the LDC.

Going back to our main theoretical question - we put forward a strong positive result, by demonstrating a compiler from standard LDC's into LDC's for edit distance, with only small losses to the parameters. In particular, the tolerated fraction of errors (typically a constant), and the code's rate are only degraded by a constant. The query complexity grows by polylogarithmic factors in the size of the codeword. The compiler is black box, in the sense that the LDC decoder for the resulting code uses the decoder of the original LDC code in a black box way (only reading and answering its queries to the purported codeword). Our main technique is reducing the task to the problem of searching an element in a large sorted list L with a constant fraction δ of corrupted values. The search should succeed with overwhelming in $|L|$ probability for all but, say, 50δ fraction of the queries into uncorrupted locations. The number of queries to the list should be polylogarithmic. We devise a comparison-based algorithm with $O(\log^{2+o(1)}|L|)$ queries for this task. This algorithm may be of independent interest, as for the more stringent setting where all uncorrupted entries should be recovered correctly, there exist polynomial lower bounds on the number of queries by comparison-based algorithms. We leave open the question of whether $O(\log(|L|))$ queries are sufficient.

Theorem 1. *(Main theorem, informal). Consider an $(\delta(n), q(n), \epsilon(n))$-LDC $L_H : \mathbb{F}_p^n \to \mathbb{F}_p^m$ for Hamming distance. Here $q(n)$ is the query complexity, and $\epsilon(n)$ is a bound on the worst case error probability in decoding a message symbol if the message is at Hamming distance $\leq \delta(n)$ from a codeword. There exists a black box transformation taking any such L_H into a $(\delta/c, q \cdot polylog(m, p), \epsilon + neg(m))$-LDC $L_E : \mathbb{F}_p^n \to \mathbb{F}_p^m$ for edit distance, where c is a (quite large) global constant. The code rate degrades by a constant. Encoding (and decoding) efficiency only degrades by a poly(n) factor.*

The transformation from Theorem 1 is black box in the following sense. Let $D_H^{w_H}, D_E^{w_E}$ denote the decoders of the original LDC (for Hamming distance) and the decoder for the LDC for edit distance that we construct, respectively. $D_E^{w_E}$ receives an input i and needs to decode x_i. For that purpose, it runs $D_H(i)$ as is, reading only the sequence of locations D_H asks to query w_H at, and answering them. To answer a query j of w_H, it simulates the answer $w_H[j]$ using queries to

---

[3] To meet the efficiency goal, we now need to incorporate the LDC decoder's randomness into the first step of generating the sampling circuit. As before, this randomness (circuit) may be public without violating privacy.

its own oracle w_E, which "induces" a codeword w_H. Finally, the output of D_H is returned.

On a high level, L_E is a composition of L_H with a standard code I for edit distance. That is, to encode a message m, it computes $w = L_H[m]$, divides w into blocks $w_1, \ldots, w_T$, and outputs $w' = (I(w'_1) \circ \ldots \circ I(w'_T))$, where w'_i is "almost" w_i. To answer a query at index i, the goal is to find the relevant block in w', and decode it to extract the relevant symbol. Even in standard codes, one central difficulty is in finding the block in w'. For this purpose, the w'_j's explicitly include their relative index: $w'_i = (i, w_i)$. This transformation is essentially the one used in SZ codes [11], where L_H is replaced by a "standard' code C. This is up to a few technical enhancements beyond using an LDC C that are required to ensure the resulting code is an LDC (see Section 1.1). The main novelty of our construction, is in demonstrating that this transformation (almost) preserves the parameters of LDC codes ([11] show that for a careful choice of block length, it preserves distance and rate of standard ECC up to a constant), by devising a suitable decoder procedure. As we explain below, just adding the indices is not sufficient for LDC codes. If the entire codeword can be read, we can just "read off" the indices of all blocks, and interpret the (decoded) (i, a) as a appearing at location i. If there are relatively few errors, this will produce a C-codeword with few erasures (duplicate and missing entries) + changes (erroneous entries we do not know of), which can then be decoded. For LDC codes, the problem is in finding a specific block w'_i by reading only $polylog(m)$ entries from the codeword (in particular, $|I(w'_i)| = polylog(m)$. Although the location of the relevant block can move up to a $\delta |W_E|$ fraction of symbols, we should find it with high probability for "most" blocks.

Our main technical tool is a new algorithm for searching an element in a sorted list L where up to a constant δ fraction of the original entries may be arbitrarily modified (and possibly out of order), looking at only $polylog|L|$ locations of the list. The algorithm performs a "clever" version of binary search, that guarantees correct recovery of $1 - c\delta$ fraction of the list entries (same set in each execution). This technique may be of independent interest. The problem of searching sorted lists with corruptions or errors in query's answers has been considered before ([10,5] to mention a few). The main difference of our setting is that we get much lower query complexity at the cost of allowing incorrect answers for some $c\delta$ of the uncorrupted entries. Without this compromise, in comparison-based algorithms (ours included), the query complexity is provably $\Omega(poly(n))$ for constant error fractions [5].

We also observe that our technique for transforming codes for Hamming distance into codes for edit distance applies to the setting of computational LDC's [8], and of Locally testable codes (see [7] and references within).

1.1   Our Technique in More Detail

Our starting point is the construction by Schulman et al [11], that converts (standard) error correcting codes for Hamming distance into ones for edit distance. Their construction is a composition of two codes.

1. Start with a standard "outer" ECC $C_1 : \mathbb{F}_p^n \to \mathbb{F}_p^m$, and apply it to the plaintext message x, obtaining y.
2. Encode y under a greedily constructed code I for edit distance as follows (denote this new code by C_2). Divide y into blocks of $\log m$ symbols each, resulting in $T = m/\log m$ blocks. Encode each block y_i at the i'th block using an "inner" (greedily constructed, exponential-time) code I, applied to (i, y_i), obtaining $w_i = I(i, y_i)$. Output $w = w_1 \circ w_2 \ldots \circ w_T$ as the codeword. The code $I : \mathbb{F}_p^{\log m} \to \mathbb{F}_p^h$ has constant rate and tolerates a constant fraction of errors. (the number of blocks is selected as such to ensure constant rate of C_2).

The resulting code $C_2 \circ C_1$ is a code for edit distance, in the sequel we refer to it as SZ.[4] Their goal is to obtain codes with efficient (in n) encoding and decoding procedures, and constant distance and rate. Thus, they plug in C_1 with constant distance and rate parameters, and $C_2 \circ C_1$ inherits these properties (due to also constant rate and distance for I). The reason that SZ do not just use I as the code for edit distance is its inefficiency of encoding and decoding, so it can only be practically applied to short blocks.

Besides constant (edit) distance, another property of the code I that they need, is that for every pair of different codewords, the distance between a prefix w_1 of w, and a suffix u_1 of u (or vise versa) of large enough (fractional) length, say 0.1, have large distance. This ensures that in a corrupted codeword w, subsequences "close enough" to different codewords do not intersect "by much". Thus, a corrupted w can be viewed as a sequence of codewords (of I) and possibly garbage between them, written one after the other (possibly up to small fractional overlaps). This way, every original w_i that was corrupted by "not too much" will be recovered when scanning a small vicinity of w_i (as is useful for LDC's), or when scanning the entire w from left to right (as is useful for standard decoding, like in SZ).

This construction suggests the following simple transformation from standard LDC's into LDC's for edit distance - plug the (standard) LDC C_1 as the outer code (instead of a standard ECC) into the construction. The code $L_E = C_2 \circ C_1$ is our LDC for edit distance! As mentioned before, there are two technical points where our construction diverges from SZ, to be noted below. A decoder for L_E acts as follows.

Simulate C_1's decoder D_1. For any query D_1 makes, decode the corresponding block (by going to its vicinity), and retrieve the relevant query by decoding I. To make blocks identifiable, we use a slightly stronger "no overlapping" property of I that is implicit in [11]'s instantiation of I (first point of divergence). At the end, output whatever D_1 outputs. If I has edit distance δ_I, then a δ_E fraction of errors will corrupt (beyond repair) a $\leq \delta_E/\delta_I$ fraction of the blocks, but the rest will be correctly recovered (if found!). If the original LDC tolerates a δ_H fraction of errors, we may set $\delta_E = \delta_H \delta_I$. As D_1 sees at most a δ_E fraction of corrupted symbols, the new decoder's decoding probability is the same as D_1's.

---

[4] In SZ, I with binary input and output alphabet is used. It is easy to modify to work over larger alphabets, possibly allowing for better (constant) parameters.

The main problem is that it is unclear how to find the required blocks. Due to deletion and insertion errors occurring before it, every block can be as far as δm symbols from its expected index (in the original sequence $w_1, \ldots, w_T$). To cope with this, we develop a clever binary search technique allowing to find it, even in the presence of corruptions. More precisely, we reduce our problem to the following problem of searching a sorted list L^* of length T (only known to us up to a factor of 2) where up to some (constant) δ fraction of the entries may have been corrupted, resulting in a list L. Entries of the list are of the form (i, a_i), where the sorting is by the unique keys i (up to duplications introduced by corruptions). One wants to learn s associated with i in L^* (or that i does not appear in it). Design an algorithm $V(i)$ that makes $polylog(T)$ queries into the list that returns the correct value s with probability $1 - neg(T)$ for at least a $1 - c\delta$ fraction of the original (i, a) entries, where c is a constant independent of δ.

The constant "loss of correctness" factor c above will just translate into a further decrease in tolerated δ_E, namely $\delta_E \leq \delta_H \delta_I / c$, so we can afford it. Roughly speaking, uncorrupted entries in L will correspond to the list of blocks $(1, w_1), \ldots, (T, w_T)$ that we not "deleted", but either modified or newly inserted. The former blocks will retain their original order, where a block's corresponding key is a blocks index i, and its payload w_i.

In Section 2.1 we present our algorithm for searching sorted lists with corruptions. In Section 3 we discuss how to adapt this abstraction to searching a symbol w_i in a codeword w of $C_2 \circ C_1$ as above (and spells out the codes' decoding algorithm). There are several technical issues that need to be carefully treated here. In particular, the type of queries we chose for the the sorted list searching abstraction are easy to (approximately) implement given w.

A second point where our construction diverges from the original construction of SZ is in the efficiency of I. As mentioned above, the inner code I is constructed in a greedy manner, with exponential complexity in the message space. In our case, this size is up to $\log m$ symbols, so encoding and decoding of that code may have complexity $m^{\log p}$ (bit operations), which is prohibitively high in the setting of LDC and ok for (non-local) decoding of the entire message for binary or constant p (although overall efficiency of decoding is a secondary goal in LDC, it is important in practice). Thus, we use a recursive version of the inner code (also mentioned in the paper), where every block (i, y_i) is encoded by a SZ code (based on, say, Reed Solomon as the outer code), so the greedy part is now applied to messages of length $\leq \log(\log m \cdot \log p)$ bits. This comes only at a constant decrease in tolerated errors and rate.

Remark 1. For some settings of parameters, one would just rather fall back to (non-local) SZ codes for edit distance, that read the entire codeword to decode. As explained above, some kind of "binary" search seems inevitable. Thus, we expect to lose a factor of $\log m$ in the query complexity (even if we were willing to give up such a factor on rate). For some codes, such as the Hadamard code, $\log m = n$, so there is no gain in query complexity. Nevertheless, the construction is non-trivial for most useful parameter settings of LDC.

1.2   Preliminaries

In this paper $\mathbb{F}_p$ denotes a finite alphabet of size p (typically, but not necessarily a finite field). We denote the Hamming distance of two strings $x, y \in \mathbb{F}_p^l$ by $dist_H(x, y)$. The edit distance between $x, y \in \mathbb{F}_p^*$, $dist_E(x, y)$ is the minimal number of insertion or deletion operations to be performed on x to obtain y (or visa versa, as $dist_E$ is a metric). We often just write "$dist(x, y)$" when the type of distance is clear from the context.

For a metric $dist \in \{dist_H, dist_E\}$, we say $C : \mathbb{F}_p^n \to \mathbb{F}_p^m$ is an error correcting code (ECC) with distance parameter d if for any pair of codewords, $C(x) \neq C(y)$, we have $dist(C(x), C(y)) \geq d$. Alternatively, we will often measure the number of errors the code can tolerate (up to $(d-1)/2$). The codes' rate is the ratio m/n.

By default, we consider families of ECC's $C : \mathbb{F}_p^n \to \mathbb{F}_p^{m(n)}$ (sometimes p depends on n as well), and discuss their asymptotic parameters.

Definition 1. *An ECC, $L : \mathbb{F}_p^n \to \mathbb{F}_p^m$ is a $(\delta(n), q(n), \epsilon(n))$-LDC (locally decodable code) for Hamming distance if there exists a decoding algorithm $D^{w'}(i)$ such that for all $i \in [n], x \in \mathbb{F}_p^n$, and all $w' \in \mathbb{F}_p^m$ satisfying $dist_H(w', L(x)) \leq \delta m$, we have*

$$Pr[D^{w'}(i) = x_i] \geq 1 - \epsilon.$$

Here D reads at most $q(n)$ locations in w'.

Definition 2. *LDC for edit distance is defined as LDC for Hamming distance (replacing $dist_H$ with $dist_E$ everywhere), with the minor difference that $D^{w'}$ is also given $|w'|$ as an additional input.*

We use the following family of codes for edit distance implicit in [11].

Lemma 1. *For every finite alphabet $\mathbb{F}_p$, there exists an integer t_0 and real $\delta > 0$, such that for all $t \leq t_0, \delta' \leq \delta$, there exists an ECC $I_{t,\delta'} : \mathbb{F}^t \to \mathbb{F}_p^m$ for edit distance tolerating up to $\delta'm$ insertions and deletions. $I_{t,\delta'}$ has constant (possibly depending on δ') rate m/t. Also, there exist a (global) constant c such that for all $I_{t,\delta'}$ as above satisfy the following "no overlapping" property. For every pair of codewords (ws_1, s_2v), if $|s_1| = |s_2| \geq 2\delta m$, then either $ws_1 = s_2v$, or $dist_E(s_1, s_2) \geq 1.5\delta m$. Furthermore, if $|s_1|, |s_2| \leq (1 - \delta)m$, then it must be the case that $dist_E(s_1, s_2) \geq 1.5\delta m$. The codes' encoding and decoding complexity is poly(m).*

See full verion for a proof.

We will need the following version of the Chernoff's bound.

Lemma 2. *Let $X_1, \ldots, X_1$ denote independent random variables, and let $X = \sum_i X_i$. Assume also that the support of each is $[0, B]$, for some $B > 0$. Then for $\epsilon > 0$, we have*

$$Pr[|X - E(X)| \geq \epsilon E(X)] \leq e^{-\Theta(\epsilon^2)E(X)}$$

2 Searching Sorted Lists with Corruptions

Some Discussion and Notation. As explained in the introduction, proving Theorem 1 boils down to the developing a search algorithm on a sorted list with (small) constant fraction $\leq \delta$ of corrupted entries, making a polylog number of queries to the list. The original list L^* list is comprised from pairs of (i, a_i) where i is a unique key (before corruptions). The input to the algorithm is a key i, and it should return a corresponding a_i in its input list L. We require that for all lists L^*, all L resulting from L^* by modifying (no indel. operations!) a δ fraction of entries, the algorithm returns a_i on query i to L with probability $1 - neg(|L^*|)$ for all but some $1 - c\delta$ fraction of the (original) entries, for a constant c independent of δ. Clearly, c can not be less then 1. In particular, if only the a_i's are modified (keys are intact), there is no way to recover the original values.

Previous work. There exist algorithms in the literature in a similar setting with stronger guarantees and worse parameters. For instance, [5,4] consider algorithms that guarantee to recover a_i for all values for which (i, a_i) was not corrupted, and if there is no key i in the sequence, corrupted or correct, the algorithm should output "not found". They prove that for such a stringent requirement, any comparison-based algorithm, that accesses some $\Omega(\log |L| + \delta \cdot |L|)$ locations errs on some input with probability at least $1/2$.[5] They demonstrate some matching upper bounds, with parameters (almost) matching the lower bound. Still, even for an algorithm matching the lower bound perfectly, for the range of parameters where δ_0 is a constant, the query complexity is $\Omega(|L|)$, which is unacceptable in our case. The key for obtaining a (comparison based) algorithm with query complexity $polylog(|L|)$, is considering a setting with relaxed correctness guarantees as above. To the best of our knowledge, this setting had not been considered before in the area of searching on sorted lists.

2.1 Our Approach

A Warmup - Random Error Locations. To gain intuition, assume that the error locations were picked at random - each entry is corrupted with probability $\delta \leq \delta_0 = 0.2$. Jumping ahead, for our application to LDC for edit distance, this would happen if the insertions and deletions occurring are at random locations.

Assume that the success requirements of the algorithm need to only hold for "most" error patters (allowing high failure rates for all queries for a small fraction of error patterns). Then the following simple variant of binary search works. Given a list of length $m = |L|$, proceed in levels, so that on every level we divide the interval at hand into three equal intervals (start with the entire list). For the middle interval, randomly and independently sample $\log^2 m$ entries, and record the fraction of keys smaller or larger then i, $(s, b = 1 - s)$ respectively (for simplicity of analysis, sample with repetitions). If some (i, a) element is found, we

---

[5] This is a certain restatement of their theorem 5, in terms of the number of elements involved in the comparison queries, rather then in terms of the number of comparisons made. The proof follows straightforwardly from their proof of that theorem.

stop and return a corresponding to the first appearance of i found immediately. Otherwise, return the corresponding a for the first such appearance and terminate). If $s, b \geq 0.4$, proceed with the middle interval recursively. Otherwise, if $s > b$ proceed with interval $(2/3, 1)$ as the new interval, if $b > s$ proceed with $(0, 1/3)$. We stop at intervals of size $\log^2 m$, and scan the entire interval; return a corresponding to the first (i, a) in the interval, or $\perp$ otherwise.

Quite straightforward analysis, implies that the above algorithm succeeds to achieve its goal for all but a small fraction of error patterns. One type of error is that of finding the wrong (i, a) and terminating the search (even if the correct (i, a) is located in a different interval). All these errors may only occur for at most $2\delta m$ of the keys i originally present in L. Those which were "duplicated" elsewhere, and those that were modified into the new duplicates, possibly erasing their own information.

For all other entries (keys) on which the algorithm may err, entries of the form (i, a) only appear in the interval that originally contains an entry (i, a) for that key, and thus this type of error may not occur. In that case, only errors due to excluding an interval originally containing i at some point along the recursion may occur - we refer to these as type 2 errors. This type of errors is slightly trickier to bound - jumping ahead, it will occur with probability $> neg(m)$ for none of these other keys for this algorithm, and account for most of the errors of the algorithm for general errors.

A crucial point is that the probability (over picking error patters uniformly at random) that the search reaches an interval with density larger then $0.25 = 1.2\delta_0$ fraction of errors for *any* searched key i is bounded by $poly(m) \cdot m^{-\Theta(\log m)} = neg(m)$ (Chernoff + union bound). Here $poly(m)$ is a bound on the number of reachable nodes (for any key i) derived from $3^{\log_{1.5}(m)} = m^{\log_{1.5}(3)} \leq m^{2.71}$.[6]

It is easy to see that if the latter happens, at every step of the recursion, the algorithm can make a type 2 error when moving to the next step of the recursion with probability at most $m^{\Theta(-\log m)}$.

This holds since if i is in the first interval, (same holds for the 3rd interval), and assuming the error density in interval 2 is indeed ≤ 0.25, then ≥ 0.75 fraction of elements in 2 are bigger then i. Thus, having $s \geq 0.4$ (necessary for $b, s \geq 0.4$) is highly unlikely - recalling (i, a) can not appear in interval 2 (we account for such keys i in type 1 errors), s has expectancy of at most most $1/3$. By Chernoff bound, $s \geq 0.4$ thus has negligible in m probability $exp(-\Theta(\log^2(m)))$. Otherwise, getting $s > b$ would require getting $s \geq 0.5$ for same expected value of 0.3 - again a $exp(-\Theta(\log^2(m)))$ probability.

Taking union bound over the path for any given key i, the overall error probability is $O(\log m \cdot m^{\Theta(-\log m)}) = neg(m)$.

---

[6] To be precise, the graph in question is the union of the algorithm's executions over all possible keys i, and all possible error patterns that were present in the original list. That is, V consists of list intervals potentially reachable at the various recursion levels ran - 3^i at the i'th level, until reaching those of size smaller then $\log^2 m$. The graph edges E connect each node at level i, to each of the three nodes at level $i + 1$ that are sub-intervals of I.

The General Case. The main difficulty is that for arbitrary error patterns, low density of errors in all intervals in not guaranteed. Thus, a more sophisticated analysis (for a somewhat more sophisticated algorithm, but quite along the lines of the one above) is required. The parameters tolerated by the above algorithm in this random errors setting are $c = 2$, and $\delta \leq 0.2$. The parameters we achieve for general errors will be worse – $c = 50$, and δ bounded correspondingly ($\delta \leq 1/c$ to obtain any non-trivial correctness guarantee).

Formal specification of the model. Let us first fully formalize the setting in which the search algorithm operates.

- The protocol is specified by an algorithm $S^L(i)$. It has oracle access to a list L, resulting from a sorted list L^* by modifying upto a constant δ fraction of elements (possibly not respecting the original order). Let m' denote an approximation on $|L|$ up to a factor of 2 (m' is available to S, while the exact $m = |L|$ is not). The input is a key i to search.
- Oracle queries: There are two types of possible queries to the list.
  1. (v_0, v_1), where (v_0, v_1) are fractional locations in the list, where $v_0 \leq v_1$. The entry (i, a) at a randomly selected location inside the interval is returned. Query cost is 1.
  2. (v_0, v_1, y). If the interval (v_0, v_1) is of (absolute) size y or smaller, the sequence of all points in the interval will be returned. Otherwise, an error is returned. Query cost is y (regardless of the query's outcome).
- Output: Given a key i, such that (i, a_i) was present in the original list (before corruptions occurred), the correct output for it is a_i.
- Goal: Maximize the worst case fraction of keys i originally present in the list (before corruptions) for which the reply is correct with probability $1 - neg(m)$. The total cost of queries made should be $polylog(m)$ - we are not trying to optimize the concrete complexity.[7]

Construction 3. *Initialize the searched interval to $I = (0, 1)$, $\Delta = 3$ (or any, other constant > 3), $T = \Delta$, $r = \log^2 m'$. Repeat:*

1. *Make a type-2 query with (I, r). If it returns a sequence of points, and one of them is of the form (i, a), return a corresponding to the first such i. Otherwise, return $\bot$. (we reached a short interval we can read completely)*

---

[7] Jumping ahead, to motivate the concrete choices in the model definition, recall searching for some key i in list L is an abstraction for searching for the i'th block in a corrupted codeword w, meant to make the analysis cleaner. The set of allowed queries into L have been selected so that in the actual decoding algorithm we are able to translate access to w' into access to L. In particular, the cost of a query q_L in the list model corresponds to the number of symbols read by the LDC's decoding algorithm in a query corresponding to q_L. In fact, to interface with the LDC's decoding process, we will need a slightly more involved, so called weighted list model (see full version). We choose to present this simpler one as the search algorithm since it captures the core ideas of searching in the weighted model. Also, our list searching abstraction may be useful for other applications, where the extra generalization is an unnecessary complication.

2. *Otherwise, divide I into T intervals $I_1, \ldots, I_T$ of equal size (up to ± 1 due to rounding). Sample r random locations in each of the intervals, resulting in $o_{i,1}, \ldots, o_{i,r}$ for the i'th interval (via type-1 queries).*

    (a) *If some sample is of the form (i, a), return a corresponding to the first such i.*

    (b) *Otherwise, for each interval, calculate the fractions $s, b = 1 - s$ of smaller and larger then i sampled elements respectively. We say that interval j votes against interval $k, k > j$ for i , equivalently votes against (I_k, i) if $b \geq 0.31$ (for $k < j$, if $s \geq 0.31$). Note that if I_j votes against (I_k, i), then it votes against all (I_h, i) for h on the same side of I_j as l_k. We then say that I_j votes against its left (right) side on i. For every interval j, we count the number of votes against (I_j, i) over all other intervals.*

       i. *If there is exactly one interval with a minimum number of votes, fix I to be that interval, and $T = \Delta$.*

       ii. *If there are two such adjacent intervals I_j, I_{j+1} let I be their union. Fix $T = 2\Delta$.*

      iii. *Otherwise, output $\perp$ and terminate.*

Theorem 2. *Construction 3 is an algorithm for searching on sorted lists (in a framework as defined above), tolerating a (small enough) constant[8] δ fraction of corruptions. For at least a $1 - 52\delta m$ fraction of the original lists' elements, it recovers them correctly with probability $\geq 1 - neg(m)$ (δ is the actual fraction of corruptions that occurred). It makes queries of total cost $O(\log^3 m)$.*

See full version for a proof, here we briefly outline the main components of the proof. Fix some list L and set of corruptions, and a searched key i. Assume for simplicity that the length of the list, m' is known, and that up to $\delta \cdot m'$ entries in the list are corrupted. There are two types of errors. The simple kind is when a corrupted (i, a) is found, for which either i or a was modified. These may lead to at most $2\delta m'$ errors (due to not finding (i, a) that was changed to (i', a), or finding (i', a) instead of a (i', b) that was originally present in the list). A more problematic kind of errors is due to not finding an uncorrupted entry (i, b) because other (corrupted) entries made the search exclude it from subsequent search at some recursion level l. These lead to the (large) constant blowup in incorrectly recovered entries (beyond $\delta m'$). Our first step is identify a set M of entries (i, a) for which an error (of either type) may occur which is independent of the algorithm's random choices. Then we bound the number of elements that fall into M due to errors of the second type. A key concept we use is that of a basic interval on a recursion level l - one Δ^l equal intervals in a partition on L (up to rounding). For any input key i, nodes of 1 or 2 contiguous intervals are considered on level l. A bad basic interval is one containing many corrupted entries (say, a ≥ 0.3 fraction). We include all entries in bad intervals in M, adding $10/3\delta m'$ entries to M. Then, we prove that at a level l with l' bad intervals, only $15 \cdot l'$ intervals I may contain uncorrupted keys for which

---

[8] Construction 3 can also handle subs-constant in $|L|$ δ with the same degradation factors, but constant δ is the most interesting parameter setting.

that interval is excluded from the search on input i (refer as "injured" entries). As the number of levels is $\Theta(\log|L|)$, naively summing over all levels results in $\Theta(\log n \cdot n) > n$ keys on which we err, which is not a meaningful bound. The second key observation is that we should count the number of entries that are injured on each level for the *first time*. To bound these, we refine the first bound, and prove that newly injured entries on level l, M_l are in fact of size $\leq 15B'_l$, where B'_l is the set of level-l bad intervals not contained in bad intervals on previous levels. The disjointness of the B'_l's for different B'_l's yields the result.

We observe that our result and technique bear only superficial resemblance to the result and technique of [3]. More precisely, one of their results is a property tester for "sortedness" (in increasing order). That is, it accepts a sorted list, and rejects a list that is $\log(|L|)\epsilon$-far in edit distance from any sorted list. Their may technical observation that a list that is $\log(|L|)\epsilon$-far from sorted contains a large fraction of "light" elements. Such elements are defined as list locations i for which a (fixed) set of some $O(\log(n))$ intervals contains at least one interval I in which a large fraction of elements of I "vote" against $L[i]$. While this observation easily induces a property-testing algorithm for ϵ-"sortedness" making $O(\log(n)/\epsilon)$ queries into L, it is unclear how to use it for searching in a list which is $\epsilon - close$ to sorted. Also, note that while the property tester is not adaptive, our searching algorithm is. Finally, the conceptual role of intervals in the two algorithms is quite different. While they look for elements with some interval "voting against it", we distinguish an interval with the least number of intervals voting against it, to continue with it to the next level of the recursion. In particular we may continue even if all intervals are voted against the "right" location for the input key i by some of the intervals. This idea seems key in allowing to search lists that are far (up to constant fraction) from sorted.

3   Transforming Standard LDC into LDC for Edit Distance

Let $C_1 : \mathbb{F}_p^n \to \mathbb{F}_p^m$ denote a (δ_1, n, ϵ)-LDC code for Hamming distance, and $C_2 : \mathbb{F}_p^m \to \mathbb{F}_p^h$ a corresponding SZ code. Let Q_1 denote a suitable decoding algorithm for C_1. To transform C_1 into an LDC for edit distance, we compose it with C_2 (as done in [11] for a standard ECC C_1, and $p = 2$).

Recall that $C_2 : \mathbb{F}_p^m \to \mathbb{F}_p^h$ on input w_1, divides it into $T = \lceil m/\log m\rceil$ blocks $w_{1,1}, \ldots, w_{1,T}$. Then there are $t = \lceil(m/T + \log m)/\log p\rceil \leq \lceil 2\log m\rceil$ symbols in a block. We let $I = I_{t,\delta}$, where $I_{t,\delta}$ is as guaranteed by Lemma 1 (we are not concerned that t needs to be "large enough", wlog. we may consider only codes starting with large enough n (m)). It outputs $w_2 = w_{2,1} \circ \ldots \circ w_{2,T}$, where $w_{2,i} = I(i, w_{1,i})$. Denote the output length of I by $m_t(= O(\log m))$.

We claim that the code $C_2(C_1)$ is a $(\delta'_1, q \cdot polylog(m), \epsilon + neg(m))$-LDC for edit distance, where $\delta'_1 = c \cdot \delta_1$, for some global constant c that depends only on parameters of I_t. The decoder Q_2 for C_2 runs a straightforward simulation of Q_1, where the crux of technical difficulty is providing answers to Q_1's oracle queries, using its own oracle. In slightly more detail.

Construction 4. *Decoding algorithm* $Q_2^{w_2'}(i)$:

1. *Run $Q_1(i)$. When a query k into w_1' is made:*
   - *Calculate the index $i \in [T]$ of the block in which the k'th position in w_2 is located ($\lfloor k/T \rfloor + 1$).*
   - *Execute $FindBlock^{w_2'}(i)$ using some $polylog(m)$ queries into w_2'. Let $v = (i', w_{1,i}')$ denote its reply. Read $w_1[k]$ from $w_{1,i}'$ and forward it to Q_1 as the reply to its query.*
2. *Output the value that Q_1 outputs.*

That is, $FindBlock^{w_2'}(i)$ locates the i'th block of w_2, decodes it via I as $some(i,a)$, where a is (hopefully) the i'th block of w_1. As mentioned before, the main difficulty is in searching for the block in w_2'. We do not know where it is located in w_2' (but only up to a distance of $\delta|w_2|$ symbols, or so).

The high level idea is to somehow interpret w_2' as a list of sorted elements with corruptions (the sorting is by the index i written in each block), and run the algorithm for sorted lists with corruptions on it. For this purpose, we should be able to make "backwards" translations of the list searching algorithm's queries into reading portions of w_2'. In particular, we show that for small enough δ_1, blocks from w_2 ($= w_2'$ before modifications) form $1 - O(\delta_1)$ of the induced list's elements, and appear in their correct order. It turns out that a slightly generalized abstraction of a *weighted* sorted list with certain restrictions on list weights emerges. Fortunately we will be able to adapt our searching algorithm for unweighted lists to this more general setting. See full version for precise details. We obtain our main theorem.

Theorem 3. *Consider an $(\delta(n), q(n), \epsilon(n))$-LDC $L_H : \mathbb{F}_p^n \to \mathbb{F}_p^m$ for Hamming distance, where $\delta(m)$ is some constant[9]. Consider a code $C_2(C_1)$ as defined at the beginning of this section (given C_1). This code is a $(c\delta, q \cdot polylog(m,p), \epsilon + neg(m))$-LDC $L_E : \mathbb{F}_p^n \to \mathbb{F}_p^m$ for edit distance, where c is a (quite small) global constant. The code rate degrades by a constant. Encoding and decoding efficiency only degrades by a $poly(n)$ factor.*

The proof of this theorem follows by the construction outlined in this section. Namely, the decoder for $C_2(C_1)$ is outlined in Construction 4. $FindBlock^{w_2'}(i)$ runs $WS^{L_2'}(i, T)$, and implements its queries using oracle access to its own oracle w_2', as outlined in the full version of the paper. The various efficiency properties of the resulting code follow from Lemma 1. The constant c is a product of two constants resulting from the $FindBlock^{w_2'}$ algorithm. The core of this algorithm is a an algorithm for searching on weighted sorted lists with corruption. This constant is comparable to the $1/52$ loss we get in the algorithm for searching unweighted lists 2. The other factor stems from the need to correct errors in I, and to make sure that the word w_2' indeed induces a list with a small ($O(\delta)$) fraction of corruptions. This part is comparable to the fraction of errors tolerated by I.

---

[9] As opposed to our construction for searching on sorted lists with corruptions, here we require that δ is not subconstant. Otherwise, the degradation in δ could be superconstant in the actual error fraction δ.

References

1. Babai, L., Fortnow, L., Levin, L.A., Szegedy, M.: Checking computations in poly-logarithmic time. In: Koutsougeras, C., Vitter, J.S. (eds.) STOC, pp. 21–31. ACM (1991)
2. Church, G.M., Gao, Y., Kosuri, S.: Next-generation digital information storage in dna. Science 337(6102), 1628–1628 (2012)
3. Ergün, F., Kannan, S., Kumar, R., Rubinfeld, R., Viswanathan, M.: Spot-checkers. J. Comput. Syst. Sci. 60(3), 717–751 (2000)
4. Finocchi, I., Grandoni, F., Italiano, G.F.: Optimal resilient sorting and searching in the presence of memory faults. In: Bugliesi, M., Preneel, B., Sassone, V., Wegener, I. (eds.) ICALP 2006, Part I. LNCS, vol. 4051, pp. 286–298. Springer, Heidelberg (2006)
5. Finocchi, I., Italiano, G.F.: Sorting and searching in the presence of memory faults (without redundancy). In: Babai, L. (ed.) STOC, pp. 101–110. ACM (2004)
6. Goldreich, O.: Combinatorial property testing (a survey). In: Randomization Methods in Algorithm Design, pp. 45–60. American Mathematical Society (1998)
7. Goldreich, O.: Short locally testable codes and proofs (survey). Electronic Colloquium on Computational Complexity (ECCC) (014) (2005), http://dblp.uni-trier.de/db/journals/eccc/eccc12.html#TR05-014
8. Hemenway, B., Ostrovsky, R., Strauss, M.J., Wootters, M.: Public key locally decodable codes with short keys. In: Goldberg, L.A., Jansen, K., Ravi, R., Rolim, J.D.P. (eds.) RANDOM/APPROX 2011. LNCS, vol. 6845, pp. 605–615. Springer, Heidelberg (2011)
9. Katz, J., Trevisan, L.: On the efficiency of local decoding procedures for error-correcting codes. In: Yao, F.F., Luks, E.M. (eds.) STOC, pp. 80–86. ACM (2000)
10. Rivest, R.L., Meyer, A.R., Kleitman, D.J., Winklmann, K., Spencer, J.: Coping with errors in binary search procedures (preliminary report), pp. 227–232. ACM (1978), http://dblp.uni-trier.de/db/conf/stoc/stoc78.html#RivestMKWS78
11. Schulman, L.J., Zuckerman, D.: Asymptotically good codes correcting insertions, deletions, and transpositions. In: Proceedings of the Eighth Annual ACM-SIAM Symposium on Discrete Algorithms, SODA 1997, pp. 669–674. Society for Industrial and Applied Mathematics, Philadelphia (1997), http://dl.acm.org/citation.cfm?id=314161.314412
12. Yekhanin, S.: Locally decodable codes. In: Kulikov, A., Vereshchagin, N. (eds.) CSR 2011. LNCS, vol. 6651, pp. 289–290. Springer, Heidelberg (2011)

The Multivariate Hidden Number Problem

Steven D. Galbraith and Barak Shani

Department of Mathematics,
University of Auckland, New Zealand
S.Galbraith@math.auckland.ac.nz, barak.shani@auckland.ac.nz

Abstract. This work extends the line of research on the hidden number problem. Motivated by studying bit security in finite fields, we define the multivariate hidden number problem. Here, the secret and the multiplier are vectors, and partial information about their dot product is given. Using tools from discrete Fourier analysis introduced by Akavia, Goldwasser and Safra, we show that if one can find the significant Fourier coefficients of some function, then one can solve the multivariate hidden number problem for that function. This allows us to generalise the work of Akavia on the hidden number problem with (non-adaptive) chosen multipliers to all finite fields.

We give two further applications of our results, both of which generalise previous works to all (finite) extension fields. The first considers the general (random samples) hidden number problem in $\mathbb{F}_{p^m}$ and assumes an advice is given to the algorithm. The second considers a model that allows changing representations, where we show hardness of individual bits for elliptic curve and pairing based functions for elliptic curves over extension fields, as well as hardness of any bit of any component of the Diffie-Hellman secret in $\mathbb{F}_{p^m}$ $(m > 1)$.

Keywords: hidden number problem, bit security, hardcore bits.

1 Introduction

The computational Diffie-Hellman assumption (CDH) states that for appropriate groups G, given values $g, g^a, g^b \in G$, the Diffie-Hellman secret g^{ab} is hard to compute. However, this assumption does not rule out the possibility that some bits of g^{ab} are predictable. This leads to interesting theoretical questions about the security of bits arising from computational problems. A useful language to express these ideas is the *hidden number problem*. Informally, the hidden number problem in a (multiplicative) group G with a (non-constant) function f defined over G is the problem of recovering a hidden element $s \in G$ given pairs $(t_i, f(st_i))$.

This problem was introduced by Boneh and Venkatesan [7] in order to study bit security (specifically blocks of most-significant bits) of the Diffie-Hellman secret. They were the first to prove hardness of bits for Diffie-Hellman key exchange. Today, this problem is studied in its own right and is of theoretical interest, and also leads to practical results, outside the scope of the Diffie-Hellman key exchange (see, for example, [10,14]). It is most desirable to prove security of the smallest possible blocks of bits (i.e., blocks of size 1).

© Springer International Publishing Switzerland 2015
A. Lehmann and S. Wolf (Eds.): ICITS 2015, LNCS 9063, pp. 250–268, 2015.
DOI: 10.1007/978-3-319-17470-9_15

Interested in the hidden number problem in (finite) extension fields, we study the following variant of the hidden number problem, which we call the *multivariate hidden number problem*. Here, the problem takes place over a ring R, on which a function f is defined, and the secret $\mathbf{s} = (s_1, \ldots, s_m)$ is an m-tuple in R^m. Informally again, the problem is recovering the secret $\mathbf{s}$ given pairs $(\mathbf{t}_i, f(\mathbf{s} \cdot \mathbf{t}_i))$, where $\mathbf{s} \cdot \mathbf{t}_i$ is the dot product of $\mathbf{s}$ and $\mathbf{t}_i$. That is, $f(\mathbf{s} \cdot \mathbf{x}) = f(s_1 x_1 + \cdots + s_m x_m)$ for $\mathbf{x} = (x_1, \ldots, x_m) \in R^m$.

This problem arises naturally from the following observation. Assume an oracle $\mathcal{O}$ gives partial information, e.g. one bit, of one (fixed) component of sx, for a secret s and a multiplier x in $\mathbb{F}_{p^m}$. One would like to learn s. First, the component can be expressed as a dot product $\widetilde{\mathbf{s}} \cdot \mathbf{x}$ for $\mathbf{x} \in (\mathbb{F}_p)^m$, a vector that represents x, and some $\widetilde{\mathbf{s}} \in (\mathbb{F}_p)^m$. If one can learn $\widetilde{\mathbf{s}}$ given $\mathcal{O}(x) = bit(\widetilde{\mathbf{s}} \cdot \mathbf{x})$, then the learner can solve the hidden number problem by computing s from $\widetilde{\mathbf{s}}$.

Previous Work

The hidden number problem has been extensively studied, and different variants have been proposed throughout the years, as well as numerous extensions (for a comprehensive overview of the different extensions, see Shparlinski's survey [18]). Boneh and Venkatesan [7] considered $G = \mathbb{Z}_p^*$ for prime p and showed that the $\sqrt{\log p} + \log \log p$ most-significant bits of the Diffie-Hellman secret g^{ab} are as hard to compute as the whole secret. Their approach uses lattice basis reduction. There is a considerable subsequent literature, including the case of extension fields, but lattice methods are unable to obtain hardness results for single bits.

Significant progress resulted from the introduction of tools from Fourier analysis (learning theory) by Akavia, Goldwasser and Safra [3] (for a complete description, see Akavia's thesis [1]). They showed that if one can find the *heavy* Fourier coefficients of a function, then one can solve the hidden number problem for that function. In addition, they built on the fundamental work of Goldreich and Levin [13] and Kushilevitz and Mansour [15] and provided an algorithm to find heavy Fourier coefficients of a function, under the *membership queries model*. This new approach allows to consider hardness of single bits, even for noisy oracles that only have a non-negligible advantage over the bias of the function in question. Since these tools work under specific query-access models, they can only be used to solve the hidden number problem when the solver has the suitable access to the function.

This new approach, involving Fourier analysis, laid the groundwork for subsequent interesting results in the study of bit security. Akavia [2] gave a solution to the hidden number problem with chosen multipliers in the multiplicative group of prime fields $\mathbb{F}_p$ for a family of functions, called *concentrated* functions, where multipliers are chosen *non-adaptively*[1]. Akavia also showed that the most-significant-bit function is concentrated. Morillo and Ràfols [16] proved that, for any integer $1 \le k \le \log_2(N)$, the k-th bit function on $\mathbb{Z}_N$ is concentrated (they

---

[1] As noted in [7], if we let "the queries be correlated" the problem already had a known solution for a block of one bit "even when the oracle is noisy".

specifically considered N a prime or an RSA modulus). This can be combined with Akavia's result on concentrated functions.

By combining the above with the work of Boneh and Shparlinski [6], Duc and Jetchev [9] showed the hardness of any single bit of elliptic curve and pairing based functions for elliptic curves over prime fields, in a model that allows the solver to change the representation of the group. In a similar model, Fazio, Gennaro, Perera and Skeith [12] gave the first single bit hardness result for Diffie-Hellman secrets in extension field – excluding hardness of the constant-term component bits – where they considered the field $\mathbb{F}_{p^2} = \mathbb{F}_p[x]/(x^2 + Ax + B)$ (with p a prime) using a polynomial basis representation. A very recent result by Wang, Zhan and Zhang [20] generalised this work to extension fields $\mathbb{F}_{p^m}$, where m is polynomial in $\log p$. As in [12], only polynomial basis representations are considered in [20].

Our Contribution

Our contribution is first and foremost of a mathematical nature. We show that if one can find heavy Fourier coefficients of a function f, then one can solve the multivariate hidden number problem for f. This is done by proving an algebraic relation between the Fourier transforms of f and $f_{\mathbf{s}}$, where $f_{\mathbf{s}}(\mathbf{x}) := f(\mathbf{s} \cdot \mathbf{x})$ as above. Using the algorithm from [1,3], we give a solution to a chosen-multiplier version of the multivariate hidden number problem for concentrated functions f over $\mathbb{F}_p$, where multipliers are chosen non-adaptively.

This allows us to generalise the solution to the hidden number problem with chosen multipliers to all finite fields $\mathbb{F}_{p^m}$ for concentrated functions, which include the k-th bit function of each component, for every $1 \leq k \leq \log_2(p)$.

We also give several application of our main results. We show how the results can be used in different models, one of which is the "representation changing" model. By constructing isomorphisms between representations of $\mathbb{F}_{p^m}$ that forms a dot product (as in the multivariate hidden number problem) in a specific component, we show that changing field representations gives the required multipliers needed to solve the multivariate hidden number problem, for concentrated functions over $\mathbb{F}_p$. Specifically, we prove hardness of any single bit of any component for Diffie-Hellman secrets in $\mathbb{F}_{p^m}$. We do not restrict only to polynomial representations. This result holds for general vector space representations and also normal basis representations of $\mathbb{F}_{p^m}$. We also give bit security results for elliptic curve and pairing based functions for elliptic curves over $\mathbb{F}_{p^m}$.

We stress that as with previous work our results are not sufficient to prove (single) bit security of the classic Diffie-Hellman key exchange. This is due to the fact that the chosen multipliers needed for these approaches cannot be obtained when attacking the Diffie-Hellman protocol. However, one can obtain bit security results for Diffie-Hellman and related schemes by considering algorithms with advice, as was done by Akavia [2], for example.

Paper Organisation. The paper is organised as follows. Section 2 gives definitions and some facts needed for our later results. Sections 3 and 4 are our main theoretical contributions. In section 3 we introduce the multivariate hidden number problem and establish our main tool, to be used in Section 4, where we give our main results: solutions to the multivariate hidden number problem over $\mathbb{F}_p$ and the hidden number problem in $\mathbb{F}_{p^m}$. Section 5 focuses on other applications. We discuss two models in which our results can be applied, by giving the appropriate background and summarizing recent results. We then show how one can use our results to prove bit security in these models, and how it relates to previous work.

2 Preliminaries

2.1 Fourier Analysis on Finite Groups

Let $(R, +, \cdot)$ be a finite ring and denote by $G := (R, +)$ the corresponding additive abelian group. We are interested in the set of functions $\{f : R \to \mathbb{C}\}$. This set of functions is a vector space (over the complex field), whose dimension is $|R|$, since, for instance, the Kronecker delta functions $\{\delta_i\}_{i \in R}$ ($\delta_i(j) = 1$ if $j = i$, otherwise $\delta_i(j) = 0$) form a basis for this vector space; every function $f : R \to \mathbb{C}$ can be written as $f(x) = \sum_{i \in R} f(i)\delta_i(x)$. Let $\overline{z}$ denote the complex conjugate of a complex number z. We define an inner product in this vector space by $\langle f, g \rangle := \mathbb{E}_{x \in R}\left[f(x) \cdot \overline{g(x)}\right] = \frac{1}{|R|}\sum_{x \in R} f(x) \cdot \overline{g(x)}$. The l_2 norm of a function f is $\|f\|_2 := \sqrt{\langle f, f \rangle}$.

A character of G is a group homomorphism taking values in the non-zero complex numbers, namely $\chi : G \to \mathbb{C}^*$ such that $\chi(x + y) = \chi(x)\chi(y)$. Since $\chi(x)^{|G|} = \chi(|G| \cdot x) = \chi(0_G) = 1$, we get that the characters take values in the complex $|G|$-th roots of unity. Moreover, there are exactly $|G|$ of them, so we associate each character χ to a group element $a \in G$, yielding χ_a. That is, denote by $\widehat{G}$ the set (group) of characters of G, and consider the map $\varphi : G \to \widehat{G}$, given by $\varphi(a) := \chi_a$. The map φ can be shown to be an isomorphism.

An alternative basis for $\{f : R \to \mathbb{C}\}$ is the Fourier basis consisting of all the characters χ. Standard facts in Fourier analysis on finite groups are: for the trivial character $\chi_0 \in \widehat{G}$ it holds that $\sum_{x \in G} \chi_0(x) = |G|$, and $\sum_{x \in G} \chi(x) = 0$ if $\chi_0 \neq \chi \in \widehat{G}$; in addition, these characters are orthogonal and have l_2 norm of 1, hence the Fourier basis is an orthonormal basis. Therefore, we can represent each function $f : R \to \mathbb{C}$ as a linear combination of the characters χ_a. This linear combination is given by $f(x) = \sum_{a \in G} \widehat{f}(a)\chi_a(x)$, where each coefficient is the Fourier transform $\widehat{f}(a) := \langle f, \chi_a \rangle$. Let $\overline{\chi}_a$ be the conjugate to the character χ_a. That is, $\overline{\chi}_a(x) = \overline{\chi_a(x)}$.

For $G = \mathbb{Z}_N$ we define the characters χ_a by $\chi_a(x) := e^{\frac{2\pi i}{N}ax}$. For $G = \mathbb{Z}_{N_1} \times \ldots \times \mathbb{Z}_{N_m}$, let $\mathbf{a} = (a_1, \ldots, a_m)$ and $\mathbf{x} = (x_1, \ldots, x_m)$; the character $\chi_{\mathbf{a}}(\mathbf{x})$ is given by $\chi_{\mathbf{a}}(\mathbf{x}) := \chi_{a_1}(x_1) \cdot \ldots \cdot \chi_{a_m}(x_m) = e^{\frac{2\pi i}{N_1}a_1 x_1} \cdot \ldots \cdot e^{\frac{2\pi i}{N_m}a_m x_m}$.

Let $f : \mathbb{Z}_p \to \mathbb{C}$ and define the function $f_s : \mathbb{Z}_p \to \mathbb{C}$ by $f_s(x) := f(sx)$, for $s \in \mathbb{Z}_p^*$. The well-known scaling property of the Fourier transform is the following relation between the Fourier transforms (with respect to the additive group $G = (\mathbb{Z}_p, +)$) of f and f_s: $\widehat{f_s}(z) = \widehat{f}(zs^{-1})$. This is a basic property of the Fourier transform, which follows from the fact that $\chi_z(sx) = \chi_{zs}(x)$. This relation inspires our approach in Lemma 13, and so we see fit to show its proof.

Lemma 1. *Let $s \in \mathbb{Z}_p^*$, let $f : \mathbb{Z}_p \to \mathbb{C}$ and define $f_s : \mathbb{Z}_p \to \mathbb{C}$ by $f_s(x) := f(sx)$ for every $x \in \mathbb{Z}_p$. The Fourier transform of f_s satisfies $\widehat{f_s}(z) = \widehat{f}(zs^{-1})$ for every $z \in \mathbb{Z}_p$.*

Proof. By definition of the Fourier transform we get that

$$\widehat{f_s}(z) = \frac{1}{p} \sum_{x \in \mathbb{Z}_p} f_s(x) \overline{\chi}_z(x) = \frac{1}{p} \sum_{x \in \mathbb{Z}_p} f(sx) \overline{\chi}_z(x) \ .$$

Since $x' := sx$ is a permutation of $\mathbb{Z}_p$, we change the order of summation and sum over x'. Therefore,

$$\widehat{f_s}(z) = \frac{1}{p} \sum_{x'} f(x') \overline{\chi}_z(s^{-1}x')$$

$$= \frac{1}{p} \sum_{x'} f(x') e^{-\frac{2\pi i}{p} z(s^{-1}x')} = \frac{1}{p} \sum_{x'} f(x) e^{-\frac{2\pi i}{p}(zs^{-1})x'}$$

$$= \frac{1}{p} \sum_{x'} f(x') \overline{\chi}_{zs^{-1}}(x') = \widehat{f}(zs^{-1}) \ .$$

∎

We now recall some definitions from [3, 9, 16]. The same definitions can be made for functions over rings R where G is their additive group.

Definition 2 (Restriction). *Given a function $f : G \to \mathbb{C}$ and a set of characters Γ, the restriction of f to Γ is the function $f|_\Gamma : G \to \mathbb{C}$ defined by $f|_\Gamma := \sum_{\chi_a \in \Gamma} \widehat{f}(a) \chi_a$.*

Definition 3 (Concentration). *A function $f : G \to \mathbb{C}$ is Fourier concentrated if for every $\epsilon > 0$ there exist a set Γ of $poly\left(\log \left(\frac{|G|}{\epsilon} \right) \right)$ characters, such that $\|f - f|_\Gamma\|_2^2 \leq \epsilon$.*

Definition 4 (Heavy coefficient). *For a function $f : G \to \mathbb{C}$ and a threshold $\tau > 0$, we say that a coefficient $\widehat{f}(a)$ (corresponding to the character χ_a) is τ-heavy if $|\widehat{f}(a)|^2 > \tau$.*

Theorem 5 (Akavia [1]). *There is a probabilistic algorithm that given a finite group G, a threshold $\tau > 0$ and oracle query access to a function $f : G \to \mathbb{C}$, finds all the τ-heavy Fourier coefficients. The algorithm runs in polynomial time in $\log(|G|)$, $\frac{1}{\tau}$ and $\|f\|_2$.*

The models of oracle access in this paper are discussed in Remark 8 below.

2.2   Finite Field Representations

Let $\mathbb{F}$ be a finite field. A known fact is that if $\mathbb{F}$ has q elements, then q is a power of some prime p, that is, $q = p^m$ for a prime p and a positive integer m. Hence, we denote that field by $\mathbb{F}_q$. Another known fact is that given a number $q = p^m$ as above, there is a unique field with q elements, up to isomorphism. Yet, $\mathbb{F}_q$ has different (all isomorphic to each other) representations. One representation of a field $\mathbb{F}_{p^m}$ is given by $\mathbb{F}_p[x]/(h)$, where $\mathbb{F}_p[x]$ is the ring of polynomials with coefficients in $\mathbb{F}_p$, the polynomial h is a monic irreducible polynomial of degree m in $\mathbb{F}_p[x]$, and (h) is the principal ideal generated by h. We emphasize that there are also other representations, like the normal basis $\{\theta, \theta^p, \theta^{p^2}, \ldots, \theta^{p^{m-1}}\}$, where θ is an element of the field such that this set is linearly independent, and $\theta^{p^m} = \theta$.

The field $\mathbb{F}_{p^m}$ is a vector space of dimension m over the field $\mathbb{F}_p$, equipped with a bilinear inner product. For an aribtrary vector space basis of $\mathbb{F}_{p^m}$ there are m^3 structure coefficients which determine the multiplication rule in $\mathbb{F}_{p^m}$. For completeness we state and prove the following standard result.

Lemma 6. *Let $\{\boldsymbol{b}_1, \ldots, \boldsymbol{b}_m\}$ be a basis of the vector space $\mathbb{F}_{p^m}$ over $\mathbb{F}_p$. For elements $u, v \in \mathbb{F}_{p^m}$, let $\boldsymbol{u}, \boldsymbol{v}$ be the coefficient vectors in $\mathbb{F}_p^m$ corresponding to this vector space basis. There exist m invertible matrices $M_1, \ldots, M_m$ such that $uv = \sum_{k=1}^m w_k \boldsymbol{b}_k$, where each coefficient is given by $w_k = \boldsymbol{u} M_k \boldsymbol{v}^T$.*

Proof. For a basis $\{\mathbf{b}_1, \ldots, \mathbf{b}_m\} \subseteq \mathbb{F}_{p^m}$, the structure coefficients determine the product of all the basis elements. That is, $\mathbf{b}_i \mathbf{b}_j = \sum_{k=1}^m c_{i,j}^k \mathbf{b}_k$, where $c_{i,j}^k$ are the structure coefficients. Then, by the bilinearity of multiplication, we get that a product of any two elements $u = \sum_{i=1}^m u_i \mathbf{b}_i$ and $v = \sum_{j=1}^m v_j \mathbf{b}_j$ is of the form

$$uv = \sum_{i=1}^m u_i \sum_{j=1}^m v_j \left(\mathbf{b}_i \mathbf{b}_j \right) = \sum_{i=1}^m u_i \sum_{j=1}^m v_j \sum_{k=1}^m c_{i,j}^k \mathbf{b}_k = \sum_{k=1}^m \sum_{i=1}^m u_i \widetilde{v_i^k} \mathbf{b}_k \ ,$$

where $\widetilde{v_i^k}$ is a linear combination of the scalars v_i with $c_{i,j}^k$ as coefficients. In other words, by representing the multiplication of $\mathbf{u}$ and $\mathbf{v}$ as linear combination of the basis elements – $\mathbf{uv} = \sum_{k=1}^m w_k \mathbf{b}_k$ – every coefficient w_k in this linear combination is of the linear form $u_1 \widetilde{v_1^k} + \ldots + u_m \widetilde{v_m^k}$, where u_i are the coefficients of $\mathbf{u}$. The existence of the matrices M_k follows.

Assume that M_k is not invertible, then there exists $\mathbf{u} \neq 0$ such that $\mathbf{u} M_k = 0$. Hence, for every $\mathbf{v}$, the coefficient $w_k = 0$. Let $u \neq 0$ be the field element corresponding to $\mathbf{u}$. We get that multiplication by u is not an injection. Therefore u is a zero divisor – a contradiction. ∎

2.3 Hidden Number Problem

The hidden number problem was introduced in [7] in order to study the bit security of Diffie-Hellman key exchange. The relation between the two is explained in Remark 9 below. The problem was introduced over the multiplicative group $\mathbb{Z}_p^*$, but it can be generalised to arbitrary finite (abelian) groups. Since our applications involve single bit functions, we present the problem with a single bit function.

Definition 7 (Hidden Number Problem (Single Bit)). *Let* $(G, \cdot)$ *be a group, let* $s \neq 0$ *be a secret element of* G *and let* $f : G \to \{-1, 1\}$. *The goal is to find the secret element* s *using oracle access to the function* $f_s(x) := f(sx)$.

Remark 8 (Access models). We use the term *oracle access* as a general term for any of the following oracle models. We follow the language from [17] in describing the oracle access models in this paper. When we write *query access* we refer to the *membership queries model*, where the learner can query the function on any input $x \in G$ and receive the sample $(x, f_s(x))$. In the *uniform distribution model*, the learner has access to a random source of samples: at each time the learning algorithm queries, a random input $x \in G$ is chosen uniformly, and the sample $(x, f_s(x))$ is returned to the algorithm.

Models of HNP. We adopt the notation from [6] and write HNP-CM for a chosen-multiplier version of the hidden number problem, which is under the membership queries model. That is, in HNP-CM the learner can query the function on any input. We emphasize that in this paper, unlike [6], any queries in this model are made *non-adaptively*. This means that the algorithm first chooses all its queries, and after receiving the response starts its process. This is opposed to adaptive queries, where the queries may depend on the secret s and are adjusted during the process of recovering s. When a solver can choose multipliers adaptively the problem already has a solution (based on the work in [5], and later [4]).

In the original (more general) variant of the hidden number problem, which we denote by HNP, the oracle access is in the uniform distribution model. That is, the solver only gets pairs $(t_i, f_s(t_i))$, for d elements $t_1, \ldots, t_d \in G$ chosen independently and uniformly at random. This is probably the most frequently discussed variant of the hidden number problem.

Unfortunately, the algorithm in Theorem 5 cannot be used in the uniform distribution model, and therefore cannot be used to solve HNP. The upside of Theorem 5 is that it is strong enough to handle oracles that only have a non-negligible advantage over the bias of the function in question. That is, the results hold even for a noisy oracle, i.e., an oracle that does not give a correct answer all the time, but with some probability. Since this work focuses on a mathematical framework, we do not elaborate on this noise model. The interested reader can look at [1, 3, 9, 16].

Remark 9. One historical motivation for the hidden number problem is the following. Given a group G, an element g in the group and the values g^a and g^b, the shared Diffie-Hellman secret s is the value $s = DH_g(g^a, g^b) = g^{ab}$. Notice that one can choose a number k and calculate g^k, then by multiplying g^k and g^a, one gets $g^a g^k = g^{a+k}$. An active attacker in the static Diffie-Hellman protocol (where Bob always uses a fixed value g^b), who has access to some bit of the shared secret, can send the value g^{a+k} to Bob, so that Bob calculates the value $(g^{a+k})^b = g^{ab} g^{bk} = s g^{bk}$ and we notice that the attacker can calculate the value g^{bk} by $(g^b)^k$, yielding the (uniformly distributed) multiplier for the secret (in the hidden number problem). The attacker's goal (computing s) is exactly the hidden number problem.

An alternative interpretation is to consider a Diffie-Hellman oracle. Suppose we have an oracle that on input g^x and g^y outputs some bits of g^{xy}. We can query this oracle on g^b and g^{a+k} for several k's, and if we can solve the hidden number problem, we can find the secret $s = g^{ab}$.

Terminology. Adopting the language from [2], we say that an algorithm (l, δ, t)-solves the (multivariate) hidden number problem if the number of queries to the oracle is at most l, the algorithm outputs the hidden number s with probability at least δ, and the running time is at most t. We say that an algorithm *solves* the (multivariate) hidden number problem if $\frac{1}{\delta}$, l and t are polynomials in $\log(|G|)$.

We now recall the main result of Akavia [2] and sketch its proof. A full proof can be found in [2] (with a different terminology of the hidden number problem; for more details see our discussion in Section 5.1). We divide the result into two parts. Theorem 10 shows that an algorithm that learns heavy Fourier coefficients of functions over $\mathbb{F}_p$, leads to a solution to the hidden number problem in $\mathbb{Z}_p^*$. Corollary 11 shows how to solve (with non-adaptive queries) HNP-CM for concentrated functions in $\mathbb{Z}_p$. The ability to choose multipliers in HNP-CM is what allows one to have the oracle query access needed in applying the algorithm from Theorem 5, which allows to solve the hidden number problem.

Theorem 10 ([2]). *Let $\mathcal{A}$ be an algorithm that learns the τ-heavy Fourier coefficients of functions defined over $\mathbb{F}_p$. For any concentrated[2] function $f : \mathbb{F}_p \to \{-1, 1\}$, there exists an algorithm that solves the hidden number problem in $\mathbb{Z}_p^*$.*

Proof sketch. Let $f_s : \mathbb{F}_p \to \{-1, 1\}$ be the function from the hidden number problem, i.e., $f_s(x) := f(sx)$. By the scaling property (Lemma 1) we know that the Fourier coefficients of f_s are simply the Fourier coefficients of f permuted by s^{-1}. One might imagine that it is easy to compute the lists of Fourier coefficents of both f and f_s and then match them up to deduce the permuting element s^{-1}. However, this is not an efficient task when p is large (in both aspects: computing and comparing). This is where the idea of using concentrated functions is crucial. Instead of computing all the Fourier coefficients we just locate the τ-heavy ones for suitable τ, using the learning algorithm $\mathcal{A}$ on both f and f_s. These lists are short (by Parseval) and so matching up the values to find the permutation factor s^{-1} is efficient. ∎

Corollary 11 ([2]). *For any concentrated[3] function $f : \mathbb{F}_p \to \{-1, 1\}$, there exists an algorithm that solves HNP-CM in $\mathbb{Z}_p^*$, where the queries are made non-adaptively.*

Akavia proved that the most-significant-bit function $MSB : \mathbb{Z}_p \to \{-1, 1\}$ is concentrated, and hence proved that HNP-CM in $\mathbb{Z}_p^*$ with the MSB function

---

[2] In [2], a different definition of concentration is taken. We use the definition from [3]. Both papers use the same method to obtain the proof of Theorem 10.

[3] See previous footnote.

can be solved. Later on, Morillo and Ràfols [16] proved that, for any integer $1 \le k \le \log_2(p)$, the k-th bit function on $\mathbb{Z}_p$ is concentrated. Therefore, HNP-CM in $\mathbb{Z}_p^*$ can also be solved with these functions.

3   Multivariate Hidden Number Problem

In this section we define our variant of the hidden number problem, which we call the multivariate hidden number problem, and then introduce the tool that helps us solve this problem.

Definition 12 (Multivariate Hidden Number Problem (Single Bit)). *Let R be a ring, let $s = (s_1, \ldots, s_m) \ne (0, \ldots, 0)$ be a secret in R^m, and let $f : R \to \{-1, 1\}$. The goal is to find the secret s using oracle access to the function $f_s(x) := f(s \cdot x) = f(s_1 x_1 + \cdots + s_m x_m)$.*

For $m = 1$ the multivariate hidden number problem is simply the hidden number problem. As noted in [18], a polynomial version of the hidden number problem (poly-HNP) can be considered. This polynomial version can be seen as a special case of the multivariate hidden number problem. As above, we write MV-HNP-CM for a chosen-multiplier version of the multivariate hidden number problem, and MV-HNP for uniformly random multipliers.

The following lemma gives a relation between the Fourier transforms of f_s and f, analogous to the relation in Lemma 1 (scaling property). This lemma may be of independent interest.

Lemma 13. *Let $f : \mathbb{Z}_p \to \mathbb{C}$, let $s = (s_1, \ldots, s_m) \in \mathbb{Z}_p^m$ be such that not all $s_i = 0$, and define $f_s : \mathbb{Z}_p^m \to \mathbb{C}$ by $f_s(x) := f(s \cdot x)$. For any $s_k \ne 0$, the Fourier transform of f_s satisfies*

$$\widehat{f_s}(z_1, \ldots, z_m) = \begin{cases} \widehat{f}(z_k s_k^{-1}) & \text{if } z_j - z_k s_k^{-1} s_j = 0, \quad \forall 1 \le j \ne k \le m; \\ 0 & \text{otherwise.} \end{cases} \quad (1)$$

Proof. Recall that a character in $\mathbb{Z}_p$ is defined by $\chi_a(x) = e^{\frac{2\pi i}{p} ax}$ and that for an element $\mathbf{a} = (a_1, \ldots, a_m) \in \mathbb{Z}_p^m$ the character $\chi_\mathbf{a}(\mathbf{x})$ is given by $\chi_\mathbf{a}(\mathbf{x}) = \prod_{i=1}^m \chi_{a_i}(x_i)$. Therefore, for $1 \le k \le m$, we have

$$\chi_{(a_1, \ldots, a_m)}(x_1, \ldots, x_m) = \prod_{i=1}^m \chi_{a_i}(x_i) = \prod_{i \ne k} \chi_{a_i}(x_i) \chi_{a_k}(x_k)$$

$$= \chi_{(a_1, \ldots, a_{k-1}, a_{k+1}, a_m)}(x_1, \ldots, x_{k-1}, x_{k+1}, x_m) \chi_{a_k}(x_k) .$$

Assume without loss of generality that $s_m \ne 0$. Then, $\widehat{f_\mathbf{s}}(z_1, \ldots, z_m) =$

$$\frac{1}{p^m} \sum_{(x_1, \ldots, x_m) \in \mathbb{Z}_p^m} f_\mathbf{s}(x_1, \ldots, x_m) \overline{\chi}_{(z_1, \ldots, z_m)}(x_1, \ldots, x_m)$$

$$= \frac{1}{p^m} \sum_{x_1,\ldots,x_m \in \mathbb{Z}_p} f\left(s_1 x_1 + \cdots + s_m x_m\right) \overline{\chi}_{(z_1,\ldots,z_m)}\left(x_1,\ldots,x_m\right)$$

$$= \frac{1}{p^m} \sum_{x_1,\ldots,x_{m-1}} \sum_{x_m} f\left(s_1 x_1 + \cdots + s_m x_m\right) \overline{\chi}_{(z_1,\ldots,z_{m-1})}\left(x_1,\ldots,x_{m-1}\right) \overline{\chi}_{z_m}\left(x_m\right)$$

$$= \frac{1}{p^m} \sum_{x_1,\ldots,x_{m-1}} \overline{\chi}_{(z_1,\ldots,z_{m-1})}(x_1,\ldots,x_{m-1}) \sum_{x_m} f(s_1 x_1 + \cdots + s_m x_m) \overline{\chi}_{z_m}(x_m) \ .$$

Since $x'_m := s_m x_m$ is a permutation of $\mathbb{Z}_p$, we change the order of summation and sum over x'_m. Therefore, $\widehat{f}_{\mathbf{s}}(z_1,\ldots,z_m) =$

$$\frac{1}{p^m} \sum_{x_1,\ldots,x_{m-1}} \overline{\chi}_{(z_1,\ldots,z_{m-1})}(x_1,\ldots,x_{m-1}) \cdot$$

$$\sum_{x'_m} f\left(s_1 x_1 + \cdots + s_{m-1} x_{m-1} + x'_m\right) \overline{\chi}_{z_m}\left(s_m^{-1} x'_m\right) \ .$$

Let $y := s_1 x_1 + \cdots + s_{m-1} x_{m-1} + x'_m$, so that $f\left(s_1 x_1 + \cdots + s_{m_1} x_{m_1} + x'_m\right) = f(y)$. We get that $\widehat{f}_{\mathbf{s}}(z_1,\ldots,z_m) =$

$$\frac{1}{p^{m-1}} \sum_{x_1,\ldots,x_{m-1}} \overline{\chi}_{(z_1,\ldots,z_{m-1})}(x_1,\ldots,x_{m-1}) \cdot$$

$$\frac{1}{p} \sum_y f(y) \overline{\chi}_{z_m}\left(s_m^{-1}(y - s_1 x_1 - \cdots - s_{m-1} x_{m-1})\right)$$

$$= \frac{1}{p^{m-1}} \sum_{x_1,\ldots,x_{m-1}} \overline{\chi}_{(z_1,\ldots,z_{m-1})}(x_1,\ldots,x_{m-1}) \cdot$$

$$\frac{1}{p} \sum_y f(y) \overline{\chi}_{z_m s_m^{-1}}(y) \overline{\chi}_{\left(-z_m s_m^{-1} s_1,\ldots,-z_m s_m^{-1} s_{m-1}\right)}(x_1,\ldots,x_{m-1})$$

$$= \frac{1}{p^{m-1}} \sum_{x_1,\ldots,x_{m-1}} \overline{\chi}_{\left(z_1 - z_m s_m^{-1} s_1,\ldots,z_{m-1} - z_m s_m^{-1} s_{m-1}\right)}(x_1,\ldots,x_{m-1}) \widehat{f}\left(z_m s_m^{-1}\right)$$

$$= \widehat{f}\left(z_m s_m^{-1}\right) \frac{1}{p^{m-1}} \sum_{x_1,\ldots,x_{m-1}} \overline{\chi}_{\left(z_1 - z_m s_m^{-1} s_1,\ldots,z_{m-1} - z_m s_m^{-1} s_{m-1}\right)}(x_1,\ldots,x_{m-1}) \ .$$

The last sum equals 0 unless the character $\chi_{\left(z_1 - z_m s_m^{-1} s_1,\ldots,z_{m-1} - z_m s_m^{-1} s_{m-1}\right)}$ is the trivial character in $\mathbb{Z}_p^{m-1}$, in which case it equals p^{m-1}.[4] Therefore we get that $\widehat{f}_{\mathbf{s}}(z_1,\ldots,z_m) = \widehat{f}(z_m s_m^{-1})$ when $z_j - z_m s_m^{-1} s_j = 0$ for all $1 \leq j \leq m-1$ and otherwise $\widehat{f}_{\mathbf{s}}(z_1,\ldots,z_m) = 0$, as stated in (1).   ∎

The interesting property of $f_{\mathbf{s}}(\mathbf{x})$ is that its Fourier coefficients are equal to zero outside the line $(x_1,\ldots,x_m) = (ts_1,\ldots,ts_m)$ for $t \in \mathbb{Z}_p$. Along this line

---

[4] Recall that $\sum_{x \in G} \chi(x) = 0$ if $\chi_0 \neq \chi \in \widehat{G}$, and for the trivial character $\chi_0 \in \widehat{G}$ we get $\sum_{x \in G} \chi_0(x) = |G|$.

the Fourier coefficients of $f_s(\mathbf{x})$ are those of $f(x)$. So it is like the graph of the Fourier spectrum of $f(x)$ is drawn along a diagonal line in the space $\mathbb{Z}_p^m$.

We now give our main tool that allows to attack the multivariate hidden number problem using Fourier learning. Denote by $Heavy_\tau(f) = \{c_i \mid |\widehat{f}(c_i)|^2 > \tau\}$ the list that represents all τ-heavy Fourier coefficients of f.

Proposition 14. *Let $f : \mathbb{Z}_p \to \{-1, 1\}$, let $s = (s_1, \ldots, s_m) \in \mathbb{Z}_p^m$ be such that not all $s_i = 0$, and let $f_s : \mathbb{Z}_p^m \to \{-1, 1\}$ be the function $f_s(\boldsymbol{x}) := f(\boldsymbol{s} \cdot \boldsymbol{x})$. Then, $Heavy_\tau(f) = \{c_1, \ldots, c_t\}$ if and only if $Heavy_\tau(f_s) = \{(c_i s_1, \ldots, c_i s_m) | 1 \leq i \leq t\}$. In other words, a coefficient $\widehat{f}_s(z_1, \ldots, z_m)$ of f_s is τ-heavy if and only if there exists $1 \leq i \leq t$ such that $z_j = c_i s_j$ for every $1 \leq j \leq m$ and $\widehat{f}(c_i)$ is τ-heavy.*

Proof. The claim follows from Lemma 13. Let $1 \leq k \leq m$ such that $s_k \neq 0$. Assume $c \in Heavy_\tau(f)$ and consider the vector $(z_1, \ldots, z_m) = (cs_1, \ldots, cs_m)$. Specifically $z_k = cs_k$, so $c = z_k s_k^{-1}$ and therefore for every $1 \leq j \leq m$ one gets $z_j = cs_j = z_k s_k^{-1} s_j$ or $z_j - z_k s_k^{-1} s_j = 0$. From Lemma 13 we get that $\widehat{f}_s(cs_1, \ldots, cs_m) = \widehat{f}_s(z_1, \ldots, z_m) = \widehat{f}(z_k s_k^{-1}) = \widehat{f}(c)$. Therefore, we get that $(cs_1, \ldots, cs_m) \in Heavy_\tau(f_\mathbf{s})$. That is,

$$|\widehat{f}(c)|^2 > \tau \implies |\widehat{f}_\mathbf{s}(cs_1, \ldots, cs_m)|^2 > \tau \ .$$

Conversely,

$$|\widehat{f}_s(z_1, \ldots, z_m)|^2 > \tau \implies \widehat{f}_s(z_1, \ldots, z_m) \neq 0$$
$$\implies z_j = z_k s_k^{-1} s_j \text{ for every } 1 \leq j \leq m$$
$$\implies z_j = cs_j \text{ for } c = z_k s_k^{-1} \in \mathbb{Z}_p$$
$$\implies \widehat{f}(c) = \widehat{f}(z_k s_k^{-1}) = \widehat{f}_s(z_1, \ldots, z_m)$$
$$\implies |\widehat{f}(c)|^2 > \tau \ .$$

That is, the coefficient $\widehat{f}_\mathbf{s}(z_1, \ldots, z_m)$ is τ-heavy if and only if there exists $1 \leq i \leq t$ such that $z_j = c_i s_j$ for every $1 \leq j \leq m$ and $\widehat{f}(c_i)$ is τ-heavy. ∎

Corollary 15. *Let f be a function defined over $\mathbb{Z}_p$, let $s = (s_1, \ldots, s_m) \in \mathbb{Z}_p^m$ be a secret, and let f_s be a function over $\mathbb{Z}_p^m$ defined by $f_s(\boldsymbol{x}) := f(\boldsymbol{s} \cdot \boldsymbol{x})$. The function f is concentrated if and only if the function f_s is concentrated.*

Proof. Let Γ be a set of characters of $\mathbb{Z}_p$, and define $\Gamma_s := \{\chi_\mathbf{a} \mid \mathbf{a} = (as_1, \ldots, as_m), \chi_a \in \Gamma\}$ to be the corresponding set of characters of $\mathbb{Z}_p^m$. The proof is evident, since $\sum_{\mathbf{a} \in \Gamma_s} |\widehat{f}_\mathbf{s}(\mathbf{a})|^2 = \sum_{a \in \Gamma} |\widehat{f}(a)|^2$. ∎

4 Main Results

In this section we show that an algorithm that learns heavy Fourier coefficients of functions over finite abelian groups, leads to solutions to the multivariate hidden number problem over $\mathbb{F}_p$ and to the hidden number problem in $\mathbb{F}_{p^m}$.

Theorem 16. *Let $\mathcal{A}$ be an algorithm that learns the τ-heavy Fourier coefficients of functions defined over finite abelian groups. For any concentrated function $f : \mathbb{F}_p \to \{-1, 1\}$, there exists an algorithm that solves the multivariate hidden number problem over $\mathbb{F}_p$.*

Proof. The proof follows from Proposition 14 and the proof of Theorem 10. Since the function f is concentrated, we can run the learning algorithm $\mathcal{A}$ (on f) in the group $\mathbb{Z}_p$. When p is very small we can just compute the list of all Fourier coefficients. When p is large we can experiment with the learning algorithm (in polynomial time) to choose a suitable threshold τ, so that one can obtain in polynomial time in $\log(p)$ a short list of τ-heavy coefficients of f.

From Corollary 15, the function $f_\mathbf{s}$ is concentrated, so running the learning algorithm $\mathcal{A}$ (on $f_\mathbf{s}$ with the same threshold τ) in the group $\mathbb{Z}_p^m$ outputs in polynomial time in $\log(p^m) = m \log(p)$ the list of τ-heavy coefficients of $f_\mathbf{s}$. We use the relation between the (τ-heavy) coefficients of $f_\mathbf{s}$ and f from Proposition 14 and follow the same process from the proof of Theorem 10 to recover the secrets $s_1, \ldots, s_m$. ∎

Since the algorithm from Theorem 5 can learn heavy Fourier coefficients for functions over arbitrary finite fields in the membership queries model, even in the presence of noise, we get the following:

Corollary 17. *For any concentrated function $f : \mathbb{F}_p \to \{-1, 1\}$, there exists an algorithm that solves MV-HNP-CM over $\mathbb{F}_p$, where the queries are made non-adaptively.*

Proof. Take $\mathcal{A}$ to be the algorithm from Theorem 5 and apply Theorem 16. ∎

We turn from the multivariate hidden number problem to the hidden number problem. Recall that the hidden number problem in the group $(R^*, \cdot)$ considers the multiplication in R, and not the dot product used in the multivariate hidden number problem. We now consider $R = \mathbb{F}_{p^m}$ as a vector space. Given a basis of $\mathbb{F}_{p^m}$ we represent an element $a \in \mathbb{F}_{p^m}$ by its components vector (related to the given basis): $\mathbf{a} = (a_1, \ldots, a_m)$. We use Lemma 6 to show that for every $1 \le i \le m$, the i-th component of the product as (for $a, s \in \mathbb{F}_{p^m}$) can be represented as $\mathbf{a} M_i \mathbf{s}^T$, where M_i is an invertible matrix. Therefore, for a function F over $\mathbb{F}_{p^m}$ we have $F_s(a) := F(sa) = F(\mathbf{a} M_1 \mathbf{s}^T, \ldots, \mathbf{a} M_m \mathbf{s}^T)$. Note that this is a general property of $\mathbb{F}_{p^m}$ as a vector space, and therefore applies to all types of field representation. Hence, the following theorem can be applied for normal bases, polynomial bases or any other vector space basis for $\mathbb{F}_{p^m}$.

Theorem 18. *Let $\mathcal{A}$ be an algorithm that learns the τ-heavy Fourier coefficients of functions over finite abelian groups. Fix $1 \le i \le m$, and let $f : \mathbb{F}_p \to \{-1, 1\}$ be a concentrated function. For any function $F : \mathbb{F}_{p^m} \to \{-1, 1\}$ given by $F(\mathbf{x}) = F(x_1, \ldots, x_m) := f(x_i)$, there exists an algorithm that solves the hidden number problem in $\mathbb{F}_{p^m}$.*

Proof. Let $s \in \mathbb{F}_{p^m}$ be the secret element in the hidden number problem, written as $\mathbf{s} = (s_1, \ldots, s_m)$ with respect to any vector space basis of $\mathbb{F}_{p^m}$. Fix $1 \le i \le m$

and consider the i-th component in $\mathbb{F}_p^m$. Lemma 6 shows that for each multiplier $a \in \mathbb{F}_{p^m}$ (written as $\mathbf{a} = (a_1, \ldots, a_m)$) in the hidden number problem we can represent the i-th component of the product as by $\mathbf{a} M_i \mathbf{s}^T = \sum_{j=1}^m a_j \widetilde{s}_j$, where $\widetilde{s}_j :=$ $\left(M_i \mathbf{s}^T \right)_j$. Therefore $F_s(x) := F(sx) = f(\widetilde{s}_1 x_1 + \ldots + \widetilde{s}_m x_m \bmod p)$. Thus, oracle access to $F_s(x)$ is equivalent to oracle access to $f(\widetilde{s}_1 x_1 + \ldots + \widetilde{s}_m x_m \bmod p)$. The latter is the multivariate hidden number problem over $\mathbb{F}_p$ with the concentrated function f. By Theorem 16 we can solve this problem to retrieve $\widetilde{\mathbf{s}} = (\widetilde{s}_1, \ldots, \widetilde{s}_m)$. Since the matrix M_i is invertible, and since $\mathbf{a} M_i \mathbf{s}^T = \sum_{j=1}^m a_j \widetilde{s}_j = \mathbf{a} \cdot \widetilde{\mathbf{s}}^T$, we can recover the secret $\mathbf{s}$ by $\mathbf{s}^T = M_i^{-1} \widetilde{\mathbf{s}}^T$, that is, $\mathbf{s} = \widetilde{\mathbf{s}} \left(M_i^{-1} \right)^T$.   ∎

Corollary 19. *Fix* $1 \leq i \leq m$, *and let* $f : \mathbb{F}_p \to \{-1, 1\}$ *be a concentrated function. For any function* $F : \mathbb{F}_{p^m} \to \{-1, 1\}$ *given by* $F(\boldsymbol{x}) = F(x_1, \ldots, x_m) :=$ $f(x_i)$, *there exists an algorithm that solves HNP-CM in* $\mathbb{F}_{p^m}$, *where the queries are made non-adaptively.*

Remark 20. One should notice that, having the ability to query the function at specific points, one can easily reduce the m-dimensional problem to m one-dimensional instances, then solve them one-by-one using back substitution of previous parts that were recovered. This is in fact how the algorithm from Theorem 5 works over direct product of groups.

Remark 21. We stress that our methods do not hold for the elliptic-curve-based hidden number problem. One of the reasons that these methods do not work in the elliptic curve case is that, unlike $\mathbb{F}_{p^m}^*$, the elliptic curve group law in $E(\mathbb{F}_q)$ is not of a bilinear form $\mathbf{s} \cdot \mathbf{x}$.

5   Applications

In this section we give several applications, under different models, of our main results. These applications generalise previous bit security results to all extension fields. In Section 5.1 we generalise the work of Akavia [2] on the hidden number problem in prime fields. In Section 5.2 we generalise the works of Fazio et al. [12] on bit security of CDH in $\mathbb{F}_{p^2}$ and of Duc and Jetchev [9] on hardness of individual bits of elliptic curve and pairing based functions for elliptic curve over prime fields. We show how to reduce each problem to the form of MV-HNP-CM. The bit security results follow from the solutions given in the previous section.

5.1   Solving the Hidden Number Problem in $\mathbb{F}_{p^m}^*$ with Multipliers of the Form g^x Using Advice

The idea of using advice to solve different variants of the hidden number problem was first considered by Boneh and Venkatesan [8]. Using advice bits, independent of the secret s, they were able to solve the hidden number problem with uniformly random samples in prime fields $\mathbb{F}_p$ for a function that outputs the $2 \log \log p$ most-significant bits. Shparlinski and Winterhof [19] modified this work to extend the result to certain subgroups of $\mathbb{F}_p$, also under the provided advice.

The terminology of Corollary 11 above is slightly different than given in [2]. There, the following variant of the hidden number problem is considered: the solver chooses values x and the multipliers for the secret s are of the form g^x. This is the original formulation of the hidden number problem in [7], which has in mind attacks on Diffie-Hellman key exchange (see Remark 9 above for more details). Clearly, this problem is harder than HNP-CM, since one has to solve certain discrete logarithms (to the base g) in order to be able to choose the right multipliers. For this reason an additional advice was considered in [2]. This short advice depends only on p and g (and not on the secret s) – it is exactly certain discrete logarithms.

Since Corollary 19 is a generalisation of Corollary 11 to extension fields, our results hold for this variant of the hidden number problem. That is, we get the following result.

Corollary 22. *Let* $1 \leq i \leq m$, *let* $f : \mathbb{F}_p \to \{-1, 1\}$ *be concentrated. For any function* $F : \mathbb{F}_{p^m} \to \{-1, 1\}$ *given by* $F(\boldsymbol{x}) = F(x_1, \ldots, x_m) := f(x_i)$, *there exists an algorithm that solves with advice the hidden number problem with multipliers of the form* g^x *in the group* $\mathbb{F}_{p^m}^*$.

As shown in [8] and then discussed in [2, 19] this result can be applied to show bit security of ElGamal's public key system and Okamoto's conference key sharing scheme.

5.2   Hardness of Every Single Bit of CDH by Changing Representations

Diffie-Hellman key exchange and many other cryptographic protocols can be considered for $\mathbb{F}_{p^m}$ with $m > 1$. Hence, it is of interest to consider bit security results in that context. It is also interesting to consider bit security for elliptic curve groups $E(\mathbb{F}_q)$.

The idea of changing representations to show hardness of bits of Diffie-Hellman secrets was first considered in [6] for Weierstrass equations of elliptic curves (defined over prime fields). They show the hardness of the least-significant bit of a Diffie-Hellman secret S in $E(\mathbb{F}_p)$ under a very strong model, in which the solver not only gets the value $f(S)$ (and therefore the value $f(S + P)$ for points $P \in E(\mathbb{F}_p)$, as explained in Remark 9 above),[5] but also gets the values $f(\phi(S))$, where $\phi(S)$ is the image of the point under an elliptic curve isomorphism $\phi :$ $E(\mathbb{F}_p) \to E'(\mathbb{F}_p)$ to a different Weierstrass model, for isomorphisms that can be chosen by the solver. This idea was followed in [9] for elliptic curves defined over prime fields, where hardness of single bits of elliptic-curve-based functions is considered, and in [12, 20] for extension fields in polynomial basis representation, where hardness of single bits of (polynomial-represented) Diffie-Hellman secrets is considered.

---

[5] In [6] the function f is the least-significant-bit function $LSB : \mathbb{Z}_p \to \{-1, 1\}$.

CDH in $\mathbb{F}_{p^m}$ with Field Isomorphisms. In [12] the field $\mathbb{F}_{p^2}$ is considered. Succinctly, when one considers the leading-coefficient component (coefficient of x), they show how one can choose multipliers by taking appropriate field isomorphisms to another polynomial basis. Let $K = k_1 x + k_0 \in \mathbb{F}_{p^2}$ be unknown (recall that $k_1, k_0 \in \mathbb{F}_p$), and suppose one is interested to learn the secret value k_1. Any isomorphism $\phi : \mathbb{F}_{p^2} \to \mathbb{F}_{p^2}$ of polynomial representations of the finite field maps K to $\phi(K) = \lambda_1 k_1 x + \lambda_0 k_1 + k_0$, for $\lambda_1, \lambda_0 \in \mathbb{F}_p$. Therefore, in a model for which one has oracle access to a single bit of the x-component after any such chosen isomorphism (therefore, chosen λ_1, λ_0), we get HNP-CM in $\mathbb{F}_p$.

The case of the constant-term component (coefficient of x^0) was left open, as well as the case of extension fields $\mathbb{F}_{p^m}$ where $m > 2$. In [20] some steps are taken to close this gap. They generalise the result of [12] to extension fields $\mathbb{F}_{p^m}$.[6] This is done by similar methods that give rise to HNP-CM in $\mathbb{F}_p$, where the secret is one of the components k_i. As in [12], the constant-term component k_0 is excluded.

For the case in which $K = g^{ab}$ is a Diffie-Hellman secret in $\mathbb{F}_{p^m}$, one can use the results involving summing functions from [11] and recover the entire secret K from the algorithm that recovers a single (fixed) component k_i.

Remark 23. Such models give some assurance that bits in the Diffie-Hellman protocol are hard. The results can be interpreted as follows: considering Diffie-Hellman key exchange over an elliptic curve (resp. a finite field), specific bits of the secret key cannot be easy to compute for all (in fact, for a non-negligble fraction of) the representations of the elliptic curve (resp. polynomial representations of the field) at once. That is, given the bit we wish to compute, there exists a representation for which this bit is hard to compute. However, this model does not prove anything about a fixed representation of the elliptic curve or finite field. It does not give any assurance of hardness of a specific bit of a specific group representation.

We show that under the representation changing model in arbitrary extension fields $\mathbb{F}_{p^m}$ one can recover directly the secret K using our solution to MV-HNP-CM. For $K = g^{ab}$, a Diffie-Hellman secret in $\mathbb{F}_{p^m}$, this shows hardness of any bit of any component, under the specified model. This result improves the results of Fazio et al. [12] and Wang et al. [20] by showing a direct reduction from the computational Diffie-Hellman assumption, with no intermediate steps. In addition, the result holds for all extension fields $\mathbb{F}_{p^m}$. This allows us to consider the case of large m, and in particular the case of fields with small characteristic.

Moreover, we do not restrict only to polynomial bases. The result holds for general vector spaces and normal bases. Polynomial bases are more restrictive and do not allow to recover the entire secret directly, since the isomorphisms restrict the multipliers of the constant term. Note that there is no particular

---

[6] In [20] they specifically consider $\mathbb{F}_{p^m}$ where m is polynomial in $\log p$. They also show that if oracle access to a single bit of the constant-term component in $\mathbb{F}_{p^2}$ is given, then one can recover the secret value k_1.

reason to choose polynomial bases to represent $\mathbb{F}_{p^m}$, so we recommend to use normal bases to get efficient field arithmetic and the strongest bit security result.

We now state our result for the Diffie-Hellman protocol. Note that in fact this result holds for any secret element in $\mathbb{F}_{p^m}$.

Corollary 24. *Let $s = DH_g(g^a, g^b) = g^{ab}$ be a Diffie-Hellman secret in $\mathbb{F}_{p^m}$. Given $g, g^a, g^b \in \mathbb{F}_{p^m}$, computing a single bit of s in a random vector space or normal bases representation of $\mathbb{F}_{p^m}$ is as hard as computing s. In other words, an algorithm that has a non-negligible advantage over a random guess in computing a single bit of s (in a random vector space or normal bases representation of $\mathbb{F}_{p^m}$) can be used to efficiently compute s.*

Proof. Let $\mathbf{s} \in \mathbb{F}_{p^m}$ be a secret with components $s_1, \ldots, s_m \in \mathbb{F}_p$. Assume one has oracle access to a bit of component j of elements in $\mathbb{F}_{p^m}$. Given $\boldsymbol{\lambda} = (\lambda_1, \ldots, \lambda_m) \in \mathbb{F}_p^m$, one needs to construct an isomorphism $\phi_\lambda^j : \mathbb{F}_{p^m} \to \mathbb{F}_{p^m}$ between representations of the finite field such that component j of $\phi_\lambda^j(\mathbf{s})$ is of the form $\lambda_1 s_1 + \cdots + \lambda_m s_m$. The result then follows.

Recall that $\mathbb{F}_{p^m}$ is a vector space of dimension m over the field $\mathbb{F}_p$, that has different types of representations. We briefly discuss the construction of a suitable isomorphism in the cases of interest.

General Vector Space $\mathbb{F}_p^m$. Let $B_1 = \{v_1, \ldots, v_m\}, B_2 = \{u_1, \ldots, u_m\}$ be two bases of $\mathbb{F}_p^m$. The mapping ϕ_λ^j of an element $\mathbf{s} = s_1 v_1 + \cdots + s_m v_m$ should satisfy

$$\phi_\lambda^j(\mathbf{s}) = (*)u_1 + \cdots + (\lambda_1 s_1 + \lambda_2 s_2 + \cdots + \lambda_m s_m)u_j + \cdots + (\star)u_m \ .$$

Consider this linear map as a matrix. One can easily see that the j-th row of this matrix should be $(\lambda_1, \lambda_2, \ldots, \lambda_m)$. In order for the matrix to be a full rank map – therefore an isomorphism – it should be nonsingular. One can easily construct such a linear map.

Normal Basis. Let $B_1 = \{\alpha, \alpha^p, \ldots, \alpha^{p^{m-1}}\}, B_2 = \{\beta, \beta^p, \ldots, \beta^{p^{m-1}}\}$ be two normal bases of $\mathbb{F}_{p^m}$. The mapping ϕ_λ^j of an element $\mathbf{s} = s_1\alpha + \cdots + s_m\alpha^{p^{m-1}}$ should satisfy

$$\phi_\lambda^j(\mathbf{s}) = (*)\beta + \cdots + (\lambda_1 s_1 + \lambda_2 s_2 + \cdots + \lambda_m s_m)\beta^{p^{j-1}} + \cdots + (\star)\beta^{p^{m-1}} \ . \quad (2)$$

Consider the linear map satisfying $\phi_\lambda^j(\alpha) = \lambda_j\beta + \lambda_{j-1}\beta^p + \cdots + \lambda_{j+1}\beta^{p^{m-1}}$ (indices for λ_k are taken modulo m such that $1 \leq k \leq m$, i.e., $\lambda_0 = \lambda_m$ and $\lambda_{m+1} = \lambda_1$). Then

$$\phi_\lambda^j(\mathbf{s}) = \phi_\lambda^j(s_1\alpha + \cdots + s_m\alpha^{p^{m-1}}) = s_1\phi_\lambda^j(\alpha) + s_2\phi_\lambda^j(\alpha)^p + \cdots + s_m\phi_\lambda^j(\alpha)^{p^{m-1}}$$

$$= s_1(\lambda_j\beta + \lambda_{j-1}\beta^p + \cdots + \lambda_{j+1}\beta^{p^{m-1}})$$

$$+ s_2(\lambda_j\beta + \lambda_{j-1}\beta^p + \cdots + \lambda_{j+1}\beta^{p^{m-1}})^p + \cdots$$

$$+ s_m(\lambda_j\beta + \lambda_{j-1}\beta^p + \cdots + \lambda_{j+1}\beta^{p^{m-1}})^{p^{m-1}}$$

$$= s_1(\lambda_j\beta + \lambda_{j-1}\beta^p + \cdots + \lambda_{j+1}\beta^{p^{m-1}})$$
$$+ s_2(\lambda_j\beta^p + \lambda_{j-1}\beta^{p^2} + \cdots + \lambda_{j+1}\beta) + \cdots$$
$$+ s_m(\lambda_j\beta^{p^{m-1}} + \lambda_{j-1}\beta + \cdots + \lambda_{j+1}\beta^{p^{m-2}}) \ ,$$

where the last equality follows from $\beta^{p^m} = \beta$ for normal bases. After collecting the terms for each β^{p^k} (with $0 \le k \le m - 1$) one gets (2). In order for ϕ_λ^j to be an isomorphism, one needs to check that $\phi_\lambda^j(\alpha)^{p^m} = \phi_\lambda^j(\alpha)$ and that the set $\{\phi_\lambda^j(\alpha), \phi_\lambda^j(\alpha)^p, \ldots, \phi_\lambda^j(\alpha)^{p^{m-1}}\}$ is linearly independent. This can be easily shown: the former property follows from $\beta^{p^m} = \beta$, while the latter from the linear independence of the basis B_2.   ∎

Remark 25 (Polynomial basis). Given a polynomial $a = a_m x^{m-1} + \cdots + a_2 x + a_1$, one looks for an isomorphism ϕ_λ^j such that

$$\phi_\lambda^j(a) = (*)x^{m-1} + \cdots + (\lambda_1 a_1 + \lambda_2 a_2 + \cdots + \lambda_m a_m)x^{j-1} + \cdots + (*)x^0 \ .$$

For the constant polynomial $1 = 0 \cdot x^{m-1} + \cdots + 0 \cdot x + 1$ one gets that the coefficient of x^{j-1} of the polynomial $\phi_\lambda^j(1)$ is λ_1, i.e., $\phi_\lambda^j(1) = \lambda_1 x^{j-1} + \ldots$. Since an isomorphism maps the identity element to the identity element, it follows that if $j \ne 1$, then λ_1 has to be 0, and if $j = 1$, then λ_1 has to be 1. Therefore, when using polynomial representations, one cannot choose multipliers for s_1 and therefore cannot recover the secret s_1 using the solution to MV-HNP-CM. One can still try to recover some, or all, of the other coefficients using the method to solve MV-HNP-CM. We leave it for future work – it is an open problem to construct isomorphisms that give rise to the required multipliers even for some coefficients.

CDH in $E(\mathbb{F}_{p^m})$ with Changing Weierstrass/ Field Representations.

Let E be an elliptic curve over a field $\mathbb{F}_{p^m}$ and let $S = (s_x, s_y) \in E(\mathbb{F}_{p^m})$ be a secret point. We wish to learn S using oracle access to some function on changed representations of S. Such results have applications for CDH and pairing functions on elliptic curves.

The simplest approach is to assume we can get a bit of a component of s_x under changes of field representation. The result then follows from the methods of Section 5.2.

If we cannot change the field representation, then we can change the Weierstrass equation as was done by Boneh and Shparlinski [6]. Suppose E is given by the Weierstrass Equation $W : y^2 = x^3 + Ax + B$. For a non-zero $\lambda \in \mathbb{F}_{p^m}$ let $W_\lambda : Y^2 = X^3 + A\lambda^4 X + B\lambda^6$. The map $\phi_\lambda : W \to W_\lambda$ that takes $P = (x, y)$ on W to $P_\lambda = (\lambda^2 x, \lambda^3 y)$ on W_λ is known to be an isomorphism of groups. The image of the point $S = (s_x, s_y) \in W$ under ϕ_λ is $\phi_\lambda(S) = (\lambda^2 s_x, \lambda^3 s_y)$.

One can see that if t is a quadratic residue in $\mathbb{F}_{p^m}$, that is $t = \lambda^2$ for some $\lambda \in \mathbb{F}_{p^m}$, then by considering only the x-coordinate, the function ϕ_λ allows to choose multipliers for the secret. That is, $\phi_\lambda(S)_x = s_x t$, where $s_x, t \in \mathbb{F}_{p^m}$. Therefore, changing Weierstrass equations allows to choose multipliers for the secret, as long as t is a quadratic residue in $\mathbb{F}_{p^m}$. Due to the work in [9] for elliptic curves defined over prime fields, this is sufficient to solve HNP-CM in $\mathbb{F}_{p^m}$. A similar approach holds for the y-coordinate. Using the solution to HNP-CM in $\mathbb{F}_{p^m}$ given in Corollary 19, this forms bit security results as in [9] for elliptic curves defined over extension fields $E(\mathbb{F}_{p^m})$. Since the solution to HNP-CM in $\mathbb{F}_{p^m}$ given in Corollary 19 does not take into account the representation of the field $\mathbb{F}_{p^m}$, this result holds for any such representation.

These arguments give the following result, which we state for the Diffie-Hellman protocol, but can also be stated for elliptic-curve-based one-way functions and pairing-based one-way functions as in [9], and in fact holds for any secret element in $E(\mathbb{F}_{p^m})$.

Corollary 26. *Let $S = DH_P([a]P, [b]P) = [ab]P$ be a Diffie-Hellman secret in $E(\mathbb{F}_{p^m})$. Given $P, [a]P, [b]P \in E(\mathbb{F}_{p^m})$, computing a single bit of S for a random representation of $E(\mathbb{F}_{p^m})$ or a random representation of $\mathbb{F}_{p^m}$ is as hard as computing S. In other words, an algorithm that has a non-negligible advantage over a random guess in computing a single bit of S (for a random representation of $E(\mathbb{F}_{p^m})$ or a random representation of $\mathbb{F}_{p^m}$) can be used to efficiently compute S.*

Acknowledgements. We thank the anonymous referees for their helpful comments.

References

1. Akavia, A.: Learning Noisy Characters, Multiplication Codes and Hardcore Predicates. Ph.D. Thesis, Massachusetts Institute of Technology (2008)
2. Akavia, A.: Solving Hidden Number Problem with One Bit Oracle and Advice. In: Halevi, S. (ed.) CRYPTO 2009. LNCS, vol. 5677, pp. 337–354. Springer, Heidelberg (2009)
3. Akavia, A., Goldwasser, S., Safra, S.: Proving Hard-Core Predicates Using List Decoding. In: FOCS 2003, pp. 146–157. IEEE Computer Society, Washington (2003)
4. Alexi, W., Chor, B., Goldreich, O., Schnorr, C.P.: RSA and Rabin Functions: Certain Parts are as Hard as the Whole. SIAM Journal on Computing 17(2), 194–209 (1988)
5. Ben-Or, M., Chor, B., Shamir, A.: On the Cryptographic Security of Single RSA Bits. In: Johnson, D.S., Fagin, R., Fredman, M.L., Harel, D., Karp, R.M., Lynch, N.A., Papadimitriou, C.H., Rivest, R.L., Ruzzo, W.L., Seiferas, J.I. (eds.) STOC 1983, pp. 421–430. ACM, New York (1983)
6. Boneh, D., Shparlinski, I.E.: On the Unpredictability of Bits of the Elliptic Curve Diffie–Hellman Scheme. In: Kilian, J. (ed.) CRYPTO 2001. LNCS, vol. 2139, pp. 201–212. Springer, Heidelberg (2001)
7. Boneh, D., Venkatesan, R.: Hardness of Computing the Most Significant Bits of Secret Keys in Diffie-Hellman and Related Schemes. In: Koblitz, N. (ed.) CRYPTO 1996. LNCS, vol. 1109, pp. 129–142. Springer, Heidelberg (1996)
8. Boneh, D., and Venkatesan, R.: Rounding in Lattices and its Cryptographic Applications. In: Saks, M.E. (ed.) SODA 1997, pp. 675–681. ACM/SIAM, Philadelphia (1997)

9. Duc, A., Jetchev, D.: Hardness of Computing Individual Bits for One-Way Functions on Elliptic Curves. In: Safavi-Naini, R., Canetti, R. (eds.) CRYPTO 2012. LNCS, vol. 7417, pp. 832–849. Springer, Heidelberg (2012)

10. De Mulder, E., Hutter, M., Marson, M.E., Pearson, P.: Using Bleichenbacher"s Solution to the Hidden Number Problem to Attack Nonce Leaks in 384-Bit ECDSA. In: Bertoni, G., Coron, J.-S. (eds.) CHES 2013. LNCS, vol. 8086, pp. 435–452. Springer, Heidelberg (2013)

11. Verheul, E.R.: Certificates of Recoverability with Scalable Recovery Agent Security. In: Imai, H., Zheng, Y. (eds.) PKC 2000. LNCS, vol. 1751, pp. 258–275. Springer, Heidelberg (2000)

12. Fazio, N., Gennaro, R., Perera, I.M., Skeith III, W.E.: Hard-Core Predicates for a Diffie-Hellman Problem over Finite Fields. In: Canetti, R., Garay, J.A. (eds.) CRYPTO 2013, Part II. LNCS, vol. 8043, pp. 148–165. Springer, Heidelberg (2013)

13. Goldreich, O., Levin, L.A.: A Hard-Core Predicate for all One-Way Functions. In: Johnson, D.S. (ed.) STOC 1989, pp. 25–32. ACM, New York (1989)

14. Aranha, D.F., Fouque, P.-A., Gérard, B., Kammerer, J.-G., Tibouchi, M., Zapalowicz, J.-C.: GLV/GLS Decomposition, Power Analysis, and Attacks on ECDSA Signatures with Single-Bit Nonce Bias. In: Sarkar, P., Iwata, T. (eds.) ASIACRYPT 2014. LNCS, vol. 8873, pp. 262–281. Springer, Heidelberg (2014)

15. Kushilevitz, E., Mansour, Y.: Learning Decision Trees Using the Fourier Sprectrum. In: Koutsougeras, C., Vitter, J.S. (eds.) STOC 1991, pp. 455–464. ACM, New York (1991)

16. Morillo, P., Ràfols, C.: The Security of All Bits Using List Decoding. In: Jarecki, S., Tsudik, G. (eds.) PKC 2009. LNCS, vol. 5443, pp. 15–33. Springer, Heidelberg (2009)

17. Mansour, Y.: Learning Boolean Functions via the Fourier Transform. In: Roychowdhury, V., Siu, K.Y., Orlitsky, A. (eds.) Theoretical Advances in Neural Computation and Learning, pp. 391–424. Kluwer Academic Publishers (1994)

18. Shparlinski, I.: Playing "Hide-and-Seek" in Finite Fields: Hidden Number Problem and its Applications. In: Proceedings of the Seventh Spanish Meeting on Cryptology and Information Security, vol. 1, pp. 49–72. University of Oviedo (2002)

19. Shparlinski, I.E., Winterhof, A.: A Nonuniform Algorithm for the Hidden Number Problem in Subgroups. In: Bao, F., Deng, R., Zhou, J. (eds.) PKC 2004. LNCS, vol. 2947, pp. 416–424. Springer, Heidelberg (2004)

20. Wang, M., Zhan, T., and Zhang, H.: Bits Security of the CDH Problems over Finite Fields. Cryptology ePrint Archive, Report 2014/685 (2014), http://eprint.iacr.org/2014/685

Lattice Point Enumeration
on Block Reduced Bases*

Michael Walter

University of California, San Diego, USA
miwalter@eng.ucsd.edu

Abstract. When analyzing lattice-based cryptosystems, we often need
to solve the Shortest Vector Problem (SVP) in some lattice associated
to the system under scrutiny. The go-to algorithms in practice to solve
SVP are enumeration algorithms, which usually consist of a preprocessing step, followed by an exhaustive search. Obviously, the two steps offer
a trade-off and should be balanced in their running time in order to minimize the overall complexity. In practice, the most common approach
to control this trade-off is to use block reduction algorithms during the
preprocessing. Despite the popularity of this approach, it lacks any well
founded analysis and all practical approaches seem to use ad hoc parameters. This weakens our confidence in the cryptanalysis of the systems.
In this work, we aim to shed light on at least one side of this trade-
off and analyze the effect of block reduction on the exhaustive search.
For this, we give asymptotic worst case bounds and present results from
both experiments and simulation that show its average case behavior in
practice.

1 Introduction

Lattice-based cryptography is a very active research area having attracted a
lot of attention in recent years. There are several reasons for this. On the one
hand, lattice problems seem very useful in the construction of new cryptographic
primitives. For example, they have been used to construct candidates for fully
homomorphic encryption [13] and multi-linear maps [12], making significant
progress on long standing open problems in cryptography. Furthermore, since
Ajtai showed in his breakthrough work [2] a worst-case to average-case reduction for lattice problems, many primitives have emerged that enjoy a strong
security reduction, see for example [23,3,28,21,22,14]. Finally, lattices have been
studied in mathematics and computer science for a long time and the hardness
of many associated problems is well understood by now. One of the most classical and prominent problems of this kind is the Shortest Vector Problem (SVP).

* Research supported in part by the DARPA PROCEED program and NSF grant
CNS-1117936. Opinions, findings and conclusions or recommendations expressed in
this material are those of the author(s) and do not necessarily reflect the views of
DARPA or NSF.

© Springer International Publishing Switzerland 2015
A. Lehmann and S. Wolf (Eds.): ICITS 2015, LNCS 9063, pp. 269–282, 2015.
DOI: 10.1007/978-3-319-17470-9_16

The SVP has been proved to be NP-hard under randomized reductions [19,24], and thus all known algorithms to solve it have a (super) exponential complexity. Unfortunately, these algorithms are not very well understood. This is demonstrated by the recurring phenomenon that, as already pointed out in [10], asymptotically fast algorithms are routinely outperformed in practice by algorithms having inferior theoretical bounds. One such example are block reduction algorithms (which actually approximate SVP, rather than solve it). In theory, slide reduction [10] seems to offer the best trade-off between running time and output quality, but is outperformed in practice by BKZ [29], as demonstrated in [11]. Such gaps between theory and practice weaken our confidence in the cryptanalysis of lattice based cryptosystems and thus hinder a wide spread adoption in practice.

Another example for such a gap are exact SVP algorithms. Sieving [4,6,26] and Voronoi cell based algorithms [25] are known to have a single exponential complexity, but they are hardly ever used to solve SVP in practice, since they are outperformed by enumeration for all practically feasible instances (see e.g. [27]), which is only known to have super exponential complexity in the worst case. Even inside the class of enumeration algorithms, such gaps exist. For example, for a long time, we only knew two kinds of enumeration algorithms that solve SVP: FinckePohst [9] (including a wide range of heuristic variants) having a worst case complexity of $2^{O(n^2)}$, and Kannan's algorithm [18] with a complexity of $n^{O(n)}$. But again, the latter is outperformed by the former in practice.

All known enumeration algorithms consist of two phases: a preprocessing that prepares the input, followed by an exhaustive search for the shortest vector. Roughly speaking, the exhaustive search is the source of the inefficiency for these algorithms and the asymptotic superiority of Kannan's algorithm stems from a very heavy preprocessing, significantly reducing the search space. However, it is also exactly this preprocessing that slows it down in practice, even though asymptotically it is dominated by the search step. Only very recently it was shown how to reduce this preprocessing step while keeping the search efficient [27]. On the other hand, it was already pointed out in [17], that spending more time on the preprocessing than the FinckePohst algorithm also makes sense in practice. To demonstrate this, a block reduction algorithm was used as the preprocessing to speed up the exhaustive search. The parameter of the reduction algorithm that controls the quality of the output can be used to trade off preprocessing time for a faster exhaustive search. A similar approach is also used in [7] and represents the state of the art. Despite the popularity of this method, to the best of our knowledge there is no well founded analysis of the trade-off that can be achieved, and all practical approaches seem to use ad hoc parameters.

Contribution. In this work, we aim to shed light on at least one side of the trade-off between preprocessing and exhaustive search in enumeration algorithms by obtaining explicit asymptotic bounds for the exhaustive search depending on the kind and parameter of the approximation algorithm used as preprocessing. We first show what a straight forward analysis might look like. While this already shows that the enumeration complexity drops from $2^{O(n^2)}$ to $2^{O((n^2 \log^2 \beta)/\beta)}$ when preprocessing the basis with block size β, we will argue that this bound is too rough by drawing a connection between enumeration on block reduced bases with large block size and Kannan's algorithm. We then build on techniques from [27] to show that the enumeration complexity in fact drops to $\beta^{O(n^2/\beta)}$. We also hint at implications these bounds have for the complexity of the entire algorithm, but leave an in depth analysis for future work. Instead, we move on to the practical side and show through a number of experiments and simulations that in practice the exhaustive search has a complexity qualitatively similar to the asymptotic bounds. We hope that this work helps to further our understanding of lattice algorithms and to ultimately lead to a wider adoption of lattice-based cryptography in practice.

2   Preliminaries

Notation. Numbers and reals are denoted by lower case letters and sets by upper case letters. For $n \in \mathbb{Z}_+$ we denote the set $\{1, \ldots, n\}$ by $[n]$. For vectors we use bold lower case letters and the i-th entry of a vector $\mathbf{v}$ is denoted by v_i. Let $\langle \mathbf{v}, \mathbf{w} \rangle = \sum_i v_i \cdot w_i$ be the scalar product of two vectors, and $\|\mathbf{v}\| = \sqrt{\langle \mathbf{v}, \mathbf{v} \rangle}$ the standard Euclidean norm. We define the projection of a vector $\mathbf{b}$ orthogonally to a vector $\mathbf{v}$ as $\pi_{\mathbf{v}}(\mathbf{b}) = \mathbf{b} - \frac{\langle \mathbf{b}, \mathbf{v} \rangle}{\|\mathbf{v}\|^2}\mathbf{v}$. Matrices are denoted by bold upper case letters. The i-th column of a matrix $\mathbf{B}$ is denoted by $\mathbf{b}_i$. Furthermore, we denote the submatrix comprising the columns from the i-th to the j-th column (inclusive) as $\mathbf{B}_{[i,j]}$. We extend the projection operator to matrices, where $\pi_{\mathbf{V}}(\mathbf{B})$ is the matrix obtained by applying $\pi_{\mathbf{V}}$ to every column $\mathbf{b}_i$ of $\mathbf{B}$ and $\pi_{\mathbf{V}}(\mathbf{b}_i) = \pi_{\mathbf{v}_k}(\cdots(\pi_{\mathbf{v}_1}(\mathbf{b}_i))\cdots)$.

Lattices. A *lattice* Λ is a discrete subgroup of $\mathbb{R}^m$ and is generated by a matrix $\mathbf{B} \in \mathbb{R}^{m \times n}$, i.e. $\Lambda = \mathcal{L}(\mathbf{B}) = \{\mathbf{B}\mathbf{x} : \mathbf{x} \in \mathbb{Z}^n\}$. If $\mathbf{B}$ has full column rank, it is called a *basis* of Λ and $\dim(\Lambda) = n$ is the dimension (or rank) of Λ. A lattice has infinitely many bases, which are related to each other by right-multiplication with unimodular matrices. With each matrix $\mathbf{B}$ we associate its *Gram-Schmidt-Orthogonalization* (GSO) $\mathbf{B}^*$, where the i-th column $\mathbf{b}_i^*$ of $\mathbf{B}^*$ is defined as $\mathbf{b}_i^* = \pi_{\mathbf{B}_{[1,i-1]}}(\mathbf{b}_i) = \pi_{\mathbf{B}_{[1,i-1]}^*}(\mathbf{b}_i)$ (and $\mathbf{b}_1^* = \mathbf{b}_1$). For a fixed matrix $\mathbf{B}$ we extend the projection operation to indices: $\pi_i(\cdot) = \pi_{\mathbf{B}_{[1,i]}^*}(\cdot)$. Whenever we refer to the *shape* of a basis $\mathbf{B}$, we mean the vector $(\|\mathbf{b}_i^*\|)_{i \in [n]}$.

For every lattice Λ there are a few invariants associated to it. One of them is its determinant $\det(\mathcal{L}(\mathbf{B})) = \prod_i \|\mathbf{b}_i^*\|$ for any basis $\mathbf{B}$. Even though the basis of a lattice is not uniquely defined, the determinant is and it is efficiently computable given a basis. Furthermore, for every lattice Λ we denote the length of its shortest non-zero vector (also known as the *first minimum*) by $\lambda_1(\Lambda)$, which is always well defined. We use the short-hand notations $\det(\mathbf{B}) = \det(\mathcal{L}(\mathbf{B}))$ and $\lambda_1(\mathbf{B}) = \lambda_1(\mathcal{L}(\mathbf{B}))$. Minkowski's theorem is a classic result that relates the first minimum to the determinant of a lattice. It states that $\lambda_1(\Lambda) \leq \sqrt{\gamma_n} \det(\Lambda)^{1/n}$, for any Λ with $\dim(\Lambda) = n$, where $\Omega(n) \leq \gamma_n \leq n$ is Hermite's constant. Finding a (even approximate) shortest nonzero vector in a lattice, commonly known as the *Shortest Vector Problem* (SVP), is NP-hard under randomized reductions [19,24].

Lattice Reduction. Lattice reduction algorithms deal with the problem of obtaining a "good" basis from an arbitrary basis for some notion of a "good" basis. The *LLL* algorithm [20] is a polynomial time basis reduction algorithm that produces a basis $\mathbf{B} \in \mathbb{Z}^{m \times n}$ such that $\delta \|\mathbf{b}_i^*\| \leq \lambda_1(\pi_{i-1}(\mathbf{B}_{[i,i+1]}))$ for all $i \in [n-1]$ and some $\delta < 1$ usually chosen close to 1.

BKZ-β [29] is a generalization of LLL to larger block size, i.e. it guarantees that the output basis satisfies $\delta \|\mathbf{b}_i^*\| \leq \lambda_1(\pi_{i-1}(\mathbf{B}_{[i,\min(i+\beta,n)]}))$ for all $i \in [n-1]$ by utilizing a SVP oracle in dimension β. When $\beta = n$, this is usually referred to as *HKZ* reduction and is essentially equivalent to solving SVP. Using Minkowski's theorem, one can prove the following bounds for $\mathbf{b}_1$ of a BKZ-β reduced basis [16]:

$$\|\mathbf{b}_1\| \leq \beta^{\frac{n-1}{\beta-1}} \lambda_1(\mathbf{B}) \tag{1}$$

$$\|\mathbf{b}_1\| \leq \beta^{\frac{n-1}{2(\beta-1)} + \frac{3}{2}} \det(\mathbf{B})^{1/n} \tag{2}$$

Note that any prefix $\mathbf{B}_{[1,i]}$ and any projection $\pi_i(\mathbf{B})$ of a BKZ-β reduced basis is also BKZ-β reduced. Unfortunately, there is no polynomial bound on the number of calls BKZ makes to the SVP oracle, but it has been repeatedly reported to behave very well in practice (see e.g. [11,7]). Furthermore, Hanrot, Pujol, and Stehlé showed in [16] that one can terminate BKZ after a polynomial number of calls to the SVP oracle and provably achieve bounds only slightly worse than (1). For these reasons, BKZ is very popular in practice and implementations are readily available in different libraries, e.g. in NTL[31] or fpLLL[5]. As the dimension and block size of BKZ grows, running it becomes more and more impractical. But since BKZ has also proved to be a very useful tool in the cryptanalysis of lattice-based cryptosystems, one would like to predict its behavior for very large instances to estimate the security of such systems. To this end, Chen and Nguyen introduced a BKZ simulator [7] that, given as input the shape of a basis and an integer closely related to the number of SVP calls, predicts the shape of the output of BKZ after the given number of calls to the oracle without the need to run it, based on heuristic assumptions. It is straightforward to modify the simulator to predict the output of BKZ by calling it repeatedly until no more change to the shape of the basis is observed.

In [10], Gama and Nguyen introduced a different block reduction algorithm, namely *slide reduction*. Similar to BKZ, it is parameterized by a block size β and uses a SVP oracle in dimension β to produce a basis with the following properties:

$$\|\mathbf{b}_1\| \leq \beta^{\frac{n-\beta}{\beta-1}} \lambda_1(\mathbf{B}) \tag{3}$$

$$\|\mathbf{b}_1\| \leq \beta^{\frac{n-1}{2(\beta-1)}} \det(\mathbf{B})^{1/n} \tag{4}$$

Moreover, every prefix $\mathbf{B}_{[1,i\beta]}$ and every projection $\pi_{i\beta}(\mathbf{B})$ is slide reduced and every projected block $\pi_{i\beta}(\mathbf{B}_{[i\beta+1,(i+1)\beta]})$ is HKZ reduced. Slide reduction has the desirable property of only making a polynomial number of calls to the SVP oracle. Unfortunately, as reported in [10] and [11], it seems to be outperformed by BKZ, despite providing better guarantees on output quality and runtime. Not surprisingly, it is rarely used in practice and we are not aware of any publicly available implementation.

Enumeration Algorithms. The standard enumeration procedure, usually attributed to Fincke, Pohst [9], and Kannan [18] can be described as a recursive algorithm: given as input a basis $\mathbf{B} \in \mathbb{Z}^{m \times n}$ and a radius r, it first recursively finds all vectors $\mathbf{v}' \in \Lambda(\pi_1(\mathbf{B}))$ with $\|\mathbf{v}'\| \leq r$, and then for each of them finds all $\mathbf{v} \in \Lambda(\mathbf{B})$, s.t. $\pi_1(\mathbf{v}) = \mathbf{v}'$ and $\|\mathbf{v}\| \leq r$, using $\mathbf{b}_1$. For each $i \in [n]$, the procedure introduces a multiplicative factor proportional to $r/\|\mathbf{b}_i^*\|$ to its complexity. So the complexity of the enumeration procedure depends on a) the upper bound r for the shortest vector and b) the shape of the basis. In fact, Hanrot and Stehlé noticed in [17] that one can estimate the complexity of enumeration based on the Gaussian heuristic by the quantity

$$E(r, \mathbf{B}) = \max_{i \in [n]} \frac{\pi^{i/2} r^i}{\Gamma(i/2 + 1) \prod_{j \geq n-i+1} \|\mathbf{b}_i^*\|} \tag{5}$$

We remark that, as already pointed out in [7], this estimate is likely to over-estimate the complexity, since it does note take heuristics like dynamic radius updates etc. into account. So Equation (5) should not be used as a precise prediction, but it is very useful to compare the expected complexity of enumeration for different inputs.

The bound r is usually chosen to be either the length of first vector $\|\mathbf{b}_1\|$ of the basis or Minkowski's bound. The shape of the basis is determined by the preprocessing strategy and there is a trade-off between preprocessing the basis and enumeration. The simplest approach, first proposed by Fincke and Pohst [9], is to apply LLL to the input and then call the enumeration procedure. This algorithm has a worst case complexity of $2^{O(n^2)}$. On the other hand, Kannan [18] proposed to use a much heavier, recursive preprocessing: alternate LLL reduction on $\mathbf{B}_{[1,2]}$ and recurse on $\pi_1(\mathbf{B})$ until no more change is observed. At this point the basis is often called *quasi-HKZ reduced*. Only then call the enumeration procedure to find the shortest vector $\mathbf{v}$ and finally recurse on $\pi_{\mathbf{v}}(\mathbf{B})$ to fully HKZ reduce the basis (which is necessary for the recursive calls to make sense). It can be shown that this algorithm runs in at most $O(n^{n/2e+o(n)})$ steps [17]. In theory, this is much better than the bound obtained for FinckePohst, but the heavy preprocessing seems to kill the performance in practice, so it is never used. It was only very recently, that a technique for interpolating both algorithms was introduced [27], providing an easy method to trade off preprocessing time and enumeration complexity. In practice, the most common approach at this point is to use block reduction algorithms to preprocess the basis before enumeration (see e.g. [17,7]), but to the best of our knowledge there is no analysis of this approach and the parameter choice is usually ad hoc.

3   Worst-Case Analysis of Enumeration After Block Reduction

Consider an algorithm that reduces an input basis $\mathbf{B}$ using a block reduction algorithm with parameter β and then runs enumeration to find the shortest vector. We are interested in the complexity of the enumeration step depending on the parameter β.

3.1   A Naive Attempt

As a warm up we will show how a simple analysis could go and argue why this result is not satisfactory. Assume for now that the enumeration bound is chosen to be $r = \|\mathbf{b}_1\|$ and that $\|\mathbf{b}_1\| \gtrsim \|\mathbf{b}_i^*\|$ for all $i \in [n]$ (which is true under a common heuristic assumption, namely the Geometric Series Assumption [30]). In this case, enumeration can be bounded by the quantity

$$\prod_i \frac{\|\mathbf{b}_1\|}{\|\mathbf{b}_i^*\|}$$

One can easily show (see e.g. [8], Theorem 1) for BKZ-β reduced bases that

$$\|\mathbf{b}_1\| \leq \beta^{\frac{\log \beta + 1}{2}(1 + \frac{i-1}{\beta - 1})}\|\mathbf{b}_i^*\| \approx 2^{(i \log^2 \beta)/2\beta}\|\mathbf{b}_i^*\|$$

which results in a bound for enumeration of $2^{(n^2/4\beta)\log^2 \beta}$. While already showing that there is at least an improvement of $(\log^2 \beta)/\beta$ as compared to FinckePohst (which corresponds to the case of $\beta = 2$), this bound seems to be too rough. Consider the algorithm with parameter $\beta = n - 1$. In this case, it has a striking similarity to Kannan's algorithm: Recall that Kannan's algorithm can be viewed as alternately calling a SVP oracle on $\mathbf{B}_{[1,2]}$ and a HKZ oracle (instantiated with a recursive call) on $\pi_1(\mathbf{B})$. The only difference between this kind of preprocessing and BKZ-$(n-1)$ is that the latter alternates between calling an SVP oracle on $\mathbf{B}_{[1,n-1]}$ and a HKZ oracle on $\pi_1(\mathbf{B})$. So a BKZ-$(n-1)$ reduced basis is also quasi-HKZ reduced and thus strictly stronger reduced than after Kannan's preprocessing. In particular, the enumeration complexity should not be larger than for Kannan's algorithm, which we know to be $O(n^{n/2e+o(n)})$. However, plugging $\beta = n-1$ into the bound we obtained above, we see that the complexity is bounded by $n^{O(n \log n)}$, which is off by a factor $\log n$ in the exponent. It follows that the analysis could be improved by at least that factor.

We remark that we do not believe that BKZ-$(n-1)$ is a suitable preprocessing for enumeration since it is even more expensive than quasi-HKZ reduction and can be expected to be at least as impractical.

3.2 ζ-Reducedness of Block Reduced Bases

Our analysis of the enumeration builds on the framework recently introduced in [27], namely ζ-reduction. We recall the corresponding definition.

Definition 1 ([27]). *Let* $\mathbf{B} \in \mathbb{Z}^{m \times n}$ *be a lattice basis[1] and* $\zeta : [n] \to \mathbb{R}_+$. *We call* $\mathbf{B}$ ζ-*reduced, if for all* $i \in [n]$

$$\|\mathbf{b}_i^*\| > \zeta(i) \det(\mathbf{B})^{1/n} \quad \Rightarrow \quad \lambda_1(\pi_{i-1}(\mathbf{B})) > \lambda_1(\mathbf{B})$$

and $\mathbf{B}_{[1,k]}$ *is* ζ-*reduced for all* $k \in [n-1]$.

In [27] it was proved that using the ζ-reducedness of a basis we can bound the enumeration step:

Theorem 1 ([27]). *Let* $\mathbf{B} \in \mathbb{Z}^{m \times n}$ *be a* ζ-*reduced basis with* $\zeta(i) \geq \sqrt{n}$ *for all* $i \in [n]$. *Then there is an efficiently computable set* $M \subset \mathbb{Z}^n$ *with* $|M| \leq 3^n \prod_{i=1}^n \zeta(i)$ *such that there is a vector* $\mathbf{x} \in M$ *with* $\|\mathbf{Bx}\| = \lambda_1(\mathbf{B})$.

It follows that in order to bound the enumeration on BKZ reduced bases, it suffices to analyze the ζ bounds that BKZ achieves. This is exactly what the following lemma does.

Lemma 1. *If* $\mathbf{B} \in \mathbb{Z}^{m \times n}$ *is BKZ-*β *reduced then it is* ζ-*reduced with* $\zeta(i) = \beta^{\frac{n-1}{2(\beta-1)} + \frac{3}{2}}$.

Proof. We prove the contrapositive and assume $\lambda_1(\pi_{i-1}(\mathbf{B})) \leq \lambda_1(\mathbf{B})$. Since $\pi_{i-1}(\mathbf{B})$ and $\mathbf{B}_{[1,i-1]}$ are BKZ-β reduced, we have

$$\begin{aligned}
\|\mathbf{b}_i^*\| &\leq \beta^{\frac{n-i}{(\beta-1)}} \lambda_1(\pi_{i-1}(\mathbf{B})) \\
&\leq \beta^{\frac{n-i}{(\beta-1)}} \lambda_1(\mathbf{B}) \\
&\leq \beta^{\frac{n-i}{(\beta-1)}} \|\mathbf{b}_1\| \\
&\leq \beta^{\frac{n-i}{(\beta-1)}} \beta^{\frac{i-2}{2(\beta-1)} + \frac{3}{2}} \det(\mathbf{B}_{[1,i-1]})^{1/(i-1)}
\end{aligned}$$

and so

$$\|\mathbf{b}_i^*\|^{i-1} \leq \beta^{\frac{(i-1)(n-i)}{(\beta-1)} + \frac{(i-1)(i-2)}{2(\beta-1)} + \frac{3}{2}(i-1)} \det(\mathbf{B}_{[1,i-1]})$$

By (2) we also have $\|\mathbf{b}_i^*\|^{n-i+1} \leq \beta^{\frac{(n-i)(n-i+1)}{2(\beta-1)} + \frac{3}{2}(n-i+1)} \det(\pi_{i-1}(\mathbf{B}))$. Multiplying those two bounds and doing some arithmetic gives

$$\|\mathbf{b}_i^*\|^n \leq \beta^{\frac{(i-1)(n-i)}{(\beta-1)} + \frac{(i-1)(i-2)}{2(\beta-1)} + \frac{(n-i)(n-i+1)}{2(\beta-1)} + \frac{3}{2}n} \det(\mathbf{B}) \leq \beta^{\frac{n(n-1)}{2(\beta-1)} + \frac{3}{2}n} \det(\mathbf{B})$$

$\square$

Using Theorem 1 we can easily deduce a runtime bound for the enumeration step.

Corollary 1. *Given a BKZ-*β *reduced basis* $\mathbf{B} \in \mathbb{Z}^{m \times n}$, *enumeration can solve SVP in* $\Lambda(\mathbf{B})$ *in* $\beta^{\frac{n(n-1)}{2(\beta-1)} + \frac{3}{2}n} 2^{O(n)}$.

---

[1] In [27] the definition covers arbitrary generating systems, not just bases. In this work however, we only consider bases, so we slightly simplified the definition accordingly.

For $\beta = 2$ (FinckePohst) and $\beta = n - 1$ ($\approx$ Kannan) we get the expected bounds up to constants in the exponent. Other values for β interpolate the two algorithms offering an improvement in the exponent of the dominating factor of FinckePohst of about $\log(\beta)/\beta$. Up to constants in the exponent, this proves that the enumeration step after BKZ is as efficient as after Kannan's preprocessing as long as $\beta = O(n)$.

Although rarely used in practice, we now also show how to apply ζ-reduction to slide reduced bases, which leads to slightly improved results.

Lemma 2. *If* $\mathbf{B} \in \mathbb{Z}^{m \times n}$ *is slide reduced with parameter* β *the* k-*th projected block* $\pi_{k\beta}(\mathbf{B}_{[k\beta+1,(k+1)\beta]})$ *is* ζ-*reduced for*

$$\zeta(k\beta < i \le (k+1)\beta) = \beta^{\frac{n-1}{2(\beta-1)} + \frac{\beta}{\beta-1} - \frac{k\beta^2}{n(\beta-1)}}$$

Proof. As before, we assume $\lambda_1(\pi_{i-1}(\mathbf{B})) \le \lambda_1(\mathbf{B})$. We start by showing the lemma for the first vector $\|\mathbf{b}_i^*\|$ of the block. In this case $\mathbf{B}_{[1,i-1]}$ and $\pi_{i-1}(\mathbf{B})$ are also slide reduced and we can apply the same approach as for BKZ:

$$\begin{aligned}\|\mathbf{b}_i^*\| &\le \beta^{\frac{n-i-\beta}{(\beta-1)}} \lambda_1(\pi_{i-1}(\mathbf{B}))\\ &\le \beta^{\frac{n-i-\beta}{(\beta-1)}} \lambda_1(\mathbf{B})\\ &\le \beta^{\frac{n-i-\beta}{(\beta-1)}} \|\mathbf{b}_1\|\\ &\le \beta^{\frac{n-i-\beta}{(\beta-1)}} \beta^{\frac{i-2}{2(\beta-1)}} \det(\mathbf{B}_{[1,i-1]})^{1/(i-1)}\end{aligned}$$

and so

$$\|\mathbf{b}_i^*\|^{i-1} \le \beta^{\frac{(i-1)(n-i-\beta)}{(\beta-1)} + \frac{(i-1)(i-2)}{2(\beta-1)}} \det(\mathbf{B}_{[1,i-1]})$$

By (4) we also have $\|\mathbf{b}_i^*\|^{n-i+1} \le \beta^{\frac{(n-i)(n-i+1)}{2(\beta-1)}} \det(\pi_{i-1}(\mathbf{B}))$. Again, multiplying those two bounds gives

$$\begin{aligned}\|\mathbf{b}_i^*\|^n &\le \beta^{\frac{(i-1)(n-i-\beta)}{(\beta-1)} + \frac{(i-1)(i-2)}{2(\beta-1)} + \frac{(n-i)(n-i+1)}{2(\beta-1)}} \det(\mathbf{B})\\ &\le \beta^{\frac{n(n-1)-2\beta(i-1)}{2(\beta-1)}} \det(\mathbf{B})\end{aligned} \qquad (6)$$

which implies $\|\mathbf{b}_i^*\| \le \beta^{\frac{n-1}{2(\beta-1)}} \det(\mathbf{B})^{1/n}$ and shows the result for the first vector of each block, because $\frac{\beta}{\beta-1} \ge \frac{k\beta^2}{n(\beta-1)}$ and so $\zeta(i) \ge \beta^{\frac{n-1}{2(\beta-1)}}$.

We now generalize to arbitrary i. Let $j = (k+1)\beta$, i.e. the end of the block. If $\lambda_1(\pi_j(\mathbf{B})) > \lambda_1(\pi_{i-1}(\mathbf{B}))$ then the shortest vector in $\pi_{i-1}(\mathbf{B})$ is in $\pi_{i-1}(\mathbf{B}_{[i,j]})$ and $\|\mathbf{b}_i^*\| = \lambda_1(\pi_{i-1}(\mathbf{B}))$, because $\pi_{i-1}(\mathbf{B}_{[i,j]})$ is HKZ reduced. It follows that $\|\mathbf{b}_i^*\|$ is ζ-reduced for all $\zeta(i) \ge \sqrt{n} \le \beta^{\frac{n-1}{2(\beta-1)}}$. Now let $\lambda_1(\pi_j(\mathbf{B})) \le \lambda_1(\pi_{i-1}(\mathbf{B}))$. Then by assumption $\lambda_1(\pi_j(\mathbf{B})) \le \lambda_1(\pi_{i-1}(\mathbf{B})) \le \lambda_1(\mathbf{B})$, so (6) holds for $\mathbf{b}_{j+1}^*$. Utilizing the fact that $\pi_{i-1}(\mathbf{B}_{[i,j]})$ is HKZ reduced and $\pi_i(\mathbf{B}_{[i+1,j+1]})$ is DSVP reduced, we easily deduce by Minkowski's theorem that $\|\mathbf{b}_i^*\| \le \kappa^{\frac{\kappa}{\kappa-1}} \|\mathbf{b}_{j+1}^*\|$

where $\kappa = j - i + 1$. Putting this and (6) together, we get:

$$\|\mathbf{b}_i^*\| \leq \kappa^{\frac{\kappa}{\kappa-1}} \|\mathbf{b}_{j+1}^*\|$$

$$\leq \beta^{\frac{\beta}{\beta-1}} \beta^{\frac{n(n-1)-2\beta j}{2n(\beta-1)}} \det(\mathbf{B})^{1/n}$$

$$\leq \beta^{\frac{n-1}{2(\beta-1)} + \frac{\beta}{\beta-1} - \frac{k\beta^2}{n(\beta-1)}} \det(\mathbf{B})^{1/n}$$

□

Again, using Theorem 1, we obtain a bound on the runtime of enumeration on slide reduced bases.

Corollary 2. *Given a β-slide reduced basis $\mathbf{B} \in \mathbb{Z}^{m \times n}$, enumeration can solve the SVP in $\Lambda(\mathbf{B})$ in $\beta^{\frac{n(n-1)}{2(\beta-1)} + \frac{(n-\beta)}{2}} 2^{O(n)}$.*

Proof. The corollary follows from a short sequence of equations:

$$\prod_{k=1}^{n/\beta} \zeta((k-1)\beta + 1)^{\beta} = \beta^{\frac{n(n-1)}{2(\beta-1)} + \frac{n\beta}{\beta-1} - \frac{\beta^3}{n(\beta-1)} \sum_{k=1}^{n/\beta} k}$$

$$= \beta^{\frac{n(n-1)}{2(\beta-1)} + \frac{n\beta}{\beta-1} - \frac{n\beta+\beta^2}{2(\beta-1)}}$$

$$= \beta^{\frac{n(n-1)}{2(\beta-1)} + \frac{\beta(n-\beta)}{2(\beta-1)}} \approx \beta^{\frac{n(n-1)}{2(\beta-1)} + \frac{(n-\beta)}{2}}$$

□

Not surprisingly, due to the better bounds achieved on $\|\mathbf{b}_1^*\|$, slide reduction yields a stronger ζ-reduction and thus improves the bound on the enumeration. However, plugging $\beta = n - 1$ into the bound[2] shows that the bound is still worse than the one for Kannan, but only by a factor $1/e$. We leave it as an interesting open question if one can achieve such a bound for block reduced bases.

Remark Recall that block reduction algorithms use a SVP oracle in dimension β. Obviously, we can use recursive calls to our enumeration algorithm (including block reduction) to implement this oracle. In the case of BKZ we can use the slightly worse bound obtained in [16] instead of Equation (1). This will give us worse constants in the exponents, but has the advantage that the number of (top level) recursive calls during the preprocessing is polynomially bounded, which bounds the overall number of recursive calls by $n^{O(n)}$. This proves that using the algorithm proposed in [16] combined with ζ-reduction, SVP can be solved by block reduction and enumeration in $n^{O(n)}$ steps by setting $\beta = O(n)$. Alternatively, we can use slide reduction instead of BKZ to achieve a similar result. To the best of our knowledge, such a bound was only known for Kannan's algorithm and the recent variant in [27], up to this point.

---

[2] Technically, this choice of parameter is not possible for slide reduction as it requires $\beta | n$. But plugging in this value should give a good estimation of how tight the bound is by comparison with Kannan's algorithm.

4 Performance in Practice

In this section we present experimental results that indicate that the bound obtained in Section 3 for BKZ is not only of theoretical nature, but that the average case hardness of enumeration on block reduced bases can be expected to follow similar bounds (with smaller constants) in practice.

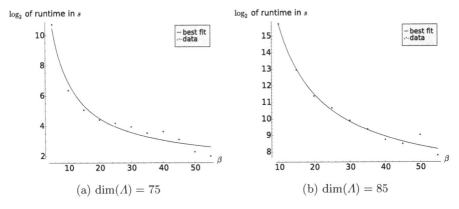

Fig. 1. Runtime of HKZ reduction after BKZ-β reduction

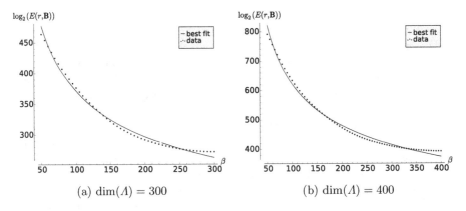

Fig. 2. Estimated runtime of enumeration (in nodes) after simulated BKZ-β reduction

All experiments and simulations were performed on random lattices in the sense of Goldstein and Mayer [15] with numbers of bit length $10n$, where n is the lattice dimension. In order to demonstrate that the enumeration follows qualitatively similar bounds in practice, we use the model $\beta^{a\frac{n(n-1)}{(\beta-1)}+bn}2^{cn}$, where n is the lattice dimension, β the block size of BKZ, and a, b, and c are parameters. We fit the model to our data using standard statistical methods and show that it is indeed a good fit.

4.1 Experiments

We used NTL's BKZ algorithm to reduce the input lattice of dimension n with varying parameter β, after which we called it again using $\beta = n$ to HKZ reduce the lattice (which is essentially equivalent to finding the shortest vector). We only measure the running time of the second call as the goal of this article is to explore the effect the reducedness has on the final enumeration. In order to obtain results in larger dimensions we set NTL's pruning parameter to 10. Still, the algorithm has its limits (both, the BKZ preprocessing and the final HKZ reduction) and we were only able to obtain meaningful results for $n \leq 85$ and $5 \leq \beta \leq 55$. We used the model for fixed n and fitted it to the data obtained by the experiments (where each data point is the average over 20 random lattices). Figure 1 shows exemplary results for $n = 75$ and $n = 85$, respectively. The results demonstrate that for fixed dimension n the running time of enumeration in practice closely follows the theoretical worst-case bound up to constants in

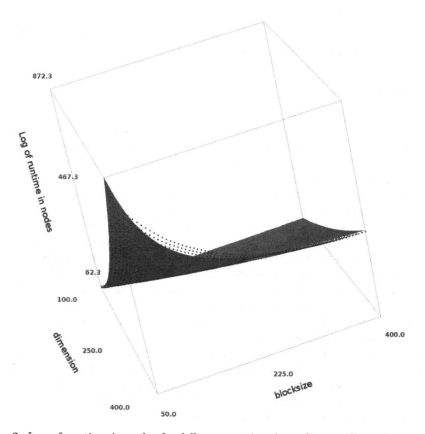

Fig. 3. Log of runtime in nodes for full enumeration depending on dimension n and blocksize β

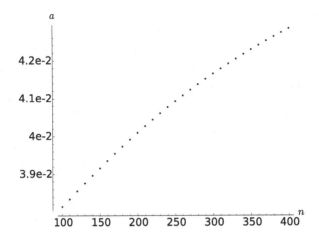

Fig. 4. Fitted value for parameter a for different $n = \dim(\Lambda)$ and fixed parameters b and c

the exponents. Curiously, the exponents for the closest curve vary for different dimensions - an issue, we will address later.

4.2   Simulation

As the experiments in the previous section are somewhat limited in scale due to resource constraints, we reverted to simulation to obtain data in larger dimensions. Specifically, we generated random lattices in dimension $n \in \{100, 110, \ldots, 400\}$ and LLL reduced them using NTL. Then we used the BKZ simulator[3] for each lattice to compute the expected shape of a BKZ-β reduced basis for $\beta \in \{50, 55, \ldots, n\}$. Finally, for each n we estimated the number of nodes that need to be enumerated using (5).

The result is shown in Figure 2. Again we see that the running time follows the theoretical bound and again we observed the phenomenon that the constants seem to depend on n. To explore this issue a little deeper, we fitted the model to the complete data set (i.e. now n and β are the variables). The result is shown in Figure 3 and indicates that for large dimensions the average case hardness can be expected to follow the model at least roughly. As we are mostly interested in the constant of the dominating term, we fixed b and c to the value obtained by this fitting and extracted the corresponding a parameter for each fixed n. Figure 4 plots the obtained a value depending on the dimension n. While the values do increase with the dimension, they do so less and less rapidly. From the theoretical analysis we know that they cannot increase indefinitely, so we conjecture that they converge at some point. We do not offer an explanation for this phenomenon and leave it for future work to explore this behavior in depth.

---

[3] Our implementation of the simulator is available at
http://cseweb.ucsd.edu/~miwalter/src/sim_bkz.sage

References

1. ACM. STOC (May 2008)
2. Ajtai, M.: Generating hard instances of lattice problems. Complexity of Computations and Proofs, Quaderni di Matematica, 13:1–13:32 (2004), Preliminary version in STOC 1996
3. Ajtai, M., Dwork, C.: A public-key cryptosystem with worst-case/average-case equivalence. In: Proceedings of STOC 1997, pp. 284–293. ACM (May 1997)
4. Ajtai, M., Kumar, R., Sivakumar, D.: A sieve algorithm for the shortest lattice vector problem. In: Proceedings of STOC, pp. 266–275. ACM (July 2001)
5. Albrecht, M., Cadé, D., Pujol, X., Stehlé, D.: fplll-4.0, A floating-point LLL implementation, `http://perso.ens-lyon.fr/damien.stehle`
6. Blömer, J., Naewe, S.: Sampling methods for shortest vectors, closest vectors and successive minima (Preliminary version in ICALP 2007). In: Arge, L., Cachin, C., Jurdziński, T., Tarlecki, A. (eds.) ICALP 2007. LNCS, vol. 4596, pp. 65–77. Springer, Heidelberg (2007), doi:10.1016/j.tcs.2008.12.045
7. Chen, Y., Nguyen, P.Q.: BKZ 2.0: Better lattice security estimates. In: Lee, D.H., Wang, X. (eds.) ASIACRYPT 2011. LNCS, vol. 7073, pp. 1–20. Springer, Heidelberg (2011)
8. Ding, D., Zhu, G., Wang, X.: A genetic algorithm for searching shortest lattice vector of svp challenge. Cryptology ePrint Archive, Report 2014/489 (2014), `http://eprint.iacr.org/`
9. Fincke, U., Pohst, M.: Improved methods for calculating vectors of short length in a lattice, including a complexity analysis. Mathematics of Computation 44, 463–471 (1985)
10. Gama, N., Nguyen, P.Q.: Finding short lattice vectors within Mordell's inequality. In: Proceedings of STOC 2008, pp. 207–216 (2008)
11. Gama, N., Nguyen, P.Q.: Predicting lattice reduction. In: Smart, N.P. (ed.) EUROCRYPT 2008. LNCS, vol. 4965, pp. 31–51. Springer, Heidelberg (2008)
12. Garg, S., Gentry, C., Halevi, S.: Candidate multilinear maps from ideal lattices. In: Johansson, T., Nguyen, P.Q. (eds.) EUROCRYPT 2013. LNCS, vol. 7881, pp. 1–17. Springer, Heidelberg (2013)
13. Gentry, C.: Fully homomorphic encryption using ideal lattices. In: Proceedings of STOC, pp. 169–178. ACM (2009)
14. Gentry, C., Peikert, C., Vaikuntanathan, V.: Trapdoors for hard lattices and new cryptographic constructions. In: Proceedings of STOC 2008, pp. 197–206 (2008)
15. Goldstein, D., Mayer, A.: On the equidistribution of Hecke points. Forum Mathematicum 15(2), 165–189 (2003)
16. Hanrot, G., Pujol, X., Stehlé, D.: Terminating BKZ. Cryptology ePrint Archive, Report 2011/198 (2011), `http://eprint.iacr.org/`
17. Hanrot, G., Stehlé, D.: Improved analysis of kannan's shortest lattice vector algorithm. In: Menezes, A. (ed.) CRYPTO 2007. LNCS, vol. 4622, pp. 170–186. Springer, Heidelberg (2007)
18. Kannan, R.: Improved algorithms for integer programming and related lattice problems. In: Proceedings of the Fifteenth Annual ACM Symposium on Theory of Computing - STOC 1983, pp. 193–206. ACM (April 1983), Journal version in Math. of Operation Research 12(3), 415–440 (1987)
19. Khot, S.: Hardness of approximating the shortest vector problem in lattices. Journal of the ACM 52(5), 789–808 (2004), Preliminary version in FOCS 2004

20. Lenstra, A.K., Lenstra Jr., H.W., Lovász, L.: Factoring polynomials with rational coefficients. Mathematische Annalen 261, 513–534 (1982)
21. Lindner, R., Peikert, C.: Better key sizes (and attacks) for LWE-based encryption. In: Kiayias, A. (ed.) CT-RSA 2011. LNCS, vol. 6558, pp. 319–339. Springer, Heidelberg (2011)
22. Lyubashevsky, V., Micciancio, D.: Asymptotically efficient lattice-based digital signatures. In: Canetti, R. (ed.) TCC 2008. LNCS, vol. 4948, pp. 37–54. Springer, Heidelberg (2008)
23. Lyubashevsky, V., Micciancio, D., Peikert, C., Rosen, A.: SWIFFT: A modest proposal for FFT hashing. In: Nyberg, K. (ed.) FSE 2008. LNCS, vol. 5086, pp. 54–72. Springer, Heidelberg (2008)
24. Micciancio, D.: Inapproximability of the shortest vector problem: Toward a deterministic reduction. Theory of Computing 8(1), 487–512 (2012)
25. Micciancio, D., Voulgaris, P.: A deterministic single exponential time algorithm for most lattice problems based on Voronoi cell computations. In: Proceedings of STOC, pp. 351–358 (2010)
26. Micciancio, D., Voulgaris, P.: Faster exponential time algorithms for the shortest vector problem. In: Proceedings of SODA, pp. 1468–1480. ACM/SIAM (January 2010)
27. Micciancio, D., Walter, M.: Fast lattice point enumeration with minimal overhead. In: Proceedings of SODA, pp. 276–294. ACM/SIAM (January 2015)
28. Regev, O.: On lattices, learning with errors, random linear codes, and cryptography. Journal of ACM 56(6), 34 (2009), Preliminary version in STOC 2005
29. Schnorr, C.-P.: A hierarchy of polynomial time lattice basis reduction algorithms. Theoretical Computer Science 53(2-3), 201–224 (1987)
30. Schnorr, C.-P.: Lattice reduction by random sampling and birthday methods. In: STACS, pp. 145–156 (2003)
31. Shoup, V.: Ntl: a library for doing number theory, http://www.shoup.net/ntl/index.html

Adaptive Key Recovery Attacks on NTRU-Based Somewhat Homomorphic Encryption Schemes

Ricardo Dahab[1,*], Steven Galbraith[2], and Eduardo Morais[1,**]

[1] Institute of Computing, University of Campinas, Brazil
[2] Mathematics Department, University of Auckland, New Zealand

Abstract. In this paper we present adaptive key recovery attacks on NTRU-based somewhat homomorphic encryption schemes. Among such schemes, we study the proposal by Bos et al [BLLN13] in 2013. Given access to a decryption oracle, the attack allows us to compute the private key for all parameter choices. Such attacks show that one must be very careful about the use of homomorphic encryption in practice. The existence of a key recovery attack means that the scheme is not CCA1-secure. Indeed, almost every somewhat homomorphic construction proposed till now in the literature is vulnerable to an attack of this type. Hence our result adds to a body of literature that shows that building CCA1-secure homomorphic schemes is not trivial.

1 Introduction

The construction of *fully homomorphic encryption* (FHE) was conjectured in 1978 by Rivest, Adleman and Dertouzos [RAD78]. Although it was immediately recognized as a very interesting possibility in cryptography, no concrete construction was known until 2009, when Gentry used ideal lattices to settle this conjecture [Gen09a].

In short, ciphertexts produced by an FHE scheme can be operated on in such a way that we obtain a ciphertext that corresponds to the addition or multiplication of the respective plaintexts. The ability to algebraically operate over ciphertexts is of great importance because we can transform any algorithm into a sequence of additions and multiplications in $\mathbb{Z}_2$. Therefore, such a scheme can evaluate any algorithm solely with access to the encryption of its input, and such that the computation returns the encryption of the output.

Since Gentry's work, many FHE constructions have appeared in the literature. However, all the proposals have a common drawback: they are not practical. Initially, the algorithms involved in the constructions, although having polynomial complexity, had high polynomial degree. Later, the asymptotic complexity became much better. Indeed, we now have constructions with polylog overhead per operation, but with terribly high constants.

* Partially supported by CNPq grant 311530/2011-7, and FAPESP Thematic Project 2013/25977-7.
** Partially supported by FAPESP Thematic Project 2013/25977-7.

© Springer International Publishing Switzerland 2015
A. Lehmann and S. Wolf (Eds.): ICITS 2015, LNCS 9063, pp. 283–296, 2015.
DOI: 10.1007/978-3-319-17470-9_17

Although fully homomorphic encryption is not practical yet, many constructions have been proposed recently, achieving a somewhat homomorphic encryption (SHE) scheme. They allow a limited "depth" of operations to be performed. These constructions are indeed very useful in practice, specially in order to provide security in the scenario of cloud computing. SHE is important also in the implementation of *private information retrieval* (PIR) protocols, which can be seen as a building block to the solution for the privacy problem that emerges when we give our data to the cloud.

In the cloud computing scenario it is natural to imagine an attacker having access to a decryption oracle (e.g., the cloud can feed invalid ciphertexts to a user and monitor their behaviour). It is obvious that a homomorphic encryption scheme cannot have security of ciphertexts under adaptive attacks. Hence, adaptive attacks are already a very serious concern in this setting. But one could hope that at least the private key remains secure in the presence of a decryption oracle. However, it is already known that this is not necessarily the case. Loftus et al [LMSV12] were the first to observe adaptive key recovery attacks, and further examples were given by Zhang et al [ZPS12] and Chenal and Tang [CT14]. By now, most schemes have been attacked, but the NTRU-based schemes remained unbroken.

Gentry's original construction is based on ideal lattices and is naturally implemented using cyclotomic rings. On the other hand, NTRU is a practical lattice-based cryptosystem, also based on cyclotomic rings, that remained without a security proof for a long time. Recently NTRU was put on a stronger foundation by Stehlé and Steinfeld [SS11], and NTRU-based cryptosystems returned as a fruitful research area. Scale-invariant homomorphic encryption was proposed by Brakerski [Bra12], presenting a construction that avoids the utilization of modulus switching technique, considerably simplifying the scheme.

In this work, we present *adaptive key recovery* attacks on NTRU-based SHE schemes. In particular, we attack the *scale-invariant* proposal by Bos et al [BLLN13].

1.1   Notation

Notation $\lfloor a \rceil$ is used to round a to the nearest integer, while notation $[a]_q$ is used to denote centralized modular reduction, i.e. reduction modulo q, but with result given in the interval $(-q/2, q/2]$. If a is a polynomial, then in order to compute $[a]_q$ we must compute a centralized modular reduction of each coefficient of a (analogously for $\lfloor a \rceil$). When working over a polynomial ring R, if $a(x) \in R$, we use the notation $a[i]$ to denote the i-th coefficient of the polynomial $a(x)$.

1.2   Paper Organization

This paper is organized as follows. In section 2 we present basic definitions and details about the security model that will be used. In section 3 we gather information about key recovery attacks on other schemes in the literature. In section 4 we describe exactly how the SHE scheme BLLN is constructed.

In section 5 we provide the main contribution of this paper, which is the key recovery attack. Finally, in section 6 we give our concluding remarks.

2 Fundamentals and Security Model

In this section we are going to present basic concepts and the security model that we will use throughout the paper.

Definition 1. Homomorphic Encryption. *A homomorphic cryptosystem is defined using four algorithms,* KEYGEN, DEC, ENC, EVAL. *The first three are conventional encryption algorithms, with plaintext space* $\mathcal{P}$ *and security parameter* λ. *The scheme is said to be* correct *if, for a given algebraic circuit* C, *every key pair* (sk, pk) *generated by* KEYGEN(λ), *any message tuple* $(m_1, \ldots, m_t) \in \mathcal{P}^t$ *and corresponding ciphertexts* $\Psi = \langle \psi_1, \ldots, \psi_t \rangle$, *that is,* $\psi_i = \text{ENC}_{\text{pk}}(m_i)$ *for* $1 \leq i \leq t$, *then we have that the* EVAL *algorithm respects the following relation*

$$\text{DEC}_{\text{sk}}(\text{EVAL}_{\text{pk}}(C, \Psi)) = C(m_1, \ldots, m_t).$$

Furthermore, the algorithms KEYGEN, DEC, ENC *and* EVAL *must have polynomial complexity and we say that the scheme is homomorphic with respect to the circuit* C.

Definition 2. Fully Homomorphic Encryption. *A scheme* $\mathcal{E} = ($KEYGEN, DEC, ENC, EVAL$)$ *is correct for a class* $\mathbf{S_C}$ *of circuits, if it is correct for each* $\mathbf{C} \in \mathbf{S_C}$. *Moreover,* $\mathcal{E}$ *is called* fully homomorphic encryption *(FHE) scheme, if it is correct for every algebraic circuit. Alternatively, we can base our construction over Boolean circuits, because both computational models are equivalent. If the scheme can deal with a restricted class of circuits, but not every one, then we call the scheme a* somewhat homomorphic encryption *(SHE) scheme.*

A cryptosystem is secure against *chosen ciphertext attack* (CCA2) if there is no polynomial time adversary $\mathcal{A}$ that can win the following game with non negligible probability.

Setup. The challenger obtains (sk, pk) = KEYGEN(λ) and sends pk to adversary $\mathcal{A}$.

Queries. $\mathcal{A}$ sends ciphertexts to the challenger, before or after the challenge. The challenger returns the corresponding plaintexts.

Challenge. The adversary randomly generates two plaintexts $m_0, m_1 \in \mathcal{P}$ and sends them to the challenger, who chooses randomly a bit $b \in \{0, 1\}$ and computes the ciphertext $c = \text{ENC}_{\text{pk}}(m_b)$. The challenger sends c to $\mathcal{A}$.

Answer. $\mathcal{A}$ sends a bit b' to the challenger and wins the game if $b' = b$.

If we allow queries only before the challenge, we say that the cryptosystem is secure against CCA1 adversaries (lunchtime attacks). As previously described, queries can be interpreted as access to a decryption oracle. If instead we only allow access to an encryption oracle, i.e., the adversary can choose any message that is distinct from m_0 and m_1 to be encrypted under the same key pair, then we say that the cryptosystem is secure against *chosen plaintext attacks* (CPA).

In homomorphic encryption, it is impossible to achieve CCA2 security, because the adversary can add an encryption of zero to the encrypted challenge, or multiply it by the encryption of one, and send it to the decryption oracle, which allows him to trivially win the game. Many FHE schemes have as public value an encryption of the private key bits, which can be sent to the decryption oracle before the challenge, which makes such schemes insecure against CCA1 adversaries. Indeed, a *key recovery* attack is stronger than a CCA1 attack and Loftus et al [LMSV12] showed that Gentry's construction over ideal lattices is vulnerable to it and presented the only SHE proposal that is known to be CCA1 secure.

Recently [CT14], Chenal and Tang showed that many SHE schemes are not CCA1 by presenting a key recovery attack. The aim of this paper is to consider such attacks in the setting of NTRU-based schemes.

From now on we are going to work over the cyclotomic ring $R_q = \mathbb{Z}_q[x]/(x^d + 1)$, where d is a power of 2. Cyclotomic rings were introduced to lattice-based cryptography in [HPS98], and have been very popular since the breakthrough work of Lyubashevsky et al [LPR13]. Lattices constructed using such rings are often called *ideal lattices*. Although there is no proof that ideal lattices maintain the same security guarantees as conventional lattices, no significant improvement in the complexity of algorithms for computational problems in ideal lattices is known.

3   Previous Constructions

We can divide homomorphic encryption schemes as in Figure 1. In the first column, we have the schemes that are based on integers, which are simpler to understand. Lattice-based constructions are separated in four categories: the initial schemes, that still depend on the Sparse Subset Sum Problem (SSSP); Brakerski-Gentry-Vaikuntanathan (BGV)-like proposals, that bring new concepts and allow better constructions in practice; asymptotically better constructions that are based on the *approximate eigenvector* method, and NTRU-based schemes, that permit to obtain ciphertexts that correspond to just one ring element, simplifying previous schemes. NTRU-based SHE offers the possibility of encoding integers in a natural way, that can be used to solve practical problems such as statistical applications [LLAN14, BLN14].

In the literature [ZPS12, LMSV12, CT14] there are adaptive key recovery attacks on many schemes and these schemes were adapted and optimized later; thus, such constructions should be assessed in order to verify whether the attacks are still feasible. Table 1 shows which schemes have been attacked by each of the previously cited works, showing also which schemes seem to be vulnerable to the same kind of attacks. Although some of them were not directly attacked, the key generation and decryption algorithms are so close to the attacked schemes, that the same strategy can be followed to compute the private key using decryption oracles.

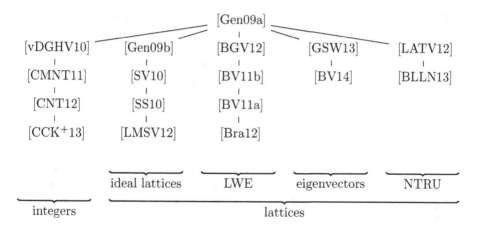

Fig. 1. Homomorphic Encryption Proposals

Table 1. Key recovery attacks

Attack	Schemes	Seems to extend to
[ZPS12]	[vDGHV10, CMNT11]	[CNT12]
[LMSV12]	[Gen09b, SV10, GS11]	[SS10]
[CT14]	[vDGHV10, BGV12, BV11b, BV11a, Bra12, GSW13]	[BV14]
this work	[LATV12, BLLN13]	-
no attack	[LMSV12]	-

4 NTRU-Based Somewhat Homomorphic Encryption

NTRU [HPS98] is an efficient lattice-based cryptographic scheme but, for many years, the lack of security proofs, reducing its security to worst-case hard lattice problems, was a serious concern. Stehlé and Steinfeld [SS11] presented such a proof, replacing the original ring $\mathbb{Z}_q[x]/(x^d - 1)$ by the previously described cyclotomic ring $R_q = \mathbb{Z}_q[x]/(x^d + 1)$, where d is restricted to a power of 2.

In 2012, López-Alt, Tromer and Vaikuntanathan [LATV12] proposed the construction of *multikey fully homomorphic encryption*, which we call the LTV scheme. The difference here is that users with distinct keys can compute ciphertexts that will be processed by a server in order to obtain the homomorphic evaluation of a determined function. It means that all the users together will be able to decrypt the function evaluation and this strategy can be followed to construct a multiparty computation scheme. Doröz, Hu and Sunar [DHS14] implemented the LTV scheme. They implemented also the homomorphic evaluation of AES, showing that it offers advantages against the BGV scheme [BGV12].

However, the LTV scheme is based on non-standard assumptions. In 2013, a scale-invariant NTRU-based scheme was proposed by Bos et al [BLLN13]. We call it the BLLN scheme. The basic scheme, $\mathcal{E}_{\text{basic}}$, can be described as follows:

Definition 3. Setup. *Given the security parameter λ construct the ring $R = \mathbb{Z}[x]/$
$(x^d + 1)$, where d is a power of two. Define $R_q = R/(q) \cong \mathbb{Z}_q[x]/(x^d + 1)$. Choose
a small integer t, real numbers σ_k and σ_e and a prime q such that $t, \sigma \ll q$.
Let $\mathcal{D}_{key}$ and $\mathcal{D}_{err}$ be distributions on R coming from discrete Gaussians on $\mathbb{Z}$
with standard deviations σ_k and σ_e respectively. The* SETUP *algorithm returns
$(t, d, q, \mathcal{D}_{key}, \mathcal{D}_{err})$.*

Key generation. *Given the output of the* SETUP *algorithm, sample polynomials
f',
$g \leftarrow \mathcal{D}_{key}$ and compute $f = [tf' + 1]_q$. Check that f is invertible modulo q,
if not choose a new f'. Compute the inverse $f^{-1} \in R_q$ and set $h = [tgf^{-1}]_q$.
The public key is $pk = h$ and the private key is $sk = f$. Algorithm* KEYGEN
returns (sk, pk).

Encryption. *The plaintext space is R/tR, so a message is given by a coset
$m + tR$. Let $[m]_t$ be a canonical representative element of the coset. Sample
$s, e \leftarrow \mathcal{D}_{err}$ and compute the ciphertext*

$$c = \text{ENC}_{pk}(m) = [\lfloor q/t \rfloor [m]_t + te + hs]_q .$$

Decryption. *Compute*

$$m = \text{DEC}_{sk}(c) = \left[\lfloor (t/q) \cdot [fc]_q \rceil \right]_t .$$

Return the message $[m]_t$.

Given the integers t and q returned by the SETUP algorithm, the plaintext
space is given by R/tR, while the ciphertext space is given by R/qR. Note that
$t \ll q$. Indeed, the last condition is important to enable as many multiplications
as possible. Thus, if t grows when compared to a fixed q, then we would be
able to execute fewer multiplications. Although the multiplicative depth of a
homomorphic encryption scheme is an important issue, it is not relevant for the
attacks we are going to present. Hence, we omit further details and we assume
that the inequalities relating t and q in Lemma 1 are respected.

The security of this scheme is based on an analysis from Gentry et al [GHS12],
which in turn used parameters presented in the work of Lindner and Peikert [LP11], showing that the scheme is secure as long as the LWE problem
parameters d, q, σ obey the inequality

$$d > \log\left(\frac{q}{\sigma}\right) \frac{\lambda + 110}{7.2}.$$

When applied with homomorphic schemes, this relation acquires a challenging
aspect. As the standard deviation increases, fewer homomorphic operations can
be evaluated, since a larger initial noise would be rapidly propagated. Thus, the
ratio q/σ determines the LWE-based cryptography security.

The distribution $\mathcal{D}_{key}$ must be chosen according to the description of Stehlé
and Steinfeld [SS11], such that the public key is close enough to the uniform

distribution, so that it reveals almost nothing about the private key. Rigorously, it reveals only a negligible fraction of the secret. Thus, $\mathcal{D}_{\text{key}}$ is a discrete Gaussian on R_q with standard deviation at least $(d\sqrt{\log 8dq})q^k$, for k in the interval $(1/2, 1)$. Furthermore, $\mathcal{D}_{\text{err}}$ is a $\omega(\sqrt{d \log (d)})$-bounded Gaussian distribution. In our attacks we may assume that q is very large in comparison with t and σ_k.

5   Adaptive Key Recovery Attacks

In a key recovery attack, we submit appropriately chosen ciphertexts to a decryption oracle in order to compute the private key. Once the private key is computed, then any ciphertext can later be decrypted. Consequently, a key recovery attack is stronger than a CCA1 attack.

5.1   Attacking the BLLN Scheme for $t > 2$ and Ternary f'

In the original paper [BLLN13], Bos et al stated that we can choose f' and g with coefficients in $\{-1, 0, 1\}$. We call this "ternary f'". We now show that in this case, and when $t > 2$, we can easily compute f' using just one query to the decryption oracle. Recall that $f'[i]$ is the i-th coefficient of the polynomial f'.

Lemma 1. *Let $f = tf' + 1$ where f' has coefficients in $\{-1, 0, 1\}$. Suppose $t \geq 3$ and $6(t^2 + t) < q$. Then,*

$$[\lfloor (t/q)[f[i]\lfloor q/t^2 \rfloor]_q \rceil]_t = f'[i].$$

Proof. Let $\lfloor q/t^2 \rfloor = q/t^2 - \epsilon$ for some $0 \leq \epsilon < 1$. Then,

$$f[i]\lfloor q/t^2 \rfloor = (tf'[i] + 1)(q/t^2 - \epsilon) = f'[i](q/t) + (q/t^2) - \epsilon(tf'[i] + 1)$$

and $[f[i]\lfloor q/t^2 \rfloor]_q = f[i]\lfloor q/t^2 \rfloor - vq$ for some $v \in \mathbb{Z}[x]$. Finally,

$$[\lfloor (t/q)[f[i]\lfloor q/t^2 \rfloor]_q \rceil]_t = [f'[i] + \lfloor 1/t - \epsilon(t^2 f'[i] + t)/q \rceil - vt]_t = [f'[i]]_t$$

since the entries of the polynomial $1/t - \epsilon(t^2 f' + t)/q$ all have absolute value $< 1/3 + 1/6 = 1/2$ (the bound $|t^2 f'[i] + t|/q \leq |t^2 + t|/q < 1/6$ is used here).   □

We introduce the informal notation $a \ll b$ to mean that b is much bigger than a (say, $b > 10^6 a$ for parameters in actual cryptosystems). Hence we can observe that $t^2 \ll q$ and so $\lfloor q/t^2 \rfloor$ is a very large integer.

Theorem 1. *Let $t > 2$ and $6(t^2 + t) < q$. Let $m_f = \text{DEC}(\lfloor q/t^2 \rfloor)$ be a polynomial in R with coefficients in $[-t/2, t/2]$, where $\lfloor q/t^2 \rfloor$ is a constant integer polynomial that can easily be computed using the public parameters q and t. Then we have that $f = tm_f + 1$.*

Proof. We have that $\text{DEC}(\lfloor q/t^2 \rfloor) = [\lfloor (t/q)[f(\lfloor q/t^2 \rfloor)]_q \rceil]_t$. Because we are multiplying f by a constant polynomial, each coefficient of f is multiplied by $\lfloor q/t^2 \rfloor$. By Lemma 1 we obtain an element in R with coefficients in $\{-1, 0, 1\}$ that equals $f' \in R$.   □

Note that the restriction $t > 2$ is a requirement for Lemma 1, but there is also a second reason why it is important. Because $-1 \equiv 1 \pmod 2$, we can't distinguish between -1 and 1 from information modulo 2. Therefore, when $t = 2$ it will be necessary to provide an algorithm to find out the sign of each coefficient.

Algorithm 5.1 uses the ideas described above. We emphasize that the attack is very fast, since it needs to perform just one query to the decryption oracle. Also, the ciphertext that we submit to the decryption oracle is trivial to construct, and the final computation is also very easy.

Algorithm 5.1. BLLN Attack for Ternary Polynomials when $t > 2$ and Ternary f'

Require: The public parameters (q, d, t).
Ensure: The private key f.
  $m_f = \text{Dec}(\lfloor q/t^2 \rfloor)$.
  return $f = t m_f + 1$.

5.2   Attacking the BLLN Scheme for General f' and $t > 2$

We now consider the case where f' is chosen from $\mathcal{D}_{\text{key}}$ and so has a wider range of possible values. The idea is to make queries on ciphertexts $c_k = \lfloor q/(kt^2) \rfloor$ for various values $k > 1$ to learn information about $[\frac{1}{k} f'] \pmod t$.

Lemma 2. *Let $f = tf' + 1$ where f' is a polynomial whose entries are integers bounded in absolute value by B such that $B^2 < q/(36t^2)$. Let $0 \le i < d$. Let $k_{\max,i} \le 2B$ be the maximal integer such that the i-th coefficient of the decryption of ciphertext $\lfloor q/(k_{\max,i} t^2) \rfloor$ is non-zero. Then, we have that, for all $0 \le i < d$,*

$$|f'[i]| = \lfloor (k_{\max,i} + 1)/2 \rfloor.$$

Proof. The proof is similar to the proof of Lemma 1. Write $c_k = \lfloor q/(kt^2) \rfloor = q/(kt^2) - \epsilon$ for $0 \le \epsilon < 1$, and note that

$$[fc_k]_q = \frac{q}{kt^2}(tf' + 1) - \epsilon(tf' + 1) - vq$$

for some $v \in \mathbb{Z}[x]$. Then,

$$u = \frac{t}{q}[fc_k]_q = \frac{1}{k}f' + \frac{1}{kt} - \epsilon t(tf' + 1)/q - vt$$

is a polynomial with rational coefficients.

We now consider rounding the coefficients of the polynomial $u(x)$ to the nearest integer. For $i > 0$ we have $u[i] = \frac{1}{k}f'[i] - v[i]t$ and so

$$\lfloor u[i] \rceil = \lfloor \tfrac{1}{k}f'[i] \rceil - v[i]t.$$

It follows that the result of the decryption query is $[\lfloor u[i] \rceil]_t = [\lfloor \frac{1}{k} f'[i] \rceil]_t$. Note that if $k > 2B \geq 2|f'[i]|$, then $|\frac{1}{k} f'[i]| < 1/2$ and so the rounded value is zero. If k is maximal, then $\lfloor \frac{1}{k} f'[i] \rceil \neq 0$ but $\lfloor \frac{1}{k+1} f'[i] \rceil = 0$, and so

$$|\tfrac{1}{k} f'[i]| \geq \tfrac{1}{2} \quad \text{and} \quad |\tfrac{1}{k+1} f'[i]| \leq \tfrac{1}{2}.$$

It follows that

$$\tfrac{k}{2} \leq |f'[i]| \leq \tfrac{k+1}{2}.$$

It remains to deal with the coefficient $f'[0]$, which has an additional error term $\frac{1}{kt} - \epsilon^\star$ where $\epsilon^\star = \epsilon t (tf'+1)/q$ is added to it. Note that, since $q \gg t(tB+1)$ and $t > 2$, we have $|\epsilon^\star| \ll 1$. However, we cannot ignore the error as we are adding it to the rational number $\frac{1}{k} f'[0]$. By the same argument as above, we compute

$$|\tfrac{1}{k} f'[0] + \tfrac{1}{kt} - \epsilon^\star| \geq \tfrac{1}{2} \quad \text{and} \quad |\tfrac{1}{k+1} f'[0] + \tfrac{1}{(k+1)t} - \epsilon^\star| \leq \tfrac{1}{2}.$$

It follows that

$$\tfrac{k}{2} \leq |f'[0] + \tfrac{1}{t} - k\epsilon^\star| \quad \text{and} \quad |f'[0] + \tfrac{1}{t} - (k+1)\epsilon^\star| \leq \tfrac{k+1}{2}.$$

Since $(k+1)\epsilon^\star < 3Bt^2 2B/q \leq 1/6$ and $1/t \leq 1/3$ we see there is no rounding error. This completes the proof.   □

Note that if $t = 2$ and $k = 1$, then we must be careful about what happens with the independent coefficient, as will be the case in the next section. However, when $t > 2$ we have that if $\lfloor \frac{1}{k} f'[i] \rceil \equiv 1 \pmod{t}$, then $f'[i]$ is positive, while if $\lfloor \frac{1}{k} f'[i] \rceil \equiv -1 \pmod{t}$, then $f'[i]$ is negative, which allows us to completely determine the private key since we know the absolute value and the sign of each coefficient.

The attack is then straightforward. Using binary search and queries to the decryption oracle one can determine $k_{\max,i}$ for $0 \leq i < d$ and hence learn all coefficients. To see that binary search is applicable, note that $|f'[i]| \leq B$ and so $|\frac{1}{2B} f'[i]| \leq 1/2$ and so decryption will generally return 0 for that coefficient. One can then query using $k = B$, and noting that $|\frac{1}{B} f'[i]| \leq 1$ and so the output of decryption is either 0 or ± 1. If the output is ± 1 then $\frac{B}{2} \leq |f'[i]| \leq B$ and one can try $k = (B + 2B)/2 = 3B/2$, while if the output is 0 then $|\frac{1}{B} f'[i]| \leq 1/2$ and one can try $k = B/2$, giving $|\frac{1}{k} f'[i]| \leq 1$, and so on. We give the details as Algorithm 5.2.

The total number of decryption oracle queries, if the algorithm is implemented naively, is $d\lceil \log_2(B) \rceil$. However, this can be improved somewhat by recycling previous oracle values and sub-dividing intervals into t sub-intervals (resulting in $\log_t(B)$ steps in the search) instead of binary splitting and $\log_2(B)$ steps.

5.3 Attacking the BLLN Scheme for $t = 2$

If $t = 2$ we can proceed as in Section 5.2, but our main problem is to find out the sign of each coefficient. Of course, if f is a valid private key then so is $-f$, so we only need to compute f up to a global choice of sign.

Algorithm 5.2. BLLN Attack for General Polynomials when $t > 2$

Require: The public parameters (q, d, t).
Ensure: The private key f.
  Let B be the largest possible coefficient of f.
  for $i = 1$ till d **do**
    Use binary search to find $1 \leq k_{\max,i} \leq 2B$ satisfying the condition of
    Lemma 2.
    $f'[i] = [\text{DEC}(q/(k_{\max,i}t^2))[i] \cdot \lfloor (k_{\max,i} + 1)/2 \rfloor]_q$.
  return $f = tf' + 1$.

  Going back to the case of ternary polynomials, we can detect with a single decryption query when the coefficients of f' are zero. But we cannot distinguish when they are 1 or -1, because we are operating modulo 2.

  The idea is to make decryption queries to ciphertexts of the form $c = \lfloor q/(t^2 k) \rfloor (1 + x^j)$ for suitably chosen k and j. We then get information about $\frac{1}{k} f'(1 + x^j)$. The point is that the i-th coefficient of $f'(1 + x^j)$ is the sum of $f'[i]$ and $f'[i - j]$ (mod d). If the coefficients $f'[i]$ and $f'[i - j]$ are both non-zero then they either cancel to zero or add to ± 2. Hence, taking $k = 2$ we can determine the signs of coefficients relative to each other. By fixing one non-zero coefficient as a "base", we can deduce the sign of all other non-zero coefficients relative to this (as before, we leave the constant coefficient to the end of the algorithm).

  When f' is ternary then the details are simple. When f' has general coefficients then the trick is to balance the sizes of coefficients so that cancellation to zero still takes place. So suppose we have run Algorithm 5.2 and determined each coefficient (except perhaps the constant coefficient) $f'[i]$ up to sign. Suppose without loss of generality that $f'[1]$ is non-zero. We will use this as our "base". For each i such that $f'[i]$ is non-zero, we consider the ciphertext

$$c = \lfloor q/(2t^2 |f'[1]| \cdot |f'[i]|) \rfloor (|f'[1]| + x^{i-1} |f'[i]|).$$

The i-th coefficient of the decryption of this ciphertext will be

$$\frac{1}{|f'[1]| \cdot |f'[i]|} \left(|f'[1]| \cdot f'[i] + |f'[i]| \cdot f'[1] \right).$$

Hence, if the signs are opposite, then we get a 0 and if the signs are equal, the coefficient is ± 1, which modulo $t = 2$ becomes 1. It follows that multiplying the absolute value by the term $(2\text{DEC}(c) - 1)$ gives us the desired result.

  Therefore, after calling algorithm 5.2, we must use algorithm 5.3 to determine the sign of each coefficient of the private key. But we still have to solve the problem of the independent coefficient, mentioned in last section. As we have seen, the term $1/t - \epsilon^\star$ can change the result of rounding to the nearest integer. For instance, considering the case of ternary f' and $t = 2$, then we have that $k = 1$ and in the case that $f'[0] = -1$, we have that

$$[\lfloor -1 + 1/2 + \epsilon^\star \rceil]_t = 0$$

Algorithm 5.3. BLLN Attack for $t = 2$

Require: The absolute value $|f'|$, and the public parameters (q, d).
Ensure: The private key f.
  Run the main part of Algorithm 5.2 to determine $|f'[i]|$ for all $0 \leq i < d$.
  Let i_0 be the smallest integer $i > 0$ such that $f'[i] \neq 0$.
  $f'[i_0] = |f'[i_0]|$.
  for $i = i_0 + 1$ till d **do**
    if $|f'[i]| > 0$ **then**
      Let $c_{i,i_0} = \lfloor q/(2t^2|f'[i_0]| \cdot |f'[i]|) \rfloor (|f'[i_0]| + x^{i-i_0}|f'[i]|)$.
      $f'[i] = (2.\text{DEC}(c_{i,i_0})[i] - 1).|f'[i]|$.
  Find three candidate values for $f'[0]$ and test the three possible values for f
  using h
  return $f = tf' + 1$.

---

and the decryption oracle returns 0 instead of 1 as expected. Then we have to distinguish between two cases: $f'[0] = -1$ and $f'[0] = 0$. But since we have arbitrarily chosen the sign of $f[i_0]$ as positive, then we must check also the case $f[0] = 1$. Hence we have three candidates for f'. We can check which of them satisfies the requirement that $(tf' + 1)h$ in R_q is a polynomial with small coefficients. This completes the attack.

There are at most $d - 1$ additional decryption oracle queries to determine the sign.

5.4   Attacking the LTV Scheme

In this section we assume that q is odd. The LTV scheme is extremely similar to the BLLN scheme. The two schemes are based on the same algebraic structure, and the key generation algorithms are essentially the same, with the only difference that LTV is restricted to the case $t = 2$. The LTV scheme is not scale-invariant, leading to simpler algorithms. Our focus is the decryption algorithm, so we explain this now.

Decryption. Compute $m = [fc]_q$. Output $m \pmod 2$.

The paper [LATV12] is vague about the exact computation of the decryption algorithm. The value m is a polynomial in R_q with small coefficients, so it is natural to interpret it as an element of $R = \mathbb{Z}[x]/(x^d + 1)$. The ambiguity comes in the next step. Does $m \pmod 2$ mean only the constant term of the polynomial modulo 2, or the whole polynomial reduced modulo 2? In our attack we assume the latter case. The former case can be reduced to the latter case by replacing a decryption query on c by d decryption queries on cx^i for $0 \leq i < d$.

The attack is therefore seen to be more-or-less identical to the attack in the previous section. Let $k \geq 1$ be an integer and consider the ciphertext $c_k = 2\lfloor q/(4k) \rfloor$. Lemma 3 shows why we can compute f' using the same strategy as before.

Lemma 3. *Let* $c_k = 2\lfloor q/(4k) \rfloor$. *Let* $k^\star_{\mathrm{max},i}$ *be the maximal integer such that* $\mathrm{DEC}(c_{k^\star_{\mathrm{max},i}})[i]$ *is non-zero. Then we have that* $f[i]$ *is given by* $k^\star_{\mathrm{max},i} + 1$.

Proof. First note that c_k is an even integer and so $(2f' + 1)c_k$ is an integer polynomial with even coefficients.

For $k \geq 1$ we have that $c_k = q/(2k) - \epsilon$ for some $0 \leq \epsilon < 2$, and decryption of c_k first computes

$$(2f' + 1)c_k = f'(q/k - 2\epsilon) + 2\lfloor q/(4k) \rfloor.$$

Note that $q/k - 2\epsilon$ is an even integer. Thus, if k is big when compared to $f'[i]$, reduction by q does not change the value, then after reducing by 2 we get zero. If $f'[i] \geq k$ then $f'[i](q/k) \geq q$ and so, as long as the error term is small enough, $f'[i](q/k - 2\epsilon) - q$ is odd. It follows that $[fc_k]_q \pmod 2$ is odd and so the condition $f'[i] > k$ can be tested using a decryption oracle query. Hence, we proceed using the same method as before. One chooses maximal $k^\star_{\mathrm{max},i}$ such that $f'[i] > k^\star_{\mathrm{max},i}$ and hence determines the value of $|f'[i]|$. For instance, we have that $|f'[i]| = k^\star_{\mathrm{max},i} + 1$. The signs and the independent coefficient are handled in the same way as above.   □

Algorithm 5.4. LTV Attack

Require: The public parameters (q, d, t).
Ensure: The absolute value of the private key f.
  Let B be the largest possible coefficient of f.
  for $i = 1$ till d **do**
    Use binary search to find $1 \leq k^\star_{\mathrm{max},i} \leq 2B$ satisfying the condition of Lemma 3.
    $|f[i]| = [(k^\star_{\mathrm{max},i} + 1)]_q$.
  return f.

---

6   Concluding Remarks

We have described adaptive key recovery attacks on NTRU-based SHE schemes. Other families of SHE schemes, as represented in Figure 1, are also vulnerable to this kind of attack, showing that CCA1 security is hard to achieve in homomorphic encryption. Adaptive key recovery attacks on homomorphic encryption seem to be realistic in certain scenarios, so they are potentially a serious problem in practice. The only homomorphic encryption scheme known to resist such attacks is the scheme by Loftus et al [LMSV12].

Acknowledgements. We thank Qiang Tang and the anonymous referees for helpful comments.

References

BGV12.   Brakerski, Z., Gentry, C., Vaikuntanathan, V. (Leveled) Fully homomorphic encryption without bootstrapping. In: Proceedings of the 3rd Innovations in Theoretical Computer Science Conference, ITCS 2012, pp. 309–325. ACM, New York (2012)

BLLN13.   Bos, J.W., Lauter, K., Loftus, J., Naehrig, M.: Improved security for a ring-based fully homomorphic encryption scheme. In: Stam, M. (ed.) IMACC 2013. LNCS, vol. 8308, pp. 45–64. Springer, Heidelberg (2013)

BLN14.   Bos, J.W., Lauter, K., Naehrig, M.: Private predictive analysis on encrypted medical data. Journal of Biomedical Informatics 50, 234–243 (2014)

Bra12.   Brakerski, Z.: Fully homomorphic encryption without modulus switching from classical GapSVP. In: Safavi-Naini, R., Canetti, R. (eds.) CRYPTO 2012. LNCS, vol. 7417, pp. 868–886. Springer, Heidelberg (2012)

BV11a.   Brakerski, Z., Vaikuntanathan, V.: Efficient fully homomorphic encryption from (standard) LWE. In: Proceedings of the 2011 IEEE 52nd Annual Symposium on Foundations of Computer Science, FOCS 2011, pp. 97–106. IEEE Computer Society Press, Washington, DC (2011)

BV11b.   Brakerski, Z., Vaikuntanathan, V.: Fully homomorphic encryption from ring-LWE and security for key dependent messages. In: Rogaway, P. (ed.) CRYPTO 2011. LNCS, vol. 6841, pp. 487–504. Springer, Heidelberg (2011)

BV14.   Brakerski, Z., Vaikuntanathan, V.: Lattice-based FHE as secure as PKE. In: Proceedings of the 5th Conference on Innovations in Theoretical Computer Science, ITCS 2014, pp. 1–12. ACM, New York (2014)

CCK+13.   Cheon, J.H., Coron, J.-S., Kim, J., Lee, M.S., Lepoint, T., Tibouchi, M., Yun, A.: Batch fully homomorphic encryption over the integers. In: Johansson, T., Nguyen, P.Q. (eds.) EUROCRYPT 2013. LNCS, vol. 7881, pp. 315–335. Springer, Heidelberg (2013)

CMNT11.   Coron, J.-S., Mandal, A., Naccache, D., Tibouchi, M.: Fully homomorphic encryption over the integers with shorter public keys. In: Rogaway, P. (ed.) CRYPTO 2011. LNCS, vol. 6841, pp. 487–504. Springer, Heidelberg (2011)

CNT12.   Coron, J.-S., Naccache, D., Tibouchi, M.: Public key compression and modulus switching for fully homomorphic encryption over the integers. In: Pointcheval, D., Johansson, T. (eds.) EUROCRYPT 2012. LNCS, vol. 7237, pp. 446–464. Springer, Heidelberg (2012)

CT14.   Chenal, M., Tang, Q.: On key recovery attacks against existing somewhat homomorphic encryption schemes. In: Latincrypt, Florianópolis-SC, Brazil (2014) (to appear)

DHS14.   Doröz, Y., Hu, Y., Sunar, B.: Homomorphic AES evaluation using NTRU. Cryptology ePrint Archive, Report 2014/039 (2014), http://eprint.iacr.org/

Gen09a.   Gentry, C.: A fully homomorphic encryption scheme. PhD thesis, Stanford University (2009), http://crypto.stanford.edu/craig

Gen09b.   Gentry, C.: Fully homomorphic encryption using ideal lattices. In: STOC 2009: Proceedings of the 41st Annual ACM Symposium on Theory of Computing, pp. 169–178. ACM, New York (2009)

GHS12.   Gentry, C., Halevi, S., Smart, N.P.: Homomorphic evaluation of the AES circuit. In: Safavi-Naini, R., Canetti, R. (eds.) CRYPTO 2012. LNCS, vol. 7417, pp. 850–867. Springer, Heidelberg (2012)

GS11.   Gentry, C., Halevi, S.: Implementing gentry's fully-homomorphic en-
             cryption scheme. In: Paterson, K.G. (ed.) EUROCRYPT 2011. LNCS,
             vol. 6632, pp. 129–148. Springer, Heidelberg (2011)
GSW13.   Gentry, C., Sahai, A., Waters, B.: Homomorphic encryption from learning
             with errors: Conceptually-simpler, asymptotically-faster, attribute-based.
             In: Canetti, R., Garay, J.A. (eds.) CRYPTO 2013, Part I. LNCS, vol. 8042,
             pp. 75–92. Springer, Heidelberg (2013)
HPS98.   Hoffstein, J., Pipher, J., Silverman, J.H.: NTRU: A ring-based public
             key cryptosystem. In: Buhler, J.P. (ed.) ANTS 1998. LNCS, vol. 1423,
             pp. 267–288. Springer, Heidelberg (1998)
LATV12.   López-Alt, A., Tromer, E., Vaikuntanathan, V.: On-the-fly multiparty
             computation on the cloud via multikey fully homomorphic encryption.
             In: Proceedings of the Forty-fourth Annual ACM Symposium on Theory
             of Computing, STOC 2012, pp. 1219–1234. ACM Press, New York (2012)
LLAN14.   Lauter, K., Lopez-Alt, A., Naehrig, M.: Private computation on encrypted
             genomic data. Technical Report MSR-TR-2014-93 (June 2014)
LMSV12.   Loftus, J., May, A., Smart, N.P., Vercauteren, F.: On CCA-secure some-
             what homomorphic encryption. In: Miri, A., Vaudenay, S. (eds.) SAC
             2011. LNCS, vol. 7118, pp. 55–72. Springer, Heidelberg (2012)
LP11.   Lindner, R., Peikert, C.: Better key sizes (and attacks) for LWE-
             based encryption. In: Kiayias, A. (ed.) CT-RSA 2011. LNCS, vol. 6558,
             pp. 319–339. Springer, Heidelberg (2011)
LPR13.   Lyubashevsky, V., Peikert, C., Regev, O.: On ideal lattices and learning
             with errors over rings. J. ACM 60(6), 43 (2013)
RAD78.   Rivest, R.L., Adleman, L., Dertouzos, M.L.: On data banks and privacy
             homomorphisms. In: Foundations of Secure Computation, pp. 169–179.
             Academia Press (1978)
SS10.   Stehlé, D., Steinfeld, R.: Faster fully homomorphic encryption. In:
             Abe, M. (ed.) ASIACRYPT 2010. LNCS, vol. 6477, pp. 377–394. Springer,
             Heidelberg (2010)
SS11.   Stehlé, D., Steinfeld, R.: Making NTRU as secure as worst-case problems
             over ideal lattices. In: Paterson, K.G. (ed.) EUROCRYPT 2011. LNCS,
             vol. 6632, pp. 27–47. Springer, Heidelberg (2011)
SV10.   Smart, N.P., Vercauteren, F.: Fully homomorphic encryption with rela-
             tively small key and ciphertext sizes. In: Nguyen, P.Q., Pointcheval, D.
             (eds.) PKC 2010. LNCS, vol. 6056, pp. 420–443. Springer, Heidelberg
             (2010)
vDGHV10.   van Dijk, M., Gentry, C., Halevi, S., Vaikuntanathan, V.: Fully homo-
             morphic encryption over the integers. In: Gilbert, H. (ed.) EUROCRYPT
             2010. LNCS, vol. 6110, pp. 24–43. Springer, Heidelberg (2010)
ZPS12.   Zhang, Z., Plantard, T., Susilo, W.: On the CCA-1 security of somewhat
             homomorphic encryption over the integers. In: Ryan, M.D., Smyth, B.,
             Wang, G. (eds.) ISPEC 2012. LNCS, vol. 7232, pp. 353–368. Springer,
             Heidelberg (2012)

Author Index